DIMENSIONS OF DYSLEXIA

Volume Two

LITERACY, LANGUAGE AND LEARNING

Edited by Gavin Reid

Dimensions of Dyslexia

Volume Two

LITERACY, LANGUAGE AND LEARNING

Edited by Gavin Reid

Moray House Publications
Holyrood Road, Edinburgh,
EH8 8AQ.

Current and forthcoming titles:

Dimensions of Dyslexia

Vol. 1 Assessment, Teaching and the Curriculum

Vol. 2 Literacy, Language and Learning
Edited by Gavin Reid

Specific Learning Difficulties (Dyslexia)
A Handbook for Study and Practice
Gavin Reid

Open Learning Courses in Specific Learning Difficulties
General Editors – Gavin Reid and Fernando Almeida Diniz

First published 1996
ISBN 0 901580 80 5
© Moray House Institute of Education

Printed and bound in Great Britain by Bell & Bain Ltd., Glasgow

CONTENTS

FOREWORD

JACKIE STEWART
Three-Time World Driving Champion

Dyslexia, or any of the derivative learning disabilities, can be one of the most mentally damaging and painful issues that the young can face. A large percentage of sufferers are abused and ridiculed by their peers, their elders, and even their teachers, in the traditional education system. The anguish and frustration and resulting lack of self-esteem can linger long in a person's life if the correct help and assistance is not forthcoming.

Dyslexia often causes the young to take the easy route – since they are often laughed at and humiliated in the circles in which they would traditionally mix at school and after school – and frequently they are dragged into the 'wrong crowd'. It can lead from truancy and crime, to alcohol and drugs. A life can be ruined or even lost. In an enormous percentage of cases, a young person with a fantastic mind can never reach true potential because they are convinced, due to the insensitivities of others and the inadequacy of the system, that they could never be achievers or successful in anything.

All of this can be avoided by understanding teachers and educators who are prepared to change the system and to accommodate a group of people that require a different kind of education which, in some cases, would only mean 'decimal points of change'. With good communication, the victims of learning disabilities, their friends and peers, could be made to understand that the ability to consume information, by either the written word, the spoken word, or even visual diagrams, cannot be done in the 'traditional manner'. It could also be emphasised that in some cases, those same individuals have skills, talents, and minds, much more expansive than the traditional 'bright' children have. If such a thing were done, humiliation could be avoided, self-esteem could be established, potential developed, a better social life created and pain and suffering avoided.

To a very large extent this difference can be created only by educators and by teachers who are prepared to be shown, and to understand that by doing things a little differently, those young minds can be taught and trained, in a large percentage of cases, to handle most of the challenges of life that otherwise might be immovable obstacles.

In the United Kingdom, it has taken a remarkable amount of time for the traditional education system to recognise that there are special needs within its domain which have to be provided for. The obstinacy of the system to fully appreciate this is extremely frustrating for a sufferer, such as myself, to accept.

What has been achieved at Moray House and what can be achieved in the future with a properly funded programme, will help innumerable people not (only of this generation, but more importantly, future generations) to contribute to and benefit our country and society in general, not to mention the possibility for dyslexia sufferers to be proud achievers.

PREFACE

This two-volume text represents a substantial update and extension to the original Moray House Course Reader *Perspectives on Practice*.

This has been necessary because of the broader scope of the concept of dyslexia and its associated dimensions and the extension of teacher training courses in dyslexia, often now at Post-Graduate and Masters level.

It is fortunate, therefore, that the authors of the chapters in these two volumes were able, despite heavy commitments, to provide the quality of insight necessary both to justify the different dimensions of dyslexia and the higher level of teacher training courses.

The contributors are drawn from a wide area throughout the UK and the United States. The Moray House Centre for Specific Learning Difficulties (Dyslexia) has organised a number of national conferences drawing established international speakers, most of whom have submitted a chapter to this book.

The contributors come from a range of backgrounds incorporating both research and practice, and this is reflected in this two-volume edition.

This book is a team effort in every respect and I wish to acknowledge all those who in some way have participated to achieve this final product. I am sure it will be greatly appreciated by all involved in the area of dyslexia.

Gavin Reid

Centre for Specific Learning Difficulties (Dyslexia),
Moray House Institute, Heriot-Watt University,
Edinburgh.

SECTION 1

INTRODUCTION

LITERACY, LANGUAGE AND LEARNING

GAVIN REID

This second volume of *Dimensions of Dyslexia* looks at issues relating to literacy acquisition, language development and other associated factors such as learning styles, motor development and self-esteem. This highlights the range of difficulties which dyslexic children can display, emphasising the need for teachers to be aware of these different dimensions.

In Section Two "Reading and Writing," Gavin Reid provides an overview of the different perspectives on reading by highlighting the models, skills and strategies which can help with the reading process. This is followed by Rhona Johnston's chapter on issues relating to the important area of phonological processing. This is also the theme of chapter four in which Meg Houston, Diane Pepper and Linda Watson discuss the results of some on-going research focusing on phonemic awareness in the nursery school.

Cyril Hellier in chapter five discusses several issues relating to literacy delay, the implications for intervention and the importance of supported and meaningful learning experiences. One well established strategy for overcoming literacy delay is paired reading and Keith Topping provides an outline of this by utilising the support of parents and peers.

This is followed by chapters from Janet Hunter and Pat Brown which look at dyslexic students' experiences with reading. Janet provides a step-by-step approach to the skilled reading and writing experience and Pat Brown specifically discusses aspects relating to the use of metacognition in reading.

Handwriting is an important area of literacy and in chapters nine and ten Mary Kiely and Jean Alston, in separate chapters, provide a detailed analysis of handwriting approaches. Both have considerable experience in this area and these chapters should provide readers with some guidelines on the teaching of handwriting.

The area of language development is an important one because of the links between literacy and language development. The next section therefore looks at different aspects of language development and particularly how these relate to literacy. Jennifer Reid and Morag Donaldson discuss the underlying causes of language disorders and describe some intervention approaches. This is followed by Marysia Nash's chapter on the connections and implications between language and literacy and in the following chapter, Marcia Mann focuses on dyslexia and its connections with language development. Language function, language system and language based learning are also discussed, and the connections between dyslexia and language are highlighted by reference to case studies.

The educational context must be considered if one is to fully understand why some programmes or strategies are more effective than others. Eileen Francis addresses this by reference to different communication styles, the importance of discussion, differentiation and curriculum issues.

An area of current interest is that of bilingualism and its effect on literacy development. This important area is addressed by John Landon in the chapter 'Reading Between the Languages' which examines some of the important issues relating to assessment and teaching.

Motor development is an area which also relates to difficulties in literacy. Adrian Dighe and Gillian Kettles provide a comprehensive survey of both research and practice with an overview of developmental dyspraxia, and Liz Stephenson and Elizabeth Fairgrieve look at the links with dyslexia and motor problems. This chapter provides some guidance on assessment, planning and implementing intervention and these aspects are clearly illustrated by reference to two case studies.

The section on Motor Development is concluded by Sheila Dobie's chapter, in which she examines factors relating to poor motor performance in the early years.

The resources available on dyslexia are obviously appreciated by professionals in the field. It is, however, important that this should not deter teachers or other professionals from ignoring the skills and strategies of learners. Section four, therefore, concentrates on aspects relating to the learner. Jane Healy begins by discussing the topical issue of attention deficit disorders. Jane is a prolific writer on a broad range of aspects relating to child development and provides a sensible insight into the area of attention difficulties based on research and practice.

Also based on practice, Vicky Hunter follows this up by describing some strategies which dyslexic children can develop for themselves to assist with reading, spelling, writing and comprehension.

Barbara Given is one of the world leaders in the field of learning styles and in her chapter, she provides a comprehensive overview of different types of learning style models which she follows up with an original addition focusing on her own work in learning systems and their implications for teaching.

The area of learning styles is further developed by Maggie Nicholson who provides a practical and insightful collection of approaches and strategies to engage the learner. In the final chapter of the section, Morag Hunter-Carsch using the principles of differentiation, provides a practical framework to help the student achieve independence in learning within the context of the curriculum.

Social and emotional considerations are extremely important and need to be considered from both the teacher's and the child's perspective. Stewart Biggar and Jenni Barr provide an interesting insight into the 'emotional world of specific learning difficulties' by discussing feelings experienced by children with specific learning difficulties. They also highlight the influence of parents and of teaching. This is followed by a chapter by Gavin Reid and John Hinton in which the demands on teachers is examined and the implications of this in relation to teacher work stress and the school system. Particular focus is also given in this chapter to stress factors which can be experienced by dyslexic children.

The final section of this volume aims to provide the reader with a broad framework of knowledge relating to current issues in the field of specific learning difficulties. Lori Muskat begins by examining the rights of the child with an insightful chapter on self-advocacy - a contemporary issue which will undoubtedly increase in importance in years to come.

Sheila Riddell, Sally Brown and Jill Duffield then discuss the results of some research on specific learning difficulties which highlight the impact of the re-definition of the role of learning support teachers. They also discuss the learning support teachers' conceptualisation of specific learning difficulties and dyslexia. In the next chapter, Linda Cumming provides a framework for practice with reference to staff development, intervention procedures and specialist provision. This is followed by parental perspectives in which Sheila Airth and Gillian Thomson provide an interesting and informative account of how they, as representatives of the Scottish Dyslexia Association, perceive the difficulties experienced by dyslexic children and their families. It is extremely important that a volume such as this takes into account the views of parents, and the two authors of this chapter, because of their long association with parents' groups and their personal experiences, both as parents and professionals, are well placed to provide these views.

The needs of dyslexic children (and how these can be met) is a question which has been the subject of on-going debates. Alan Dyson and David Skidmore, in the chapter 'Contradictory Models: The Dilemma of Specific Learning Difficulties' provide a clear analysis of the issues which relate to this dilemma and provide a model for specific learning difficulties provision. This model provides a conceptualisation of specific learning difficulties with a clear rationale of providing access to the mainstream curriculum. The essence of this is captured in the four aims of the rationale - differentiation; building self-esteem; building learner autonomy and developing skills. The chapter closes by relating the model to government policy.

Gavin Reid concludes this volume with a discussion on the positive side of dyslexia. The work of Jane Healy and Tom West in particular are discussed, which shows that the skills and talents of dyslexic children may lie in areas other than literacy, and it is important that these talents are recognised. It is fitting to end this two-volume text on this positive note. It is important that teachers and professionals everywhere recognise these talents, build on them and help dyslexic students develop a positive attitude to learning. Tom West (1991) perhaps sums this up best when he suggests:

> *"We ought to begin to pay less attention to getting everyone over the same hill using the same path. We may wish to encourage some to take different routes to the same end. Then we might see good reasons for paying careful attention to their descriptions of what they have found. We may wish to follow them some day."*

It is hoped, therefore, that this two-volume text provides many different paths for teachers and other professionals to follow and that all dyslexic children and adults will benefit from this.

SECTION 2

READING AND WRITING

PERSPECTIVES ON READING

GAVIN REID

The research literature on the process of reading can provide useful insights to indicate why some approaches may be successful while others may not. It can also provide some theoretical frameworks which can help guide the teacher through the morass of programmes and philosophies, and it can help to identify the nature of reading, the fundamental principles and concepts, and the importance of the role of the learner in the reading process.

This chapter will therefore examine perspectives on reading by focusing on the following: Models and Methods; Principles and Practices; Skills and Strategies; Concepts and Comprehension; Learning and the Learner.

MODELS AND METHODS

It has been asserted (Reason *et al.*, 1988) that a dichotomy exists in reading research between cognitive psychologists who focus on the single word and elements of words, and teachers and educational psychologists, who appear more concerned with the wider aspects of literacy and in particular, those aspects related to instruction. Methods of teaching reading have therefore been of more concern to teachers and educational psychologists. However, it should be appreciated that such methods owe their existence to the models which have been devised and developed following extensive and continuing research in the field of reading.

Methods of teaching reading lie within a continuum of approaches, ranging from the systematic and sequential acquisition of sub-skills of reading at one end to the osmotic enrichment of language experience at the other end. These two approaches broadly represent the 'bottom-up' and the 'top-down' models of processing information and each presents specific methodologies embodied within a theoretical framework.

The 'bottom-up' model implies that the reader processes graphemic information, then moves to individual letters, then larger chunks, and that only after the word has been processed is meaning inferred by the reader (La Berge and Samuels, 1974).

The top-down model, on the other hand, which gathered impetus from the work of Smith (1979) and Goodman (1967), assumes that readers move from the higher (cognitive) to the lower (perceptual) mental processes. This model, therefore implies that good readers do not need to decode and make sense of the shapes of letters because they initially focus on the whole word. It is from focusing on the whole word that readers abstract meaning. The lower, perceptual elements, according to the 'top-down' theorists, are used only to confirm the original 'guess'. Goodman (1967) called this model the 'psycholinguistic guessing game' and it clearly places an important function on the role of context and language experience.

There are, however, arguments against both these models (Stanovich, 1984, 1992). It has been asserted that fluent readers do not necessarily rely on context but are more fluent because they are more adept at recognising text. It has also been shown that the rate of reading is affected by the readers' inferences and the use of context, so at least an element of 'top-down' processing is occurring in fluent reading.

Stanovich theorises that reading actually utilises both 'bottom-up' and 'top-down' processes and his 'interactive compensatory approach' implies that readers use compensatory strategies to assist with reading. Readers, therefore, with poor word recognition (decoding) would be more reliant on context than readers with good decoding skills. The implication of this view is that the teaching of reading should promote flexibility and recognition of the child's individual strengths and weakness in addition to the learning preferences.

Stanovich, focusing on the specific difficulties in reading experienced by dyslexic children, provides evidence for cognitive differences between dyslexic readers and other poor readers. This is encapsulated in the 'phonological-core variable-difference model' (Stanovich 1988, Stanovich and Siegel, 1994). According to this model, dyslexic children display a phonological difficulty which is specific to the reading task and does not pervade other domains of cognitive functioning. Stanovich agrees, however, that a continuum of phonological-core difficulties exists from one end of the spectrum (where the deficits will be located only in phonological processing) to the other end of the continuum (where the reader will have 'a host of cognitive deficits' and a cognitively immature profile.) He terms the readers at this end the 'garden variety poor readers'. This model helps to explain why dyslexic children often show secondary problems in addition to a phonological processing deficit (Holligan and Johnston, 1988). All dyslexic children, except those positioned at the uni-dimensional, phonological processing end of the continuum, will show multi-dimensional cognitive difficulties which may affect performance across a range of tasks.

Frith (1985) describes models of reading development as 'stage models'. The initial stage being the logographic phase when children recognise words based on visual features and contextual cues; the reader then moves to an alphabetic phase in which the letter-sound correspondence is the principal feature and finally to an orthographic phase when the reader becomes fluent and can relate his reading skills to the accurate spelling of words. Dyslexic children find the transition from the logographic to the alphabetic stage problematic because a degree of phonological skills are necessary to cope with the letter-sound relationships which are a feature of the alphabetic stage.

Goswami (1993) argues that reading development should be conceived as an interactive developmental process rather than as a series of stages. Progress in reading, therefore, will in turn affect changes to the child's level of phonological knowledge. She suggests that children develop phonological knowledge through the use of an analogy model of reading by using the 'onset' and 'rime' parts of words to help in word recognition. She further argues that dyslexic children may not spontaneously develop analogous reading strategies, but would benefit from being taught such a strategy.

Augur (1990) believes that while a substantial amount of children will not respond to the essentially visually based methods emanating from psycholinguistic theorists such as 'look and say' and 'real books', dyslexic children will almost certainly encounter difficulty. This is because the memory difficulties encountered by the dyslexic child mean that new words are not easily stored in memory and such new words need to be constantly used otherwise they are forgotten. Additionally, according to Auger, dyslexic children often confuse words which look similar such as 'one' and 'once'. She suggests a highly structured phonics approach (Auger & Briggs, 1992) based on the original programme devised by Hickey (1977 which teaches children the fundamental concepts of sound, letter and written shape relationship. The programme begins with only a small combination of carefully selected letters to avoid unnecessary confusion.

Reason (1988) attempted to obtain some consensus on the teaching of reading through the formation of an interest group consisting of twenty specialist support teachers and educational psychologists and concluded that the two approaches are not 'mutually exclusive' Most children would usually acquire literacy through the language experience model with programmes such as 'The Apprenticeship Approach' (Waterland, 1986) which allows children to benefit from enriched reading experiences through a psycholinguistic orientation and peer and adult assistance. For some children, however, this method would need to be supplemented by a step-by-step method of skill acquisition. The balance of these two types of instruction needs to be examined in the light of the individual child's learning history, current learning context and learning style. The choice is not, therefore, either/or; instead, a focus must be placed on the holistic needs of the learner, not only to be able to tackle the reading process, but to receive pleasure from the reading text.

PRINCIPLES AND PRACTICES

Although there are a considerable number of reading programmes and strategies available for use with dyslexic students, it is now generally accepted that many of those programmes share similar principles. It is recognised that dyslexic students present difficulties in many aspects of phonological processing and in short- and long-term memory processes. These difficulties deprive the learner of automatic access to the decoding of print. To help overcome these difficulties, programmes suggested to help deal with the problem of dyslexia, usually incorporate the following:

- Multi-sensory techniques;
- automaticity and over-learning principles;
- a structured and cumulative approach.

The context and form of programmes may vary but the underlying aims of accessing all the senses and attempting to enhance automaticity by the essentially repetitive processes of over-learning can be seen in many programmes which have been developed to deal with dyslexia.

Multi-Sensory

Multi-sensory techniques involve visual, auditory, kinaesthetic and tactile reinforcement. The rationale of such techniques appear to stem from the view that kinaesthetic activities help to establish visual-auditory associations in grapheme and phoneme correspondences, in addition to reinforcing left to right letter progression (Orton, 1966). It is also suggested that multi-sensory activities can help to retrieve words from long-term memory (Slingerland, 1971)

The manner in which multi-sensory techniques are utilised appears to vary depending on the programme used. For example, Orton believes that individual phonic sounds should be pronounced as the child traces a word, Gillingham feels that individual letter names should be called out, while Fernald argues that words should not be broken up artificially and that whole words should be said aloud while tracing or writing (Clark, 1988).

Why should multi-sensory techniques work? Although there is evidence to suggest that the techniques have considerable merit (Clark, 1988), there is no real evidence available to suggest they work, or indeed which specific skills that enable facilitation of the reading process are enhanced by multi-sensory work. Hulme (1981) found that tracing letters helps children with reading difficulties remember words visually. Since poor readers tend to rely on visual memory, this kind of exercise helps to reinforce visual memory and could prove beneficial for such readers. It has also been recognised that children benefit from multi-sensory techniques because it strengthens the visual-perceptual area and therefore increases proficiency at recognising letter shapes.

Lane (1990) developed a multi-sensory programme focusing on the following factors: Aural – Read – Respond – Oral – Written (ARROW). This technique utilises the child's own voice replayed through high fidelity recording equipment and this relationship between the child and his voice helps to explain, according to Lane, the success of the programme. Rowe (1987) examined the use of the ARROW technique and noted improvement in clustering skills. A one-year study Lane, 1987) provided impressive improvements in reading and spelling attainment. Similar results have been found in other studies (Bellamy and Long, 1994; Lane, 1994).

There are, however, some considerations to note in accepting such findings, such as the selection of the sample and the acknowledged difficulty in isolating the precise components of the programme which accounted for its apparent successes. There are indeed many variables within the ARROW technique which could account for such successes. For example, there is considerable interaction with adults, considerable reading practice, application of the written mode and the provision of withdrawal facilities.

Some hold a view that multi-sensory learning requires a cognitive focus which has to be learnt over time and especially from an early age. Chasty (1990) argues that a teaching strategy which incorporates both visual and auditory modes simultaneously may be unsuccessful because the child's memory systems have not received sufficient practice in using the two modes purposefully and in linking these two elements together and storing them in long-term memory as a recallable unit. The implication of this view is that purposeful multi-sensory training should be incorporated from the early stages and particularly in nursery education. This would help the child develop the complex memory processes for efficient multi-mode learning.

Automaticity

Automaticity is an important aspect of the learning process. After a period of learning, skills usually become internalised and automatized. This is clearly an economy-saving device which liberates one's cognitive capacities to concentrate on the organisation and mastering of new skills and not relearning old previously learned skills. In reading at the word level, the process of automaticity frees the working memory to allow for more efficient processing at the sentence and passage levels of text (Stanovich, 1984).

Chasty (1990) sees automaticity as a learned process which consolidates the sub-skills in reading, thus freeing the working memory processes to focus on variables other than the mechanics of reading. Chasty argues that children with specific learning difficulties find automaticity more difficult to achieve and it is this which helps to explain their difficulties in mastering reading sub-skills and acquiring literacy.

To help the child master automaticity, three aspects should be taken into account: processing time, presentation and consolidation of learning material and memory training.

It has been recognised that dyslexic students are slower at word recognition than good readers. Reid (1986) showed the importance of instructional time and the pacing of instruction to prevent information overload. Bryant (1990) also identified this aspect of slow speed of processing information as well as difficulty automatizing information learned. Experimental studies (Fawcett and Nicolson, 1990) have confirmed this difficulty of automatization with dyslexic students. Clearly therefore, it must be recognised and appreciated that dyslexic students will need more time to process and learn information than other children who may not share similar difficulties mastering automaticity.

The work of Fawcett and Nicolson (1990) illustrates that presentation of learning tasks singularly is more effective in terms of facilitating automaticity than the presentation of simultaneous tasks which may result in competing demands on the memory's resources. There may be some justification, therefore, for a systematic review of previously learned material at the beginning and end of each lesson. This perhaps repetitive form of consolidation may be necessary for children with dyslexic difficulties to help them achieve some degree of automaticity.

Chasty (1990) argues that automaticity can be achieved by actually teaching the skills involved in remembering information. Thus, he argues, more focus should be placed on the facility of memory as opposed to the product of reading. There may well be a case for arguing that children will not benefit fully from the experience of reading until they have acquired appropriate memory skills.

Over-learning

Perhaps one way to help to achieve automaticity and improve the memory processes is to adopt the principle of over-learning. This can be achieved through repetitive presentations of the same material and is in fact a method frequently utilised with dyslexic children. According to Thomson (1990), such a strategy helps to strengthen the memory processes and alleviate some of the difficulties associated with attentional difficulties. Thomson also suggests that teachers should be aware of the variations in performance of dyslexic children from day-to-day and argues that the long-term effects of this may be minimised by structured over-learning. While benefits may be recognised for over-learning, one has to be cautious that this does not result in boredom and monotony, thus making the learning task unexciting and mechanical. Effort should therefore be made to introduce some variety so that the same principles and concepts may well be presented, but the different forms of presentation will vary, thus minimising monotony.

Structured and Cumulative

Many successful programmes for dyslexic students are highly structured involving a step-by-step approach. They also incorporate a cumulative approach beginning with basic aspects of literacy acquisition such as sounds and letter names and once these have been mastered, moving on to more complex reading sub-skills. It is, however, a point to note that not all students are suited to a highly structured approach and some recognition should be made of the students learning style before deciding on the approach to be used.

SKILLS AND STRATEGIES

Developmental Perspective

It has been recognised that the skill of reading is a developmental one which is acquired over a number of years (Chall, 1983). From this developmental perspective, therefore, the first stage includes language awareness, recognition of names and letters, and reading concepts such as the purpose of books and the relationship between written and spoken words (Chall, 1983). The child then integrates graphic and contextual factors, a developmental stage which may be restricted by limited phonic knowledge, limited experience with language and lack of reading practice. The implication of a developmental model such as the one proposed by Chall is that readers become more flexible in the use of reading strategies as they become more proficient. This emphasises the holistic nature of reading and the necessity to incorporate strategies and techniques which draw on both top-down and bottom-up models. It is clearly important, therefore, that the learner be provided with a broad range of reading strategies since even accomplished readers may need to utilise bottom-up processing when faced with mastering new types of information, perhaps some technical words, or new concepts.

Although developmental models can provide some useful insights into the acquisition of skills, it is important that developmental stages should not be accepted too rigidly. Thomson (1994) suggests that an important aspect of the developmental perspective is the expectation of change over time. Sometimes, therefore, dyslexic children develop at a consistent rate, but it is more usual for the development to occur in a more haphazard learning curve, with 'sudden spurts' of progress followed by an extended period of plateaux in performance. It is therefore necessary to adopt a flexible and individual perspective in implementing reading programmes with dyslexic children.

Reading Words by Analogy

Ehri and Robbins (1992) provide evidence which highlight the strategy of analogous reading. This involves decoding new words not by phonemic segmentation but by using 'onset' and 'rime' strategies and the familiarity of known words. Thus, to read the word 'peak' by analogy, the reader will search his memory store to obtain a word which has the same rime pattern as 'peak' e.g. 'beak' and will break that word into onset – 'b' and rime 'eak'. The widespread use of this strategy has been documented in a number of other studies (Goswami, 1988, 1992, 1993). She found that analogous reading develops earlier than phonological decoding and that the strategy was of particular benefit to non- and poor readers. Goswami investigated the recognition of onset and rime syllables by beginning readers and found evidence that the ability to divide words into onset and rime sub-units may be a crucial factor which will enable beginning readers to read words by analogy (Goswami and Bryant, 1990; Goswami, 1993). If, as these studies suggest, analogous reading is an important strategy for non- and beginning readers, there is a strong case for focusing the early teaching of reading towards assisting children to grasp the inherent patterns in rime words and recognising the sub-units of 'onset and rime'. (See Fig. 1).

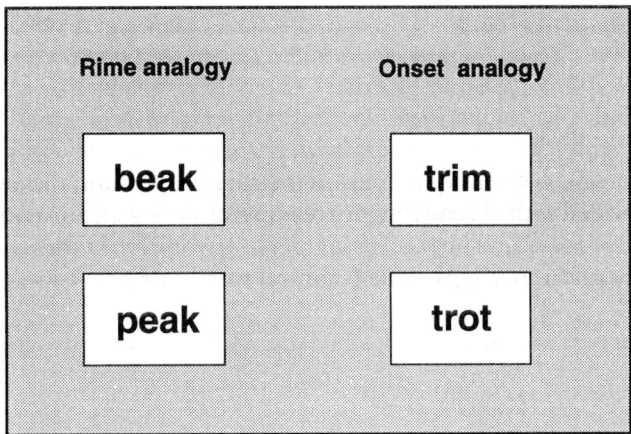

Reproduced by permission (Goswami, 1994)

Ehri and Robbins (1992), however, found that although it was easier for beginning readers to process information words by analogy than by phonological decoding, some basic underlying knowledge of phonological decoding was necessary in order for beginning readers to recognise words using the strategy of analogy. Additionally, Bruck and Treiman (1992) found that although they learnt words quicker and easier using analogy strategies, they were less able to generalise their new learning. Whilst they acknowledge that rime-based analogies do have a role to play in teaching children new words, they nevertheless maintain that such instruction is not a 'panacea' and that the relationships between individual graphemes and individual phonemes are of fundamental importance.

Ehri and Robbins (1992) suggest that phonological decoding skills can assist beginning readers to read new words by analogy to known words, helping in the process of segmenting words into onset and rime sub-units and in forming appropriate connections between graphemes and phonemes. This finding, though important, still leaves the crucial question unanswered in relation to whether analogous reading is a temporary initial strategy for beginning readers which will be complemented or replaced by phonological decoding once this has been mastered, or whether analogy reading actually underlies decoding skills and indeed facilitates the development of phonological decoding skills. The beginning reader may not, therefore, be blending phonemes when tackling new words but merely accessing from memory already formed sub-units of 'onsets and rimes'.

There clearly seems to be some value in learning to read words using the 'onset' and 'rime' strategy. Wise *et al.* (1990) found that beginning readers who learned to read words by segmenting them into onset and rime sub-units remembered how to read the words better than readers who segmented the words into other types of sub-units. Ehri, however, suggests that in order for such programmes to be successful it is important for the reader to acquire some phonological skills at the outset, in order to appreciate how letters symbolise sound as this would help the reader recognise the onset and rime and sub-units in new words.

Phonological Skills

Phonological factors appear to be of considerable importance to the process of reading. Indeed it has been argued (Liberman and Shankweiler, 1985; Pennington *et al.*, 1987) that phonological processing occurs at all levels of reading and that all letter recognition requires letter sound access or phonological decoding. This may not always be apparent, especially in the case of proficient readers. There is, however, considerable agreement among researchers that a certain level of phonological skills is necessary for reading and that most dyslexic children have a specific deficit in phonological reading (Ellis, 1991). The evidence for this comes from studies in phonological awareness, phonological analysis and phonological segmentation as well as studies in analogous reading (Ehri *et al.*, 1992; Goswami, 1993). In relation to phonological awareness (Bradley and Bryant, 1985) found that pre-readers' sensitivity to rime and alliteration correlated with later reading achievement. Fox and Routh (1983) studied children tackling tasks which required phonological analysis – asking children to say only part of a particular word – and were able to identify from this children who would have difficulty in reading. Studies in phonological segmentation (Liberman *et al.*, 1977; Fox and Routh, 1980, *et al.*) have found correlations between children being able to tap out the phonemes (sounds) in a word and learning to read.

Although there appears to be a clear relationship between phonological processes and reading, there is still some debate as to whether this relationship is causal or reciprocal. For example, Bradley and Bryant (1985) and Bradley (1990) displayed evidence of a causal relationship between sound categorisation and reading. This means that phonological awareness must precede reading since it has a direct causal influence on the child's progress in reading. Studies by Ehri and Wilce (1985) and Jorm and Share (1983) show a reciprocal relationship between phonological processing and reading. These studies revealed the linguistic insight which children develop as a result of an awareness of print and from the experience of matching speech to print.

Rack, Snowling and Olsen (1992), however, examine the role of phonological processing in reading, and argue it is more prudent to talk of levels of phonological processing rather than dividing reading into phonological processing and direct lexical route. This view also underlines the individual differences among dyslexic students rather than discrete subtypes.

A case can, however, be made that phonological processing and reading have both a causal and a reciprocal function. While it is true that young children who have developed phonological skills are quicker to grasp the alphabetic principle, it is also the case that exposure to print, the growing awareness that written words correspond to spoken words, and the experience of matching letters with sounds help children become competent and familiar with phonological elements in words.

Indeed Ehri *et al.* (1992) suggest a vitally important role for phonological processing throughout the course of reading development. Ehri's model displays a close link between phonological skills and sight word recognition since she believes that the development of sight word recognition is dependent on subject's phonological skills. This would mean that dyslexic readers would encounter problems at all stages of reading development because of their phonological difficulty. Rack, Snowling and Olsen (1992), however, argue that there is a degree of independence between the skills associated with phonological processing and sight word recognitions. Perhaps phonological focusing may well be the central component, but that does not necessarily compromise the role of the other factors. Rack, Snowling and Olsen present the case that many dyslexic children acquire word recognition skills beyond the level that would be predicted from their phonological skills. Thomson (1990), however, believes that teaching the sub-skills of reading – phonetic teaching – is of vital importance because meaning and comprehension appear to develop out of the teaching of sub-skills such as phonic awareness, syllabification and the relationship between sound and symbol.

Thomson (1994), in part, suggests that one of the cases of dyslexic children's weak syllable skills may be due to problems in phonemic awareness as well as inability to retain phoneme sequences in short-term memory.

Johnston (1994) argues however that for beginning readers it is necessary to complement phonemic awareness training with training in alphabetic skills involving letter knowledge. In part, she suggests that her studies indicate that the main predictor of reading at age five from the measures taken at age four was knowledge of the alphabet.

Strategies

Arnold (1990) presents a case for making reading real and puts forward the view that scanning is a reading skill which can be taught and used effectively by poor readers. She suggests that the use of the strategy of scanning can help release poor readers from the burden of attempting to read every word. The practice of scanning can be developed by the child through exercises and games. Arnold suggests an activity such as asking children questions about a reading passage without giving them time to read it fully. This facilitates the selection of key words. The use of the technique of scanning also helps to facilitate meaning through this identification of key words.

Waterland (1986) proposes the view that reading should be purposeful and meaningful and that a child can read effectively without necessarily acquiring competence in the sub-skills of reading. This apprenticeship approach to reading (Waterland, 1986) assumes that the acquisition of written language is comparable to spoken language. Thus, it is important for the child to benefit from enriched reading experience in the same way that enriched language expression is necessary for the acquisition of language. Adult and peer support and imitation and modelling are therefore important ingredients in the teaching of reading.

Although this approach can be highly commended in its view of reading as a meaningful and pleasurable activity, in its use of language experiences and the use of the adult role model, it can still be argued that the acute decoding problems of children with dyslexic difficulties prevents them from fully accessing the benefits from programmes like the apprenticeship approach. Indeed, Cashdan and Wright (1990) distinguish between the general context of literacy behaviour and the specific context of the sentence and the word and argue that it is access to the specific components of reading which allows the reading skills to develop. This view implies that some focus and attention should be placed in teaching and accessing the components of reading in order that the child gains full benefit from the reading experience. It might also be argued, however, that abstracting meaning from text, possible even with faulty decoding, is an important component of reading and one which the dyslexic child has skills to access.

There are a number of studies which illustrate reading gains through teaching methods focusing on teaching sub-skills and, in particular, phonological processing skills (Thomson, 1990, 1994; Farrall, Thomson and Watkins, 1994). In one study, Thomson conducted a daily programme aimed at teaching syllables using a syllable analysis training programme; he found significant gains among a group of poor readers with weak performance in multi-syllable words. The gains were particularly significant in their performance in reading two and three syllable words.

It was also found (Thomson, 1994) that dyslexic children made more progress following a programe of teaching syllable types as opposed to copying the whole word out. The same study also showed the success of the multi-sensory method (Simultaneous Oral spelling) for dyslexic children.

Johnston and Thomson (1989) carried out an interesting piece of research comparing the reading progress of 8-year-old Scottish and New Zealand children. The Scottish sample were taught through a phonics approach while the New Zealand children were taught through a structured book experience approach which used context and language expression. This study suggested that the Scottish children had a significant advantage over the New Zealand group in their abilities to decode words. This may provide strong evidence to support the effectiveness of phonics teaching.

Some programmes analyse the tasks involved in reading and tackle the teaching of reading from a behaviourist perspective (Solity and Bull, 1987). These programmes propose a reading hierarchy of target objectives to be mastered by the reader. The objectives are broken into smaller and smaller steps until a step-size is reached where the child can succeed. Criterion Referenced tests are used to establish the child's level and identify and monitor those areas where the child can succeed. This is basically a record-keeping system but by identifying the areas of difficulty, it may help the teacher compile a suitable programme. This approach does not specify any particular method of teaching so therefore the teacher can adopt a variety of methods and approaches to help the child achieve mastery.

It appears that no one approach can be successful for every child. Reason (1988) used the term the 'scattergun approach' to describe reading intervention strategies which draw on a number of approaches and do not attempt to use any specific programme to develop specific sub-skills. Even though there does seem to be some agreement that many dyslexic-type difficulties result from problems in phonological awareness and memory difficulties, there is no real agreement on how to deal with these difficulties in terms of a reading programme. Reason describes this 'scattergun approach' as a balanced reading programme which acknowledges that individual children may respond to different methods and strategies. This view is supported by the extensive research into reading and learning styles (Carbo *et al.*, 1986; Dunn and Dunn, 1992) which acknowledges the individualism of children in relation to the learning task. A balanced reading programme, therefore, should contain elements of programmes aimed to establish enjoyment and meaning from text and language-based reading experiences, as well as dealing with the phonetic aspects of reading.

CONCEPTS AND COMPREHENSION

Children with dyslexic difficulties usually display comprehension skills well in advance of their decoding abilities. At the same time, however, there is evidence to suggest that these decoding difficulties restrict the child's competencies and performance in comprehension tasks (Stanovich, 1986). Although one would expect to find a discrepancy between dyslexic children's reading comprehension and decoding skills (Aaron, 1989), a view has been put forward that dyslexic children generally receive little actual training in reading comprehension because the main focus of teaching is placed on the decoding difficulties (Maria, 1986). If it is the case that the child's decoding difficulties restrict competencies in comprehension, as Stanovich suggests, then it is extremely important for the teacher to take account of this and develop teaching approaches aimed not just at improving decoding, but also fostering appropriate comprehension skills.

Important factors which can facilitate the development of reading comprehension are an awareness of the importance of schema activities which can enhance metacognition, and an understanding of the value of the interactive process between teacher and student. These three factors, therefore, schema theory, metacognition and student/teacher interaction, will be discussed below in relation to the development of reading comprehension of students with dyslexic difficulties.

Role of Schema

The development of a set of schema helps the student build concepts and this consequently facilitates reading comprehension. The reader embarks on the reading process with a number of schemas based on his or her background knowledge. These schemas can be seen as providing the learner with a framework based on both background knowledge and cognitive development. Echwall and Shanker (1983) describe schema as 'pre-suppositions about the meaning of text'. Thus, beginning readers will understand reading material if it can be accommodated to their existing schema even if it requires the schema to be modified or developed in some way. There is, therefore, a reciprocal relationship between the reader's background knowledge and the reading text, since both interact and enhance the other. For example, practice at reading will increase the reader's background knowledge and an extended background knowledge will facilitate comprehension of text. It is therefore important for the teacher to ensure that the reading text can be accommodated within the learner's schema and that the reader's schema is a relevant one for the text.

Maria (1986) views the readers' background knowledge as one of the most important aspects of the understanding and interpretation of text, and thus of the development of reading schema. One of the main concerns, therefore, is the necessity to bridge the gap between the reader's background knowledge and the information in the reading text. Many strategies have been attempted to achieve this and there is still considerable debate on the most effective method. Pre-reading discussion, however, is an approach which has been well evaluated in relation to helping to bridge this gap (Au *et al.*, 1985). Such discussion should help to clarify the extent of the reader's background knowledge and help to shape and develop knowledge framework so helping the reader obtain appropriate meaning from the text.

This view is supported by McKeown, Beck *et al.* (1992) who examined the contribution of prior knowledge to reading and reading comprehension. They found that students who were provided with background knowledge as a primer to reading the text recalled more material from the text and significantly answered more questions than students who read the text without the additional background knowledge.

It is therefore important to consider the view that if the child has no schema the text is not understood and if the reader finds schema other than those intended, the text is misunderstood (Rumelhart 1980). There is, therefore, sound argument for a 'prior knowledge' lesson before introducing the reading text. This can be of significant importance to the subsequent comprehension of the text, and for dyslexic readers such a lesson would also assist in the decoding process because they would be able to use context more efficiently.

Metacognition

Metacognition has been defined as 'the knowledge and control the child has over his or her own thinking and learning activities' (Baker and Brown, 1984). Baker and Brown see 'knowledge' as an awareness of the demands of the task and 'control' as the ability to plan and monitor one's own activities while reading.

Metacognition is therefore not about teaching individual skills, but rather it is concerned with teaching knowledge and control strategies which can be generalised by the student across other learning tasks in different contexts. A strategy, as opposed to a skill, can therefore be viewed as a 'problem-solving behaviour'. Baker and Brown acknowledge that many of the strategies which can be utilised to enhance metacognitive skills are essentially study skills, but they point out that the main difference is that in teaching metacognitive strategies, one is not first teaching the skill but the rationale for applying that skill and how the learner feels about using a particular strategy. Maria (1986) makes the very valid point in relation to reading comprehension, that it is more important for the teacher to know how students arrived at their answers than to determine whether or not the answers are correct. Thus, the teacher is facilitating the process of understanding.

There are a number of different approaches in relation to building metacognitive skills, some of which are outlined below.

Reciprocal Teaching

The main aspects of reciprocal teaching (Palincsar and Brown, 1985) include generating questions about the text, summarising the text, predicting what will happen next and clarifying what the students have read. An additional component of reciprocal teaching is the interactive dialogue between teacher and student and eventually among the students themselves. During this interaction, the teacher guides the students through the processes outlined above. Thus the teacher will ask questions which will generate further questions from the students and perhaps provide the students with additional background information and some predictions about what will happen next. The student and the teacher are, therefore, reciprocating and sharing knowledge by the building of 'scaffolds' to help develop an understanding of the process of learning and comprehension on the part of the student. Initially, the teacher may well have to feed in more information than will be fed back by the student, but this should diminish as the student takes more control over his own learning.

Main Idea Identification

Williams (1986) has developed some interesting approaches in relation to assisting students identify and select main ideas. According to Williams, the principal skill required in selecting main ideas from text is the skill of being able to classify themes, pictures and objects from the text. Hence, Williams encourages practice in studying sentences and words to obtain clues which will help to identify main ideas.

Comprehension through Imagery

An interesting piece of research has been conducted by Bell (1986,1991) using Gestalt imagery as an aid to comprehension among children with decoding difficulties. Students with weak Gestalt imagery are only able to process 'parts' rather than 'wholes' from either verbal or written verbal stimuli. Students with decoding difficulties would be utilising their cognitive resources to decode the actual print and may, by default, find themselves with a weaker Gestalt, unable to process the meaning of the written word. Bell argues that weak decoding can be a primary contributor to weak Gestalt imagery and that a phonological disorder can cause image distortion which interferes with comprehension. Therefore, according to Bell it is crucial that specific Gestalt training is provided to help support comprehension and to overcome the disadvantages of decoding difficulties such as weak vocabulary. Bell has developed a Gestalt programme 'Visualising and Verbalising for Language Comprehension and Thinking'. The programme begins with picture to picture exercises which involve the student describing to the teacher a given picture, then the student moves on to describing in detail a picture of the visual images conveyed, firstly by single words, sentences and paragraphs.

The clinical data provided by Bell's study seems promising, although Clark (1988) argues that some students are simply unable to process verbal information visually because of their particular learning style. Nevertheless what does seem convincing is the link between Gestalt imagery and reading comprehension and the adverse effect of poor decoding skills, such as those experienced by the student with dyslexia, on both Gestalt imagery and reading comprehension.

In a similar manner, Hunter-Carsch (1990) developed a programme which aimed to enhance visual imagery in reading. The programme is based on a number of steps which aim to facilitate both visual imagery and comprehension in reading. These steps include:

- Attending and abstracting, which facilitates the holding on to an idea.
- Decoding, which involves the discussing of words, spellings and meanings.
- Encoding, which focuses on the construction of words.
- Extending, which utilises phrases and definitions.
- Differentiating, which focuses on concepts and assimilation.
- Communicating and translating, which is directed to the different uses of words.

The key principles of this programme appear to be both its practical nature, which involves the child writing out letters and words, and the element of reciprocity between teacher and child, which facilitates the child moving through the stages from the initial one of attending to the more complex skill of interpreting and translating.

Niklasson (1993) argues that any stifling of creativity will impede progress in reading. Niklasson's model of teaching is based on the three aspects of expression, experience, and cognition and on developing perceptual awareness in children through specific physical exercises. Niklasson argues that these promote openness and confidence, which benefit creativity, concentration and reading.

Interactive Process

The value of the interactive process between teacher and student, and indeed student and student, has been encapsulated in the discussions on the approach known as Reciprocal Teaching (Palincsar and Brown, 1984). This approach provides a good example of the facilitative value of the teacher or peer tutor in enhancing the development of schema and metacognitive strategies. Another approach widely used to help develop metacognitive skills, is the mediated learning experience, a central component of Reuven Feuerstein's Instrumental Enrichment. This maintains that early learning is very much influenced by parent-child interactions which helps to guide children through problem-solving activities (Blagg, 1991).

LEARNING AND THE LEARNER

Chasty (1990) presents a case that more attention should be directed to developing the teaching of skills which can facilitate effective learning and thus competent reading. Some of the skills he outlines as necessary are learning skills, including working memory training and visual-auditory perceptual training; language skills, including oral language, language organisation, concepts and labelling; and study skills and thinking skills.

A good case can be made for directing teaching programmes to help develop learning and thinking skills. These programmes, however, should also help the learner develop self-awareness skills. Such skills can help learners appreciate the demands of the task and facilitate the selection of appropriate strategies. Some attention must therefore be directed to examining how the student actually learns.

The implication of this for children with dyslexic difficulties is the necessity to broaden one's teaching perspective from one directed to the acquisition of sub-skills to a holistic one which looks at the complete task in the learning context. It is important that a learning framework be developed to help with the teaching of reading. This framework could incorporate aspects relating to the goals of the exercise, skills and information necessary to fulfil the goals, the value of the outcome of the task for the learner, and the degree of transfer of learning to other tasks and contexts. Such a reading programme, which focuses on the development of contextual and appropriate schema, can meet the needs of a much wider variety of children's learning styles than to a highly structured specific reading programme which focuses on the acquisition of reading sub-skills as the primary learning outcome. Chasty (1990) believes that by advocating a broader approach to the teaching of reading one is allowing children to be 'active interrogators of the learning and thinking process' as well as the text. Cashdan and Wright (1990) agree with this view that it is the learning task that needs to be analysed rather than the teaching programme.

This view emphasises that children with specific learning difficulties usually find it difficult to acquire mastery of reading sub-skills and this in turn may restrict their learning opportunities. The development of the learning programme should focus on the specific skill content of the task and on the process which is necessary for the learner to acquire that skill. The main aim of such a programme is to teach children to be 'self-running' and to help them acquire control over their own learning.

Recently, considerable attention has been directed to children's learning styles and to how teaching styles and programmes can be modified to take children's learning styles into account (Dunn and Dunn, 1992). Carbo, Dunn and Dunn (1986) present an argument that phonic teaching does not work for every child and they identify three kinds of reading styles –

- Those who need phonics to become good readers;
- those who can learn phonics but who do not need phonics to read well; and
- those who are unable to master phonics.

They distinguish between auditory/analytical and global reading styles and argue that those who need phonics will have a strong auditory/analytical reading style but will not be able to distinguish word patterns unless taught to do so. Children who can learn phonics but do not need phonics to read well are usually competent in both auditory/analytical and global reading styles, and their global strengths, intuitively supported by abilities to learn and master the principles of phonics, will enable them to develop both a sight vocabulary rapidly and a knowledge of word patterns. This group would learn most successfully through activities such as writing stories, listening and talking about stories, and reading books of their own choice. The third group, those who are unable to master phonics, need a carefully planned individual programme which focuses on comprehension in order that enjoyment of text will motivate the child to read for pleasure. Carbo points out that good readers exist who have never mastered phonics.

Carbo further argues that too much emphasis is placed on decoding tests to assess the level of a child's reading progress and decoding is only one aspect of reading. Some children who can read fluently and with good comprehension do poorly on sections of reading tests which focus on decoding. Carbo argues that children with strongly global learning styles can learn to read well without mastering any of the sub-skills on which children may be tested in reading tests. She argues that poor readers tend to be tactile, kinaesthetic learners with a global learning style and this should be taken into account when devising a teaching programme.

CONCLUSION

The important comment which should be made in relation to dyslexia and the teaching of reading is that no one approach can be held up as having an exclusive role for the remediation of reading difficulties. It is, therefore, important to be aware of a variety of approaches and to appreciate the principles underlying these approaches. At the same time, one must acknowledge that there are different varieties and degrees of difficulty among dyslexic children and this needs to be considered in the planning and implementation of a teaching programme.

As with any teaching programme, one must identify and access the learners' strengths. Strategies such as scanning can therefore be of enormous value to dyslexic children. Scanning not only makes reading less arduous, it also brings more meaning to the text, which in itself reinforces the pleasurable aspects of reading. There is also an important role for fostering comprehension skills to prevent the decoding difficulty experienced by dyslexic children from further disadvantaging them in relation to text comprehension. Thus, the building of appropriate sentences and other preparatory pre-reading work are very important in order to provide dyslexic children with a sufficient textual knowledge base, both to aid decoding and enhance the use of context. Therefore, concepts such as metacognition, which focus on the process of learning rather than the product, are of supreme importance since they underline the holistic nature of learning and of reading. Reading is not just 'cracking the code' but appreciating the meaning and purpose of text and the application of this to other situations and contexts. One should not be focusing, therefore, on the teaching *of* reading, but on the teaching *about* reading.

In assessing the individual learning and reading styles of dyslexic children, it is important to recognise that a 'common core' difficulty lies in the area of phonological processing, and teaching programmes should also reflect this, but not to the exclusion of the other factors mentioned, such as comprehension, language experience, development of schema, imagery and modelling.

It is interesting to note that the key principles of many specially prepared programmes for dyslexic children, multi-sensory teaching and overlearning can be recommended for use in teaching programmes for all children. This underlines the important fact that effective teaching programmes for reading should cover a broad range of perspectives and not just coach the learner to acquire some basic, but perhaps essential, sub-skills of the reading process.

REFERENCES

Aaron, P. G. (1989). *Dyslexia and Hyperlexia.* Kluwer Academic Publishers, Norwell, M.A.

Arnold, H. (1990). 'Making Reading Real' in *Children's Difficulties in Reading, Spelling and Writing.* Pumfrey, P. and Elliott, C. (Eds.). Falmer Press.

Au, K. H. (1985). 'The role of research is a successful reading programme.' In *Reading Education,* Osborn, J., Wilson, P. F. and Anderson, R. C. (Eds.) pp. 275-292. Lexington M.A. D. C. Heath.

Augur, J. (1990). 'Dyslexia – have we got the teaching right?' In *Children with Literacy Difficulties.* Pinsent, P. (Ed.). David Fulton Publisher. London.

Augur, J. and Briggs, S. (Eds.) (1991). *The Hickey Multi-Sensory Language Course.* Whurr, London.

Baker, L. and Brown, A. L. (1984). 'Metacognitive Skills and Reading' In Pearson, P. D. (Ed.) *Handbook of Reading Research.* Longman, New York.

Bell, N. (1986). *Visualising and Verbalising for Language Comprehension and Thinking.* Paso Robles, C A: Academy of Reading Publications.

Bell, N. (1991). 'Gestalt Imagery: A Critical Factor in Language Comprehension' in *Annals of Dyslexia,* Vol. 4, (1991).

Bellamy, H. and Long, L. A. (1994). Joint paper presented at the first Arrow Conference, Frenchay Hospital, Bristol.

Blagg, N. (1991). Feuerstein's Instrumental Enrichment Programme: A Comprehensive Evaluation of *Can We Teach Intelligence.* Erlbaum, USA.

Bradley, L. (1990). 'Rhyming connections in learning to read and spell'. In Pumfrey P. D, and Elliot C. D. (Eds.). *Children's Reading Spelling and Writing Difficulties. Challenges and Responses.* Falmer, Lewes.

Bradley, L. and Bryant, P. E. (1980). 'Why children sometimes write words which they do not read.' in Frith, V. (Ed.) *Cognitive Process in Spelling.* London: Academic Press.

Bradley, L. and Bryant, P. E. (1985). Rime and Reason In *Reading and Spelling.* Ann Arbor, M.I.University of Michigan Press,USA.

Bruck, M. and Treiman, R. (1992). 'Learning to pronounce words: The limitations of analogies.' *Reading Research Quarterly,* Vol. 27, No. 4, pp. 375-389.

Bryant, P. (1990). 'Phonological Development and Reading'. In Pumfrey, P. D. and Elliott, C. D. (Eds.). *Children's difficulties in reading, spelling and writing.* Falmer Press, London.

Carbo, M., Dunn, K. and Dunn, R. (1986). *Teaching students to learn through their individual learning styles.* Prentice Hall.

Cashdan, A. and Wright, J. (1990). 'Intervention strategies for backward readers in the primary school classroom' in *Children's Difficulties in Reading, Spelling and Writing.* Pumfrey, P. and Elliott, C. (Eds.).

Chall, J. S. (1983). *Stages of Reading Development.* New York: McGraw Hill.

Chasty, H. (1990). 'Meeting the Challenge of Specific Learning Difficuties' in *Children's Difficulties in Reading, Spelling and Writing.* Pumfrey P. and Elliott C. (Eds.). Falmer Press.

Clark, D. B. (1988). *Dyslexia: Theory and Practice of Remedial Instruction* York Press, Maryland.

Dunn, R. and Dunn, K. (1992) *Teaching elementary students through their individual learning styles.* Allyn & Bacon,Massachusetts (1992).

Echwall, E. E. and Shanker, J. L. (1983). *Diagnosis and Remediation of the Disabled Reader.* Boston: Albyn & Bowan.

Ehri, J. C. (1987). 'Learning to Read and Spell Words.' *Journal of Reading Behaviour,* 19: 5-31.

Ehri, J. C. and Robbins, C. (1992). 'Beginners need some decoding skill to read words by analogy.' *Reading Research Quarterly,* pp. 12-26.

Ehri, L. C. and Wilce, L. S. (1985). 'Movement into Reading:Is the first stage of printed word learning, visual or phonetic?. *Reading Research Quarterly, 20, 163-179.*

Ellis, N. C. (1991). 'Spelling and Sound in Learning to Read'. In Snowling, M. and Thomson, M. *Dyslexia, Integrating Theory and Practice.* Whurr Publishers.

Fawcett, A. and Nicolson, R. I. (1990). 'Automaticity – a new framework for Dyslexia Research' in *Meeting Points in Dyslexia,* Hales, G. (Ed.). B.D.A.(1990).

Fox, B. and Routh, D. K. (1980). 'Phonemic analysis and severe reading disability in children' *Journal of Psycholinguistic Research, 9:115-19.*

Fox, B. and Routh, D. K. (1983). 'Reading disability, phonemic analysis and dysphonetic spelling. A follow up study.' *Journal of Clinical Child Psychology,* 12: 28-32.

Fox, B. and Routh, D. K. (1984). 'Phonemic analysis and synthesis as word attack skills: Revisited' *Journal of Educational Psychology, 76:1059-64.*

Frith, U. (1985). 'Beneath the surface of developmental dyslexia' in *Surface Dyslexia in Adults and Children,* Marshall, J. C., Patterson, K. E. and Coltheart, M. (Eds.). London: Routledge & Kegan, Paul.

Goodman, K. (1967). 'Reading: a psycholinguistic guessing game' *Journal of the Reading Specialist,* 6. 125-35.

Goswami, U. (1988). 'Orthographic analogies and reading development.' *Quarterly Journal of Experimental Psychology,* 40: 239-268.

Goswami, U. (1992). Towards orthographic analogy model of reading development. Decoding vowel graphemes. In *Beginning Reading.* Submitted to Journal of Experimental Child Psychology.

Goswami, U. (1993). Orthographic analogies and reading development. *The Psychologist, Vol.6, No.7, July 1993.*

Goswani, U. (1994). The Role of Analogies in Reading Development, *Support for Learning,* Vol. 9, No. 1, pp. 22-26.

Goswami, U. and Bryant, P. (1990). *Phonological Skills and Learning to Read.* Hillsdale, New Jersey: Erlbaum Assoc.

Hickey, M. (1977). *Dyslexia: A Language Training Course for Teachers and Learners.* Better Books, Bath.

Hulme, C. (1981). *Reading Retardation and Multi-Sensory Teaching.* London: Routledge & Kegan Paul.

Hunter-Carsch, M. (1990). 'Learning strategies for pupils with literacy difficulties. Motivation, meaning and imagery' in *Children's Difficulties in Reading, Spelling and Writing*. Pumfrey, P. and Elliott, C. (Eds).

Johnston, R. S. (1994). The importance of letter knowledge to the emergence of phonemic awareness in pre-school children: implications for learning to read in Links 15, Vol. 1, No. 3, pp. 29-31.

Johnston, R. S. and Thomson, G. B. (1989). 'Is dependence on phonological information in children's reading a product of instructional approach?' *Journal of Experimental Child Psychology*, 48: 131-45.

Jorm, A. F. and Share, D. L. (1983). 'Phonological Recording and Reading Acquisitions.' *Applied Psycholinguistics*, 4: 103-47.

Lane, C. H. (1987). 'Aiming Arrow at Learning Targets' *British Journal of Special Education*, 14, 3, 99-101.

Lane, C. H. (1990). 'ARROW: Alleviating Children's Reading and Spelling Difficulties' in *Children's Difficulties in Reading, Spelling and Writing*. Pumfrey, P. and Elliott, C. (Eds.). Falmer Press.

Lane, C. H. (1994). Paper presented at the first Arrow conference, Frenchay Hospital, Bristol.

La Berge, D. and Samuels, S. J. (1974). 'Toward a theory of automatic information processing in reading.' *Cognitive Psychology*, 6: 293-323.

Liberman, I. Y. and Shankweiler, D. (1985) Phonology and the problems of learning to read and write. *Remedial and Special Education*, 6:8-17.

Liberman, I. Y., Shankweiler, D., Liberman, A. M., Fowler, L. and Fischer, F. W. (1977). 'Phonetic segmentation and recording in the beginning reader' in *Toward a Psychology of Reading*, Robert, A. S. and Scarborough, D. L. (Eds.). Erlbaum Assoc.

Maker, L. and Brown, A. L. (1984). 'Metacognitive skills in reading.' in *Handbook of Reading Research*, Pearson, P. D. (Ed.). 353-94. New York: Longman.

Maria, K. (1986). *Adapting the new comprehension techniques for the learning disabled child*. Paper presented to the 13th Annual Conference of the N.J. Branch of the Orton Dyslexia Society. New York.

McKeown, M., Beck, I., Sinatra, G. and Loxter Mann, J. (1992). 'The contribution of prior knowledge and coherent text to comprehension.' *Reading Research Quarterly*, pp. 78-93.

Niklasson, M. (1993). *Adding Meaning to Life – A Matter of Experience*. Paper presented at 5th European Conference of Neuro-Developmental Delay in Children with Specific Learning Difficulties. Chester, England.

Orton, J. (1966). 'The Orton-Gillingham Approach.' in *The Disabled Reader*. Money, J. (Ed.). 119-46. Baltimore. The John Hopkins' University Press.

Palincsar, A. and Brown, A. (1985). 'Reciprocal Teaching: A means to a meaningful end.' In *Reading Education*, Osborn, J., Wilson, P. T. and Anderson, R. C. (Eds.). 199-310 Lexington MD:DC Heath.

Pennington, B. F., Lefly, D. L., Van Orden, G. C., Bookman, M. O. and Smith, S. D. (1987). 'Is Phonology by-passed in normal or dyslexic development? *Annals of Dyslexia*, 37:62-89.

Rack, J., Snowling, M. and Olsen, R. (1992). 'Reading Deficit in Developmental Dyslexia.' *A Review: Reading Research Quarterly*, pp. 28-53.

Reason, R., Brown, B., Cole, M. and Gregory, M. (1988). 'Does the "Specific" in "Specific Learning Difficulties" make a difference to the way we teach?' *Support for Learning*, Vol. 3, No. 4., pp. 230-236.

Reid, E. (1986). 'Practicing Effective Instruction.' *Exceptional Children*, 52: 510-519.

Rowe, M. (1987). 'Arrow in Free Flight.' *Teacher of the Deaf*, 11,2. pp. 42-54.

Rumelhart, D. R. (1980). 'Schemata: The building blocks of cognition.' in *Theoretical Issues in Reading and Comprehension*, Spiro, R.J., Bruce, B. T. and Brewer, W. I. (Eds.). 33-58. Lawrence Erlbaum Assoc.

Slingerland, B. H. (1971). 'A Multi-Sensory Approach to Language Arts for Specific Language Disability Children.' *A Guide for Primary Teachers.* Cambridge M.A. Education Publishing Service.

Smith, F. (1989). 'Conflicting Approaches to Reading Research and Instruction.' in *Theory and Practice of Early Reading*, Vol. 2. Beswick, L. B., Weaver, P. A. and Goodman, L. (Eds.). Erlbaum Assoc.

Solity, J. and Bull, S. (1987). *Special Needs – Bridging the Curriculum Gap.* Open University Press. Milton Keynes.

Stanovich, K. E. (1984). 'The interactive-compensatory model of reading. A confluence of developmental, experimental and education psychology.' *Remedial and Special Education,* 5:11-19.

Stanovich, K. E. (1986). 'Mathew effects in reading: Some consequences of individual differences in the acquisition of literacy. *Reading Research Quarterly, 21:360-407.*

Stanovich, K. E. (1988). 'Explaining the difference between the dyslexic and the garden-variety poor readers: the phonological core model'. *Journal of Learning Disability* 21, 10, 590-604.

Stanovich, K. E. (1992). 'Speculations on the causes and consequences of individual differences in early reading acquisition.' In Gouch, P. B., Ehri, L. C. and Treiman, R. (Eds.). *Reading Acquisition,* pp. 65-106. Hillshale, N.J. Erlbaum.

Stanovich, K. E., Nathan, R. G. and Zolman, U. E. (1985). 'The Developmental Lag Hypothesis in Reading.' *Child Development,* 59: 71-86.

Thomson, M. (1990). 'Evaluating Teaching Programmes for Children with Specific Learning Difficulties.' in *Children's Difficulties in Reading, Spelling and Writing.* Pumfrey, P. and Elliott, C. (Eds.). Falmer Press.

Thomson, M. E. (1994). How children with dyslexia respond to specialised teaching; some practical and theoretical issues in Hales, G. (Ed.) *Dyslexia Matters.* Whurr Publishers.

Waterland, L. (1986). *Read with Me: An Apprenticeship Approach to Reading.* The Thimble Press, Stroud.

Williams, J. P. (1986). 'Teaching children to identify the main idea of expository texts.' *Exceptional Children* 53: 163-68

Wise, B. W., Olson, R. K. and Treiman, R. (1990). 'Subsyllabic units in computerised reading instruction. Onset rime vs. post vowel segmentation.' *Journal of Experimental Child Psychology,* 49: 11-19.

READING DISORDERS – DO POOR READERS HAVE PHONOLOGICAL PROBLEMS?

RHONA JOHNSTON

INTRODUCTION

There is currently a major debate in research into specific reading disorders – the issue is whether or not the problems experienced by poor readers can be characterised as being due to a phonological disorder. This has led research in recent years to concentrate heavily on the phonological aspects of reading and the phonological skills which underlie learning to read, to the detriment of the understanding not only of the visual processes involved in reading but also of the interaction between visual and phonological processes.

THE DUAL ROUTE MODEL

The dual route model of skilled adult reading has had a major impact on the theorising about developmental reading problems (Coltheart, 1978). This proposes that there are two routes to skilled reading. There is the direct visual route, which gives direct access to a word's meaning or pronunciation. This is similar to the idea of a 'sight' vocabulary. It must operate with irregular words such as 'aisle', and can also operate with regular words such as 'hand'. Regular words, on the other hand, might also be read by the indirect phonological route, which operates by converting letters and letter sequences into sounds. This must occur for unfamiliar words and non-words, e.g. 'poast', for which the direct route would be ineffective. This route is similar to a phonic approach. The dual route model is intuitively appealing, and seems to fit well with the idea that some children's problems in reading seem to be on the visual side, whereas others seem to have problems on the phonological side. However, the model has had the unfortunate consequence, in developmental studies, of leading us to imagine that learning to recognise words by sight, and learning to 'sound out' unfamiliar words, are two separate processes.

RESEARCH

There are two areas of research which have led to the view that children's success in reading is largely determined by the development of their phonological skills.

The first of these relates to the development of phonological awareness. A number of studies have shown that pre-school phonological awareness skills, e.g. the ability to detect the odd word out in auditorily presented sequences of words such as 'hat, hill, hub, rug', were predictive of later reading development (e.g. Bradley and Bryant, 1983). Several studies have been carried out to train pre-school and school age children in phonological segmentation tasks to see whether this enhances reading ability (e.g. Bradley and Bryant, 1983; Lundberg, 1988; Hulme *et al.*, 1992). Successful enhancement of reading skill in such studies has led to the view that reading difficulties are due to poor readers having impaired phonological skills. There are a number of reasons for suggesting that this is too simplistic a view.

Firstly, the majority of these programmes have been successful only when the children were taught about sounds in relation to letters (e.g. Bradley and Bryant, 1983; Hulme *et al.*, 1992). The paper by Bradley and Bryant (1983) is probably the best known of these studies, but it is widely misreported. In this study, children who had weak pre-school phonological awareness skills were trained to categorise sounds. In one condition, this was carried out purely auditorily, and in another condition, the children were shown plastic letters when trained on the sounds. Only in the latter condition was there a significant increment in reading ability. Hulme *et al.* (1992) similarly found that phonological training alone did not enhance reading performance. These studies point to the importance of teaching children with reading problems how to map letters and letter sequences onto sounds; they do not support the view that training in the auditory analysis of words alone is efficacious.

A further problem is the evidence that learning to read itself contributes to phonemic segmentation ability. Morais *et al.* (1979) found that Portuguese adult illiterates who had started to learn to read as adults could do phoneme deletion tasks, e.g. they could say what sound is left if you take the 'f' from 'flat'. However, adults from a similar background who had not learnt to read could not do the tasks.

The idea that all developmental reading problems can be ascribed to a causative underlying phonological disorder is therefore in severe difficulty. There would appear to be a reciprocal relationship between the development of phonological skill and learning to read, not a simple causal one.

The second major area of research which implicates phonological problems as a cause of reading difficulties involves examining the performance of poor readers on reading tasks. For a while, the evidence in this area, based on several case studies describing poor readers with severe phonological problems (e.g. Johnston, 1983; Temple and Marshall, 1983), weighed heavily in favour of the phonological deficit explanation. Case studies, however, do not tell us how typical phonological reading problems are, although group studies in the early 1980s did suggest that such problems were widespread. These group studies asked poor readers to read non-words in order to assess their phonological reading skill. (This task is a pure test of decoding ability; with real words there is the possibility that the item may be in their sight vocabulary.) The poor readers' performance on these non-words was compared with that of reading age controls, i.e. younger normal readers reading at the same level as the poor readers. The argument is that if poor readers read non-words less well than their reading age controls, despite being matched on word reading ability, then this provides evidence of a phonological reading disorder. Studies such as Snowling's (1981) did find poor readers to be impaired in reading non-words for reading age; however, other studies have failed to find this deficit (e.g. Treiman and Hirsh-Pasek, 1985; Johnston *et al.*, 1987a). This has posed severe difficulties for the hypothesis that most poor readers have problems with the phonological aspects of reading.

THE WAY FORWARD

In an attempt to resolve this issue, Rack *et al.* (1992) reviewed the ten studies which have shown this deficit, and the six which have not. Their approach was to focus on what they believed to be the methodological weaknesses in the six studies which did not find a non-word naming deficit. They suggested, for example, that non-words of insufficient complexity were used in these studies since Snowling (1981) had found that poor readers' difficulties were most pronounced with complex polysyllabic non-words, whereas some of the studies failing to find a non-word naming problem used simple one syllable non-words. However, Rack *et al.* overlooked the fact that some studies which found a non-word naming deficit used the same non-word stimuli as studies which did not find a non-word naming deficit, e.g. Holligan and Johnston (1988) versus Johnston *et al.* (1987a). This suggests that there is variation in the kinds of problems experienced by different groups of poor readers.

Rack *et al.* also failed to deal with the fact that the dual route model predicts that if a phonological approach is being taken to reading, then regular words should be read better than irregular words so that poor readers suffering from a phonological deficit should not show a regular word advantage. However, in most studies, poor readers show an advantage in reading regular words. Furthermore, in the study by Holligan and Johnston (1988) the poor readers had problems in reading non-words but showed a normal regular word advantage compared with their reading age controls. According to the dual route model, this should not happen, as the indirect phonological route is said to be responsible for the reading of both regular words and non-words. If this route is deficient then there should be evidence for this in both tasks.

In trying to resolve these problems in the literature, I have taken the view that we should be examining children's visual as well as their phonological skills, as both of these processes are used in reading and they may well interact. Marjorie Anderson and I assessed both the visual and phonological segmentation skills of poor readers. In order to test phonological ability, we used two tasks. One of them was a version of Bradley and Bryant's (1983) odd word out task, and the other was a phoneme deletion task, where the child is asked to say what sound is left if you take the 'f' sound from the word 'flat'. Visual segmentation skills were measured by asking the children to detect shapes embedded in pictures, e.g. finding a triangle hidden within a clown's face.

So far, we have studied 80 poor readers with an average age of 10, comparing them with normal readers aged 10 (the chronological age controls) and normal readers aged 8 (the reading age controls). In addition to the visual and phonological segmentation tasks, we asked them to read regular and irregular words, and one and two syllable non-words (e.g. 'mip', 'daspog'). The first result to strike us was that the poor readers performed appropriately for reading age on the two phonological segmentation tasks. We therefore had to conclude that there was no evidence that these children were suffering from an underlying phonological disorder which was causing their reading problems.

However, a different picture emerged when we looked at the reading tasks. Although the poor readers showed a regular word advantage, the effect was smaller than it should have been for reading age. Furthermore, the poor readers were impaired at reading both the one and two syllable non-words for their reading level. There was evidence, therefore, of phonological reading problems. How could this be explained if their phonological skills in the auditory domain were appropriate for reading age?

We found the answer to lie in the poor readers' visual segmentation skills. The poor readers performed normally for chronological age on this task, this skill apparently developing independently of reading ability. We showed that absolute levels of visual segmentation ability were associated with the extent to which a regular word advantage was shown. Those poor readers who were good at the visual segmentation task showed a very small regular word advantage. It was the disparity between visual and phonological segmentation ability, however, which accounted for the non-word naming deficit. Those poor readers who had a strong advantage on the visual task compared to the phonological task had the most difficulty in reading non-words. Poor readers who did not have this imbalance used a phonological approach to reading.

This suggests that we need to look at the interaction between visual and phonological segmentation ability in order to explain how individual poor readers approach reading tasks. We believe that poor readers with good visual segmentation ability adopt a rather global visual approach to reading, i.e. they read to their strengths. It seems that they find it hard to read by a phonological approach because these skills are relatively weak, not because these skills are deficient in absolute terms. Visual segmentation ability is known to be associated with IQ, so these children are likely to be the most intellectually able children. Less able children do not have this disparity between visual and phonological ability, and are better able to use a phonological approach to reading.

However, this pattern of performance was only found in reading. The approach the poor readers took to spelling was unaffected by the disparity between their visual and phonological segmentation ability, and they produced as many phonologically accurate spelling errors as their reading age controls.

SOME INTERIM CONCLUSIONS

Our current work is focused on trying to find out more about the visual approach to reading that seems to be adopted by the brighter poor readers. However, in the meantime we offer a number of conclusions:

1   Most poor readers' problems are not due to an underlying phonological disorder. Although many bright poor readers do have difficulty with a phonological approach to reading, this is due to relatively good visual skills rather than to impaired phonological skills.

2   Training in sound analysis alone is unlikely to enhance reading skill in poor readers.

3   The teaching method most likely to help poor readers is a multi-sensory, phonic technique which shows children frequently occurring spelling patterns and how they sound. This is not a form of phonological training as such, and should not be confused with going

from sound to spelling, as in the Elkonin method advocated in Reading Recovery.

4   The imbalance between visual and phonological segmentation ability in poor readers will be fairly small in the early stages of schooling. However, visual skills develop with increasing chronological age, whereas phonological segmentation skills are tied to reading development. An imbalance will therefore develop in many of these children as they get older. This would suggest that remedial help of a phonics type should be given as early as possible, as it may reduce the number of poor readers who adopt a global visual approach to reading. At the same time, the phonics approach should also help the less able poor readers, who we found were able to use a phonological approach to reading.

We do not argue that phonological skills are unimportant – children need to be able to use a phonological approach to reading as this enables them to decode unfamiliar words when reading text. It is not surprising, therefore, that phonological skills correlate with reading attainment. The performance of the lower ability children in our study, however, shows that being able to use a phonological approach to reading does not mean that reading will develop at the normal rate. What, then, is the cause of reading disorders in most poor readers? Clearly we need to look more closely at other areas of difficulty that poor readers are known to have. We know that consistent weaknesses have been found in short-term memory, and that poor readers often performing like their reading age rather than their chronological age controls on these 5 tasks (e.g. Johnston *et al.* 1987b). However, an area worthy of further investigation is long-term memory. We know that one of the major failings of poor readers is that they do not recognise words to which they have been repeatedly exposed. This is clearly a long-term memory failure, which may be related to the short-term memory deficit, yet it is an area which has received very little consideration in the literature.

REFERENCES

Bradley, L. and Bryant, P. E. (1983). 'Categorising sounds and learning to read – a causal connection.' *Nature,* 301, 419-421.

Coltheart, M. (1978). 'Lexical access in simple reading tasks' in Underwood G. (Ed.), *Strategies of Information Processing.* London. Academic Press.

Holligan, C. and Johnston, R. S. (1988). 'The use of phonological information by good and poor readers in memory and reading tasks.' *Memory and Cognition,* 16, 522-532.

Hulme, C., Hatcher, P., and Ellis, A., (1992). 'Improving literacy skills in poor readers – the importance of integrating the teaching of phonological and reading skills.' *International Journal of Psychology,* 17, 65.

Johnston, R. S. (1983). 'Developmental deep dyslexia?' *Cortex,* 19, 133-139.

Johnston, R. S., Rugg, M. D. and Scott, T. (1987a). 'The influence of phonology on good and poor readers when reading for meaning.' *Journal of Memory and Language,* 26, 57-68.

Lundberg, I., Frost, J., and Petersen, O. P. (1988). 'Effects of an extensive programme for stimulating phonological awareness in pre-school children.' *Reading Research Quarterly,* 23, 263-284.

Morais, J., Cary, L., Alegria, J., and Bertelson, P., (1979). 'Does awareness of speech as a sequence of phonemes arise spontaneously?' *Cognition,* 7,323-331.

Rack, J. P., Snowling, M. J. and Olson, R. K. (1992). 'The non-word reading deficit in developmental dyslexia – a review.' *Reading Research Quarterly,* 27, 28-53.

Snowling, M. J. (1981). 'Phonemic deficits in developmental dyslexia.' *Psychological Research,* 43, 219-234.

Temple, C. M. and Marshall, J. C. (1983). 'A case study of developmental phonological dyslexia.' *British Journal of Psychology,* 74, 517-533.

Treima, N R. and Hirsh-Pasek, K., (1985). 'Are there qualitative differences in reading behaviour between dyslexics and normal readers?' *Memory and Cognition,* 13, 357-364.

PHONEMIC AWARENESS AND CONCEPTS OF PRINT IN THE NURSERY SCHOOL

MEG HOUSTON
DIANE PEPPER
LINDA WATSON

The massive body of evidence linking reading skills to underlying phonological skills has come from a variety of sources, including studies of dyslexic children. Phonological awareness has been determined as being a powerful predictor of reading ability.

Research findings indicate that children become aware of rhyme and alliteration before they go to school and that this can significantly influence their eventual success in learning to read and spell.

Recent work in the field would suggest that simply to teach the alphabet or to teach phonemic segmentation in a 'skill and drill' way is not enough to significantly affect reading development, but that if all aspects of phonemic awareness are presented in a purposeful metacognitive way the effect can be greatly enhanced.

Understanding of the concepts about print and understanding of the link between the spoken and the written word are also elements that pave the way to success in reading.

Research into general literacy development and research into specific difficulties with print seem to come to their closest relationship in the area of phonological awareness.

Teachers of the nineties have stopped the pendulum of the great reading debate midway and are acknowledging that polarised views are not helpful. 'Top-down' and 'bottom up' approaches sit happily together, and the mix can be adjusted to meet the real needs of each individual child. The many aspects of phonological awareness can be promoted in a meaningful and enjoyable way that meets all the criteria for child-centred good practice.

RATIONALE

'Early Intervention', 'Recovery Programmes' and 'Phonological Awareness' are now familiar concepts in our classrooms, but they seem to be initiated after a child has experienced some degree of failure. Despite very convincing evidence relating to phonological skills in pre-school children, our nursery classes are not realising the full implications of the research.

Logic tells us that if an intervention is to be 'early' it must start in the nursery. If young children are aware of alliteration and rhyme before they go to school, then, surely, we should capitalise on this phonological awareness by fostering, promoting and extending it. If, as a result, reading difficulties are reduced, then Recovery Programmes will be needed for far fewer children.

Much guidance has been offered on the form, structure and pacing of interventions designed to help children with reading difficulties. Little guidance has been offered on the form-structure and pacing of interventions designed to promote phonological awareness, letter identity knowledge and concepts about print in the nursery. Of the little that is offered, nothing matches the degree of clarity and specificity for work with older failing readers.

AIM

The aim of our project is to develop, within the framework of sound nursery philosophy and practice, a range of activities and approaches which children will enjoy and which will involve them in playing with words and sounds. It is hoped to develop children's sensitivity to sounds to a level which will prevent or greatly reduce reading difficulties at the primary stage. The development of practice to improve phonological awareness will be accompanied by activities to develop awareness of the forms, functions and uses of print and to develop letter identity knowledge.

Research would suggest that an initiative such as this in the nursery class should create a very sound foundation from which to approach beginning reading in P1. It should also assist, concurrent with other indicators, in the early identification of children with specific learning difficulties.

THE PROJECT

The project is planned over four years and the nursery intervention is to be assessed quantitatively and qualitatively by measuring various outcomes at P1, P2 and P3, and by other observations, interviews and questionnaires.

There is a comparison group in the nursery's base school and a matched control group in another nursery.

THE INTERVENTION

August to October

Nursery Rhymes as often as possible but at least one session every day for both the morning and the afternoon class.

Particular concentration on five Nursery Rhymes with all children:

> Jack and Jill
> Humpty Dumpty
> Baa Baa Black Sheep
> Twinkle Twinkle
> Hickory Dickory Dock

> Also: Singing Games
> Poems
> Finger Play Games
> Daily story using a Rhyming or Alliterative Book.

Examples:

Games and Action Songs –	Farmer's in his Den
	Ring-a-ring-a-roses
	Heads, Shoulders Knees and Toes
	In and out the Dusty Bluebells
	Eyes Nose Cheeky Cheeky Chin
Counting Songs and Rhymes	One Two Buckle my Shoes
	Old Joe Braddleum
	One Man went to Mow
	One, two, three, four, five
Songs	Lavenders Blue
	London Bridge
	London's Burning
	In a Cottage in a Wood

Poems	When we were Very Young
	Now we are Six
Stories	Terrible, Terrible Tiger
	Each Peach Pear Plum
	Peepo
	Dr Seuss Books
	Two Shoes, New Shoes
	My Cat Likes to Hide in Boxes.

November to December.

As August to October, plus:

Work with small groups randomly chosen.
Each group given 2 x 10 minute sessions per week.

Format:

1   Nursery Rhyme chosen to say or sing together.

2   Oral cloze.

3   Start a rhyme and group finish it.

4   Take a word from the rhyme and ask for words that sound like it:

   'What sounds like sheep?'

   'What sounds like hill'' etc.

   Words and non-words valued equally, but differentiated.

5   Use of Rhyme Readers and Silly Rhyme Cards:

   e.g.   'A crook trying to cook a book on a hook'
      'What words sound the same?'
      'What words look the same?'

   Introduction of Games like:
      Snap
      Happy Families
      Animal Lotto
   to reinforce rhyming and add expressive rhyming.

   Art work linked to Nursery Rhymes:
      'Guess which Rhyme I've painted!'

   Identification of Initial Letters.

   Words and Names that start with the same sound.

Literacy, Language and Learning

Size of Words – big and small.

Counting letters in words.

Counting words in sentences.

January to April

As November to December, plus:

Targeting the four year olds for:

1   Revision of previous work.
2   Encouraging automaticity with the body of knowledge.
3   Establishing a wider understanding of 'words that sound the same.'
4   Extending the use of oral cloze.
5   Odd one out game – using Lynette Bradley's 3 conditions:

e.g. cat	hat	fan	rat
pat	fit	bat	hat
rod	rot	box	rock

Singing and clapping to investigate word length.

Clapping and stamping syllables, especially with own names.

Using Alphabet books to teach the name and sound of letters.

Looking at the letters in own name.

Concepts, format and function of print.

Language of books – beginning, end, title, author, picture, print, etc.

May to June

As before, plus:

The introduction of a BBC computer into the nursery giving children daily opportunities to use an Alphabet Programme

Examples of Qualitative Data collected at the halfway stage of the Project (2 years on)

Timed observations of free play in the experimental nursery were undertaken by the Nursery Teacher. Additional observations by the NSO and by an independent professional were undertaken.

Some examples of the child/child interactions in the free play situation involving various children from both a.m. and p.m. groups are as follows:

- Book and clock matching with one child leading a group who were looking at the Time book and setting the clock accordingly.

- Three boys using sticklebricks to make letters F H and L.

- Using a woodblock in the music corner to 'tick' while singing Hickory Dickory Dock.

- Writing names in the glueing corner.

- One child reading a notice on the wall 'Well it's my name and it's something about me.' She then copied it down on a piece of paper.

- Two boys reading from the wall. 'It says 'Fraser' cos its got a F and two r's.'

- Katrina writing all over a piece of paper.

- One boy asks for his address to be written down as he needs it to fill in an application form on a cornflakes packet.

- One child made a treasure map with a big X on it and said, 'X marks the spot.'

- One child 'reading' a rhyme book to a group, holding up the book and pointing to the words.

- Glueing area – Lynsay writing her name and saying 'L for Lynsay.'

- Two children reading 'What's the Time Mr Wolf' – saying the words together and pointing to them together, self correcting as they went along.

- Two children reading all the names on flags in the crispie corner.

- Glueing corner – a group singing nursery rhymes to each other as they worked.

- One child spelling out another's name for him to write.

- A group making initial letters in the sand tray.

- 3 girls matching words in Hey Diddle Diddle book to the same words on the wall chart.

- Two boys singing nursery rhymes to each other in the glueing area. 'I'll miss out words and see if you can get them.'
  Took turns at this then started changing the rhyme to make it funny.

Observations in the control nursery showed language and imaginative play typical for the age group. There was much talk and interaction around babies, policemen, cars and robots.

Nursery rhymes, and name writing were teacher-led and were not observed to transfer to free play.

Written notices were small and were used to identify childrens' paintings and models.

This nursery shows normal good practice where a great deal of input is given to extending language and concepts and socialisation.

Interviews with P1 teachers suggested that the children who had had the nursery intervention were indeed making a very good start to beginning reading. There was the normal spread of achievement but unusually there were no distressed or 'stuck' children.

Unexpected bonuses came in their reports that the children were using their automaticity with nursery rhymes to display discussion skills, Socratic dialogue and thinking skills far beyond what might be expected in P1.

The teachers stated a qualitative difference in listening, retaining knowledge, in working together, in the sense of belonging to a group, in turn taking, in the curiosity and interest shown.

One interesting example is when asked to give other words beginning with a certain letter these children took joy in producing a vast list and adding to it in an on-going way all day, in the cloakroom, after lunch, after playing and even the next day.

A significant comparison can be made with statements by the teachers of the control group. On the one hand to get nursery children to realise that work should be completed and certain tasks and activities must be done and that the child-centred 'choosing' approach does not happen all day in P1 and with statements by the P1 teachers of the experimental class that these children did not have the 'I don't want to do that' syndrome, but were happy to engage in set group, individual, or class activities.

Parent questionnaires showed that the phonemic awareness intervention had promoted a very high level of carry over from nursery to home. The children were constantly making statements about, asking questions about, and playing with words and sounds and print.

CONCLUSIONS

All concerned feel that the intervention has been successful on many levels. The daily format was greatly enhanced by the nursery teacher's ability to pick up on and respond appropriately to the many opportunities presented by the children to promote, foster and enhance rhyming, alliteration, letter knowledge and concepts about print. Her watchword over the two years has been – 'A chance missed is a chance lost!'

Nursery teachers who make the decision to bring print, phonics and the alphabet into the nursery will quickly join us in the realisation that we can make a significant difference to the future literacy skills of a great many children, if we guide them through their puzzlement and wonder, join them in the fun and joy of playing with words, accept the fact that for part of the day, at least, most children enjoy organised, purposeful activities and try never to underestimate the knowledge and abilities that children bring to school with them.

Over the next two years we hope that our measures of outcomes will give positive quantitative feedback to our intervention.

IMPLICATIONS

We feel we have made a start in providing a 'How to' to answer the 'Why to' of the researchers.

If more nursery teachers join us, then the intervention can be made more finely tuned and more effective.

The results of the parent interviews would suggest that much could be gained from involving parents in a more constructive way.

The intervention cost nothing in monetary terms. Personal reading from the mass of available literature helped us to form the philosophy and rationale that underpins the work.

The biggest hurdle for some people to overcome may be the dispelling of the myth that print has no place in the nursery.

Lothian Region has, at this point, agreed to fund a video of the intervention. We hope to show that activities related to print and phonological awareness can be infused into normal good practice. We hope to highlight that a nursery teacher can guide, direct and respond to opportunities without losing the child-centred ethos. We hope to show the fun and enjoyment nursery children can have in group work and whole class work where chants, rhymes and rhythms related to print are the focus.

The skills and knowledge particular to nursery teachers in terms of classroom management, differentiation, diagnostic assessment and sheer range of approaches are not always acknowledged by their colleagues in other sectors. They are well placed to promote phonemic awareness in a way that could make a significant difference to the educational future of many children.

COMPENSATING FOR LITERACY DELAY: PROVIDING MEANINGFUL EXPERIENCE FOR DELAYED LEARNERS

CYRIL HELLIER

Current consideration of effective intervention in the event of reading difficulty focuses on phonological processing. As Sylva and Hurry (1995) conclude:

"On the basis of current knowledge it seems likely that if there is a specific cause for reading disability at all, it resides in the area of phonological awareness."

Reason and Boote (1994) distinguish the three interwoven and multiplying areas of fluency, meaning and phonic skills in considering intervention/teaching strategies. This paper develops the theme of closing the gap for delayed literacy learners in Hellier (1994). It focuses upon meaningful experience in all areas of literacy, but acknowledges the crucial part played in the other two areas. The author believes the further area of motivation to be critical, and suggests that to a large extent, it can be dealt with by the timely provision of planned and meaningful literacy experience.

Skilled and unhindered readers can read individual letters, whole words, use context to decipher unfamiliar words, follow strings of meaning and process complex information automatically; they possess phonemic awareness and skills of analysis, which are increasingly recognised as lacking in those experiencing reading difficulties, however characterised. The majority spend considerable periods of time applying, practising and developing their skills in their own time and outside of school settings. Sylva and Hurry (*op cit*) acknowledge this to be a major factor in developing vocabulary, understanding and skills.

It is, therefore, a fundamental paradox that the poor or delayed reader is doubly disadvantaged by both his (the literature suggests that it far more likely to be a boy, hence my use of 'he') inferior literacy skills and the compounding factor of cumulative lack of experience of reading as a meaningful and rewarding activity. The poor reader lacks the skills and often the confidence to spend time in unrewarding activity and so the experience gap develops. This is particularly the case for the child with specific learning difficulties/dyslexia.

The literature on this group, makes for confusing reading, given the differences in definition; incidence is dependent on differing parent, professional discipline, legal and political opinion. It is probably safe to conclude that children experiencing severe literacy, and other associated learning difficulties, range from one to four per cent of the pupil population. The literature would suggest that many pupils remain unidentified. Beyond this category, a significant minority of students finish formal education, lacking functionally independent use of literacy skills and the desire to continue to utilise them. The scale of this problem in the western world, Kozol (1985), should not be underestimated. Although my focus is on specific literacy difficulties/dyslexia, I would argue that this paper has relevance to the teaching of literacy delivered in every classroom.

My own view is that the question often asked by the practitioner as to who exactly we are talking about, can only be answered in functional terms using a full description of the child's history and his strengths and weaknesses. Given that the practitioner's primary goal is to teach as effectively as possible according to the individual's needs, then the debate concerning definitions and labels can appear rather sterile at the coal face. In their wide ranging inquiry into specific learning difficulties/dyslexia, Pumfrey and Reason (1991), provide backing for such a view:

> *"It is now better appreciated that studies using chronological age or mental age matched controls, as opposed to reading age matched controls are confounded by intractable 'chicken and egg' problems of interpretation concerning causality. Proposed symptoms and deficits could just as likely be a consequence of reading experience as a cause of reading difficulty."*

Whatever the criteria applied in distinguishing those with specific learning difficulties from 'backward readers', it is most likely the case that all groups of poor or delayed readers share a lack of adequate and positive reading experience.

Much of the literature on teaching dyslexi, tends to focus on individualised and cumulative multi-sensory programmes which aim to minimise the risk of failure, through a step-by-step approach. Such painstaking 'bottom up' strategies which develop analytic subskills, (Lewis and Fowell-Jones, 1993), are designed to ensure that learning occurs successfully, albeit slowly. Meaning is subservient to technical competence.

By way of contrast, Reading Recovery, an extension of mainstream teaching, the central plank of support delivered as early intervention to all unsuccessful children at the end of one year of schooling, is not focused upon any particular sub-group. Contrary to its narrower title, it aims to concurrently teach individual children, global understanding of the purposes of literacy, as well as specific skills in reading, writing and spelling. This approach, recently evaluated in England and Wales, Sylva and Hurry (*op cit*) appeared to be utilised patchily but was widely referred to across Australia, when I worked there as an educational psychologist in 1992. At the very least, I believe that in the UK context, a focus on mechanical reading skill, to the exclusion of wider pragmatic understanding of a child's situation, is ineffective and likely to lead to a less supportive response from teachers and parents. Although a child has particular difficulty in dealing with the mechanical aspects of decoding, it is important not to overstress this to the exclusion of focus on the reader's wider understandings and use of text. There are, however, advantages and disadvantages in all systems. The student in an Australian school, unlucky enough not have the expensive Reading Recovery programme available, may lack phonemic awareness and explicitly taught structures to acquire literacy skills; he also faces potential learning difficulties. Ideally, a balanced teaching programme needs to be in place in any setting. Current research previously cited, which has elucidated the skills used in effective reading, demands this if all identified factors are to be promoted.

Fads, trends, schools of thought and zeitgeists all result in changes of approach, however, resulting in possible polarisation of view. The recent politicised debate in England and Wales around the 'real books' issue is one example. One advantage in Scotland has been relative stability and slow speed of change resulting in the maintenance of more traditional methods in this area, as new methods are considered and tried. Phonics still figure large in the average Scottish Primary classroom. By contrast, in South Australia, I was struck by the rejection of old fashioned methods and the consequent lack of structured language approaches; no phonics were taught, spelling was left up to the individual to invent and literacy was developed through a guided experience model. Reading was encouraged through the use of graded and structured real book reading materials; many children, my Primary 1 son being one, learned to read very quickly. However, a significant minority of children desperately lacked effective structures and strategies to develop literacy skills. Assigning the label of Dyslexia had fallen out of fashion, resulting in increasing numbers of parents seeking diagnosis of Attention Deficit Disorder instead.

As a practitioner working for 17 years, I have frequently received referrals of pupils experiencing specific learning difficulties; children identified in this situation tend to share various similar attributes which are enduring across different cultural contexts. These include varying degrees of insight into their difficulties, such that they can talk about their difficulties. The intellectually more able child usually develops a greater degree of self-awareness earlier on; the growth of defensive strategies to protect themselves against the gradual awareness that they do have a problem, and the expression of frustration is often in an indirect manner. Initially, this is most apparent at home in the presence of family members, with whom they are less guarded and to whom they are more inclined to express feelings.

Much remains to be written about the effective response to specific learning/ difficulties, as Biggar and Barr (1993) suggest in their plea for 'differentiation of the interpersonal to match differentiation of the curriculum'.

If left unrecognised and there is a lack in support to deal with genuine learning difficulties, then secondary problems often arise, usually of a social nature. Peers may be unsympathetic, parents may exert undue pressure, and teachers may perceive their difficulties in inappropriate terms; these include explanatory hypotheses such as 'unrealistic' or 'overprotective' parents, 'lazy' or 'low potential' pupils.

Numerous variables affect the response of the child to his situation; these include:

- The age at which difficulties have been recognised and responded to;
- the degree of sympathy and understanding they have experienced in coming to terms with their learning difficulties;
- the degree of parental support,` as opposed to pressure;
- the teacher's attitude and response in terms of modified curriculum;
- peer responses;

and above all:

- the child's developing self-image and sense of self-esteem.

PRESENTING FEATURES

Following on from the variables outlined above, various presenting features may arise when pupils with specific learning difficulties are referred:

- **Evidence of significant literacy (and sometimes Maths) skills gaps** with no other obvious causal factor such as a sensory/medical impairment or a troubled home situation. One does have to be wary as other contributory factors may co-exist and be viewed as the sole ones!

- **A discrepant skill profile** as the student may appear to have adequate or good skills in areas including oral discussion, reasoning and artwork.

When further assessed, he may reveal an uneven profile with, significantly depressed reading age and a relatively superior comprehension age – many referred pupils who struggle with analytic and phonological aspects of text still manage to extract a superior degree of meaning. Pupils scoring reading ages of between six and seven years invariably display superior reading comprehension ages, by six to 24 months. A minority however, spend so much time and energy processing the technical demands of text, that their comprehension is equal to or behind their reading age.

Bakker (1992) hypothesises two distinct groups of dyslexia, 'L' and 'P', mediated by left and right cerebral hemispheres respectively. Clinical experience of the author is consistent with this view; pupils in the hypothesised L group, may appear to read rather impulsively and to be desperately in search of meaning, making guesses based on approximations of the superficial aspects of each word. They **are** able to extract some meaning from context, utilising metacognitive strategies, but are held back from good performance by poor word recognition and word attack skills. This inevitably also results in delayed spelling, pupils lacking adequate phonic structures and decoding skills to differing degrees.

In contrast, in the P group, children reflect earlier neurological development; they may read laboriously slowly using analytic strategies, decoding with the phonic knowledge which they have struggled to acquire; and meaning is usually lost as a result of the processing demands of decoding. Spelling skills remain poorly developed. What distinguishes the two groups is the differing facility to use left brain processes to extract meaning, over and above the right brain ones, which focus on letter and sound recognition.

- A presentation where **the child is cast as lazy or lacking in motivation**; this is especially the case for the older pupil of third year of schooling onwards. I was struck by the relatively early age of referral in Australia, many children appearing with literacy difficulties by the end of first year at school. This is a result of significant differences in mainstream teaching methodology, I believe – the downside of a change in emphasis to global strategies, to the exclusion of analytic/phonic methods in classrooms. Australia still has its share of literacy failures throughout the age ranges, in school and beyond, despite the current zeitgeist!

- **Adjustment difficulties** which initially often figure at home; the school may or may not be aware of these. Some referrals are parent-initiated against the wishes of the school, who may be unsympathetic.

If they are present at school, adjustment difficulties can reflect the full range of diversionary and avoidance strategies, from withdrawal to active disruption. Over time, social problems may develop at school and these may be the first signs which alert teaching staff to make referral to outside agencies. At the earliest, these appear in my practice in Scotland by the second year of school and may include work avoidance in specific tasks and/or minor social difficulties. In the most extreme cases, late referral of disaffected secondary pupils is the first indication to outside agencies. Referrals are, on occasion, made in the wake of a prolonged sequence of behaviour management practices. When reading a pupil's school file, in such cases, a focus on learning issues although raised by relatively sympathetic class teachers historically, has often been displaced over time by focus on social and behavioural matters.

IMPLICATIONS FOR INTERVENTION

In aiming to close the gap as far as possible, assessment should focus on functional aspects of a child's performance in areas of difficulty. Close scrutiny of strengths and weaknesses in the actual areas of skill application provide the best assessment, allowing intervention to follow directly on. Kemp (1987) typifies this approach.

The typical scenario in the UK includes the situation where the child's functional literacy skills, matched by stage appropriate material, result in an increasing gap developing between these, his interests and oral understandings; the challenge is to help provide experience as early as possible, to offset the cumulative losses which otherwise accrue. These may include lowered self-esteem, lack of general knowledge and failure to make adequate progress in the wider curriculum.

To minimise such effects, the student needs:

- **Early identification** by the second year at school, ideally speaking. Although the literature reflects that we are at an early stage of being able to define predictive measures to anticipate failure, it is the case that once difficulties are visible, the experience of failure should be minimised for all children at risk. The need is for all involved to be aware; Pumfrey and Reason (*op cit*) recommend that:

"Educational psychologists and teachers continue to develop skills and methods to effect early identification of children who are at risk of poor literacy development."

Clearly there are needs for mainstream staff to receive in-service training, to make them more aware of these issues, and to help them to be more effective in identifying such pupils. Such support has been patchy to date e.g. Hellier *et al.* (1991). The advantage of the global approach in Australian mainstream schools, was that children could be identified more obviously at a younger age, this being, in part, the result of few analytic strategies being present in mainstream class teaching. However, teachers, when faced by a failing student in her class, found it difficult to have explanations or effective strategies in response.

• **Supported reading experiences** of preferred material using a range of reading material, consistent with the child's age and interests:

a)   Graded and reduced demand texts, although unfashionable in some schools of thought and particularly so in Australia, do provide the opportunity to the student to experience relative success as an 'independent' reader. Pupils identified early on, by their second year at school, benefit from personalised 'organic' texts based around their world knowledge and language; these can include personalised reading material using photos of himself, familiar people, family, teaching staff, class peers etc. and familiar places and events. However, the tendency of teachers to structure and to limit experiences which may be perceived to be too difficult for the poor reader can result in very restricted experiences, especially if they are the main or the only intervention. Teaching only high frequency words, for example, which tend to lack inherent meaning, fails to capitalise on a child's knowledge of the familiar and the idiosyncratic; such factors may help a pupil to maximise his learning. An additional problem arises that judgements made about a pupil's competence when reading prepared and restricted material can result in a falsely positive impression. Wider experiences provide more challenge, interest and assessment information.

b)   Graded texts do not, however, provide adequate interest and information to older pupils and so it is essential to have regular experience of age appropriate and interest-feeding material chosen by the pupil, from the outset. The skill of actually choosing will not develop unless opportunities are made available to permit this to occur. Paired reading offers a stress-free and highly effective, research validated methodology to provide supported reading experience which fulfils many of these needs. This well documented technique, widely reported and utilised in the UK, was totally lacking in practice in South Australian schools – the bones of the technique called 'neurological impress' were present in the literature, Kemp (*op cit*), but were not used widely in the way outlined in this paper.

Supported reading experience needs to made available daily; a range of different people might be able to provide it. Peers, either age equivalent or cross age could be organised at school on a timetabled basis (Thompson 1992, for example); if times are set aside for silent reading then these would provide ideal opportunities. Settings could include reading centres in classrooms or resource libraries. The research evidence is clear that both tutors and tutees gain from such organised experiences (Topping and Lindsay, 1992). Tutors would need some training in these circumstances. Parent volunteer help could also be utilised; a further step being the training of parents themselves as part of a parental involvement programme.

c)   Earlier reference was made to phonic / analytic methods. In this respect, Australia can boast the creation of interesting innovation, using coded phonics or diacritical marks, Solomon (1992), which have now been successfully piloted in Scotland, Hellier (1993), Hellier (1995). The use of diacritical marks to reduce ambiguity between spoken and written language has been documented for over a century; however this user-friendly system represents a new and innovative attempt to reduce literacy failure, having reflected on the relative efficacy of other attempts. It teaches an unambiguous pronunciation code, principally focused on vowels, which permits accurate and secure word attack in the event of encountering unknown or confusing words. The diacritical marks based on international pronunciation marks, include a dot, a stroke or minute graphic symbol and are placed above or below normal printed text. A filled-in dot above any letter is always pro-nounced 'i' as in pig, for example; in this way the word 'busy' would be coded with a dot above the 'u'. The code is relatively simple, is always available on a card with a pictorial reminder when reading takes place, and can be ignored if the child can decode without it. In addition, the techniques used within the system promote phonemic recognition and understanding so that existing phonic knowledge is utilised more effectively. Once learned and the trained procedures followed, then a child can read any level of text that he chooses, provided that it is overwritten with the diacritical codes. In time, the need for the codes fades. Such support can significantly reduce onset of literacy failure in many pupils, and provide valuable opportu-nities to prevent associated anxiety by reducing confusion arising from the discrepancies between the spoken and the written form of language. The exciting possibility with this method is that independent reading of any material is a relatively quick prospect when overwritten with the learned codes. In this way, both technical aspects of reading are dealt with as well as allowing the extraction of meaning.

- **Supported writing experiences** need to be provided regularly with the same aims, namely to permit the pupil to experience personal written language at a level consistent with his age and abilities, rather than his skill level. Obviously, the age of the child results in different expectations, ranging from early literacy work in an infant depart-ment to examination performance in secondary education and beyond. Copying skills are usually relatively unimpaired (it may be a slow process), and are depended on by pupil and teacher. However, I am arguing for additional support, elements of which include:

  Paired writing – developing the theme so commonly associ-ated with reading, an adult or peer can provide the role of scribe to ensure that the pupil's ideas are put down relatively quickly and correctly spelt. This is possible on both an indi-vidual and a small group basis.

  Use of tape recorder – through experience, a pupil can learn to express himself on audiotape, the results being subse-quently written up by a third party (parent help could be enlisted on occasion). It would be possible in some situations for the pupil to copy the written work in his own handwriting. The end result would be for the pupil to experience the satisfaction of his ideas well written up for display purposes, to show to others. A folder of all such examples (photocopied) could then allow for a cumulative record of positive writing experiences.

Computer technology – there are numerous opportunities to utilise new technology for pupils with severe literacy difficulties.

These include:

a) The concept keyboard with personalised vocabulary overlays of the child's own world knowledge and language. This technology is particularly appropriate for the younger child or for the more delayed learner, given its limitations on vocabulary size (up to 128 words/phrases per overlay). In effect, it allows a pupil to write using only word recognition and discrimination skills. Spelling skills are not required; the advantage in the UK is that this technology is widely available in most schools. (In contrast, there was considerable diversity in mainstream schools in South Australia; the concept keyboard and other technical supports were more likely to be available in special school settings).

b) Predictive word processors which, although originally devised for those with physical disabilities, by significantly reducing the number of key strokes, do help those with spelling difficulties. In effect they provide a far more sophisticated form of the support described in (a) and an extension to the increasingly prevalent spell checkers (in word processors and hand-held equipment). The writer reads/selects a word from a list on screen which is generated by his own attempts e.g. the initial letter of a word. The sophistication arises due to the software's reference to past experience by that writer and to syntax, in offering choices. The word can be copied or printed directly on screen in mid-sentence depending on the pupil's choice. PAL (Booth 1991) is the most commonly quoted programme of this type.

c) Audio feedback built into word processors and spell checkers is rapidly becoming commonplace. As a result, attempts to write using available spelling knowledge can be checked against the sound of what has been written ('I drink m**u**lk'). If it sounds incorrect when read back by the computer, further attempts can be made until it tallies with recognised pronunciation ('I drink m**i**lk'). The advantages arising to assist reading and spelling do not need elaboration. Technology which writes when spoken to is now available and will be utilised far more in the near future, I predict.

In conclusion, it is important to recognise the need for a balanced programme of response to a student experiencing considerable frustration in the face of literacy difficulties wherever s/he may be educated . The above (largely top down) strategies go some way to offset such frustrations through the provision of meaningful compensatory experiences, and although relevant to any child who is underachieving or delayed in reading acquisition, are particularly relevant to those with specific learning difficulties/dyslexia. Each child facing the challenge of such long term difficulties, needs a balance of tuition which tackles phonological /analytic strategies , and global understandings through delivery of the ideas in this paper.

REFERENCES

Biggar, S. and Barr, J. (1993). The Emotional World of Specific Learning Difficulties. In Specific Learning Difficulties (Dyslexia), Gavin Reid (Ed.). Moray House Publications.

Bakker (1992). Neuropsychological Classification and Treatment of Dyslexia. Journal for Learning Difficulties, Vol. 25, No. 2, Feb.

Booth, L. (1991). Having a Pal in the Classroom. TASK Magazine. Spring. No 9.

Clay, M. (1987). Learning to be Learning Disabled. New Zealand Journal of Educational Studies. 22, 155 - 173.

Hellier, C. (1993). Reading unscrambled. Times Educational Supplement. September 3, p14.

Hellier, C. (1994). Closing the Gap. Compensating for literacy delay in children with specific learning difficulties/dyslexia. Support For Learning Vol. 9, No. 4, p162.

Hellier, C. (1995). Reading For Sure – The Verdict. Times Scottish Educational Supplement. March 10, Platform. p18.

Hellier, C., Kaye, P. and Barron, I. (1991). Specific Learning Difficulties/Dyslexia. Introduction and background literature for TEPS in-service mainstream staff. Tayside Region.

Kemp, M. (1987). Watching Children Read and Write. Thomas Nelson, Sydney.

Kozol, (1985). Illiterate America. New York: Doubleday.

Lewis, G. and Fowell-Jones, M. (1993). Dealing with Dyslexia. Special Children. June/July No. 67.

Pumfrey, P. Reason, R. (1991). Specific Learning Difficulties/Dyslexia. Challenges and Responses. NFER.

Reason, R. and Boote, R. (1994). Helping Children with Reading and Spelling. A Special Needs Manual. Routledge. London and New York.

Solomon, J. (1992). The use of diacritical marks to reduce anxiety in the reading of English. International Journal of Psychology, V27 3/4, p596.

Sylva, K. and Hurry, J. (1995). Early intervention in children with reading difficulties: An evaluation of Reading Recovery and a phonological training. Thomas Coram Research Unit. Prepared for School Curriculum And Assessment Authority. February.

Thompson, P. (1992). Raising reading standards: The reader-leader scheme. Support for Learning 7. No 2.

Topping, K. and Lindsay G. (1992). Paired Reading: a review of the literature. Research papers in Education 7.

PARENTS AND PEERS AS TUTORS FOR DYSLEXIC CHILDREN

KEITH TOPPING

INTRODUCTION

What do children with specific reading difficulties need? It might be presumed that by definition all regular methods of literacy instruction have already failed, so whatever is needed must be new, different, exotic and highly technical.

Yet those who work with these children know all too well that the problem is rarely solely within the child's cognitive abilities. In many cases anxiety, poor self-image, poor attention span associated with social or emotional difficulties, lack of confidence, learned helplessness and other affective factors play a large part.

While 'high-tech' methods of remediation may have the virtue of stimulating interest through novelty and can sometimes give the child a sense of importance, dependence on such methods can create major problems of generalisation of skills to everyday life. Furthermore, such methods may require substantial capital investment in equipment, high levels of specialist training and very favourable and therefore expensive teacher-pupil ratios. The result in some areas has been that not all children in need can be helped, with those who fall through the net unfortunately often being children from families of lower socio-economic status.

Attempts to address the non-cognitive aspects of the problem of specific reading difficulty have also been subject to constraints of cost. While Lawrence (1972) has shown that counselling of weak readers can be as effective in terms of raising reading age as some other interventions targeted directly on reading skills, counselling takes time and time is money. In recognition of this, 'counselling' has sometimes been given by low-paid non-teaching assistants, with no less effect than that given by trained teachers.

For some SpLD children, their anxiety, the grinding arduousness of their attempts to read and their all-consuming fear of failure lead them to devote much energy to evading reading – at times almost as much as they would have devoted to reading. Of course, the more they avoid reading, the less practice they have, and the less practice, they have the slower their progress and the smaller the likelihood of any sense of achievement. The associated learned helplessness leads some children to wait for the requisite skills to be pumped into them in a quasi-medical fashion, rather than attacking texts themselves as best they can and finding their own idiosyncratic pathways to extracting the meaning.

What if a way could be found to increase the amount of reading practice such children have while simultaneously making reading easier and reducing anxiety, giving children more self-confidence and placing them much more in control of their own learning? What if this could be done by some form of supported reading which enabled children to attack texts nearer their own interest level rather than being confined to their current independent reading level, while making reading feel less effortful and creating a sense of achievement by accelerating progress in terms of numbers of books read? What if this could be achieved at very low cost in teacher time and other resources?

The Paired Reading technique sets out to do exactly this.

PAIRED READING

Paired Reading is not any old thing that two people do with a book. It is a very specific structured technique, designed for parents, peers and other volunteers to use when tutoring reading. At first sight, it can seem very simple, this being unsurprising in a method designed for use by non-professionals, but in use it proves both subtle and powerful in its effects.

It has been in use since 1976, and is now deployed with mixed ability and reading delayed groups of all kinds, including those with severe learning difficulties and adult literacy students. It is flexible and responsive and ascribes 50 per cent of the control to the tutor and 50 per cent to the tutee, intending to be both democratic and empowering. Most importantly, it is a kind of supported reading which enables the delayed reader to tackle much more mature reading content than would otherwise be the case. In the vast majority of cases, it reduces anxiety and promotes greater self-confidence. It also substantially raises the total amount of reading practice undertaken without stressing the tutee.

METHOD

The child (tutee) chooses high interest reading material irrespective of its readability level, from school, the community library or home. Newspapers and magazines are fine. There is no requirement to finish the book, but if children keep changing in midstream maybe they need to take more care choosing.

Pairs commit themselves to an initial trial period in which they agree to do at least five minutes Paired Reading on five days each week for about eight weeks. This time can be found in any part of the day and the frequency of usage enables them to become fluent in the method and is sufficient for them to begin to see some change in the child's reading. Other tutors (grandparents, siblings, friends and neighbours) can be encouraged to help but must all use the same technique – the target child is deliberately asked to quality control the tutoring they receive.

The usual advice about finding a relatively quiet and comfortable place applies. It is important that both members of the pair can see the book equally easily – tutors who get neck-ache get irritable! Likewise, the usual advice about talking about the book (or whatever it is) applies, but in Paired Reading the child is more likely to want to talk about a book **they** have chosen and talk is also more necessary given the (probably) greater difficulty of the text, as a check on comprehension.

A very simple and ubiquitously applicable correction procedure is prescribed. When the child says a word wrong, the tutor just tells the child the correct way to say the word, has the child repeat it correctly and the pair carry on. Saying 'No!' and giving phonic or any other prompts is forbidden. However, tutors do not jump in and put the word right straight away – the rule is that tutors pause and give the child four or five seconds to see if they will put it right all by themselves. (The exception to this rule is with the sprint reader, who five seconds after making an error could be three lines along and have made more errors – in this case, earlier intervention and a finger point from the tutor to guide racing eyes back to the error word is necessary).

So how is the child going to manage this difficult book s/he has chosen? Tutors support children through difficult text by **Reading Together** – both members of the pair read all the words out loud together, with the tutor modulating their speed to match that of the child, while giving a good model of competent reading. The child must read every word and errors are corrected as above.

When an easier section of text is encountered, the child may wish to read a little without support. Tutor and tutee agree on a way for the child to signal for the tutor to stop Reading Together. This could be a knock, a sign or a squeeze. When the child signals, the tutor stops reading out loud right away while praising the child for being so confident. Sooner or later, while **Reading Alone** the child will make an error which they cannot self-correct within four or five seconds. Then the tutor applies the usual correction procedure **and** joins back in **Reading Together.**

The pair go on like this, switching from Reading Together to Reading Alone to give the child just as much help as is needed at any moment, according to the difficulty of the text, how tired the tutee is, and so on. Children should never 'grow out of' Reading Together; they should always be ready to use it as they move on to harder and harder books.

Praise for good reading is essential. Tutors must **look** pleased as well as saying 'good' and other positive things. Praise is particularly required for good reading of hard words, getting all the words in a sentence right and putting wrong words right before the tutor does (self-correction). Nagging, fussing and complaining are forbidden, but PR does not rely on negative commands for effectiveness – these undesirable behaviours are engineered out by engineering in incompatible positive behaviours.

The framework of the technique is outlined in Figure 1. Of course, there is nothing new about it – some elements of long-standing practice have merely been put together in a particularly successful package. A few teachers have difficulty accepting the technique for philosophical reasons. Forget that, just try it. Remember PR does not constitute the whole reading curriculum, but is designed to complement it without interfering with it. Further details will be found in Topping and Wolfendale (1985) and Topping (1995).

ORGANISATION

PR is widely used with children of all reading abilities and it makes sense to try it out initially on a range of students rather than attempt to solve all your worst reading problems overnight. This will also help to avoid stigmatisation of your first effort. Choose a small group of fairly well motivated tutors and tutees to practise on, but not so small or scattered that there is no sense of group solidarity or togetherness (around 10 would be good). Ensure that the children have easy and frequent access to a wide range of books available for the project.

Invite all potential tutors to a launch or training meeting, together with the children who will be the tutees, since pairs are trained together from the outset. At this meeting, after an introduction designed to create an air of novelty and excitement (some people like to put on a little play about how NOT to do reading at home), training in the technique commences. Tell the group about the basic structure of the technique **and** give a demonstration of how to do it. The demonstration can be on video, live by role play between teachers or by a teacher with user-friendly child, or by a graduate pair from a previous programme. Demonstrate **Reading Together** and **Reading Alone** separately to start with, then in normal alternation. Take especial care to highlight the correction procedure, the four to five second pause and lots of praise.

Now have the pairs go ahead and practise the technique, offering them necessary space and privacy. Remember that to practise Reading Together at all sensibly, the pair will need a book above the child's current independent readability level, so it is highly desirable to have the tutees choose books for the practice in school before the meeting so you can keep an eye on this. Left to themselves, the children will choose easy books for the purpose of making a good impression! As the pairs practise, circulate to diplomatically check on technique, offering further advice, coaching or re-demonstration with the individual child where necessary – and don't forget the praise! Remember that you can't advise or coach unless you have tried out the technique yourself on a few tame children.

After the practice, feed back your observations to the group, take questions, outline the day to day operation of the project, and offer refreshments if appropriate. Pairs should keep a PR Diary, noting the date, what was read, for how long, with whom and any comments about how well the child did. Some tutors have trouble thinking what to write in the last column, so some schools provide them with a dictionary of praise – children are always happy to offer suggestions for this. The diary should be checked by the co-ordinating teacher each week, who should add their own positive comment and sign it officially, perhaps also issuing a new sheet for the next week. This is a means for the child to get a double dose of praise – and is also a mutual accountability device, of course.

You will also need to advise pairs about the different places from which they may borrow books. Give pairs an easily read handout to remind them of the technique and to show to other potential tutors (this may need to be in more than one language). Some schools offer Paired Reading badges, balloons, and other such nonsense beloved by children – all helping to advertise the programme. You may wish to have the pairs contract into the programme more or less formally.

When discussing diaries with children in the ensuing weeks, check if all is going well. If it is not, you may wish to call in the pairs for a brief conference about the programme and to see if they are still 'doing it right'. In a parent tutored project, if you can find the time, a home visit is even better. In all cases have the pair show you how they are doing it and check the difficulty level of the books chosen (these may be consistently too hard or too easy).

After the initial period of commitment, gather the pairs together again for a feedback meeting. Tell them how you think things have gone and seek their opinion on the technique and organisation of the project. Some present will say little and some will not attend, so you might also wish to have feedback questionnaires for the participants (see Topping and Whiteley, 1990, for examples). You might wish to test the children's reading before and after the project so you can feed back the overall results to the group, but avoid giving out individual scores as one score is unlikely to accurately reflect the complexity of what has occurred. You might want to offer the group further tangible indicators of the school's approval at this point.

The main purpose of the meeting is to regenerate enthusiasm and group cohesion, since you do not want anyone to think this is 'the end'. Encourage everyone to say where they want to go from here: go on with PR five days a week, go on but only two or three days a week, go on with reading at home but in a different way, or stop for a rest and perhaps start again later. Children may wish to go on keeping the diary and you will have to decide how often you can find time to see this in the longer run.

Further information and advice about the organisation of parent tutoring will be found in Topping and Wolfendale (1985), about peer tutoring in Topping (1988) and about both in Topping (1995).

The idea that parent, peer or other volunteer tutors might succeed where professional teachers have failed is challenging. Surely some parents of children with specific reading difficulties are themselves poor readers and would not be able to serve as tutors. Equally, surely some of them would be so anxious about their child's problem that the effect could be negative.

Both of these questions require consideration. Certainly if the parent is extremely tense, there is a risk of negativity creeping into the tutoring situation. Yet many such parents cannot avoid trying to do something, whatever the school may advise. Paired Reading is designed so that the opportunity for negativity is engineered out – if the parent is determined to do something, PR may be the safest thing for them to do. In the few cases where the parent / child relationship seems hopelessly pathological, tutoring by other volunteer adults or by peers is likely to be more successful.

Paired Reading is designed for cross-ability tutoring. In other words, the tutor must be a more able reader than the tutee. Remember that the readability level of the books used needs to be controlled only to the level of the tutor, not that

Fig. 1

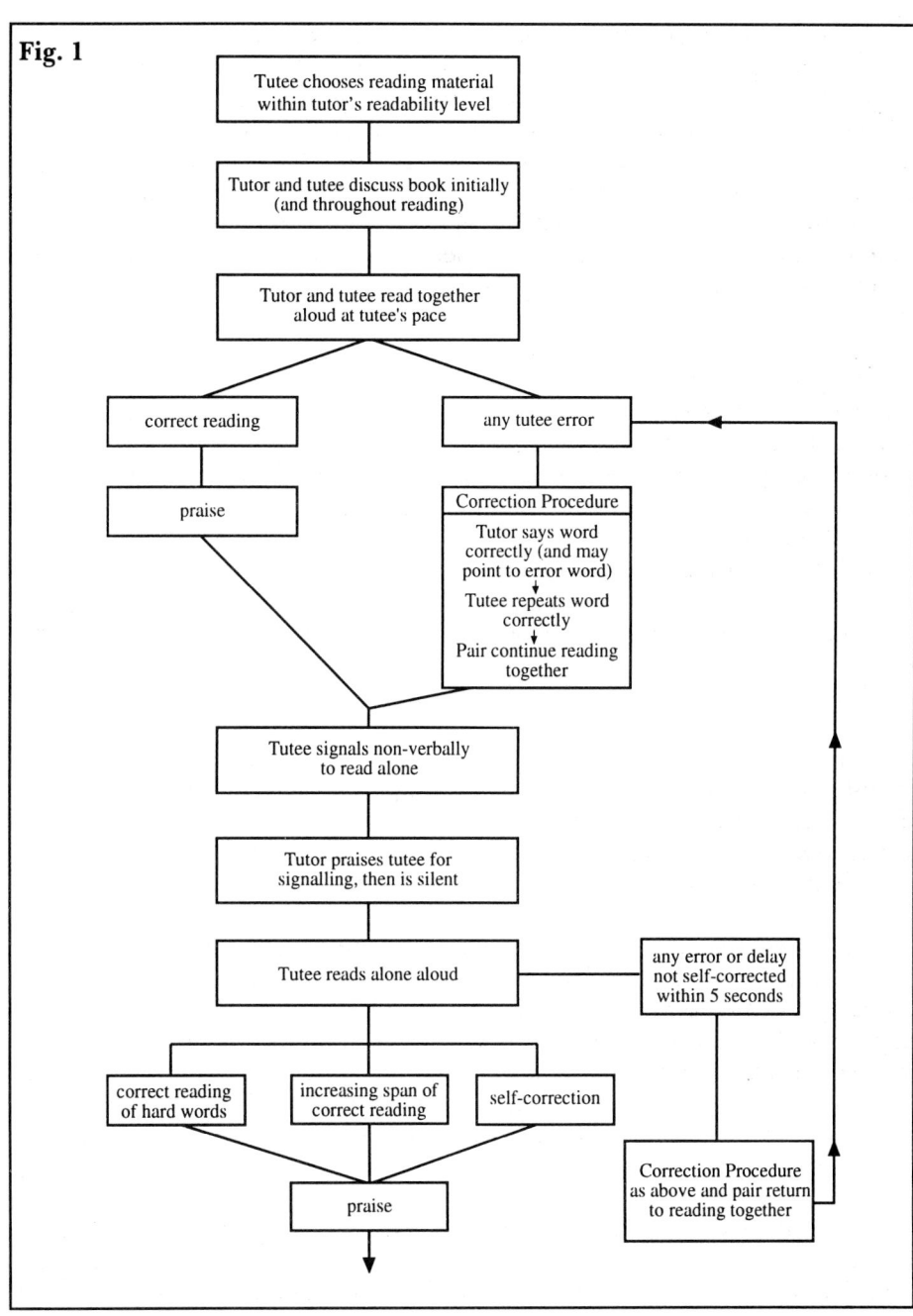

Tutee chooses reading material
within tutor's readability level

Tutor and tutee discuss book initially
(and throughout reading)

Tutor and tutee read together
aloud at tutee's pace

correct reading

any tutee error

praise

Correction Procedure

Tutor says word
correctly (and may
point to error word)

Tutee repeats word
correctly

Pair continue reading
together

Tutee signals non-verbally
to read alone

Tutor praises tutee for
signalling, then is silent

Tutee reads alone aloud

any error or delay
not self-corrected
within 5 seconds

correct reading
of hard words

increasing span of
correct reading

self-correction

Correction Procedure
as above and pair return
to reading together

praise

of the tutee. Especially in peer tutoring, but also in parent tutoring where the parent's literacy level is low, books must not be used which are too difficult for the tutor to read accurately – we certainly do not want tutees learning errors. However, a differential in ability of only two years of reading age in the pair is adequate, so some parents of restricted literacy are entirely capable of using the method, given the establishment of a choice of books within an appropriate readability ceiling. For these parents, PR with their child gives them a socially legitimate reason to read low readability material and is likely to raise the confidence and skills of the tutors also, through the extra practice involved for both.

GENERAL EFFECTIVENESS

Paired Reading has been the subject of a very large amount of research, starting in the UK and now internationally, and this has been reviewed by Topping and Lindsay (1992).

Much of the evaluation has been in terms of gains on norm-referenced tests of reading before and after the initial intensive period of involvement. Published studies do not always reflect the reality of ordinary life in the classroom, but with PR it is possible to compare the results of 60 published (and therefore selected) studies of projects with outcome data from 155 unselected projects operated in one local authority. In the published studies, involving a total of 1012 children, for each month of time passed the average Paired Reader gained 4.2 months in reading age for accuracy and 5.4 months for comprehension. In the 155 unselected projects, involving 2372 children, for each month of time passed the average Paired Reader gained 3.3 months in reading age for accuracy and 4.4 months for comprehension.

Of the published studies, 19 included control or comparison groups, while of the unselected projects, 37 included control groups. Although the control groups often also made gains greater than would normally be expected, the PR groups on aggregate did far better, although the differential was greater in the published projects.

But do these gains last? Published reports on five projects with follow-up data are available, but of the unselected projects, 17 included such evidence. In the latter, up to 17 weeks after the initial project intensive period, 102 children in seven projects were still gaining over two months of reading age per chronological month elapsed for both accuracy and comprehension. At longer term follow-up, 170 children in 10 projects were still gaining well over one month of reading age per month elapsed in both accuracy and comprehension. Thus it seems that while the initial startling acceleration does not continue indefinitely, the gains certainly do not 'wash out' subsequently, and follow-up data from control group projects confirms this (Topping, 1992).

The data from the unselected projects further suggested that well-organised projects yielded better test results, that participant children from lower socio-economic classes tended to show higher gains, that home visiting by teachers increased test scores and that boys tended to accelerate more than girls. Also, second language Paired Readers accelerated more than first language Paired Readers in accuracy but less in comprehension (while of course accelerating a great deal more than non-Paired Readers of either type).

Taking another approach to evaluation, the subjective views of parents, children and teachers in the unselected projects have also been gathered by structured questionnaire, enabling responses to be summarised (Topping and Whiteley, 1990). In a sample of over 1000 parents, after PR, 70 per cent considered that their child was now reading more accurately, more fluently and with better comprehension. Greater confidence in reading was noted by 78 per cent of parents. Teachers reported better reading in the classroom in a somewhat smaller proportion of cases (about eight per cent less). Of a sample of 964 children, 95 per cent felt that after PR they were better at reading and 92 per cent liked reading more. Eighty-seven per cent found it easy to learn to do, 83 per cent liked doing it and 70 per cent said they would go on doing it.

Paired Reading has also been used in an Adult Literacy context, with spouses, friends, neighbours and workmates acting as tutors. The advantages of being able to use more appropriate and more readily available reading material and receive tutoring on a little and often basis closely linked to everyday life are extremely important, especially for the majority of adults with literacy difficulties who cannot or will not attend a class.

Scoble, Topping and Wigglesworth (1988) reported the evaluation of a six-week project of this type, noting average gains of 10.4 months in reading age for accuracy and 13 months for comprehension for those students who could register on the scale at pre-test. On miscue analysis, most tutees showed a striking increase in self-correction. Once PR is applied in a more complex Family Literacy context, it soon becomes very difficult to evaluate, since there are problems establishing who is doing what and with which and to whom. (Wolfendale and Topping, 1995).

RESEARCH WITH DYSLEXIC CHILDREN

Of 59 published PR outcome studies reviewed by Topping and Lindsay (1992), 45 targeted children whose reading was delayed. However, data from multiple-site field trials in one local authority suggested a much higher proportion of mixed ability pupils were increasingly being included in such projects on an equal opportunity basis. In this latter context, there was some evidence that during PR the weaker readers tended to make slightly greater gains on reading tests than the better readers. The method was, however, originally devised for use with weak readers and has indeed been used successfully with populations with very severe problems, including special school children with physical handicap, severe learning difficulties, moderate learning difficulties and emotional and behavioural difficulties, as well as travelling children and children for whom English was not their first language.

This of course brings us to the thorny perennial – when is a weak reader truly 'dyslexic'? If we take as a definition recognition as such by the Dyslexia Institute, just two studies have reported on such samples. These two will be focused on here, although many other studies of PR with delayed readers might be regarded as relevant.

In 1984, Evans reported a study of six children aged 10 to 13 years whose retardation ranged from 1.5 to 5.5 years of reading age. Parent tutors were deployed and two training meetings were held, with a view to establishing Reading Together before training Reading Alone. During the seven week initial period of commitment, home-school record sheets were used to keep a diary of activity and progress. An initial home visit was made to introduce the project and weekly home visits were made during the seven week period. Some difficulties were encountered with access to appropriate books. Pre- and post-testing on the Neale Analysis of Reading Ability indicated means gains of 2.8 months in reading accuracy and 15.5 months in reading comprehension, while understanding of vocabulary as measured by the British Picture Vocabulary Scale increased by the equivalent of nine months.

Thus, while the reading accuracy increase was less than two months for each month of the project (an indifferent result compared to the outcomes of many other PR studies), doubtless this reflected something of a triumph for the children and parents concerned and other outcome results were much more substantial. The inclusion of weekly home visits is a luxury many teachers will not be able to afford. The wider research picture (see Topping and Lindsay, 1992) suggests that although home visits do tend to improve the effectiveness of a project as measured by reading test gains, nevertheless very good results are obtainable with no home visits whatsoever.

A larger scale project was reported by Young and Tyre (1983) in their excellent book 'Dyslexia or Illiteracy? – Realising the Right to Read'. Fifteen children between the ages of 8 and 13 years took part, all at least two years retarded in reading. Here Paired Reading was used by parents in combination with other approaches in the context of a complete intervention 'package', and it is thus difficult to tease out which aspects of the project resulted in which elements of the overall gains made.

A number of variations of Paired Reading were utilised simultaneously or sequentially according to the needs of individual participants and supported by parent-tutored writing and spelling activities and three one-week 'holiday schools'. Some supportive home visits were incorporated. Over one year, a matched control group advanced on average 0.8 years on reading tests, the dyslexic experimental group 1.8 years and a matched comparison group of reading delayed but not dyslexic children 2.0 years. The authors emphasise that whether or not the children were classified as dyslexic made no difference to the benefit they derived from the project.

There has been no published study of peer tutored Paired Reading with specific reading difficulty pupils under the definition used above (an opportunity for someone here), but there is a great deal of work on PR peer tutoring with reading delayed pupils not so categorised. The general finding is that peer tutoring is as effective as parent tutoring in the short term while the tutoring takes place, but there is less certainty regarding longer term gains once the tutoring is discontinued than is the case with parent tutoring (see Topping, 1992).

ALTERNATIVE APPROACHES

Of course, Paired Reading is just one of the techniques which have been used by non-teachers to remediate reading delay. A review of research on 'Parents as Reading Tutors for Children with Special Needs' will be found in Topping (1989). Techniques referred to include various versions of 'Shared Reading ,' the Pause Prompt Praise technique, parent workshops, token reinforcement procedures, precision teaching methods and Direct Instruction programmes. Some of these have also been delivered by peer tutors in some circumstances. These are described in more detail in Topping and Wolfendale (1985) and a review of progress in parental tutoring of reading over the last decade will be found in Wolfendale and Topping (1995).

Methods similar to Paired Reading have been devised for other areas of the curriculum, and user-friendly but structured techniques such as Cued Spelling and Paired Writing have been successfully used by both parent and peer tutors (see Topping, 1993 and 1995 for details). Extension to other areas has included the development of Paired Maths and Paired Science, although these latter are very much intended for dissemination on a mixed-ability basis.

Accepting that children with specific reading difficulties can often seem an intractable group with which to work, there are clearly methods and techniques here which merit exploration. Parents and peers can be made part of the solution instead of being regarded as part of the problem. Solutions need to be more simple rather than more complex. In terms of cost-effectiveness in an era of shrinking resources, this represents a viable way forward.

REFERENCES

Evans, A. (1984). *Paired Reading: a Report on Two Projects.* Division of Education, University of Sheffield (unpublished paper).

Lawrence, D. (1972). *Counselling of Retarded Readers by Non-Professionals.* Educational Research 15, 48-51.

Scoble, J., Topping, K. and Wigglesworth, C. (1988). 'Training Family and Friends as Adult Literacy Tutors.' *Journal of Reading* 31 (5) 410-417.

Topping, K. J. (1988). *The Peer Tutoring Handbook: Promoting Co-operative Learning.* London: Croom Helm; Cambridge, MA: Brookline.

Topping, K. J. (1989). 'Parents as Reading Tutors for Children with Special Needs'. in: Jones, N. (Ed.). *Special Educational Needs Review*, Vol. 1. London: Falmer Press.

Topping, K. J. (1992). 'Short- and Long-Term Follow-up of Parental Involvement In Reading Projects.' *British Educational Research Journal,* 18 (4) 369-379.

Topping, K. J. (1993). *Techniques for Family Literacy.* Viewpoints (ALBSU) 15, 22–33.

Topping, K. J. (1995). *Paired Reading, Writing and Spelling: The Handbook.* London. Cassell.

Topping, K. J. and Lindsay, G. (1992). *Paired Reading: A Review of the Literature.* Research Papers in Education 7 (3) 1-50.

Topping, K. J. and Whiteley, M. (1990). *Participant Evaluation of Parent-Tutored and Peer-Tutored Projects in Reading.* Educational Research 32 (1) 14-32.

Topping, K. J. and Wolfendale, S. W. (Eds.) (1985). *Parental Involvement in Children's Reading.* London: Croom Helm; New York: Nichols.

Wolfendale, S. W. and Topping, K. J. (Eds.) (1995). *Family Involvement in Literacy: Effective Partnerships in Education.* London; Cassell.

Young, P. and Tyre, C. (1983). *Dyslexia or Illiteracy? Realising the Right to Read.* Milton Keynes: Open University Press.

Note

The Paired Reading and Paired Learning Bulletins are available on microfiche from ERIC (1985 ED285124, 1986 ED285125, 1987 ED285126, 1988 ED298429, 1989 ED313656), as is the Ryedale Paired Reading Adult Literacy Training Pack (ED290845). A Teacher's Manual and NTSC training video titled 'Paired Reading: Positive Reading Practice' is available from the North Alberta Reading Specialists' Council, Box 9538, Edmonton, Alberta T6E 5X2, Canada, and is also distributed by the International Reading Association. A video entitled 'Setting Up a Paired Reading Programme' has been produced by the Partnership in Education Project of Strathclyde Regional Council. A video training pack about Paired Reading and Accelerated Reading is being produced by the Institute for Academic Excellence, Madison, Wisconsin, USA. Details about the Paired Science Pack are available from the author at the address in the notes on contributors.

The Centre for paired learning may be contacted by email at cpl@dundee.ac.uk – details of an Internet list server on peer tutoring are available from here.

BRIDGING THE GAP – EXPERIENCING SKILL IN READING AND WRITING

JANET HUNTER

INTRODUCTION

This chapter looks at two techniques which may be used as part of the cocktail of strategies which Reason (1994) suggested be brought together to meet the needs of the individual child with a specific learning difficulty.

THE DYSLEXIC EXPERIENCE

It is well recognised that the bottom up literacy skills which non-dyslexic children 'apparently acquire automatically from reading (as if by osmosis!)' (Thomson and Watkins, 1990) must be carefully taught in a structured and repetitive way to the child with SpLD. It is then necessary to try to help the child transfer the knowledge acquired in this controlled way into independent reading and writing.

Teachers are all too familiar with the child who may have grasped a particular spelling rule, for example, but can only use it successfully in exercises focused on that rule. Reading, or writing for that matter, 'is an incredibly complicated job' (Morgan, 1986), which requires the integration of many sub-skills for success in dealing with or producing text. Due to lack of automaticity, the dyslexic has difficulty integrating these skills. When writing, he may opt to use only a very safe and basic spelling vocabulary, producing a simplified piece of work which does not express his more complex ideas; or when reading, may rely too heavily on contextual cues and pay insufficient attention to graphic information (Stanovich 1980), thus failing to read either competently or accurately.

One solution is to work on two levels. Independent reading and writing are restricted to the child's competence level by only presenting him with structures previously over learned, as in the Hickey programme (Augur and Briggs, 1991); by reducing the amount of text and enlarging the print on each page thus allowing a greater amount of time for processing (Reid, 1994); or by working to strengths in supporting contextual cues with pictures, taped text or working in partnership.

For the child to access text at his ability level requires intermediary support – scribing for example, or having material read to him.

The disadvantage of only interacting with print on these two levels is that the dyslexic child never experiences directly the stimulation and motivation open to the non-dyslexic at first hand, often from an early age (Meek, 1982). Reading and writing at the SpLD child's accuracy level is an exercise in improving competence. Interaction with author or audience at ability level is a mediated experience.

BRIDGING THE GAP

Skilled Experience Reading and Writing seek to bridge this gap. These approaches aim to give the dyslexic child the immediate experience of skill in reading and writing, whilst at the same time providing the opportunity to practise successfully integrating or organising the various sub-skills within a meaningful context. To this end the following factors need to be taken into consideration:

- **Interest and motivation**

    An American Commission on Reading, Anderson *et al.* (1985) considered that one of the important elements in developing skilled reading was motivation to read through, seeing it as a useful and enjoyable activity. It follows, therefore that the texts used must be meaningful, relevant and interesting to the child.

- **Reduction of stress**

    As far as possible, the activity should take place in an environment where the child is relaxed and comfortable, since anxiety has been shown to reduce working memory or processing capacity (Eysenck, 1979, 1982; Darke, 1988). Hodges (1985) indicates that when students are taught in a compatible learning environment, they feel more relaxed and can perform better. Carbo (1986) recognised that, compared to good readers, poor readers tend to need softer lighting and are more likely to benefit from sitting in an informally designed area. Reading aloud was also identified by Pumfrey and Reason (1991) as one of the stressors inhibiting successful learning, therefore should be avoided.

- **Parental involvement**

    If parents are being encouraged to partner their children in reading at home, ideally the method should be easily explained, simple to carry out, enjoyable for both partners, and sustainable. The positive attention focused on child and parent in the tuition and backup necessary for a relatively complicated method such as Paired Reading, will undoubtedly have a beneficial effect (see Lawrence, 1985). However, motivation is inherent in the reading activity itself when it leads to 'enjoyable, interesting, exciting, pleasurable and useful experiences for the individual' (Pumfrey, 1991) and 'parents report much more relaxed and enjoyable reading with their children when the story itself rather than the child's reading performance is the issue' (Obrist and Stuart, 1990).

- **The apprenticeship approach**

  Reason (1994) reminds us that it was not enough for apprentices just to watch a craftsman produce the finished article (in this context, listening to a skilled reader reading), they also had to actively practise their craft. The following two methods combine modelling for the child of skilled reading and writing, along with responsibility by the child of actively practising these skills himself.

SKILLED EXPERIENCE READING

There are three requirements for the child and his partner.

1 **The child is instructed to read silently, while his partner reads aloud.**

   Reading silently frees the child from any negative evaluation, either his own or his partner's, about his performance. An adult partner, although aware of the need to praise the child, may still be inwardly evaluating the child's reading in a negative way and conveying this underlying message to the child. In reading silently, the focus is on interacting with the text rather on how well the child is progressing.

2 **The child is instructed to follow the words with his eyes, while his partner runs her finger along beneath the text. If the child looks away from the text, the adult stops reading and waits until he looks back.**

   The adult's finger movement, corresponding to her oral reading, is a visual representation of her fluency and attention to the cohesiveness and structure of the text, pausing at full stops, for example, or at the end of a clause. It is perfectly acceptable for the child to look away from the print – he may want to think about what he has just read, talk about it or look at a picture. If that happens, the adult stops immediately and waits until the child's eyes return to the text before continuing to read. There is no need for any additional verbal instruction.

3   **The child is instructed to listen inside his head to the words he is reading.**

'The depressed reading performance of dyslexic readers is due to difficulties associated with the processing of the phonological features of the language' (Aaron, 1989), with phonology and syntax closely intertwined. Bakker (1990) describes two types of dyslexic readers: those who read slowly, accurately and in a fragmented way and those who read hurriedly with many errors. With this third instruction the latter child is being asked to attend to decoding accurately, with grapheme/phoneme awareness and attention to grammatical words.

These indicators of success show motivation, enjoyment, interaction and comprehension:

- The child asks to continue reading for longer at the end of a session. He may also not want the book to end, and will check to make sure there are no more pages to read.
- He reacts to the text by, for example, laughing and turning to his partner to share his enjoyment. He may also talk about the plot or characters and predict a possible outcome.
- He looks relaxed and happy when reading.
- Parents report the child voluntarily picking up books to read at home, something he avoided doing in the past.

SKILLED EXPERIENCE WRITING

This can be practised individually or in a small group. To begin with, the child works from a text. This should have content of interest to the child but be within his comprehension range, since this technique focuses on process rather than content. Usually the text is worked on one paragraph at a time, but this can be adjusted to suit the individual child.

STEP 1: **The child's attention is directed to content, structure and language in one paragraph of the text.**

This may be done in a variety of ways.

- Skilled Experience Reading, with the children reading silently and the teacher reading aloud.

- As above, with the addition in a prepared text of a choice of words at regular intervals, for example:

  'Then the body (saw, was) rolled in bits of (cloth, clop). Good luck spells were put (on, in, up) the rolls of (sloth, cloth).' The children ring the word which they hear the teacher read.

  'Then the body *was* rolled in bits of *cloth*. Good luck spells were put *in* the rolls of *cloth*'.

- Scanning activities, perhaps counting the number of sentences and highlighting the full stops.

- Checking for words which may be difficult to remember how to write, and practising spelling them in a variety of different ways.

STEP 2: **The text is covered and the teacher dictates the paragraph one sentence at a time for the children to write – as fast as they can.**

Recall, particularly of sequential information, is often a problem for dyslexic children. The teacher can help them learn to hold the sentence more successfully by utilising as many senses as possible, and in particular their preferred one (see Reid, 1994, on learning styles). They might watch the teacher's lips, 'switch on' to listening with attention, vocalise by repeating and involve kinaesthetic/tactile senses by tapping fingers or feet or counting off the words on their fingers.

Working with one whole sentence at a time brings a greater awareness of punctuation, the structure of the sentence and how more than one together build into a paragraph. If the sentence is too long for the child to remember before writing, the teacher must read the whole sentence first before dictating it in smaller parts, each time reminding the child that this is only part of the sentence.

Speed in writing is essential. As soon as the child stops to think about how to spell a word or correct a mistake, he is likely to forget what he intended to write. He needs to understand that, at this stage in the writing process, all that matters is getting an indication of the content down on paper which he can edit and perfect later. If he cannot remember how a word is spelled, for example, he either puts in the letters he knows or leaves a space and keeps moving on. In effect, the dyslexic child is being shown how to separate the different processes in writing, that is: expressing ideas, spelling correctly, structuring the language, punctuating and writing legibly – and tackle one after the other, rather than try and fail to combine them in one attempt.

STEP 3:   S.O.A.P.

SOAP stands for Spelling, Omissions and Additions, and Punctuation, the editing skills necessary to produce a perfect piece of prose, which must be checked each in turn. These are essential skills for the dyslexic child; nevertheless, only too often, he sees editing as something someone else does to his writing, pointing out to him the mistakes he has made. Using SOAP in this controlled context, where he checks through each constituent part in turn, finally checking and ticking off each word and item of punctuation with the text, shows him that he can take responsibility himself. It also means that having an 'off' day, when his hand seems determined to get letters or words wrong, is an inconvenience rather than a disaster. He can see that cultivating good editing skills enables him to produce a perfect piece of prose regardless of how poorly integrated he is on any particular day. Younger children like the idea that their hand does not have a brain, is liable to do something different to what they were expecting, and therefore always needs to be checked up on carefully.

Metacognition

It is important that the children understand the value of applying these skills and start transferring what they are learning into any writing they do. At the start of each session, in a similar way to starting a Reciprocal Reading session (Brown, 1993), the teacher selects one of the skills about to be practised, showing its function and the need for it . For example, she may choose punctuation, and start a discussion by reading out a passage for the children to listen to, first randomly punctuated so that it does not make sense, then correctly punctuated.

Positive self-evaluation

Equally important at the start of each session, is evaluation by each child, helped by the teacher, of his strengths in the process and, not weaknesses, but areas in which he needs to focus. Again, at the finish, the child reviews what he did to make his piece of writing perfect, and is reminded to continue paying attention to these aspects in any other writing he does that day. The emphasis is on praise, recognition, self-empowerment and responsibility.

Legibility

Legibility, the final step in producing written work, is not addressed in the Skilled Writing sessions, but needs to be looked at as a separate issue. Some children can produce good handwriting, with work neatly set out if they can concentrate on that alone in a separate step; others are able to develop handwriting skills with help, either in school (Kiely, 1993) or from an Occupational Therapist: along with proficiency in word processing this is an essential part of the curriculum for the dyslexic child.

STEP 4:   Independent writing

In the final sessions, once the child shows confidence with the process in working from a text, he practises applying these skills when expressing himself in his own writing. Now the text is internalised rather than externalised in front of him, but the process is the same. First, he must focus on what it is he wants to write, in the same way that he attended to the text. Then he writes quickly so that he stays focused and remembers, and this applies whether it is a plan for a longer piece of work or just one sentence in entirety. He finally applies SOAP and evaluates his work with the help of his teacher.

CONCLUSION

Working out a teaching plan to target the dyslexic child's needs cannot be done in isolation in the mainstream school. 'The art of making effective curricular provision lies in integrating the programmes of the individual or small group with the curriculum of the class or school' (Scottish Office Education Department, 1994). Skilled Experience Reading and Writing are examples of techniques based on a general framework and of use to a range of children in developing literacy skills, within which the individual dyslexic child's specific strengths and weaker areas can be addressed.

In addition, these techniques seek to provide metacognitive strategies and self-understanding which will be of use to the individual with a specific learning difficulty, not just as a young child in the classroom, but in dealing with literacy throughout adolescence and into maturity.

REFERENCES

Aaron, P. G. (1989). Dyslexia and Hyperlexia. Kluwer Academy.

Anderson, R. C., Heibert, E. H., Scott, J. A., Wilkinson, I. A. G. (1985). Becoming a Nation of Readers: The Report on the Commission on Reading. US Government Printing Office.

Augur, J. and Briggs, S. (Eds.) (1991). The Hickey Multi-sensory Language Course. Whurr.

Bakker, D. J. (1990). Neuropsychological Treatments of Dyslexia. In: Hales, G. *et al.*, (Eds.) *Meeting Points in Dyslexia*: Proceedings of the First International Conference of the British Dyslexia Association. B.D.A.

Brown, P. (1993). The Learner – Metacognition in Reading. In Reid, G. (Ed.) Specific Learning Difficulties (Dyslexia): Perspectives on Practice. Moray House Publications.

Carbo, M., Dunn, R., Dunn, K. (1986). Teaching Students to Read Through Their Individual Learning Styles. Englewood Cliffs, N. J. Prentice Hall.

Darke, S. (1988). 'Anxiety and working memory capacity'. Cognition and Emotion 2.

Eysenck, M. W. (1979). 'Anxiety, learning and memory: a reconceptualisation'. Journal of Research in Personality, 13.

Eysenck, M. W. (1982). Attention and Arousal (Cognition and Performance). Springer Verlag.

Hodges, (1985). 'An analysis of the relationships among preferences for a formal / informal design, one element of learning style, academic achievement and attitudes of seventh and eighth grade students in remedial mathematics classes in a New York City junior high school'. Doctoral Dissertation, St John's University. Dissertation Abstracts International 45, 2791A.

Kiely, M. (1993). Handwriting – Skills, Strategies and Success. In Reid, G. (Ed.) Specific Learning Difficulties (Dyslexia): Perspectives on Practice. Moray HousePublications.

Lawrence, D. (1985). 'Improving self esteem and reading'. Educational Research, 27,3.

Meek, M. (1982). Learning to Read. Bodley Head.

Morgan, R. (1986). Helping Children Read: The Paired Reading Handbook. Methuen.

Obrist, C. and Stuart, A. (1990). The Family Reading Groups Movement. In Unter-Carsh, M. *et al.* Primary English in the National Curriculum. Blackwell Education.

Pumfrey, P. D. (1991). Improving Reading in the Junior School: Challenges and Responses. Cassell Education.

Pumfrey, P. D. and Reason, R. *et al.* (1991). Specific Learning Difficulties (Dyslexia). NFER-Nelson.

Reason, R. (1994) Paper presented at Specific Learning Difficulty Conference, Edinburgh. Moray House Publications.

Reason, R. and Boote, R. (1994). Helping Children with Reading and Spelling: A Special Needs Manual. Routledge.

Reid, G. (1994). Specific Learning Difficulties (Dyslexia): A Handbook for Study and Practice. Moray House Publications.

Scottish Office Education Department (1994). Effective Provision for Special Educational Needs: A Report by HM Inspectors of Schools. The Scottish Office Education Department.

Stanovich, K. E. (1980). 'Toward an interactive - compensatory model of individual differences in the development of reading fluency.' Reading Research Quarterly, 16.

Thomson, M. E. and Watkins, E. J. (1990). Dyslexia: A Teaching Handbook. Whurr.

METACOGNITION IN READING

PATRICIA BROWN

INTRODUCTION

'Learning is a process which starts at birth, continues in school and extends through life.'

This short statement from an article by Simpson (1988) is neither contentious or novel. In fact educationalists would generally agree with these aspirations. It does, however, simplify the underlying complexities of this variable concept of learning which has been the focus of much research over the years.

Historically, psychologists have attempted to formulate general laws of learning valid for all humans. The ultimate aim has been to improve teaching and classroom learning but this has remained an elusive goal. No single, generally acceptable model has been developed for analysing learning effectiveness and the contributing factors. Contrasting explanations of classroom learning have been developed by different psychologists holding different philosophical positions. Each of them, whether they be behaviourist, psychometric or humanistic, contain important and correct explanations of some aspects of certain kinds of learning, but all are partial in that each theorist has concentrated on a limited range of learning situations and so has utilised a restricted range of evidence (Entwistle, 1987). Gradually, therefore, research has shifted to an acceptance that it is important to understand learning from the pupil's perspective within the context of the classroom. Psychologists appear to have accepted the importance of this social context and the significance of the complex interaction between pupil, teacher and task.

There is little doubt that children, especially in their pre-school years, are able to acquire considerable knowledge and skills as a result of 'incidental' learning. This learning takes place in the context of everyday occurrences and interactions. However, with the transition into formal schooling, the emphasis changes to 'intentional' learning and problems may arise. Pupils are now expected to learn for the purpose of recall and are subsequently expected to apply that information in the context of some problem-solving activity. Intentional learning contrasts with incidental learning. As Palincsar and Klenk explain (1992), it is an achievement which results from 'the learner's purposeful, effortful, self-regulated, and active engagement'. They outline three requirements for successful learning in this context. Firstly, the pupil must possess the ability and awareness to monitor and control learning activities. Secondly, it is necessary for the pupil to access a repertoire of appropriate strategies; and finally, the pupil requires motivation through success and feelings of self-worth.

The concept of 'self-regulation' (which occurs when a pupil monitors and controls the active process of learning) is a major component of metacognition and is central to this chapter. As children mature, they acquire self-regulatory skills. However, these skills develop at different rates and to different degrees. They form the basis for success across the curriculum in a variety of learning contexts from mathematical problem-solving to reading and are crucial for 'adaptive, planful learning'. Unfortunately, they are not always easy to acquire and are not generally explicitly taught in classroom situations (Borkowski, 1992).

The aim of this chapter, therefore, has been to present a balanced view of metacognition, one which is relevant within an educational setting and which pinpoints the strengths and identifies the limitations. Although the concept of metacognition has consistently been described as abstract and elusive by a variety of researchers, it has generated an abundance of innovative research which has an intuitive appeal to teachers. From this research, it has become apparent that those learners who have poor metacognitive skills are at a disadvantage in all subject areas and, as a result, practical classroom applications have developed. Initially, the research focused on reading comprehension skills which are central to the curriculum but the research field has now widened to include, for example mathematical problem-solving (Montague, 1992).

METACOGNITION IN READING

Metacognition, as Brown, Armbruster and Baker (1986) point out, plays 'a vital role' in reading. The term is a relatively new label for a large amount of theory and research which considers learners' knowledge and their directed use of their cognitive abilities. Recently, those involved in educational research have appreciated the importance of metacognition in helping to describe the reading process. Garner (1987) explains the reasons behind this. Firstly, the theory and research can help explain the differences in performances of readers of various ages and secondly, this theoretical framework can be used for devising instructional interventions to promote greater strategy use among readers.

The work of Flavell, who is credited with first using the term metamemory (that is, knowledge about one's own memory), has been fundamental in shaping research into metacognition. He developed a model of cognitive monitoring (1979) in an attempt to capture the complexities of metacognition as well as clarify a concept which he himself indicates could be 'fuzzy'. The components of his model, metacognitive knowledge, metacognitive experiences, cognitive goals (or tasks) and cognitive actions (or strategies), interact and cause the monitoring of a wide variety of 'cognitive enterprises'.

Flavell differentiates between metacognitive knowledge and metacognitive experience. For example, metacognitive knowledge would be child's belief that he or she is better than another at reading or spelling while metacognitive experiences would be as Flavell explains 'conscious cognitive or affective experiences that accompany and pertain to any intellectual enterprise'. An example could be a sudden feeling that you do not understand something that has been said or which you have read. Garner describes clearly the links between these concepts by explaining that metacognitive knowledge can serve as a base for metacognitive experiences which, in turn, trigger strategy use. All are influenced by the goal or task which is the objective of the cognitive enterprise.

Flavell has studied metacognition and cognitive monitoring in a variety of situations, especially in relation to oral communication skills. His model has been influential and his research is constantly referred to by many working in the field of reading. Most of the studies discussed in this chapter use the work of Flavell and/ or his terminology when describing metacognition.

RECENT RESEARCH INTO METACOGNITION IN READING

There are many examples of research into the reading process which focus on these metacognitive aspects. The terminology varies but terms such as metacognition, cognitive monitoring and comprehension monitoring are often used interchangeably by researchers. However, some researchers differentiate between these terms and claim they are hierarchically related concepts. For example, Baker and Brown (1984) maintain that comprehension monitoring is one type of cognitive monitoring while cognitive monitoring itself is a component of metacognition.

The research field has divided into two main areas. In one, the focus is on children's *metacognitive knowledge* about reading, especially their verbalised knowledge of various aspects of reading. The other area studies the *regulation and control of this knowledge* while reading for different purposes. As Baker and Brown comment, each of these two perspectives, although not conceptually exclusive, has developed its own research approach. The former employs interviews while the latter investigates regulatory behaviour across a variety of tasks.

The problems associated with interviews are clearly and fully discussed by Garner (1987) who states, 'Because of limited language skills, confusion about general processes being queried, or inability to speculate about hypothetical events, young children may be at a disadvantage in responding to interview probes.'

Her concerns are that the interview can either underestimate or even overestimate the stable knowledge a child has about person, task and strategy aspects of a wide variety of cognitive processes. She does offer alternative methods to collecting data which may eliminate some of these problems. One alternative method, for example, is cross-age tutoring where older learners without adult supervision are encouraged to externalise their knowledge to assist younger children to read and answer detailed questions about a text. The externalisation allows observers to assess the metacognitive knowledge displayed by the tutor.

In spite of the inherent problems researchers have experienced with interviews, two main results have emerged consistently from such studies. The first, proposed by Baker and Brown (1984), is: 'Younger and poorer readers have little awareness that they must attempt to make sense of text; they focus on reading as a decoding process, rather than as a meaning getting process.' The second is detailed by Garner (1987) when discussing a study she carried out in 1981 with Reis: 'Younger children and poorer readers are unlikely to demonstrate that they notice major blocks to text understanding. They seem not to realise when they do not understand.'

Greater understanding of children's metacognitive knowledge is only one important facet of metacognition in reading. Bearing in mind the interactive meaning-getting model of the reading process, the other (already briefly mentioned) consists of the self-regulatory mechanisms used by an active learner during reading. They include planning, checking the outcomes of any strategy used, and monitoring the effectiveness of any attempted action, as well as testing, revising and evaluating one's strategies for learning (Armbruster and Brown, 1984).

Brown has tried to capture this complexity in a tetrahedral model of learning. According to this model, four major variables enter into the learning situation:

1   *Text:* the nature of the material to be learnt.

2   *Task:* the purpose for reading which learners commonly meet in school.

3   *Strategies:* the activities learners engage in to understand and remember information.

4   *Characteristics of the learner:* prior experience, background knowledge, interests and motivation.

The goal of an effective learner is the control or self-regulation of these four variables. He or she must co-ordinate their complex interaction to be successful.

This model provides a useful framework for studying the research into the regulation and control of metacognitive knowledge. In the next few paragraphs, therefore, pertinent examples using the model will be included. They illustrate both the developmental and performance differences (Brown, Armbruster and Baker, 1986).

•   Text

When considering the text, readers must be able to distinguish between the central ideas in a text and those that are peripheral. Even young children at primary school are commonly asked to concentrate on main ideas when reading. A study by Brown and Smiley (1977) highlights the problems that may arise. Although young children may be able to identify the main character and sequence of events in a simple story they experience difficulties in more complex texts. In their study, Brown and Smiley asked 8, 10, 12 and 18-year-olds to rate the ideas of complex folk stories according to their importance to the theme of the passage. Only 18-year-olds could reliably distinguish four levels of importance or centrality to the theme. Eight-year-olds could make no reliable distinction between levels of importance. Even 12-year-olds had difficulty deciding on the relative importance of text elements. This has important implications for learning. It is not sufficient to simply be aware of the necessary knowledge; a child must be able to apply the knowledge where and when appropriate to achieve a successful outcome.

•   Task

The fundamental task, however, for any reader is knowing that the primary goal of reading is to understand the content. As stated earlier, the novice reader can have problems even with this basic notion. If children are unaware that reading is supposed to lead to understanding rather than simply decoding, they will find great difficulty adjusting their behaviour depending on the task at hand. A simple strategy such as slowing down when encountering difficulties and speeding up when the material is trivial may not be applied when necessary.

Skimming, for example, is one activity again often demanded within classroom contexts which reflects a pupil's understanding of adjusting the reading rate depending on the purpose of the task in hand. A study by Myers and Paris (1978) concluded that 12-year-olds understood that the purpose of skimming was to pick out the informative words. The 8-year-olds, however, thought that skimming was reading all the easy words. One possible interpretation of this result may be that it is a reflection of their conception of reading as meaning getting and word decoding respectively, which in turn affects their ability to control their behaviour.

• Strategies

According to Brown's model, reported in an article by Brown, Armbruster and Baker (1986), the crucial variable is 'strategies'. She claims that when comprehension fails the child must make several important strategic decisions and he or she must choose from the following options: 'store the problem in memory as a pending question in the hope that clarification will be forthcoming; reread the text; look ahead in the text; or, if necessary, consult another source.' These strategies, which have been called 'fix-up' strategies (Alessi, Anderson and Goetz, 1979), are critical for efficient reading.

• Characteristics of the learner

The final variable in Brown's tetrahedral model is possibly the most influential and least susceptible to manipulation in the learning environment. It is the 'characteristics of the learner'. This particular variable appears to have received the least attention in Brown's work because of the inherent problems associated with attempting to design instruction aimed at altering these characteristics. Motivation, for example, clearly plays an important role when reading. Paris *et al.* (1984) express this succinctly when they explain that strategies have components of 'both skill and will'. Therefore, unless a learner wants to succeed in a task and attain the goals, he or she will never spend the time and energy to engage in metacognitive strategies. In the short-term, external incentives can produce effort but it is doubtful whether they will continue and have long lasting effects.

Another crucial influence on successful reading is the background knowledge which a reader brings to the task. The child may lack the requisite knowledge of the world to understand texts that presuppose adequate background experience. As Baker and Brown (1984) explain: 'If the text deals with topics unfamiliar to the reader, it will be difficult for her to understand the significance of the material, to select main points, and to disregard trivia.'

One solution is to select texts which deal with familiar material and gradually increase the introduction of new knowledge. However, this would be difficult to implement in the practical everyday life of the classroom when children are constantly exposed to a great wealth and variety of reading materials. Another solution detailed by Baker and Brown is to 'increase the reader's store of information'. This can be achieved by a programme of enrichment although this again may prove difficult since every programme would need to be devised to meet the needs of each individual child.

In conclusion therefore, much of the research into the self-regulatory mechanisms of children reading for meaning can be accounted for within Brown's model of learning. The four variables are interdependent and children differ in their control of text, task and strategies depending on their own characteristics. The research itself illustrates the differences in control between learners of differing ages and differing reading achievement. The convergent findings from recent research into metacognition generally, whether it be knowledge or control, have been summarised by Garner (1987) when she states: 'Young children and poorer readers are not nearly as adept as older children and good readers, respectively, in engaging in planful activities either to make cognitive progress or to monitor it.'

Therefore, poorer readers are clearly at a disadvantage in school because of deficiencies in their knowledge and application of metacognitive strategies. They are not nearly as resourceful in completing the variety of reading tasks necessary in academic settings.

STRATEGY TRAINING IN READING

In the last section of this chapter, I have indicated some of the problems which children may experience when reading and which can result in a poorer understanding of text. Awareness of these difficulties can be the preliminary step to attempting some form of remediation. Three main ways of improving comprehension have been detailed by Oakhill and Garnham (1988). Firstly, additions or changes can be made in the text to enhance comprehension without requiring any active effort by the reader. For example, the addition of pictures, titles and summaries. Secondly, activities such as note-taking, underlining and writing summaries can all improve comprehension. These are often referred to as 'study aids'. The third set of aids to comprehension are processing strategies which children can be taught to apply as they are reading. They can help children think about the text and whether they understand it. These strategies mainly attempt to enhance comprehension and they differ from the first two types of aids in that they rely entirely on what goes on in the reader's head rather than on 'external' aids to comprehension.

Research has focused almost exclusively on training these processing strategies for two main reasons. Firstly, if successful, these procedures can be applied to any text, and secondly, poor readers cannot easily provide their own illustrations or text organisation or even make effective use of traditional study aids. The aim is therefore to give poor readers the skills that better readers naturally use. There is also evidence (Garner, 1987) that poor comprehenders' problems arise partly because they fail to monitor their comprehension, or at least they make less use of monitoring strategies. In consequence, therefore, a great deal of research has been devoted to identifying then training these strategies. According to Garner, the strategies taught have been 'academically fundamental' (all children appear to need them) and 'differentially exercised' (some children appear not to use them spontaneously).

Success has been measured against three criteria which were identified by Belmont *et al* (1982):

1   Was there an immediate improvement of performance?
2   Were the instructional effects durable?
3   How successful was the transfer of the instructed activity to new situations?

For example, immediate improvements in performance can be evident either in qualitative changes or in quantitative changes. Durability of effects can be measured by maintenance of acceptable performance over a time interval without further instruction. Successful transfer demands acceptable performance in situations that are related but still different from the original training sessions. These three criteria are clearly dependent on each other and essential for successful strategy training.

Brown, Armbruster and Baker (1984) discuss three general types of training studies to illustrate the need for readers to be actively involved. They maintain that this is essential for training to be effective.

'Blind training' instructs children to perform particular activities but without explaining the significance of such activities. They are told what to do but not why. Although these procedures are sufficient for some children because they can infer the significance of the strategy, poorer readers especially are at a disadvantage. For example, rereading is an effective aid to comprehension but for children to use the strategy they must believe in its effectiveness and efficiency. The consequences of this type of instruction for poor readers are detailed by Paris and Oka (1986): 'Passive inattention in the classroom or obedience rule-following are negative tactics that students often use to appear involved in tasks, yet these approaches avoid learning altogether.'

The other two types of training studies detailed by Brown, Armbruster and Baker have added metacognitive supplements. They are 'informed training' and 'self-controlled training'. Both have met with success but the latter is viewed as superior in addition to including information about the strategy readers have been instructed to use, there is explicit instruction in how to monitor and evaluate the strategy used.

DIRECT CLASSROOM APPLICATION OF STRATEGY TRAINING IN READING

One particular procedure to improve comprehension which incorporates both 'informed' and 'self-controlled' training is Reciprocal Teaching. It has developed into a flexible instructional approach which has direct applications in a variety of learning contexts. Reciprocal Teaching (which takes place in a group or paired situation) features guided practice in the application of four concrete strategies aimed at comprehending a section of text (Palincsar and Klenk, 1992). The four strategies identified by Palincsar and Brown in their initial study in 1984 were questioning, clarifying, summarising and predicting. According to Palincsar and Brown, these four activities serve a dual purpose, they are both comprehension fostering and comprehension monitoring. That is, they enhance comprehension while allowing the pupil to check whether it is occurring.

The hallmark of this form of instruction is that it is interactive in nature, with each pupil and adult taking turns to be 'teacher'. No passive inattention here! The text can be read aloud in sections, depending on the decoding skills of the pupils, following which the 'teacher' leads discussion by asking questions. Other participants respond to the questions and generate additional questions if necessary. The 'teacher' then asks for clarifications which encourages further discussion on ambiguous sections of the text. Then the 'teacher' summarises the section and, if appropriate, generates predictions regarding upcoming content in the text. Finally, a new 'teacher' is selected who leads the discussion on the next section of text.

The results from their first study in 1984 were impressive. The three criteria for success outlined earlier had been met. Firstly, there was an improvement of performance. The children involved, aged 12, who were at least two years behind in comprehension, made gains quantitatively in daily tests of comprehension and in a standardised reading test. They also made qualitative gains in the content of their daily dialogue with the researchers. An analysis of the dialogue showed main idea questions increased during the period of reciprocal teaching and main idea summaries increased substantially. Secondly, the effects were durable. The children involved maintained their improvements at the final follow-up visit eight weeks after the study had finished. Finally, the skills generalised to other areas of the curriculum such as social studies and science classes.

Moore (1988) identified four main theoretical elements of reciprocal teaching which he considers were instrumental in its success.

The first and most influential is that of 'scaffolding' (Palincsar and Brown 1984) which has been derived from Vygotskian developmental theory. It refers to the support given to a novice by an expert through the use of dialogue to model and explain cognitive processes. The amount of scaffolding is varied to suit individual differences. As Brown and Palincsar explain: 'The teacher should model the desired comprehension activities, thereby making underlying processes overt, explicit and concrete.'

Garner (1987) outlines the work of Vygotsky (1978) which she suggests is a solution to the problem of low durability in some strategy training. She details his notion of 'zone of proximal development' by which Vygotsky suggested that cognitive functions appear, first on the social (inter-psychological) level, and only later on the individual (intra-psychological) level. This zone of proximal development is the distance between the level of independent problem-solving and the level of problem-solving in collaboration with an expert. Vygotsky explained: 'What children can do with assistance of others might be in some sense more indicative of their mental development than what they can do alone.'

The second element described by Moore is 'fading' of the expert's role in modelling these reading comprehension strategies. This allows the learner to take over more responsibility slowly while gaining confidence, and has been shown to be an important feature of successful strategy training.

The third element is 'active involvement' which within reciprocal teaching means the learner has to assume an active teacher role. The 'passive inattention' detailed by Paris and Oka (1986) which they describe as 'avoiding learning altogether' is not possible when the learner is forced into such an active role.

The final element is the 'provision of feedback' to the learner regarding the efficiency of the strategy and the value of using a strategy in that context. It is important to know the utility of a strategy; for example, when to use it, how to use it and how to monitor the success. Moore concludes by stating, 'In short, reciprocal teaching demonstrates that through active involvement in real reading contexts, strategies can and do make a difference.'

The success of the Palincsar and Brown studies (1984) is not an isolated phenomenon. There have been other training studies which have demonstrated that metacognition can be promoted through direct instruction in the classroom. One such study which appears both relevant and practical in an education setting was reported by Paris, Cross and Lipson (1984). This involved 8 and 10-year-olds in an experimental curriculum of 'informed strategies for learning' (ISL) which was designed to increase children's awareness and use of effective reading strategies.

Fourteen comprehension strategies (e.g. skimming, locating main ideas, monitoring comprehension, making inferences, etc.) were taught over a period of four months. The strategies were taught using concrete metaphors such as 'Be a reading detective', 'Stop – say the meaning in your own words' and 'Dead end – go back and read the parts you don't understand'. The three modes of instruction were classroom lessons which included modelling of a particular strategy as well as how, when and why to use it; the bulletin board, which colourfully illustrated the metaphors, included questions that focused on how, when and why and served as a reminder during normal class work; and suggestions for classroom teachers on how to use the strategies within their every day work.

The children who participated in ISL made gains in cloze and error detection tasks compared with a control group. In interviews, they also revealed a greater understanding and awareness about reading strategies and the goals of the task. Paris *et al* .(1984) concluded, 'The theoretical value of this study lies in the demonstration that group instruction can be used to transmit information about reading strategies and more importantly that children can be convinced to use the strategies on their own.'

However, strategy training in reading has not been without its critics and it is wise to be aware of the more important cautions which have been expressed. Firstly, the basic assumption made by most researchers is that poor readers will benefit from being taught to use strategies that skilled readers use naturally. Although this may appear fairly obvious, the fact that poor comprehenders have not acquired these strategies may indicate they are, in some cases, unable to acquire them. As Oakhill and Garnham (1988) state, training children to ask questions about cause and effect should enhance comprehension because it helps children to find connections between events. But if some readers are not capable of identifying those connections, they will not benefit from such training. It therefore cannot be assumed that poor comprehenders will automatically become good ones if they are 'taught' the skills.

Another realistic caution expressed about strategy training has been outlined by Garner (1987) and is based on research by Peterson and Swing (1984). They point out that children have to carry out cognitive processing 'in real time'. This means that given the nature of the activity flow in most classrooms, pupils cannot work slowly enough to incorporate unpractised metacognitive strategies. In consequence, pupils who are worried about 'being left behind' in task completion often revert to less mature, more rehearsed routines. Garner emphasises ,therefore, the need for plenty of guided practice so strategies become 'more personalised and more routinised'.

There is one danger, however, which must be considered when attempting strategy training and that is the problem of being too prescriptive. We do not yet know enough about skilled reading generally or reading strategies specifically to state with any confidence the 'right' way to read or for that matter, the 'right' strategies children should adopt to be successful. Research by Pask (1976) for example, has identified two distinctive styles of learning – holist and serialist – which represent consistent preferences for using certain learning processes while other research on cognitive styles has differentiated between convergent and divergent thinking. Differences in styles of learning will, in turn, affect children's approaches to learning and this needs to be taken into account so that strategy training is not implemented too mechanically. Ultimately, children must be encouraged to be flexible in their approach to reading in order to satisfy the task in hand, whether it be educational or social. As Palincsar (1986) claims: 'In conducting metacognitive instruction, one aspires to teach students to plan, implement and evaluate strategic approaches to learning and problem solving. Students, therefore, assume control of their own learning.' This 'control' by the pupils themselves must be the ultimate goal of strategy training.

CONCLUSION AND DISCUSSION

This chapter has set out to describe the recent research into strategy training which has its basis within the wider context of metacognition. The literature has illustrated that the training of cognitive skills to enhance comprehension can be successful with poorer readers. Consequently, there are educational implications for all teachers. They are in an ideal position to foster metacognitive skills within the context of their everyday teaching. Strategy instruction can be intertwined with subject area instruction and has been successful when applied over a continuous period of time (Garner, 1987). As well as the structured programmes described, such as Reciprocal Teaching and ISL, there are many ways teachers can assist pupils to improve their metacognitive skills and become more successful learners. For example, while completing tasks, teachers can make covert metacognitive processes overt by thinking aloud and modelling appropriate strategies. They can demonstrate that the same strategy can transfer successfully to a variety of learning situations and (importantly) provide pupils with opportunities to practise strategies so they become personalised and routine. The classroom can be a place where cognition is discussed.

Some pupils with specific learning difficulties may also be at risk from poor metacognitive knowledge and strategy use. Their obvious difficulties in acquiring the necessary literacy skills have resulted in intensive direct instruction over prolonged periods of time to develop competence. This, however, may result in failure to utilise self-regulatory skills flexibly or spontaneously. As Wright and Cashdan (1992) explain, 'Although the approaches are essentially well-designed, there may be more to successful reading and spelling remediation than appropriate skills acquisition alone.'

Bearing this in mind they designed a pilot study aimed at 'young backward readers with poor decoding abilities' which attempted to address this problem by combining phonological skills training with explicit instruction in the meta-linguistic, metacognitive aspects of reading and spelling. The skill component incorporated a direct teaching model adapted from the Simultaneous Oral Spelling method advocated by Bryant and Bradley (1985), while the metacognitive element included the development of concepts about reading and spelling and strategy development as well as self-regulation and monitoring of thinking. Although the formal test results were inconclusive, Wright and Cashdan observed improvements in phonological abilities as well as the ability to approach reading/ spelling tasks strategically through co-ordination of plans, strategies and verbalisation. They claimed that, 'During the intervention period, the children moved from passive, anxious, unsystematic learners at baseline to keen active participants in the teaching sessions.'

It is interesting to note the choice of words used by the researchers to describe their learners: 'Passive and anxious' at the beginning of this intervention while becoming 'keen, active and interested' as the study progressed. This change

in behaviour which can readily be observed when pupils are involved in Reciprocal Teaching (Brown, 1992) is essential for success learning. Pupils who have a specific learning difficulty are often characterised as 'passive' and are without doubt 'anxious'. They may have negative motivational attributes and beliefs which in turn influence their approaches to learning.

Metacognitive strategy training does have important motivational consequences. Reciprocal Teaching, for example, through guided practice and scaffolding can control frustration and decrease the risk inherent in problem solving. Among other things it reduces the numbers of steps in the process to a manageable amount and relies on the teacher to make overt any mismatch between the pupil's response and more appropriate strategy use. Therefore, pupils gradually gain independence in a supportive learning situation.

As Borkowski (1992) explains, 'Teachers do not merely deliver content to students but rather model strategic processing.' He himself advocates that Reciprocal Teaching could be extended into the realms of motivational retraining in order to provide pupils with the 'energising factors necessary for independent reading and thinking.' Borkowski also claims that teachers who are consciously aware of metacognitive skills are, 'In a good position to reshape self-defeating beliefs, enhance feelings of self-efficiency, foster interests in learning for its own sake and associate such changes in the motivational-self systems with the emergence of independent self-regulatory skills.'

This may seem a formidable challenge, but learning has to be seen as both cognitive and emotional in content and it is wise in a chapter devoted to the learner that this important aspect is not overlooked. Teachers have a crucial role to play in encouraging pupils to become more successful learners in the classroom. The awareness and positive fostering of metacognitive skills is indispensable.

REFERENCES

Alessi, S., Anderson, T. and Goetz, E. (1979). An Investigation of Lookbacks during Studying. Discourse Processes, 2, 197-212. Cited in Garner, R. (1987) *Metacognition and Reading Comprehension*. Norwood, NJ: Ablex Publishing Corporation.

Armbruster, B. and Brown, A. (1984). Learning from Reading: The Role of Metacognition. In Anderson, R., Osborn, J. and Tierney, R. (Eds.), *Learning to Read in American Schools*. Hillsdale, NJ: Lawrence Erlbaum Associates.

Baker, L. and Brown, A. (1984). Metacognitive Skills and Reading. In Pearson, P. D. (Ed.), *Handbook of Reading Research*. New York: Longman.

Belmont, J., Butterfield, E., and Ferretti, R. (1982). To Secure Transfer of Training Instruct Self Management Skills. In Determan, D. and Sternberg, R. (Eds.), *How and How Much Can Intelligence Be Increased.* Norwood, NJ: Ablex.

Borkowski, J. (1992). Metacognitive Theory: A Framework for Teaching Literacy, Writing, and Math Skills. *Journal of Learning Disabilities, 25,* 253-257.

Brown, A., Armbruster, B. and Baker, L. (1986). The Role of Metacognition in Reading and Study. In Orasanu, J. (Ed.), *Reading Comprehension: Form Research to Practice.* Hillsdale, NJ: Lawrence Erlbaum Associates.

Brown, A. and Smiley, S. (1977). Rating the Importance of Structural Units of Prose Passages: A Problem of Metacognitive Development. *Child Development, 48,* 1-8.

Brown, P. (1992). Reciprocal Teaching: An Approach to Improving Reading Comprehension by Training Metacognitive Strategies. In Satow, F. and Gatherer, B. (Eds.), *Literacy without Frontiers.* Great Britain: UKRA.

Bryant, P. E. and Bradley, L. (1985). *Children's Reading Problems.* Oxford. Markwell.

Entwhistle, N. (1987). *Understanding Classroom Learning.* London: Hodder & Stoughton.

Flabell, J. H. (1979). Metacognition and Cognitive Monitoring. *American Psychologist,* Oct., 906-911.

Garner, R. (1987). *Metacognition and Reading Comprehension.* Norwood, NJ: Ablex.

Montague, M. (1992). The Effects of Cognitive and Metacognitive Strategy Instruction on the Mathematical Problem Solving of Middle School Students with Learning Disabilities. *Journal of Learning Disabilities, 25,* 230-248.

Moore, P. (1988). Reciprocal Teaching and Reading Comprehension: A Review. *Journal of Research in Reading, 11,* 3-14.

Myers, M. and Paris, S. (1978). Children's Metacognitive Knowledge About Reading. *Journal of Educational Psychology, 70,* 680-690.

Oakhill, J. and Garnham, A. (1988). *Becoming a Skilled Reader.* London: Basil Blackwell Ltd.

Palincsar, A. (1986). Metacognitive Strategy Instruction. *Exceptional Children, 53,* 118-124.

Palincsar, A. and Brown, A. (1984). Reciprocal Teaching of Comprehension Fostering and Comprehension Monitoring Activities. *Cognition and Instruction, 1(2),* 117-175.

Palincsar, A. and Klenk, L. (1992). Fostering Literacy Learning in Supportive Contexts. *Journal of Learning Disabilities, 25,* 211-225.

Paris, S., Cross, D. and Lipson, M. (1984). Informed Strategies for Learning: A Programme to Improve Children's Reading Awareness and Comprehension. *Journal of Educational Psychology, 76,* 1239-1252.

Paris, S. and Oka, E. (1986). Self Regulated Learning Among Exceptional Children. *Exceptional Children 53,* 103-108.

Pask, G. (1976). Styles and Strategies for Learning. *British Journal of Educational Psychology, 46,* 128-148.

Peterson, P. and Swing, S. (1983). Problems in Classroom Implementation of Cognitive Strategy Instruction. In Pressley, M. and Leven, J. (Eds.), *Cognitive Strategy Research: Educational Applications.* New York: Springer-Verlag.

Simpson, M. (1988). Improving Learning in Schools – What Do We Know? A Cognitive Perspective. *Scottish Educational Review, 20,* 22–31.

Vygotsky, L. (1978). *Mind in Society: the Development of Higher Psychological Processes.* Cambridge, MA: Harvard University Press. Cited in Garner (1987).

Wright, J. and Cashdan, A. (1992). Training Metacognitive Skills in Backward Readers: A Pilot Study. *Educational Psychology in Practice, 7,* 153–162.

HANDWRITING – SKILLS, STRATEGIES AND SUCCESS

MARY KIELY

INTRODUCTION

Handwriting

Every craftsman, whatever his trade, needs a tool. If the tool is less than satisfactory, the end result can never fulfil the original aim in its entirety. Handwriting is the tool with which the writer presents his ideas. It is important to write legibly and at speed. It is a skill that can be taught to practically all children and will be of enduring benefit to them. Many children, including those with specific learning difficulties, find it extremely difficult both to write legibly and at an appropriate speed. These skills can be taught and need to be seen as an important area both in Primary and Secondary School.

There has also been a tendency to regard the teaching of handwriting as the prerogative of the Primary School – the Secondary School it seems, has more important things to attend to and 'it may be too late anyway'. There may also be some confusion as to who carries the responsibility for improving a pupil's handwriting, since it crosses all subject boundaries.

The cause of the apparent reluctance to do much about bad handwriting in the Secondary School, apart from the occasional admonition to 'tidy up your handwriting', has probably lain in a lack of appreciation of the effect of bad handwriting on the pupil himself. Whereas most teachers would agree that poor presentation of work has a bad effect on the self-esteem of the child, it would appear most unlikely that any significant number appreciate the sheer magnitude of the destruction of self-esteem that can ensue; there may even be a feeling that, if pupils were so worried, they would do something about it – showing also a lack of appreciation that some pupils, such as those with specific learning difficulties, are unable to do anything about it themselves and need considerable help to effect any improvement.

When a pupil's handwriting has improved his self-esteem can soar, often successfully helping him to tackle much more of his other school work with greater zeal and determination.

AN AGENCY FOR CHANGE: THE WRITING ROOM

A major obstacle to the improvement of handwriting in a secondary school is that there is usually no one with specific responsibility for it and there may be no specific policy on handwriting. At Dumfries Academy, the writing room was introduced to remedy deficiencies in basic English such as sentence structure, punctuation, spelling and handwriting. Pupils were released for periods of approximately 20 minutes per week to attend and they were extracted at different times each week so that their absences were not always from the same subject. Initial referrals were by members of staff.

Much of the work in the writing room focuses on handwriting and the successes achieved encouraged a major influx of self-referrals from pupils. Peer recognition of success was responsible for much of this. The considerable increase in morale and self esteem amongst pupils, consequent upon the dramatic improvement in the presentation of their work, is worthy of note. It is on the results achieved in this writing room that the present chapter is largely based.

PRE-PROGRAMME CONSIDERATIONS

While it may be possible to take children for handwriting instruction in small groups, handwriting is such an individual process and the errors which a pupil has acquired are so particular to himself that it is only through highly individualised tuition that these errors can be fully eliminated.

When I first see a pupil, the main requirement is that he should be well motivated. He must be keen to improve his handwriting. That is why I am so much encouraged by the fact that so many of my pupils are self-referred. Such motivation, however, can never be taken for granted; it must be nurtured and enhanced, together with the confidence and self-esteem which are so closely related to it.

Therefore, when I see a pupil initially, I must convince him that his handwriting can be improved comparatively easily. I show him specimens of 'before and after' handwriting and tell him that such improvements have been effected in a short period. I try to ensure that the process consists of a large number of short-term gains so that the pupil is continually meeting success.

Initially, I photocopy a sample from the pupil's normal class-work and I ask him to write a short piece for me in order to observe his writing action closely. Together, we look at these samples of his handwriting; I praise wherever I can and then we discuss aspects of it that he would like to change so that the pupil is very much involved in his own learning.

PLANNING THE PROGRAMME

Having identified the areas of concern in the pupil's handwriting, I plan an individualised programme for him; I decide on which difficulties to concentrate and allocate my areas of priority accordingly. I begin by making a few specific suggestions for improvement and get the pupil to concentrate on these, practise them and incorporate them in a piece of writing. The pupil immediately sees an improvement, albeit on the small side, but this motivates him sufficiently to go away and practise this assiduously during the following week so that it becomes automatic. He is expected to practise every night and to incorporate the teaching points made into the writing of his ordinary class-work. By the time he next attends the writing room, the improvements are so noticeable as to encourage and motivate him further; this facilitates the repetition of the process. After a number of such visits to the writing room, the improvement is normally large enough to discontinue tuition. A few months later, the pupil's progress is reviewed. In the majority of cases, the improvement is sustained; in the few regressions which occur, they can normally be remedied comparatively easily by repetition of the tuition; in some cases, there is further improvement, usually where the pupil's own style has developed. The key to success here is undoubtedly the number of short-term gains that are continually built into the learning process to sustain motivation which allows the pupil's own natural style to develop.

HANDWRITING SKILLS

It is not the purpose of this chapter to provide a detailed treatise on handwriting but rather to indicate how, within the context of the modern comprehensive school, bad handwriting can be comparatively painlessly improved to an acceptable (not necessarily perfect!) standard, within a short space of time so that the pupil's motivation can be easily maintained. However, it is appropriate to explain briefly the main faults which I attempt to eradicate.

* **Pencil Grip**

Firstly, it soon becomes obvious if handwriting is an effortless relaxed activity for the pupil. One prime inhibiting factor is a faulty grip on the pen or pencil. A faulty grip can cause tiredness, tension or even pain when having to write at length and too much or too little pressure can obviously effect the handwriting; a faulty grip can also prevent good letter formation. It can be difficult to change and can be time consuming but it is very important to do so. Pupils have told me how they hated writing and subjects involving a lot of written work because of this problem. To change the grip, experimenting with different types of pens or pencils to see which suit the pupil best will probably be necessary. Pupils tend to enjoy this and the element of choice involved.

I encountered one pupil who had no problems with handwriting until he was required to write at speed or length, which he resisted, and it became obvious that he tired easily because of his faulty grip. A three sided pencil, instead of the usual barrel shaped pencil, produced no improvement; however, the 'GRIPPY', a simple unobtrusive rubber device to attach to the pencil or pen (readily available on the market) which is shaped and slightly hollowed, proved effective and after practising with the 'GRIPPY' for several weeks, he was able to discard it, hold an ordinary pencil correctly and write effectively at speed or length. It should be mentioned, however, that if a child has an unorthodox grip with which he is managing to write legibly, quickly and effortlessly, then no attempt is made to change that grip.

- **Positioning**

  Whilst sitting comfortably is obviously important, the correct positioning of the paper is perhaps less evidently so. However, it can be very inhibiting to have the paper squarely in front of the writer as this can restrict movement. To ensure fluent, speedy handwriting the paper should be positioned on the same side of the body as the writing hand and, for right handers, it should be suitably slanted slightly to the left with the left hand on the paper for steadying purposes (and vice-versa for left handers).

- **Paper**

  Lined paper provides a structure of base lines to which the pupil can relate his letters and gauge their size, and also keep his writing straight. Some pupils have to be constantly encouraged to make this appropriate use of the lines. When unlined paper is in use, heavily lined paper underneath can be used as a guide.

- **Spacing**

  One of the notable features of the writing room experience is the pupil's participation in his own learning, an invaluable ingredient for maintaining motivation. When we initially examine the pupil's handwriting together, an obvious error often becomes apparent in our discussion, that of bad spacing; this has the virtue of being easily remedied and making a considerable transformation so quickly that the pupil feels he is really making progress. Poor or little spacing between words is a very common fault and is easily corrected by comparing a model of good spacing with the pupil's own work and asking him to copy the former. Once a pupil becomes aware of this error he normally has little difficulty in eliminating it from his own class-work. Similarly, when uneven spacing occurs between letters in words, the pupil is again shown a correct model to compare with his own; he is asked to write words with and without appropriate spacing and observe the difference, thus heightening his awareness. Once this has registered, the pupil has little difficulty in practising and reinforcing this in his on-going writing.

- **Letter Formation**

Good letter formation is of prime importance. Pupils have to be taught to form letters correctly, practising together letters which are similar in size and shape. Groups in which letters can be conveniently taught and practised together can be as follows:

- Letters which have a rounded pattern –

$$c \quad \sigma \quad a \quad d \quad g \quad q \quad s$$

- which seem to cause more difficulty –

$$e \quad f$$

- letters which are more linear–

$$i \quad t \quad l \quad u \quad y \quad j$$

$$r \quad n \quad h \quad m \quad b \quad p \quad k$$

- letters which are more zig-zag –

There can be a certain overlap between these groups.

- Letters need to be of the correct height and certain ones need to be practised –

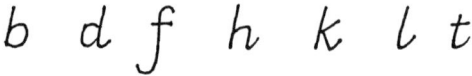

- Similar practice has to be given to letters which go below the line –

Capital 'P' and small 'p' frequently cause some difficulty.

It has to be stressed to pupils that letters have to be fully completed so that it can be seen where one letter ends and another begins. In particular

$$a \quad b \quad d \quad e \quad g \quad o \quad p \quad q$$

are completely closed. It is especially important to complete 'o' 'a' and 'd' completely, otherwise 'o' can look like 'u;' 'a' can look like 'u' and 'd' can look like 'c l.'

Attention should also be paid to reversals of letters, 'b' and 'd' being particularly important. It should be pointed out that only the letters 'd' and 'e' begin in the middle, all others start at the top. It should be emphasised that 'b' begins at the top with a vertical line. If 'o' is incorrectly formed in a clockwise direction it causes problems for joining; a similar problem arises with 's' if it is started in the wrong place.

It is essential that pupils acquire proper letter formation and a knowledge of where letters should start and finish before joining begins. At the secondary stage, some children have developed their own system of joining which will correspond to a greater or lesser extent with the generally accepted methods, and these can be modified to suit their particular requirements.

Letters can then be grouped into those joined horizontally and those joined diagonally.

LETTERS WHICH CAN JOIN HORIZONTALLY

σ v w

For example:

σσ σc σd σi σy

LETTERS WHICH CAN JOIN DIAGONALLY

a c d e h i k l m n t u

There are the following types of diagonal joins:

1. Diagonal joins to letters of similar heights, for example:

am an im in ip is

2. Diagonal joins to taller letters, for example:

ah it il ik

3. Diagonal joins to 'e', for example:

ae de ce me ee le

4. Diagonal joins which help to form the next letter. These are the most difficult and need particular emphasis and practice, for example:

ad ca ma na ag ng ao co

With letters that are traditionally difficult to join or even with letters that the pupil finds difficult to join for some reason of his own, the best course is not to join them but to put the two letters close together so that they appear to be joined. I would also do this where capital letters are involved.

Letters which my pupils found difficulty in joining are:

b g j p q r s x y z

Other points which have to be attended to are the size of the writing, which should not be too large or too small, with adequate definition, the development of a consistent forward slant and the evolution of a smooth flowing, rhythmic style.

- **Writing at Speed**

Even when the pupil has been taught to write correctly and legibly, there is the question of writing at speed to consider. As far as the slow writer is concerned, problems of grip, comfortable seating and appropriate positioning of paper have been already discussed. If these have been attended to, the key to development of writing at speed is to practise spacing, letter formation and joining so that their correct implementation becomes automatic and the writer can transfer his thoughts to paper without giving attention to the writing process. It is essential to encourage a smooth steady progression across the paper with minimal lifting of the hand. I find it is helpful to have ligatures (ticks) at the end of words, where appropriate, because this promotes a flowing progression to the next word. Experience has also shown me that a forward consistent slant helps a pupil to introduce a rhythmic and fluent progression across the paper. After these points have been dealt with, the development of writing at speed will usually come naturally with practice. However, if an unsuitable style has been acquired this might have to be changed. In handwriting, as with many other skills, it is often the simplest that is the best. Occasionally, a pupil's handwriting can be illegible because of writing too fast. If such requirements as good letter formation, joins, slant and spacing are fulfilled, a simple reduction in speed is often enough to effect considerable improvement.

CASE STUDIES:

Having summarised the main principles of good handwriting, it is instructive to consider how these principles can be applied to transform bad handwriting, at the Secondary School stage, into something that is legible, reasonably attractive and can be written fluently with some semblance of style. It should be emphasised that this is not an attempt to produce near-perfect handwriting but just to produce something that will serve as an effortless, expeditious tool for the expression of the written word in an attractive manner, enabling a pupil to take justifiable pride in his presentation of work. Improvements have to be effected quickly in a way which will facilitate a continuous series of successful outcomes for the pupil so as to maintain the initial motivation and to encourage him to undertake the considerable amount of practice required.

*   **Barry (aged 12)**

Initial Sample:

> Animals that dont are star iish whale
> plaice crab
> Pangolin dont know
> cow horse hare
> crab whale starfish plaice
> Pangon dont konw

Final Sample:

> Most of the things we use everyday are made in factories. The factories are specially organised so that a lot of the same sort of things can be made very quickly. This factory makes bicycles. People in factories see the nurse if they are ill. They eat in the canteen.

Barry's initial sample shown was given me as typical of his class-work. Barry was unhappy about his writing but did not know how to improve it. His spacing, both between and within words, was poor. His letter formation was inconsistent and the sizing of his letters needed attention. He wrote the letter 's' in reverse. The writing had no joins except for a few diagonal ones. He wrote in staccato, jerky movements with the paper straight in front of him.

On his first visit we concentrated on spacing and on improving his letter formation, which was not too bad. Some practice was given on letter sizing with particular reference to ascenders (tall letters) and descenders (letters partly below the line). Barry practised these points at home during the following week and in his class-work and had made a marked improvement by the time of his second visit. At Barry's second visit and for the following few weeks we concentrated on different joins. At the second visit I also introduced the correct positioning of paper and we started to develop a smooth fluent rhythmic style, paying particular to ligatures (ticks) at the end of suitable letters which added to the fluency of movement. Barry practised diligently at home and incorporated the suggestions into his class-work. His regular and marked improvement sufficed to motivate him greatly and the final sample of handwriting was produced on his fifth visit to the writing room.

- **Peter (aged 13)**

    Initial Sample

    > The witches is told by the boy is
    > 13 on holiday with his gran. When he
    > The witches is caught up in a meeting of witches.
    > plan to turn all the children in
    > he world into mice. he is caught
    > by them and turned into a mouse.

    Sample on the sixth visit

    > Lonnie Zamora was chasing a speeding car when he heard a roar and
    > saw a blue flash in the sky. The flaming ball was slowly coming down
    > not far away.

Due to his bad handwriting, Peter had difficulty in completing assignments, not because of lack of ability for the task, but because his hand became easily tired and he had difficulty writing at length.

As the specimen shows, his writing slanted in different directions and he had difficulty in keeping to base lines. Spacing was irregular and some of his letters, such as 'd', involved loops.

His writing was punctuated by sudden bursts of speed at the end of a line and he seemed to have difficulty moving across the page. Besides rectifying the usual errors, the first priority with Peter was to modify his grip. His wrist movements were also very restricted. The vital development of more flexible movement was greatly facilitated by positioning his paper slightly to the right, angling it to suit him, and positioning his non-writing hand on the paper. Because his writing went up and down so much, Peter also had to practise positioning his writing relative to the base lines. He retained some of his loops, for example in 'y' and 'g' but discarded them in 'l' and 'h'. Achieving a smooth writing movement across the page necessitated a large amount of practise but eventually Peter got into his rhythm and, with a sudden breakthrough, achieved the second sample illustrated on his sixth visit to the writing room. Peter has maintained this improvement and is much more confident in his work across the curriculum.

- **John (aged 14)**

  Original Sample:

  > The only difference between the two experiments is that in our the magnesium is being added to a diluted hydrochloric acid and the other is being added to Hydrochloric acid. which is more concentrated

  Second Sample:

  > An M.P. can reply to letters and enquiries from his constituents. He represents his constituents by doing such things as investigating complaints about income tax or social security.

Review Sample:

Hundreds of travellers who vanished without trace in the sixteenth century Galloway sparked of one of Galloways most baffling mysteries.

    John is a pupil with considerable academic potential but it was considered that he would be handicapped, particularly in external examinations, by his handwriting. He was keen to improve it and particularly to join his handwriting. In the original sample John was able to form his letters confidently and well, although the letter 'f' needed attention and the letter 'd' could look like 'cl'. Spacing, the relative sizing of letters and joining all needed some attention, whilst assistance with the flow and speed of writing was also required. John worked very hard at remedying these defects with the main priority on joining. Because of his lack of experience of this, it took about four weeks for it to become automatic without having to think about it. It was at this stage that the second sample was produced. This shows that John had then improved his letter formation, mastered cursive writing to some extent and developed a slant. John was now anxious to develop a style, and, although he did not attend the writing room again until two months later, when the third sample was taken, he continued to practise hard and this third sample shows further improvement and development of his writing with adequate speed and fluency. This improvement in his handwriting, favourably commented on by many of his teachers, gave John much more self-confidence overall and his grades have improved in subjects across the curriculum.

- **Andrew (aged 15)**

Week One

What you were trying to do, how you went about it eg and what your solution was like. you may like to get your parents to read drafts of your report

Week Two

trying to do, how you went about it and What your solution was like. You may like to get your parents to read drafts of your report.

Week Three

His soul flew from him betrayed and unwanted, replaced by the blackness, sucked in through the pores, draining his very lifeblood. None could quench his burning rage, only the power of the gauntlet could relieve this burden.

This case study is provided to show how a pupil, with a small amount of guidance, can, in three weeks, transform his handwriting to a much more mature style. The initial sample shows an immature style, lacking in slant and definition. On the first visit to the writing room attention was paid to the following letter formations in the sample. In the first line the letter 'o' has no horizontal join and is not joined to the next letter. Nor is the letter 'u' completed with a ligature (tick). In the word 'went' the letters 'e' and 'n' are incomplete and just merge. In the second line, in the word 'and' the 'a' is not closed and looks like the letter 'u'. Also the 'a' and 'n' merge. The formation of the letter 'd' in the third line also needs attention. Discussion also took place on the development of slant and of the smooth movements of the writing hand across the page to develop a rhythmic pattern and abandon jerky movements. All the teaching points were practised and reinforced at home and applied in the normal class-work until the end of the following week, when the next visit produced the much improved second sample.

As well as emphasizing original teaching points, it was suggested that the writing could be made smaller and a further week's practice produced the third sample, a fluent, acceptable style, produced at a good speed with free and flowing movement. Andrew is delighted with the improvement in his handwriting and is particularly proud of the much more mature impression it conveys.

CONCLUSION

It is to be hoped that this chapter has firmly established the importance of commitment and motivation in the improvement of handwriting. The key to success is undoubtedly pupil-motivation, which is necessary to undertake the considerable amount of practice involved. The process is basically a partnership. There is much discussion and the pupil is encouraged to assess his own work and discuss suggestions for improvement. He does, in fact, take a great deal of responsibility for his own learning, thus cultivating the more mature approach in which the pupil recognises his own difficulties and then attempts to do something about them.

It is only when the effects of improved handwriting are seen that one begins to comprehend the full extent of the problems created by bad handwriting. When a pupil's self-esteem and morale are vastly enhanced, his written work takes on a much greater appearance of maturity and his whole attitude to school changes for the better; one really begins to appreciate what must have been missing before and how much greater priority Secondary Schools should give to the improvement of handwriting.

Where handwriting has improved, teachers tend to value a pupil's work more highly and pay greater attention to it. Improved handwriting also tends to make weaknesses in spelling, punctuation and sentence construction more easily detectable.

The handwriting samples in this chapter, typical of many on record, show the extent of the actual improvement of handwriting achieved. Perhaps the last word on evaluation should be with those most intimately associated with improved handwriting, the pupils themselves.

'The writing room has helped me to rejuvenate my writing technique. This was vital as I am sitting my final exams soon and it could improve my grade as much as from a grade 3 to a grade 2.'

'Changing my handwriting really allowed me to express my personality on paper as well as giving me more self-confidence.'

'Some people see writing as sort of eyes because if you see untidy writing you think that person is untidy and not trustworthy.'

'When my writing was bad I didn't like other people to read it.'

'To me better writing means a better job and hopefully further education.'

'I find it easier to revise my notes because I can now read them.'

'Looking back on what I used to write like and what I write like now shows you what you can achieve with a bit of help and a lot of work.'

However, improved handwriting can also be a disadvantage!

'I had to bring an extra I.D. to the bank to prove my identity because my signature had altered so much.'

REFERENCES

Alston, J. and Taylor, J. (1985). *The Handwriting File: Diagnosis and Remediation*. LDA Wisbech.

Alston, J. and Taylor J. (1987). *Handwriting: Theory, Research and Practice*. Croom Helm.

Pumfrey, P. D. and Reason, R. (1991). *Specific Learning Difficulties (Dyslexia) Challenges and Responses*. NFER Routledge.

Sassoon, R. (1986). *Helping your Handwriting*. Arnold Wheaton.

Committee on Primary Education (1986). *Report of the Project: Foundations of Writing. Consultative Committee on the Curriculum*.

Raban, B. and Postlethwaite, K. (1988). *Classroom Responses to Learning Difficulties*. MacMillan Education.

ASSESSING AND PROMOTING HANDWRITING SKILLS

JEAN ALSTON

TEACHING HANDWRITING: 1970 TO 1995

Handwriting, in some schools in the United Kingdom, has not been well taught during recent decades. As in the teaching of reading, where the emphasis has sometimes been upon developing a love of books and neglect of word attack skills, in writing, the concern has been with creative and expressive writing rather than with the craft of writing, which requires the teaching of handwriting and secretarial skills. Handwriting has often been regarded as a literacy skill that would develop spontaneously, so long as the child is given sufficient encouragement and stimulation. Some of our more able children have seen the logic of having good letter forms, and have been able to teach themselves. However, for children with learning difficulties, specific or general, the demise of the teaching of handwriting, often throughout the 1970s and 1980s, has led to parents, teachers, and the children they teach, experiencing handwriting difficulties which could have been avoided.

Handwriting, of course, is a motor skill, which has its foundations in letter formation. There are 26 lower case letters, the ones most commonly used in early education. If the movements are taught well in early educational stages, there will be good foundations for the development of all literacy. If the movements are not taught, a sizable proportion of pupils will experience handwriting difficulties for many of their years in school. Young teachers, themselves untrained in the development and teaching of handwriting, have little knowledge or experience with which to assist their pupils. All children are disadvantaged when the teaching of handwriting is neglected. However, children with difficulties, specific or general, fare worse than most. They are left with weak writing foundations, and may never recover throughout their educational years.

There are 26 lower case and 26 capital letters. In the early stages of education, emphasis tends to be placed on developing the lower case letters, with perhaps use of the occasional capital letter for the beginnings of children's names. With this situation in mind, we can concern ourselves principally with the 26 lower case letters. Children may not be aware that there are just 26 lower case letters to contend with. The complexity of written language in both reading books, and for writing requirements, makes the whole task of writing seem quite daunting, and leads to the view by some children that writing is beyond their capacity.

PUPILS' WRITING IN THE 1990s

What are the grounds for asserting that the teaching of handwriting has been neglected, and what has children's writing looked like during recent years. Are there lessons to be drawn from observing what has gone wrong? Figure 1. shows Esther's writing about the ear, a competent piece of written work, which shows how badly let down its writer is by her teachers.

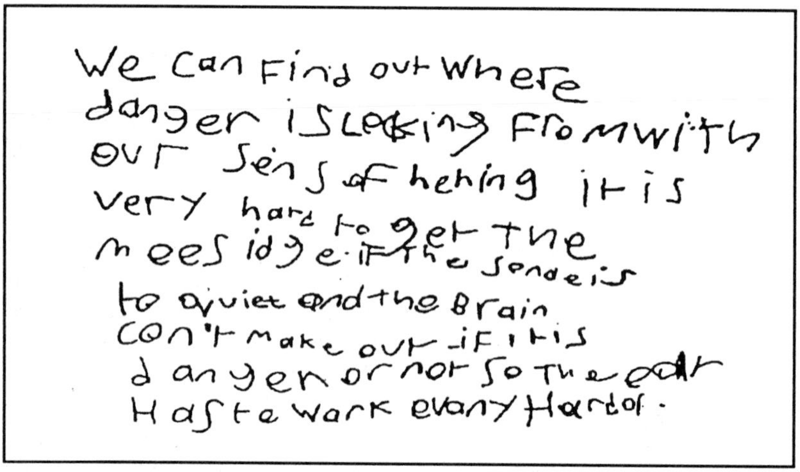

Figure 1. Esther writes about the ear's function.
Content is good but handwriting leaves something to be desired.

Esther is an intelligent girl, who writes well about what she wishes to say to her reader. She is making some progress in spelling and has a reasonably good bank of correctly spelt words for her writing task. She is prepared to write words that she does not yet spell correctly. Observation of Esther's writing shows us that letters such as 'a' 'g' 'n' 'o' 'q' 'u' have inaccurate or unconventional letter formation, that letter sizes are extremely irregular, and that writing is poorly aligned.

Figure 2. shows Christopher's writing. His intellectual assessment showed that he is within the top 10 per cent of the population. He, too, has been let down by his teachers.

Christopher has specific learning difficulties, so the teaching omission has been particularly disastrous for him.

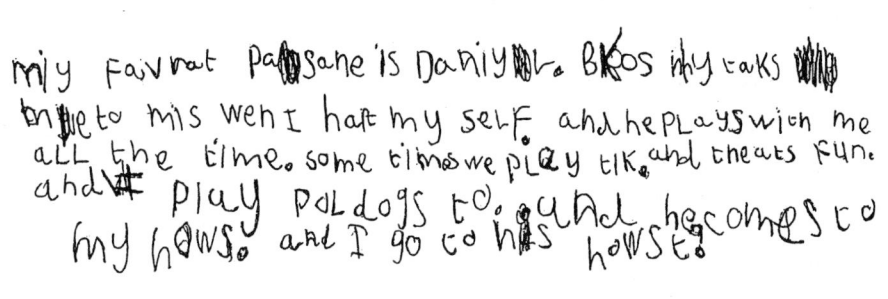

Figure 2. Christopher, almost eight years of age, writes about his favourite person

Christopher's writing shows all the difficulties shown in Esther's writing. However, he has the additional difficulty of having few word attack skills for spelling.

The first requirement for writing is that children should have complete mastery of the letters of the alphabet. They should learn letter sounds and letter movements from the beginning, and letter names too, unless the teacher believes that the three bits of information about each letter will be too much for some children. Letter names are learnt in songs about the alphabet, and the alphabet is often displayed on the nursery or reception class wall. After all, I have a name, the child has a name, and children will easily understand that letters also have names. The names are very useful when spelling skills begin to develop. They allow us to talk about letters and to feel in control of them.

WHICH LETTERS SHALL WE TEACH?

In our concern about handwriting, we need to identify the most appropriate letters for success. One reason for poor handwriting in our schools has been the persistent use of print script throughout the infant years. After all, the movements for printed letters can be quite different from those for cursive letters, which can be written in a form so that letters will join easily. Print script is usually upright, consisting of vertical marks and circles. Cursive script, in contrast, has oval forms and slightly sloping uprights, which help the writer to move more quickly and fluently across the writing page. I am selecting two scripts which provide good foundations from the beginning. Both encourage writing with a slight slope and have letter bodies which have an oval form. Christopher Jarman's script establishes 'skeleton' letters without the 'ready for joining stroke' in the early stages, and adds the 'exit hooks' later. Prue Wallis Myers shows how a fluent writing movement can be introduced from the beginning.

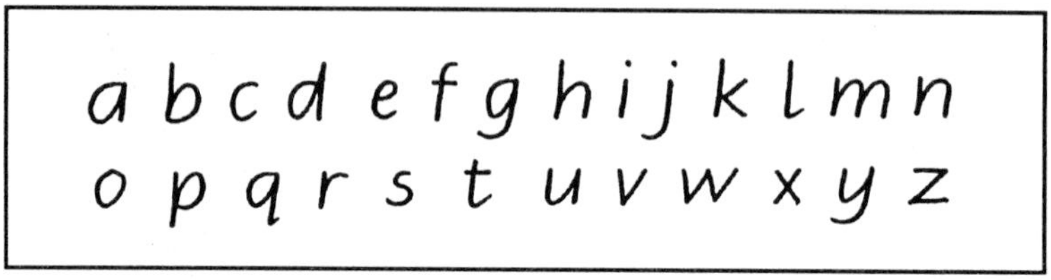

a b c d e f g h i j k l m n
o p q r s t u v w x y z

Figure 3a. Christopher Jarman's skeleton alphabet for first letters.

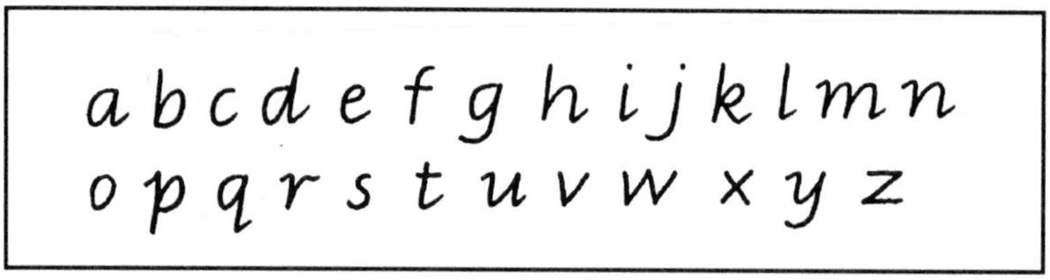

a b c d e f g h i j k l m n
o p q r s t u v w x y z

Figure 3b. Christopher Jarman's skeleton alphabet with added hooks.

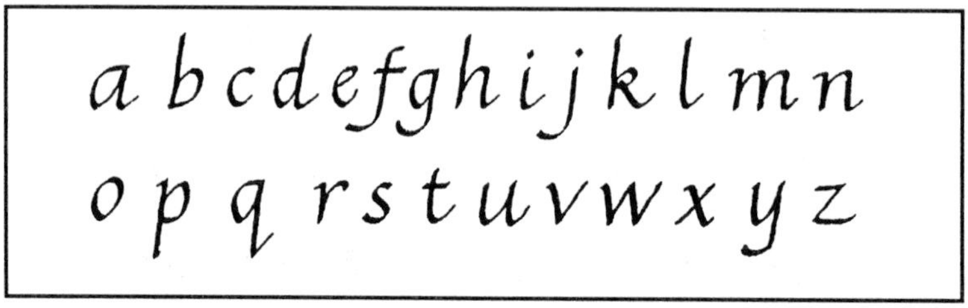

a b c d e f g h i j k l m n
o p q r s t u v w x y z

Figure 4. Prue Wallis Myers' Movement in Writing alphabet, which has full letter movements from the beginning.

For those with severe directionality difficulties, such as those displayed in Neil's writing, a fully cursive, joined handwriting script is often indicated.

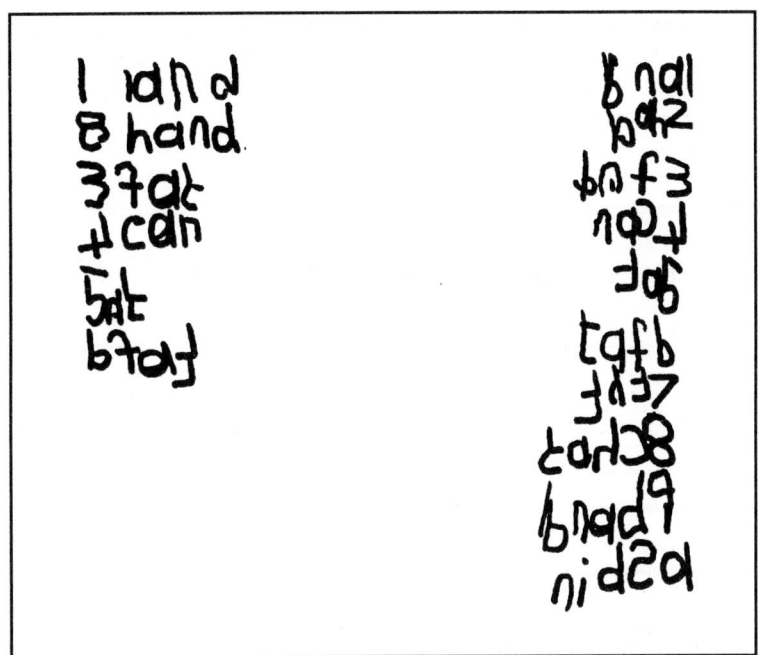

Figure 5.

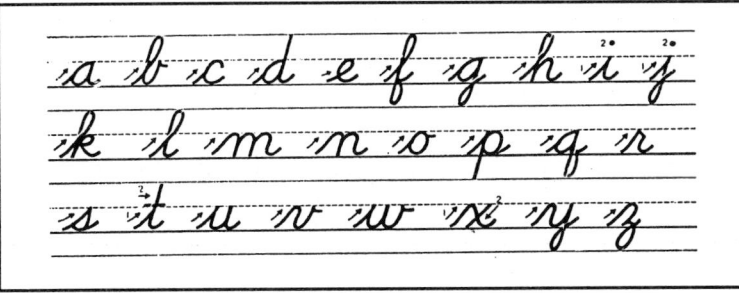

Figure 6a. The Dealian cursive script, similar to those advocated for use with dyslexic pupils.

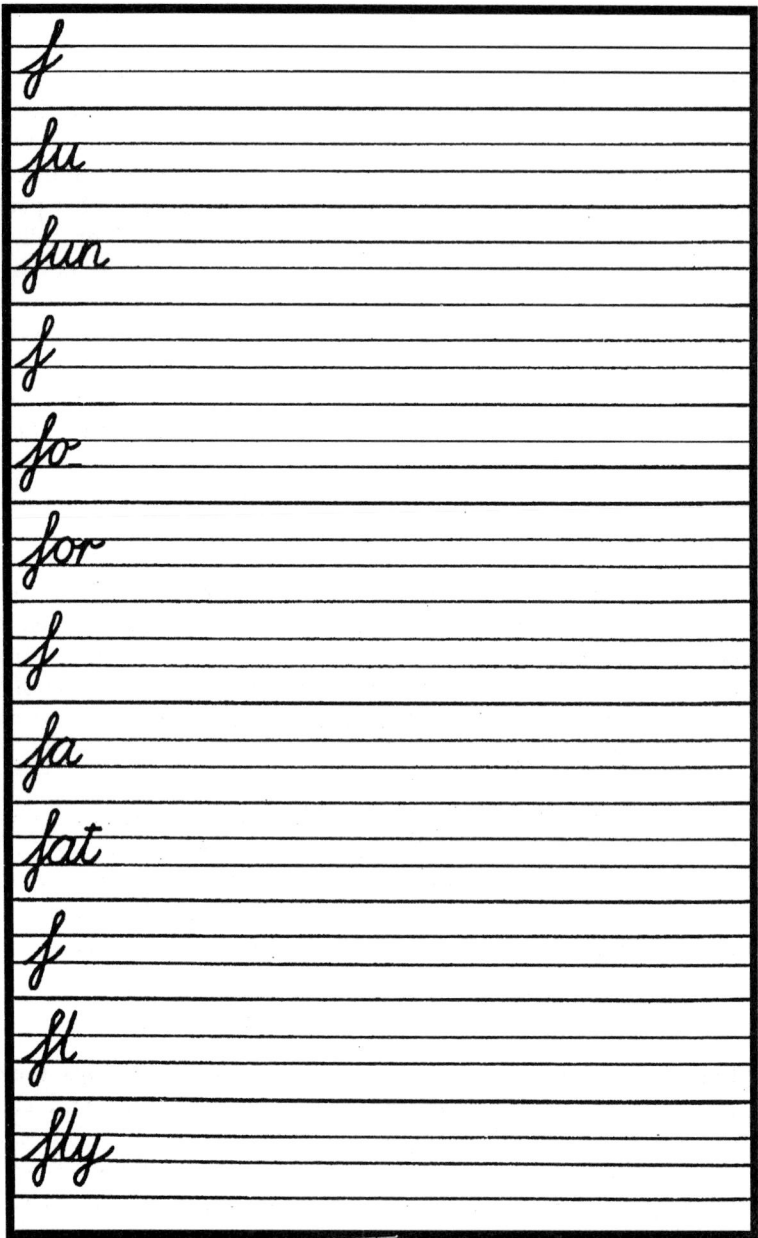

Figure 6b. The St Boniface writing scheme, which has a fully cursive script and lined paper formats.

The major advantage of using a fully cursive script is that the movement for each letter is begun on the baseline. For the child with spatial and directionality difficulties, this is very helpful. He does not have to remember where to begin each letter, as that becomes a constant when every letter is begun on the line, and he does not have to lift the pen or pencil from the writing surface when he is in the middle of a word. For the child with problems, every time he lifts his pen, he is uncertain where he should begin to write the next letter. This problem is precluded when he is taught using a fully cursive script. The fully cursive handwriting script is usually taught in a mult-sensory manner. The letter is written at the same time as other senses are engaged in the learning process, i.e. the child says the name of the letter, writes the letter, listens to the name as he says it, and looks at the movement as it occurs. There is no doubt that this procedure succeeds for children. However, the fully joined script has more movements than most handwriting scripts require. If the child has an established script, the change to full cursive should be considered in the light of other factors.

FORMING LETTERS CORRECTLY

Regardless of the handwriting script selected, the fact that handwriting is a movement skill should always be borne in mind. Movements, once learned, are difficult to change. Once we learn to swim, or to ride a bike, the skills remain with us. Imagine what would happen if the gear positions in the gearboxes of our cars changed from time to time. There could be serious traffic problems before we were completely adapted.

Some handwriting programmes suggest that letters should be correctly formed before the child attempts free written work. Bill Michael, author of the Scottish writing project, has persuaded many reception class teachers to adopt this policy. When this occurs, correct handwriting movements are established right from the beginning, and years of corrective teaching are avoided.

PENCILS AND PENS

There are now many pencils and pens in our stationery shops. It is difficult to choose from the extensive displays, and many of us arrive home and realise that, once again, we have chosen inappropriately. For younger children, probably the best product on the current market, is the Handhugger Pencil from Berol. This matt finished pencil has a wooden barrel which will sharpen easily, and an unexpectedly soft HB lead. There are Handhugger pencil crayons, which young children also like to use. It is always advisable to ask if a pen can be tried before purchase. Ball points are not good for the encouragement of handwriting skills, as the writer sometimes has little control over the direction that the pen will take. Fibre tips are better, and cartridge pens give us a wide range to choose from. W. H. Smith have their own product, which has a soft plasticised area above the nib so that the writer has more control. In the more expensive range the LAMY pencil and pen, available from The Pen Shop, based in a number of locations, has a triangular shaped barrel and works very successfully for some pupils. There is also a LAMY pencil, which has a similar barrel, and fulfils the same function. Pens with nibs require the writer to hold them at quite a different angle from modern pens. The latter write best when they are held in a relatively upright position. The hand needs to have much more control with modern pens than with traditional pens. As we observe from the pictures of mediaeval scribes who wrote with quills, the traditional pen determines the angle at which it must be held for writing.

PAPER POSITION AND POSTURE

Good posture is important for writing. Many children with handwriting difficulties peer closely at the paper and give evidence of visual binocular instability and or convergence difficulties. Optometrists are much more aware of the problems of children with literacy difficulties than they used to be. However, it is important to identify one in your area who is particularly skilled in this sphere. Some will advise about eye exercises, or even give short exercise sessions. This is important to assist some children with handwriting difficulties.

The position of the paper for writing should be comfortable for the writer. In general, the right hander has the paper sloping towards the left, and the left hander has the paper sloping towards the right. With good posture, the forearm for writing will remain roughly parallel to the vertical edge of the paper.

For left handers, the task of writing from left to right can be a difficult one. They inevitably cover the letters as they write. Because they push across the body with pen or pencil, rather than moving away from the body midline as right handers do, some left handers hold the paper securely, by placing the right hand at the left side of the paper. If they do this, left handers cross hands when writing, which creates a further difficulty for seeing the words they have written. When this occurs, the inverted hand posture, so often seen in left handers, quickly develops. Once established, the inverted hand posture is difficult to change.

Some children with handwriting difficulties find great benefit when they are provided with a sloping board for writing. Those with directionality problems, perhaps also experiencing binocular convergence difficulties, find the sloping surface particularly beneficial. Simple sloping boards are available from P. Wallis

Myers, who has made them available as part of the Movement into Writing handwriting programme.

Whether young children should be provided with lined paper is always a question for debate. Figures 1 and 2 show how writing develops when lined paper is not provided. The first research, to examine the benefits or otherwise, of teaching infants to write using lined paper, was conducted by Burnhill *et al.*, in 1975. It showed quite clearly that six-year-olds write more legibly when they are given lined paper. However, little attention has been paid to that research, and children up to the age of eight are sometimes expected to produce legible and attractive writing when paper is unlined. Of course, the teacher needs to assess readiness for lined paper, and many teachers do so. Children with spatial and directionality difficulties, our dyslexic pupils among them, find unlined paper extremely difficult to use. After all, each lower case letter has a relationship to the writing baseline. It is difficult to know how letters can become regular in size unless relationship to the writing baseline is clearly understood.

CHILDREN WITH HANDWRITING DIFFICULTIES

Some children with handwriting difficulties have not been taught good letter formation in the early years. Their incorrect movements then create problems in later education. However, there are also children affected by Developmental Co-ordination Disorder (Dyspraxia). These are the children who have difficulty with many physical skills, so that they are late beginning to walk, dress themselves with extreme difficulty, and have problems with running, hopping, ball skills, and most physical activities. Handwriting is difficult for virtually all affected children. They often read well, so that whether they have specific learning difficulties is not questioned by their teachers. It can be several years after they begin school before the real extent of their difficulties are recognised. Good letter formation, the judicious use of lined paper, and exercises to assist the development of fine and gross movement skills are all needed for these children. Figure 7 shows writing by Marcus, a six and a half year old boy, who has Verbal Intelligence equal to 136, placing him at above the 99th Centile, compared with children in his age group. He reads at the greater-than 9 years level. Marcus will eventually transfer to keyboard writing, though schools, particularly at the junior age range, are reluctant to arrange for pupils to have use of a keyboard. In secondary schools, there is also a reluctance to arrange transfer to keyboard skills, principally because of financial implications.

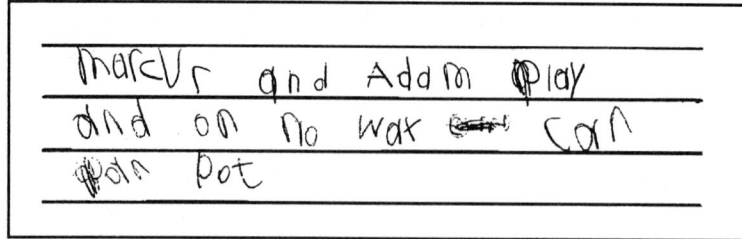

Figure 7. Marcus's writing at the age of six and a half years. The use of unlined paper in his infant school, has not helped him to develop regularly sized handwriting.

Figure 8. shows Jonathan's writing. Compared with Marcus, whose problems are confined almost exclusively to fine movements, Jonathan has perceptual and short-term memory difficulties. His writing shows irregular letter size, inability to write on lines, and crossings out which are caused by his inability to plan the movement he intends to make.

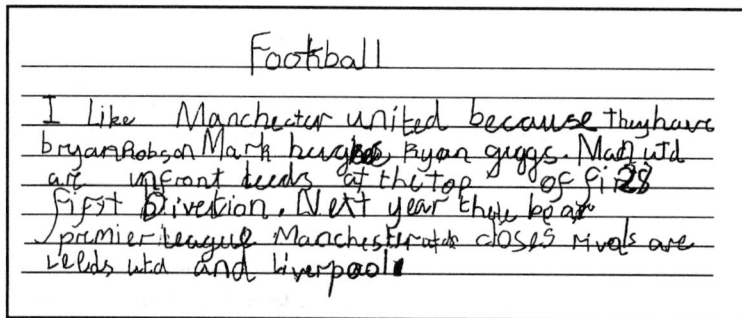

Figure 8. Jonathan's writing at almost ten years of age.

INTERVENTION FOR HANDWRITING SKILLS

Although handwriting difficulties can be complex, often leaving the teacher quite bemused about how she can assist, there are some conventions that need to be followed. For example, letters must be correctly formed, or letters within words cannot be easily joined. When letters are correctly formed from the early stages, the joins will easily follow:

Joins after letters which end on the baseline join to the next letter through diagonal joins. The following letters finish at the baseline 'a' 'c' 'd' 'e' 'h' 'l' ('g' 'j' 'y'). Diagonal joins can be seen in the following words:

it at all ill in

Letters which finish at the top join horizontally. The following letters finish at the top 'o' 'r' 'v' 'w.' Words which have horizontal joins include:

on for wood win van run

Even when letters are correctly formed, the 'over and back' join must be taught. The 'over and back' join precedes letters such as 'a' 'c' 'd' 'g' 'o' 'q' 's' can be seen in the following words:

mat cat hat sat and land sand

A quick assessment of joining skills can be completed by asking the child to write four words. They are:

the and from girl

The four words include virtually all the kinds of joins that the writer needs to make.

Writing has many vertical letter strokes. When the strokes are irregular, as they are in James' writing, the writing has an untidy appearance. James can be shown how the uprights of his letters differ. His problem can be easily corrected.

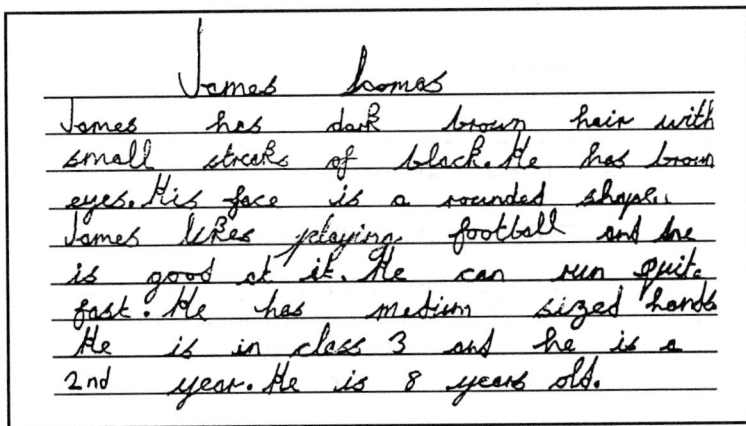

Figure 9. James' handwriting has irregular uprights

Irregular writing size can only be corrected through provision of lines. If the 'bodies' of letters are as tall as the uprights, or if they are generally irregular, either drawing in an extra line to show the upper limits of small letters, or the provision of writing paper with the extra line, should help to solve the problem.

Word spacing may also be irregular. However, if relative letter size is corrected, word spacing is often corrected spontaneously.

An easy way to discuss handwriting correction is to encourage pupils to remember four Ss. They are:

Slope Size Space Sitting on the line

When the four Ss are corrected, handwriting should be greatly improved.

ASSESSING AND MONITORING WRITING SKILLS

Handwriting is just a part of the more complex task of writing. Writing, as such, should be monitored from time to time. Without monitoring, some pupils make little progress. A timed piece of writing (20 minutes for pupils up to the age of 12 years, and 30 minutes for older pupils) is a useful measure of writing status and progress. Students with specific learning difficulties (dyslexia or dyspraxia), are likely to seek special examination arrangements when they reach GCSE or Scottish Examination Board levels. There has been a considerable amount of research on writing speeds. However, the writing which simulates examinations best is likely to be the free written work described above. For primary aged pupils, the following titles are suitable, and writing should be conducted for a twenty minute period (Alston, 1994).

My Favourite Person
Someone I know very well
Something in which I am very interested

Dutton (1990; 1992) used the title My Life History and requested pupils to write for thirty minutes. A timed piece of written work, such as that conducted by Alston and Dutton, allows one to compare student output with what he or she was able to write on a previous occasion, and to compare individual output with what is known about the output of students in general, at different stages of educational progress. Written output is a broad measure. However, assessing writing speeds is a complex task. Written output is probably the best measure that we have at present. Figure 10. shows a standardised piece of writing by Kyle, who writes for 20 minutes about his interests.

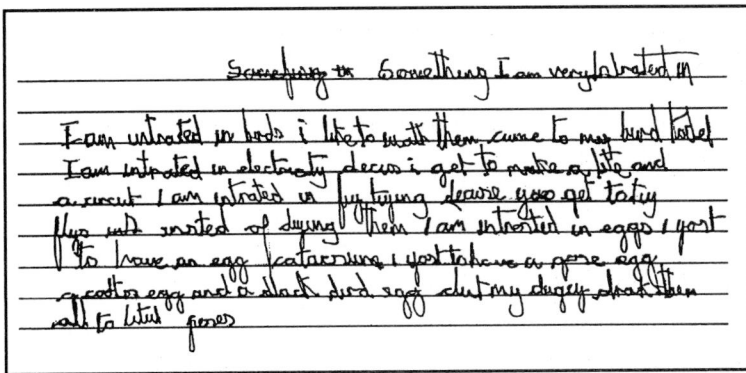

Figure 10. Ten year old Kyle writes for 20 minutes, about his interests

CONCLUSION

There are major principles to be adopted in the teaching and correction of handwriting. They are especially important for children with specific learning difficulties. It is essential that correct letter movements should be well established when the child begins to write. Without this, there can be eleven or more years of school in which handwriting needs to be corrected. Joins can be introduced early, as soon as good letter forms are written. Handwriting conventions, such as regularity of relative letter size, spacing, and slope, need regular perusal, and monitoring of writing progress, through standardised free writing, allows us to monitor progress as the child moves through the educational system. Appropriate teaching, assessment and monitoring, ensure that handwriting and general writing skills move on, making writing by hand a medium for functional use, and as a means of expression, throughout the educational years.

REFERENCES

Alston, J., Taylor, J. (1990). *Handwriting Helpline*. Manchester: Dextral Books.

Alston, J. (1994). Written Output and Writing Speeds. *Dyslexia Review,* Vol. 6, No. 2. pp 6 - 12. Available from The Dyslexia Institute, 133 Gresham Road, Staines, Middlesex, TW18 2AJ.

Alston, J. (1995). Assessing and Promoting Writing Skills. Amington, Tamworth: NASEN.

Brolly, J., Tedman, J. (1993). *St Boniface Writing Scheme*. Ventnor, Isle of Wight: St Boniface Primary School.

Burnhill, P., Hartley, J., Fraser, S., Young, N. (1975). Writing lines: an exploratory study. *Programmed Learning and Educational Technology*, 11, pp84-87.

Dutton, K. (1990). *Writing under Examination Conditions: Establishing a Baseline*. Scottish Education Department/ Regional Psychological Services, and in Handwriting Review, 1992.

Jarman, C. (1993). *The Development of Handwriting Skills*. Cheltenham: Stanley Thornes.

Michael, B. (1993). *The Foundations of Writing Project*. Glasgow: Jordanhill College.

Myers, P. Wallis. (1994). *Movement into Writing*. Available from P. Wallis Myers, 2 Richmond Court, Richmond Road, Bowdon, Altrincham, WA14 2TZ.

Thurber, D. N. (1980) *D'Nealian Handwriting*. Glenview Illinois: Scott Foresman.

RESOURCES

Dyspraxia Trust, P.O. Box 1270, Gerrards Cross, Bucks, SL9 OSF.

Handwriting Interest Group, 6 Fyfield Road, Ongar, Essex, CM5 OAH.

Sloping Boards for Desk Top. From: P. Wallis Myers, 2 Richmond Court, Richmond Road, Bowdon, Altrincham, WA14 2TZ.

Handhugger Pencils and Pencil Crayons, Berol Ltd., Oldmedow Road, King's Lynn, Norfolk, PE30 4JR.

SECTION 3

SPEECH AND LANGUAGE

SPECIFIC LANGUAGE IMPAIRMENT: EXPLANATIONS AND IMPLICATIONS

JENNIFER REID and
MORAG L. DONALDSON

WHAT IS SPECIFIC LANGUAGE IMPAIRMENT?

A child who fails to develop language[1] normally while making otherwise unexceptional developmental progress may be said to have a specific language impairment (SLI)[2]. Diagnosis of this condition is usually carried out by excluding other conditions associated with language and/or communication difficulties, that is, if the child cannot be shown to be suffering from general learning difficulties, physical disability, hearing loss, emotional or behavioural disorder, autism, environmental deprivation or any other condition which could explain the language problems, then a diagnosis of 'specific language impairment' is made.

The unsatisfactory nature of a definition which refers only to the absence of a clear aetiology has inspired much research over the past 20 years or so, involving children with SLI. However, the search for features which are uniquely characteristic of children with SLI has not been particularly successful (Bishop, 1992; Miller, 1991). While such children, by definition, show grossly normal development in non-linguistic areas, when compared to normally developing children, they nevertheless show subtle difficulties and differences in some aspects of non-linguistic ability, especially when assessed in experimental conditions. However, as we will argue in the following section, it is not always clear whether such non-linguistic difficulties are causes or consequences of the linguistic problems.

Language not only fulfils a variety of important communicative functions, but it can also be a powerful cognitive tool, serving as a means of mental

---

1 We use the term 'language' to refer primarily to spoken language, and 'language development' to the ability to both understand and produce spoken language. Spoken language ability involves the integration of knowledge at a number of levels, namely speech sound system (phonology), grammatical system (syntax and morphology), word and sentence meaning (semantics) and communicative functions (pragmatics). We prefer 'language production' or 'expressive language' to the term 'speech' which tends to be more closely associated with the speech sound system rather than the other levels.

2 Other terms may be used to refer to the condition. 'Developmental language disorder' is a term widely used, particularly by practising speech and language therapists. 'Developmental dysphasia' or 'developmental aphasia' were terms widely used in the past but, although still popular in continental Europe, they have largely passed out of favour among practitioners in the UK.

representation and hence influencing children's thinking, memory and learning. Non-linguistic skills which are usually acquired with the help of language may be less well developed in children with a language impairment. Thus, the consequence of SLI will not necessarily be restricted to the area of communication.

RESEARCH DESIGN ISSUES

One problem with some of the extensive literature on possible causes of SLI concerns issues of research design. These issues are neither trivial nor restricted to research in this area, therefore we consider some discussion to be relevant here[3].

In the search for an underlying cause for language impairment, the abilities of language-impaired children have been compared with those of normally developing children of the same age[4]. However, caution is required in interpreting the findings from such comparisons. For example, if we observed that language-impaired children tended to be more socially immature than normally developing children of the same age, we could not use this finding to argue that social immaturity causes language impairment. When a child has poor language skills, it is likely that the ability to communicate verbally with other people will be affected. Lack of experience in communicating verbally with other people may lead to a degree of social immaturity. Thus, the social immaturity of the SLI group may be the result of language impairment rather than a cause.

In order to overcome this problem with research designs which compare on the basis of chronological age, some studies compare the performance of the SLI children with younger, normally-developing children whose language development is at a similar level (NLD children). Such designs are not without their own problems, not the least of which lies in the choice of language measure. The measure chosen may be one of language comprehension, language production, or a composite measure. Since many children with SLI will have widely discrepant receptive and productive language, the choice of a measure for language matching will have a very significant effect on the nature of the NLD group, and therefore also on the results of any comparison of the two groups.

SLI: A SINGLE UNDERLYING CAUSE?

If there is a single cause of SLI, we might begin by asking whether the source lies within the child or within the child's environment. A common lay assumption is that failure to develop language at the normal rate in the early years comes about

---

3 Methodology is discussed by Bishop (1992), and similar issues are discussed with reference to research in reading by Bryant and Bradley (1985) and Gathercole and Baddeley (1993).
4 Studies which use such comparisons are referred to as having a 'chronological age-matched design', in the terminology of experimental psychology. The comparison group of children is referred to as the 'control group', hence 'chronological age-matched controls'.

because of some inadequacy in the child's communicative environment. There are two main variations of this argument, both of which are sources of parental anxiety and guilt well-known to practising speech and language therapists.

The first is that a child with a language delay does not talk because s/he has no need to. The home environment does not provide the opportunities or motivation to communicate, or other people 'talk for' the child. The second account comes in several guises, but typically assumes that language input to the child is lacking in some respect, either in quantity or in quality.

There is no doubt that children who experience extreme environmental deprivation suffer adverse consequences for language as well as other abilities (Skuse, 1992). On the other hand, it seems that the ability of the young child to develop language is extremely robust, even in settings which in terms of adult input may appear relatively impoverished. Research studies have produced no evidence that all, or even the majority of, children with language impairments have significantly adverse communicative environments. This literature is reviewed comprehensively by Leonard (1987).

Adults modify their language when they talk to young children. There is an extensive literature on the characteristics of this 'child directed speech', or 'motherese', which, it is hypothesised, serves to facilitate language learning (Snow, 1986). The characteristics of child directed speech include modifications at a variety of levels, such as voice quality, intonation, vocabulary and grammatical structure. In particular, utterance length and complexity appear to reflect the child's current language level.

A number of studies have demonstrated differences in the communicative behaviours of parents of SLI children compared to those of parents of NLD children of the same age[5]. However, a different picture emerges when comparison is made with NLD children of similar language levels. Very few studies using language-matched controls show any differences at all in the language and communicative behaviours of the two groups of parents. It seems that the parents of SLI children, like other parents, are sensitive to their children's language comprehension and production abilities[6]. Even if we find that for some language-impaired children, environmental factors have influenced their developmental progress, there is little case for arguing for an environmental cause for SLI.

The alternative position is that factors underlying SLI are intrinsic to the child, and that environmental factors serve to influence the effects of the condition

5 See the review in Leonard (1987), pp 2-10.
6 For a discussion of some of the bi-directional influences on conversation with language-impaired children, see Conti-Ramsden (1985, 1991).

on individual children's histories. There have been several proposed theories of SLI which fit this general position. We shall sketch out a couple of the more influential theoretical positions, but the interested reader should refer to the more detailed reviews presented in Leonard (1987), Miller (1991) and Bishop (1992).

AN AUDITORY PERCEPTUAL DEFICIT?

Eisenson (1972) was an early attempt to present a unitary account of SLI, or 'developmental aphasia', as he called it. He hypothesised that SLI resulted from a fundamental difficulty in auditory (speech) perception. Expressive problems were construed as resulting from inadequate processing of linguistic input. Different varieties of SLI arose from varying degrees of severity of the underlying impairment. He proposed a continuum of severity ranging from mild phonological or grammatical difficulties to profound receptive aphasia.

The notion of a fundamental auditory perceptual disorder has fared rather better as a result of research findings than many other theoretical accounts. The work of Tallal and her colleagues[7] has been particularly influential. A central finding is that SLI children are at a disadvantage in tasks requiring the perception of brief or rapid acoustic events, and this has been replicated in a number of forms in many studies and using different groups of children. Unfortunately, most of this work has been conducted using chronological age-matched controls and is therefore insufficient evidence of a causal link from auditory perception to language.

The basic design of the experimental task in the above studies is one in which children are required to distinguish and sequence two complex tones which are presented with varying time intervals between them. It is not immediately obvious how limited language might influence the development of the ability to perform this task. However, one might ask if the SLI children performed as younger NLD children. This appears not to be the case. Tallal, Stark and Curtiss (1976) presented some evidence of qualitative differences in the performance of SLI children and younger NLD children. However, they also found that NLD children under 4:6 years were not very successful on the experimental task. This finding makes it difficult to interpret the findings from the SLI children, given that in many instances, their language abilities fell below this developmental level.

Despite these findings of interesting qualitative differences in the perceptual abilities of children with SLI, we are left wondering what it means. To date, the verdict on a causal link between the two must remain not proven.

7 There are several important papers, see, for example, Tallal, Stark and Mellits (1985), but this work is also comprehensively reviewed in Bishop (1992).

A MORE GENERAL COGNITIVE DEFICIT?

Another line of research has been the investigation of non-verbal cognitive abilities in children with SLI. Given that SLI children have, by definition, non-verbal abilities within the normal range, it is perhaps surprising that investigations have uncovered apparently significant differences and difficulties in non-linguistic activities.

Piaget viewed language acquisition as one aspect of the development of the ability to use symbols (Piaget and Inhelder, 1969). Early symbols usually resemble the real object, such as when a child uses bricks as food while pretending to cook. As children's symbolic understanding develops, they are able to use more arbitrary symbols, which have no physical resemblance to the object or event they denote. Words may be viewed in this light as symbols, the meanings of which are shared by speakers of the language, but are essentially arbitrary. Poor symbolic function has been proposed as the cause of language difficulties, but research in this area has also resulted in a mixture of contradictory findings and unconvincing evidence. For example, some investigators have suggested that children with SLI show rather impoverished symbolic play compared to their peers. However, Terrell, Schwartz, Prelock and Messick (1984), using a comparison group matched on expressive language ability, found that the SLI children showed a higher level of symbolic play than these younger NLD children. Poor symbolic play may therefore be the result of language impairment.

Other postulated theories have involved, for example, deficits of short-term memory, sequencing or hypothesis testing. In a review of research in this whole area, Johnston (1988 p. 705) concludes,

> 'Research on the cognitive abilities of language-disordered children presents a convincing picture of substantial impairment. At many ages, across visual, auditory and tactile stimuli, across many domains of knowledge, in symbolic and non-symbolic activities, in tasks with little to no explicit verbal demand, language-disordered children perform below age expectations.'

A few years later, the same author urges a move away from research designed to 'document low performance in yet another mental task. . .' (Johnston, 1991 p. 300). In her view, we need to know what distinguishes children with SLI from children with more general, or other sorts of learning difficulties, in other words, their strengths as well as their weaknesses. Those working with SLI children quote anecdotal evidence for such strengths, such as 'overdeveloped visual skills' or 'compensatory learning strategies', but hard evidence of such strengths across numbers of children is lacking as yet.

It is perhaps rather odd that most of the theories of SLI discussed so far have postulated underlying deficits in non-linguistic abilities. In much of the research to date, despite a general consensus that SLI children present a range of different sorts and severities of linguistic impairments, the linguistic characteristics of individual or groups of children have been relatively neglected. Children with SLI are treated as a relatively homogeneous group, whose difficulties result from some, as yet undiscovered, common, underlying deficit. To therapists and teachers working with SLI children, this assumption may seem quite unreasonable in the face of so much evidence of individual differences. The only common factor for lumping these children together seems to be the existence of some significant degree of language impairment. Is this sufficient evidence for homogeneity?

UNTANGLING THE LINGUISTIC CHARACTERISTICS

In clinical and educational practice, most of the advances of the past 20 years or so have come, not from searching for elusive causes, but from detailed attention to the particular language difficulties faced by individual children. In the 70s and early 80s, the seminal work of Crystal and colleagues (Crystal, Fletcher and Garman, 1976) on grammatical disability, and of Ingram (1976) and Grunwell (1982) on phonological disability brought about a revolution in the conception and remediation of disorders of language structure, and the appearance of a new field of academic endeavour, clinical linguistics (Crystal, 1981; Grundy, 1989). More recently, attention has shifted away from structural aspects of language towards the communicative context of language use, the 'pragmatic' aspects of language. The 'pragmatic revolution' was fuelled particularly by the work of Prutting in the USA (Gallagher and Prutting, 1983). Two volumes on clinical pragmatics have recently appeared in the UK (McTear and Conti-Ramsden, 1992; Smith and Leinonen, 1991).

Such developments have had a major impact on the assessment and remediation of language impairments in children. They have opened up new possibilities for dealing with individual and group differences among children with SLI. Not only this, but the focus on pragmatics and issues of language use has led to the 'discovery' of a new type of language impairment, that of pragmatic disorder.

HETEROGENEITY: DIFFERENT TYPES OF SLI?

The general consensus now seems to be that SLI may be nothing more than a convenient umbrella term, bringing together a range of types of impairment which may or may not be mutually exclusive. The most influential work in this area has been that of Rapin and Allen in the USA (Rapin and Allen, 1983; 1987). Their clinical typology is probably the one to which most frequent reference is made. Their categories include:

Verbal auditory agnosia (or 'word deafness' as described originally by Worster Drought and Allen in the 1930s), characterised by inability to comprehend language presented to the auditory channel.

Verbal dyspraxia[8], characterised by dysfluent, effortful speech, short utterances with defective phonology in contrast to adequate or even normal comprehension.

Phonologic programming deficit syndrome, characterised by speech which is more fluent than in verbal dyspraxia, with longer utterances but poor intelligibility (usually called phonological disorder in the UK).

Phonologic-syntactic deficit syndrome: these children have dysfluent speech, phonological deficits and speak in short utterances with grammatical deficits affecting closed class words (e.g. a/the; in/on/ under; is/was/were) and morphology (e.g. word endings such as plural forms or past tense endings) (phonological-syntactic disorder in the UK).

Lexical-syntactic deficit syndrome: these children are late to begin talking but have normal phonology for their age. They are characterised by severe word retrieval deficits, immature syntax (sentence construction) and language formulation difficulties (lexical-syntactic disorder).

Semantic-pragmatic deficit syndrome, characterised by deviant language processing and use in the context of fluent, well-formed language with adequate speech intelligibility. These children are often verbose and have large vocabularies, yet have comprehension deficits for the meaning of verbal messages, particularly questions and non-literal language. They have pragmatic deficits seen as impaired ability to obey the rules of conversation, such as in turn-taking and topic maintenance. They may perseverate and chatter

---

8 This impairment may also be referred to as 'articulatory dyspraxia', or just 'dyspraxia', but the latter should perhaps be avoided since it may be confused with conditions affecting non-speech motor systems such as limb or eye movements.

incessantly. They may be echolalic and use overlearned scripts rather than language which is appropriate to the context. In the UK, this impairment tends to be called 'semantic-pragmatic disorder' (Bishop, 1989).

These potted descriptions pay only lip service to the natural history of SLI, i.e. how the profile of a child with SLI (or another condition) changes with age, and the effects of differential severity. They are clinically derived, that is, derived from careful observation of large numbers of children with language impairments. Their validity in terms of unique and/or mutually exclusive characteristics has not been systematically tested. However, they appear to have some ecological validity, for they have found favour with many clinicians.

INTERVENTION ISSUES

To be effective, intervention strategies must be geared to the needs of the individual child and therefore must be closely integrated with thorough, on-going assessment procedures. Few would disagree with this statement, although there is less agreement about exactly how information from diagnostic assessments should be translated into intervention strategies. For example, should the main aim be to develop a child's strengths so as to compensate for her/his weaknesses, or should the emphasis be on developing the skills in which s/he is weakest? Whatever the answer to this question is, it is clear that the more general question of 'What is the best intervention strategy for SLI?' is too simplistic. Instead, we need to ask a series of more specific and more complex questions concerning the effectiveness of particular intervention techniques in achieving particular goals, for particular types of children, with particular types of language impairments, in particular sets of circumstances. The following sections aim to give a flavour of some approaches to intervention for children with SLI and to consider some of the evidence which can be used in addressing questions of effectiveness. (For a more detailed review, see Donaldson, 1992).

Intervention strategies vary along several dimensions, including those corresponding to the following questions:

(1)   What should be taught or developed?

(2)   How should the intervention be carried out?

In other words, there is variation in the goals of intervention and in the techniques used to achieve these goals.

GOALS OF INTERVENTION

An intervention will usually have a variety of goals, ranging from very general goals to more specific goals or objectives. Typically, goals are arrived at through assessment procedures which are rather different to those through which the initial diagnosis of SLI was made. Assessment for the purposes of diagnosis will probably be made using norm-referenced, standardised tests, which involve comparing the child's performance with that of a representative sample of other (usually normally-developing) children and the assignation of an age-equivalent or other standardised score. Such norm-referenced assessments are not usually sufficiently detailed or informative for the purposes of planning intervention. For this purpose, clinicians may turn to criterion-referenced procedures, in which the child's performance is compared to a more detailed set of criteria or goals. These are typically organised as developmentally-sequenced levels, and the child's abilities are matched to a developmental level or other standard, either through observation or through testing (which may be informal or standardised). Examples of assessments used for planning treatment would be the Detailed Test of Comprehension, from the Derbyshire Language Scheme (Knowles and Masidlover, 1982), which is an unstandardised test and the Pragmatics Profile (Dewart and Summers, 1988), in which information on developmental level is gained through a structured interview with the child's parents or carers. Linguistic profiles (Crystal, 1982) are derived through the analysis of elicited speech samples, and these are used in particular by therapists working with children who have more complex and persisting impairments and who are receiving intensive remediation, for example, in a language unit.

Developmental goals are selected to help a child achieve those aspects of language which would be the next to appear according to some generally agreed developmental sequence, based on the literature on language development in normal children. This approach works rather better for those aspects of language about which there is a large literature, such as the acquisition of grammatical tense inflections, but can be problematic in areas about which less developmental information is available, such as the acquisition of conversational rules. In fact, developmental goals may not be particularly functionally relevant to a given child in her/his own circumstances. The selection of appropriate goals may therefore be influenced by functional considerations, so that the language skills acquired suit the individual needs of the child and are more likely to lead to pragmatic gains.

Although different types of intervention goals are far from mutually exclusive, there has been a historical shift away from an emphasis on the structure of language towards an emphasis on language as a tool for communication. The relative emphasis on these two types of goal also varies according to the nature of a child's language problems. For instance, for a child with a phonological-syntactic disorder, intervention is likely to focus on language form, although not in isolation from function, whereas for a child with a semantic-pragmatic disorder, intervention is more likely to focus on the communicative functions of language, although not in isolation from the linguistic tools required to achieve communicative goals.

At a more specific level, intervention may target phonological, syntactic, semantic or pragmatic aspects of a child's language, or non-linguistic skills which are felt to provide some of the relevant underpinnings for more efficient language learning, such as attention to sound, turn-taking, representational play or matching and sorting. Within each of these aspects even more specific goals will usually be formulated to guide intervention (Fey, 1986; Harris, 1990; Lees and Urwin, 1991).

In reviewing studies evaluating the effectiveness of language intervention, Nye, Foster and Seaman (1987) found that the largest improvements occurred for syntactic characteristics and the smallest for pragmatic characteristics (although the difference was not statistically significant).

INTERVENTION TECHNIQUES

A vast range of intervention techniques are used with children who have SLI, since most clinicians devise individualised programmes based on the needs of the particular child, combined with their own experience of what has proved successful in the past. Nevertheless, these techniques can be grouped into three broad categories: behavioural approaches, naturalistic approaches and 'compromise' approaches.

Behavioural approaches to language intervention are based on the principles of learning theory and hence on the assumption that language can be learned through such processes as imitation, reinforcement, shaping, modelling and prompting. For example, if the goal is to teach a child to use personal pronouns (such as 'he' and 'she') appropriately, exercises might be presented in which the child is shown a picture (e.g. of a girl swimming) and is asked a question (e.g. 'What is the girl doing?'). The question could then be followed by a prompt ('Say, "She is swimming" ') to encourage the child to imitate the appropriate response. A correct imitation could then be reinforced by praising the child. Modelling is similar to imitation, but the child is not asked to reproduce the therapist's utterance immediately. Instead, the child is asked to listen carefully to the therapist producing utterances containing the linguistic forms which are the target of intervention. Then the child is given a turn at speaking in a context similar to the one in which the therapist has modelled the relevant linguistic forms. For instance, the therapist and child may take turns at describing a set of pictures.

There are a number of studies indicating that behavioural techniques can be effective in improving the production of various linguistic forms in children with a specific language disorder (for a review, see Leonard, 1981). However, children often experience difficulties in generalising what they have learned to related linguistic constructions. Hegde, Noll and Pecora (1979) taught children to use 'is' in sentences beginning with 'he' and found that although the children successfully generalised their use of 'is' to other sentences beginning with 'he', they failed to generalise to sentences beginning with 'she'.

Problems can also arise in generalising to situations which differ from the training situation. Leonard (1981) outlines four of the ways in which situations may differ from the training situation: in terms of the visual stimuli talked about (e.g. real situations versus pictures), in terms of the verbal stimuli used as prompts (e.g. open-ended versus explicit questions), in terms of the setting (e.g. home versus clinic), and in terms of the co-conversationalist (e.g. parent versus therapist). On the basis of several studies investigating generalisation effects, Leonard concludes that use of a trained linguistic form is usually successfully generalised to situations which differ from the training situation in only one or two of these respects, but that problems in generalising tend to arise when situations differ in three or four respects. It is therefore important for behavioural training to be conducted in a variety of contexts.

Naturalistic approaches to language intervention are based on the assumption that children will learn language best in situations where it is being used to serve genuine communicative purposes and where it is closely integrated with real life activities. This assumption is often accompanied by the assumption that children's language problems can be resolved through incidental learning. Thus, the role of the therapist or teacher is not to improve the use of particular linguistic behaviours through explicit teaching, but rather to facilitate incidental learning of linguistic behaviours in meaningful communicative contexts by providing appropriate linguistic input and opportunities for use of the targeted linguistic behaviour. One way of making communicative contexts meaningful is to base them around activities and topics which are of interest to the child and which relate to her/his experiences. Therefore, naturalistic intervention programmes need to be tailored to the interests of individual children, as well as to their need for an emphasis on a particular type of linguistic input. Another way of ensuring that interventions occur in meaningful, relevant contexts is to carry them out within real-life settings, such as the classroom, playground or home, rather than withdrawing the child to a separate room or to a speech therapy clinic. This, in turn, encourages collaboration with significant people in the child's life, such as parents, siblings, peers, class teachers and nursery nurses. (Of course, collaboration with at least some of these people can also be encouraged in a clinic setting, but in a more contrived way.) Advocates of naturalistic approaches include McLean and Snyder-McLean (1978) and Lahey (1988).

Since the naturalistic approach involves intervening either in everyday settings or in settings designed to mimic everyday settings, problems of generalising what is learned from the therapeutic situation to real-life situations are avoided or substantially reduced. Bochner *et al.* (1980) present two case studies which highlight typical differences between the naturalistic approach and the more traditional behavioural approach. One 5 year old who had a language disorder and suspected mild mental retardation received language intervention based on the behavioural approach, whereas another 5 year old who had similar problems received intervention based on the naturalistic approach. Both children made progress in language skills, but the nature of this progress differed between the two children. The child who had received behavioural intervention acquired the skills she had been drilled in, such as labelling pictures and objects and answering direct questions, but she did not succeed in generalising these skills to normal conversations with her teachers and peers when she moved from a special education class into a mainstream class. In contrast, the child who had received the naturalistic intervention did acquire spontaneous language skills which generalised to the new setting of a mainstream class. Bochner *et al.* see their findings as evidence for the claim that 'children learn what they are taught' (1980: p. 100). Although this conclusion is based on a qualitative study of only two children, it is broadly consistent with the conclusion reached by Leonard (1981) on the basis of more extensive evidence (from a review of studies). He concludes that training which focuses only on particular linguistic forms tends to yield effects limited to the child's use of these forms, whereas training with a more general focus usually results in broader linguistic gains.

When considering issues of generalisation, it is important to remember that the contexts in which children are likely to have to deploy linguistic skills are not restricted to low-structure, informal contexts in which language is closely linked to their own immediate purposes and concerns. It is true that such contexts predominate in the life of a young child, but if the child is to progress successfully in the educational system, s/he will also have to cope with more formal contexts in which language is 'disembedded' from immediate purposes (Donaldson, 1978). In particular, the ability to use and understand language in disembedded contexts, and perhaps also to reflect on the formal properties of language, is likely to be crucial to the acquisition of literacy. Such considerations become especially significant in the light of the evidence indicating that children with spoken language disorders are at risk of encountering reading problems (Silva, 1987).

The naturalistic approach has considerable intuitive appeal since it is consistent with contemporary theories of normal language acquisition. Although such theories differ in whether they emphasise innate knowledge of the structural properties of language (Chomsky, 1986) or the acquisition of language within supportive social contexts (Bruner, 1983), they have in common an eschewal of the role of explicit language teaching by adults. However, despite the superficial plausibility of the argument that intervention procedures for children with language disorders should aim to mimic the processes by which language is normally acquired, some caution is called for. It does not necessarily follow that the 'normal' developmental route is the best route for all children. The very fact that children with language disorders have not made normal progress in acquiring language 'naturally' suggests that an alternative approach may be beneficial or even necessary.

Of course, most naturalistic intervention approaches are alternative approaches in the sense that they aim to adapt normal interactions to the child's needs, by for example providing extra opportunities to observe and practise linguistic forms or functions which are posing problems. However, as Conant *et al.* (Conant, Budoff, Hecht, and Morse, 1984) point out, a potential difficulty is that opportunities to work on particular problem areas may not arise sufficiently frequently in natural situations. Furthermore, considerable skill and ingenuity on the part of the teacher or therapist is required in order to exploit naturally occurring opportunities for intervention.

Conant *et al.* devised an intervention programme which aimed to combine the advantages of traditional behavioural approaches with those of incidental learning approaches. Their programme consisted of a set of communication games in which particular features of syntax, vocabulary or articulation could be focused upon, but in which these features served the same pragmatic functions as in normal conversation. In these games, the roles of speaker and hearer were alternated between the child and the teacher. For example, hiding games were used in which the child and the teacher took turns at guessing where an object was hidden. The materials for this game could be constructed in such a way as to encourage the use of particular linguistic forms in the guesses. The feedback which the child received related not to arbitrary standards of 'correctness' but to the communicative adequacy or inadequacy of his messages (e.g. whether the child succeeded in communicating his guess to the adult so that she could look for the object in the place the child had intended). Conant *et al.* found that children who received their intervention programme over a period of four months made more progress (in terms of the quality of their spontaneous speech) than an untreated control group. This effect applied to children whose language disorder was accompanied either by a moderate cognitive delay or by no cognitive delay. It did not hold for children who had a severe cognitive delay. Conant *et al.*'s findings illustrate the effectiveness of 'compromise' approaches which combine features from the behavioural and naturalistic approaches to intervention. Similar approaches have been devised by several other authors. For example, the Metaphon approach to treating phonological disorders (Howell and Dean, 1994) also employs communication games as a means of focusing intervention on particular phonological contrasts within pragmatically appropriate contexts. Howlin (1987; 1989) reports that in recent years, behavioural approaches to intervention have become less artificial and that behavioural techniques are now usually employed in communicatively meaningful contexts. She further suggests that the degree of structure which is appropriate in a language intervention approach will depend on characteristics of the child. In particular, she proposes that more highly structured programmes may be best suited to children with very limited linguistic skills or those with limited motivation to communicate (e.g. severely autistic children).

In summary, most of the available intervention techniques have been shown to produce some positive effects, but no particular technique stands out as being more effective overall than other techniques (Leonard, 1981; Nye *et al.*, 1987). The literature also suggests that different techniques produce different types of positive effects and that different techniques are probably appropriate for different types of children. However, clear and detailed evidence is lacking on which techniques are best suited to which children.

AN ILLUSTRATIVE CASE HISTORY

The eclectic approach which is preferred by the majority of practising clinicians is perhaps best illustrated with a potted case history. J was referred by her health visitor to a speech and language therapist at the age of 2:10 years. She was reported to be a healthy child, the youngest of three children of professional parents. At that time, she showed little interest in verbal communication with her family, spoke very little and then only in single words or stereotypical phrases, her play was poorly developed and she showed a rather unsettling independence for her age. She attended for her first block of intervention from just after her third birthday (6 weekly 45 minute sessions of individual therapy with J and her mother). The goals for this period of intervention included both pre-linguistic and early language behaviours such as response to sound, attention to speech, turn-taking in a simple game, selecting everyday objects by name and carrying out simple commands. A number of the more behavioural techniques such as modelling, shaping and chaining were employed, particularly as her attention span for any one activity was relatively short at this stage. However, attention was also paid to providing opportunities for J to experience success in simple communicative functions, such as requesting desired, but out-of-reach objects or otherwise influencing the actions of adults through the use of language.

J made rapid and sustained progress during and immediately after the period of therapy, and on review at age 3:6 years, she was noted to be a much more communicative child, whose play and social interaction had matured to a near age-appropriate level in many areas. Not only was she responding to other people's communicative attempts but she was also initiating conversations with others. However, her language comprehension and production were still well below age-appropriate level, therefore she attended for a second block of weekly intervention, this time with much more specifically linguistic goals. Structured activities were selected in order to build up J's ability to make sense of longer and more complex sentences. New vocabulary, particularly in the area of verbs and adjectives, was taught by focused stimulation during therapy sessions and follow-up consolidation activities at home. Although comprehension of new vocabulary items was primarily targeted, production was also stimulated, as encouraging J to produce new words appeared to aid learning (Connell, 1987). New grammatical forms were introduced using 'old' vocabulary, in order to allow J to focus attention on the targeted structure without competing demands from the need to process less well-established vocabulary. While some turn-taking was always preserved, it was often felt necessary to minimise any communicative element to the activity, again in order not to overload J's linguistic system. Consolidation of new words and forms was facilitated by gradually increasing the linguistic or communicative demands during the activity. She received a total of between 6 and 8 hours of therapy over a 3-4 month period.

By the age of 4:6 years, J's comprehension was within the normal range for her age on standardised testing, and the focus of attention shifted to language production. She spoke in largely well-formed sentences but made little or no use of complex, multi-clause structures. She also had persistent problems with some of the language of space, in particular the prepositions 'behind' and 'in front of', despite previous work in this area. This time, intervention took the form of paired therapy with another child of the same age and with similar difficulties. Most of the activities during the sessions were 'communicative', that is, they were devised to provide opportunities which led to successful communication if the targeted linguistic form was used (or failure if it was not used). For example, barrier games (Bunce, 1989) were used, in which one child had to describe a scenario using miniature toys, or one picture from a set of highly similar ones, for the child on the other side of the barrier to copy or select. Instant feedback on the success or not of the communication is achieved merely by removing the barrier. Such activities provide enormous motivation for children of this age and older, and success is inherent in the activity, allowing the child to take responsibility for monitoring her own language.

An interplay of both developmental and functional goals, and a variety of therapeutic techniques is evident in this intervention history, and it serves to illustrate the eclectic yet principled approach which is aimed for in therapy for children with SLI.

CONCLUSION

Specific language impairment is something of a paradox. On the one hand, the problems encountered by children who have a specific language impairment are by definition specific to language, in the sense that they cannot be adequately explained in terms of a single underlying cause such as low general intelligence. On the other hand, these children's linguistic difficulties are sometimes accompanied by more specific and subtle non-linguistic difficulties, for example with auditory processing or symbolic play.

One possible explanation for this paradox may be that the non-linguistic difficulties are at least in part effects (rather than causes) of the linguistic problems. Since language is an important cognitive and social tool, it would not be surprising if language impairments in the developing child interfered with some other aspects of development. However, on the basis of the available research evidence it is difficult to distinguish between the causes and the effects of specific language impairments. Indeed, it may well be that the causal relationships will prove not to be simple unidirectional ones, but rather that a complex pattern of two-way influences and interactions between linguistic and non-linguistic difficulties will be found in future research.

The elusiveness of a single underlying cause for specific language impairment may be partly attributable to the heterogeneity of the linguistic problems which are covered by the diagnostic label 'SLI'. The linguistic problems which characterise children with SLI vary not only in severity but also in whether they affect comprehension, production or both, and in terms of which linguistic levels (i.e. phonological, syntactic, semantic or pragmatic) they influence.

The picture which we have presented of the nature of SLI has several implications for intervention. Firstly, since the problems encountered by children with SLI are primarily linguistic and since the nature of these problems varies across children, assessment procedures should aim to identify which specific aspects of language are problematical for a particular child, so that appropriate goals of intervention can be formulated. Secondly, despite this emphasis on linguistic goals of intervention, it is also important to recognise that various types of non-linguistic difficulties may be associated with SLI (either as causes or as effects), and that these may need to be taken into account in planning intervention. Thirdly, in view of the heterogeneity of the problems associated with SLI, the goals of intervention will vary from child to child and should be used as a basis for devising individualised programmes of intervention. Finally, regarding intervention techniques, we advocate a compromise approach which combines features of the behavioural and naturalistic approaches. Such an approach is useful in targeting those specific aspects of language which are posing problems for an individual child, while at the same time retaining an emphasis on the communicative and cognitive functions which language fulfils in the child's everyday life.

REFERENCES

Bishop, D. V. M. (1989). 'Autism, Asperger's syndrome and semantic-pragmatic disorder: Where are the boundaries?' *British Journal of Disorders of Communication*, 24(2), 107-121.

Bishop, D. V. M. (1992). 'The underlying nature of specific language impairment.' *Journal of Child Psychology and Psychiatry*, 33(1), 3-66.

Bochner, S., Price, P., Salmon, L., Yeend, G. and Orr, E. (1980). 'Language intervention: a classroom report.' *British Journal of Disorders of Communication*, 15, 87-102.

Bruner, J. S. (1983). *Child's Talk: Learning to Use Language*. Oxford. Oxford University Press.

Bryant, P. and Bradley, L. (1985). *Children's Reading Problems*. Oxford. Blackwell.

Bunce, B. H. (1989). 'Using a barrier game to improve children's referential communication skills.' *Journal of Speech and Hearing Disorders*, 54, 33-43.

Chomsky, N. (1986). *Knowledge of Language*. New York. Praeger.

Conant, S., Budoff, M., Hecht, B. and Morse, R. (1984). 'Language intervention: a pragmatic approach.' *Journal of Autism and Developmental Disorders*, 14, 301-317.

Connell, P. J. (1987). 'Teaching language form, meaning and function to specific-language-impaired children', in Rosenberg, S. (Ed.). *Advances in Applied Psycholinguistics: Disorders of First Language Development* (Volume 1). Cambridge. Cambridge University Press.

Conti-Ramsden, G. (1985). 'Mothers in dialogue with language-impaired children.' *Topics in Language Disorders*, 5, 58-68.

Conti-Ramsden, G. (1991). 'Mother-child interactions with language-impaired children and their siblings.' *European Journal of Disorders of Communication,* 26, 337-354.

Crystal, D. (1981). *Clinical Linguistics.* Vienna. Springer Verlag.

Crystal, D. (1982). *Profiling Linguistic Disability.* London. Edward Arnold.

Crystal, D., Fletcher, P. and Garman, M. (1976). *The Grammatical Analysis of Language Disability.* London. Edward Arnold.

Dewart, H. and Summers, S. (1988). *The Pragmatics Profile of Early Communication Skills.* Windsor. NFER-Nelson.

Donaldson, M. (1978). *Children's Minds.* Glasgow. Collins/Fontana.

Donaldson, M. L. (1992). *Children with Language and Communication Disorders: A Review of the Literature.* Edinburgh. Edinburgh Centre for Research in Child Development.

Eisenson, J. (1972). *Aphasia in Children.* New York. Harper & Row.

Fey, M. E. (1986). *Language Intervention with Young Children.* London. Taylor & Francis.

Gallacher, T. M. and Prutting, C. A. (Eds.). (1983). *Pragmatic Assessment and Intervention Issues in Language.* San Diego. College Hill Press.

Gathercole, S. E. and Baddeley, A. D. (1993). *Working Memory and Language.* Hove, East Sussex. Lawrence Erlbaum.

Grundy, K. (Ed.). (1989). *Linguistics in Clinical Practice.* London. Taylor and Francis.

Grunwell, P. (1982). *Clinical Phonology.* London. Croom Helm.

Harris, J. (1990). *Early Language Development: Implications for Clinical and Educational Practice.* London. Routledge.

Hegde, M., Noll, M. and Pecora, R. (1979). 'A study of some factors affecting generalisation of language training.' *Journal of Speech and Hearing Disorders,* 44, 301-320.

Howell, J. and Dean, E. C. (1994). *Treating Phonological Disorders in Children: Metaphon-Theory to Practice.* London, Whurr.

Howlin, P. (1987). 'Behavioural approaches to language', in Yule W. and Rutter M. (Eds.), *Language Development and Disorders.* Oxford. Blackwell/MacKeith Press.

Howlin, P. (1989). 'Changing approaches to communication training with autistic children.' *British Journal of Disorders of Communication,* 24, 151-168.

Ingram, D. (1976). *Phonological Disability in Children.* London. Edward Arnold.

Johnston, J. R. (1988). 'Specific language disorders in the child', in McReynolds, L. and Yoder, D. (Eds.), *Handbook of Speech-Language Pathology and Audiology* (pp. 685-715). Philadelphia. B.C. Decker.

Johnston, J. R. (1991). 'Questions about cognition in children with specific language impairment', in Miller, J. F. (Ed.), *Research on Child Language Disorders* Austin, Texas. Pro-Ed.

Knowles, W. and Masidlover, M. (1982). *Derbyshire Language Scheme* (Revised ed.). Ripley, Derbyshire. Educational Psychology Service.

Lahey, M. (1988). *Language disorders and language development.* London. Collier Macmillan.

Lees, J. and Urwin, S. (1991). *Children with Language Disorders.* London. Whurr.

Leonard, L. B. (1981). 'Facilitating linguistic skills in children with specific language impairment.' *Applied Psycholinguistics,* 2, 89-118.

Leonard, L. B. (1987). 'Is specific language impairment a useful construct?' in Rosenberg, S. (Ed.), *Advances in Applied Psycholinguistics: Disorders of First-Language Development.* Cambridge. Cambridge University Press.

McLean, J. E. and Snyder-McLean, L. K. (1978). *A transactional approach to early language training.* Columbus, Ohio. Merill.

McTear, M. M. and Conti-Ramsden, G. (1992). *Pragmatic Disability in Children.* London. Whurr.

Miller J, F. (1991). 'Research on language disorders in children: a progress report', in Miller, J. F. (Ed.), *Research on Child Language Disorders: a Decade of Progress.* Austin, Texas. Pro-Ed.

Nye, C., Foster, S. H. and Seaman, D. (1987). 'Effectiveness of language intervention with the language/learning disabled.' *Journal of Speech and Hearing Disorders,* 52, 348-357.

Piaget, J. and Inhelder, B. (1969). *The Psychology of the Child.* London. Routledge and Kegan Paul.

Rapin, I. and Allen, D. (1983). 'Developmental language disorders: nosological considerations', in Kirk, U. (Ed.), *Neuropsychology of Language, Reading and Spelling* (pp. 155-184). New York. Academic Press.

Rapin, I. and Allen, D. A. (1987). 'Developmental dysphasia and autism in preschool children: characteristics and subtypes', in *Proceedings of the First International Symposium on Specific Speech and Language Disorders in Children,* (pp. 20-35). University of Reading. AFASIC.

Silva, P. A. (1987). 'Epidemiology, longitudinal course and some associated factors: an update', in Yule, W. and Rutter, M. (Eds.), *Language Development and Disorders.* Oxford. Blackwell/MacKeith Press.

Skuse, D. (1992). 'The relationship between deprivation, physical growth and the impaired development of language', in Fletcher, P. (Ed.), *Specific Speech and Language Disorders in Children.* London. Whurr.

Smith, B. R. and Leinonen, E. (1991). *Clinical Pragmatics.* London. Chapman & Hall.

Snow, C. E. (1986). 'Conversations with children', in Fletcher, P. and Garman, M. (Eds.), *Language Acquisition.* Cambridge. Cambridge University Press.

Tallal, P., Stark, R. and Curtiss, S. (1976). 'Relation between speech perception and speech production impairment in children with developmental dysphasia.' *Brain and Language,* 3, 305-317.

Tallal, P., Stark ,R. and Mellits, D. (1985). 'Identification of language-impaired children on the basis of rapid perception and production skills.' *Brain and Language,* 25, 314-322.

Terrell, B., Schwartz, R., Prelock, P. and Messick ,C. (1984). 'Symbolic play in normal and language-impaired children', *Journal of Speech and Hearing Research,* 27, 424-429.

LANGUAGE AND LITERACY: CONNECTIONS AND IMPLICATIONS

MARYSIA NASH

INTRODUCTION

This chapter explores the relationship between literacy and language disorder and considers both theory and practice. This relationship is important to teachers and speech and language therapists because some children with language disorders have significant difficulties with reading and spelling and some with dyslexia have language difficulties. The chapter is divided into three sections.

1   Language disorders as precursors to problems with literacy
2   The relationship between the type of language disorder and type of literacy difficulty
3   Language deficits in dyslexia

LANGUAGE DISORDERS AS PRECURSORS TO PROBLEMS IN LITERACY

Children learning to read and write need a reasonable foundation of verbal language skills. Stackhouse (1988) suggests that an 'intact facility for speech and language development appears to be a necessary prerequisite for satisfactory reading and spelling development'.

Webster and McConnel (1987) state that many children with early spoken language difficulties will go on to have problems with literacy, while those at the severe end of the spectrum will undoubtedly face problems.

EVIDENCE FROM RESEARCH STUDIES

Longitudinal studies such as Fundudis *et al.* (1979), Richman *et al.* (1982), Silva *et al.* (1983) as reported in Howlin and Rutter (1987) provide evidence that the spelling and reading scores of language delayed children were much lower than those of controls.

Making predictions for children with specific language disorders on the basis of these findings is difficult, however, because the research did not differentiate children with specific developmental language disorders from those with global cognitive delay. It is therefore impossible to know how much of the educational differences were as a result of the earlier language deficit and how much as a consequence of low IQ.

Data from a study by Aram *et al.* (1984) reported in Howlin and Rutter (1987), who followed up a small group of children identified as language disordered pre-school, suggested a greater incidence of poor educational attainments even in children who did not have a low IQ.

Children with both language problems and low IQ had the worst educational outlook.

More recently, the Bishop and Adams (1990) longitudinal study investigated the reading attainments of children identified as having specific language impairment pre-school.

The children's language had been assessed at $4^1/_2$ years and again at $5^1/_2$ years, Bishop and Edmondson (1987). At eight years six months, in addition to other tests, reading and writing were also assessed.

Among the results was the finding of a link between early language difficulties and later problems with literacy. The authors were surprised to find, however, that the children whose language impairments had resolved by five years six months continued to progress well and had no significant impairments on language or literacy measures and that their use of phonics to read and spell non-words was as good as other $8^1/_2$ year olds.

Children with persisting language impairments were poor readers at $8^1/_2$ years but this was not an isolated difficulty. Problems with reading occurred in the context of widespread verbal deficits and poor non-verbal skills. Reading comprehension was much more of a problem than reading accuracy.

While it seems that language impairment is related to success with literacy, it is clearly not the whole story.

Magnusson and Naucler (1990) also make this observation. They state, in relation to children with language disorders, 'Even if a majority of them have reading and writing problems, some of them seem to acquire written language in much the same way as linguistically normal children. Furthermore, the children who seem to have the most serious speech problems are not necessarily the ones for whom reading and writing will be the most problematical, while children whose language problems are not particularly severe may have grave difficulties in learning to read and write.'

To investigate this paradox, Magnusson and Naucler (1990) undertook a longitudinal study to look at the importance of, and relationships between, linguistic, meta-linguistic and non-linguistic factors for reading and spelling. Initial findings were reported for language disordered children and normal children on linguistic and linguistic awareness tasks, one year before starting school and the beginning and end of the first grade. Performance on reading and spelling tasks was measured at the end of the first grade.

Their study allowed them to consider:

1   The role of linguistic competence in general for reading and spelling development.
2   The role of certain aspects of linguistic awareness as a possible prerequisite for reading and spelling acquisition. Tasks included rhyming, segmentation of syllables and phonemes, identification of phonemes and also a task requiring judgment of syntactic acceptability.
3   The possibility of predicting reading and spelling achievements in the first grade from pre-school data.

Results suggested that **as a group** the language disordered children had poorer language, linguistic awareness and reading and spelling abilities than the normal children. However, some individual language disordered children performed better than their matched normal peer group on some measures. For example, some language disordered children performed better on one or more of the linguistic awareness tasks than the matched normal, and some were better readers and spellers.

Furthermore, even when some of the disordered children's reading and writing scores were compared to an absolute standard, there were language disordered children not only at the lowest reading and spelling level but also among the best. In addition, some normal children were among the poorest. This does not mean that language competence is irrelevant for reading and writing development, because the study found that both the language disordered children who were good at reading and spelling and the normals who performed well gained high scores on language comprehension and syntactic production tasks and, most importantly, high scores on linguistic awareness tasks.

Conversely, the normals who performed poorly were similar to the other poor performers, who were language disordered, by having low scores on these tasks.

Thus, these authors concluded that both linguistic abilities and also linguistic awareness are required for the development of reading and spelling.

Syntactic competence seemed the most important linguistic prerequisite, while rhyming and the ability to identify phonemes are the most important aspects of linguistic awareness and the best predictors for reading and spelling **at least in the first grade.**

While the findings of this study are interesting, the authors acknowledge that some children assigned to the normal group may have had language problems that were overlooked. This, together with importance of certain linguistic abilities and linguistic awareness for attainments in literacy, may have accounted for the difference within and between the two groups.

IMPLICATIONS FOR PRACTICE

Research has highlighted the importance of language levels and linguistic awareness for learning to read.

The following suggestions are offered in relation to practice.

Children with persisting language impairment entering school should have their progress in literacy monitored. Liaison between speech and language therapist and teacher is particularly important in the early years, to discuss management should problems occur.

An Educational Psychologist's assessment of the child's non-verbal ability will help ascertain to what extent any lack of progress is compatible with IQ.

The importance of linguistic awareness for literacy should be recognised. We need to be more aware of the status of these skills in language impaired and normal children and to consider ways in which they can be assessed.

Stackhouse (1988) considers that the speech and language therapist has a critical role with pre-school children in identifying the 'at risk' child and promoting pre-reading and pre-spelling skills since she claims that some of the dyslexics of the future are in speech therapy clinics now.

Nursery teachers should consider whether there is a case for screening 'normal' children's linguistic awareness. Mann (1984) suggests that skills which may predict first grade reading ability might be tested as part of a kindergarten screening battery.

Whether a decision is made to target all children, or to identify and intervene with those who have problems, it seems that developing these skills is important.

Bryant (1985) suggests that skill with sounds can and should be fostered in young children and can be an enjoyable activity. He says that young children love nursery rhymes etc and that this kind of activity which happens naturally should be encouraged to help children's progress with literacy at a later stage.

Similarly, Stackhouse (1990) suggests that speech therapy intervention should address the link between spoken and written language problems and that activities can promote pre-reading and pre-spelling skills as well as improvements in verbal language. For specific suggestions, see Stackhouse (1985). Mann (1984) feels most optimistic about remediating deficiencies in phonological sophistication. She suggests that phonological awareness may be helped, if not brought about, by some experience which encourages the child to manipulate phonological structure. Some children may need some systematic training in order to achieve the level of sophistication about phonemes and phonological rules that is required for skilled reading. She makes a number of suggestions for indirect methods such as teaching nursery rhymes and poetry or encouraging secret languages like talking backwards, and at a later stage for direct awareness training.

It seems that encouraging linguistic awareness is important for all children, language disordered, normal or dyslexic. Perhaps teachers and therapists should be co-operating to develop this skill in children at both the pre-school and early school stage.

THE RELATIONSHIP BETWEEN THE TYPE OF LANGUAGE DISORDER AND THE TYPE OF LITERACY DIFFICULTY

Children with language disorders are not a homogenous group and they may experience varying difficulties with literacy.

There have been a number of attempts to classify language disorder into different sub-types, Rapin and Allen (1987) and Bishop and Rosenbloom (1987).

Three of the sub-types from the Bishop and Rosenbloom (1987) classification, viz: Developmental apraxia of speech, Phonologic-syntactic syndrome and Semantic pragmatic disorder, will be considered in relation to literacy.

DEVELOPMENTAL APRAXIA OF SPEECH (VERBAL DYSPRAXIA)

This is a pronunciation disorder which can vary in severity but where children have a motor programming deficit for speech. The main symptoms are summarised by Tate (1991), as follows:

- Inconsistent articulatory production.
- Difficulty in selection and sequencing of phonological and articulatory movements.
- Increased difficulty with increased complexity of sequences.
- Altered prosodic features.
- Difference between voluntary and involuntary movements.
- Possible concomitant expressive language disorder.
- Possible concomitant learning disability and general motor problems.

With regard to literacy, Stackhouse (1985) states that in dyspraxia there may be no systematic relationship between sounds and meaning. Pronunciations of words may be very variable. Reading and spelling difficulties are to be expected as a result of such inconsistency, since written language will be laid down onto a faulty spoken language base.

Stackhouse looked at the nature of the reading and spelling processes of children with dyspraxia aged 7 - 11 years and found that in reading they were unable to utilise a sound by sound approach to reading unfamiliar words. Their errors e.g. 'canary' read as 'competition' seemed to be guesses prompted by individual letters in the word. It appeared that they were increasing their reading age by relying on a visual reading strategy without phonological skill.

Their spelling errors were bizarre and did not follow the normal processes identified in spelling development.

In another study, Snowling and Stackhouse (1983) noted that in dyspraxic children there was not a direct relationship between pronunciation and spelling. However, great difficulty was observed in segmenting a word prior to spelling. It appeared that mistakes occurred early in the spelling process when speech sounds were analysed prior to sound-letter translation.

Although not all children will be so severely impaired, the case of Michael, Stackhouse and Wells (1991), illustrates the range of difficulties which can be experienced.

Michael 11 years
Verbal Dyspraxia and language problems

Marked phonological processing difficulties.

Reading was at seven year level and the approach to written language tasks indicated that Michael relied on visual strengths to overcome his difficulties with auditory processing. He had great difficulty with phonological strategies, he made visual errors in reading and was unsuccessful in applying phonics. His spelling age was six years eight months and here his difficulty with phonological strategies was even more obvious. He made predominantly bizarre or non-phonetic errors.

The authors presumed that his difficulties with making progress beyond a visual approach to reading and spelling were a consequence of his marked phonological processing difficulties (his auditory discrimination, rhyme and segmentation skills were all poor). His inconsistent speech output compounded the problem.

PHONOLOGIC – SYNTACTIC SYNDROME

According to Bishop and Rosenbloom (1987), this is the most common type of developmental language disorder.

Severity varies. Characteristics include:

- Pronunciation errors arising from problems learning the rules of the English sound system and resulting in a spectrum from complete unintelligibility to occasional mild immaturities. (Problems confined to pronunciation of this type are commonly labelled phonological disorder.)
- Syntactic structure may be behind age level.
- Possible concomitant comprehension difficulty.

There is some evidence, Bishop and Adams (1990), that isolated phonological problems in pre-literate children were not predictive of reading difficulties at eight years six months. Children with severe and persistent phonological problems may have a different outlook, however. Certainly for the children in the Bishop and Adams' study it was difficult to ascertain the severity of the phonological impairment at five years six months and the stage at which it resolved. (The data suggests that almost all the children had no phoneme problems by eight years six months.) This may mean that generalising the findings to all children with isolated phonological disorders may not be appropriate.

Robinson Beresford and Dodd (1982) suggest that children with phonological disorders are at risk for dyslexic difficulties.

They compared the spelling of 11 children with phonological disorder with a group or normal children matched on age, sex and reading ability and found that the phonologically disordered children made significantly more errors and unlike the control group, did not find the spelling of regular words easier than irregular words. The two groups were also qualitatively different. Unlike the control group, the phonologically disordered group made non-phonetic spelling errors.

Furthermore, the speech disordered children made as many spelling errors on words they pronounced correctly as on words they mispronounced.

It is interesting that the spelling difficulties described are reminiscent of those described in dyspraxic children and it appears that some of the children in the study may also have had symptoms of dyspraxia.

SEMANTIC PRAGMATIC DISORDER

This subtype of language disorder was first described by Rapin and Allen (1983) and is one where children have problems with language use and content but relatively little problem with language form (grammar and pronunciation). Often other behavioural and cognitive abnormalities co-exist with the language difficulty, many of which resemble mild forms of the deficits found in autism.

In relation to literacy, Bishop and Rosenbloom (1987) observe that ,'Unlike other language disordered children, a few of these children learn to read at the normal age or even earlier. However, their comprehension for what they read tends to be poor.'

Rapin and Allen (1986) also suggest that this group may have problems with reading comprehension.

Two research studies give some insight into the development of literacy in this group. The first, a single case study by Conti Ramsden and Gunn (1985), describes a boy, Tony, with a conversational disability/semantic pragmatic disorder.

The longitudinal study describes how Tony between the ages of four years four months and four years nine months enjoyed reading and had a small sight vocabulary. This may not seem surprising until we consider that his verbal comprehension as measured by the Reynell Developmental Language Scale was two year two months and his understanding of vocabulary was below a 1:5 year level. At a later stage, between four years nine months and five years two months, and still with very poor scores on verbal comprehension tests, Tony had a sight vocabulary of about 40 words and could write simple sentences without help. The discrepancy between verbal comprehension and mechanical reading ability persisted so that aged five years seven months, and with a verbal comprehension of one-two years behind his chronological age (depending on the test), Tony was observed to have a mechanical reading ability well above his chronological age. The way in which Tony made progress in literacy is not clear, however, and it is not possible to know whether his was a predominantly visual approach or whether he was using phonics.

A slightly larger study, Spence *et al.* (1989), looked at the reading of seven children (mean age 12 years five months) with high level semantic difficulties which might also be referred to by some as Semantic Pragmatic Disorder. These authors did not feel, however, that all their children had pragmatic problems.

In addition to their verbal language difficulties, the children displayed a discrepancy between their reading accuracy and their reading comprehension, with accuracy better than comprehension.

In the study, the children were given a reading passage followed by a series of questions. The passage was read aloud easily and many of the children did so with normal prosody. This, the authors felt, could create the impression that what was read was also understood. However, although their response to the standardised questions was better than expected and superficially correct, with further probing it appeared that the children had not grasped the precise meaning.

Furthermore, their scores on the Neale Analysis of Reading Ability were interesting in that although comprehension was well below their chronological age, the mean score for accuracy was also depressed, albeit to a lesser extent. In response to this observation the authors suggest that there is a need for further investigation into 'whether mechanical reading skills eventually plateau, because poor comprehension adversely affects the use of predictive strategies'.

IMPLICATIONS FOR PRACTICE

While some language disordered children may be more at risk for reading comprehension problems, others have problems with decoding text and great problems with spelling.

The more severely affected children with Semantic Pragmatic Disorder tend to have marked difficulties with verbal comprehension. These may still be apparent when they start school and they are likely to be placed in language units. While many have great problems with attention, they may show a considerable interest in numbers, letters and reading. Nishio (1981), as quoted in Rapin and Allen (1986), suggests that in some, reading can be used as a means for improving the comprehension of oral language. It may, therefore, be possible to use the written word to focus attention on language you may wish to teach using, for example, either Language Through Reading Level 1 and/or ideas based on it.

At a later stage, Language Through Reading Levels two and three, which specifically target the comprehension of 'Wh' questions, pronoun reference, inferencing etc., may be useful as these children often have problems in these areas.

Throughout their reading development, it will be necessary to monitor comprehension carefully as this is likely to pose greater problems than accuracy.

Helping the child to identify areas where comprehension is a problem, coupled with strategies by which the child addresses this, may be helpful for older children, and ideas based on the work of Dollaghen and Kaston (1986) and applied to reading may be useful.

Children with dyspraxia and phonological disorders who have problems decoding and spelling because of poor phonological processing skills may be helped to progress from the visual approach to the alphabetic phase of literacy development. Intervention aimed at strengthening auditory processing skills may be helpful. (See Stackhouse (1985)).

For many language disordered children, including those with semantic pragmatic disorder or phonologic syntactic disorder, the choice of reading scheme/book is important.

When comprehension is impaired significantly, it is important to assess the level of understanding required – whether the book requires understanding at sentence or discourse level. Where comprehension relies on understanding discourse (i.e. several sentences linked together to form a bigger unit of meaning such as a story), some children may have considerable difficulty.

In addition it is important to note the extent to which inference is required so that problems may be avoided or overcome. During inference, world knowledge is brought to bear in comprehension to 'fill in' information which is not explicitly stated. Children with semantic pragmatic disorder may find this process of inference particularly difficult.

The vocabulary is also important. Children who have poor receptive vocabulary may have reading comprehension difficulties as a result of their failure to understand certain words and figures of speech such as 'fell out' etc. Knowledge of vocabulary will also affect the child's ability to make predictions to assist in decoding.

For the child with very delayed grammar, the choice of a reading book/ scheme should involve consideration of the grammar in the text. For example, a book may require him to read sentences considerably outwith his grammatical competence. As a result, his ability to use 'top down' processes, i.e. knowledge of language to assist decoding, may be considerably reduced. A text with structures more at his grammatical level, may be more helpful for developing reading and reinforcing language work.

LANGUAGE DEFICITS IN DYSLEXIA

Although not all dyslexics have speech and language problems, a proportion have subtle undiagnosed language difficulties that may only become recognised if the child is also seen by a speech and language therapist.

Stackhouse (1991) describes how some dyslexics may have had speech therapy in the past but have been discharged and are then re-referred with a query as to whether their earlier spoken language problems are relevant to their lack of progress with literacy. Other dyslexics, despite having some degree of language difficulty, may never have been recognised as such, perhaps because their problems went unrecognised or there was a lack of opportunity for referral.

Some children are referred to a speech and language therapist, when the educational psychologist identifies a verbal-performance discrepancy on IQ tests with the verbal score significantly poorer than the performance score.

Whatever the reason for the eventual referral to speech and language therapy, on assessment the following deficits may be identified:

Receptive vocabulary – Some children with specific learning difficulties score at or in advance of their age on tests such as the British Picture Vocabulary Scale while others may score below, Klein (1985).

This author also suggests that higher level comprehension may be affected and that there may be problems understanding age appropriate syntax or with absurdities, puns, proverbs etc.

Naming difficulties are common. Findings from a study by Snowling *et al.* (1988) suggested that dyslexics perform more poorly on object naming tasks than their age and intelligence suggests and their difficulty was not associated with inadequate knowledge of word meaning. It appears that the dyslexics may have some difficulty acquiring precise phonological representations for words.

Because the children may possess faulty or impoverished representations of some words, these will tend to be mispronounced and/or be difficult to access. The authors quote an error which illustrates this: 'ack, ac, aquarine, fishtank' for aquarium.

A study by Stirling and Miles (1986) showed that dyslexic children distorted words more frequently than controls when they tried to say them e.g. buckle – buttle, bustle, bucker etc., and these errors seem in keeping with the explanation put forward by Snowling *et al.* (1988) and cited above.

Klein (1985) states that dyslexics may have difficulty communicating in a fluent, creative and interesting manner and suggests ideas for assessment and management. Stirling and Miles (1986) investigated dyslexics' fluency when asked to explain the meaning of a particular word. Among other ways, the dyslexics differed from the controls by producing more incomplete sentences and more frequent use of 'um', 'er', and 'well'.

Verbal Memory Deficits may also be apparent and Klein (1985) suggests a number of areas where problems may arise including learning sequences such as the days of the week and months of the year, retaining a sequence of verbal information such as the rules of a game, learning tables etc.

In addition a reduced digit span and difficulty with repetition of, in particular, polysyllabic words can occur.

Stackhouse and Wells (1991) describe how a dyslexic child may have problems with unclear speech due to speech sound omissions together with imprecise articulation. Difficulty may no longer be in pronouncing individual consonants but at a less obvious level. Full assessment of speech by the speech and language therapist may therefore be appropriate.

Poor auditory skills may be present in dyslexia, Stackhouse and Wells (1991), and the following areas should be assessed: auditory discrimination (including complex non-words), rhyme detection and production and syllable and phoneme segmentation.

The child's ability to apply alphabetic skills to reading and spelling tasks should also be assessed. For a case study of a dyslexic boy with a range of higher level language problems, the reader is referred to Stackhouse and Wells (1991).

IMPLICATIONS FOR PRACTICE

The recognition that dyslexics often have some degree of language difficulty suggests that there is a role for the speech and language therapist in their assessment and management. See Robinson (1993), this publication, (chapter 26).

Stackhouse (1991) states that it is important to use appropriate psycholinguistic tests in investigating older children with subtle speech and language difficulties and that there is a need to develop better assessments for the more subtle speech and language deficits in older children. Furthermore, there is a need for teachers, therapists and educational psychologists to collaborate in assessment and intervention.

The work of Snowling *et al.* (1988) provides insight into dyslexics' naming difficulties which may be usefully generalised to children with more obvious language disorders.

Naming deficits, often described as word finding difficulty, are recognised in the language disordered population. These difficulties have been so called because the child is unable to provide a word he very often understands. The exact reason for the difficulty and hence the most appropriate remediation for it are still not fully understood.

The research with dyslexics suggests that impoverished or faulty phonological representations may affect accurate naming even when there is good semantic knowledge. This emphasises the phonological aspects of word learning, a neglected area in therapy. Assessment of any child with vocabulary problems should therefore consider both phonological and semantic knowledge in order to target remediation as appropriately as possible.

CONCLUSIONS

Research indicates that language disordered children may be at risk for problems with reading and spelling, that different types of difficulty may be experienced, and that dyslexics may have high level speech and language disorders. In the light of these relationships, the need for speech and language therapists to collaborate with teachers in assessing and managing such children is desirable.

REFERENCES

Bishop, D. V. M and Adams, C. (1990). 'A Prospective Study of the Relationship between Specific Language Impairment, Phonological Disorders and Reading Retardation.' *Journal of Child Psychology and Psychiatry.* 31(7).

Bishop, D. V. M. and Edmundson, A. (1987). 'Language Impaired 4-year olds: Distinguishing Transient from Persistent Impairment.' *Journal of Speech and Hearing Disorders,* 52, 156-173.

Bishop, D. V. M. and Rosenbloom, L. (1987). 'Childhood Language Disorders: Classification and Overview.' In Yule ,W. and Rutter, M. (Eds.) *Language Development and Disorders.* MacKeith Press.

Bryant, P. (1985). 'The Question of Prevention.' In Snowling, M. J. (Ed.) *Children's Written Language Difficulties.* NFER-Nelson.

Conti Ramsden, G. and Gunn, M. (1986). 'The Development of Conversational Disability: A Case Study.' *British Journal of Disorders of Communication,* 21(3).

Dollaghan, C. and Kaston, N. (1986). 'A Comprehension Monitoring program for Language Impaired Children.' *Journal of Speech and Hearing Disorders,* 51, 264-271.

Gillies, M. and Hutt, E. (1985). *Language Through Reading, Parts I, II, III.* Developed by John Horniman School Staff.

Howlin, P. and Rutter, M. (1987). 'The Consequences of Language Delay for Other Aspects of Development.' In Yule, W. and Rutter, M. (Eds.). *Language Development and Disorders.* Mac Keith Press.

Klein, H. (1985). 'The Assessment and Management of Some Persisting Language Difficulties in the Learning Disabled.' In Snowling, M.J. ed. *Children's Written Language Difficulties*. NFER-Nelson.

Magnusson, E. and Naucler, K. (1990). 'Reading and Spelling in Language Disordered Children-Linguistic and Meta-linguistic Pre-requisites: Report on a Longitudinal Study.' *Clinical Linguistics and Phonetics*. 4(1).

Mann, V. A. (1984). 'Longitudinal Prediction and Prevention of Early Reading Difficulty.' *Annals of Dyslexia*. 34.

Rapin, I. and Allen, D. A. (1983). 'Developmental Language Disorders: Nosologic Consideration.' In Kirk, U. (Ed.) *Neuro-psychology of Language Reading and Spelling*. Academic Press. New York.

Rapin, I. and Allen, D. A. (1986). 'Communication Disorders in Early Childhood.' In Flemhig, I. and Stern, L. (Eds.) *Proceedings of the 2nd European Symposium on Developmental Neurology*.

Rapin, I. and Allen, D. A. (1987). 'Developmental Dysphasia and Autism in Preschool Children: Characteristics and Sub-types.' In *Specific Speech and Language Disorders in Children*. AFASIC.

Snowling, M. J. and Stackhouse, J. (1983). 'Spelling Performance of Children with Developmental Verbal Dyspraxia.' *Developmental Medicine and Child Neurology*, 25, 430-437.

Snowling, M. van Wagtendonk ,B. and Stafford, C. (1988). 'Object Naming Deficits in Developmental Dyslexia.' *Journal of Research in Reading*. 11.

Spence, L., Fleetwood, A., Gelvit, J., Wrench, B., Earles, L. and Searby, C. (1989). 'A Descriptive Study of a Subgroup of Moor House School Children with High Level Semantic Difficulties.' In Grunwell, P. and James, A. (Eds.) *The Functional Evaluation of Language Disorders*. Croom Helm.

Stackhouse, J. (1985). 'Segmentation, Speech and Spelling Difficulties.' In Snowling, M. J. (Ed.) *Children's Written Language Difficulties*. NFER-Nelson.

Stackhouse, J. (1988). 'Relationship between Spoken and Written Language Disorders.' In Mogford, K. and Sadler, J. (Eds.) *Child Language Disability: Implications in an Educational Setting*. Multilingual Matters Ltd.

Stackhouse, J (1990). 'Phonological Deficits in Developmental Reading and Spelling Disorders.' In Grunwell, P. (Ed.) *Developmental Speech Disorders*. Churchill Livingston.

Stackhouse, J. and Wells, B. (1991). 'Dyslexia: The Obvious and Hidden Speech and Language Disorder.' *Speech Therapy in Practice* 7 (1).

Stirling, E. G. and Miles, T. R. (1986). 'Oral Language of Dyslexic Adolescents.' *Child Language and Teaching Therapy*. 2 (2).

Tate, M. (1991). 'Developmental Dyspraxia – a sibling case study.' *Speech Therapy in Practice*. Vol. 7, No. 1, 1991.

Webster, A. and McConnel, C. (1987). *Children with Speech and Language Difficulties*. Cassell.

ROLE OF THE SPEECH THERAPIST

NICOLA ROBINSON

INTRODUCTION

A community speech therapist provides a service in a local area to all those suffering from a variety of communication disorders. This includes young pre-school children with slow development of speech and language through the whole age range to elderly people with acquired problems following neurological damage. Our job is to offer assessment, to attempt a diagnosis and to suggest appropriate treatment and management. The involvement of a speech therapist with dyslexic children is appropriate if it can be shown that there are links between written and spoken communication. This involves consideration of how the human brain is functioning during language development, whether there might be a neurological cause of dyslexia and whether speech is an important foundation for written language. It is also necessary to review the skills which will normally have been learnt by the time a child is ready for reading and writing, to look for evidence that may indicate that particular kinds of early spoken language difficulty are predictors of later literacy failure and to discover the extent of spoken language problems among children with dyslexia.

THE ISSUES

In considering whether it is justifiable to involve a medically trained and employed speech therapist in the management of a learning disordered child whose problems appear to lie in the realm of reading and writing rather than in speech (Fig 1), a number of questions can be asked:

- What type of links exist between verbal communication and written communication and is there any reason for one type of disorder to coexist with or affect the other?

- Is there any evidence that the child with dyslexia may suffer verbal or oral language problems as well as literacy difficulties?

- Does the child with dyslexia have a hidden verbal deficit which only becomes obvious once more complex language tasks are tackled?

- Is there evidence that children presenting spoken language problems early on then go on to have problems with literacy?

- Is it possible that dyslexia is a distinct and special kind of language disorder?

- Are the speech disordered and the reading disordered population one and the same?

- Are there faulty underlying processes accounting for failure in both types of language function?

- Do all speech and language disordered children develop dyslexia or only those with specific difficulties in translating visual experience into speech, i.e. those with verbal coding problems?

- Does the condition of dyslexia involve complex difficulties with the auditory processing channel as well as the visual?

- Is it therefore possible to identify a distinct group of children with both spoken and written language disorders who justify particular lines of treatment?

- If so, how can these children be identified and what help do they require and when?

- If dyslexia is caused by an underlying pathological process in the development of the central nervous system, is it helpful to include a speech therapist in the team, bearing in mind that speech therapy is normally a health service based profession?

Speech therapists with their training in medical neurology, child development, speech and language pathology, and linguistic and phonetic analysis, should be able to provide a service to a learning support team. They may be able to provide relevant information on the child's early language development. By using their assessment techniques they should be able to identify any underlying processes which are faulty, and so to help in the planning of remedial treatment.

Fig. 1

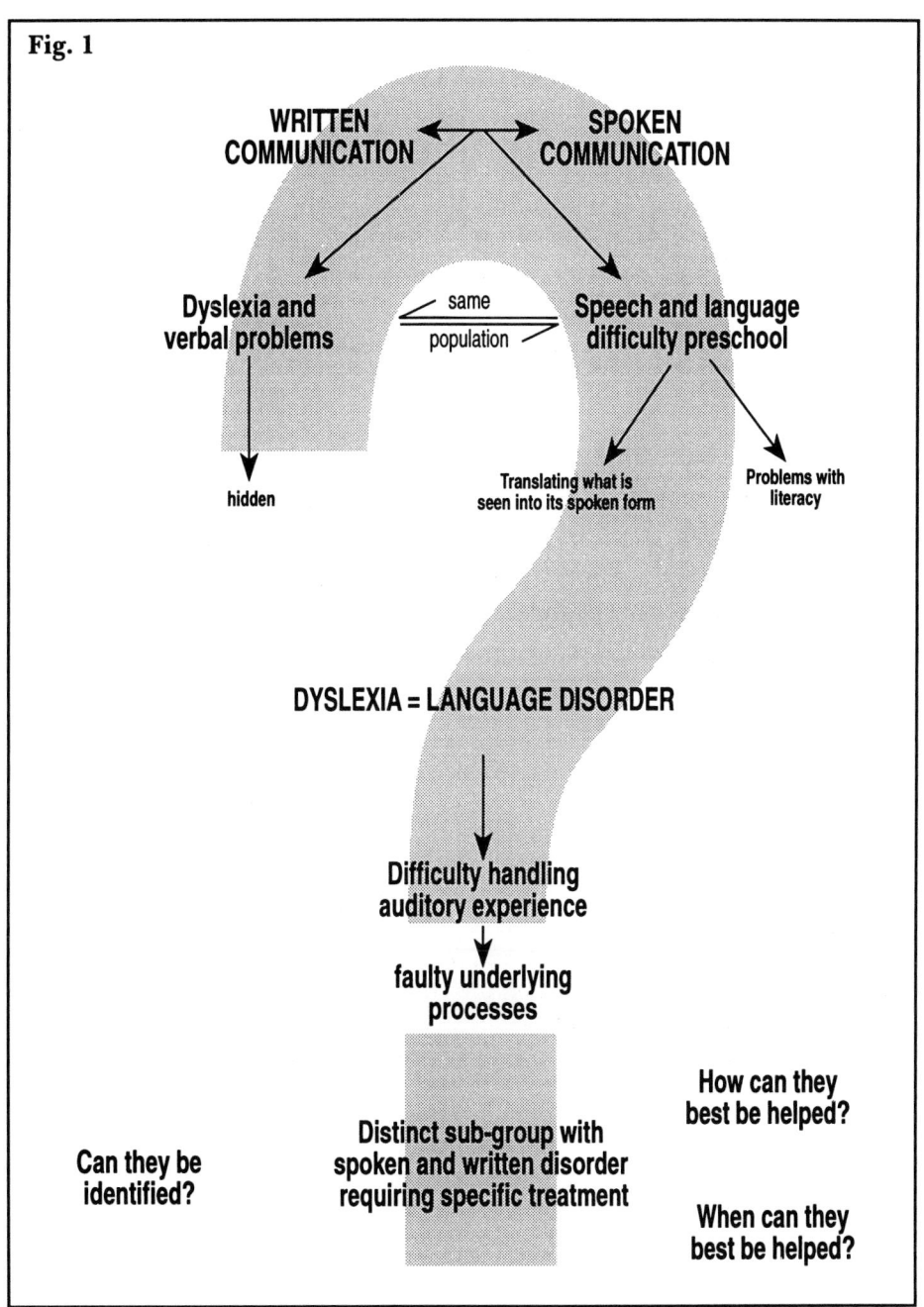

WRITTEN COMMUNICATION

SPOKEN COMMUNICATION

Dyslexia and verbal problems

same population

Speech and language difficulty preschool

hidden

Translating what is seen into its spoken form

Problems with literacy

DYSLEXIA = LANGUAGE DISORDER

Difficulty handling auditory experience

faulty underlying processes

Can they be identified?

Distinct sub-group with spoken and written disorder requiring specific treatment

How can they best be helped?

When can they best be helped?

LANGUAGE AND LITERACY

Crystal (1986) tells us that language is the most complex piece of behaviour a human being ever learns. Spoken English has over 40 sounds used in over 300 combinations to produce over 7000 syllables. These are used in a vocabulary of around 50,000 reasonably common words. These words are combined into sentences by over 1000 grammatical rules along with several dozen prosodic patterns of intonation, pitch, stress and volume – all of which will be used in a variety of social and educational settings.

Spoken language is a genetically determined faculty evolving historically nearly 60,000 years before written language was invented, a skill dependent on learning from older members of the group and so more vulnerable to personal or social disruption.

For language processing to take place, both in understanding and in responding, the brain must receive, interpret and organise information adequately in order to connect what we see with what we hear.

Complex associations must take place between adjacent parts of the brain within the language area if the functions of speech, understanding, reading and spelling are to take place (see fig. 2a).

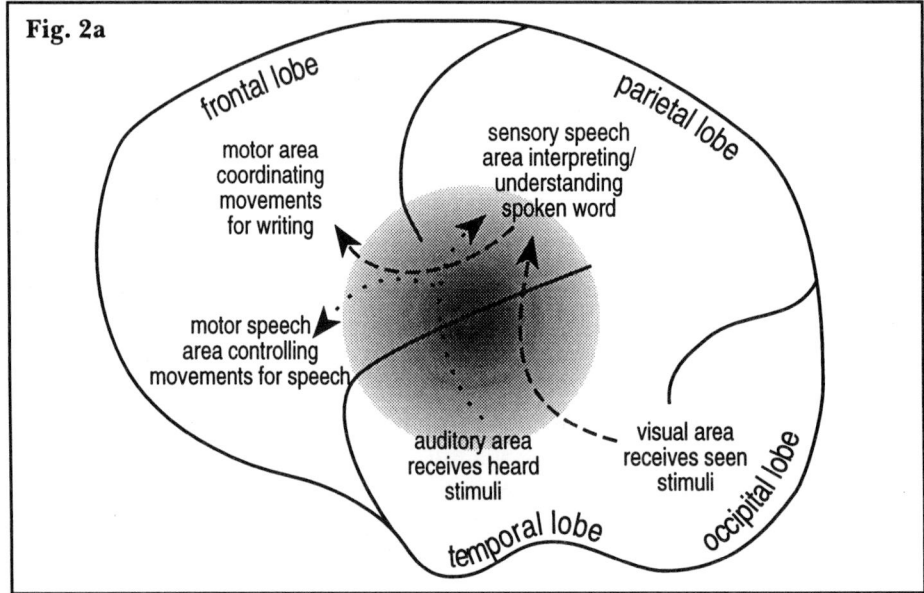

Fig. 2a

frontal lobe

parietal lobe

motor area coordinating movements for writing

sensory speech area interpreting/ understanding spoken word

motor speech area controlling movements for speech

auditory area receives heard stimuli

visual area receives seen stimuli

occipital lobe

temporal lobe

Reading a written text and spelling out written words both relate to the representation of language. When reading aloud, we convert visual symbols into spoken language and when spelling, we convert speech into visual patterns. We can therefore predict that such correlated behaviour will share common brain mechanisms (Duane, 1991) and problems with both are likely to share a common base.

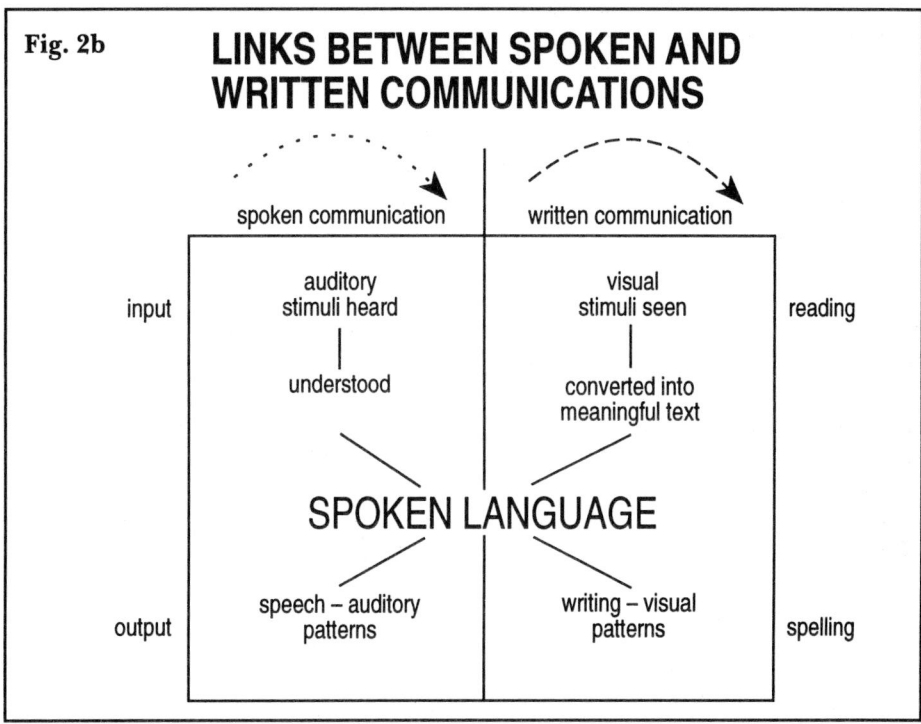

Fig. 2b

LINKS BETWEEN SPOKEN AND WRITTEN COMMUNICATIONS

spoken communication — written communication

input — auditory stimuli heard / visual stimuli seen — reading

understood / converted into meaningful text

SPOKEN LANGUAGE

speech – auditory patterns / writing – visual patterns

output — spelling

Semrud (1989) suggests that dyslexia may be related to some underlying defect of a neurological nature in the brain upsetting the normal asymmetry necessary for establishing language skill. Hornsby (1984) states such a subtle disturbance in the arrangement of brain cells could result in two language areas referring messages across for analysis, leading to jamming and confusion. This anomaly of brain development, interacting with environmental and hereditary factors, would result in a developmental difficulty with language.

Normal development of the nervous system, and presumably of the brain too, may well occur only in response to the developing organism's life experience. If vital experiences do not occur at the critical times, there may be permanent structural and functional defects.

Mann (1984) states that an unusual arrangement of brain cells may make them less efficient in language processing, resulting in greater problems when recognising shapes, giving them sounds, stringing them together, transferring sounds to shapes and writing them down. Sequences of sounds and shapes may not be easily remembered or expressed in a logical order. Mann reminds us that any attempt to explain the causes and manifestations of these problems can only be speculative due to our limited knowledge of cerebral processes. However, dyslexia is perhaps best thought of as a symptom, not a disease, a symptom of a large number of language disorders, or even a symptom-complex in itself.

Having discussed the links between spoken and written communication, shared brain mechanisms, and parallel language processing, it will now be useful to consider the importance of speech as a necessary foundation for reading and spelling. If the ability to read and write is related to competence in spoken language, it may be expected that factors which make for competence in speech will improve literacy.

Children learn to read and write after they have learnt to say almost anything they need or want to say. Literacy is then a secondary skill learnt once a child has learnt to talk, to understand what is said, to recognise words as separate units of meaning, to hear sounds correctly and to blend them in his or her own speech. A child needs to be able to retrieve names of items rapidly – to have a vocabulary – and to have some syntactic knowledge of how words can be combined, and also the ability to code information phonetically according to its sounds. In addition, literacy requires a more conscious level of awareness of phonology, semantics and syntax (Snowling, 1985).

EARLY LANGUAGE DEVELOPMENT

A closer examination of the linguistic skill which a child has normally developed by school age will help us to identify and understand the deviations that can occur, both before the development of literacy and associated with dyslexia during the school years. Figs 3 and 4 describe the levels of language.

Phonology refers to the sounds of a language. Spoken language is made up of collections of sounds strung together in a sequence of contrasts to form words. Sounds are what we hear as opposed to letters which are the alphabetic name we give to some sounds. These sound contrasts distinguish between words of different meaning and make up the phonology of a language. By school entry, children normally have an almost complete phonological system with fully intelligible speech, having acquired the system following a developmental pattern.

Articulation refers to the physical ability to produce the sounds accurately with the tongue, lips and oral musculature moving appropriately. This is not a language skill. Children at school entry often have residual minor difficulties pronouncing the more complicated sounds such as 'th' and 'r' and will substitute with more easily articulated sounds. The term 'phonetic' refers to the way sounds of speech can be transcribed using phonetic symbols as opposed to letters, to cover sounds not directly correlated with our alphabet. Speech therapists are familiar with the International Phonetic Alphabet which enables all speech to be transcribed and identified in an accurate and true form. Each phonetic symbol has an associated three term label which describes its voicing, place and manner of production. (Fig. 3)

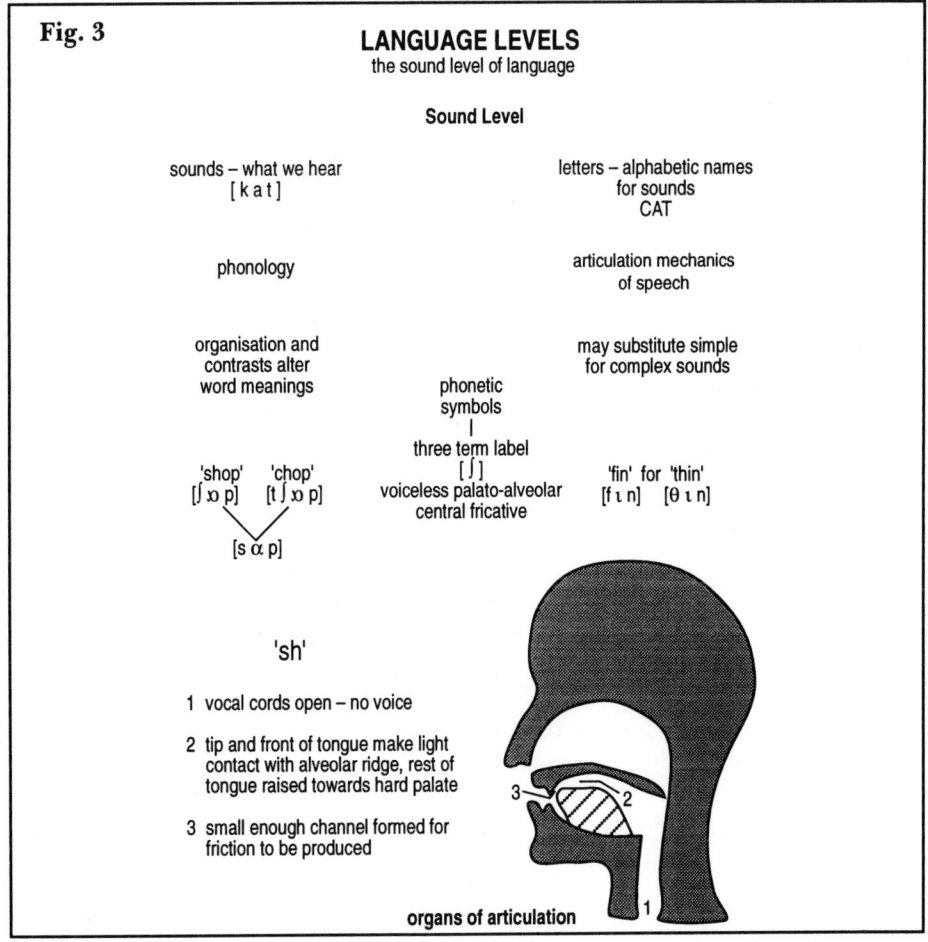

Fig. 3

LANGUAGE LEVELS
the sound level of language

Sound Level

sounds – what we hear
[k a t]

letters – alphabetic names
for sounds
CAT

phonology

articulation mechanics
of speech

organisation and
contrasts alter
word meanings

may substitute simple
for complex sounds

phonetic
symbols
|
three term label
[ʃ]
voiceless palato-alveolar
central fricative

'shop'   'chop'
[ʃ ɒ p]   [t ʃ ɒ p]

'fin' for 'thin'
[f ɪ n]   [θ ɪ n]

[s ɑ p]

'sh'

1 vocal cords open – no voice

2 tip and front of tongue make light
contact with alveolar ridge, rest of
tongue raised towards hard palate

3 small enough channel formed for
friction to be produced

organs of articulation

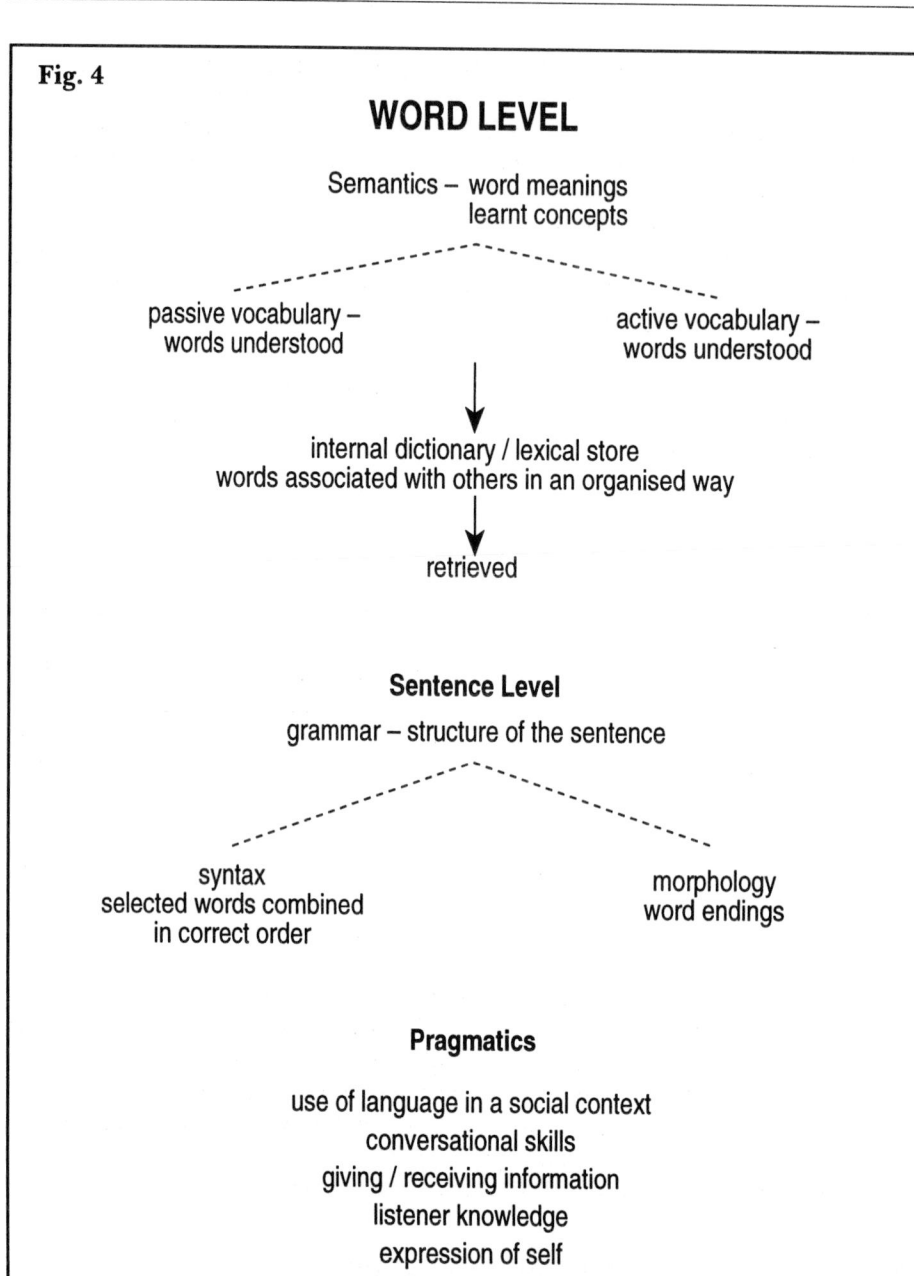

Fig. 4

WORD LEVEL

Semantics – word meanings
learnt concepts

passive vocabulary –
words understood

active vocabulary –
words understood

internal dictionary / lexical store
words associated with others in an organised way

retrieved

Sentence Level

grammar – structure of the sentence

syntax
selected words combined
in correct order

morphology
word endings

Pragmatics

use of language in a social context
conversational skills
giving / receiving information
listener knowledge
expression of self
control over environment

Semantics (fig. 4) refers to the meaning of words, the concepts behind the labels which we attach to the entities around us. These labels or words make up our vocabulary. We have a passive vocabulary (words we understand the meaning of) as well as an active vocabulary (words we use). We learn new vocabulary by learning how new words are associated with words we already know; for example, with similar or opposite meanings, or as members of the same category. This makes up our 'internal dictionary' or lexical store. By school entry, a child may have a vocabulary of many thousands of words but this number will double before the child enters Secondary School.

At the sentence level words are combined according to syntactic rules governing word selection, word ending and word order. At school entry, children are still increasing their understanding of complex sentences as well as learning the use of irregular syntactic rules in their own speech.

Pragmatics refers to the use of language in a social context, and refers to our skill at conversation, our ability to give and receive information, our awareness of listener knowledge and the way we use language to express ourselves and control our environment. By school entry, a child is still learning the more subtle ways of using language; how, for instance, to recognise such features as sarcasm, persuasion, implied requests and inference. It is the pragmatic aspect of language that is of particular relevance for the older age group. Many of these skills do not normally develop before the age of eight to twelve. This means that difficulties at the pragmatic level may not be obvious until later.

It is therefore vital to realise how much language development continues beyond the age of five years if we are to distinguish between normal and deviant features in a child's speech and language beyond this age.

Prior to five, some children will struggle to acquire many of these skills. Some will progress through the expected order of acquisition but at a much slower rate, exhibiting a delay in language development at any or all levels. Others show different patterns of development with atypical features suggesting a disorder. Not all of these children will go on to have difficulties with reading and spelling but there is increasing evidence that particular kinds of verbal language difficulty are better predictors than others of later literacy failure.

PREDICTING LEARNING DIFFICULTIES

Bishop and Edmondson's (1987) study of prognostic indicators established that the likelihood of reading impairment in language disordered children depends upon the type and severity of the disorder. Those with isolated phonological disorder at the age of four are less at risk than those with semantic and syntactic as well as phonological impairment. Provided a child's language problem has resolved by the age of five and a half, there should be little risk of a later literacy problem. However, persisting specific language impairment at this age will be likely to show itself in reading and spelling difficulty. Phonological difficulty becomes a more reliable predictor if still present at a later age.

Further studies looking at predictive behaviour have been carried out. Wiig, Semel and Crouse (1973) found that syntactic difficulties were significant precursors of reading failure. Stark (1984) states that children who have apparently recovered from early language impairment frequently go on to become late readers. Hornsby (1984) suggests that 60% of dyslexics were late or poor talkers. Mann (1984) found that tests of letter-naming, short-term memory, word repetition and phonological processing skill are better predictors of reading failure than IQ tests.

Snowling (1987) suggests that the ability to deal with speech at the level of the phoneme (i.e. at the sound level) is a good predictor of later reading development. Bradley (1980) suggests that phonological processing problems contribute significantly to reading failure.

Exactly what skills are of particular concern? The child needs to be able to segment the sound stream he hears into the component sound elements (phonemes) i.e. to divide words heard into their constituent sounds. This constitutes phonological processing. It renders the child capable of detecting initial, medial and final sounds in words, as well as identifying common or shared sounds in different words and so to have a sensitivity to rhyme and alliteration. This skill allows analysis of words into their component sounds and the blending of sequences of sounds into words, an important skill to be acquired before letter knowledge.

Snowling (1985) suggests that such phonological skills are vital as prerequisites for literacy, although other authorities such as Morais (1991) Integrating Theory and Practice consider that such skills develop as a consequence of exposure to the alphabet. Certainly, learning to read enhances phonological skills. Goswami and Bryant (1990) suggest that children are not interested in analysing words into smaller units until at least six years of age. However, they consider that the child's obvious and early natural interest in rhyme is based on the ability to hear the opening and closing of words – which constitutes a type of phonological skill of importance to reading success.

Bradley (1980) devised a training programme during which six to seven year olds were taught to be aware of the sounds in words and how these were linked to rhyme. By eight to nine years, these children were eight to ten months further ahead in reading and seventeen months further ahead in spelling than controls who were taught to concentrate on the meaning. By twelve to thirteen years, the children were reading at their appropriate age and were two years ahead of controls in spelling. Training in sound categorisation was more effective when it involved an explicit connection with the alphabet.

Speech sounds occur in a continuous, rapid flow of co-ordinated movements affected by neighbouring sounds rather than one sound fully articulated after another. Similarly, words have unnoticed boundaries in connected speech. A child's auditory processing skill allows her or him to understand the nature and boundaries of words, syllables and sounds. It is vital that this should occur before the learning of letter rules for reading and spelling.

Fig. 5 shows three stages of phonology: input, segmentation and output. Breakdown at each of these stages leads to particular difficulties for the child. (Snowling 1985).

Input refers to the awareness of salient features of sounds and the ability to discriminate between words which sound similar. The child who is unable to do this will confuse words by not being aware of subtle but important differences.

Segmentation is the intervening stage during which the child analyses words into sounds before translating these into letters and recognising shared sounds in different words. To analyse in this way, the words must be held in the memory in a phonological form or code. Problems at this stage prevent children from segmenting and building words from sounds.

Output refers to the production of words; the pronunciation of words based on the retrieval of instructions that direct the necessary mouth movements. Problems at this stage render the child unable to pronounce some words accurately and consistently or to repeat words heard.

Symptoms of poor phonological processing will include a poor internal representation of sounds, inaccurate pronunciation of words, a slow increase in vocabulary with poor retrieval of words and poor acquisition of grammatical structure. In addition, there will be difficulty in transferring to the alphabetic stage of literacy development and with the indirect route to literacy.

Having ascertained that phonological processing problems are likely to interfere with the child's progress in learning how to read and spell, and that

Fig. 5

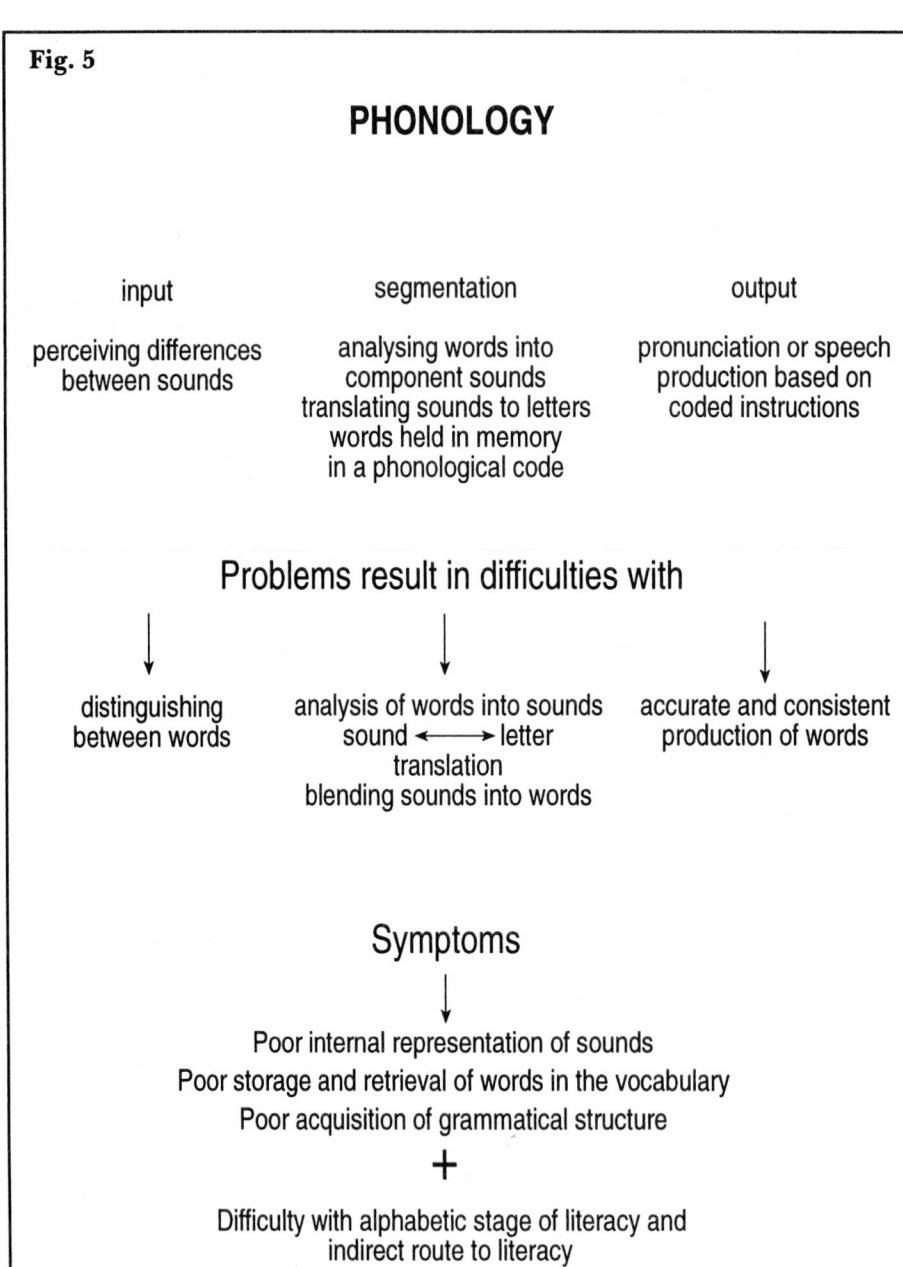

PHONOLOGY

input	segmentation	output
perceiving differences between sounds	analysing words into component sounds translating sounds to letters words held in memory in a phonological code	pronunciation or speech production based on coded instructions

Problems result in difficulties with

distinguishing between words

analysis of words into sounds
sound ⟷ letter translation
blending sounds into words

accurate and consistent production of words

Symptoms

Poor internal representation of sounds
Poor storage and retrieval of words in the vocabulary
Poor acquisition of grammatical structure

+

Difficulty with alphabetic stage of literacy and indirect route to literacy children requiring speech therapy at the pre-school stage are more likely to be poor at these skills when at school, it is now important to consider dyslexia at school age.

DYSLEXIC PUPILS OF SCHOOL AGE

Is there any evidence that dyslexic children experience spoken language difficulty ? If there is this would provide further evidence that dyslexia may be a symptom of generalised deficit in verbal language. Obviously, not all children with dyslexia will have a problem with spoken language but those who do may have high level problems which are only identifiable by more complex language tasks and which are easily missed.

Snowling (1987) suggests these children are slower at retrieving words, use circumlocutions and have difficulty with category labels.

Renaldi (1991) suggests that word-finding difficulties may be evidenced in continuous speech by hesitations, revisions, discontinued utterances and even interruptions as the child struggles to use the utterance before it is forgotten. The older child will fail to organise his expressive language efficiently and will avoid social situations where there is a need to initiate conversation. These children will fail to understand ambiguous statements such as 'pull your socks up' and they will fail to appreciate the linguistic aspects of humour.

Thompson's (1984) evidence shows that children with dyslexia are liable to use less descriptive words and to use simple grammatical forms, with irregular verb tense errors.

Pavlidis and Miles (1981) suggest that children with dyslexia fail to understand more complex linguistic structures and need information put in a readily usable form to integrate with their own general knowledge.

German (1985) states that the child's failures are due to difficulty in attaching labels to incoming visual information – a verbal labelling difficulty. The child struggles to remember the articulatory-motor patterns of sounds in words affecting word-retrieval.

Renaldi (1991) suggests that gaps in the child's vocabulary reflect a difficulty in the understanding of certain concepts. Language serves as a 'learning bridge' to bring abstract concepts such as time within the child's reach. If language is made simple and used to represent familiar events, the child will eventually be able to understand the concept itself. Renaldi adds that these linguistic problems are frequently linked to emotional and cognitive factors, and that these difficulties are more specific and more severe than would be expected in a child with general developmental delay.

So it appears that children with dyslexia may have very subtle problems. These may show as deficiencies in their semantics, syntax and pragmatics. Phonology may also be impaired, resulting in inadequate processing of auditory signals. All these may have an adverse effect upon their development of vocabulary and on the ability to label words.

READING AND SPELLING ACQUISITION

How do these difficulties with words influence the development of literacy?

To explore this we must first understand how a child learns to read and spell from his or her first experiences with written language (see fig. 6). Reading is the process by means of which we attend to a written text, recognise letters and convert these to sounds, rehearse the sounds in a sequence either to ourselves or aloud and extract the sense of the text. To do this we need to develop a sight vocabulary – a store of words in memory that we rapidly recognise. We also need to develop a knowledge of our spelling system and our alphabet in order to decode or analyse words.

We can define two routes to this process, a direct visual route whereby we recognise the visual pattern of words and can rapidly attach a spoken label to it; and an indirect auditory route involving a process of deciphering the strings of letters in words and translating these to sounds. We can see how these two routes operate by looking at Frith's three phases to the acquisition of reading skill. These three phases are the logographic phase (matching the visual appearance of a written word to its spoken counterpart), the alphabetic phase (in which words are broken down into smaller units and letters are translated into sounds) and the orthographic phase (in which chunks of words are automatically recognised, only unfamiliar words having to be decoded letter by letter).

Frith also defines a pre-reading phase during which the child begins to learn about print and speech sounds, gradually recognising that letters represent specific sounds, and so building up a sight vocabulary. The fluent reader then becomes quicker at decoding and learns to recognise common spelling patterns. Reading to learn is the final stage when more efficient comprehension increases the reader's general knowledge from what has been read.

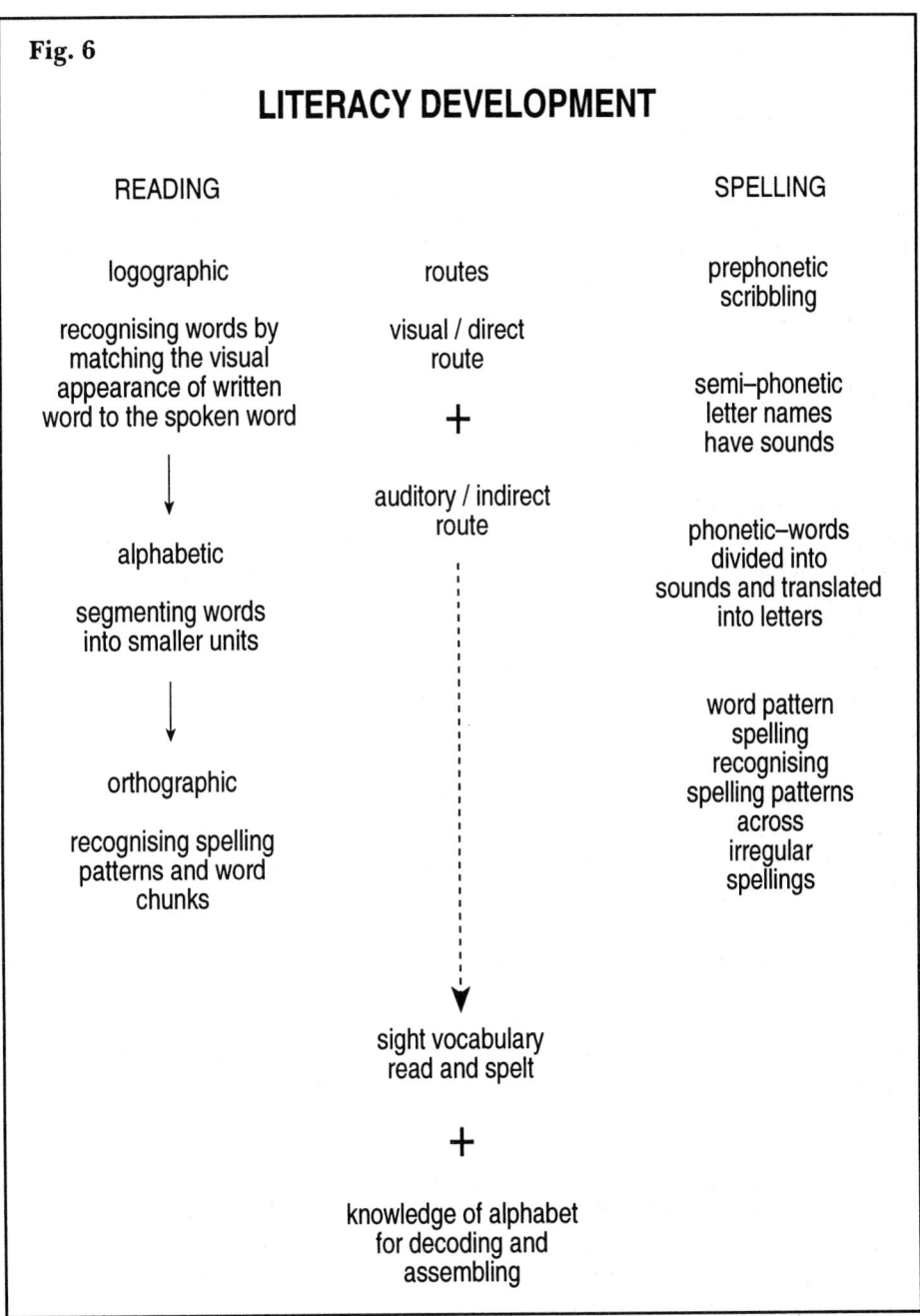

Fig. 6

LITERACY DEVELOPMENT

READING	routes	SPELLING
logographic		prephonetic scribbling
recognising words by matching the visual appearance of written word to the spoken word	visual / direct route	
	+	semi–phonetic letter names have sounds
	auditory / indirect route	
alphabetic		phonetic–words divided into sounds and translated into letters
segmenting words into smaller units		
		word pattern spelling recognising spelling patterns across irregular spellings
orthographic		
recognising spelling patterns and word chunks		

sight vocabulary
read and spelt

+

knowledge of alphabet
for decoding and
assembling

Spelling is the process by which we select exact letter representations of what we say to put on paper. Two routes are again used: a direct visual route where learned spellings of words are retrieved or addressed from the memory store; and an indirect phonic route when words are assembled letter by letter and spelt as they sound. Ehri (1991) describes a pre-phonetic stage of scribbling attempts at letters and numbers, a semi-phonetic stage when the child is aware that the names of letters have a sound to them, a phonetic stage when the child segments words into sounds and translating sounds into letters, and finally a word-pattern spelling when the child is able to distinguish common patterns of spelling common to many words, as well as learning irregularly spelt words.

We can therefore see that both reading and spelling require a decoding or phonic skill when words have to be segmented into sounds, sounds have to be recognised and discriminated, translated to and from letters, blended and pronounced. We know already that these are phonological skills which may well be impaired in children with dyslexia. In addition, we know that reading and spelling depend on primary oral skills of vocabulary development, grammatical knowledge and comprehension skills that may also be lacking in the child with dyslexia.

Reading and spelling are complicated processes: phonological, visual, orthographic and contextual skills are all needed, at different times. Bryant and Bradley (1986) suggest that some children use the wrong skill at the wrong time. Perhaps the dyslexic reader copes with whole word 'visual' methods in developing a sight vocabulary but due to phonological difficulty fails to translate letters to sounds, or to remember letter-sound associations. The child fails to reflect upon the sound level of language and struggles to retain the phonological form of words in memory. Other readers with poor language skills may fail to use semantic, syntactic or contextual cues and although able to work out words from sounds may confuse meanings of word and fail to understand what has been read.

So we can see that the poor reader will present with a variety of reading and spelling problems. These will reflect different deficiencies in processing language and also different strategies in trying to compensate for those deficiencies.

ASSESSMENT

Is it possible to discover exactly what is going wrong by looking carefully at the presenting characteristics of the child's reading and spelling ? It seems that we need to study more than the reading process and to check the spoken language skills as well.

An assessment will help us to make a diagnosis, to identify learning problems leading to the disability and to assist in the planning of remedial treatment.

An assessment must be able to distinguish between normal development and deviations from it. This requires a knowledge of normal language development particularly in its later stages. We need to analyse the presenting symptoms and to investigate their underlying nature. There is no "classic dyslexic". The nature of the dyslexic's difficulties change with time and with the child's development. We must adopt a descriptive approach to these children, rather than attempt to attach labels which mean different things to different people.

It is important, as with all language impairment, to understand the child with dyslexia in relation to his or her whole personal development. Emotional difficulties may either be the cause of a communication problem or may result from it. Subtle disorders may be missed or misconstrued. Failure to reason or understand may lead to a behaviour reaction which may be dismissed as disobedience. We must try to assess to what extent the child is distressed, lacks confidence, or is depressed and withdrawn.

Before commencing assessment, a full case history will be taken from the parents. This will provide useful information regarding other indicators of dyslexia such as undetermined or crossed laterality, clumsiness, lack of concentration or poor pencil control in addition to signs of speech and language difficulty. Once at school, the teacher can provide information on the child's written and spoken language skills to give the therapist a wider view of how the child copes in a variety of speaking situations. If a psychological assessment has been carried out, such information will also be of great importance, as will pertinent information regarding any medical conditions such as hearing loss.

ASSESSING SPOKEN LANGUAGE

When assessing language skills, both formal standardised assessments and informal assessment procedures are useful. Formal assessments give objective measures of ability comparing the child's performance with an age related standard. Speech therapists have a variety of standardised methods for assessing vocabulary, comprehension and the use of grammatical rules; although regrettably few that cover the adolescent years.

These are best combined with tasks given to check the child's conversational skills, descriptive and explanatory ability, and word association. The latter includes word selection tasks which reveal the child's storage and retrieval skills.

In addition, phonological or auditory processing skills can be assessed using a variety of standardised tests of auditory memory, discrimination and organisation, as well as a variety of tasks to check segmentation, blending, rhyme and sound-letter conversion.

A speech therapist could conduct an oral examination if necessary and general intelligibility of speech will be checked. It is important to detect such conditions as dyspraxia, a motor programming problem with a characteristic picture of speech and written language impairment. Stackhouse (1991) reminds us that when children with speech and language problems do have reading and spelling problems as well, this may be for a variety of reasons: speech problems arising out of poor health, physical problems such as cleft lip or palate or cerebral palsy, or fluctuating hearing and attention problems. Such children, however, are no more at risk than the normal population for 'specific' reading and spelling problems and so need to be diagnosed as such.

ASSESSING WRITTEN LANGUAGE

The child's written language performance also needs assessment. There are standardised tests giving age norms for reading and spelling. Error analysis may also be helpful in deciding whether there is a defect in the auditory or the visual pathways – where there is no detectable hearing or visual loss but the child appears unable to process heard or seen experiences. Thompson (1984) gives the following guide to an error analysis. An auditory channel deficit will have some of the following consequences for reading: substitution of sounds, poor sound blending, knowledge of letter names but not of their sounds, mispronunciations, wild guesses at words, poor 'sounding out' or phonic attack, substitution of words with similar meaning and poor sound-letter conversion. A visual channel deficit will result in reversals and inversions of words and letters, loss of place in text, omission and addition of words, ignored punctuation, substitution of visually similar words, confused order of letters, poor knowledge of spelling patterns and words spelt as they sound.

In the case of spelling, an auditory channel deficit will have the following symptoms: ends of words omitted, synonyms substituted, second letter of blends omitted, substitution with voiced/voiceless counterpart, confusion between high frequency sounds and those perceptually similar, confusion or omission of vowels, poor identification of middle part of word and wild guesses at spelling with at times no relation between sounds of words and letters chosen. With a visual channel deficit, the speller will spell phonetically, mixing upper and lower case letters, reversing and inverting letters and producing words with incorrect letter sequences.

Children may perform adequately on testing but fail to transfer their ability to the classroom. They may be making poor use of their capabilities and instead of needing to learn new skills, they should receive help with those which they already possess.

Can a speech therapist assess the performance of pre-school children at a pre-literacy stage in order to identify the child who is at risk? If so, those with problems can be brought to the attention of the teacher at school entry by the speech therapist. Of course, not all children starting school with impoverished language skills will have been referred to a speech therapist. Similarly, not all children who have received speech therapy will be later candidates for learning support. Many parents will understandably wish their child to start school with no labels attached or special treatment awaiting them. The speech therapist will discuss the matter with parents if it is suspected that there may be reading difficulties. If phonological awareness and pre-reading skills appear to be lacking, the therapist can suggest suitable advice regarding pre-literacy activities.

During therapy, note can be made of the child's awareness of sounds, letters and rhyme as well as skills of listening and concentration. Speech therapy should of itself promote listening skills by concentrating attention on the sound of the words and by increasing the knowledge of how they are produced. Part of the therapy programme will be to show the parents how to stimulate the child's interest in the sound of letters, rhyme and rhythm. Certain play activities may help to alleviate some of the difficulties in the early school years.

PLANNING REMEDIATION

This leads to the third function of assessment: its role in planning remedial treatment. Having described the dyslexic child's individual reasons for failing, his or her strengths, weaknesses and compensatory strategies, it becomes possible to plan a remedial programme.

We can see with which modalities the child functions best: auditory, visual, vocal or motor, and we can use these senses to improve weaker areas. Snowling (1985) reminds us that the child may have been amenable to training in a way that has masked their underlying true reasons for failure. We are faced with the choice: either we apply treatment directly to the area of weakness or we promote an alternative strategy in an attempt to compensate. It is vital that we relate educational strategies to the individual's needs.

Can the child's needs be met with extra tuition alongside other poor readers, or does he require special teaching methods on his own? Thompson

(1984) suggests a different approach according to the type of dyslexia: helping an auditory channel deficit by working through the visual modality with some training of auditory skills, and helping a child with visual deficit by working through the auditory modality with some training of visual skills. The dyslexic child with a mixed picture requires a multi-sensory approach strengthening all senses: visual, auditory, tactile, and kinesthetic.

The speech therapist's training in phonetics as well as in linguistics has been shown to be beneficial to the successful management of the dyslexic child. Understanding what the sounds of speech are all about, by getting to know how we make them, can help with the difficult task of making sense of seemingly abstract sequences of noise heard at speed in a continuous flow of speech, especially if there are no clear breaks to distinguish where one sound ends and the next begins. Phonological problems need to be tackled individually, using the different senses to help the child find some way of representing and remembering speech at the sound level. One way of helping the child to link a spoken sound to its letter symbol and to remember this association for recall, is to link the sound with its oral movement, that is the auditory-articulatory relationship. Kinesthetic and tactile feedback can be a useful part of a multi-sensory strategy. The child can be shown whether or not his vocal cords are moving, what part of the mouth the sound is made in and with what movement, and whether there is contact made or not, or a narrow gap allowing friction to occur. This phonetic knowledge will sharpen the child's pronunciation of words and help the sounds become controllable units. Where similar sounds are confused, as in the case of vowels, high frequency sounds, and blends, learning the 'feel' of the sounds will help to distinguish between them, for example, what mouth shape is assumed for which vowel. Watching the oral movements on another speaker's face may help a child to remember the 'visual appearance' of sounds when they are spoken. Children can be shown how to help themselves, by being aware of their own speech and giving them clues about the required sounds and the word boundaries.

Experimenting with articulation and encouraging the child to talk things through, trying out words aloud while writing them, working rules through by saying them aloud in their own words, all these will help engage kinesthetic, visual and memory pathways.

Rehearsal of pronunciation of polysyllabic words by splitting them into syllabic units, each syllable beginning with a consonant sound if possible, will enable the child to see a long, difficult word as a series of short, easy units and enable the planning and sequencing aspects to become instinctive. New vocabulary can be introduced in this way too. When working on phonic skill with a child with a phonological problem affecting spoken word production, the therapist can advise the teacher on the order of acquisition of the sound system, so that the introduction of sounds and their correlated letter forms can be in an appropriate order of complexity.

There are various ways of helping a child to become aware of sound patterns and so to memorise them. For instance, he or she can be shown how vowel sounds determine rhyme (and the letters which are involved.) Showing how different words share common sounds whether initially, medially or finally will help the child to be aware of sound patterning in words and to retain these patterns by linking into memory.

Such sound categorisation practice will help with auditory discrimination and perception (or input phonology), with the intervening stage of sound segmentation and blending, and with pronunciation (or output phonology). This in turn will help with the holding of the phonological form of words in memory and with the decoding processes of literacy.

The speech therapist's role in helping to plan support for the dyslexic with more subtle high level language problems begins with the careful identification of these. It should perhaps include increasing the ability of teachers to detect such problems. Once any problems have been identified, specific advice should be given regarding the linguistic experiences the child faces in the classroom. This might include encouraging the teacher to use readily understandable language and controlling sentences for length and complexity.

A child should be encouraged to let others know when she or he has not understood. Less obvious language such as metaphors should be explained and the child encouraged to read 'between the lines'.

New vocabulary should be carefully explained by relating to previously known words. All these measures help to produce an organised 'internal dictionary'. Teaching cueing-in methods to help with a word retrieval problem and encouraging the child to self-cue or substitute may also be helpful. A tape recorder can be very useful in developing listening, speaking and self-monitoring skills. The child's ability to judge his or her own speech performance is always worth encouraging.

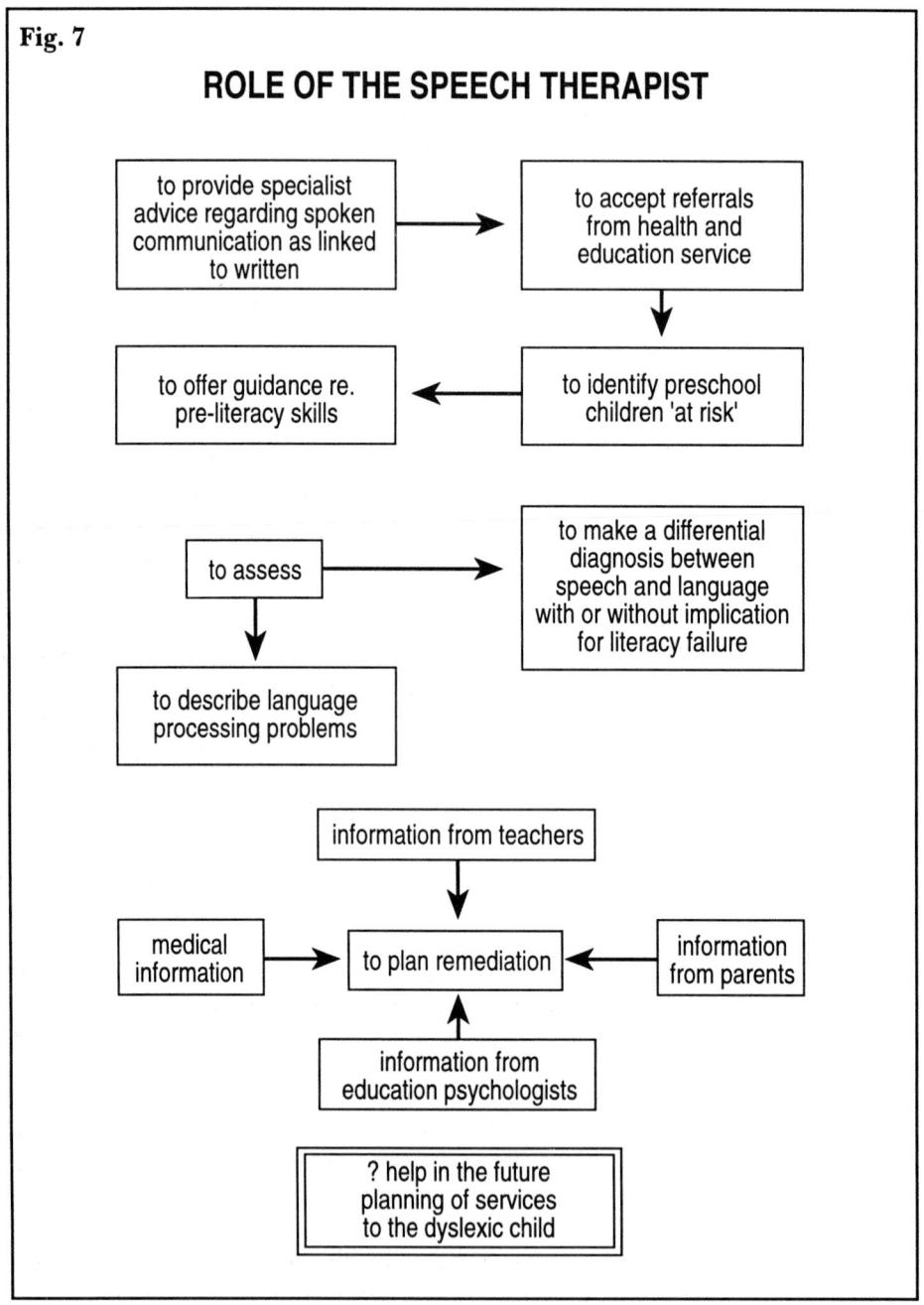

Fig. 7

ROLE OF THE SPEECH THERAPIST

to provide specialist advice regarding spoken communication as linked to written → to accept referrals from health and education service

to accept referrals from health and education service ↓

to identify preschool children 'at risk' → to offer guidance re. pre-literacy skills

to assess → to make a differential diagnosis between speech and language with or without implication for literacy failure

to assess ↓ to describe language processing problems

information from teachers ↓

medical information → to plan remediation ← information from parents

information from education psychologists ↑ to plan remediation

? help in the future planning of services to the dyslexic child

CONCLUSION

Since there appears to be links between spoken and written language it would follow that a specialist in speech should have a place in the management of a written language problem where a spoken component may exist.

Children with dyslexia do appear to suffer from a language disorder which sometimes affects spoken as well as written communication.

Evidence suggests that the child with dyslexia may have difficulties with spoken communication that are only noticed at a later stage by a skilled observer.

Dyslexia is not a condition that erupts at the reading and writing age in absence of early symptoms. Instead, children at risk can be identified before they go to school if already presenting with speech and language delay. If dyslexia has precursors in the faulty language development of pre-school children, there may be useful preventative measures which can be undertaken at that age, which will have consequences for parents and for doctors and health visitors who are responsible for routine developmental care of children.

Once identified, there follows the responsibility of early management to prevent the frustration and anxiety that may otherwise come. Assessment and guidance for parents and nursery teachers is a role the speech therapist already has. It should perhaps be extended to include specific advice regarding pre-literacy skills where necessary. Therapists should make and maintain contact with the relevant school for as long as required.

Therapists have a range of tests and skills at their disposal for accurate assessment of a child's performance. This allows a distinction to be made between a child showing normal features of later language development and one showing delayed or disordered development, also between a child showing speech impairment which has no implication for literacy failure and one with underlying or more hidden language problems of significant relevance to literacy failure.

A description rather than a label should be provided for the benefit of the learning support team. This will detail results of standardised tests and task performances, based on the speech therapist's expertise in phonetic and linguistic analysis.

A reading and spelling error analysis will illustrate the effect of these problems and show at what stage their development has been arrested.

If dyslexia is a learning problem which is due to the absence of good reading and spelling models, and if suitable experiences given at an appropriate age can help, then it follows that a speech therapist's experience in the identification and correction of these difficulties may be very valuable in the learning support team.

If dyslexia reflects a difference in learning then it requires a difference in teaching. The question of who carries out remediation is a debatable one. In my own experience, the speech therapist's role has been an advisory one with the learning support teacher implementing suggestions. This has been inevitable due to the limitations on my time and I have attempted to monitor developments after the initial referral. The question of how to provide a useful service to the secondary school is a difficult one, reflecting, I presume, the lack of attention given to children with language problems in this age group. Literacy development is often presumed to be complete by secondary school entry, at a time when many demands are placed upon it. Some language problems are only revealed at this stage in the child's education, and may surface as academic, social or behavioural problems.

Programmes of remediation are best based on the pooled knowledge of phonetics, linguistics, psychology and education. By sharing information derived from the various disciplines, a greater understanding of the child's unfolding difficulties will be achieved. Speech therapists have experience of methods which are likely to be a considerable help to some of these children. Such methods should be used to supplement a teacher's own skills in the identification and care of language-disordered children in the classroom.

The speech therapist is in a very favourable position, being a professional accepted equally as part of the health and education services and so able to receive referrals from many sources.

Speech therapists do have special skills based on theoretical knowledge and clinical experience that can contribute to the management of children with dyslexia, although the extent to which they can fulfil the role I have described will perhaps depend on a degree of specialist knowledge not normally covered in basic training.

There is much to be learnt regarding the best age to concentrate intervention and the best ways of providing remedial treatment given the time constraints and the implications for the use of professional resources. Ultimately, these constraints are often financial ones.

In the future it may be advantageous for the speech therapist to be included in planning the service to this client group. This would require changes in the way speech therapy services are currently resourced and organised.

REFERENCES

Bishop, D. V. M. and Edmondson, A. (May 1987). 'Language impaired 4 year olds: distinguishing transient from persistent impairment. *Journal of speech and hearing disorder.* Vol. 52.

Bradley, L. (1980). *Assessing reading difficulties: a diagnosis and remedial approach.* Macmillan.

Bryant, P. and Bradley, L. (1986). *Children's reading problems.* Blackwell.

College of Speech and Language Therapists (1991). *Communicating quality professional standards for speech and language therapists.*

Crystal, D. (1986). From 'The nature of specific language disorders in children and its assessment: The linguistic angle.' *Advances in working with language disordered children.* I.C.A.N.

Ellis, A. W. (1991). *Reading, writing and dyslexia.* Open University Press.

German, D. (1985). 'Semantic word category in disnomia,' *British Journal for Disorders of Communication,* Vol. 20, No. 2.

Goswami, V. and Bryant, P. (1990). *Phonological skills and learning to read.* Erlbaum Assoc.

Hales, G. (Ed.) (1989). *Meeting points in dyslexia.* Proceedings of first International Conference on Dyslexia.

Heaton, P. and Winterson, P. (1986). *Dealing with dyslexia,* Better Books.

Hornsby, B. (1984). *Overcoming dyslexia.* Pub. M. Dunitz Ltd.

Mann, V. (1984). 'Longitudinal prediction and prevention of early reading difficulty: Annals of Dyslexia.

Mogford, K. and Sadler, J. (1989). 'Child Language Disability,' *Multilingual Matters.*

Newton, M. J., Thompson, M. E. and Richards, I. R. (1978). *Readings in dyslexia.* L. D. A.

Pavlidis, G. Th. and Miles, T. R. (Eds.) (1981). *Dyslexia research and its applications to education.* Wiley.

Quin, V. and Macauslan, A. (1986). *Dyslexia: what parents ought to know.* Pelican Health Books.

Renaldi, W. (Aug. 1991). *The Meaning of moderate learning difficulties at secondary school age.* College of Speech and Language Therapists Bulletin.

Semrud, Hynd, G. and Semrud-Clikeman, M. (1989). 'Dyslexia and brain morphology.' *Psychology Bulletin.* Vol. 106.

Snowling, M. and Thomson, M. (Eds.) (1991). *Dyslexia – integrating theory and practice.* 'Neurological issues in dyslexia,' Duane, D.; Metaphonological abilities and literacy,' Morais, J.; 'The development of reading and spelling in children: an overview,' Ehri, L.; 'Dyslexia: The obvious and hidden speech and language disorder,' Stackhouse, J. and Wells, B. Proceedings of the second International Conference on Dyslexia. Whurr.

Snowling, M. (1985). *Children's written language difficulties,* extract – quoting Wigg, Semel and Crouse (1973); and Frith. Stackhouse – Segmentation speech and spelling difficulties. Windsor. NFER Nelson.

Snowling, M. (1987). *Dyslexia: A Cognitive Developmental Perspective.* Blackwell.

Snowling, M. *et al* (1986). 'Segmentation and speech perception in relation to reading skill: a developmental analysis.' *Journal of Experimental Child Psychology.* Vol. 41.

Snowling, M., Stackhouse, J. and Rack, J. (1986). 'Phonological dyslexia and dysgraphia – a developmental analysis,' *Cognitive Neuropsychology,* No. 3.

Snowling, M., Van Wagtendon, B., Stafford, C. (1988). 'Object naming deficits in developmental dyslexia,' *Journal of Research in Reading,* Vol. 11, No. 2.

Stackhouse, J. (May 1982). 'Investigation of speech and reading performance in speech disordered children.' *British Journal of Disorders of Communication.* Vol. 52.

Stackhouse, J. (1988). 'Relationship between spoken and written language disorders' in Mogford and Sadler's *Child's Lang Disability,* Vol. 1, Implications in an educational setting. Multilingual Matters.

Thomson, M. (1984). *Development Dyslexia, It's Nature's assessment and remediation.* Arnold.

Young, P. and Tyre, C. (1990). *Dyslexia or illiteracy.* Open University Press.

LANGUAGE IN CONTEXT

EILEEN FRANCIS

INTRODUCTION

In the early 1970s, little attention was paid to language in education issues and even less to the issue of communication in the classroom. The publication of texts by the Open University in the mid-seventies (1972) and the Bullock Report 'A Language for Life' (1975) increased interest in language across the curriculum. The development of understanding provided by the disciplines of applied linguistics and social psychology, in relation to verbal and non-verbal communication, meant that the 1970s was the decade when communication became an issue for Scottish education. Teacher educators and subsequently teachers were able to claim that communication had intrinsic value as well as instrumental value for education. The subject of teacher talk and student talk became legitimate areas of study.

During the 1980s, communication was subsumed into the wider concern for personal and social development programmes in the curriculum. In the 1990s, communication is back on the agenda in the context of discussion about values in education – 'communication' and 'respect for others' are key words in the values statements being produced by schools.

This chapter asks you to consider the concept of language in context, from the perspective of your own experience. How near or far from your own assumptions and expectations are the statements contained in this chapter?

THE SCHOOL IS A SPEECH COMMUNITY

Lakoff and Johnson (1980) have described the conceptual system, in terms of which we both think and act, as being fundamentally metaphorical in nature. They explain that we are not normally aware of our conceptual system and that we think and act automatically along certain lines for reasons which are not obvious. 'Concepts structure what we perceive, how we get around in the world and how we relate to other people. Our conceptual system thus plays a central role in defining our everyday realities.' Understanding our own conceptual system is the primary task of education and language is an important source of evidence.

Communication is based on the same conceptual system that we use in thinking and acting. Education, being a human enterprise taking place in relationships, needs to take the dialogue metaphor as a paradigm.

In the past, the transmission metaphor in education has been dominant in Scotland. Progress was made with a dialogical approach to education in the 1980s, but recently the transmission metaphor has begun to compete for attention again as teachers discuss more efficient ways of increasing information flow to the student. The vocabulary of packing, sending, targeting and receiving tends to mask interpersonal aspects in education.

Tiberius (1986) has described the nature of the tension which exists between dominant and competing metaphors in education: 'Proponents of different metaphors tend not to confront each other; they talk to each other. However, they are like people talking different languages. They see different things when they look from the same point in the same direction. There is a tendency for misunderstanding as similar terms, concepts and experiments are used to convey new meanings in new contexts and in new relationships with each other.'

Those who promote the study of educational discourse tend to use specific terminology to inform other educationalists about their priorities in education. Such phrases as 'School is a place where the learner is empowered'; 'a community of learners'; 'and induction into a life-long learning process', give the impression that the school aspires to be an ideal speech community.

Saville-Troike (1982) describes speech communities as holding knowledge and behaviours in common. The speech community is characterised by patterns of language use, interpretation, rules of speaking and attitudes concerning language which are identifiably specific. What is of interest in the speech community is the range of interactional functions and domains present and the processes which separate, unify or stratify them. Effective communication requires individuals to orientate themselves by applying a set of rules in any given situation. Teachers need to identify the verbal and non-verbal forms appropriate to the community and to understand how they define and constrain interpersonal interaction in communication situations.

THE CLASS IS A GROUP

The school is a communication system within which groups are constantly forming and reforming for the purpose of carrying out a variety of learning tasks. The teacher has two main functions: to maintain the group and to help the group to work. Learning tasks will not be achieved if the teacher gives greater attention to maintaining the group. It is helpful if the teacher has a sense of the group as a dynamic process and has developed process thinking skills (Bramley, 1979) so that the double task of managing the group and managing the task is in balance.

Teachers and students are inextricably linked in the group process. It is for the teacher to decide which sessions during the day will highlight the process objectives of an activity and which will focus on content objectives. A class group in which both teachers and students have developed process thinking skills will be able to work effectively.

Process thinking enables us to understand that there are significant elements of the communication process which can be under the teacher's conscious control: the physical arrangement of the context in which learning is to take place; the organisation of the group within that context; the leadership style which will be adopted to accomplish the task. The imagery of the physical setting conveys the communication rules.

The student entering the classroom receives messages about the learning context. Tables and chairs are spaced for individualised learning, grouped for content-orientated work, placed in table-free circles for process-orientated work. Learning tasks need to be considered in relation to the most appropriate communication style to meet performance criteria: individualised work; paired work; groups of different sizes and compositions. In any one day, the students will move through a series of different communication contexts. It is the teacher's task to observe how each is handled. Students will show different strengths and weaknesses in communication and individual preferences for specific learning contexts.

The leadership style of the teacher will be adapted accordingly, providing directive leadership when information-giving is required and a variety of styles which facilitate different types of groupwork (Francis, 1985). The significant factor is for teachers to be aware that at one and the same time they are members of their groups as well as leaders. It is as if a semi-permeable membrane separates the leadership and membership regions of the group which allows initiating roles in communication to emerge from either region. When students initiate, teachers mediate the communication, maintaining responsibility for helping the students to manage themselves and the learning task.

While these three 'process shapers' (physical setting, group composition and leadership style) are under conscious control, groups have a dynamic of their own and function accordingly. Teachers need awareness and insight to analyse the dynamics of the group, understanding that the personal histories of the students and their expectations and assumptions about the learning process will affect the way in which the group works. These issues are addressed in the literature on psycho-dynamics, a body of knowledge concerning human functioning which gives priority to the role of emotional development and its effects on physical, social and intellectual growth.

COMMUNICATION STYLES ARE DIFFERENT

Individuals bring a variety of communication styles to the group. They need the capacity to analyse aspects of communication style which influence the group dynamic. How does a group member influence the group process: is the group 'pushed' towards completion of a task or 'pulled' towards a resolution? Skilled communicators will use a combination of both styles.

Affiliative behaviour in a group helps it to work. Trower, Bryant and Argyle (1978) described affiliative behaviour as a combination of controlling and rewarding behaviours which communicate assertiveness and rapport. When the balance is inappropriate, some participants appear aggressive, autocratic, or inappropriately dominant, while others, conversely, may appear indecisive, lacking in conviction or submissive.

Facial expression, eye contact and voice quality are more significant than verbal behaviour in communicating affiliative behaviour. One experiment (Mehrabian, 1977) provided the statistic 38% voice, 55% face and 7% verbal expression, to describe the relationship between verbal and non-verbal features in interpersonal communication. This statistic can be reassuring to students who are low contributors in groups. The way in which we listen to others can assert competence in learning as effectively as the amount of talk produced.

Research on discussion in Scottish classrooms (Francis, 1990) indicated that low contributors in the class group gain much from working together. They become more effective contributors as a result. High contributors, when placed with similar students, have to address their own communication style and realise that listening is as significant as talking when completing a discussion task.

Swift, Gooding and Swift, in Dillon, (1988) describe the important of 'wait-time' between student-student and teacher-student interventions to encourage thoughtful responses. They observed that an increase in wait-time between contributions in a discussion had the effect of raising the cognitive level of a discussion.

Recently Tannen (1992) has described communication style in terms of a combination of features. She describes the way in which we communicate considerateness as 'rapport talk' and high involvement as 'report talk'. In practice, teacher education appears to be more concerned with developing a communication style characterised by high involvement and report talk than with considerateness and rapport talk. Teachers are role models for students and they may project ambivalence in the learning context about communication styles characterised by sensitivity, perceptiveness and the capacity for reflection.

The value placed by teachers and students on different communication styles in the classroom will convey attitudes to aggressive behaviour, for example, in communication between boys and girls, between those from different ethnic backgrounds, and in a lack of tolerance of those who are observed as silent members of the group.

DEVELOP COMMUNICATION IN CONTEXT

If change is to occur in learning relationships, teachers will need genuine commitment and the inner belief that classroom discourse can be improved. In some schools, the constraints are physical – group size and physical space communicate that student talk is of lesser significance than the role of the curriculum or of the teacher in classroom interaction. In these settings, discussion activity may be marginalised and the emphasis placed on individualised or resource-based learning.

Parents and students still expect teachers to be the centre of classroom practice. Teachers are expected to be in control. Research on discussion shows that many students undervalue talk in education because they feel it is not as open to scrutiny as the written word. They distrust the transient nature of oral communication.

The discipline which helps educationalists understand language in context is applied linguistics. Literature produced by English language teachers for foreign language learners and by speech therapists working in clinical settings provides frameworks which are helpful in school-based learning environments. The pedagogical descriptions of applied linguistics, however, have been resisted by many educationalists who adopt a content-orientated rather than a process orientated approach to education.

Recently it has been encouraging to observe that there are attempts to reassess the contribution of applied linguistics in education. The establishment of the project on specific learning difficulties, sponsored by the Scottish Dyslexia Trust at Moray House Institute and research initiated by the SOED on the role of the speech therapist in education indicates that this resistance is under review.

LANGUAGE IS CENTRAL TO THE LEARNING PROCESS

Nisbet, speaking at the National Forum for Educational Research in Scotland in 1991 stated:

'Learning results from a personal construction of knowledge: learning is not something that happens to students: it is something that happens by students. We need to give more attention to the motivation to learn, to the affective and social elements in learning . . . building confidence is a crucial step in learning: student's perceptions of the task and of themselves, their self-image, influence their learning profoundly. Our current focus on the cognitive aspects of learning needs to be balanced by the recognition of the learner as an active, feeling participant in the learning process.'

Educationalists who agree with this analysis have applied a range of alternative approaches to learning, based on pedagogical descriptions which are different from those contained in familiar curriculum guidelines. Three approaches are provided here as an illustration.

(i) **Making thinking explicit: the metacognitive approach:**

This approach (influenced by the work of Feuerstein, De Bono and Lipman) states that where motivation and achievement are below the national norm we should look carefully at pupils' attitudes to their education. We need to encourage pupils' feelings of ownership and control of their education and this can be done by helping them to develop awareness and control of their own thinking processes. Students can develop thinking frameworks which can be applied across the curriculum as a strategy to tackle difficulties and to increase their ability for philosophical enquiry.

Students are encouraged to think explicitly using a self-questioning procedure. When defining the task they can ask themselves: 'What am I supposed to be doing?' Next they might consider the transfer of learning experience: 'Have I done something like this before?' 'What will help me this time?' At the planning stage, the questions to be addressed are: 'What will I need?' 'How will I go about it?' Later, when evaluating their performance, they ask: 'Did I do what I was supposed to do?' 'How could I do better next time?' 'What do I need to work on?'

Cross-curricular programmes based on this approach are now being implemented in a number of schools in Lothian region and will become a feature of the new 5-14 curriculum.

(ii)   **Learning to discuss**

The Standard Grade curriculum development programme provided the context for an experiment which aimed to make the discussion process explicit in the learning environment. It was suggested that the development of explicit understanding of the constituent elements of discussion skill should be on the agenda of all schools. A discussion profile of each student was produced on the basis of behavioural evidence (what did the students do in discussions?); cognitive evidence (how were the students thinking in discussion?); affective evidence (how did the students feel in discussion?) and interpersonal evidence (how were relationships managed in the discussion group?). The skills which were monitored for behavioural evidence included organising self for discussion; attending to others in discussion; listening to the content of the discussion; contributing to the discussion; responding to the contributions of others; observing and showing awareness of the roles others take; adopting different roles in discussion appropriate to context, and enabling the group to complete a discussion task.

The discussion development programme demonstrated how each of these skills could be further refined. For example, the components of 'contributing skill' could be developed in the direction of proposing an idea; building an argument; supporting an argument; seeking information from others; giving information to others; disagreeing appropriately in argument. A range of activities and self-assessment measures to help students with their own personal development of discussion skills were piloted in schools and made generally available to teachers in publications produced during the 1980s.

A teacher reporting on the effectiveness of the discussion programme commented on a particular task to improve contribution rate:

'It is quite clear that the pupils are learning about and improving their discussion skills. The task demonstrated that the quieter pupils are very capable of discussing ably but are clearly often submerged by the louder, more aggressive members. The success of the experiment was highlighted by the obvious enjoyment of the low contributors' group. The group with the highest contribution rate particularly enjoyed the challenge of the new group. They found it much harder work and made a real effort to observe discussion skill rules. When asked about the re-constituted groups, everyone was pleased or just as happy as they had been previously – there were no negative comments.'

Taking the view that successful discussion is within the reach of teachers and pupils at all levels of schooling, Dillon (1994) in a comprehensive treatment encourages educators to learn how to use discussion in their own practice.

As the use of 'learning to discuss' programmes increases, more attention will be placed on the cognitive dimension of discussion. Learning objectives will focus on monitoring the quality of discussion performance. For example, the quality of reflectiveness – how thoughtful, reflective and searching do the students show themselves to be? Or the quality of consistency – how do the students demonstrate coherence, consistency and consecutiveness in though and argument?

(iii)   Differentiating language in context

The metacognitive approach and the learning to discuss programme are finding a place within the framework of 5-14 developments for students of every ability. It is to be hoped that attention to these approaches will generate greater awareness and sensitivity to the needs of individual students, particularly those with specific language difficulties. The study of language in context challenges our assumptions on the traditional view of ability. Some potentially able learners show significant differences in their ability to process language. There is a need to re-consider our approach to language work with able and less able learners alike.

There are some students – labelled as having problems in terms of motivation and ability – who conceal a learning difficulty. Language difficulties are subtle, they do not always announce their presence. They may not be documented in the school records. They may, however, affect potentially able students and interfere with their educational development.

Differentiating the language curriculum is dependent on developing accurate observation skills. Assumptions about the abilities of children should not be based on impressionistic observations. All observation is subjective and tends to encourage the use of value judgments: 'he lacks confidence,' 'she is talkative'. What do these descriptions mean and on what evidence are they based? When a teacher observes 'lack of confidence,' are they referring to a child who contributes little in class? Whose face lacks expression? Who sits on the edge of the group? Who stares at the worksheet before beginning to work? Who fails to complete the work sheet in the time allowed?

Language investigations are ineffective if interpretations are based on psychological and social assumptions derived from observation of non-verbal and interaction behaviour. Difficulties with verbal behaviour which affect the capacity for learning may be masked by inappropriate attention to the psychological overlay of social interaction.

Studies carried out in schools in connection with the Moray House Special Educational needs course (Francis, 1979,1985) showed that specific language assessment activities carried out during a 40 minute session could provide the teacher with useful information about the language processing abilities of a class group. Some students were revealed as highly able in their understanding of vocabulary and others less able. Some students had little difficulty in understanding a series of instructions while others showed problems in understanding and failed to complete tasks. Findings for receptive language abilities e.g. listening and understanding in context, were not necessarily matched by those for expressive language. The logic of cause and effect used in a story sequence might be observed in some students, but not in others. The amount and quality of the language produced in story telling was variable. Findings on auditory memory tended to be most variable. For example, some students were able to remember ten digits with ease, others had difficulty in remembering six.

Observations of students during a discussion activity provided a different perspective. Some of those who failed to sequence logically or to use complex and varied language constructions spoke a great deal in discussion.

The learning support service in schools should be able to demonstrate a range of specialised strategies which provide the evidence required for diagnostic assessment. However, teachers should also consider developing a series of activities based on the vocabulary of the existing curriculum, the instructions required by the curriculum and a sample of specific tasks to assess the language differences within a class group.

Evidence from observations of student language should have an effect on the teacher's own use of language. The language of explanation can be considered more critically when there is an awareness that some students are less able to understand verbal complexity. Efforts can be made to ensure that instructions are succinct and carefully phrased. Instructions should be repeated if there is evidence of genuine misunderstanding rather than as a matter of course.

Research has shown that increased use of statements by teachers stimulates student interaction. Questions should be used to obtain information. Questioning as part of a ritual classroom game should be avoided. Communication is being used purposefully when there is an increase in the listening ability of the teacher and a greater understanding of the different learning styles in the class group. Deep structure learning needs to be valued more highly than surface structure learning based on memory.

APPLICATION TO A SPECIFIC CURRICULUM CONTEXT

The Geography curriculum at Standard Grade provides a specific context in which to test the application of the statements contained in this chapter. The 'Lurcher's Gully Enquiry' is a case study which is used for the investigation of conservation and economic issues to encourage understanding of the nature and purpose of environmental education. The investigation is based on groupwork, resource based-learning and discussion.

Understanding of the discussion process ensures that the groups are organised around low and high contributors: those who need more time to process language work together, while those who process language more quickly also work together.

During the simulation of the Lurcher's Gully enquiry, those who are linguistically able handle complex documents on conservation and economic issues on behalf of their peers. Those who are less able recreate the arguments of the conservationist, the developer or the ski-lift owner at an anecdotal level. The teacher mediates the experience so that each student constructs the argument at a particular reporting level – verbatim, process or conceptualised reporting. Students meet in pairs differentiating the arguments or matching similar arguments. Each level is valued as a different kind of contribution which needs to be considered for a thorough investigation of the topic. The different language levels of the debate can be highlighted and the need to integrate the various points of view emphasised.

In writing, the differentiation of the class group's work is developed in a similar way. As in any organisational system, those who are able to be responsible for the routine completion of questionnaires and worksheets are regarded as performing as valuable a function as those who create journalistic reports or speeches to Ministers of State or leaders of concerned bodies.

The language of 'core' and 'extension', which is often applied to the development of the curriculum for use in differentiated learning contexts, has no relevance in this example – the work of every student is regarded as 'core' work.

Self-assessment strategies which are included as a part of this learning system are vital so that students document the differences between one argument as compared to another and learn to understand the difference between anecdotal, verbatim and conceptualised reporting.

SUMMARY

This chapter emphasises that appropriate language in context is the key to the effective differentiation of learning. There is a need to understand the content of the student's language – their ideas, their formulation, their management in thinking. To understand the capabilities of the student in terms of the form of spoken language – the process of articulation, the amount and quality of vocabulary and syntax. To understand the use of language – in one-to-one, small group and large group interaction, and to understand the communicative context, not only of the learner, but also of the teacher and of the curriculum.

REFERENCES

Bramley, W. (1979). *Group tutoring: Concepts and case studies*. Kogan Page.

Bullock, A. (1975). *A Language for Life*. HMSO.

Cashdan, A., *et al* (1972). *Language in Education*. Open University.

Dillon, J. T. (1994). *Using Discussion in Classrooms*. Buckingham. Open University Press.

Francis, E. (1979). *Social Skills Training in Education*. Education in the North. Aberdeen.

Francis, E. (1985). *Learning to Discuss*. SCCC.

Francis, E., Gillon, M., McKay, C. (1985). 'Communication for Special Educational Needs: A Multi-disciplinary Approach.' *British Journal of In-service Education*. Vol. 12.

Francis, E. (1988). 'Group Processes' in Dillon, J. T. (Ed.). *Questioning and Discussion: a Multi-disciplinary study*. Ablex Publishing Corporation. New Jersey USA.

Francis, E. (1990). 'Working Together on Discussion' in Brubacher, M., Payne, R. and Rickett, K. (Eds.) *Perspectives on Small Group Learning: Theory and Practice*. Rubicon, Ontario, Canada.

Lakoff, G. and Johnson, M. (1980). *Metaphors We Live By*. Chicago University Press.

Mehrabian, A. (1972). *Non-Verbal Communication*. Aldine-Atherton. Chicago.

Saville-Troike, M. (1982). *The Ethnography of Communication*. Basil Blackwell.

Swift, Gooding and Swift, (1988). 'Questions and Wait-time' In Dillon, J. T. *Questioning and Discussion: A Multi-disciplinary Study*. Ablex Publishing Corporation, New Jersey, USA.

Tannen, D. (1990). *That's Not What I Meant*. Virago. London.

Tiberius, R. (1986). 'Metaphors underlying the improvement of teaching and learning.' *British Journal of Educational Technology*. Vol. 17. No. 2.

Trower, P., Bryant, B. and Argyle, M. (1978) *Social Skills and Mental Health*. Methuen.

LANGUAGE AND DYSLEXIA

MARCIA MANN

Language is the most complex of all human functions. It is the most recent of nature's creative innovations, the last in the evolutionary ladder to develop, and that which we like to point to as a demonstration of humankind's superiority over the other species with which we co-habit this earth. While we do not question the ability of our furred, feathered or flippered neighbours to communicate, we understand that it is the facility with spoken and written language, and the ability to think about language, which sets us apart from other creatures.

Humans are born with the genetic blueprint for developing language (Rawson, 1992) and need only the neural and mechanical 'hook-ups' functioning smoothly and co-operatively, to become good communicators and successful language users. Pinker (1994) views language as an 'instinct . . . a distinct piece of the biological makeup of our brains'. He supports the concept of a genetic predisposition or 'wiring-up' that is separate and aside from the influences of external factors. Dickinson and McCabe (1991) describe the language continuum as a braid, rather than a sequential process, consisting of multiple strands which are added to and interwoven with the whole at various points in the developmental process.

LANGUAGE FUNCTION

Views of the language function are as varied as there are thinkers and writers on the subject. Skinner (1957) speaking for the experimental psychologists down-plays, perhaps discards, the biological aspects of language. Environment is everything! The neuro-scientists, on the other hand, may prefer to concentrate on efforts to understand and explain language on the basis of neuronal organization and cortical functioning (Galaburda, 1989). Still other writers make a very good case for the necessity of an intimate relationship between language and conceptualization. Edelman (1992) believes that critical factors in developing the self-concept depend on the ability for long-term storage of symbolic relations, which the individual has acquired through interactions with others of the same species. The interaction between phonemic and symbolic sets of memories, together with conceptual value-category memories, he believes, allow for a modeling of the world. Others note that the language function tends to change as a function of time, and view the language continuum in terms of the types of academic complaints which become apparent at various ages, beginning with delayed onset of language to poor test taking skills and the need for more time to process linguistic information.

LANGUAGE SYSTEM

Where consensus does appear among various writers, it is in the agreement that the language user must have a reliable system for receiving linguistic information, and then for interpreting, integrating, storing, retrieving and finally expressing this information when needed.

In November 1982, ASHA (The American Speech-Language-Hearing Association) Committee on Language adopted the following definition of language:

Language is a complex and dynamic system of conventional symbols that is used in various modes for thought and communication. Contemporary views of human language hold that:

- Language evolves within specific historical, social, and cultural contexts;
- language, as a rule-governed behaviour, is described by at least five parameters – phonologic, morphologic, syntactic, semantic and pragmatic;
- language learning and use are determined by the interaction of biological, cognitive, psychosocial, and environmental factors;
- effective use of language for communication requires a broad understanding of human interaction including such associated factors as non-verbal cues, motivation, and sociocultural roles.

The child learns two languages; first an oral language, and then a written language which is superimposed on the oral structure. Taking into account the ASHA definition, it may be said that language is the process by which meanings are exchanged between individuals through a system of symbols. In an alphabetic system, such as English, the letters are assigned certain sounds, the sounds are strung together in a systematic way to make words, and the words are strung together, according to rules, to make sentences. (see Fig.1).

By the time a child is 6 years old, oral language ought to be set and developed as a usable tool for communication. At the age of 6, the demands of school, i.e. academic learning, and the demands of social learning are such that information must be funnelled through a well developed, intact language system.

Fig. 1

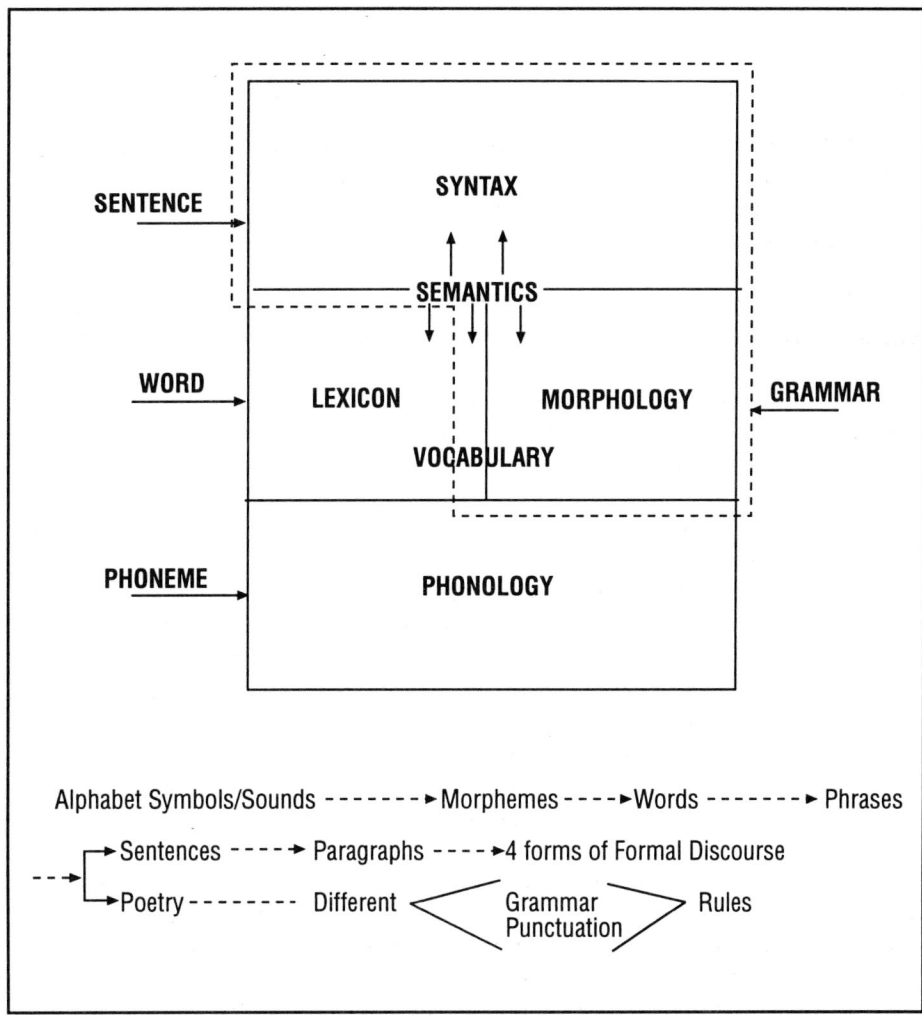

LANGUAGE BASED LEARNING

By the sixth year, the child generally has a repertoire of about 2,500 words (Templin, 1957). All the very complex articulatory movements necessary to produce the phonemes of the English language have been mastered, and the rule structure has been successfully internalized. The child should have reasonable facility with the morphological and semantic aspects of the language, and is able to use grammatic forms correctly. The intact 6 year old no long says 'we goed to the store'. He or she has learned that the past tense of the irregular verb form 'go', is 'went'.

The youngster with no 'system glitches' in his or her language function can just 'get it', without being specifically taught the information. When there are disruptions or malfunctions in the ability to process linguistic information, the child begins to experience learning difficulties resulting from this basic language disorder. These language-based learning disorders, we refer to as dyslexia. Dyslexic children must be taught the language, both oral and written, in a very well organized, structured, systematic and multi-sensory manner, in order for the information to 'stick': that is, for the information to be properly received, interpreted, integrated, stored and later retrieved.

LANGUAGE AND DYSLEXIA

The study of dyslexia in the United States began with the work of Samuel T. Orton in the 1920s. In his seminal work in the field, 'Reading, Writing and Speech Problems in Children', Orton drew some very interesting conclusions based on several years of careful research. Strephosymbolia, or what we refer to as dyslexia, was by no means merely a 'reading disorder'. He speaks of adolescents 'who have acquired a good vocabulary but who have great difficulty in gaining the meaning from reading of long sentences or paragraphs'. He goes on to say that frequently 'such a patient will be able to define accurately and without hesitation all the words in the material read and yet fail to grasp the significance of the sentences into which they are combined'. We see many youngsters today, particularly in the upper grades, who can decode reasonably well, but, because of their inability to make appropriate semantic associations, have particular 'complaints' about not understanding what they read.

Orton also found that oral reading was apt to be a 'jerky', word by word affair, with apparently little use of, or understanding of, the suprasegmentals of language – the linguistic suprasegmentals being inflection, pauses, stress, pitch and rate of articulation. In the years since Orton did his research and writing, we have come to understand that about 50% of the meaning in the English language is carried by the decoding of phonemic elements, and other 50% by the suprasegmental. As I like to explain to the youngsters with whom I work, choppy, word by word, laborious reading is very boring, and 'turns your brain off' to the reading material. The result? 'I haven't the foggiest notion what that paragraph is about. And besides, its boring!' There is certainly a lot to be said for the 'old fashioned' procedures of having children read aloud, with expression.

Rawson (1992) talks of Orton as a neuropathologist and psychiatrist, intimately involved in studying both brain and mind. She says that, 'Orton made it clear in his first public statement in 1925 that he was concerned not just with reading, but with the whole of the human language function. As a result, we are presented with small 'relevancies', unique and individual pieces of information, which ought not to be viewed in isolation, but as markers pointing toward a more encompassing perspective.'

It has become clear, since the early work of Liberman (1985) and other researchers, that the ability to process phonological information is essential in the process of developing literacy. It should not be taken as gospel, however, that this is the only marker for predicting language learning disorders.

While statistics vary among researchers, it is estimated that 10-20 percent of the population suffers from this hidden handicap. Dyslexia mystifies the unenlightened, and often plays havoc among the scientific community, in their efforts to arrive at a definition. The Orton Dyslexia Society recently put forth two definitions: one for the researchers, emphasizing phonological processes, and another developed by a committee of members, intended for more general usage. The members' definition states that:

> *"Dyslexia is a neurologically-based, familial disorder which interferes with the acquisition and processing of linguistic information. Varying in degree of severity, it is manifested by difficulties in receptive and expressive language, including phonological processing, reading, writing, spelling, and sometimes arithmetic. Dyslexia may occur concomitantly with other limiting conditions such as lack of motivation, sensory impairment, or inadequte instructional or environmental opportunities, but is not a result of these conditions. Although dyslexia is lifelong, individuals with dyslexia successfully respond to timely and appropriate intervention."*

Dyslexia is the only medically handicapping condition where the prescribed treatment must be educational. Rawson (1992) explained it best when she said:

> *"The differences are personal.*
> *The diagnosis is clinical.*
> *The treatment is educational.*
> *The understanding scientific."*

In looking for the commonality, i.e. those patterns consistent among dyslexics, the only similarities we can find are the dis-similarities... the basic linguistic inconsistencies . . . the unexplainable highs and lows in performance. The youngster who gets a 95% on a spelling test today and can't spell the same words tomorrow! The adult who studies French for two years, becomes reasonably fluent, and then forgets everything. The adolescent who spends years learning to read and write Hebrew, and after being away from the language for a period of time, is no longer able to decode the symbols or understand the words.

CASE STUDIES

Rawson (1992) describes a fictionalized 10 year old boy who complains, 'What's wrong is my words . . . Sometimes I couldn't think of the right words. Sometimes I still can't . . . and after a while the right ones sometimes pop up . . . Either I can't learn them, or I work very had and do learn them, only I forget them right away'.

Janet, a bright 10 year old, once remarked to her teacher, 'I have a problem with the words. Sometimes I know them, but other times, they just seem to fly out of my head'.

Richard, a very apt and curious 11 year old, whose writing was characterized by large, poorly formed letters, with no systematic or organized method for spacing words, exhibited speech patterns quite analogous to his writing. While his letters seemed to march across the page, jostling and bumping each other, the words just tumbled out of his mouth, pushing and shoving at each other on the way, often tripping up his articulators en route. Richard, diagnosed as a clutterer, had speech patterns that were slurred and often unintelligible. He was like a locomotive speeding along and finally derailing, because of the loss of control at such excessive speeds. A discrepancy perhaps, between a thinking mind working at top speed, and a linguistic 'mechanical' system unable to keep up.

Cluttering is often seen in the dyslexic population, as well a...
a variety of articulatory disorders. Youngsters may exhibit a...
difficulties in producing phonemes accurately. Quite often, a...
language, the error patterns will be inconsistent. There may be ...
child is able to produce difficult sounds, and other days when he ...

Once we understand that dyslexia is a disorder that may affe...
areas of language functioning, it becomes easier to see patterns of ...
efforts, whether on paper or in speech. Errors of omission, addition, ...
of sounds, syllables, words, or even phrases, may occur on paper or ...
language. Sequencing difficulties, in recalling and re-telling a series of ...
understanding directions, in using time, place, and directional words are ...
pitfalls for the dyslexic. The little girl who loves to play the 'penan...
'pisghetti', or walk on a 'limolemum' floor is well know to us. The ...
elements are consistent, only the manner of expression may change.

The person with dyslexia is one who has great difficulty in storin...
retrieving information. Things are always just 'on the tip of my tongue'. Nam...
impossible. One very well thought of and popular college professor, o...
occasion of his retirement, said that although he missed the students, he was **so**
relieved not to have to worry over remembering all their names.

'It's like digging around in the bottom of my closet,' said Charles, a cheery
9 year old. 'Sometimes I can find what I'm looking for, even thought it takes a little
longer, but sometimes I just can't! Even though I know it's in there.'

These are the children who may have been seen for speech therapy at an
early age, perhaps to correct an articulation problem or because of a language
delay, and then discharged as 'corrected'. They very often attract our attention in
Junior or Senior High School because they have been placed in special classes for
the learning disabled. Most of these youngsters have 'no problems', other than 'a
little trouble getting their thoughts down on paper', or 'horrible handwriting', or
'simply awful spelling, but he can use a spell check on the computer', or need, as
one mother put it, 'just a little fine-tuning'.

In cases like these, the initial complaint is usually analogous with the tip of
the iceberg. Like the iceberg, the great mass of the problem, the underlying
language disorder, has been covered over with this myriad of small issues. It is
quite usual to find that the bright dyslexic adolescent has coped successfully with
earlier language difficulties. As the academic demands require greater linguistic

proficiency, however, the system begins to falter. Small complaints become larger ones and academic disaster becomes commonplace.

The story of Robert serves as a good illustration of the subtleties one finds when dealing with bright dyslexic children. This young man was diagnosed at the age of 12 when he was put out of the 'gifted' class at school, for failing to meet the academic criteria. Because of his high intelligence and very good social skills, Robert was able to mask the underlying language disorder until the academic demands 'overloaded' his linguistic capabilities.

During the assessment, the mother reported that Robert's oral language was delayed. He didn't begin speaking until about 2F(1,2) years of age. Robert did not appear to be speaking English, however, but seemed to have developed 'his own language'. He continued with this highly structured private language for about 6 months, until about the age of 3, when he began to speak in 'English' phrases and soon after, sentences.

Robert's mother, confused and somewhat awed by this sudden gushing forth of adult language, reported that she felt foolish telling nursery rhymes and singing nursery songs to this child who appeared so suddenly mature in his language functioning.

Robert's continued development was unremarkable. He entered kindergarten and did well, but began having 'behaviour problems' in the first grade. Becoming the class clown, Robert enjoyed tremendous popularity among his peers, but did not win accolades from his teacher. As he continued in elementary school, Robert's good intellect and well developed social skills helped to mask the academic problems he was beginning to have. Report cards reflected average work, 'but could do better if he applied himself', with occasional highs on some tests. Maths and science were Robert's best subjects, and, as one would assume, reading was boring.

As he grew, Robert exhibited good mechanical ability and very poor graphomotor skills. He could take anything apart and fix it, the mother reported, but his handwriting was terrible. Letters remained poorly formed and generally illegible. Robert still prefers to print, rather than use cursive writing. Reading is slow, spelling errors abound, and there continue to be problems with directionality and word retrieval.

With an I.Q. in the superior range, and educational therapy to address the basic language processing problems, Robert has gone on to become a very successful orthopaedic surgeon.

The language difficulties never disappear. They simply change as a function of time. Sometimes, as in the case of Robert, the signs of language differences are very subtle. At other times, the markers are glaring and call attention to the youngster, as someone in need of help.

CONCLUSION

These are the children who may hear, but may have difficulty understanding what they hear. They may be very quick on the athletic field, but painfully slow in making appropriate verbal responses. They may have delayed speech, articulatory disorders, and difficulty with storing and retrieving information. They may be clutterers or stutterers. They may have problems in formulating and expressing their ideas, either orally or on paper. The common factor is language, and the syndrome can be called dyslexia.

REFERENCES

ASHA Committee on Language (1983). *Definition of Language*. ASHA, 25, 44.

Dickinson, D. and McCabe, A. (1991). 'The Acquisition and Development of Language.' In Kavanagh, J. (Ed.) *The Language Continuum*, York Press, Maryland.

Edelman, G. (1992). *Bright Air, Brilliant Fire*. Basic Books, New York.

Galaburda, A. (Ed.) (1989). *From Reading to Neurons*. MIT Press, Cambridge.

Liberman, I., and Shankweiler, D. (1985). 'Phonology and The Problems of Learning to Read and Write' In *Remedial and Special Education*, 6, 8-17.

Orton, S. (1937). *Reading, Writing and Speech Problems in Children*. W.W. Norton & Company, New York.

Pinker, S. (1994). *The Language Instinct*. William Morrow & Company, New York.

Rawson, M. (1992). *The Many Faces of Dyslexia*. The Orton Dyslexia Society, Baltimore.

Skinner, B. (1957). *Verbal Behaviour*. Appleton-Century-Crofts, New York.

Templin, M. (1957). *Certain Language Skills in Children*. The University of Minnesota Press, Minneapolis.

READING BETWEEN THE LANGUAGES: BILINGUAL LEARNERS AND SPECIFIC LEARNING DIFFICULTIES

JOHN LANDON

THE UK EDUCATIONAL CONTEXT FOR BILINGUAL DEVELOPMENT

A significant number of schools in Britain have bilingual learners on their rolls. Accurate statistics are not available; the government does not require them. Nor do many schools voluntarily record the home languages of pupils in their databases. Those that do rarely include details of the level of competence in the child's first language(s) or the range and functions of its/their use. The fact is that the regular use of a language or languages other than English within the homes and communities of tens of thousands of British school children is not considered educationally relevant. For example, a quick glance through the indexes of books on reading development is unlikely to yield a single reference to bi-literacy (that is, literacy in two or more languages) or to learning to read and write in a second language. Few university departments of education provide any initial training in bilingual development. A child's competence in a language other than English is unlikely to be discussed in the case notes of an educational psychologist (Desforges, 1995) or a speech therapist (Stokes and Duncan, 1989). In spite of four decades of immigration of cultural and linguistic minorities into Britain, bilingualism is still not on the educational map.

In this regard, Britain is out of step with much of the rest of the world. The majority of the world's population speaks more than one language and in many countries, bilingual development features prominently in educational provision. In most countries of northern Europe, there is considerable investment in staff and resources so that the first languages of migrant groups can be taught within the mainstream school to children from those linguistic backgrounds. In the US, two-way or dual language bilingual education occurs, where English and the minority language are both used in the classroom as media of education for minority and majority students alike. In both types of programme, bi-literacy is as much an aim as full bilingualism, with literacy being acquired in both languages either simultaneously or with an initial emphasis on first language literacy (Baker, 1993). Thus, the majority or second language is added to the language of the minority community, without any threat to the latter.

In Britain, however, although some minority indigenous languages receive this kind of support in certain regions, and although bilingualism with bi-literacy is the aim in the teaching of prestigious Western European languages, in the case of the first languages of minority groups there is no such commitment to maintenance or development. On the contrary, the benefits of bilingualism which are claimed for Welsh- and Gaelic- medium programmes and for the teaching of French or German are disavowed in the case of Punjabi, Urdu, Cantonese or Somali (Landon, 1993). First language maintenance is rather viewed as problematic to second-language development and to integration. The experience of most children whose home language is other than English is thus subtractive, as the first language is marginalised and reduced in favour of the second (Lambert, 1974)

THE EFFECTS ON THE BILINGUAL CHILD'S LINGUISTIC AND COGNITIVE DEVELOPMENT OF NEGATIVE AND POSITIVE RESPONSES TO BILINGUALISM

Children from minority ethnic groups grow up in Britain within a society and educational system which are not positively disposed towards the languages of their communities, nor, by extension, it may be assumed, towards their cultures or values. Such a negative climate places enormous pressures upon the vitality of minority community languages. This reveals itself in language shift (Romaine, 1983, 1989) whereby there is a gradual reduction in the use of the minority language across generations of speakers and a gradual increase in the use of the majority language. The minority language used in the home and community becomes influenced in its grammar and lexis by borrowings from the majority language. In literate communities, the extent of literacy in the minority language declines, leading to destandardisation and linguistic instability. The functions for which the language is used also are reduced and become confined to social interaction in which the relationship between the participants and the familiarity and immediacy of the subject matter contribute as much, if not more, to the conveyance of meaning as the language itself. These consequences of low linguistic status, lack of educational support for minority language development and, in some cases, the dissipation, or absence, of a viable linguistic community have serious implications for the language experience of the child before entry to school, for the linguistic and cognitive basis of the child's subsequent learning and for the commitment of the minority community and family to the mainstream educational process.

This is the worst case scenario. However, it must be said that, in spite of the difficulties, many families strive to maintain their first language at home and by sending their children to community-led supplementary language classes. Also, after the failure to support minority languages during the primary school years, some secondary schools offer them as modern foreign languages up to examination level. In these cases, as the language develops, beyond social usage, as a medium of reasoning and learning and as the child becomes literate in the first language, the benefits of bilingualism in terms of general intellectual and linguistic development may manifest themselves.

Bilingualism is not itself the problem. As has been shown, it is the societal circumstances which create under-developed languages which cause problems for many potentially bilingual learners. When this potentiality is realised, the two linguistic systems do not, as is commonly believed, operate separately causing cognitive confusion and linguistic interference. Rather, the research evidence suggests that the bilingual has an integrated whole linguistic system which manifests itself in two languages (Duncan, 1989). Cummins (1981) illustrates this phenomenon in the form of two icebergs. The icebergs appear as two separate peaks above the surface, but beneath the surface they are fused. In the same way, both languages operate through the same central processing system, although their surface features are different.

Therefore, when learning takes place through the medium of one language, it is stored within the central processing system. The concept or skill does not need to be learned again in order for it to be expressed in the second language; it merely needs to be encoded within a different linguistic system. If a child learns to read in the first language – the most appropriate language for the development of initial literacy since it is the stronger oral language and the main language of the child's pre-reading experience – that child does not have to learn to read again when s/he begins to function in a second language. S/he has to adapt the operation of a familiar skill to the linguistic rules, and often the subject matter, of an unfamiliar language and culture. This is quite different from acquiring a new skill through a new language.

Research also shows that well-developed bilingualism is attended by other cognitive advantages. Many of these advantages may have a direct impact on reading ability. Because a bilingual will have two or more ways of comprehending or expressing a single idea, a number of studies (Carringer, 1994; Cummins, 1976) suggest that 'the ownership of two or more languages may increase fluency, flexibility, originality and elaboration in thinking' (Baker, 1993). Other studies (Cummins, 1976; Ben Zeev, 1977) indicate that bilingual children, in their contrastive 'observation of two languages and in their endeavour to keep them apart, come to pay more attention to language itself, its structures and the central properties defining it, than do monolingual children' (Skutnabb-Kangas, 1981). These advantages have been illustrated well by using the analogy of the effect of wearing differently tinted lenses (SCCC, 1993). The wearer has the choice of how to view the world - through yellow or blue tinted lenses. He can compare his different perceptions of the world with the different shades and tones which the different lenses highlight. He can also wear the yellow and blue lenses at the same time and experience the merging of colours, and recognise that one's perception of the world depends very much on the lenses through which one views it. If applied to reading, this is a powerful metaphor for skills in interpretation, analysis, criticality and evaluation.

Failure, through the education system, to develop bilingualism or to support the maintenance of first languages at home is, therefore, a significant potential cause of reading failure amongst bilingual children. However, as many educational programmes worldwide have shown, most notably the Rock Point Navajo Project (Rosier and Holm, 1980), a subtractive bilingual context which promotes the acquisition of literacy skills through the poorly developed second language can be transformed into an additive situation, with the resultant reversal of poor performance in second language reading and writing and the addition of literacy in the first language. At Rock Point, and in other bilingual intervention programmes, literacy is initially acquired in the child's first language, that is the language of the home and of early learning. It is only when first language literacy is firmly established that reading in the second language is introduced. It is unlikely that educational policy-makers in UK will adopt this practice. However, schools can support literacy development in the first language at home by encouraging parents to read to their children in the home language and, if necessary, by providing the necessary resources. Since the absence of first language literacy is a key indicator of reading underachievement in the second language, it is necessary for schools to gather and record data on the child's competence in the first language. The Primary Language Record (Barrs *et al.*, 1988) and materials from the London Borough of Tower Hamlets (Hall, 1995) are useful in this respect. Information on the role which first language literacy plays in the home should also be obtained. This may be a key area for intervention if literacy support is eventually required.

LEARNING TO READ IN A SECOND LANGUAGE

The processes underlying the development of literacy in the first and second language are interdependent (Cummins, 1981). The cognitive processes which have been developed through the one language will transfer to use in the other. The child who is already literate in the first language will be able to draw on understandings of the nature of reading and approaches to reading which have been used in the processing of texts in the first language when s/he is sufficiently competent in the second language to read texts in that language.

The corollary to this is that only those processes which have been developed through the first language will be transferable. If the skills required to read the first language involve top-down processing, because that is the way the child has been taught to access first language text or because the script is not alphabetic or phonemic and does not allow of any other approach, that is the only cognitive process which will transfer. If a child has been taught to decode text without comprehension, or to interpret meaning at the sentence level and not across text, it is only these processes which will transfer.

Goswami and Bryant (1990) in their critical studies of research into the degree of phonological awareness and sensitivity to onset and rime of illiterate groups and of those, like Chinese and Japanese, who have learned to read a logographic, and not an alphabetic, script have concluded that these groups have poorly developed phonological segmentation skills. Their lack of training in alphabetic literacy has meant that these skills are undeveloped (Read *et al.*, 1986) and are not transferable to approaches to English reading based on the ability to recognise phonological segments or onset and rime. However, decoding skills which depend on whole character recognition and not upon concurrent vocalisation (that is, the sounding out of phonemic segments) (Kimura and Bryant, 1983) will transfer to the reading of English. Therefore, the inability of children who come from homes in which they are exposed to non-alphabetic approaches to reading to achieve in segmentation tasks or to detect rhyme is not necessarily an indicator of a specific learning disorder or physical impairment, although these are accepted indicators of underachievement in native English-speaking children (Bradley and Bryant, 1978). Indeed, if the evidence is that a child is able to comprehend text in the first language, there can be no question that the child has a specific learning difficulty. Underachievement in reading in the second language is more likely to indicate an inadequacy in the approach adopted for the teaching of reading within the school or some other trauma, for example anxiety or racial harassment, which has no cognitive aetiology.

Traditional approaches to the teaching of reading which are common in village schools in the developing world value the ability to decode at the sound-symbol level. Reading aloud, without any check on comprehension, is a widely used method of teaching. In mosque schools (madrasahs) the ability to read the Q'uran in Arabic, without necessarily understanding it, is considered a valuable spiritual exercise and, therefore, of educative worth. Indeed, any attempt to interpret or evaluate the text would be considered contemptuous. These traditional approaches to reading are often found in community-run first language classes in Britain and may well influence attitudes to the teaching of reading held within religiously conservative families. If a child has learned to read in this way, no higher order comprehension skills will transfer to reading in the second language. Indeed, when reading for meaning is introduced in the second language there may be a misunderstanding, or even suspicion, of what is required. Therefore, if a child has difficulty with reading for understanding in the second language, in spite of the ability to decode at the sound-symbol level, this may be the result of previous training. Support within the classroom will require to concentrate on introducing new understandings of the nature of reading which emphasise comprehension and interpretation rather than on developing decoding skills at the phonetic level.

A third factor underlying difficulties which bilingual learners might experience when developing second language reading skills relates to the level of competence they have achieved in the second language. Cummins (1984) has demonstrated that language proficiency can be conceptualised along two continua. First is a continuum relating to the range of contextual support available for expressing or interpreting meaning. Thus, meaning can be expressed with a high degree of contextual support on the one hand, or very little contextual support, on the other. Where communication is highly context embedded, there are many more para-linguistic and situational cues to meaning than the linguistic medium alone. When extra-linguistic cues are not present, in contextually unsupported communication, expression or comprehension of the message depends more heavily on knowledge of the language. In terms of written text, contextually supported material is that which shares content with the everyday experience of the reader and uses language and storyline which is highly predictable. Folk tales and the more naturalistic 'real books' and reading scheme materials are good examples. Written communication characterised by language demands at the context-reduced end of the continuum consists of novels and the transactional discourse of many of the reference texts used in the classroom.

The second continuum rests along a line of relative cognitive demand. At one end are communicative tasks and activities requiring little active cognitive involvement for effective performance. This would include superficial decoding of simple texts, or blank-filling exercises where a few given alternatives or a wide range of possible options are available. At the other end are tasks which require active cognitive involvement – for example, hypothesizing the outcome of a story plot or argument, deducing meaning or critically evaluating an author's style.

Cummins has shown from analysis of bilingual children's performance of a range of tasks along both these continua, that, on average, children are able to perform tasks which are cognitively undemanding and contextually supported at the level of their monolingual peers on average after approximately eighteen months instruction through the second language. However, the same level of performance in cognitively demanding and contextually unsupported activities takes approximately five to seven years. Recent research (Collier, 1989) has suggested much longer, between eleven and thirteen years, that is – much of the average child's school life. It should be noted, in line with earlier discussion, that those learners who are able to undertake contextually unsupported and cognitively demanding tasks successfully in their first language are able to transfer these cognitive and linguistic processes more rapidly to communication in the second language. However, for children whose first language is not so highly developed, no such transfer is possible.

Children in this latter category may well be able to perform comprehension tasks which are undemanding and firmly embedded in a meaningful context after a short period of second language instruction. This may coincide with the first two years of primary school. However, when the comprehension demands of the curriculum increase as longer, more complex discourse covering less familiar subject matter is introduced, the children may begin to lose ground to their monolingual peer group and exhibit considerable reading difficulties. Intervention by the teacher to support reading development may exacerbate the difficulty if that intervention employs methods which concentrate on decoding below the level of meaning (for example, phonic drills) or use of materials which are essentially meaningless (texts constructed on the basis of graded phonic patterns or readability scales rather than of relevance and interest to the reader). In such circumstances, teachers may well explain the cause of the learner's reading difficulties as organising or learning difficulties which affect the processing of information, instead of taking steps to support the child's second, and if possible first, language development by providing contextually supported materials and activities at the appropriate cognitive level.

A fourth aspect of the problems which children from minority language backgrounds may experience in comprehending text is the cultural context of the text itself. A familiar cultural context supports the communication of meaning. As Carrell (1983) says: 'The text itself does not carry meaning. A text only provides guidance for listeners and readers as to how they should construct the intended meaning from their own previously acquired knowledge'. Without the relevant background knowledge, the child may fail to construct any meaning at all from the text in the second language, or using his/her own cultural knowledge as the basis for understanding may totally or partially misunderstand the author's intentions. The degree of cultural congruence between the author and the reader will not only affect final comprehension but also the process leading up to it: the ability to recognise, interpret and predict certain kinds of phenomena or behaviour described in texts (Wallace, 1986). Cultural misunderstandings may reveal themselves in totally surprising ways both in classroom reading and in reading tests and give rise to suspicions that the reader is experiencing problems at the level of cognitive processing, rather than at the level of cultural familiarity.

Finally, the difficulties with reading already described may lead to frustration in a teacher unfamiliar with the processes of bilingual development. S/he may feel that the child is not trying hard enough, especially if the child is a fluent speaker of the second language in social situations. S/he may blame the child's linguistic or cultural background. S/he may equate language difficulties with learning difficulties. S/he may concentrate too heavily on graphophonic miscues – for example, omission of plural and tense morphemes, and fail to recognise that the child is predicting items of structure and deducing meaning from context quite effectively (Wallace, 1986). In each of these ways, the teacher may communicate dissatisfaction with the pupil's performance, which may increase the learner's anxiety. Anxiety, in turn, will reduce the child's facility in processing text. Reading tests and screening procedures may well be used to confirm the teacher's inaccurate diagnosis, especially if data about the child's linguistic background, research into the process of bilingual development and consideration of the appropriateness of reading approaches and materials are not taken into account. As Cummins (1989) has stated: 'Professionals involved in assessment and support need to become advocates for minority students by focusing primarily on the ways in which academic difficulty is a function of interactions within the school context rather than legitimising the location of the 'problem' within the students themselves'.

TESTING HYPOTHESES TO CONFIRM OR REJECT SPECIFIC LEARNING DIFFICULTIES AS AN EXPLANATION OF READING FAILURE AMONGST BILINGUAL LEARNERS

As has been shown, the societal and educational context in which children develop, or fail to develop, as bilinguals in UK, as well as the process of bilingual development itself, generate a number of behaviours which may be interpreted, in most cases wrongly, as demonstrating a learning difficulty in general or dyslexia in particular. As Mattes and Omark (1984) emphasise:

'Second language learners who perform poorly in the school setting because of limited familiarity with English and/or cultural differences need to be distinguished from children who demonstrate communicative disorders and/or abnormalities that require special education intervention.'

Professionals clearly face a dilemma. On the one hand, they must avoid diagnosing a learning difficulty where none exists. If a misjudgement is made, the bilingual child may be labelled, and assigned a mode of instruction or learning environment which is not suitable, and is likely to be counterproductive. On the other hand, they must not fail to identify early any learning difficulty which does exist, and, thereby, deprive the bilingual child of appropriate support at an early stage.

Many bilingual learners will face problems in accessing the curriculum through the medium of their second language. They require the provision of appropriately demanding teaching materials and learning opportunities which mediate the language demands of the curriculum and facilitate bilingual development. A few bilingual learners will, in addition, have specific learning difficulties. As well as support to meet the linguistic demands of the curriculum, they will also require specific programmes and strategies which have been developed to teach pupils who have organising, or learning, deficiencies which restrict their competencies in information processing, in motor skills and working memory (Reid, 1994).

One method of addressing this dilemma is to use a hypothesis testing approach developed in Surrey for the psychological assessment of bilingual pupils with reported learning difficulties (Wright, 1991). It relies on the school collecting as much information as possible about the child's background, including details of linguistic development and language use in each of his/her languages and data on home, school and community experiences. It also uses conventional assessment and screening processes. However, it recognises that these were standarised, most probably, on Western monolingual populations, and that accepted interpretations of results are based on similar populations. A hypothesis-testing approach asks what further information the professional needs to collect in order to eliminate some of the possible reasons for the concern about the child's level of performance, bearing in mind that the child is developing as a bilingual and is a member of a cultural and ethnic minority group. It uses this information to test, and if necessary, to revise earlier explanations.

Some of the principles underlying the additional questions which would need to be asked in relation to a bilingual child have already been discussed. The questions may be general and hypothesise that the child is learning more slowly than others because the ethos and curriculum of the school are experienced as threatening and alien, rather than welcoming and accommodating. Additional information required to confirm or reject this hypothesis would focus on the ethnic and linguistic composition of the school, the staff, and the pupil population. Questions also would need to be asked of the school's policy on equal opportunities and implementation of anti-discriminatory practice. The investigation should involve parents and members of local minority ethnic communities, as well as school staff. It may well be that taken-for-granted practices and procedures within the school, although not intentionally discriminatory, may have unintentional discriminatory effects, in that they exploit, exclude, misrepresent or hurt children from minority backgrounds and their families (Landon, 1994).

Other hypotheses may focus on linguistic or cognitive causes, including the notion that the bilingual learner has a specific learning difficulty. As has been discussed, indicators of a specific learning difficulty, which include poor reading and spelling, left/right confusion, orientation problems, sequencing difficulties, poor short-term memory, confusion over punctuation and grammar, difficulty in naming objects and problems with letter formation (Crombie, 1993) may easily be confused with poor performance arising from the child's experience of language loss in the first language, the timescale involved in second language development, or the classroom environment in which second language learning has been taking place.

Evidence would need to be gathered about the child's exposure to different languages from birth, reports of early language development, the current range of use of different languages by the child and evidence of progress in first and second language learning. Information on first language needs to come from a native speaker's analysis of the child's proficiency and from reports from community language classes. The vital importance of this kind of data for making accurate diagnoses clearly indicates the need for education authorities to recruit and train minority language speakers for this purpose. If a child is experiencing a loss of contact with the first language, this is more likely to be an explanation for difficulties experienced in the development of the second language than a specific language disorder. Similarly, if a child is exhibiting signs of poor performance and has been learning the second language for a relatively short time, the timescale is more likely to be significant as the cause of difficulty.

CONCLUSIONS

It is hoped that the hitherto invisible role of bilingualism and its relationship to learning will gain a much higher profile in school policies on record-keeping, assessment and language development. For this to be achieved, it is necessary for every class teacher, support teacher and professionals, like educational psychologists and speech therapists, to receive training in the nature of bilingualism and patterns of bilingual development in the current subtractive bilingual context of Britain. The consequences of such training are empowerment for teachers and equity for minority language pupils and their parents.

Many professionals feel inadequate, in the present climate, when faced with a bilingual pupil who appears to be having difficulties with accessing the curriculum. They either doubt their own professional competence, or, more often, perceive the deficit within the child or his/her linguistic and cultural background. With greater awareness, the teacher will see that a supportive and culturally and linguistically inclusive classroom and school environment is the most effective basis for academic success for the vast majority of bilingual learners. There is abundant evidence for this in many schools. For those learners whose difficulties are not related to the process of bilingual development, a school whose procedures and staff leave this option open to full investigation will make early identification of the true causes of academic failure a reality.

REFERENCES

Baker, C. (1993). *Foundations of Bilingual Education and Bilingualism*. Clevedon: Multilingual Matters.

Barrs, M., Ellis, S., Hester, H. and Thomas, A. (1988). *The Primary Language Record Handbook*. London: Centre for Language in Primary Education.

Ben-Zeev, S. (1977). The influence of bilingualism on cognitive strategy. *Child Development*, 48, 1009-1018.

Bradley, L. and Bryant, P. E. (1978). Difficulties in auditory organisation as a possible cause of reading backwardness. *Nature*, 271, 746-747.

Carrell, P. (1983). Some issues in studying the role of schemata or background in second language comprehension. *Reading in a Foreign Language*, 1, 2, 81-92.

Carringer, D. C. (1974). Creative thinking abilities of Mexican youth: the relationship of bilingualism. *Journal of Cross-Cultural Psychology*, 5, 492-504.

Collier, V. P. (1989). How long? A synthesis of research on academic achievement in a second language. *TESOL Quarterly*, 23, 509-531.

Crombie, M. (1993). The role of the teacher. In Reid, G. (Ed.) *Specific Learning Difficulties (Dyslexia): Perspectives on Practice*. Edinburgh: Moray House.

Cummins, J. (1976). The influence of bilingualism on cognitive growth: a synthesis of research findings and explanatory hypotheses. *Working Papers on Bilingualism*, 9, 1-43.

Cummins, J. (1984). *Bilingualism and Special Education: Issues in Assessment and Pedagogy.* Clevedon: Multilingual Matters.

Cummins, J. (1989). *Empowering Minority Students.* Sacraments, CA: California Association for Bilingual Education.

Desforges, M. F. (1995). Assessment of special educational needs in bilingual pupils. *School Psychology International,* 16, 1, 5-17.

Duncan, D. M. (Ed.) (1989). *Working with Bilingual Language Disability.* London: Chapman & Hall.

Goswani, U. and Bryant, P. E. (1990). *Phonological Skills and Learning to Read.* Hove: Lawrence Erlbaum.

Hall, D. (1995). *Assessing the Needs of Bilingual Pupils: Living in Two Languages.* London: David Fulton.

Kimura, Y. and Bryant, P. E. (1983). Reading and writing in English and Japanese. *British Journal of Developmental Psychology,* 1, 129-144.

Lambert, W. E. (1974). Culture and language as factors in learning and education. In Aboud, F.E. and Meade, R. D. (Eds.) *Cultural Factors in Learning and Education.* Bellingham, Washington: 5th Western Washington Symposium in Learning.

Landon, J. (1993). Bilingualism: two languages or forked tongue? the 5-14 position discussed. *Scotland's Languages,* 1, 4-5.

Landon, J. (1994). *A Question of Balance: Unintentional Discrimination in the Daily Life of Schools.* Edinburgh: Moray House.

Mattes, L. and Omark, D. (1984). *Speech and Language Assessment for the Bilingual Handicapped.* San Diego, CA: College Hill Press.

Read, C., Zhang, Y., Nie, H., and Ding, B. (1986). The ability to manipulate speech sounds depends on knowing alphabetic spelling. *Cognition,* 24, 31-44.

Reid, G. (1994). *Specific Learning Difficulties (Dyslexia): A Handbook for Study and Practice.* Edinburgh: Moray House.

Romaine, S. (1983). Collecting and interpreting self-reported data on the language use of linguistic minorities by means of 'language diaries'. *MALS Journal,* 9, 1-30.

Romaine, S. (1989). *Bilingualism.* Oxford: Blackwell.

Rosier, P. and Holm, W. (1980). *The Rock Point Experience: A Longitudinal Study of a Navajo School.* Washington, D.C: Center for Applied Linguistics.

SCCC (1993). *Languages for Life: Bilingual Pupils and 5-14.* Dundee: Scottish Consultative Council on the Curriculum.

Skutnabb-Kangas, T. (1981). *Bilingualism or Not: The Education of Minorities.* Clevedon: Multilingual Matters.

Stokes, J. and Duncan, D. M. (1989). The challenge of working with minority languages. In Duncan, D. M. (Ed.), *Working with Bilingual Language Disability.* London: Chapman & Hall.

Wallace, C. (1986). *Learning to Read in a Multicultural Society: the Social Context of Second Language Literacy.* Oxford: Pergamon.

Wright, A. (1991). The assessment of bilingual pupils with reported learning difficulties. In Cline, T. and Frederickson, N. (Eds.). *Bilingual Pupils and the National Curriculum.* London: University College.

SECTION 4

MOTOR DEVELOPMENT

DEVELOPMENTAL DYSPRAXIA
– AN OVERVIEW

ADRIAN DIGHE
GILLIAN KETTLES

Clumsiness in children is not a new phenomenon; however, the special educational needs of children with motor learning difficulties have, until now, been relatively neglected. Recent years, since the advent of the 1981 Education Act, have seen a growing interest in and awareness of the problems faced by children with a variety of specific learning difficulties. The most widely studied group within this category are dyslexic children who have a specific difficulty learning to read and spell, independent of intellectual disability, gross sensory impairment, inappropriate teaching or emotional disturbance. The recognition of children with specific motor learning difficulties has been more gradual but is certainly growing.

Children are not clumsy by nature, indeed, once the toddler stage has passed, many develop a fluidity of movement that inspires admiration. Children whose movements are awkward and ungainly present an unhappy contrast. They may be mistaken to be of low ability, to be badly behaved or simply to lack motivation. Only when their movement skills are markedly discrepant with their chronological age and perceived intellectual ability will a specific type of developmental disorder be considered. As with dyslexia, these children are often defined by exclusion.

The ability to perform skilled, purposeful movement is often taken for granted within every day life. Only when we watch a child with a physical disability struggle to perform a simple sequence of actions can we begin to appreciate the complexity of processes underlying the development and acquisition of learned movement and the significance of this in gaining mastery over the environment becomes clear.

The importance of motor competence as a prerequisite for accessing the school curriculum is becoming increasingly obvious. Modern teaching methods involve children in more practical work than before. There has been a return to the formal evaluation of handwriting skills. Participation in sports and games is actively encouraged as part of an emphasis on developing a more healthy lifestyle. Motor inco-ordination can present a significant barrier to a child's progress and have a deleterious effect on everyday functioning both at home and at school.

This chapter presents an overview of developmental dyspraxia (one of the terms currently in vogue to describe children with specific motor learning difficulties). It is our intention to alert professionals to some of the possible causes, characteristics and educational consequences of the condition as well as to suggest some practical strategies for intervention.

HISTORICAL CONTEXT

The medical literature reflects a long history of interest in the more obvious movement disorders such as the choreas and cerebral palsy. It was not until the early years of the 20th century that attention began to shift towards describing and explaining the more subtle motor dysfunctions, including physical awkwardness, which were experienced by maturing children when attempting reasonably complex tasks.

As early as 1911, Dupre (cited in De Ajuriaguerra and Stamback, 1969) described a 'motor deficiency syndrome' in children which was characterised by signs including awkwardness of voluntary movement, excessive tendon reflexes, mild hypertonicity (increased muscle tone) and associated movements. Dupre considered the syndrome to be distinguishable from other major motor disorders in which paralysis or muscle weakness was a significant feature by the subtle nature of its neuropathology which affected 'the motor functions in their adjustment to everyday life'.

The clumsy child syndrome was first formulated in the 1930s by observers of children evidencing post-encephalitic complications (Schain, 1972). Initially, physical awkwardness was considered to be related to mild but traditional neurological medical problems such as cerebral palsy. Oseretsky (1931) was one of the first to recognise motor awkwardness as a discrete neuro behavioural entity.

Orton (1937) who studied poor co-ordination among dyslexic children, is credited as being one of the first to recognise the multidimensional nature of motor dysfunction. He wrote that motor co-ordination could reflect both a neurological disorder of praxis (motor planning problem) and also a difficulty caused by poor visual spatial recognition, independent of neural pathologies. Orton was also the first to illuminate the social emotional accompaniments of motor inco-ordination. His description of these children remains easily recognisable today:

"Such children are somewhat delayed in learning even the simpler movements such as walking and running, and have great difficulty learning to use their hands and to copy motions shown to them. They are slow in learning to dress themselves and are clumsy in their attempts to button their clothes, tie their laces, handle a spoon and in other simple tasks."

(Orton, 1937)

Orton was of the opinion that children with what he considered to be 'minimal brain damage' could overcome their difficulties and become proficient in their skills purely by practice and training in the motor tasks they found so difficult. He advised parents to adopt attitudes of 'tolerant amusement' towards such episodes and to view the condition as a constitutional disability as opposed to undue carelessness.

After World War II, interest in awkward children expanded, as motor ineptitude appeared as a symptom in several syndromes. Walton *et al.* (1962) presented case studies of five children referred for assessment who shared the principal feature of severe clumsiness which was serious enough to interfere with essential everyday movement activities such as dressing, feeding, walking, writing, drawing and copying. These children showed no obvious signs of neurological abnormality.

Walton *et al.* (1962) felt that the defects in cerebral organisation evidenced by these children implicated cerebral pathways concerned with the organisation of skilled movement or with the recognition of tactile and other sensory stimuli. They suggested there was a problem with neurophysiology (brain function) rather than brain damage. Further observation suggested that it was never really possible to completely distinguish apraxia from agnosia, for defects of recognition invariably lead to defects of execution. Developmental agnosia and apraxia thus came to be seen as part of a spectrum of developmental disorders affecting speech, reading, movement and spatial orientation which was slowly being better defined. The presumption that children only had to try harder to acquire motor skills was, however, still well entrenched (and to a certain extent remains so even today).

During the 1960s, the concept of 'minimal cerebral dysfunction' was still in favour. This term, which was used to describe a heterogenous group of behaviour syndromes, learning disorders and motor disabilities, served a useful purpose in drawing attention to a large group of children who were often in urgent need of help, but said little about the individual difficulties these children faced, such as language delay, defects in perception or motor organisation and hyperactivity or emotional immaturity, often in a variety of combinations. Such terminology proved unsatisfactory, not only through lack of specificity, but also because of an erroneous supposition that abnormal behaviours were linked to some discrete anatomical brain abnormality. Rarely could the specific site of this 'anatomical abnormality' be demonstrated, indeed, on standard neurological assessment, only minimal signs were present.

Bax and MacKeith (1963) argued cogently that the term 'minimal cerebral damage' should be discarded and research directed towards identifying such children more precisely through more detailed diagnosis. Walton, in a forward to Gubbay's 1975 study, suggested it would be preferable to identify the specific deficits in each child and to describe these under the generic title of 'specific learning difficulties'.

Since Walton *et al.* (1962) published their earlier case studies, several authors have published descriptive clinical material concerning the characteristics shown by clumsy children (Gubbay *et al.* 1965; Dare and Gordon, 1970; Gubbay, 1975; Henderson and Hall, 1982 and Johnston *et al.* 1987). These different authors, by emphasising different core features or constellations of characteristics, have reinforced the realisation that the clumsy child syndrome is made up of several sub-classifications of children including those with and without associated learning problems; those whose problems appear within several task areas versus those whose dysfunctions are more specific; and those whose problems appear to be the result of immaturity versus those whose problems appear to be more long lasting (Silva and Ross, 1980).

Contemporary research into the etiology and diagnosis of clumsiness in children has proceeded slowly. Productive work in the 1980s included an exploration of the sensory perceptual processes that underlie motor awkwardness, the development of more useful assessment instruments and the establishment of studies exploring improved strategies for change. There remains a need for studies designed to clarify causation in order to inform more productive 'syndrome specific' strategies for remediation. The reader is referred to Hulme and Lord (1986) and Kalverboer (1990) for a review of contemporary research.

TERMINOLOGY

(Despite the many arguments for and against labelling children, parents and professionals need an umbrella term to encompass the various difficulties a child may have. A variety of terms have been used throughout this century to describe children with specific motor learning difficulties (see Figure 1). In this chapter we use (developmental) dyspraxia and clumsiness interchangeably as these are the terms we encounter most frequently in schools. Regardless of terminology, it is important to recognise that clumsy children do not form a homogenous group but vary in terms of the pattern, extent and severity of their difficulties.

Fig. 1

congenital apraxia (Orton, 1937) congenital maladroitness (Ford, 1960) developmental apraxia and agnosia (Walton *et al.*, 1962) clumsy child syndrome (Walton *et al.*, 1962 and many others) minimal cerebral dysfunction (Paine, 1968) motor impaired (Whiting *et al.*, 1969) visuomotor inco-ordination (Wilson, 1974) developmental apraxic ataxia (Gubbay, 1975) developmental dyspraxia (Lesny, 1980a) developmental clumsiness (Hulme and Lord, 1986) perceptuo motor dysfunction (Laszlo *et al.*, 1988) specific developmental disorder of motor dysfunction (WHO, 1992) developmental co-ordination disorder (American Psychiatric Association DSM IV, 1994).

Developmental dyspraxia is a relatively recent term. It combines the notion that the disorder has a constitutional origin, possibly resulting from underlying restrictions within the developing brain and nervous system, with the notion that the cognitive drive to organise and plan movement as a response to the perception of sensory input (via sight, sound, smell, vestibular awareness and kinaesthesis) is somehow impaired.

It is not helpful to think of developmental only in the sense of an immaturity, as this implies that with the passage of time, the problem will self-correct. There is mounting evidence to suggest that clumsy children continue to experience difficulties throughout their school career, even into adulthood (Levine, 1984; Gilberg *et al.*, 1989; Geuze and Borger, 1993 and Losse *et al.*, 1991) and that these difficulties can have a profound effect on other areas of family life (Chesson *et al.*, 1990. In other words, children do not just grow out of it.

The terms agnosia, apraxia and dyspraxia have traditionally been used in the field of adult neurology to describe the effects of acquired cerebral lesions in adults. In this sense, these terms would be used to denote loss of a well established function. The use of the term 'developmental' as a prefix is intended to describe interference with the development of a particular function in the first place.

Agnosia is an inability to interpret sensory perceptual input when peripheral pathways bringing such information to the brain are intact. The perception of an object is achieved through integration of sensations from one sensory channel with those obtained from other channels and with memories of sensations derived from previous experience, including actions in response to that sensation. Perception is faulty if this secondary process fails to develop normally.

Apraxia is an inability to carry out purposeful movements requiring the integration of several body parts in the absence of obvious sensory difficulties, mental retardation and/ or other peripheral muscular skeletal problems. There is no memory for patterns of movement, therefore; although the physical ability remains adequate for their performance, the organisation to do so is lacking.

These terms indicate the two main categories of disability affecting the dyspraxic child: defects of perception and motor organisation. In individual cases the child may show a predominance of one or other (in some cases, both).

A key feature of dyspraxia is a delay or inordinate difficulty in learning complex motor acts that require a sequence of movements. Eventually when engrams of the movements do become encoded in the brain, the brain is able to perform learned tasks automatically with improved speed and finesse. Although now successful with this one task, the child will still have difficulties learning other new skills. It is this difficulty in automating complex movements and concomitant difficulty with generalising a learned movement to other tasks or movement sequences that suggests a disorder of cognitive functioning must play a part in the overall problem i.e dyspraxia is a type of specific learning difficulty.

DEFINITION

"The clumsy child is mentally normal, without body deformity; physical strength, sensation and co-ordination are normal on routine testing; there is an impaired ability to perform skilled, purposeful movement."

(Gubbay 1963)

"Clumsy children are a heterogeneous group whose perception of sensory input, organisation of balance or fine movements and mechanism of establishing symbolic or kinaesthetic memory is impaired out of all proportion to their general intelligence yet do not have frank cerebral palsy or other gross neurological deficits."

Miller (1986) described dyspraxia as: *"a disorder of the higher cortical processes involved in the planning and execution of learned, volitional, purposeful movements in the presence of normal reflexes, power, tone, co-ordination and sensation."*

Clarke (1991) defined dyspraxia as: *"a disorder of the quality of movement i.e. the efficiency of co-ordination."*

Deul and Doar (1992) define dyspraxia as: *"an inability to learn or perform serial, voluntary movements with the proficiency expected for age and/ or verbal intelligence, in the absence of abnormalities of volition, strength, co-ordination, motor speed or sensation that are sufficient to explain the poor performance."*

What all clients with dyspraxia have in common is a deficit in motor planning that results in motor clumsiness (Cermak, 1992).

The Dyspraxia Trust (1991) defines dyspraxia as: *"an impairment or immaturity in the organisation of movement which leads to associated problems with language, perception and thought."*

Movement

Dyspraxic children show a marked discrepancy between their movement abilities and age and have inordinate difficulty learning complex motor skills that require a sequence of movements. Gross motor skills (walking, running, throwing and catching) are delayed and they have great difficulty learning to use their hands to copy movements shown to them. Consequently, fine motor skills (eg. threading, buttoning drawing and writing) are hard to learn, difficult to retain and generalise, and hesitant and awkward in performance;

Language

Language may be late to develop and speech articulation may be immature or even unintelligible in the early years due to difficulty making and co-ordinating the precise movements of the speech apparatus (lips, tongue, larynx , soft palate etc.) necessary for clear speech. Language delay may lead to associated learning difficulties with reading and spelling

Perception

Dyspraxic children show impaired understanding of the messages that their senses convey and difficulty relating these messages to actions. This manifests itself through poor concentration and listening skills, poor visual and auditory perception; a lack of spatial and directional awareness and poor perception of self within the environment.

Thought

Dyspraxic children of average intelligence may have great difficulty formulating an idea and/or conceptualising a plan of action as well as organising and sequencing their thoughts. This can make it hard for them to reason through problems or even to know how to begin a task.

Defects of perception and motor organisation are the two main categories of disability affecting the dyspraxic child and the child may show a predominance of one or the other.

HOW DOES IT FEEL?

In order to appreciate the feelings of frustration felt by many dyspraxic children take a few minutes to try the following experiment. Hold a mirror at eye level to reflect a double lined star and then, looking only through the mirror, take a pen in your non-preferred hand and draw a line between the existing lines. Try not to lift your pen off the paper.

Fig. 2

HOW DOES THE CHILD FEEL?

It is important to learn to interpret the child's response carefully for they may not say what they really mean. The actual response is often more subtle and takes considerable discernment to work out, for example, one child accounted for a dislike of team games with the comment, 'everyone is taller than me'.

- It doesn't matter how hard I try, I never win, It's no use, I can't do it.
- It's impossible.
- It's always too difficult.
- My hands forgot what they were supposed to do.
- Playtime is boring.

(Adapted from 'The Child with Motor Learning Difficulties: A Guide for Parents and Teachers, Occupational Therapy Dept., Royal Aberdeen Children's Hospital)

WHY ARE THEY CLUMSY?

Dyspraxia is thought to be caused by a failure of the Central Nervous System (CNS) to organise and plan purposeful motor actions as a response to adequate interpretation, integration and processing of incoming sensory information. It produces a delay in the development and acquisition of motor skills. There is no demonstrable interruption to the message pathways from the brain to muscles and joints via nerves. The precise etiology in individual cases is often unknown.

Lack of Movement Skill

Restricted exposure in early years to motor tasks, particularly within the context of emerging social skills, can present as an apparent developmental motor impairment. In the long term, however, the motor skills of such children seem minimally affected by deprivation and improve rapidly with practice and training.

Specific Pathologies

There are also claims that clumsy children may have suffered brain damage, either prior to, during or after birth. The doctor presented with the child who may be dyspraxic must therefore undertake a thorough developmental and neurological examination to rule out certain pathologies (eg. mild cerebral palsy, cerebellar tumours, hydrocephalus, muscular dystrophy, lower motor neuron disease, visual defects and epilepsy). In some rare progressive conditions, deterioration is slow and may not match the rate of normal maturational rate of a young child, so that some developmental progress is observed.

Acquired Dyspraxia

The term dyspraxia was traditionally used within the field of adult neurology to describe the effects of acquired cerebral lesions in adult stroke patients. Studies of their dyspraxic symptoms led to the formulation of two theoretical models designed to explain the processes contributing to and detracting from efficient motor planning and sequential behaviour. The centre or 'specific lesion' theory proposes that dyspraxia stems from lesions to the specific centres in the brain which are responsible for programming and controlling motor behaviour. Lesions to the motor cortex, for example, have been linked to ideomotor apraxia (difficulties in the ordering and sequencing of sub movements contained within complex skills).

Other researchers (eg. Basso *et al.*, 1980; Alexander and Schmidt, 1980) have argued that specific lesions do not always correspond to predictable patterns of disruption to motor behaviour. They propose an alternative 'disconnection theory' which suggests that dyspraxic symptoms stem from an interruption in pathways linking areas involving information processing centres which mediate the execution of movements. Lesions to the fibres of the corpus callosum, which disrupt communication between the two cerebral hemispheres, have been linked with various motor co-ordination difficulties (Geschwind, 1975). It is probable that insults to pathways as well as subtle lesions to various neural centres combine to cause the various forms dyspraxia and apraxia seen developmentally as well as in adult stroke patients (Cratty, 1990). The following review of the CNS and control of motor skill highlights some of the possible areas where disruption might occur.

THE CENTRAL NERVOUS SYSTEM (CNS) AND CONTROL OF MOTOR SKILL

Neuro behavioural explanations of dyspraxia require an elementary understanding of brain function and organisation.

To perform a skilled movement the brain must first receive the right sensory information (sensation) and then interpret and process this information (perception) before a suitable response can be planned, initiated and effected efficiently by the motor system.

Various parts of the CNS play an important part in the control of body movement, including the spinal cord, medulla, basal ganglia, lower brain (brain stem and cerebellum) and higher brain (cerebral cortex).

Fig. 3

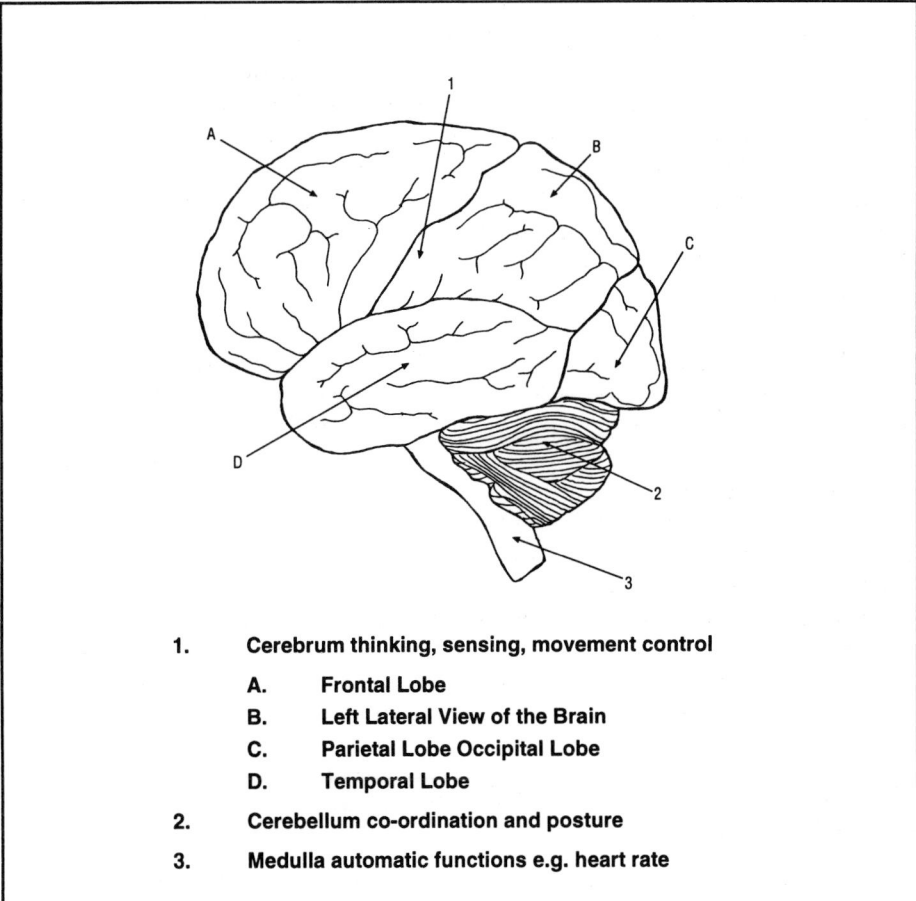

1. **Cerebrum thinking, sensing, movement control**

    A. **Frontal Lobe**
    B. **Left Lateral View of the Brain**
    C. **Parietal Lobe Occipital Lobe**
    D. **Temporal Lobe**

2. **Cerebellum co-ordination and posture**

3. **Medulla automatic functions e.g. heart rate**

Fig. 4

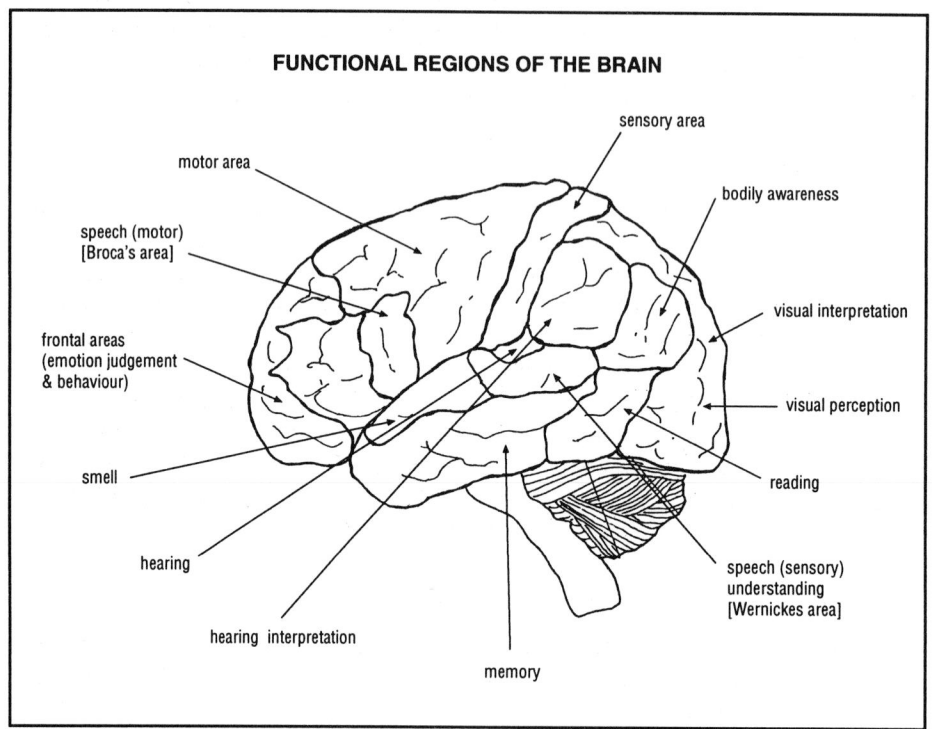

FUNCTIONAL REGIONS OF THE BRAIN

sensory area

motor area

bodily awareness

speech (motor)
[Broca's area]

visual interpretation

frontal areas
(emotion judgement
& behaviour)

visual perception

smell

reading

hearing

speech (sensory)
understanding
[Wernickes area]

hearing interpretation

memory

Sensory Receptors

The human CNS contains a vast number of neurons (nerve cells) linked to receptors which are primed to detect stimuli such as light, sound, pressure of touch, temperature, position and rate of movement. Sensory information is transmitted to the sensory cortex of the brain by way of synapses and dendrites (interconnections). When a nerve fibre of a particular modality is stimulated, the type of sensation felt is determined by the point in the CNS at which that particular nerve fibre terminates.

Somatic Sensory Cortex

Sensory signals of all modalities terminate in an area of the brain called the somatic sensory cortex which corresponds, by and large, to the parietal lobe. The exceptions are visual signals which terminate in the occipital lobe and auditory signals which terminate in the temporal lobe. The somatic sensory cortex has a distinct spatial orientation for the reception of nerve signals from various parts of the body. Each side of the cortex receives sensory information from the opposite side of the body, with communication between the two cerebral hemispheres taking place via the nerve fibres of the corpus callosum. The sensory cortex integrates all the messages before forwarding them to the motor areas of the cortex where decisions are taken as to the kind of response to make.

Motor Cortex

The motor cortex houses an extremely large memory and works in association with other parts of the CNS to fine tune what would otherwise be quite coarse and imprecise motor activities. The motor cortex can be subdivided into the primary motor area (part of the frontal lobe) which is concerned primarily with controlling the hands and speech muscles; the premotor area (located immediately in front of the primary motor area) which has a similar representation of muscle groupings and is concerned with the patterning of muscle movements; and the supplementary motor area which is thought to act in unison with the premotor area to provide attitudinal movements, fixation of parts of the body, positioning of the head and eyes and other manoeuvring movements that facilitate finer control of the hands and feet by the primary motor area.

Transmission from Brain to Muscles

The most important output pathway is the pyramidal tract, the nerve fibres of which originates 30% from the primary motor cortex, 30% from the premotor and supplementary motor areas and 40% from the somatic sensory area. The pyramidal tract travels from the motor cortex right down through the lower brain and brain stem to form part of the spinal cord. On route, most of its nerve fibres cross over to the opposite side of the spinal cord, thus motor representation in the cortex of the left cerebral hemisphere comes from the right side of the body and vice versa.

Extrapyramidal System

Some of the nerve fibres from the motor cortex project directly to other areas of the lower brain, including links to the cerebellum and direct feedback loops to the motor cortex. The term 'extrapyramidal system' is given to these parts of the brain which contribute indirectly to motor control and are not part of the direct corticospinal pyramidal system. The extrapyramidal system has an important function in controlling many of the body's subconscious movements such as breathing, posture and equilibrium.

Cerebellum

Working in association with the motor cortex, the cerebellum plays a major role in co-ordinating patterns of movement involving peripheral body parts (especially the hands, fingers and feet) as well as in sorting out the timing and sequencing of motor responses in preparation for action. The cerebellum receives continuously updated information regarding the desired programme of muscle contractions from the motor control areas of other parts of the brain. It also receives continuous sensory information from peripheral body parts so that it can determine the sequential changes required in each part of the body relating to position, rate and force of movement. If the two sets of data do not compare favourably, signals are immediately transmitted to instruct the motor cortex to increase or decrease the levels of activity required in the muscles concerned. The cerebellum also helps the cortex to plan the next sequential movement a fraction of a second in advance, while the present movement is still being executed as well as to modify the force of a movement where necessary, in order to achieve smooth progression from one movement to another.

Basal Ganglia

The basal ganglia, like the cerebellum, do not function by themselves but in association with the motor cortex and the pyramidal tract. Most of the input signals come from the motor cortex and most of the output is signalled back to the motor cortex directly. One of the main roles of the basal ganglia is to function with the pyramidal tracts to control complex patterns of motor activity (eg. cutting with scissors, passing a football, throwing a ball). They play an important role in the cognitive control of motor activity which determines the speed, pattern and sequence of movement required to achieve a desired response.

CAUSES OF DEVELOPMENTAL DYSPRAXIA

The causes of developmental dyspraxia in children have not been as clearly identified as have lesion behavioural relationships among adult stroke patients, partly because damage to the developing brain is rarely focused or localised in the way damage to an adult brain may occur. Furthermore, children with developmental dyspraxia have no obvious physical or neurological abnormality to explain their condition and typically manifest a more diverse set of symptoms than children with organic brain damage (Lehmkuyl 1984).

Developmental dyspraxia is widely believed to result from a more diffuse disruption of brain anatomy and function. The most likely explanation is that some form of neurological dysfunction has occurred at a microscopic cellular level due to underlying restrictions or limitations within the developing nervous system. Immature neurone development as a consequence of low birth weight and other perinatal stresses (eg. anoxia at birth, viral infections and the effects of toxins) has been offered as a possible explanation (see Gordon and McKinley, 1980).

Brain Growth and Development

Brain development occurs in a complex but predictable sequential pattern. The effect of any insult is therefore dependent on its timing in relation to the events of brain growth with the most severe forms of disruption occurring during the early stages of pregnancy.

During the first three to four weeks after conception a flat plate of cells forms the neural tube. Disruption during this critical early stage may lead to gross abnormalities such as spina bifida or anencephaly and the foetus is unlikely to survive (Nishimura, 1970).

During the third and fourth months of gestation cells along the neural tube divide to create neurons (nerve cells). Although they will continue to grow in size and migrate to eventual locations, the majority of the brain's nerve cells are present midway through pregnancy. Damage at this stage has been associated with severe forms of mental retardation, including spastic cerebral palsy and microcephaly (disproportionately small brains).

The next phase of brain development (the 'brain growth spurt') heralds the rapid growth and development of many neural processes. These include the formation of dendrites (thin projections of the nerve cell body which interconnect with other nerve cells across synapses); an increase in the number of glial cells (provide various support functions including nutrition); and myelination (the formation of lipid insulating sheaths round nerve fibres to speed conduction of electrical discharges). The first two processes start midway through pregnancy and continue for the first two years of life. Myelination begins late in pregnancy and continues until around the time a child begins school. Problems occurring during cellular level processes underlying the maturation of neurological structures may be manifest in numerous ways, including various forms of developmental dyspraxia.

Numerous developmental deficits may be attributable to anomalies in cell migration (the microscopic, neural developmental process by which various types of neurons are transported and relocated to form networks, structures and connections to sensory receptors). Although the precise, biochemical mechanisms facilitating this process have yet to be fully understood, cell migration is known to proceed at different rates in various components of the CNS. Within the cortex, it is normally completed between the 32nd and 34th weeks of gestation, although in other central structures, including the cerebellum, it continues to take place after birth. The cerebellum has been shown to be disproportionately susceptible to processes affecting brain growth in late pregnancy and early infancy (Dobbing and Smart, 1973).

It has also been suggested that disturbance of brain development during the growth spurt may lead to limitations in the numbers of dendrites or glial cells. As a consequence, incoming sensory information may be inaccurately received and/or transmitted and thus fail to achieve the desired effect in terms of motor control or response. Another popular theory behind dyspraxia is that complex interconnections within motor cortex have somehow become mixed up, again causing information to be processed in a random and haphazard way.

Recent researchers have begun to speculate that faulty neural regression (the process by which the developing nervous system eliminates extraneous and apparently unneeded neurons and neural networks) may lead to various forms of unwanted behavioural consequences, including the disruption of perceptual processes, speech difficulties, distractability and excessive motor activity (Carlson, Earls and Todd, 1987). It has been suggested that an over-abundance of nerve cells and neural networks may lead to inefficient use of available biochemical nourishment within the brain. The process of neural regression when completely understood should result in the better understanding of children who may be hyperactive motorically and/or hyper reactive sensorially (Cratty, 1994).

It seems there are various forms of dyspraxia and therefore possibly several causes. A pioneer study of the associations between specific neural insults and behavioural disruptions in children speculated that both brain injuries and cerebral immaturity contribute in various combinations to forms of developmental apraxia and dyspraxia seen among children (Knuckey *et al.*, 1983).

Psychological Accounts of Motor Development

As Henderson (1986) points out, much of the work on defining and describing motor impairments has been undertaken by the medical profession. Existing psychological accounts of motor development are as yet inadequate as models on which to base classification, and without accurate classification, models for causation are difficult to elaborate and test. There are however some useful pointers.

There is an assumption underlying much research on movement control that an entire movement may be centrally represented within the brain in the form of a motor program. The motor program has two phases, one concerned with program construction and the other concerned with implementing the response. Construction of the program involves establishing the end goal of the movement and setting specifications for the movement itself (eg. the muscles to be involved, the timing of the sequence of muscle events and force parameters for the individual muscles). In this way, sensory information is processed, stored and used to determine skilled motor activity.

This suggests there may be three primary points at which skilled motor behaviour may break down: a) in the integration of incoming sensory information, b) centrally in the activation and construction of the program and c) peripherally in the implementation of the motor program.

The work of Ayres (1972) suggests learning and behavioural problems in many children may be due to inadequate sensory integration at a subcortical level. It is assumed that in normal sensory motor development there is a sequence of development in which the tactile and vestibular mechanisms play a primary role. Later developing sensory systems are dependent on adequate integration of earlier ones. Ayres has pioneered a treatment programme (Sensory Integration) that provides and reinforces sensory information to ensure that integrating mechanisms are stimulated to a normal response level.

Hulme *et al.*, (1982) have explored the possible functional importance of perceptual impairments as determinants of clumsiness in children. Visual perceptual input is a prerequisite for skilled movement, particularly perception of distance and spatial relationships. Adequate kinaesthetic perception (the ability to discriminate the position of body parts and the amplitude and direction of their movements) is also necessary. The integration of these cross modal linkages between visual and kinaesthetic modalities, which improves as the child matures, is suggested to be an important determinant of motor skill. In clumsy children, this cross modal linkage has been found to lag behind development in the other sensory modalities. In their experiments, Hulme *et al.*, (1982) found that clumsy children had a basic problem in coding visually perceived length (they had to make successive judgements about the length of straight lines). There was, however, no correlation between the kinaesthetic judgement of length and motor skills generally. This suggests that clumsy children may only display deficiencies in kinaesthetic judgements when attempting reasonably complex tasks (Hulme and Lord, 1986). It has been suggested that kinaesthetic training can improve kinaesthetic perception and kinaesthetic memory (Lazlo and Bairstow, 1983) as well as promote changes in social behaviour (Lazlo and Bairstow, 1988; Lazlo *et al.*, 1989) although not all would agree that it necessarily improves motor performance (Hoare and Larkin, 1991; Polatajko 1995).

There is also evidence to suggest that construction of the central motor program is problematic for some dyspraxic children and that an important component in this is a deficient timekeeping mechanism (Williams, Woollacott and Ivry, 1992). We have already discussed the key role of the cerebellum in timing and central timekeeping mechanisms. Thus, there is a move away from the notion that fixed brain damage or static dysfunction is responsible for the observed difficulties in clumsy children. Further study of the problems exhibited by clumsy children may help to provide more detailed insight into the way the brain normally constructs its plans for motor performance and subsequently lead to the development of appropriate intervention strategies (Deuel and Doar, 1992).

INCIDENCE

Various estimates put the incidence of dyspraxia in school children between 5 15% depending on the definition adopted and identification procedure used (see Henderson S. E., 1992; Gordon N. and McKinley I. 1980). Boys are four times as likely as girls to be affected although girls when affected do appear to have significantly greater problems. Most primary school teachers are likely to have one or two children with such problems in their current classes.

RATIONALE FOR REMEDIATION

Sugden and Henderson (1994) suggest a number of reasons why professionals should concern themselves with the problems of developmental dyspraxia:

1. It can be extremely distressing to children and their families. In many ways, the fact that the children look physically normal makes it more difficult to cope with than if the child were more obviously impaired, hence the term 'hidden handicap' (Sugden and Keogh, 1991).

2. It is widely accepted that the development of sensory motor behaviour (controlled movement) has a part to play in the development of cognitive abilities (thinking and understanding). Children need to experience movement in order to learn about themselves, the relationship to the environment, and the interaction of the two (French and Lee, 1994).

3.   If the condition is not addressed appropriately, it often stays with the child throughout his/ her school career. Unresolved difficulties in the area of sensory motor behaviour have been found to contribute to the development of educational underachievement, emotional and be-havioural difficulties and low self concept (Losse *et al.*, 1991).

ASSESSMENT

"Accurate assessment and successful management go hand in hand. Without a detailed assessment, an intervention programme cannot be geared to the individual needs of the child. Without a well formulated intervention programme, a detailed assessment is only of limited value."

(Sugden and Henderson, 1994)

School teachers, given appropriate INSET training, are in an ideal position to identify clumsy children and to refer on to outside agencies where appropriate. They may obtain evidence about a child's movement difficulties through systematic observation of a child's demeanour and approaches to particular tasks within school and in the playground. Additional information may be obtained from parents as well as by the use of checklists and other informal methods of assessment. Professionals who may give advice and help in assessing and planning remediation of motor co-ordination difficulties include:

- Paediatrician/ School Doctor
- Physiotherapist
- Occupational Therapist
- Speech Therapist
- Educational Psychologist
- PE Specialist

PRESENTATION OF THE DYSPRAXIC CHILD IN SCHOOL

Dyspraxic children may experience a variety of problems in gross or fine motor co-ordination, motor planning and organisation and may differ in the extent to which they are affected by them. The following section is intended to give a general indication of how dyspraxia may manifest itself within the school setting:

Gross Motor Problems

Dyspraxic children can perform basic skills (eg. walking, running, catching, kicking) at a rudimentary level but have difficulty using these skills flexibly and automatically. Many have difficulty with balance as well as with balancing items. They lack awareness of themselves in space and often bump into chairs and tables within the classroom or trip and fall over in the playground. Many have a propensity to get lost in large school complexes. It is not surprising that many are reluctant to participate in team games and other physical activities.

Fine Motor Problems

Poor gross motor skills in turn affect fine motor co-ordination. Some children may perform gross motor movements more competently than fine motor movements and vice versa. Early signs may include undecided hand dominance and difficulties using fingers to button clothes, handle cutlery or play with constructional toys. By school age, the dyspraxic child may not have mastered many of the prerequisite skills necessary to participate fully in everyday classroom and playground activities. They typically have an immature pencil grasp, poor pencil control and difficulty learning to use equipment such as scissors and rulers.

Problems with Written Work

Dyspraxic children are slow to learn to write and experience problems with the presentation and organisation of their written work. They may learn to write neatly at the expense of speed although it generally requires a disproportionate amount of effort to achieve the necessary muscle control. Excessive muscle tension and slow speed of writing are causes of extreme anxiety, particularly when time constraints are imposed as in examination situations.

There is an overall untidiness in the presentation of written work with evidence of frequent rubbing or crossing out. Letter formation and alignment is often erratic, due to an inability to integrate and place letter parts in their proper spatial perspective. They may overrun when composing individual letters due to excessive muscle tension and often appear to have no perception of line and margin. Copying from the blackboard is a particularly arduous task for dyspraxic children with visual perceptual problems who lose their place transposing letters between vertical and horizontal planes.

In addition to problems with the presentation of written work, dyspraxic children have problems formulating their thoughts and ideas for written expression. If offered direction and a plan, they may be able to get on with the story but often have problems sequencing their ideas and show no understanding of beginning, middle or ending. They show a poor concept of time and often confused tenses; punctuation is poor and words may be written backwards or spelt in several different ways. Generally speaking, written work takes a long time to complete and rarely reflects the true verbal potential of the child.

Specific Learning Difficulties with Reading and Maths

"The brain that cannot organise sensory input cannot organise letters and numbers."

(J. Ayres)

Not all dyspraxic children have difficulty learning to read although some have spelling problems associated with immature speech articulation. A delay in reading skills can sometimes occur due to visual memory difficulties or poor visual spatial discrimination eg. analysing the shapes of letters. Some dyspraxic children have difficulty using both eyes to scan a line of print smoothly. As a consequence, key words may be omitted, words or letters may appear in reverse order along a line or may appear to be in wrong line.

Visual perceptual difficulties and problems with sequencing can lead to problems with numeracy: some dyspraxic children have difficulty recognising or copying shapes or figures; remembering number patterns; and laying out arithmetic in the appropriate columns (see Gordon, N. and McKinley, I. 1980 for a fuller explanation).

Memory Impairments

Many dyspraxic children have problems absorbing and recalling information and responding to and carrying out instructions within a busy classroom environment. Children with visual perceptual deficits may have difficulty copying from the blackboard as they are unable to memorise what they have seen on the board and transpose it to the paper on the desk. As well as this they are being asked to rotate this visual image through 90 degrees from the vertical to the horizontal and to transpose the size of the letters involved.

Emotional and Behavioural Difficulties

"Repeated failure in front of their peers to match normal expected performance of skills in the lesson produces and gradually hardens an attitude of failure. They can't play, nobody wants to dance with them; they are never chosen or are last to be chosen for teams; classmates laugh at their inability to cope. This situation reinforces their feelings of inadequacy and their self-esteem and self-image are destroyed."

(Russell, 1988)

Dyspraxic children of average intelligence frequently underachieve academically due to low self-esteem and a lack of confidence. To a certain extent the socio-emotional effects of dyspraxia are related to the child's own personality or character. The timid child may develop a sense of failure and become introverted and depressed. The more outgoing child typically gives up trying and adopts the role of class clown as a way of gaining peer group credibility. The short tempered child, through sheer frustration may become hostile, aggressive and sulky whilst the anxious child may develop non-organic pains and move towards neurosis.

Children with low self-esteem are far more likely to attribute success in any particular task to external factors beyond their own control, so, for example, they will say it was due to luck rather than hard work on their part. One child, when praised for successfully completing a bead threading task replied, 'these beads were easier to thread than the other ones'. The obvious implication is that dyspraxic children need to be told they have made progress for they will not perceive improvement for themselves.

Within class, the dyspraxic child may display disruptive, distractable and inappropriate attention seeking behaviour. Often impulsive, they seem to have no regard for the consequences of their actions. Their inconsequential behaviour together with poor physical co-ordination, has considerable repercussions within their peer group Such children are frequently ostracised from games and sports and can become the victims of playground jokes and bullying.

Dyspraxic children have difficulty establishing friendships within their own age group and are often regarded as loners. A familiar pattern is for friendship to be sought with younger or older children or with adults. Factors creating barriers seem to include: reluctance to take part in sport and other physical activities; poor performance at games together with difficulties understanding the rules; problems sharing and being part of a team; lack of awareness of social rules; and the child's own aggression and impulsive behaviour.

SUMMARY OF PROBLEMS

With clumsy children the difficulty lies in having and using the necessary organisational skills to achieve an intended action rather than in understanding what is required of them or what they want to do.

By definition, the problem lies not with simple tasks but with complex tasks, particularly those involving set sequences of action or response. Within the context of daily living these children face immense difficulties as most complex tasks have many components that are automatically carried out in the correct sequence and frequently simultaneously.

The degree to which an individual child has any or all of the above problems varies a great deal. Unless the problems are very severe they will not prevent the child from learning but they will slow the learning process and make certain areas of the curriculum more difficult to master.

INTERVENTION

"The primary objective of all methods of intervention must be to improve the child's ability to function in everyday life. This involves equal concentration on the child's movement whilst at the same time addressing the issues of coping, adapting and compensating for difficulties that may be hard to remedy. Thus, it may not be realistic to claim to cure clumsiness but to help children make maximum use of their existing resources by opening up new avenues of skill acquisition and developing coping strategies."

(Sugden and Henderson, 1994)

It is difficult to suggest an overall treatment programme as each child will have different problems which will need to be addressed in different ways. Intervention must, above all, be age appropriate, match ability levels and be geared to the child's individual needs and learning style. Emphasis should be placed on: prioritising the skills that the child needs or wants to learn; helping them to develop compensatory strategies to circumvent more persistent problems; and building their confidence and self-esteem. The following sections are intended to offer some practical strategies for dealing with some of the more common problems.

Physical Skills

Dyspraxic children need to be taught physical skills in such a way as to ensure that they can achieve success and thus gain confidence. This requires a more prescriptive, stage by stage approach than might ordinarily be used with frequent opportunities for practice, overlearning and reinforcement. Involving the child in planning and monitoring his own programme should encourage an increased sense of personal commitment and confidence.

Planning Differentiated PE Activities

There are many ways in which physical education activities can be differentiated to meet the needs of the dyspraxic child (Knight, 1991):

1. Wherever possible, efforts should be made to avoid competitive activities such as team sports where a dyspraxic child's lack of skill will distinguish them from their peers. Activities such as stations (see Russell, 1988), circuit training or running where a child is encouraged to improve upon his own performance, or activities such as dance, music and drama are preferable. Parental involvement in activities such as horse riding or swimming is also to be encouraged.

2. PE equipment should be kept to a minimum to avoid clutter, and materials selected which are appropriate for the situation and level of performance of the child. Large, brightly coloured balls and beanbags can be introduced to simplify throwing and catching techniques. Plastic bats are lighter and easier to manage in one hand. Provision should also be made for dyspraxic children to work on apparatus at lower levels eg. benches and mats, as opposed to horses during gymnastics.

3. Working in pairs or small groups is preferable to whole class situations for games, as children get more turns this way. Where group work is unavoidable, membership and team leaders should be varied to allow children the opportunity to mix. Staff may wish to consider grouping children according to their levels of motor ability and forming lunchtime clubs. Many dyspraxic children will benefit from short, daily sessions of targeted practice, gradually increasing the degree of movement difficulty required.

4. It is important to ensure that children can see and hear the teacher and understand the language that they use. Information should be stated clearly with instructions given one at a time. It helps to reinforce and practise the meaning of STOP at the beginning of each lesson. Visual cues and practical demonstration may be used to reinforce auditory verbal information across the whole curriculum.

5. The size of the playing area can be made smaller by, for example, creating artificial boundaries using hoops or lines, thereby reducing the amount of gross motor activity proportionately. Individual mats can give structure to a PE lesson, security to the timid child and firm boundaries to the lively child who is here, there and everywhere! The length of a pitch or distance from targets in aiming or throwing activities can be reduced in similar ways. Substituting beanbags for balls decreases the distance the implement travels and reduces the play area accordingly.

6. Children should be given plenty time to work out their ideas and realistic time limits for the completion of tasks.

7. Give lots of praise for effort as well as actual achievement but encourage the child to talk about their feelings of frustration if they do fail. Above all, try to make activities fun as well as functional for if you enjoy yourself, chances are the children will too.

8. Changing for swimming or PE may present additional problems for the dyspraxic child. Parental involvement should be sought in teaching the child a set system for removing clothes and dressing eg. always start with the shoes and socks. Look at small steps needed to achieve goal and teach systematically, starting with undressing first. Make sure the child is correctly positioned eg. has chair to sit on when removing shoes and socks. Avoid clothes that are too tight; use velcro on shoes rather than shoe laces and choose clothes with a distinctive front and back eg. V neck jumpers or labels on back.

Fine Motor Co-ordination

Young children will benefit from activities which involve manual dexterity, particularly those which involve a speed element to encourage automatic activity. Possible activities include:

Bead Threading	Pastry Cutters and Playdough
Picking up Small Articles	Dressing and Undressing
Connect a Straw	Brick Building
Construction Toys	Finger Games (Church and Steeples)
String Games	

When selecting activities for older children it is important to teach and practise skills which will have a beneficial effect on other skills and improve the child's ability to function independently in everyday life. A programme of perceptual motor activities will, for example, be more beneficial for developing a child's early handwriting skills than a course of bead threading. Perceptual motor activities might include:

Shape and Pattern Copying	Copying Pegboard Designs
Mazes, Spot the Difference,	Drawing around Stencils
What's Missing?	Finishing Shapes
Tracing	

Colouring In

Writing with Eyes Closed

Doodles on the Blackboard

Pre-Writing Patterns

Writing Letters in Air/Sand/Feely Double Letters

Figure of eight in air with preferred hand/non-preferred hand/both hands simultaneously.

Handwriting

It is important to judge dyspraxic children against their own best efforts and to constantly praise and encourage them to progress in their own way and in their own time.

1.   A structured handwriting programme practised for a few minutes on a daily basis will help to encourage the development of a more automatic and less cortical handwriting style. When children can write and join letters automatically, they are free to concentrate on the intellectual components of spelling, sentence structure and creative composition.

2.   Multi-sensory teaching methods and practice in pre-writing skills (see above) should be used to draw attention towards the motor components of handwriting (as opposed to perceptual problems). Encourage the child to verbalise the nature and directions of strokes while tracing and drawing individual letters.

3.   Teaching a cursive handwriting style will help with aspects such as word spacing and help to reinforce the kinaesthetic memory of words. For difficult cursive letters, it may be necessary to work initially on component parts of letters and gradually build these up to whole letter forms.

4.   Correct sitting posture (i.e feet firmly on the floor, bottom squarely on the chair and some form of support at the bottom of the spine) is very important as an aid to learning the motor control of writing. Good postural training means starting with appropriate furniture for an individual's size. A sloping writing surface encourages pupils to move their shoulders backwards and sit up straighter, thereby attaining the desired focal length for close work. Commercial ones are available although a large atlas propped up on a few books or a ring binder sloping towards a child can be just as effective.

5. Appropriate paper position aids posture and ensures that writers can see what they are doing without twisting either their hand or their own body. Paper is usually best placed to the side of the hand that writes, which means allowing sufficient desk or table space for each child. Alternatively, if the work to be copied is fixed to the top of a sloping board it will all come within the same visual field.

6. A wide variety of pens and pencils should be made available to enable children to choose which suits then best. Pencil grips are available commercially and triangular shaped pencils are also available from LDA. An unconventional penhold need not necessarily be corrected. Older children with poor motor control may have found something that gives them more support and works reasonably well for them.

7. Efforts should be made to avoid excessive written work, especially work which involves copying from the blackboard as dyspraxic children frequently lose their place transposing letters between planes. It is preferable, although admittedly more time consuming, for work to be written in the child's workbooks or for worksheets to be provided.

8. Dyspraxic children may require extra time to complete written work. Where appropriate, they should be encouraged to take brief notes, write key words or to annotate diagrams in place of copious notes. Special arrangements may be required when taking examinations.

9. Typewriters, word processors or computers can be helpful in some cases to supplement, but not to take the place of handwriting. Such machines may take the pressure off children and enable them to get their ideas down with a satisfying and more acceptable presentation. Discretion should be used as some children with co-ordination difficulties may also have difficulty locating keys and learning to type.

Reading

The dyspraxic child who is struggling with reading may have difficulty controlling his/her eye muscles. In this case, parents should be encouraged to take the child to an orthoptist or opthamologist to advise on appropriate exercises for remediation. If the child has difficulty directing his or her eyes, cardboard windows or coloured overlays may help to minimise visual distractions. Systematic, structured, multi-sensory teaching approaches, which are well described elsewhere in the present publication, are most beneficial.

Memory

Dyspraxic children may have difficulty directing their attention within a busy classroom:

1.   Keep instructions clear and concise and ensure you have the child's attention before starting to speak. It can help to preface instructions with a warning (eg. John, in a moment I am going to ask you) to ensure that the child is ready to listen.

2.   Encourage the child to repeat back key points as well as to talk through tasks as their own voice will help to direct their motor movements and serve as a useful tool to memory.

3.   Visual cues and practical demonstrations may be used to supplement auditory verbal material. In some cases, written checklists or pictorial reminders may be beneficial.

Self-Esteem

Teachers can significantly influence the development of a positive self-image by providing experiences that can enhance a child's confidence and self-esteem:

1.   All staff should be encouraged to develop a sympathetic attitude towards the child with dyspraxia and to show positive expectations of their work and behaviour.

2.   Changing self-esteem requires an intense focusing on individual attributes, accentuating the positives and rewarding effort as well as actual achievement with genuine praise.

3.   The child should be provided with opportunities to carry out relevant tasks where success is guaranteed. This may necessitate breaking tasks down into smaller, more realistic and achievable steps, allowing extra time to complete written work and expecting less in terms of quantity.

4.   It helps to have the child seated near the teacher so that she can readily observe how much effort is being put into work, less obviously

help to keep the child on task and know when to intervene and change the activity before frustration boils over.

5. Communicate to the child the attitude that doing your best is what counts, not always doing better than others. Teaching and reinforcing positive self-talk can help to counteract any negatives the child may engage in (e.g. I'm not a failure because I didn't make it, I'm a success because I tried).

6. Give the child some responsibility within the classroom to develop their self-esteem and increase their social profile amongst their peers. Involving children in setting their own targets helps to ensure motivation and self-confidence. Parents can also help to find opportunities outside the classroom to acknowledge the child.

Social Integration

The teacher must also accept that the child's behaviour is neither a reflection of his/ her ability to control or to motivate children nor the result of bad parenting. The dyspraxic child lacks foresight and may not have the necessary structure and planning to achieve the desired behaviour.

1. Avoid using rewards as incentives as the child with dyspraxia has a physical problem and is probably already trying as hard as they can. They need to be told where they are going wrong and given structure to regulate and modify their behaviour.

2. Tell other children about dyspraxia to help them understand why the dyspraxic child behaves as he does and is not always reprimanded.

3. Staff on playground duty should be aware of the child's apprehension/risk of bullying and observe carefully from a distance.

4. Provide quiet areas where children can sit and chat as an alternative to charging around the playground.

5. Consider asking an interested teacher in school to organise a very low key 'lunch club' to provide children with appropriate movement activities and to encourage social interaction.

CONCLUSION

Although dyspraxia is not curable, evidence suggests the child will improve in some areas with growing maturity and can be helped to a large extent with appropriate teaching, understanding and encouragement to overcome the continuing problems they will face.

Dyspraxic children, often of average ability, are generally underachievers primarily because they are misunderstood and give up the struggle to achieve. If help is sought, there is a great deal that can be done to help these children achieve their full potential.

Early identification is essential and teachers are in an ideal position to observe any motor difficulties in the classroom. Even just by improving self-esteem and confidence, improved school performance can be achieved.

FURTHER INFORMATION

Further information can be obtained by contacting:
The Dyspraxia Trust
PO Box 30
Hitchin
Hertfordshire
SG5 1UU
Tel: 01462 454986.

REFERENCES

American Psychiatric Association (1994). *Diagnostic and Statistical Manual of Mental Disorders*, 4th Edition, Washington DC, American Psychiatric Association.

Ayres, J. (1972). *Sensory Integration and Learning Disorders*. Western Psychological Services, Los Angeles.

Alexander, M. P. and Schmitt, M. A.(1980). The aphasia syndrome of stroke in the left anterior cerebral artery territory. *Archives of Neurology*, 37, 97-100.

Basso, A., Luzszatti, C. and Spinler, H. (1980). Is ideomotor apraxia the outcome of damage to well defined areas of the left hemisphere? Neuropsychological study of CAT correlation *Journal of Neurology, Neurosurgery and Psychiatry*, 43, 118-126.

Bax, M. and MacKeith, R. (1963). Defining the Concept of Minimal Brain Damage, In *Minimal Cerebral Dysfunction, Clinics in Developmental Medicine*, 10, Bax, M. and MacKeith, L. Ú. R. (Eds.). Spastics International London.

Carlson, M., Earls, F. and Todd, R. D. (1988). The importance of regressive changes in the development of the nervous system: toward a neurological biological theory of child development. *Psychiatric Development* , 7, 1-12.

Chesson, R., McKay, C. and Stephenson, E. (1990). Motor Learning Difficulties and the Family. Child Care, Health and Development, 16, 123-138.

Clarke, W. (1991). Occupational Therapy and the Dyspraxic Child in *Praxis Makes Perfect*, Dyspraxia Trust, Hitchin, Herts.

Cratty, B. J. (1994). *Clumsy Child Syndromes: Descriptions, Evaluation and Remediation.* Chur, Switzerland, Harwood Academic.

Cratty, B. J. (1990). Motor development of infants subject to maternal drug use: Current evidence and future research directions, *Adapted Physical Activity Quarterly* , 7, 110-125.

Cermak, S. (1985). Developmental Dyspraxia in Roy, E. A, *Neuropsychological Studies of Apraxia and Related Disorders* , 225-243, North Holland, New York.

Curry, D. (1991). Breaking the cycle of failure. *Special Children* , 49, 10-12.

Dare, M. T. and Gordon, N. (1970). Clumsy children a disorder of perception and motor organisation. *Developmental Medicine and Child Neurology*, 12, 178-185.

De Ajuriaguerra, J. and Stambeck, M. (1969). Developmental dyspraxia and psychomotor disorders. In *Handbook of Clinical Neurology* (Vol. 4) Vinken, P and Bruyn, G., (Eds.). Amsterdam.

Deul, R. K. and Doar, B. P. (1992). Developmental Manual Dyspraxia: A Lesson in Mind and Brain. *Journal of Child Neurology* 7, 99-103.

Dyspraxia Trust (1991). *Developmental Dyspraxia Explained*, The Dyspraxia Trust, Hitchin, Herts.

Dyspraxia Trust (1991). *Praxis Makes Perfect*. Dyspraxia Trust, Hitchin, Herts.

Geschwind, N. (1975). The apraxias: Neural mechanisms of disorders of learned movement. *American Scientist*, 63, 188-195).

Gillberg, I. C .and Gillberg, C. (1989). Children with preschool minor neurodevelopmental disorders IV: Behaviour and school achievement at age 13. *Developmental Medicine and Child Neurology*, 31, 3-13.

Gordon, N. and McKinley, I. (1980). *Helping Clumsy Children*. Gordon, N. and McKinley, I. (Eds.). Churchill Livingston, London.

Grimley, A. M. D. and McKinley, I. A. (1977). *The Clumsy Child,* Association of Paediatric Chartered Physiotherapists.

Gubbay, S. S. (1975). *The Clumsy Child a Study of Developmental Apraxia and Agnosic Ataxia*. Saunders, London.

Gubbay S. S., Ellis, E., Walton J. N. and Court, S. D. M. (1965). Clumsy Children: A Study of Aparxic and Agnosic Defects in 21 Children, *Brain* 88, 295-312.

Hall, D. M. B. (1988) Clumsy Children, *British Medical Journal* ,296,375,376.

Henderson, S. E. (1986). Problems of Motor Development Some Practical Issues. *Advances in Special Education*, 5, 187-218.

Henderson, S. E. and Hall, D. (1982). Concomitants of clumsiness in young school children, *Developmental Medicine and Child Neurology*, 24, 448-460.

Hulme, C. and Lord, R. (1986). Clumsy children a review of recent research. *Child Care, Health and Development,* 12, 257-269.

Kalverboer, A. F. (Ed.) (1990). *Developmental Biopsychology Experimental and observational Studies of Children at Risk*, Ann Arbor MI University of Michigan Press.

Knight, E. (1991). The Dyspraxic Child In and Around School in *Praxis Makes Perfect,* 8, 2731. The Dyspraxia Trust, Hitchin, Herts.

Knuckey, N. W., Apsimon, T. T, and Gubbay, S. S. (1983). Computerised axial tomography in clumsy children with developmental apraxia and agnosia. *Brain and Development* 5,14-19.

Laszlo, J. and Bairstow, P. (1989). Process Orientated Assessment and Treatment of Children with Perceptuomotor Dysfunction. *Clinical and Abnormal Psychology*, Lovibond, P. and Wilson, P. (Eds.). North Holland Elsevier Science.

Laszlo, J. and Bairstow, P. (1983). Kinaesthesis: its measurement, training and relationship to motor control. *Quarterly Journal of Experimental Psychology* , 35A, 411-421.

Lehmkuyl, G. (1984). Ideomotor and Ideatory Apraxia in Childhood. *Acta Paedopsychiatrica* 50, 97-110.

Lesny, I. A. (1980a). Developmental Dyspraxia and Verbal Dyspraxia. *Developmental Medicine and Child Neurology*, 22, 407.

Lesny, I. A. (1980b). Developmental dysgraphia dysgnosia as a cause of congenital children's clumsiness, *Brain and Development*, 2, 69-71.

Levine, M. D. (1984). Cumulative Neurodevelopmental Debts: Their Impact on Productivity in Late Middle Childhood. In Levine, M. D. and Satz, P. (Eds.) *Middle Childhood: Development and Dysfunction.* Baltimore, University Park Press.

Losse, A., Henderson, S. E., Elliman, D., Hall, D., Knight, E. and Jongmans, M. (1991). Clumsiness in Children Do they grow out of it? A 10 year Follow up Study. *Developmental Medicine and Child Neurology*, 33, 55-68.

Marieb, E. N. (Ed.). *Human Anatomy and Physiology*, Chapter 12, The Central Nervous System, 387, Benjamin, Cummings Pub. Co (USA).

Orton, S. T. (1937). *Reading, writing and speech problems in children.* Norton Co., New York.

Oseretsky, N. A. (1931). Methoden der untersuchung der motorile, Heft 57. Beihefte Zur Zeitschrift Fur Ange Wandte Psychologie, Barth, Leipzig.

Paine, R. S. (1968). Syndromes of 'minimal cerebral damage', *Paediatric Clinics of North America,* 15, 779-801.

Russell, J. P. (1988). *Graded Activities for Children with Motor Difficulties.* Cambridge University Press.

Schain, R. J. (1972). *Neurology of Childhood Learning Disorders.* Baltimore, Williams & Wilkins.

Stephenson, E. (1986). Children with motor learning difficulties. *A Guide for Parents and Teachers.* Occupational Therapy Department, Royal Aberdeen Children's Hospital, Aberdeen.

Sugden, D. A. and Henderson, S. E. (1994). Help with Movement. *Special Children* , 75, Back to Basics 13.

Sugden, D. A. and Keogh J. F. (1991). *Problems in movement skill and development.* Columbia: University of South Carolina Press.

Walton, J. N., Ellis, E. and Court, S. D. M. (1962). Clumsy Children, a study of developmental apraxia and agnosia, *Brain*, 85, 603-612.

Whiting, H. T. A., Clarke, T. A. and Morris, P. R. (1969). A clinical validation of the Stott Test of Motor Impairment. *British Journal of Social and Clinical Psychology*, 8, 270-274.

WHO (1992). *The ICD 10 Classification of Mental and Behavioural Disorders: Clinical Descriptions and Diagnostic Guidelines.* WHO, Geneva.

Williams, H. G, Woollacott, M. H. and Ivry, R. (1992). Timing and Motor Control in Clumsy Children. *Journal of Motor Behaviour* , 24, 165-172.

Wilson, R. G. (1974). The Clumsy Child. *Midwife and Health Visitor* , 10, 53-55.

DYSLEXIA AND THE LINKS WITH MOTOR PROBLEMS

LIZ STEPHENSON
AND ELIZABETH FAIRGRIEVE

INTRODUCTION

By no means do all dyslexic children experience motor difficulties but a significant proportion do. It has been estimated that approximately 50% form a sub-type who have some motor dysfunction. (Regehr and Kaplan, 1988). Similarly not all children with mild motor dysfunction (Developmental Co-ordination Disorder) experience dyslexic-type learning difficulties. Whilst links between the temporal aspects of linguistic ability and hand movements are accepted, the reasons remain unclear. As yet no direct relationships between development of functions can be inferred. The domains appear related functionally but further clinical research is essential. Nevertheless, we are required to meet the needs of these children and fuller understanding and more accurate assessment is required of those professionals involved.

It has been suggested that developmental dyslexia is a symptom of a more general and pervasive deficit. (Nicholson and Fawcett, 1990). Quoting from the British Child Health and Education Study (1985), they state that close observation of dyslexic children and reports from their parents indicate that there is often impairment of basic skills masked by coping strategies and increased attention to tasks i.e. these children 'work harder than normal children'.

Over the years three main theoretical frameworks have emerged.

1. **Left Hemisphere Dysfunctions**

    Because of its relationship with linguistic functions, this assumes the left hemisphere to be preferentially pre-programmed for control of timing processes in language plus temporal resolution of perceptuo-motor information and more general motor output.

2. **Inter-Hemispheric Collaboration Deficit**

    (Corpus callosum disorder)

There is much conjecture about how information is passed between hemispheres. Variations in the dynamics of this interaction may be a factor.

It has been suggested that there is a possible interaction between 1 and 2. (Gladstone and Best, 1989).

3.   **Cerebellar-Vestibular Theory**
Levinson (1980, 1984) first considered a possible cerebellar-vestibular link with dyslexia. Whilst many of the signs he described are consistent with those commonly found in dyslexia, to date, scientific research has not universally supported this.

The experience of this chapter's authors suggests that dysfunctions seen in dyslexic children may fit any one of these three theoretical frameworks. However there may be some children in whom the problem is mainly visuo-spatial and more likely to be linked with right hemisphere dysfunction.

LINKS BETWEEN DYSLEXIA AND SPECIFIC PROBLEMS

Many authors describe specific types of motor problems which link with dyslexia. These correspond with the authors' clinical experience and with the motor problems described in the classifications developed by Ayres (1972, 1979) and Fisher, Murray and Bundy (1991).

The following are the most common motor features to be discussed:

Poor Bilateral Integration

This is one of the most common features, and is considered by several authors to be a problem associated with dyslexia. Marshall, Gladstone *et al.* (1989) state that 'bilateral motor abnormalities have been clinically observed for many years in reading disordered children' and go on to say that their own findings support the hypothesis that 'dyslexics manifest intermanual co-ordination deficits'.

Other authors go further and acknowledge not only a link between bimanual co-ordination and speech and language, but suggest that bimanual co-ordination may be the most 'direct precursor of speech and language' (Wolff, Michel, Orrut 1990), surely good reason to consider bilateral integration in relation to dyslexia.

Many other authors focus on bilateral integration problems. Hoffman (1980), in a study of children with specific learning difficulties, found that 45.8% had bilateral integration problems; and Wolff, Michel and Orrut (1990) found that the bilateral integration problems demonstrated by approximately 50% of dyslexics suggested a 'subgroup' who showed this feature. They, like Rousselle and Wolff (1991), describe the major difficulty as being related to asynchronous, asymmetrical bilateral tasks.

Wolff, Michel and Orrut propose that problems with interaction between the cerebral hemispheres may be a factor which accounts for both interlimb timing deficits and the difficulties in learning to read which are found in dyslexics. Rousselle and Wolff similarly describe interhemispheric transfer problems which may be 'outwardly expressed as an interference with interlimb co-ordination for functionally specific tasks'.

Lack of clearly established hand dominance

This has also been considered, over the years, in relation to dyslexia. Certainly in the authors' experience there appears to be a relationship between the two. As long ago as 1937, Orton first described the importance of 'mixed dominance', and Rice (1969) suggested that children with poorly established dominance also have directional confusion and reversal of letters, numbers and words.

Problems with direction and orientation

These are also described by several authors. Hoffman, in his study of children with specific learning difficulties, found as many as 78.3% had problems with directionality, and Levinson (1980 and 1984) described many dyslexic children as showing right/left directionality confusion, in addition to associating it with balance problems due to a possible cerebellar/vestibular link with dyslexia. Morrison and Sublett (1980) also described a subgroup of children with specific learning difficulties who, in addition, had problems associated with balance and corresponding disorders in visuo-motor integration. Hoffman similarly described a very high proportion (81.3%) of children with visuo-motor integration problems in his specific learning difficulties study.

Timing, rhythm and sequence difficulties

'One of the defining features of good motor co-ordination is good timing.' (Geuze and Kalverboer 1994.) Wolff, Michel and Orrut (1990) suggest that the problems of tempo, prosody and rhythm experienced by dyslexics in relation to language and reading also apply to writing and other skilled manual tasks. Rousselle and Wolff (1991) also state that many dyslexics have difficulty in performing manual and motor skills requiring timing, precision and serial action.

Eye movement problems

Another well discussed area is the relationship of 'abnormal' eye movements to dyslexia, though as Fagan *et al*, (1985) point out, the results of research on the nature and prevalence have been inconsistent. Several studies do, however, describe abnormal or erratic eye movements in children with reading difficulties (Regehr and Kaplan, 1988). Hoffman, in his 1980 study of children with specific learning difficulties was also interested in the link between visual problems and specific learning difficulties. Recently it has been suggested that 'what children see affects how they spell' (Cornellison *et al*, 1994); the authors link unstable binocular control with limited visual memories for letter strings resulting in phonologically plausible, but erroneous spelling. Clinical experience of the authors, again, substantiates a link.

ASSESSMENT

The literature has illustrated the fact that many dyslexic children have motor problems (Regehr and Kaplan, 1988); and clinical experience of the authors suggests that many children with Developmental Co-ordination Disorder have specific learning difficulties. A pilot study by one of the authors (Stephenson *et al*. 1989, 1990, 1991) found that 23/31 children with Developmental Co-ordination Disorder were receiving learning support, 15 specifically for reading, writing and spelling i.e. 50% of the total. The study also indicated that most referrals to Occupational Therapy were initiated by educational psychologists. It therefore follows that teachers must be key people in the identification process.

Peer problems were common in these children and behaviour problems were frequent, though only four children were still experiencing the latter following identification and intervention.

The teacher's role is therefore critical, and probably best summed up by the key 'Recommendations' made in the same paper:

1.   Education staff should be the key people in identification, remediation and changing attitudes.
2.   Teachers have an essential role in identification from the day the child enters school. This should be acknowledged.
3.   Teachers should initiate the referral process.
4.   Teachers need the knowledge and understanding to do this.

The role of this chapter is to provide this in order to enhance the teacher's ability to identify, thereby leading to remediation or referral.

Liaison between education professionals and therapists enhances the child's potential for learning and for increased self-esteem.

Clinical experience of the authors suggests that the motor problems commonly seen in dyslexic children closely relate to those included in 'Vestibular – Bilateral Integration Dysfunction' (Ayres 1972, 1979) or more recently 'Postural Ocular and Bilateral Integration and Sequencing Disorder' (Fisher, Murray and Bundy, 1991). In either case, the clinical signs and performance symptoms described are similar. Ayres' classification also includes 'Vestibular Language Disorders' i.e. problems with articulation and language. The literature, as previously discussed, strongly supports these links. Solan, an optometrist, described children with specific learning difficulties as often having had histories of clumsy motor skills (e.g. skipping, laces, buttons, cutting) in kindergarten and first grade; and proposed that these problems were suggestive of a child with potential specific learning difficulties (Solan, 1979).

Teachers need, therefore, to be able to recognise these motor features, which are frequently more pronounced in younger and pre-school children and may act as early predictors of possible dyslexic-type problems.

These signs (clinical) and symptoms (performance) include the following:

(NB They are set out with a clinical bias (i.e. as they most commonly present to the clinician). Those features which have been previously discussed as frequently occurring in the literature regarding motor links with dyslexia are asterisked.)

Low muscle tone
A feeling of softness in the muscles; floppiness; a 'rag doll-like' quality.

Poor co-contraction
An inability to stabilise a joint (by simultaneously contracting the muscles around it). Co-contraction allows us to control a movement throughout its range, or to stabilise the joint whilst performing another movement. (e.g. stabilising posture and shoulder joint whilst moving the wrist and fingers in order to write).

Clumsy, inflexible movement
Resulting from the child's need to fix his otherwise 'wobbly' joints, in an attempt to achieve stability.

Immature postural responses

Lack of the automatic righting, equilibrium and saving reactions which are required for balance. These responses let us correct head position in relation to body movement, adjust posture in subtle ways and save ourselves by protective extension of our arms when falling.

> NB. The last can be a conscious, learned response which children use to compensate for lack of spontaneous righting reactions and adjustments.

Persistence of some primitive reflexes

Some of the basic, automatic motor patterns which a baby requires in order to develop, persist and interfere with the acquisition of more sophisticated postural responses and movement e.g. when a baby turns its head, its body follows. This enables it to roll. If, however, this reflex persists and the child's body continues to turn with its head, this inevitably limits the development of sophisticated, segmented movement.

Slumped sitting posture

Resulting from many of the above factors, and largely outwith the control of the child, often interpreted by teachers as laziness or unwillingness to apply himself to a task.

Unclear hand preference*

Inconsistent choice of hand. This needs to be noted during many activities; not simply pencil skills.

Avoidance of midline crossing*

An inability to cross the midline of the body thereby being unable to work in the opposite side of space. The child will use a variety of strategies to avoid crossing the midline e.g. changing hands at midline; turning the body when reaching to the opposite side; leaning far over to the side; placing all materials to one side of the desk. Always check carefully, therefore, to see whether the child actually does cross its own midline.

Ipsilateral hand use*

A tendency to use each hand on its own side of the body, again avoiding crossing the midline.

Poor ocular-motor control across midline*

Observed as a blink or 'skip' at the midline during attempts at smooth visual pursuit; or a complete loss of the visual stimulus at the midline. May cause the child to skip words, skip a line, or completely lose his place in a text.

Right/left confusion*
Confusion over right and left, of own body and space.

Bilateral integration problems*
Difficulty with the co-ordination of body sides. Often, particular difficulty with reciprocal (i.e. alternating) bilateral movement, or asymmetrical movement i.e. integrating two body sides when each is performing a different movement (as required for tying laces, using cutlery etc.) Recently, particular difficulty with bilateral projected action sequences has been described e.g. performing consecutive jumps; catching a ball on the rebound etc.

These clinical signs are commonly linked with the following 'symptoms':

–   Reading difficulty (including reading backwards).
–   Problems with rote learning (tables, months of year, days of week etc.).
–   Confusion of orientation of letters, numbers, words, shapes (i.e. reversal or inversion).
–   Confusion over right and left in space and in relation to direction.
–   Problems with P.E. and games.
–   Intolerance of stress; frustration and, inevitably, low self-esteem.

It is essential to link the signs and symptoms and never to consider them in isolation. Always consider any child with known speech and language problems, which may be early predictors. If concerned, balance the extent of motor difficulty with any specific learning difficulty, and refer on if the motor component seems significant.

Referral procedures vary from area to area, but the teacher's first resource is usually the educational psychologist or school doctor who will refer on to the appropriate medical facility. A paediatrician's opinion is important in order to exclude any more serious neurological, or muscular condition. Some areas have developed standard screening systems e.g. Grampian has a motor-learning difficulties clinic which comprises a medical examination followed by occupational therapy screening assessment.

Results of therapy assessment usually fall into clusters of signs which link with specific performance symptoms. This, in its turn, can help the decision regarding the need for direct therapy (and its nature) balanced against the option of consultation or a school or home-based programme as possible alternatives.

THERAPY INTERVENTION

Assessment is the essential precursor to therapy and may be the only intervention required. Continued involvement can take several forms which, to maximise effects, involves liaison with home and school. Occupational therapists and/or physiotherapists have become increasingly involved in recent years. The extent varies according to locality. Therapists focus on sensori-motor skills and the impact of problems on the child's abilities at home and school.

Claims made in earlier research on positive outcomes following specific therapy interventions have been questioned and largely refuted (Polatajko, Law, Miller, Shaffer, McNab, 1991; Polatajko, Kaplan, Wilson, 1992). Inherent problems in conducting research into the effects of therapy are many. The group of children are broad and heterogeneous with problems ranging from Developmental Co-ordination Disorder (DCD) to dyslexia. Most studies have focused on the DCD group. (Law, Polatajko, Shaffer, Miller, McNab, 1991; Kaplan, Polatajko, Wilson, Faris, 1993).

Theoretical frameworks underlying specific therapy approaches have been questioned as well as research methods. Nevertheless, those involved with these children seek the best possible intervention package. At the present state of research comparing therapy approaches, no one method emerges as the method of choice. (Humphries, Wright, Snider, McDougall, 1992; Wilson, Kaplan, Fellowes, Gruchy, Faris, 1992; Humphries, Snider, McDougall, 1993; Kaplan, Polatajko, Wilson, Faris, 1993). Therefore, the optimal approach appears to be multi-faceted and inter-disciplinary.

Types of Therapy Involvement

1. Consultation – interpretation of results related to child's needs is the essential aftermath of assessment. Thereafter, continued access for parents and teachers to a consultation service may be the most appropriate input. Programmes already initiated within schools can be entirely appropriate.

2. Direct Therapy – may be appropriate for a stated period. Three main models are identified (Table II), each designed to meet comprehensive needs. In practice, an integrated approach is more usual.

3. School Programme – devised and graded by therapist in collaboration with school and implemented by teachers/support staff; can be integrated into child's total educational programme; requires regular review by all concerned.

4.   Home Programme – devised and graded by therapist in collaboration with parents, implemented within family and reviewed as
needed; may include activities for specific needs and/or recreational
pursuits.

These are not exclusive. For instance, a child receiving weekly therapy may
also have activities incorporated into home and school life.

Criteria influencing type of intervention

Decisions regarding the most appropriate programme involve balancing a
variety of factors affecting the child, his/her family and school as well as local
therapy resources. The range of these are outlined in Table I. The natural
assumption is that direct therapy will yield better outcomes. In the experience of
the authors, indirect therapy can prove just as effective though we do not know of
research in this sphere.

TABLE 1 – PLANNING THERAPY INPUT – FACTORS TO CONSIDER				
THERAPEUTIC		**CHILD**	**ENVIRONMENTAL**	
ASSESSMENT	**RESOURCES**		**FAMILY**	**SCHOOL**
Type of disorder	Service model	Age	Structure and size	Type of school
Degree of disorder	Experienced therapists	Perceived competence	Location/space/ resources of home	Class size
Balance of motor and academic learning problems	Treatment facilities	Impact on self-esteem	Perceived effect on child	Learning support + auxiliary resources
Impact on child's daily life	Ancillary resources e.g. – Other services – Toys/equipment library	Desire for help	Attitudes to child versus siblings	Perceived effect on child
Perceived impact on home/school life	– Recreational		Commitment towards intervention	Attitudes to child
				Comittment towards intervention

In broad terms, if assessment results indicate significant motor problems,
direct therapy may be the approach of choice. But even so, the psycho-social
impact of difficulties on child, family and school may lead to an indirect approach
being more appropriate. Conversely, when the child's specific learning difficulties
are more significant than motor difficulties, the indirect approach is generally

favoured. Again, psycho-social factors may mitigate against this. (McLean, 1991; McLean, Chesson, 1991).

Long-term studies have underlined the effects of 'Clumsiness in Children' over 10 years (Losse, Henderson, Elliman, Hall, Knight, Jongmans, 1992) concluding that difficulties do not disappear but that impact and effects change. With this in mind the degree and type of therapy input should be adjusted to meet changing needs as the child matures.

Description of Therapy Applications

Processes involved in learning have been described in both neurology and psychology. Influences of rehearsal/practice in consolidating learning are emphasised as is the importance of pleasure through achievement. Therefore, an important issue is how to ensure success so the child is motivated to practise skills that present problems. In some instances, by-pass strategies may be appropriate.

Another factor is that many postural and movement functions are achieved without thought. Attention is focused on the activity and not the process involved. Many of these children have to concentrate on all aspects of activities. Therapy programmes, therefore, need to find ways to help a child towards more automatic adaptation of posture and movement within skills.

Table II outlines the treatment models most often applied in an integrated therapy approach for children with dyslexia. Each approach addresses issues regarding learning but from different perspectives. To be competent in all of these, therapists need post-graduate training and experience. These are becoming available.

A growing range of publications are available which, used with discretion to meet individual needs, can be valuable resources.

Some are more biased to education (Russell, 1988; Alston, Taylor, 1988) and others to therapy (Fink, 1989) In addition, models have been devised for home programmes (McLean-Manning 1994). They have value for all concerned.

The following case studies illustrate two applications of therapy input to meet differing needs.

TABLE II –
APPROACHES USED IN THERAPY PROGRAMMES : APPLICATIONS TO DYSLEXIA

THERAPY APPROACH	DESCRIPTION	REFERENCES	APPLICATIONS	COMMENTS
SENSORY INTEGRATION Based on the hypothesis that motor learning problems in some children result from inefficient sub-cortical integration of sensori-motor aspects of posture and movement; considered a foundation for learning	Child centred approach. Activities are 'fun,' providing a carefully graded developmental sequence. Encourages 'automatic' responses. Provides achievable challenges. Self-motivating	Ayres, 1972 Ayres, 1979 Fisher, Murray and Bundy, 1991	Postural/ocular movement disorders (vestibular dysfunction) with bilateral integration difficulties or – Mild dysfunction where emotional reactions inhibit participation in homes/school programmes	– Individual – 1 Hour per week. Specified period – Specialist therapy approach – Precautions necessary
PERCEPTUAL-MOTOR Based on the premise that motor-learning provides a foundation for symbolic learning	Requires conscious attention to tasks. Follows a developmental sequence of gross to fine motor activities focusing on observed motor deficits and spatial problems	Barsch, 1967 Frostig, 1970 Kephart, 1971	Development of bilateral arm and hand function – Development of sequence and timing – Development of spatial skills (in space and on paper)	– Common to education and therapy – Individual or group – Appropriate for home and or school programmes
COGNITIVE BEHAVIOURAL Based on a problem-solving approach to specific difficulties	Requires conscious and active co-operation. Uses specific strategies to help child structure, plan and execute functional skills. Success promotes motivation	Sugden, 1989 Henderson and Sugden, 1992 Wilcox, 1991 Wilcox and Polatajko, 1994 Polatajko, 1995	– Teaching specific functional skills, e.g. shoelaces – Writing programmes – Teaching by-pass strategies, e.g. word processing	– Common to education and therapy – Individual or group – Appropriate for home and/or school programmes

CASE STUDY: I

Jane was referred to Occupational Therapy aged 7.5 years. Birth history was uncomplicated and early development considered normal, her dislike of playground equipment and anxiety on stairs and escalators ascribed to her timid, shy personality. Concerns arose shortly after starting school when she was slow learning to read and write. She had been referred to ENT and Ophthalmology. Regular input from a Learning Support teacher was available at school but continued slow progress, particularly related to writing, led to referral to a Paediatric Neurologist and from there to Occupational Therapy. Her difficulties with writing, particularly spacing and spelling, were thought to be related to visuo-motor and/or visuo-perceptual problems.

During assessment, Jane was quiet and at first quite anxious, very aware of difficulties but co-operated throughout. She responded appropriately to instructions and was able to express herself verbally. Results of assessment were linked with her difficulties with everyday skills and were broader than the reason for referral.

The following emerged:

1. **Marked Postural Insecurity**
   - Slightest movement or distance from the ground increased postural tension and inappropriate fear interfering with efficiency of her balance reactions.
   - Her timidity in P.E., playground etc. therefore likely to be a self-protective strategy.

2. **Problems related to Bilateral Integration**
   - Right hand preference for pencil but otherwise used either hand
   - Mid-line crossing often avoided
   - Bilateral function immature in gross and fine motor skills
   - The above difficulties were seen at home and school e.g. ball skills, craftwork, fastenings and cutlery

3. **Pencil Control**
   - Very immature grasp
   - Total movement of the arm
   - Heavy pressure

- Letters large, angular, irregular in shape and spacing but no reversals
- Spelling appeared phonetic but letter sequence often incorrect

Following post-assessment liaison with parents and school, Jane was referred to the Dyslexia Association. Auditory discrimination problems were identified and guidance given to school. Weekly therapy commenced for six months to address the motor aspects of her difficulties.

Therapy initially used a Sensory Integration approach, focusing on diminishing Jane's postural insecurity, improving balance and bilateral integration. Activities carefully graded the amount and speed of movement generated, the height of equipment and the amount of control she had over external factors. Bilateral activities were incorporated progressing from similar to assistive and reciprocal arm and hand function. She responded quickly and began to set herself challenges.

After two months, a home programme started focusing on pencil skills, using a cognitive approach and self-guidance strategies towards more mature pencil grasp and finer motor control over shapes, size and spacing.

Half way through the therapy period, horse-riding was suggested. This helped Jane socially and enabled her to test her confidence away from parents' anxious gaze.

Six months later Jane amazed all by her new found confidence and willingness to 'have a go'. She had mastered riding a bike, skipping and was more adventurous in playparks. She resented parents' advice to 'take care'. She was more competent with cutlery and fastenings. At school, she was making friends and rarely held back from taking part. The quality of pencil control had improved though the spelling problems remained. She continued to receive regular Learning Support.

Formal therapy was discontinued with a home programme of games to encourage bilateral hand skills. Riding was to continue. When seen six months later improvements in function and self-confidence had continued. Mild motor problems remained but Jane's positive attitude minimised their effect. One year later it was agreed that no further review was needed. At school, her need for Learning Support had decreased to minimal support in the classroom.

CASE STUDY: 2

'It seems reasonable to accept Rudel's (1985) conclusion that any motor skill deficit tends to be with newly acquired skills, and to be largely outgrown by age 9-10 years.' (Nicolson and Fawcett, 1990).

The following case study illustrates this point.

Paul was referred to Occupational Therapy aged 11 years. The primary concern was related to his difficulty with reading and writing which persisted despite Learning Support help. There was a strong family history of spelling problems.

Paul was a highly articulate boy with well above average verbal and language skills, but failure to achieve expected school progress.

Occupational Therapy Assessment

On assessment, he was willing, co-operative and tried extremely hard, demonstrating motivation and determination. He had a realistic acceptance of his problems, describing his drawing as 'often rubbish; I keep having to rub out', and his writing as 'printed because I can do it quicker, and I don't join it the way the teacher likes'.

Results of assessment, linked with the history, confirmed the following:

1. **Clear Specific Learning Difficulty**
    - Significant reading difficulty (but good comprehension of text read to him)
    - Spelling problems: letter sequence errors; letter omissions; poor visual recall of words
    - Poor written work: very basic compared with good verbal ability

2. **Problems related to Bilateral Integration**
    - Frequent failure to use assistive hand
    - Inconsistent midline crossing
    - Problems with bilateral skills. (Some persisting; many only recently resolved) e.g. cycling, cutlery, laces, ball skills, jumping, swimming, action sequences

3.   Problems with Pencil Skills
- Excess effort required; pressure excessive
- Drawing content limited for age and ability level
- Writing problematic: difficulties with spelling, letter sequence, letter formation and linking. Early reversal of letters, small words, number order
- Design copying poor: clear problems with direction change, resulting in constant rotation of the page

Intervention
The Occupational Therapist met with Paul's class teacher and Learning Support Teacher to discuss priorities.

Motor Skills
Teachers confirmed that his 'co-ordination' had improved considerably, and agreed with the Occupational Therapist that direct therapy, focusing on remaining motor problems, would not be appropriate at this stage. It would probably simply reinforce low self-esteem resulting from awareness of lack of motor competence.

Alternative Strategies
Paul had been receiving extra help with spelling. It was suggested that he should improve his keyboarding skills, using 'Predictype' or a similar system to increase speed. A Spellmaster could also be used to assist spelling when writing.

Writing
As a backup to word processing, or to increase self-esteem, an occupational therapy writing programme was offered. This type of programme takes place after school and during the holiday prior to secondary school, so as to interfere minimally with school work. Commitment is essential, therefore it needs discussion and a 'contract' agreed between child, parents and therapist. The approach aims to enhance direction of letter formation, flow and automaticity in the writing process, thereby allowing the child to attend more to spelling, sequence and content. Despite such a programme resulting in enhanced writing skills, scribing, a word processor, or extra time may be needed for exam purposes.

Therapy Ideas for Home
Everyday activities were suggested to enhance bilateral skills and projected action sequences e.g. trampolining, swimming, cycling, punchball, bilateral ball skills (graded within capabilities and ensuring success).

Secondary School Liaison

The Occupational Therapist arranged to meet with secondary school staff – guidance and learning support – to consider subjects where difficulty could be anticipated. This would include practical subjects requiring bilateral integration such as Technical, Home Economics, PE and Games.

Once Paul is established in his first term, more in-depth discussion should take place between the Occupational Therapist and specific subject teachers to address any problems which may arise.

This case study demonstrates the value, particularly with older children, of consultation, re-framing and use of alternative strategies, in addition to, or instead of, direct Occupational Therapy.

CONCLUSIONS

Therapists and researchers recognise the problems in measuring progress in motor skills. Assessment tools are not sufficiently sensitive to detect subtle quantitative and qualitative changes in childrens' abilities or in their self-percepts. Some indicators for better outcomes are emerging; age being significant and early detection important. Hence, teachers' role in identification is crucial.

Although measurement of change is problematic, improvements in childrens' abilities to cope with everyday experiences are reported. Nicolson and Fawcett (1989) suggested that many of the specific difficulties dyslexic children experience are 'symptoms of a more general deficit – the failure to fully automatise skills'. Experience suggests that intervention may assist this process so that motor skills are less dependent on focused concentration thereby allowing the child to cognitively attend to learning.

REFERENCES

Alston, J., Taylor, J. (1985). *The Handwriting File: Diagnosis and Remediation of Handwriting Difficulties.* Learning Development Aids.

Ayres, A. J. (1972). *Sensory Integration and Learning Disorders.* Western Psychological Services, Los Angeles.

Ayres, A. J. (1979). *Sensory Integration and the Child.* Western Psychological Services, Los Angeles.

Barsch, R. (1967). *Achieving Perceptual Motor Efficiency.* Special Child Publications.

Chesson, R., McKay, C., Stephenson, E. (1991). 'The Consequences of Motor/Learning Difficulties for school-age children and their teachers: some parental views'. *Support for Learning,* 6 (4)173-177.

Chesson, R., McKay, C., Stephenson, E. (1991). *Children with Motor-Learning Difficulties: A Study Report for Parents*. Occupational Therapy Dept., Royal Aberdeen Children's Hospital.

Child Health and Education Study (1985). *Report to the Department of Health and Social Security I. Clumsy Children*. Department of Child Health. University of Bristol.

Cornelisson, P., Bradley, L., Fowler, S., Stein, J. (1994). 'What children see affects how they spell.' *Developmental medicine and child neurology*, 36 716-727.

Fagan, J .E., Kaplan, B. J., Raymond, J .E., Edgington, E. S. (1988). 'The Failure of Anti-motion sickness medication to improve reading in developmental dyslexia: Results of a randomised trial.' *Developmental and Behavioural Paediatrics*, 9 (6) 359-366.

Fink, B. E. (1989). *Sensory Motor Integration Activities*. Therapy Skill Builders, Arizona.

Fisher, A. G., Murray, E. A., Bundy, A. C. (1991). *Sensory Integration Theory and Practice*. F. A. Davis, Philadelphia.

Frostig, M. (1970). *Movement Education; Theory and Practice*. Follet, Chicago.

Geuze, R. H., Kalverboer, A. F. (1994). 'Tapping a Rhythm: A problem of timing for children who are clumsy and dyslexic?' *Adapted Physical Activity Quarterly*, 11 203-213.

Gladstone, M., Best, C. T., Davidson, R. J. (1989). 'Anomalous Bimanual Co-ordination among dyslexic boys.' *Developmental Psychology*, 25 (2) 236-246

Henderson, S. E., Sugden, D. A. (1992). *Movement and Assessment Battery for Children Manual*. Psychological Corporation.

Hoffman, L. G. (1980). 'Incidence of vision difficulties in children with learning disabilities.' *Journal American Optometry Association*, 51 (5) 447-451.

Humphries, T. W., Wright, M., Snider, L., McDougall, B. (1992). 'A comparison of the effectiveness of sensory integrative therapy and perceptual-motor therapy in treating sensory integrative function in children with learning disabilities.' *Developmental and Behavioural Paediatrics*, 13 31-40.

Humphries, T. W., Snider, L., McDougall, B. (1993). 'Clinical evaluation of effectiveness of sensory integrative and perceptual motor therapy in improving sensory integrative function of children with learning difficulties.' *Occupational Therapy Journal of Research*, 13(3) 163-182.

Kaplan, B. J., Polatajko, H. J., Wilson, B. N., Faris, P. D. (1993). 'Re-examination of Sensory Integration Treatment: A Combination of Two Efficacy Studies.' *Journal of Learning Disabilities* 26 (5) 342-347.

Kephart, N. C. (1971). *The slow learner in the classroom*. Charles E. Merrill, Columbus.

Law, M., Polatajko, H. J., Shaffer, R., Miller, J., McNab, J. (1991). 'The impact of heterogeneity in a clinical trial: motor outcomes after sensory integration therapy.' *Occupational Therapy Journal of Research*, 11; 177-189.

Levinson, H. N. (1980). *A solution to the riddle dyslexia*. Springer-Verlag, New York.

Levinson, H. N. (1984). *Smart but feeling dumb*. Warner Books, New York.

Losse, A., Henderson, S. E., Elliman, D., Hall, D., Knight, E., Jongmans, M. (1991). 'Clumsiness in children – do they grow out of it? A 10-year study.' *Developmental Medicine and Child Neurology*, 33; 55-68.

McLean, M. F. (1991). 'Parents as co-therapists for children with motor learning difficulties; A review of the literature.' *British Journal of Occupational Therapy*, 54 (2).

McLean, M. F. Chesson, R. (1991). 'Factors affecting parents' role as co-therapists; A pilot study of parents of children with motor learning difficulties.' *British Journal of Occupational Therapy*, 54 (7).

McLean-Manning, U. (1994). 'Pandora's Boxes; A home training scheme in gross and fine motor skills for the "clumsy child".' *Proceedings 11th Congress World Federation of Occupational Therapists*, 1; 207.

Morrison, D., Sublett, J. (1986). 'The effects of sensory integration on nystagmus duration, equilibrium and visual-motor integration in reading retarded children.' *Child: Care, Health, Development*, 12 (2) 99-110.

Nicolson, R. I., Fawcett, A. J. (1990). 'Automaticity: A new framework for dyslexia research. *Cognition* 35; 159-182.

Orton, S. (1937). *Reading, writing and speech problems in children.* Norton, New York.

Polatajko, H. J., Low, M., Miller, J., Shaffer, R., McNab, J.(1991).'The effect of a sensory integration programme on academic achievement, performance and self esteem in children identified as learning disabled: results of a clinical trial.' *Occupational Therapy Journal of Research* 11 (3) 155-176.

Polatajko, H. J., Kaplan, B. J., Wilson, B. N. (1992). 'Sensory integration treatment for children with learning disabilities; Its status 20 years on.' *Occupational Therapy Journal of Research,* 12 (6) 323-341.

Polatajko, H. J. (1995). 'Clinical trial of a process oriented treatment approach for children with developmental co-ordination disorder.' *Developmental Medicine and Child Neurology.*

Regehr, S. M., Kaplan, B. J. (1988). 'Reading disability with motor problems may be an inherited subtype.' *Paediatrics,* 82 (2) 204-210.

Rice, J. (1969). 'Confusion in laterality: a validity study with bright and dull children.' *Journal of Learning Disability,* 2 (7) 112-121.

Rousselle, C., Wolff, P. H. (1991). 'The dynamics of bimanual co- ordination in developmental dyslexia.' *Neuropsychologia,* 29 (9) 907-924.

Russell, J. P. (1988). *Graded activities for children with motor-learning difficulties.* Cambridge University Press.

Solan, H. A. (1979). 'Learning disabilities: The role of the developmental optometrist.' *Journal American Optometry Association,* 50 (11) 1256-1266.

Stephenson, E., McKay, C., Chesson, R. (1990). 'An investigative study of early developmental factors in children with motor/learning difficulties.' *British Journal of Occupational Therapy,* 53 (1) 4-7.

Stephenson, E., McKay, C., Chesson, R. (1991). 'The identification and treatment of motor/learning difficulties: parents' perceptions and the role of the therapist.' *Child: Care, Health and Development,* 17 91-113.

Sugden, D. A. (1989). *Cognitive approaches in special education.* Falmer Press.

Wilcox, A. (1993). 'Verbal self-guidance as a treatment technique for children with developmental co-ordination disorder.' *Canadian Journal of Occupational Therapy,* 59 (1).

Wilcox, A., Polatajko, H. J. (1994). 'The impact of verbal self- guidance on children with developmental co-ordination disorder.' *Proceedings 11th Congress World Federation of Occupational Therapists,* 3 1518.

Wilson, B. N., Kaplan, B. J., Fellowes, S., Gruchy, C., Faris, P. (1992). 'The efficacy of sensory integration treatment compared to tutoring.' *Physical and Occupational Therapy in Paediatrics,* 12 (1) 1-36.

Wolff, P. H., Michel, C. F., Ovrut, M. (1990). 'Rate and timing precision of motor co-ordination in developmental dyslexia.' *American Psychological Association Inc.,* 26 (3) 349-359.

PERCEPTUAL MOTOR AND NEURO-DEVELOPMENTAL DIMENSIONS

SHEILA DOBIE

INTRODUCTION

Many children display severe limitations in their motor abilities. There is much evidence in any classroom of children adopting compensatory measures to cope with the wide ranging demands placed upon them by the school environment. They have failed to develop the physical competencies so essential in the everyday management of themselves and the tasks which comprise the educational process.

Maeland (1992) and Lerner *et al.* (1987) identify the mastery of many school subjects and everyday activities as dependent on the acquisition of skilled movement. Lerner indicates that academic and cognitive problems may be due to insufficient motor experiences and gaps in motor learning.

It is further suggested,

"One fact remains, motor activity is essential in order to learn; the child must stabilise his body and govern its movements in order to obtain real learning."

(de Quiros and Schrager, 1979).

BIRTH FACTORS

Much debate presently focuses on influences which impinge upon children reaching their optimal performance. At risk factors, both biological and environmental, have been the concern of Garwood and Sheehan (1989). Low birth weight has been identified by Hunt *et al* .(1982) and Klein (1988) as a potential risk factor for developmental difficulties.

Studies by Abel Smith and Knight-Jones (1990) confirm previous findings that low birth weight children, compared with full term infants, were inferior in intelligence, had significantly lower motor performance, verbal, quantitative and memory scores. In a further study, Astbury *et al.* (1990), of 110 children, of whom 57 survived, six children had physical disabilities, five had sensory disabilities and six had developmental delay. Some 47% of the surviving population were found at two years to have evidence of hyperactivity, impulsivity or distractability; and three children were deemed to be withdrawn or passive.

Cotrell (1992) examined 135 cases of learning disabled children and adults, concluding that in every case there was some form of interference at birth. Major contributing factors appeared to be early or premature birth, 35% of the children and 45% of the adults. The second factor was that of precipitate birth, 41% of the children and 22% of the adults. Other factors included late delivery, forceps delivery, caesarean section, breech delivery, foetal anoxia, and induced labour. Associated learning problems were identified as chronic.

Swanson *et al.* (1992) confirm the importance of differential developmental profiles of all at risk babies, including consideration of ethnic variations, infants with chronic lung disease and the normal pre-term infant or those exposed to drugs or alcohol in utero.

Escalating developmental problems in babies as a consequence of maternal drug use are reported by Cratty (1990) and perhaps understandably, poverty, low maternal education, or age and low support systems are reflected in the concerns of Abraham and Scott (1988). Whatever the origins, the difficulties which confront children are both troublesome and diverse.

THE IMPORTANCE OF MOTOR DEVELOPMENT

In consideration of the evidence concerning children who are underachieving, or present behavioural problems, some of the underlying factors frequently reported include limitations in motor skill development, poor co-ordination, perceptual motor difficulties, clumsiness and visual-motor integration problems. Klein (1988) and Cowden and Eason (1991) advocate early intervention to ameliorate presenting problems and prevent school failure.

It should be noted that,

". . . developmental movement and gross motor deficiencies are a special case for intervention strategies and that movement problems may be more difficult to eliminate than other deficiency classifications."

(Cowden and Euson, 1991).

Sherrill and Pyler (1985) have established that as many as 75% of children with learning difficulties have moderate motor difficulties. Cermak and Henderson (1989) provide an estimation of 60-90% for children with learning difficulties who also have co-ordination problems.

Looking at pre-school neuro-developmental disorders and subsequent profiles at ages 10 and 13, Gilberg *et al.* (1989) showed that almost 25% of all children with school achievement problems at 10 and almost 40% of such children at 13 had motor perception dysfunction and attention deficit disorders.

A higher frequency of learning difficulties, particularly in spelling, writing and also in reading and maths, was identified in a sample of clumsy children than in a comparative group, (Sovik and Maeland, 1986). Children with specific developmental language disorders are recognised, Cermak *et al.* (1986) and Rintala and Palsio (1993) to have accompanying problems with motor skills.

Motor deviance as a marker for dysfunction in other areas is identified by Capute *et al.* (1981) and studies by Gilberg *et al.* (1989), Losse *et al.* (1991) and more recently, Geuze and Borger (1993); all reflect that contrary to the expectations of many professionals, the problems of inept motor performance do not diminish with maturity, and are thought to be associated with a high prevalence of learning difficulties and psychological problems.

> *Motor learning problems have been shown to be persistent characteristics associated with educational failure, social isolation, anxiety, withdrawal and depression persisting into adolescence.*
>
> (Russell, 1988).

INTERVENTION PROGRAMMES

It is significant that Furth and Wachs (1975) see movement and thinking as interdependent, claiming that many children perform academic tasks inadequately because they have failed to master the contributory movement control which supports learning. Considerable controversy exists in the determination of the efficacy of different interventional programmes and attempts have been made to evaluate their effectiveness.

Kavale and Mattson (1983) examined the most popular perceptual motor training programmes and found that all programmes evidenced small treatment affects. However, from an analysis of 180 studies, the primary findings indicated that,

> *"Perceptual motor training is not an effective intervention technique for comparing academic, cognitive or perceptual motor variables."*
>
> (Kavale and Mattson, 1983).

In a study of the effectiveness of a sensory integration therapy programme for children with perceptual motor deficits, Densen *et al* (1989) found no greater gains in language development, in perceptual motor development or in handwriting – than a parallel physical education programme or no treatment at all. In a further study looking at motor treatments and learning disabilities, Humphries (1992), examined sensory integration, perceptual motor and non treatment groups adopted for 133 children with learning difficulties. The findings supported improvement using either of the intervention strategies, including gains in motor planning and gross motor functioning but without any carry over into other functional activities.

Support over time has been afforded various interventional approaches including the development work based on the movement theories of Rudolph Laban, promoted by Veronica Sherbourne and reported in her publication Developmental Movement for Children (1990).

Other interventions include:

Therapeutic intervention of specific motor therapy following assessment. Godfrey and Kephart (1969).

Occular-motor integration through visual perceptual skills. Frostig (1970).

Sensory integration approaches using the basic input systems, visual kinaesthetic, vestibular tactile and auditory. Ayres (1980).

Goal directed intervention approaches through short term objectives and task analysis. Wessel (1980).

The generalisation of motor patterns using extensive movement exploration and participation in multiple variations of motor situations. Kiphard (1981).

Developmental strategies with a remedial approach. McClenaghan and Gallaghue (1982).

Evaluation of kinaesthetic abilities. Laszlo and Bairstow (1985).

Early paediatric intervention. Eason (1991).

Consideration of the learning environment including modification and adaptation of techniques. Cutforth (1991).

Adaptation of physical activities. Sherrill (1986).

EVALUATION OF INTERVENTION

Despite all these treatment strategies, the perplexing problem has remained that, although many assessments may be made, the root cause of the presenting problems and deficiencies remains unidentified. The programmes may produce improvement for some children but whether this is generalisable and influential in alleviating associated learning has been considered to be uncertain.

It has come to be accepted – Caputo *et al.* (1981) – that practice of individual gross and fine motor skills will have no demonstrable influence on cognitive development. Single isolated competencies may improve, but without generation.

In taking cognisance of the reflected reservations and in the general acknowledgement that the problems which underlie the motor, and in many cases, associated learning difficulties, are variable amongst children, professionals have sought informed solutions to the problems. In consideration of why some children regardless of how much they practise never become as skilled as their peers, Sveistrup *et al.* (1992) suggest that,

> *"Identifying the system which is dysfunctional rather than the skill the child is having problems with will allow the development of a remedial programme for teaching the underlying deficit versus training the specific task."*

A process orientated approach of diagnosis and treatment is advocated by Laszlo and Bairstow (1985) who focus on the development of kinaesthetic acuity and perception and memory.

THE ROLE OF REFLEXES

A substantial body of knowledge Rider (1972), Ayres (1972), de Quiros (1976), Blythe and McGlown (1979), Morrison (1985), Auxter and Pyfer (1989), Field (1990), Blythe (1992) and Eichstaedt and Kalakian (1993) point to the influences of sensory integration systems and reflex patterns in supporting efficient movement.

In other circumstances,

> *"Abnormalities in the early modification of primitive reflexes and the development of a broad range of coordinated motor behaviours appear to be causal factors in the learning problems of a variety of children."*

> (Morrison, D., 1985).

Rider (1972), in an investigation to establish the relationship between postural reflexes and academic performance, compared a group of children who exhibited learning problems and who had been referred for a perceptual motor learning programme with a group of normal children. The prevalence of abnormal postural reflexes was compared between the two groups and the children referred for the motor programme were identified as having significantly more abnormal reflex responses than the normal group. An additional factor which emerged showed that within the normal group, those children who exhibited abnormal reflexes were found to score lower on achievement tests than did others in the group who exhibited no abnormal reflexes.

Blythe (1992) asserts that,

"The continued presences or absence of a cluster of aberrant reflexes causes writing and copying difficulties, reading and spelling problems, impaired short-term memory, the inability to sit still and concentrate, excessive day dreaming, clumsiness and awkwardness and to a lesser degree mathematical problems."

(Blythe, P. 1992).

Furthermore, Morrison (1985) points out that failure to inhibit the primitive reflexes and establish adequate responses to gravity has been constantly associated with varying degrees of behavioural disturbance. Fortunately, processes of intervention are possible. Pyfer (1988), Nelson (1988), Fisher and Murray (1991) all point to the potential for change in any individual afforded relevant developmental experiences. Pyfer (1988) supports skilful evaluation of reflexes and sensory systems, followed by intervention.

Fisher and Murray (1991) speculate that enhancement of the function of the nervous system is feasible through tactile, vestibular and proprioceptive inputs. Nelson (1988) sees the central nervous system as an unhappy system,

"Just waiting for the message that it needs to activate the normal response that is obscured by the effect of damage or disruption."

In alleviating the concomitant difficulties, which may be associated with the vestibular, kinaesthetic, tactile, visual auditory or reflex systems, particularly in those children who exhibit motor control, learning or behavioural difficulties, it is proposed that a systematic neuro-developmental approach should be adopted.

CONCLUSION

The responsibility for intervention should be cross-curricular and multi-professional with the starting point being derived from the maturational status of individual pupils. Participation in specially individualised and differentiated activities would provide the basis for amelioration of the underlying neurological dysfunctions. Interesting varied physical activities are not in themselves sufficient to ensure functional change which will alleviate motor or other associated problems.

In situations where neuro-development is delayed critical control is necessary to compensate for the lack of voluntary movement, therefore directing attention to the motor control rather than the learning process. It is known that,

> "... *language development, language internalisation, speech, reading, writing and other symbolic processes progress as the child is able to exclude from the conscious or awareness level a great amount of body information or external information transmitted through body receptors.*"

(de Quiros, 1979).

Dysfunctions which prevent the automisation of perceptual skills, impede learning, and dictate a potential vulnerability for distractability and concentration must be of concern to educators.

Neuro-developmental remediation is a viable strategy which allows motor skills to emerge and generalise with practice, thus allowing the child to optimise their full learning potential.

REFERENCES

Abel Smith, A. E. and Knight-Jones, E. B. (1990). 'The abilities of very low birthweight children and their classroom controls', *Developmental Medicine and Child Neurology*. 32. 590-601.

Astbury, J. and Orgill, A. A., Bajuk, B. and Yu, V. H. (1990). 'Low Birthweight Survivors. How soon can we tell?' *Developmental Medicine and Child Neurology*. 32 582-589.

Auxter, D. and Pyfer, J. (1989). *Principles and Methods of Adapted Physical Education and Recreation*. Times Mirror/Morsby Pub. 6th Ed.

Ayres, A. J., Mailloux, Z. and Wendlere, C. (1987) 'Development Dyspraxia – Is it a unitary function?' *Occupational Therapy Journal of Research* 7. 93-110.

Ayres, A. J. (1972). *Sensory Integration and Learning Disorders*. Los Angeles. Western Psychological Services.

Ayres, A. J. (1972). 'Types of Sensory Integrative Dysfunction Among Disabled Learners'. *A J Occupational Therapy*. 26. 13-18.

Ayres, J. (1980). *Sensory Integration and the Child*. Western Psychological Services.

Blyth, P. and McGlown, D. (1979). *An Organic Basis for Neuroses and Educational Difficulties*. Insight Publications.

Blythe, P. (1992). *A Physical Approach to Resolving Learning Difficulties*. Presented – 4th European Conference of Neuro-developmental Delay in Children with Specific Learning Difficulties. Chester.

Capute, A., Shapiro, B. and Palmer, F. (1981). 'Spectrum of Developmental Disabilities.' *Orthopedic Clinics of North America.* No 1 June 1981.

Cermak, S., Ward, E. and Ward, L. (1986). 'The relationship between articulation disorders and motor co-ordination in children.' *The American Journal of Occupational Therapy.* 40. 546-550.

Carmak, S. and Henderson, A. (1989). 'Learning Disabilities.' In *Neurological Rehabilitation.* C. V. Mosby.

Chandler, L. S., Andrew, M. S. and Swanson, M. W. (1980). *Movement Assessment of Infants.* Rolling Bay, W A.

Cotrell, S. (1992). 'The Effect of Obstetric Problems on Neuro-Developmental Delay.' 4th European Conference on Neuro-Developmental Delay. March 1992.

Cowden, J. E. and Eason, B. L. (1991). 'Pediatric Adapted Physical Education for Infants, Toddlers and Pre-Schoolers.' *Adapted Physical Activity Quarterly.* (8) 263-279.

Cratty, B. J. (1975). *Remedial Motor Activity for Children.* Philadelphia. Lea and Febiger.

Cratty, B. J. (1979). 'Perceptual and Motor Development 'in *Infants and Children.* 2nd edition. NJ Prentice Hall.

Cratty, B. J. (1986). 'Perceptual and Motor Development 'in *Infants and Children.* 3rd edition. NJ Prentice Hall.

Cratty, B. (1990). 'Motor development of infants subject to maternal drug use. Current evidence and future research strategies.' *Adopted Physical Activity Quarterly.* 7. 101-125.

Cutforth, N. (1991). 'The under-achieving child. Implications for Physical Education.' *Bulletin of Physical Education.*

Densen, J. F., Nuthall, G. A., Bushnell, J. and Horn, J. (1989). 'Effectiveness of a sensory integrative therapy programme for children with perceptual motor deficits.' *Journal of Learning Disabilities.* 22. 221-229.

de Quiros, J. and Scharger, D. (1979). *Neuro-Psychological Fundamentals in Learning Disabilities.* Novato, C A Academic Therapy Publications.

de Quiros, J. (1976). 'Diagnosis of vestibular disorders in the learning disabled.' *Journal of Learning Disabilities.* 9(50-57).

Eason, B. L. (1991). 'Adapted physical education delivery model for infants and toddlers with disabilities.' *Journal of Physical Education and Recreation and Dance.* 2(6) 41-43.

Eichstaedt, C. and Kalakian, L. (1993). *Developmental/Adapted Physical Education. Making Ability Count.* Macmillan Pub Co 3rd ed.

Fisher, J. G. and Murray, E. Chapter 1 in *Sensory Integration Theory and Practice.* F A Davies Co. Philadelphia 1991.

Furth, H. and Wachs, H. (1975). *Piaget's Theory in Practice. Thinking Goes to School.* Oxford University Press.

Gallahue, D. (1982). *Developmental Movement Experiences for Children.* John Wiley.

Garwood, S. G. and Sheenan, R. (1989). 'Designing a Comprehensive Early Intervention System.' *The Challenge of Public Law.* 99-457. Austin TX Pro Ed.

Gillberg, I. C., Gillberg, C. and Groth, J. (1989). 'Children with pre-school minor neuro developmental disorders v neuro developmental profiles at age 13.' *Developmental Medicine and Child Neurology.* 31 14-24.

Godfrey, B. and Kephart, N. (1969) *Movement Patterns and Motor Education* Appleton Century Crofts.

Graham, M. A .and Scott, K. G. (1988). 'The Impact of Definitions of High Risk on Services to Infants and Toddlers.' *Topics in Early Childhood Special Education.* 8(3) 23-38.

Geuze, R. and Borger, H. (1993). 'Children who are clumsy: five years later.' *Adapted Physical Activity Quarterly.* (10)10-21.

Humphries, T., Wright, M., Snider, M., McDougall, B. (1992). 'A comparison of effectiveness of sensory integrative therapy and perceptual-motor training in treating children with learning disabilities.' *Development and Behavioural Pediatrics.* Vol 13, No 1.

Hunt, J., Toole, W. R., Halvin, D. (1982). 'Learning disabilities in children with birthweights. 1500 grams.' *Perinatology* (6) 280-287.

Klein, N. K. (1988). 'Children who were very low birthweight. Cognitive abilities and classroom behaviour at five years of age.' *Journal of Special Education.* Vol. 22, (No 1), 1988.

Kavale and Mattson, P. D. (1983). 'One jumped off the balance beam. Meta-analysis of perceptual motor training.' *Journal of Learning Disabilities.* 16. 165-173.

Kephart, N. (1960). *The Slow Learner in the Classroom.* Columbus. O. H. Merrill.

Kiphard, E. (1981). 'Adapted Physical Education in Germany.' Proceedings of International Symposium on Adapted Physical Activity. New Orleans.

Laszlo, J. and Bairstow, P. (1985). *Perceptual motor behaviour. Developmental assessment and therapy.* Praeger Scientific.

Lerner, J., Mardell-Czudnowski, C. and Goldenburg, D. (1987). *Special education for the early childhood years.* 2nd ed. Englewood Cliffs. NG Prentice Hall.

Losse, A., Henderson, S. E., Elliman, D., Hall, D., Knight, E. and Jongmanns, M. (1991). 'Clumsiness in Children – do they grow out of it? A 10-year follow up study.' *Developmental Medicine and Children Neurology.* 33,55-68.

Maeland, A. F. (1992). Identification of Children with Motor Co-ordination Problems. *Adapted Physical Activity Quarterly.* (9) 330-342.

McClenaghan, B. and Gallahue, D. (1978). *Fundamental Movement. A Developmental and Remedial Approach.* Philadelphia Saunders.

Morrison, D. C. (1985). *Neurobehavioural and Perceptual Dysfunction in Learning Disabled Children.* C. J. Hogrefc Inc. N I Toronto.

Nelson, C. (1988). 'Infant Movement. Normal and Abnormal Development.' *Journal of Physical Education Recreation and Dance.* September.

Pyffer, J. (1988). 'Teachers don't let your students grow up to be clumsy adults.' *Journal of Physical Education, Recreation and Dance.* January.

Rider, B. (1972). 'Relationships of postural reflexes to learning disabilities.' *American Journal of Development Therapy.* Vol. 26, No 5. July/Aug (239-243).

Rintal, A. and Palsio, N. (1993). 'Effects of Physical Education Programmes in Children in Learning Disabilities.' Paper presented at the 9th International Symposium on Adapted Physical Activity. Yokohama, Japan.

Russell, J. (1988). *Graded Activities for Children with Motor Difficulties.* Cambridge University Press.

Sherbourne, Veronica (1988). *Developmental Movement for Children in Mainstream, Special Needs and Pre-School.* Cambridge University Press.

Sherrill, C. and Pyler, J. (1985). 'Learning Disabled Students in Physical Education.' *Adapted Physical Activity Quarterly.* 2.283-291.

Sherrill, C .(1986). *Adapted Physical Education and Recreation. A Multi-disciplinary Approach.* Dubuque, I. A .William C. Brown.

Sovik, N. and Maeland, A. (1986). 'Children with Motor Problems. (Clumsy Children).' *Scandinavian Journal of Educational Research.* 30,1.39-53.

Stott, D. H., Moyes, F. A. and Henderson, S. E. (1984). 'Test of Motor Impairment'. London Psychological Corporation.

Sugden, D. (1991) 'Assessment of Children with Movement Skill Difficulties.' *The British Journal of Physical Education.* Summer.

Sveistrup, H., Burtner, P. and Wollacott, M. H. (1992). 'Motor control approaches that may help to identify and teach children with motor impairments.' *Pediatric Exercise Scheme.* Vol. 4, (3).

Swanson, M., Bennett, F., Kirkwood, S. and Whitfield, M. (1992). 'Identification of neuro-development abnormality at four and eight months by the movement assessment of infants.' *Development Medicine and Child Neurology.* (34) 321-337.

Tingle, M. (1990). 'The Motor Impaired Child.' *Practical Integration in Education.* NFER London.

Wessel, J. A. (1980). 'I Can.' *Primary Skills.* Northbristle, I. L. Hubbard.

SECTION 5

THE LEARNER

WHY CAN'T THEY PAY ATTENTION? – ATTENTION DEFICIT DISORDERS AND LEARNING DISABILITIES

JANE HEALY

The reason our children don't follow directions is that they're tuned out. These children don't listen. They have so much stimulation – they're used to the TV blaring, the stereo, the household commotion. I'm not sure so many are ADHD; they're just restless because they don't have anything inside. They're so used to being entertained.

> – EIGHTH-GRADE TEACHER,
> SUBURBAN SCHOOL, GEORGIA

They have a much better store of general information than children twenty years ago. If they listen, they can follow directions, but it is difficult to keep their attention long enough to explain what to do.

> –TEACHER,
> UNGRADED RURAL SCHOOL, MINNESOTA

The kids are sharp and intuitive, but – listening skills? Not as good as students in the past. Some seem to have forgotten how to learn without visual stimulation and affirmation of what they hear. Concentration and memory are just not as important to them. They seem to have their own agendas in life, and school gets in the way sometimes.

> – FIFTH-GRADE TEACHER,
> URBAN SCHOOL, OREGON

THE PROBLEM OF ATTENTION

Although 'attention deficits' are involved in the vast majority of learning-disability referrals, teachers of all students complain more about diminished attention spans than about any other characteristic of their students. As soon as I began to talk with educators, I discovered that merely mentioning the word 'attention" opened a floodgate of response. To my surprise, I also heard the same concerns expressed from abroad, although outside the United States the diagnosis of 'learning disability' and ADHD are much less prevalent.

In Tours, a large city southwest of Paris, the director of a primary school and an instructor in the highly esteemed École Normale (Teachers' College), told me, 'The teachers here complain a lot; they say the children don't listen any more, they are restless. This is only my personal opinion, but I think one learns not to listen when one watches television. I think the children get in the habit and then when the teacher talks, they don't hear her either.' She went on to describe other concerns remarkably similar to those I was hearing at home about hurried lifestyles, over programmed children, and the decline of thoughtful conversations around the family dinner table. 'Personally, I don't think the parents encourage calmness or listening,' she mused.

It is clear from the preceding comments that declining listening abilities are the main symptom, but most teachers sense that they also reflect students' problems with focusing and maintaining internal control of attention in any situation. Overall mental restlessness and inability to persist in solving problems, reading 'hard' books, or doing work perceived as 'boring' are even more serious symptoms. In the United States, a national crisis in 'problem-solving ability' – the ability to stay focused long enough to reason out and solve a mental challenge – has become the primary agenda item of the National Council of Teachers of Mathematics and the Association for Supervision and Curriculum Development.

Could these trends simply represent inevitable signs of progress? Will children be better off if they learn early to respond to the pace of the contemporary world. Certainly, to be adapted to today's surroundings, young brains need to deal with a lot of rapid-fire stimuli. To reason effectively and solve problems, however, growing minds also need to be able to retain and connect these 'bits.' Perhaps most importantly they need to learn what it feels like to be in charge of one's own brain, actively pursuing a mental or physical trail, inhibiting response to the lure of distractions.

Attention determines how and what an individual learns.[2] It enables us to make choices and to maintain control over what we notice, absorb and remember. Children with attention problems fall into two general categories: some are too mentally active, with their focus jumping from one thing to another, while others behave as if their brains were underactive. Those in the latter group frequently are termed 'spaced out,' but they are much less frequently diagnosed than the 'hyper' ones, who respond impulsively to whatever can be touched or seen in their environments and have particular difficulty internalising personal controls.[3] Those with serious disorders often grow up to be impulsive adults; ADHD is statistically linked with delinquency and antisocial behavior. If our society wants citizens who can reflect as well as respond, who can come up with solutions to the problems of a complex world, it must teach its children to stop, listen and think, as well as to react.

How can we help children learn to direct their mental energies? How much can the environment affect patterns of attention, listening, and problem-solving? Let us consider first what is known about attention and why physicians prescribe drugs for some children who lack it. Then we will start to take a look at what environments, both physical and mental, have to do with the way it develops – or fails to – during childhood.

WHAT IS AN ATTENTION DEFICIT?

Attention, like learning disability, is not a single measurable quantity Although psychologists are far from agreeing on an exact definition they have generally believed, as far as learning is concerned, that *selective attention* – the ability to concentrate and stay focused on a particular task – is the critical issue.[4] But selective attention has proven hard to measure. Like memory, it is 'task specific', changing according to the job the brain is asked to do and the underlying motivation to do it. For example, many teachers who complain that students can't pay attention and listen in class also notice that the same children will concentrate on a computerised video game for long periods of time. In these two situations, there are clear differences between both motivational and cognitive factors such as auditory or visual attention, saliency (attention-grabbing quality) of the stimulus, requirements for memory, physical involvement, and the pace of the activity, all of which affect attention.

For all learners, attention varies from situation to situation, and it is difficult to determine the fine line between normal restlessness and pathology. Now that so many children seem out of sync with the attentional demands of their classrooms, the problem is compounded. Even the extreme diagnosis of 'ADHD' – which assumes that the child has some sort of organic brain dysfunction – depends on rather vague criteria, since there are no sure-fire neurological tests to prove its existence.

To diagnose a child as pathologically inattentive, most doctors depend mainly on behavior checklists filled out by teachers and parents; the official diagnosis is often subjective. A certain proportion of items like the following must be checked:

- Failure to finish things he or she starts.
- Failure to listen.

- • ▪ Difficulty in concentrating or sticking to an activity.
- • ▪ Acting before thinking.
- • ▪ shifting between one activity and another.
- • ▪ Difficulty in organisation.
- • ▪ Calling out in class/difficulty awaiting turns.

To earn the additional designation 'hyperactive,' the child must also show excessive physical activity (e.g. run or climb excessively).

Since all children exhibit these behaviors at times, the diagnosis is supposed to be restricted to problems that are unusually severe for the child's age and level of mental development. Curiously, however, doctors are told that the child may seem perfectly normal during the office visit, since ADHD children are often able to control themselves in novel or one-to-one situations.[5]

CONTROLLING ATTENTION: FROM INSIDE OR OUTSIDE?

Ritalin and other drugs prescribed for ADHD are variations on the type of stimulants, or amphetamines, banned in over-the-counter diet pills. They help heighten and sharpen attention – even in many 'normal' people. Some children with organic difficulties seem to benefit from carefully regulated doses that enable them to focus appropriately, listen more carefully to the teacher, and complete more work. In fact, moderate doses would have the same effect on almost anyone – at least for a while – and many doctors complain that the number of children treated is much larger than it should be. Some physicians, parents, and teachers are too eager, they say, to give children drugs with well-recognised negative side effects, instead of working to help them learn to manage their own behavior.

Many children diagnosed as having attention deficit disorder are extremely intelligent, but there is some reason to doubt the overall benefit of drug treatment alone in helping them use that intelligence productively. Students who take their medication do become more tractable, completing more repetitive 'work' such as worksheets with fill-in answers and drills on maths problems. In most studies conducted thus far, however, drugs per se do not make them score better on tests of academic achievement or of higher-level thinking and problem-solving.[6] Some studies have even shown that the level of dosage needed to make teachers approve a child's behavior is so high that it actually dulls reasoning ability. These findings raise questions, not only about the type of 'work' dominating many classrooms, but also about the real source of the problem.[7]

Lasting improvement is generally not seen after the drug treatment is stopped. A few children appear spontaneously to 'outgrow' attention problems around adolescence, probably because of nervous system maturation, but many retain problems of self-control that persist into adulthood.

'Curing' attention problems seems to be close to impossible. Teaching students to talk through problems, thus developing conscious strategies for self-control, is the only therapy used thus far that appears to produce results lasting after drugs are discontinued.[8-10] In fact, this sort of 'cognitive therapy' – using language to control behaviour – has been shown to help even without drug treatment. Some professionals have gone so far as to suggest that the real disability is a lack of this type of teaching – both at home and at school.

MISFITTED ATTENTION: WHAT IS THE REAL PROBLEM?

Since most of the 'epidemic' of inattention cannot be linked to proven organic dysfunction of the central nervous system, other factors that create a misfit between the children's development and the demands of the schools are being considered. According to the newest research, a small percentage of problems called ADHD may be covering up basic anxiety or depression.[11] Many more may be related to other, environmental causes. Overall a confusing picture emerges.

In her book, *When Children Don't Learn*, Dr Diane McGuinness expresses scepticism about the validity of the diagnosis itself. 'Problems in the control of attention could result from deficiencies in the central nervous system, which could produce distractibility, failure to sustain attention to a task, inability to plan actions, and a diminished attention span. However, similar difficulties could be created by an environment that is either *too overwhelming or insufficiently compelling* [emphasis added],' she states.[12] Dr McGuinness, who confesses she is irate about the amount of Ritalin being prescribed today, believes that many children thought to be 'hyperactive' are really normally vigorous children 'who refuse to abide by adult admonitions to sit still and conform to rules set by adults for their own convenience'. She makes the point that children's bodies are designed by nature to be active, and the overly wiggly ones may really know what is good for them more than the docile types 'who are overly conforming and remain for hours in sedentary positions'.

Under some circumstances (such as in the doctor's office), even children labelled ADHD are able to control their attention – but only if the situation is novel, one-on-one, and they get frequent and continuous rewards and reinforcement of some kind. For example, they can pay excellent attention to computer activities with frequent token rewards (e.g. a laser gun blows up a space invader every time the student gets a maths problem correct), and their schoolwork improves noticeably when someone works individually with them. In one interesting study, children diagnosed ADHD were paid to respond quickly and accurately to a test on which they had previously scored quite poorly when no reward was offered. Much to the experimenter's surprise, promise of money brought their performance up to the level of a normal control group.[13]

These findings and others have led a number of professionals to begin rethinking their views. Dr Russell Barkley, nationally noted authority and author of *Hyperactive Children*, recently told a large group of educators that he is changing his mind about what an 'attention deficit' really is.[14] 'If you have an attention deficit, shouldn't it show up everywhere? If language is impaired, we see language impairment anywhere the child needs to use language. How can this be an attention deficit? Don't we need to look for something else that explains this variation? Why do they do better with novel situations, with rich schedules of reinforcement [frequent rewards]? People are seriously questioning whether this is really an attention deficit.'

One theory, according to Dr Barkley, is that the ADHD children have particular trouble with what he calls 'rule-governed behavior.' When the environment demands adherence to a rule, especially one with few consequences, trouble begins. 'So when a teacher says, 'He's not paying attention,' what she really means is he's not listening, he's not following the rule. 'I told him to go back to his desk, get out his maths problems, and work on them, and he didn't do the rule.'

'It's been shown that when ADHD children are paying attention to what they like, they don't have an attention deficit,' he emphasised. 'So if they brought a car from home, or a transformer, or they're doodling war pictures on the corner of that reading workbook – their attention span for war pictures is phenomenal! But it isn't for the stuff you ask them to do. The problem, then, is not attention, it's a disability in rule-following.'

However, even these children can follow rules if there is an immediate reward, Dr Barkley has observed. 'In adults, we are the only animal that operates on a very sparse schedule of reward; I only get a paycheck once a month, but I show up at work every day. There is something fascinating about the human brain that allows it to be exquisitely sensitive to extremely sparse schedules of reward, but that is something that has to develop. Young children can't do it. You can tell a young kid you'll take him to Disneyland in February, and that won't do it. These ADHD kids are like younger kids; they need immediate feedback and reinforcement.'

Why might this be the case? Dr Barkley suggests, for some children, underlying differences in the motivational-control systems of the brain may not be operating normally; thus they need a much stronger external impetus to concentrate on the task at hand. They simply don't respond as other children do to 'social approval'.

'Somehow, neurologically, these children have a threshold for what rewards them that is set too high; it takes a more powerful reinforcer to get them to do what they are told. That is why they require the money, food, bikes, toys, privileges, bribes – to work. Because the subtle rewards – love of learning, grades, teacher approval –don't motivate these kids at all. You can say 'good boy, good boy' all you want and that isn't going to work.'

'They can understand what you say to them,' he points out, 'they just don't act on it. *It's really a problem with how language governs behavior* – the connections between the linguistic and the motor systems'.[15]

Dr Barkley suspects there is a genetic cause for these brain differences, possibly related to the way chemicals (neurotransmitters) help different parts of the brain work together. Children who develop the most severe forms of ADHD so that they become openly 'oppositional' and often delinquent, tend to come from families with a history of alcohol abuse, delinquency, and antisocial behavior, which he thinks may reflect some overall type of inherited problem. We can't blame parents for the fact that they have a difficult child, he insists, but we must acknowledge that a child's environment helps determine how the problem is expressed. As with bad table manners that seem to run in families, no one has been able to measure exactly how much living with impulsive adults in poorly structured ~social~ situations contributes to the problem.

Obviously, no clear-cut answers about the 'why' of attention problems are available. Perhaps neurology is just struggling to catch up with common sense, for it seems foolish to deny that the way a child is taught and shown to behave has a lot to do with whether or not he learns to manage himself without an immediate reward. A number of practical, real-life studies show that children's adult models may be a significant, but frequently unappreciated, variable.[16] ~Variable~

FURNISHING THE EXECUTIVE SUITE: HOW BRAINS LEARN TO PAY ATTENTION

Both physical and mental environments help develop the ability to pay attention. Because attention requires the use of many different areas of the brain, any severe trauma, 'insult,' or biochemical abnormality may affect it. As we all know, even transient emotional states can knock this delicately balanced block off the tower of learning abilities.

Attention systems grow in several directions in the brain: side to side, bottom to top, and inside to outside. Here's a brief summary of how they are formed.

Activating the Hemispheres

The side-to-side connections are mainly in the *corpus callosum*, that tough and busy band of fibres that carries messages between the hemispheres and lets the two sides of the cortex work efficiently together. Several prominent neuropsychologists believe that brains with attention and learning problems have trouble getting an idea into the appropriate hemisphere and keeping it there long enough to be processed efficiently.

One recent study measured electrical brain waves in right and left hemispheres of LD (in this case, reading disabled) children when they were doing different types of learning tasks; the measurements were then compared with brain-wave recordings from a group of good students doing the same activities. The good students showed the expected changes in hemispheric activation depending on whether the task was a verbal or non-verbal one, although overall they tended to favor left-hemisphere strategies. The LD children showed different patterns: (1) they had less overall left-hemisphere activation, even in verbal tasks, and (2) they showed significantly smaller shifts from one hemisphere to the other when the tasks required different processing strategies.[17]

If children have not had a chance to develop strong connections between the two sides or enough practice using left-hemisphere systems for careful listening, they certainly might have more trouble concentrating, getting their brains quickly and efficiently into gear for school tasks, and finding the best way to study and remember things they are supposed to learn.[18]

Three Levels of Attention

The up-and-down axis of brain maturation, which is probably the major route by which children learn to pay attention, may be particularly at risk in today's environments. Although, technically, this 'attention circuit' cannot be separated from the hemispheres, since it crosses through them, it is, in many respects, a separate apparatus. Imagine, if you will, a circuit that runs from the base of your skull at the back of your head all the way up through the middle of the brain to the front of your forehead and back down again. This is similar to the main route from which higher-level systems receive information about where and how attention should be focused. These higher centres, in turn, decide what is to be done and then instruct the rest of the brain in how the behavior (including learning) is to be directed.

This attention loop has three layers that develop from bottom to top and inside to outside the brain. The first, primitive stage of the circuit lies near the top of the spinal cord, where it joins the skull, in brain structures that closely resemble those of other animals. It is responsible for basic alertness (e.g. staying awake when it is appropriate), screening out or letting in various types of stimuli (e.g. focusing without being distracted by background sights or sounds), filtering information, and getting the higher centres of the cortex 'in gear.'

awake.
screen out
distract
in gear

Second come centres for emotion and memory, which are located in the middle of the brain in an area technically called the *limbic system*. In these 'subcortical' areas, the incoming stimuli are connected with motivation (how important is it for me to pay attention to this right now?) and some centres for memory. I find it particularly interesting, although not intuitively surprising, that attention, emotion, motivation, and memory have such a close physical link in the nervous system.

emotion
memory

NB.

Developmental influences on the limbic system are one of the great, barely unfolded mysteries of the brain. How do children acquire the neural foundations of motivation? No one really knows, but the central role of these midbrain connections imply that they must be important indeed.

At the very top of the circuit lie the *frontal lobes of the cortex*, comprising the frontmost parts of both right and left hemispheres. This part of the brain, which is the human animal's unique neural possession, is often called the *executive of the brain* because it is responsible for planning and regulating behavior. It consists of the *motor cortex*, which helps plan and implement physical movement, and the *prefrontal* areas, which, when (and if) fully developed, become the 'boss' of thinking. (The terms 'frontal' and 'prefrontal' are used interchangeably.)

The neural groundwork for attention abilities is laid early in prenatal life, when the bottom layer of primitive 'alerting' areas are developing. After birth the child must collaborate with nature and the motivational system to build the connections that put the thinking brain in charge. Because the higher centres can't take over immediately, young children are notoriously 'stimulus-bound' – at the mercy of any new sensory experience or idea. Thus they tend to be highly distractible.

During the years of childhood, especially between the ages of three and six, most youngsters work hard on learning to screen out both external and internal distractions and marshal their attention at will. Any environmental force that severely interferes with this important learning has the potential to disrupt the system. Sometime during adolescence, most brains are sufficiently mature to start to attend to future goals and use more complex forms of mental control (please notice, parents, I said 'most'). It's a long process, indeed, and demands continued support from concerned and persistent (if often exasperated!) adults.

Attention and the Brain's Executive

Prefrontal development is not completed at least until late adolescence, or even adulthood. Thus, the way a child learns to use executive functions is doubtless highly dependent on the experiences the environment provides. Adults who show children how to put thought ahead of action, delay gratification, and use language as a tool for thinking and planning help provide the fundamental training ground for the brain's executive.

support

Curiously, this 'highest' level of the brain's functioning does not seem to be measured by standard IQ tests. The rest of the cortex serves as the *storehouse* for taking in information, which it associates and connects into the intellectual data bank that constitutes a lifetime of learning. The frontal systems have a different responsibility: seeing that the data gets used effectively, the reason why they are referred to as the executive. When experts give advice about boosting mental skills, they are usually referring to the most efficient ways of filling up the storehouse. Unfortunately, they too often forget that merely trying to shovel in information will serve little purpose unless children also learn how to use their brains to stay mentally focused, put information into perspective, reflect on meaning, plan ahead, and follow through constructively – the fundamental components of problem-solving. For this reason, 'competency tests' that measure only the accumulation of data may seriously mislead us about children's real learning abilities. Without an efficient 'executive,' real-life competency is jeopardised.

Despite its critical importance in learning – as well as in life – there is little research on the way prefrontal development can be influenced. It appears that the way the brain learns to talk to itself may be a major factor in building its internal connections and learning to control the workings of both mind and body.[19]

For now, let us consider some of the interrelated factors that can cause trouble at any of the three levels of the attention system. Outright trauma, either before or after birth, is probably responsible only for a relatively small percentage of attention problems, but increasing numbers of children are currently seen as being at risk because of greater loads of environmental toxins and better survival rates for low-birthweight infants. Other more subtle factors, from 'noise pollution' to biochemical effects of junk food, may tip the brain's attentional balances either before or after birth.

Several types of hazards in contemporary life should be specifically mentioned:

1. Toxic substances and foods that may predispose children to attention problems.

2. 'Noisy' environments that cause children to tune out rather than tune in.

3. Sedentary lifestyles.

4. Failure by adults to act as constructive, thoughtful 'coaches' for children.

HOW BRAINS GET INSULTED: ENVIRONMENTAL HAZARDS FOR ATTENTION AND LEARNING

Before birth, some children suffer specific types of damage or so called 'insult' to attention-regulating systems. Brains are at risk both before and soon after birth by overt damage from illness, accident, or exposure to toxins (e.g. lead, solvents, medications, etc.). Anything that deprives the brain of oxygen, particularly during times of rapid development, can also subtly jeopardy attention abilities. For example, children whose mothers smoked during pregnancy, who were premature, or who suffered various types of birth trauma tend to have a higher rate of attention problems and related learning disabilities than other youngsters.

Even after the foundation systems are in place, the brain can be disrupted by anything that interferes with the proper workings of the limbic system or the higher centres in the cortex, particularly the frontal areas. Sometimes these effects are so subtle that no one connects the cause with the resulting learning problem. One reason is that the brain has built-in mechanisms to protect itself, which may work well until they become overtaxed.

A good example of a built-in protection system is the so-called *blood-brain barrier,* which screens out brain-damaging materials that may be circulating in the rest of the bloodstream. Some potentially injurious substances are able to sneak across this barrier, and it can also be weakened, or made more permeable, by environmental factors, such as prolonged exposure to toxins or an unbalanced or inadequate diet.

Once across the barrier, troublesome agents can affect brain functioning in at least two ways that are, as yet, only generally understood. First, they may be directly toxic and create overt, permanent damage, as in the impairments inflicted on the foetal brain by alcohol. More subtly, they may cause temporary changes in the fine chemical balance that makes thinking possible. Brains can be either intolerant or frankly allergic to certain substances, but it is difficult to pin down the culprits.

HEREDITY, ENVIRONMENT, AND 'EXCEPTIONAL' BRAINS

Children with divergent learning styles are particularly at risk for attention problems because their preferred modes of learning do not fit with the demands of a traditional classroom. Scientists are trying to get more specific about how nature and nurture affect such patterns of learning ability. They have found that 'exceptionality' (such as musical, mathematical, or linguistic talent, as well as some categories of learning disability) may be related to inherited differences in the way brains are constructed. Nevertheless, the effects of environments created by family members with particular interests can't be discounted, say Drs. Lorraine Obler and Deborah Fine in their fascinating book *The Exceptional Brain*. 'Stating that a talent or disability is biologically or genetically based does not mean that it will necessarily develop or fail to develop regardless of the conditions under which a child grows up. Certain environmental factors are crucial for the manifestation of talent as they are for the manifestation of disability.'[10]

GENES, DYSLEXIA, AND THE FETAL BRAIN

It is difficult and highly technical work to sort out the respective effects of genes and family habits, agrees Dr Bruce Pennington of the University of Colorado. Dr Pennington is director of a large study searching for specific genes by which language, reading, and learning disabilities can be transmitted from parent to child. Just because many members of a family have a certain trait, he says, we cannot assume it is necessarily genetic. Parents who enjoy reading and conversation will tend to surround their children with a literacy-rich environment and extensive listening experiences, and vice versa.

Nevertheless, Pennington's research, the largest family learning disability study ever conducted, has confirmed that some specific types of learning difficulties, including language disorders such as stuttering, speech, and some reading problems, are genetically influenced. Members of these families, interestingly enough, are often distinguished by talents in other areas. As researchers work to clarify definitions and probable causes, they are uncovering some fascinating clues about why this might be true.

The term 'dyslexia' has often been used as a garbage can for any kind of problem with reading. Current research, however, has limited the use of the term to describe a brain-based disorder in putting together the sight and sound of printed language in reading, spelling, and writing (e.g. looking at a letter and saying its sound; remembering how to write *said*). Dyslexic children, who compose only one special segment of the entire LD population, may also have difficulty with some aspects of oral language, such as coming up quickly with the word they want to say or getting the order of the sounds and syllables straight. Because they tend to mix up the order of letters and words when they read (and sometimes the order of numerals when they do arithmetic), people used to think the problem was in their eyes. Now it is suspected that the culprits really are deficits in left hemisphere systems responsible for analysing and arranging things in sequential order and linking sound with written symbol.

Even with their genetically 'different' brains, dyslexic children who come from homes where they have been exposed to books and good examples of language often learn to read reasonably well. Although their spelling is often 'atrocious,' these youngsters may escape diagnosis as they learn to compensate for, or cover up, their difficulties. They also prove that 'disability' is a relative term, as they are often talented in more predominantly right-hemisphere skills, such as visual arts, mathematical reasoning, music, mechanical aptitude.[12]

Attention problems in school frequently accompany dyslexia, but dyslexics often have excellent visual attention for details of things they see (other than printed words!), and they can spend long hours in activities such as working on an engine or a design. They are youngsters who might be academic stars in a culture with a different set of intellectual priorities.

How are these brains different? Studies using new computerised pictures of brain areas in action show that dyslexic children seem to use different neural systems for reading than do 'normal' readers.[13] A second line of evidence suggests that this mix-up takes place because certain brain areas developed differently before birth. Because the young brain is so plastic, it manages to reorganise itself around reading, but academic skills still suffer to some degree.

'A TERRIBLE-LOOKING BRAIN'

Not long ago, the late Dr Norman Geshwind and his colleague Dr Albert Galaburda, of Harvard University, began intensive work on the brains of several dyslexics who had willed them for study. All of these brains differed in particular ways from the 'normal' pattern of cell organisation, especially in one general language area of the left hemisphere. Microscopic analysis pinpointed the origin of the differences at a certain period of prenatal cell migration. Instead of finding their intended homes, groups of neurons ended up in peculiar places and arrangements. Moreover, areas in the right hemisphere – the ones, in fact, that would probably underlie visual, mechanical, or other creative abilities – were proportionately larger in these people.[14]

Given the growing evidence that dyslexia tends to run in families and to be more evident in males, Dr Geshwind decided to interview families of dyslexics. When he uncovered repeated prevalence of left-handed relatives and auto-immune, or allergic, disease, he developed a theory. He speculated that imbalances of hormones or antibodies secreted by the mother at different times during pregnancy might subtly rearrange the infant's brain in ways that would make it less adept at reading and language, more talented in visual-spatial skills, and more likely to be left-handed.[15]

No final answers are yet available, but this research is being continued by Dr Albert Galaburda. Until more is known, these studies provide powerful evidence that even though baby brains are born with differences, they can eventually learn to accomplish a complex learning task (in this case, reading) with brain systems different – and perhaps geographically far removed – from the ones best suited for the job. The scientists working on these projects agree that the *way dyslexics – or anyone else – uses their brains is a critical factor in modifying them.*

I had an opportunity to chat with Dr Galaburda after a recent speech in which he emphasised 'the Darwinian-like interaction' between the environment and the growing brain. Genes provide the environment with 'a range of structures to choose from,' he explained, 'and the environment chooses from this range of possibilities. The structure of your brain determines that you can dance, but it doesn't permit you to fly,' he said, smiling. 'There are some things the genes just don't permit. But on the other hand, the brain is not pre-wired to act just one way; instead it gives the environment certain flexibility in selection. I think even if children have not quite the best wiring diagram for something, you can make it look better or less well depending on the environment.[17]

'Different kinds of environmental factors, from chemicals to societal pressures . . . are potentially capable of resulting in abnormal brain interactions,' explained Dr Galaburda. On the other hand, his studies of dyslexic brains have reminded him that we should never underestimate the ability of the brain, given the right kind of support, to compensate for innate difficulties. 'If you change the brain [before birth] you probably change the range of possibilities that are available to this brain in some sense, but the range of possibilities is still very great. One of our dyslexics was a very distinguished, famous, brilliant psychologist and she had a *terrible looking brain!*'[18]

THE FLIP SIDE OF DYSLEXIA: NON-VERBAL LEARNING DISORDERS

Scientists are hot on the trail of brain differences that lie behind another difficulty, termed 'non-verbal learning disorder,' which seems to stem from the opposite problem: insufficient right hemisphere power.

People with right-hemisphere disabilities may be quite competent at linear, sequential skills like spelling, reading out loud, or doing basic maths equations, but have trouble when they must comprehend abstract ideas, relate to people socially, or reason in a visual-spatial format (e.g., maps, charts, three-dimensional puzzles, architectural drawings). They have trouble understanding the relationship of their bodies in space or the ideas in literature or social studies. They almost invariably run afoul of more advanced maths courses. Their primary difficulty is one of seeing the 'whole picture' of a situation: sizing up meaning when they read or when they deal with others, for example. They may have trouble interpreting the emotional quality of people's facial expressions and do or say inappropriate things in social situations.[19]

[**A Cautionary Note:** Most of us lean toward one 'style' or another but are still well within the normal range; just because any of these descriptions sound like someone you know does not mean they have a brain disability, just that they are at a different point on a continuum than someone else. The fact that we all have unique patterns of talents keeps us supplied with people who want to be proofreaders as well as those who prefer architectural design.]

Serious cases of non-verbal learning disorder, in which the individual's abilities are obviously affected, are just now receiving professional attention. Little is known about causes or treatment, but researchers suggest early intervention to help the brain develop connections for manipulating the physical world and understanding other people's reactions and the principles behind ideas.

Children who show this type of learning profile may not look 'disabled' in early grades and are often, in fact, viewed as quite advanced because of large vocabulary, facility on the computer, early reading of words, and good maths computation skills. The tipoff is that they tend to pursue linear kinds of learning, like computer math or spelling drills, as obsessively as they avoid such visual-spatial challenges as video games, team sports, or mechanical puzzles.'[20] Since the child's family may share some of the same characteristics, manual and interpersonal abilities may not have high priority at home.

Non-verbal learning disorders and dyslexia are just two of the many conditions that get lumped under the term 'LD' (and which may or may not include 'attention deficit' problems), but they are among the major ones for which specific, and possibly inherited, brain differences have been suggested. No one knows how many 'learning disabilities' are caused by environments that interact with more 'normal' brain patterns to make children unprepared for school learning. Most experts agree, however, that this number is probably growing. Because the types of technology needed to look, literally, at the learning brain are only now being developed and are expensive, it will be a long time before we fully understand the normal learning process, let alone all its variations. A few scientists have already begun the quest.

LOOKING INSIDE THE BRAIN

At Michigan State University, Dr E. James Potchen, chairman of the Department of Radiology, works at the forefront of these efforts. He directs a project in which magnetic-resonance imaging, a method of seeing the working brain in 'exquisite detail,' as he says, is being used to probe the relationship of brain structure and learning disability.

Dr Potchen has looked at 18,000 brains, and says that 'we are all abnormal because all brains are so different. It's amazing we do as well as we do.' Having brain differences should not necessarily be viewed as having a disease, he maintains, and there can be tremendous changes in the architecture of the brain from learning. He guesses the child's brain is always in the process of being rewired.

Dr Potchen tells of both animal and human brains that have restructured themselves significantly on the basis of learning experiences. Some types of birds even develop new neurons when they learn to sing. In a human experiment he showed pictures of a stick figure to doctors and artists while their brain activity was being scanned. Different areas of the cortex would 'light up' depending on the individual's profession. The artists, looking at the drawing, showed brain patterns indicating greater complexity of association and understanding.

NOISY BRAINS

"Nowadays when the parents bring these kids in the morning, we have to spend at least a half hour either waking them up or calming them down. They come from houses where the TV is going all the time, ride in cars with the music blaring – it's no wonder some have blocked it out and others are bouncing off walls. We used to be able to start our activities as soon as the children arrived, but now we always begin with a nice long transition period to get them tuned in."

– NURSERY SCHOOL TEACHER, TEXAS

"Could stereo headphones change children's brains? Obviously there's the potential for that. One could argue one of two things: either that it will make them more auditorily responsive or that it's going to produce some kind of weird dissociation between modalities [hearing and seeing] because they're chronically dissociated by the use of those things."

– DR WILLIAM T. GREENOUGH

What does noise bombardment do to children's brains? How much may it account for kids who can't pay attention, listen to 'talk,' and tune in appropriately to learning? One line of research has centreed on the irreplaceable structures in the ear that are especially vulnerable during early years. It has been proven that they can be damaged by certain loud noises, including music.

Another group of studies has shown that environments not considered particularly noisy by adults may interfere permanently with the development of language, listening, and even reading abilities.[46]

Other interesting avenues of speculation are also being discussed behind the closed doors of neuropsychological conferences. Three of these involve the effects of a preponderance of musical stimulation on the development of the hemispheres and the connections between them, some additional ideas about what heavy doses of 'beat' might do to growing brains, and the effects of an overload of sensory input on a nervous system that has not yet developed effective mechanisms to defend itself.

Brain studies have repeatedly shown that music, for everyone but highly trained musicians, is processed predominantly in the right hemisphere in areas directly opposite those responsible for most language processing. Most of us listen and respond primarily in a holistic, 'feeling' way to melody (right hemisphere's speciality), while musicians are trained to listen analytically to the technical sequence of notes and other features that must be handled by the left hemisphere.[47,48] The relaxed state often induced by music is reflected in changes in brain-wave patterns: the more vigorous beta waves that characterise active mental processing yield to slower alpha waves, which are more commonly associated with relaxation. When parts of the brain are 'in alpha,' they are essentially switched off from active thinking or learning.

[handwritten margin note: alpha — relax / switched off]

Why do some teenagers insist they can concentrate better on their homework with a background of music? We might speculate that music as background generates enough alpha in the right hemisphere to enable left hemisphere language areas to lead the attack on academic work. No one really understands all the ramifications of hemispheric byplay. Moreover, what works for one brain may be annoying or distracting for another. When music stops being background and becomes foreground, concentration probably suffers.

Increasing questions are being raised as to whether too much loud music might induce in a growing brain not real relaxation, but instead a habit of defensively 'tuning out' to active thought ('going into alpha'). A related question is whether large quantities of uncritical listening may rob left-hemisphere language systems of the developmental time and space they need for fine-tuning. Certainly, the lyrics of much contemporary music are definitely not designed as linguistic models. 'For every song that stands or falls by its words, there must be a hundred that thrive in spite of them . . . and sound often has the edge over sense,' commented Jon Pareles, acerbic *New York Times* music critic.[49] Like other serious musicians, he expresses concern over declining interest by listeners in responding to more complex analytic forms of the art. Much popular music, he says, 'eliminates the most complex, time-consuming, mentally draining part of musical experience – paying attention'.[50]

No one would recommend depriving adults of badly needed relaxation and harmless – for them – pleasures. Yet there are many adult pleasures that are handled successfully only by the mature brain. For children, challenge is the stimulus for the hemispheres to get their act together by strengthening the physical connections between them. Anything that either forces or induces the brain into a non-learning state for extended periods of time could certainly interfere with this process.

Young brains are particularly sensitive because they haven't yet developed automatic screening devices. The normal human brain has built-in mechanisms for moderating incoming sensory stimulation levels that keep it sufficiently 'aroused' without becoming overwhelmed. Children's brains, however, have not had time to refine these filtering systems; when overwhelmed, they either 'tune out' or their behaviour becomes unmanageable. Even normal adults exposed long enough to abnormally high or low levels of sensory stimulation may start to act like hyperactive children![51] We all learn to screen out a great deal of background noise (e.g., canned music in stores, office etc.), but at some point the unconscious effort involved takes its toll and we become habitually stressed out without understanding why. For youngsters, it is even harder to sort out such effects.

Dr Susan Luddington-Hoe, an authority on infant stimulation, points out that even before birth, tender young brains show a distinctly negative response to certain kinds of noise. She cites one example of a professional pianist who, when pregnant, found she could no longer play Chopin because her infant started to thrash around so violently. This foetus, however, seemed to love Mozart. 'The fetal heartbeat changes significantly to different types of music,' says Dr Luddington-Hoe. 'Both before and after birth, babies are really bothered by strong beat and loud music but they love soft music and are especially thrilled by Vivaldi.' In another case, a foetus who was taken to a rock concert kicked so hard, apparently in consternation, that he broke one of his mother's ribs.[52]

'My guess is the biggest problem with learning-disabled children is that their sensory thresholds are so low because they've had such a history of bombardment,' says Dr Luddington-Hoe. 'Their brains are letting in too much input because they're overwhelmed.'

HOOKED ON ALPHA?

When considering children whose attention problems seem to relate more to underactivity, some professionals wonder whether these children are learning to swaddle their brains in sensation-dulling music as an escape from excesses of stimulation in everyday life. Is it possible to be neurologically addicted to alpha rhythm? Certainly, headsets do seem to be on their way to replacing books and magazines for the young.

When I shared some of these questions with Dr Jerre Levy, an expert on hemispheric development who teaches at the University of Chicago, she admitted she had been wondering about this issue herself. 'It's the nature of the music they're listening to, this popular music,' she said. 'It is different from other kinds of music in that the tempo is exactly like a metronome: beat, beat, beat. Studies have shown that flashing lights at a fixed frequency (flash, flash, flash) sets up a

rhythm in the brain that interferes with normal processing. The same may be true of the auditory system', she suggests.

'When a person is simply sitting doing nothing', Dr Levy went on, 'brain waves are regularly synchronised: boom, boom, boom. (This is the case in relaxed states such as alpha). If the person is given a mental problem to solve, the brain's rhythm becomes "desynchronised" because the rhythm is broken by being forced to think.

'Now, if in your waking hours you have something coming in that's going beat, beat, beat,' she explained, 'my own feeling is that you're going to make kids space out because it's putting the brain into a loop; if it's in the loop, it can't desynchronise and therefore it can't think. You're really *blocking the capacity for thinking*.'[53]

Scientists have become sufficiently concerned to initiate animal studies of other kinds of rhythmic variables. Researchers at Fairleigh Dickinson University reared mice either in a quiet environment, one with soft classical background music, or one with equally soft but rhythmic drumbeats. The first two groups developed normally, but the latter animals showed difficulty navigating a standard maze, hyperactive and vicious behavior, as well as significant abnormalities in growth of brain cells in centres for learning and memory. Thus, it appears that continual exposure to other kinds of rhythms may also irritate the brain, irrespective of volume.[54]

In summary, it does not seem unreasonable to suggest that the brain needs time and quiet space in which to develop the ability to manage itself. To gain enough inner control to enjoy the quality of its own mental life, a child's mind should be furnished with some pieces of quiet thought, not the tacky trappings of constant noise.

SUMMARY: LIFESTYLES AND LEARNING

Attention and learning abilities depend both on the way the brains of the learners are innately structured and the uses for which they are trained. The success of any learning experience depends on the interaction between a brain's strengths and weaknesses and the demands of the learning situation. Some children's learning abilities are damaged by overt or subtle environmental impairment, but the term 'learning disability' now often simply describes an unexplained misfit between child and school. Attention deficit disorder (ADHD) and dyslexia are examples of disabilities that may sometimes have a genetic component but that also reflect strong effects of environmental training.

The growing brain is resilient, but may eventually be compromised by combinations of factors ranging from exposure to toxic substances, over- or understimulation, or lack of availability of appropriate adults to provide scaffolds for intellectual growth. Particularly important are inner speech, attention, and problem-solving strategies attributed to prefrontal development in the brain.

Environments can cause problems if (1) the specific demands they place for learning are misfitted to the brains of the learners, or (2) if they fail to instill in developing minds the fundamental skills of attention and reasoning. Increasing numbers of children today show evidence of weakness in attention, language, and reasoning, yet teachers continue to assume the presence of these skills and tend to blame the students for their unwillingness to pay attention to content and method for which their brains have been poorly adapted.

If adults in a society have things they want children to pay attention to, they must make available the consciousness that will develop the habits of mind – and thus the structures of the brain – to make it possible.

* This chapter is adapted from *Endangered Minds* by Jane Healy.

REFERENCES

1   Aubin, M. Personal communication. October 1988.

2   Picton, T. *et al.* 'Attention and the brain.' In Friedman, S., *et al. The Brain, Cognition and Education.* New York: Academic Press, 1986.

3   Posner, M. 'Attention and the control of cognition,' In Friedman, S. *et al. Op cit.*

4   Johnston, W. and Dark, V. 'Selective attention.' *Annual Review of Psychology* 37, 1986, pp 43-75.

5   Ceci, S. (Ed.) *Handbook of Cognitive, Social and Neuropsychological Aspects of Learning Disabilities*, Vol. II Hillsdale, NJ: Lawrence Erlbaum Associates, 1987.

6   Whalen, C. and Henker, B. *Hyperactive Children.* New York: Academic Press, 1980.

7   Bigler, N. *et al.* 'Educational perspectives on attention deficit disorder.' Paper presented at the international ACLD conference. Las Vegas, February 1988.

8   Whalen, C. and Henker, B. *Hyperactive Children.* New York: Academic Press, 1980.

9   Kirby, E. and Grimley, L. *Understanding and Treating Attention Deficit Disorder.* New York: Pergamon, 1986.

10   Pelham, W. 'The combination of behaviour therapy and methylphenidate in the treatment of attention deficit disorders: A therapy outcome study.' In Bloomingdale, L. (Ed.) *Attention Deficit Disorder*, Vol. 3, Oxford, Pergamon, 1988.

11   Silver, L. 'The confusion relating to Ritalin,' *ACLD Newsbriefs*, September 1988.

12   McGuinness, D. *When Children Don't Learn*. New York: Basic Books, 1985, pp. 200-2-1.

13   Cohen, N. 'Physiological concomitants of attention in hyperactive children.' Unpublished PhD. dissertation, McGill University, 1970.

14   Barkley, R. 'Attention-deficit hyperactivity disorder.' Address presented at symposium: The Many Faces of Intelligence. Washington, D. C., Kingsbury Centre, September 1988.

15   Barkley, R. 'An overview of attention deficit and related disorders in childhood and adolescence.' Address presented at course: Neurodevelopment and Its Implications for Attention, Emotion and Cognition: California Neuropsychology Services. Long Beach, CA, November 1988.

16   Jacobvitz, D. and Sroufe, L. 'The early caregiver-child relationship and attention deficit disorder with hyperactivity in kindergarten: A prospective study.' *Child Development*, 58, 1987, pp. 1496-1504.

17   Mattson, A., *et al.* '40 Hertz EEG activity in LD and normal children.' Poster presentation, International Neuropsychological Society. Vancouver, BC, February 1989.

18   Best, C. T. (Ed.). *Hemispheric Function and Collaboration in the Child*. New York: Academic Press, 1985.

19   Welsh, M. and Pennington, B. 'Assessing frontal lobe functioning in children: Views from developmental psychology.' *Developmental Neuropsychology* 4 (3), 1988, pp. 199-230.

20   Brody, J. 'Widespread abuse of drugs by pregnant women is found.' *New York Times*, August, 30, 1988.

21   *Education Week*, June 1, 1988.

22   'Get the lead out of your water.' *PTA Today*, February 1988.

23   *New York Times,* April 12, 1989, p.1.

24   Hartman, D. *Neuropsychological Toxicology*. New York: Pergamon, 1988.

25   Flax, E. 'Pesticides in schools: Focus shifting from indifference to concern.' *Education Week*, April 20, 1988.

26   'In California district, chemicals are used as last resort.' *Education Week*, April 20, 1988.

27   Levine, A. and Krahn, D. 'Food and behavior.' In Morley, J., *et al.*, (Eds.) *Nutritional Modulation of Neural Functioning*. New York: Academic Press, 1988.

28   Wurtman, R. and Wurtman, J. *Nutrition and the Brain*, Vols. 4, 6 and 7. New York: Raven, 1979, 1983, 1986.

29   Winick, M. *Nutrition in Health and Disease*. New York: Wiley, 1980.

30   Winick, M. *Malnutrition and Brain Development*. New York: Oxford University Press, 1976.

31   Kane, P. *Food Makes the Difference*. New York: Simon & Schuster, 1985.

32   Chollar, S. 'Food for thought.' *Psychology Today*, April 1988, pp. 30-34.

33   Conners, K. *Feeding the Brain: How Foods Affect Children*. New York: Plenum Press, 1989.

34   Conners, K. 'The phenomenology and neurophysiology of attention: Foods, drugs and attention in children.' Address presented at course: Neurodevelopment and Its Implications for Attention, Emotion and Cognition: California neuropsychology Services. Long Beach, CA, November 1988.

35   Wurtman, R. and Ritter-Walker, E. *Dietary Phenylalanine and Brain Function*. Boston: Birkhauser, 1988.

36   *Nation's School Report* 14 (2), 1988.

37   'Army softens basic training.' Cleveland Plain Dealer, April 17, 1989, p.1.

38   Allen, G. 'Why we need to improve youth fitness.' *PTA Today*, February 1987.

39   *Nation's School Report* 14 (2), 1988.

40   Miller, N. and Melamed, L. 'Neuropsychological correlates of academic achievement,' Poster presentation, International Neuropsychological Society, Vancouver, BC, February 1989.

41   Philips, S. 'The toddler and the preschooler.' Unit for Child Studies, Selected Papers, No. 29, New South Wales University, 1984. (ED 250 097).

42   Ayres, A. J. *Sensory Integration and Learning Disorders*. Los Angeles Western Psychological Services, 1972.

43   Ayres, A. J. 'Improving academic scores through integration.' *Journal of Learning Disabilities* 11, 1978, pp. 242-45.

44   Weikart, P. *Round the Circle: Key Experiences in Movement*. Ypsilanti, MI: High Scope Press, 1986.

45   Weikart, P. Personal communication, November 1988.

46   Pennington, B. 'Genotype and phenotype analysis of familial dyslexia.' Address presented at the Annual Meeting of the Orton Dyslexia Society. Tampa, FL, November 1988.

47   Vail, P. *Smart Kids with School Problems*. New York: Dutton, 1987.

48   Duffy, F. and Geshwind, N. *Dyslexia*. Boston: Little Brown, 1985.

49   Obler, L. K. and Fein, D. (Eds.), *Op cit.*

50   Geshwind, N. 'The brain of a learning disabled individual.' *Annals of Dyslexia,* 34, 1984.

51   Geshwind, N. and Behan, P. 'Left-handedness: Association with immune disease, migraine, and developmental learning disorder.' Proceedings of the National Academy of Sciences, USA, 79, 1982, pp. 5097-5100.

52   Galaburda, A. Personal communication. November 1988.

53   Galaburda, A. 'Ordinary and extraordinary brains: Nature, nurture and dyslexia.' Address presented at the Annual Meeting of the Orton Dyslexia Society. Tampa, FL, November 1988.

54   Duane, D. D. 'Dyslexia: pure and plus: A model behavioral syndrome.' Address presented at the Annual Meeting of the Orton Dyslexia Society. Tampa, FL, November 1988.

55   Rourke, B. 'The syndrome of nonverbal learning disorders.' *The Clinical Neuropsychologist* 2 (4), 1988, pp. 293-330.

56   Mills, J. 'Noise and children.' *Journal of the Acoustical Society of America* 58 (4), 1975, p. 776.

57   Deutsch, D. (Ed.). The Psychology of Music. New York: Academic Press, 1982.

58   Breitling, D., *et al.* 'Auditory perception of music measures by brain electrical activity mapping.' *Neuropsychologia* 25 (5), 1987. pp. 765-74.

59   Pareles, J. 'What'd they say? A wop-bop a loo-bop.' *New York Times*, August 8, 1988.

60   Pareles, J. 'New-age music booms softly.' *New York Times*, November 29, 1988.

61   Zentall, S. and Zentall, T. 'Optimal stimulation: A model of disordered activity and performance in normal and deviant children.' *Psychological Bulletin* 94 (3), 1983, pp. 446-71.

62   Luddington-Hoe, S. 'Infant development and care.' Symposium sponsored by Symposia Medicus. Cleveland, November 1988.

63   Levy, J. Personal communication. November 1988.

64   Schreckenberg, G., and Bird, H. 'Neural plasticity of MUS musculus in response to disharmonic sound.' *Bulletin of the New Jersey Academy of Sciences* 32, 1987, pp. 77-86.

STRATEGIES FOR EFFECTIVE LEARNING

VICKY HUNTER

INTRODUCTION

What makes learning effective for children? Many writers have recently considered different kinds of learning and their effectiveness. For example, the idea of deep, surface or strategic learning (Entwistle, 1987).

Surface learning is quickly forgotten; deep learning has more lasting effects because it has relevance for the learner; strategic learning is what is often called for in school, namely learning for an ulterior objective, usually that of passing exams. It is not the purpose of this chapter to explore these aspects of learning but simply to acknowledge their existence and set the following ideas in that context.

The fundamental premise is that for learning to be effective it must be relevant to the learner and must fit in with his or her learning style.

Generally the best way to achieve this is to listen to, observe and respect the pupil. Having stated these preliminaries, the following observations and strategies are offered as suggestions that help us to help children to learn more effectively. The context is that of mainstream secondary schools.

READING

(a) Decoding

There are many class teachers (and parents) who consider that the only way to ascertain whether a pupil is coping with reading is to listen to him reading aloud. In fact, oral reading and silent reading are rather different skills. Although pupils often share the view that the only true test of reading ability is to be able to read in front of one's peers, they become incredibly frustrated with their own inability to do so. They are so nervous the words get all jumbled up; the teacher corrects a mistake and makes them feel even more conspicuously incompetent; other pupils start reading over them. In order to escape from this humiliation, they attempt to get the whole thing over in record time – with even more disastrous consequences. The annoying thing is that they often understand the passage. Why else do they sometimes read 'high' for 'low' or 'up' for 'down'. That is not a decoding error. It is amazing how children can stutter and stumble over the detail of a passage and yet somehow have a fuller understanding of the content than the teacher who has been intent on conducting an error analysis and has studiously noted omissions, hesitations and repetitions while failing to take in the substance of the story.

(b)   Comprehension

There are some pupils who rely heavily on context clues and comprehension skills rather than decoding skills. Many are adept at the strategies of gleaning information and predicting the likely progress of a story. Unfortunately, if a pupil's decoding skills are too poor, he can construct a story on a completely wrong premise – e.g.. the pupil who read 'peat bog' as 'pet dog' had great difficulty in then getting the rest of the passage to make any sense at all.

Some pupils have become masters of reading the teacher's face. They know the nod and the smile that mean everything is correct and the frown that means a word is wrong. Their tactic, then, is to guess at a word and then check the teacher's face for the signal. When they return to the text they have lost the place and a great commotion of wriggling, sniffing and coughing ensues while it is found.

STRATEGIES

The first strategy, as always, is to observe the pupil, note how he is behaving and discover what kind of learning is currently being effective for him. The kinds of situations outlined above should be explored in order to help the pupil adjust his learning to a more effective mode. Often the pupils who are nervous and embarrassed about reading aloud in the class are the same ones who feel stigmatised because the teacher never asks them to read!

Strategies which could benefit **all** pupils include:

(a)   Decoding

(i)   Group reading

Pupils can be arranged in social or ability groups and encouraged to find the way of reading that best suits them. They may choose to read silently; or to read in unison; ask their best reader to read; take turns; ask for teacher support. (Group work is often facilitated by the presence of a learning support teacher or, in secondary schools, by the recruitment of senior pupils to assist in this way). This strategy enables them not only to handle the reading, but to develop effective strategies for determining their own favourite way of learning.

(ii)   Listening to tapes

Commercially produced tapes or (good) home-made ones. Pupils can sit at a listening centre together, but another strategy is to use Walkman-type tape players. Although this requires multiple tapes it does get rid of the potential for sabotage with a centre. The existence of taped material is also useful if a pupil has been absent and finds difficulty in catching up if reading on his own.

(iii)   Teacher and pupil reading

Teacher reading aloud and pupils reading part silently. It is important in this case to summarise what has been read and/ or check out comprehension.

(b)   Comprehension

(i)   Discussion

In pairs or groups, pupils can discuss topics such as:
How did the main character feel?
Has anything like this ever happened to you?
What happens next, etc?

(ii)   Illustrations

Pupils can be referred to the appropriate page to draw pictures of the setting, the characters, a plan or a map of the area etc. They can look through magazines to find pictures of people to represent the characters in a poster. This activity leads to discussion, e.g. No, that girl's too young/too pretty/too posh to be that character.

(iii) Written answers

True/False, Yes/No variety.

A selection of summaries with the task being to select the correct one – again, discussion makes this work even better, a list of events to put in the correct order; close passages.

(iv) Spidergrams/key word diagrams e.g.

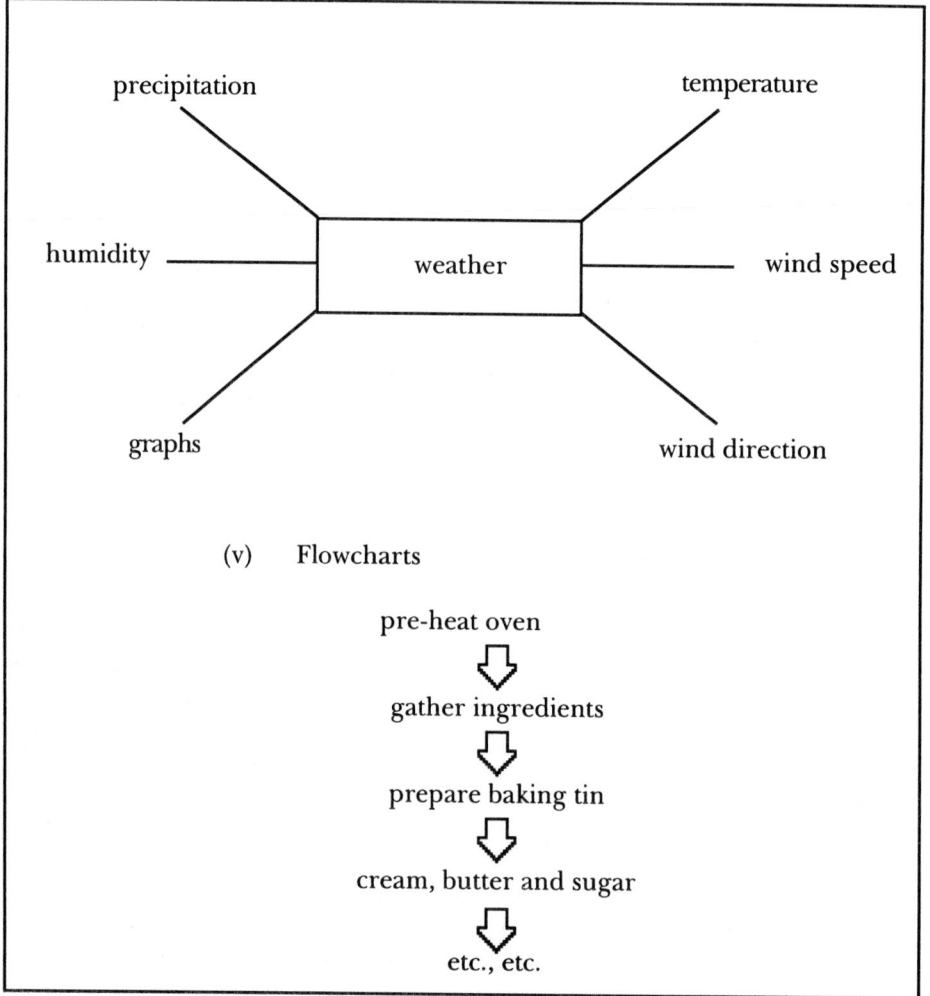

(v) Flowcharts

WRITING

A boy wrote on the topic of 'My Best Friend':

'He's not very briny but niram I sow that's OK.'

(He's not very brainy, but neither am I, so that's OK)

What is writing? It is about communicating one's ideas on paper and this is what children need to be encouraged to do. By secondary school, many of them have restricted their output because they are weary of being corrected for spelling, handwriting and punctuation.

The aim must always be to continue to develop these technical skills while continuing to value content and creativity.

(a)   Handwriting

By secondary school, handwriting is a very difficult thing to change. Many pupils have developed personal styles and idiosyncratic pencil grips which have become ingrained over a number of years. Many able pupils face problems when they are required to do more and more writing as they face exams and the style that served them well enough when younger becomes inefficient for lengthy writing sessions.

STRATEGIES:

(a)   Changing handwriting grip and/or style

If a pupil really wants to change he can be offered pencil grips, specially designed pencils and lessons showing the correct way to form and join letters. However, in my experience, not many pupils have the motivation or determination to do this, particularly as the demands on them in general are constantly increasing. I would, however, stress that the best solution is to get everything right at the start if at all possible.

(b)   Take the pressure off

Many pupils appear to have been nagged about their handwriting all their school career. Parents complain about it, teachers go on about it. Some youngsters feel that they could submit an investigation unravelling the mystery of the universe and it would be returned with

'Your handwriting requires attention' scrawled across it by teachers who, incidentally, often do not present very positive role models.

(c) **Set realistic standards**

For some pupils, particularly early in secondary school, all that is needed is a reminder that neat handwriting is called for. Many Primary teachers are horrified at what their Secondary colleagues appear to be accepting, while the Secondary staff are simultaneously commenting on the poor standard of handwriting in the new intake. The pupils are just trying it on!

(d) **Alternative solutions**

(i) Use of a word processor/lap top computer

This is not generally the panacea some people think it will be. First of all pupils need practice in key-boarding skills and in the operation of the computer. Even with this, their output is generally slower than that of their peers and of their own written attempts.

Then there is the fact of being different by using this aid. Some children, of course, revel in the kudos, but others feel stigmatised and conspicuous. These aids are useful for finished work but may have limited value on a day-to-day basis.

(ii) Use of a scribe

This, too, is a skill which needs to be practised, particularly if it is to be used for external exams. Again, individual pupil needs and feelings need to be taken into consideration. Some love the sound of their own voice and the freedom to express themselves fully, others are mortified at having to articulate ideas that they are not too sure about anyway.

(iii) Use of tape recorder/dictaphone (for later transcription)

Again, depending on how a pupil feels about speaking into a machine, this can be a useful tool. If it is to be used in class it can be disturbing to other pupils and so arrangements have to be made to overcome this. Transcribing the words is a time consuming task for someone.

SPELLING

There are plenty of books offering advice on ways of teaching spelling and a number of diagnostic tests to help teachers determine the nature of a pupil's difficulty – e.g. poor visual memory, poor auditory memory, lack of phonic knowledge, lack of knowledge of serial probability etc. Self-image as a speller can also be assessed (NFER Nelson Diagnostic Spelling).

It is undoubtedly the case that by secondary stage the view of oneself as a poor speller is one of the major stumbling blocks to improvement. Many dyslexic pupils deliberately restrict their output to the words they can spell or restrict the quantity of their written work to minimise the number of corrections they will have to make at the redrafting stage. For some the self-image problem is so great that they hate the idea of using error analysis as a vehicle for learning spelling. They prefer the objectivity of using spelling books or programmes.

It is thus important to find ways of improving spelling while also encouraging creativity and depth in written work.

STRATEGIES

(a) Error Analysis/Personal Word Bank

Provided the pupil is not like the few described above who find the process threatening, this can be an effective way of valuing the pupil. The pupil is asked to highlight words in his own writing that he thinks are wrong and attempt corrections. If the word is still wrong or he is unsure, that word is added to the word bank. It is important to go through this self-correction process. If it is just left to the teacher to find the words, the pupil will be quick to say it was just carelessness/laziness which led to the mistake.

(b) Other Methods

Looking at the word with meaning; look, cover, write check methods; (Peters) building up letter strings; using computer programs; combining handwriting with spelling; using a dictaphone to practise spellings . . . the list of strategies goes on and on. Whatever method is used, it is important to value the pupil's own learning style and offer myriad opportunities for success.

(c) Alternatives

As with handwriting, in order to maintain the depth and creativity of response, use can be made of techniques such as scribing and taping where the need for correct spelling can, for the moment, be forgotten.

MOTIVATION AND LEARNING STYLES

Bearing in mind the maxim that in school 'no-one ever learns nothing', it is interesting to consider how much pupils with learning difficulties have learned in terms of developing coping strategies. Unfortunately for some of them, these strategies are destructive – disruption, truancy, detachment. Some coping strategies are conventional and approved of by teachers on the whole – e.g. using pictures to aid understanding, asking the teacher for help. However, many pupils in our classrooms are investing an enormous amount of time and effort first in devising strategies and then in concealing them from the teacher.

The most obvious strategy in this category, of course, is 'asking your pal'. For some teachers this is still beyond the pale but fortunately many more are now accepting that peer discussion is a most effective learning tool. The student doing the explanation has his own understanding deepened by the very process of having to make something clear to another.

Children have several spelling strategies that they try to conceal. If they are having to transfer a word from one context to another they scribble it on their hand, their desk, their folder in order to copy it down later. Because this process is surreptitious the word is often illegible anyway. All these pupils need is permission to use scrap paper to conduct this exercise – and praise for having thought of it.

This piece of scrap paper can also be used for trying out the spelling of a word. This is an effective strategy used by successful adult spellers, but for some reason many pupils are ashamed of their need to test themselves in this way. Again, permission and praise are required.

Another example of this phenomenon was the pupil whose method of working out number problems was effective for her because she simply could not remember number bonds. She spent hours of her life in the Maths class flicking her jotter backwards and forwards as she concealed her nefarious practice:

$$13 - 7 = 6 \qquad 1 \ 2 \ 3 \ 4 \ 5 \ 6 \ \cancel{7} \ \cancel{8} \ \cancel{9} \ \cancel{10} \ \cancel{11} \ \cancel{12} \ \cancel{13}$$

She wrote down the numbers 1-13 and then crossed off 7 numbers from the right hand side. She was helped by having her jotter ruled off to allow working; by being valued for her ability to work out this strategy; and of course by being given an addition/subtraction square and a calculator!

For many pupils with specific learning difficulties, school is one long experience of failure and frustration. And when they do finally master something they are pushed on to the next task, the next challenge. We can help them by setting smaller, achievable targets and by giving them the chance to enjoy their success. Ten new spelling words learned thoroughly and then tested achieving full marks is more motivating than twenty words half learned and a test score of ten.

Alongside the processes of teaching, there must go genuine respect for the pupil and understanding of his feelings.

CONCLUSION

Effective learning always relies on matching the task to the learner. This requires careful thought as to the level and type of learning experience to offer, but it also requires that teachers value pupils and seek to construct learning situations which enhance their self-esteem and develop in them the belief that they can do it.

> 'When I got up this morning
> I thought the whole thing through
> Say, who's the master, the king of the universe?
> * Christopher, it's you.'
> * (Substitute the name of your pupil.)

REFERENCES

Entwhistle, N. (1987). *Understanding Classroom Learning,* Pub. Hodder & Stoughton.
Denis, V. and Caydon, J. (1992). *Diagnostic Spelling Test.* NFER, Nelson.
Peters, M. (1985). *Spelling: Caught or Taught.* Routledge.

THE POTENTIAL OF LEARNING STYLES

BARBARA K. GIVEN

That children with learning difficulties make one and a half to four years reading gain in one year causes most teachers to stop and ask questions, yet that is what research revealed when children were taught through their individual learning styles (Carbo, Dunn and Dunn, 1986; Dunn *et al.* 1995). Research consistently reveals that when students are taught through their preferred versus their non preferred learning style they demonstrate: 1) statistically significant improvement in their attitudes toward instruction, 2) increased tolerance for cognitive diversity, 3) statistically significant increased academic achievement, 4) better discipline/behaviour, and 5) greater self-discipline for homework completion (Andrews, 1990; Butler, 1986; Brunner and Majewski, 1990; Dunn, Griggs, Gorman, Olson and Beasley, in press; Elliot, 1991; Gadwa and Griggs, 1985; Klavas, 1993; Lemmon, 1985; McCarthy, 1990; Orsak, 1990; Stone, 1992). Even so, critics argue that factors other than style-responsive instruction may account for academic gains (Curry, 1987,1990; Davidson, 1981; Kavale and Forness, 1987; Snider, 1992). In this chapter, I focus on learning style models that spawned identification instruments, why style-responsive instruction is effective, and scientific support for the learning style construct.

LEARNING STYLE MODELS

Learning style is described as a set of '. . . traits that serve as relatively stable indicators of how learners perceive, interact with, and respond to the learning environment' (Keefe, 1982, p. 44). Over 100 learning style models exist and most can be grouped into one or more of the following five categories: 1) personality and emotional models, 2) psychological, cognitive and information models, 3) social models, 4) physical models, and 5) environmental and instructional models.

Emotional/Personality Models of Learning Style. In the early 1900s, Carl Jung launched the concept of psychological types when he divided major emotional and personality characteristics into four bipolar clusters: extraversion/intraversion, sensation/intuition, thinking/feeling, and judging/perceiving. Later, Isabel Myers (Myers and Briggs, 1976) and her mother Katherine Briggs expanded Jung's work and produced the Myers-Briggs Type Indicator with sixteen combinations of the four types. David Kolb (1984) took a different tack. He combined Jung's psychological types with concepts from Piaget, Dewey and Lewin to form crossed bipolar continua to represent how individuals perceive information and how they process information once it is received. [See figure 1 for a comparison of three Jungian-based models.] When crossed, these two continua created four major learning styles: diverger, assimilator, conveger, and accommodator. Kolb described corresponding learning behaviours as engaging in concrete experiences, reflecting on that experience from different perspectives, creating abstract concepts, principles or theories, and using the theories as guides for active experimentation.

Fig. 1

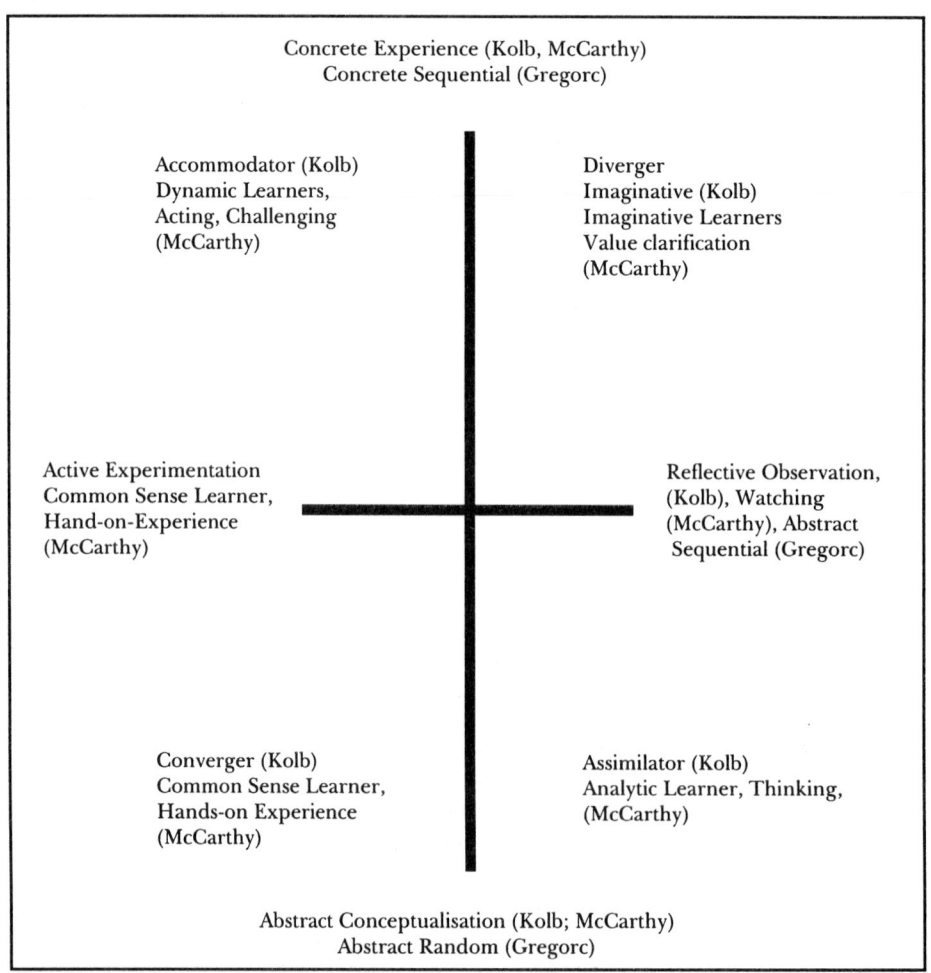

Concrete Experience (Kolb, McCarthy)
Concrete Sequential (Gregorc)

Accommodator (Kolb)
Dynamic Learners,
Acting, Challenging
(McCarthy)

Diverger
Imaginative (Kolb)
Imaginative Learners
Value clarification
(McCarthy)

Active Experimentation
Common Sense Learner,
Hand-on-Experience
(McCarthy)

Reflective Observation,
(Kolb), Watching
(McCarthy), Abstract
Sequential (Gregorc)

Converger (Kolb)
Common Sense Learner,
Hands-on Experience
(McCarthy)

Assimilator (Kolb)
Analytic Learner, Thinking,
(McCarthy)

Abstract Conceptualisation (Kolb; McCarthy)
Abstract Random (Gregorc)

Anthony Gregorc (1982) combined Jungian concepts with phenomenology to study underlying causes of learning behaviours. His metaphysical model included four 'mind channels': concrete sequential, abstract sequential, abstract random, and concrete random. The philosophical principle of his model was that 'the primary purpose of life is to realise and actualise one's individuality, spirituality, and collective humanness' (p. v). Gregorc believed that individuals can learn to behave through non dominant channels for adjustment to varying circumstances so long as the dominant style is permitted opportunity to develop.

Like Gregorc, Susan Dellinger (1989) interpreted Jung's contribution in an individualistic way. She assigned a geometric shape – circle, square, triangle, and squiggle – to each of Jung's four types and added an extra shape, a rectangle, to indicate characteristics of exploration and experimentation experienced when individuals are in new or unusual circumstances. [See figure 2.] Although playful in approach, Dellinger's shapes offer an interesting way to introduce the learning style concept.

Fig. 2

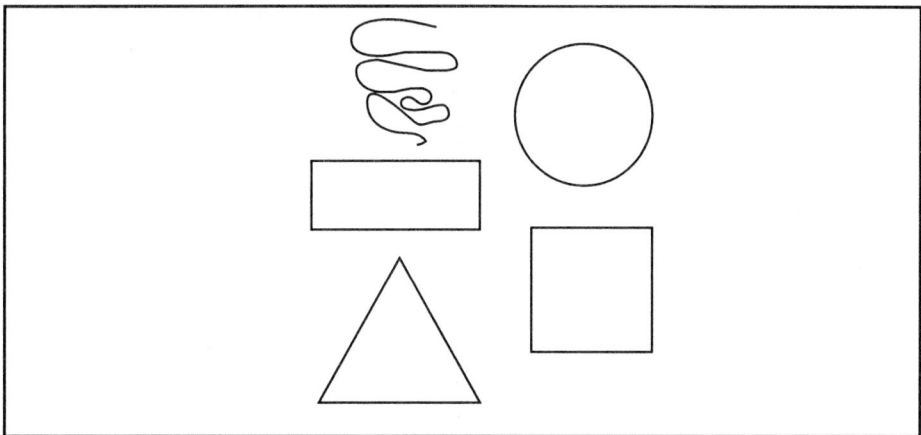

In the emotional domain, Dunn and Dunn (1993, 1994) were more concerned with how students are motivated, how persistent they are when pursuing a task, and the level of responsibility assumed for completing the task. [See figure 3.] They focused on the source of motivation as coming from internal desires, authority figures or peers. Responsibility centred on staying power and task completion; some students stick with a task whereas others take frequent breaks and have many activities started before finishing one. They also included the difference between an individual's need for specific, well defined structure for task completion versus preference for a broad explanation with freedom to impose one's own structure or lack thereof upon the task.

Fig. 3

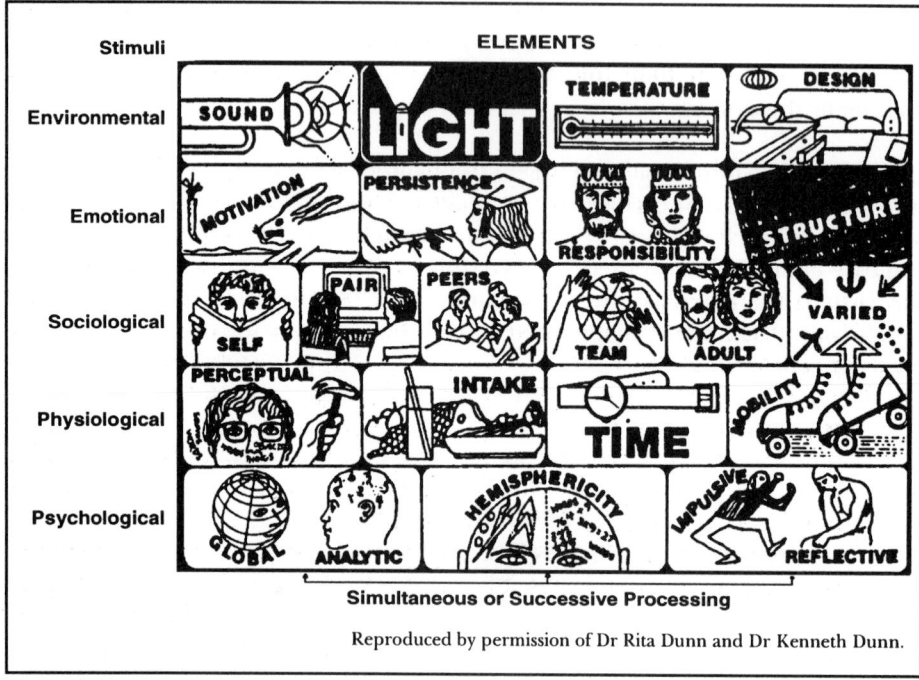

Reproduced by permission of Dr Rita Dunn and Dr Kenneth Dunn.

Psychological Approaches to Learning Style. In an attempt to understand the complexities of learning, cognitive psychologists used bipolar dimensions such as field independent vs field dependent (Witkin, 1976) and sequential vs simultaneous (Kaufman and Kaufman, 1984). Letteri (1982) compiled several bipolar models into a synthesised whole and identified Type I, Type II, or Type III learners based on individual preferences. A Type I profile correlated highly with academic success and represented an analytic, focused, narrow, complex, reflective, sharpened, and tolerant cluster of characteristics. Letteri then designed instruction to assist Type II and Type III learners to become similar to Type I, since Types II and III were identified as lower in academic achievement.

The Dunn and Dunn (1994) model included three bipolar psychological styles: global/analytic, left brain/right brain hemisphercity, and impulsive/reflective response patterns. The Dunns described global/analytic and left brain/right brain as synonymous for instructional purposes.

Many researchers and practitioners focused on modality preferences (visual, auditory, tactile and kinaesthetic) as the primary ways information is received and as indicators of learning style. It is common to hear someone say, 'Don't tell me. Show me; I'm a visual learner.' Or 'If I write it, I can tell if it's spelled right.' Some shun written directions and either follow the diagrams or begin assembling a bicycle or luggage rack by figuring it out on their own: 'I learn best when I do it myself.' Others want to be told new information: 'I get confused with maps, just tell me how to get there.'

To determine modality strength, Barbe and Swassing (1979) developed a set of plastic shapes for learners to assemble in sequence after seeing them, feeling them with closed eyes, or hearing someone read the sequence (circle, square, triangle, cross). Grinder and Bandler (Grinder, 1993) extended an analysis of modality preferences to include attention to eye movements, language usage, the pace of language delivery, body movements, and reactions to learning experiences. In their Neuro Linguistic Programming (NLP), they paid close attention to verbs used in conversation as signals for modality strengths. 'I see what you mean,' suggests a visual learner. 'I hear you,' suggests auditory preferences while, 'I get what you mean,' or 'It feels right to me,' suggest tactile or kinaesthetic learning preferences. The Dunns also included perceptual modalities in their model, but they considered them as elements of the physical domain because of their biological bases. Also the Dunns (K. Dunn, personal communication) attributed deeper meaning to statements. For them, statements such as 'Let me try it' suggest a need for tactual, visual, interactive learning with a reliance on doing the task for oneself. 'We need a walk through' represents kinaesthetic, feeling through doing, and a need for visual input and interaction. 'I need a written memo' suggests a need for a word oriented visual input that can be analysed then reflected upon.

Social Approaches to Learning Style. Social learning styles pertain to preferences and consistent behaviour patterns used for interacting with others. Dunn and Dunn (1993) focused on the learner's preference for working alone, with one or more peers, in a team, with an adult or authority figure or in a variety of social groupings. Grasha (1972) developed learning style scales which included: independent, dependent, collaborative, competitive, participant, and avoidant learning patterns. As with researchers in the above sections, these researchers matched teaching styles to learning patterns as defined in their models and found that students learned best in settings where their social-emotional needs were met.

Brandt (1983) cautioned about some danger in always matching social preferences. He studied functional and dysfunctional family-oriented social interactions and identified three styles that demonstrated dysfunction: acquiescent, self-important, and deprived. The acquiescent style reveals a history of parental over direction and intrusiveness which results in a loss of inner direction, excessive reliance on approval, expectations to satisfy others rather than self, and disappointment in self for failing to measure up to others' expectations. A person with this style may be overly dependent upon authority figures for direction and validation.

A self-important style has a history of high levels of gratification and high levels of expectation that others will maintain in other social groups his/her favoured position within the family. This person demonstrates a grandiose sense of self whose self-worth is linked to performance. Expectation of the self-important person is entitlement to special treatment for continual gratification. This person is disappointed, according to Brandt, when there is a loss of specialness at school or in not getting what is thought to be rightfully deserved.

By contrast, the person with a deprived style reveals a history of emotional and physical deprivation resulting in fear of rejection, fear of abandonment, a sense of neediness accompanied by a despair that his or her needs will never be met. This person expects the worst and acts accordingly as a defence against hurt feelings. This is a common style of incarcerated adolescent girls who have a history of physical and sexual abuse (Boo, 1995). Brandt believed these dysfunctional styles can be changed to healthy styles, but Boo (1995) warned that change may take years. In the meantime, each of these social styles can have a deleterious effect on learning, thus instruction needs to be skilfully presented to help the learner move into more healthy interactions.

Physical Approaches to Learning Style. Except for modality preferences noted earlier, Dunn and Dunn (1993, 1994) appear to be the only learning-style advocates to include physiological considerations of style in their model. These include snacking while studying, walking or moving about when learning and studying, or taking tests during preferred time of day. These characteristics correlated highly with characteristics of global learners whereas sustained focus, remaining seated and on task until task completion correlated with analytic style and higher achievement (Dunn and Dunn, 1993, 1994). Stone (1992) and Andrews (1990) studied elements of style with elementary students and found that when students chewed gum, snacked, and/or moved around during class, global students' achievement increased.

While not identified as learning style advocates, Dennison and Dennison (1989) designed a series of physical exercises to integrate the brain hemispheres for more effective cognitive functioning and receptivity – a consistent aim of learning style approaches. Their educational kinaesthetic or brain gym exercises were designed to strengthen left-to-right eye movements, binocular and peripheral vision, spatial awareness, visual discrimination, eye-hand coordination, auditory alertness, auditory receptivity, and clarity of thought. Their program has a strong reliance on neuro-anatomy and brain functioning research. The importance of consuming ample drinking water, eliminating caffeine intake, and reducing refined sugar consumption support the Edu-K curriculum. Few research reports exist, but those that do are impressive (Hannaford, in press).

Environmental/Instructional Approaches to Learning Style. The Dunns determined that many students have definite preferences for bright versus dim light, sound versus quiet, formal versus informal furniture design, and warm versus cool classroom and study environments. When students were allowed to work in environments consistent with their preferred environmental needs, they achieved at higher levels than when working in mismatched environments (Dunn and Dunn, 1993, 1994).

Marie Carbo (Carbo, Dunn and Dunn, 1986), a former remedial reading teacher, adapted the Dunn and Dunn model to guide reading instruction. She also developed a structured procedure for recording books to help students develop reading vocabularies and reading fluency while gaining information about something of high interest to them. She focused on specific considerations in addition to interest level: the book must be of high interest to the student. It must be recorded with full expression and careful pacing to allow time for the student to focus on the words while listening, and provision must be made for repetitive listening to short segments that are later read to the teacher.

Reid (1994) advocated the use of teacher observations rather than use of a standardised instrument for identification of learning style preferences. He based his series of classroom observations on how students interact, communicate, move, organise themselves and their materials, attend, understand and succeed. He found that teachers who match instruction to observed student preferences increased student interest in instructional tasks.

Bernice McCarthy (1987) studied the relationship between learning style approaches and research on brain behaviour. She borrowed heavily from Kolb and others to develop a quadrilateral model for instructional design. She then divided each quadrant into left brain/right brain characteristics to create an eight-step approach for lesson planning: 1) creating an experience – right mode, 2) reflecting, analysing experience – left mode, 3) integrating reflective analysis into concepts – right mode, 4) developing concepts, skills – left mode, 5) practising defined 'givens' – left mode, 6) practising and adding something of oneself – right mode, 7) analysing application for relevance, usefulness – left mode, and 8) doing it and applying to new, more complex experience – right mode. McCarthy promoted experiential learning and teaching to match each student's learning style at least part of the time.

Kathleen Butler (1984) also translated theory into practice by designing specific instructional recommendations for Gregorc's four 'mind styles'. She expanded his model to include instructional procedures consistent with Bloom's levels of thinking. Renzulli and Smith (1978) took a different instructional approach. They designed a questionnaire to assess learners' preferences for various types of learning experiences: projects, simulations and acting, drill and recitation, peer teaching, discussion, teaching games, independent study, programmed instruction, and teacher talk or lecture. Their research with students identified as gifted or talented revealed that teaching through instructional preferences resulted in more positive attitudes toward school.

MULTIPLE INTELLIGENCES

On the surface, Gardner's (1985) multiple intelligences – musical, spatial, bodily-kinaesthetic, mathematical/logical, interpersonal, intrapersonal, or verbal/linguistic – resemble learning styles. This, however, is easily clarified. Learning style implies consistency of preferences and use across contexts and intelligences. Multiple intelligences suggested the ability to shift in the use of an ability contingent upon context. Different circumstances require the use of different intelligences according to Gardner's schemata. Learning styles are applicable across the various intelligences; however, as in learning styles, one or more of the intelligences is generally stronger than the others. Because of this, Gardner (1985) suggested that teachers 'need to adapt . . . curricula as much as possible to the particular learning styles and strengths of students' (p. 79).

LEARNING STYLE FRAMEWORK

There is an old axiom: 'the more complex something is, the greater the need to make it simple.' This tendency to organise complexity into simple systems is clearly demonstrated in attempts to understand the learning process and the role learning styles play in that process. The question remains, 'Is there one model more valid and reliable than others for the initiation of a styles-responsive instructional program?' To answer this question, I attended training programs presented by several of the models' designers and enrolled in graduate coursework over the last several years. I experimented with each model in graduate level classes and with children, adolescents and adults enrolled in a campus-based program for individuals with learning difficulties. I then began combining various models until a combination of the best of each model emerged for me. This paper describes the evolutionary thinking that took place.

Each of the models tends to focus on only one or two slices of the learning style pie. Only the Dunn and Dunn model offers a comprehensive approach with major elements found in each domain. New and replicated research to support the Dunns model is extensive which makes it the best researched, strongest and most comprehensive model available. Extensive resource materials, workshops and institutes are available for beginners to advanced learners.

McCarthy's model has strong user appeal, but it has far less research to support its use than does the Dunns 'model. It appears to be a simpler model with four quadrants versus five domains and 22 elements. The **4Mat** System, however, is deceptive in its apparent simplicity. Like Kolb's experiential model upon which McCarthy based much of her theory, full understanding of **4Mat** requires extensive study, application and reflection on hemisphericity literature and McCarthy and Kolb's publications. Nonetheless, because it offers a visual format for constructing lesson plans that include experiential learning and the use of all perceptual modalities, **4Mat** is a viable model for novices and for those who wish to delve deeper into theoretical issues. Colourful support materials, a computer-based lesson plan data base, and training workshops support its use.

Butler's interpretation of Gregorc's model provides a rich but hypothetical composite of instructional ideas and rationale. Availability of research to support her suggestions is limited, but her recommendations seem well-grounded in theory and best practice. Butler offers publications, training sessions and workshops as does her mentor, Anthony Gregorc.

To build interest in a short amount of time, to get my foot in the cognitive door, and to lay a foundation for moving to greater depth, I found Dellinger's psycho-geometric shapes a useful place to introduce the learning style concept. Primary children to adults of all ages relate to shapes. A playful introduction promoted rapid, superficial knowledge of style and served as a motivator for more in-depth learning.

When organised in a framework with Dunns' domains and Kolb-like quadrants, a rich framework emerged [figure 4]. The environmental domain was placed in the middle to show connections with all other domains, to indicate that everything is done within a context, and to convey that context plays a key role in determining which domain will be most influential at any one time. It also fosters the concept that transitions from one style to another occur within the environment.

Fig. 4

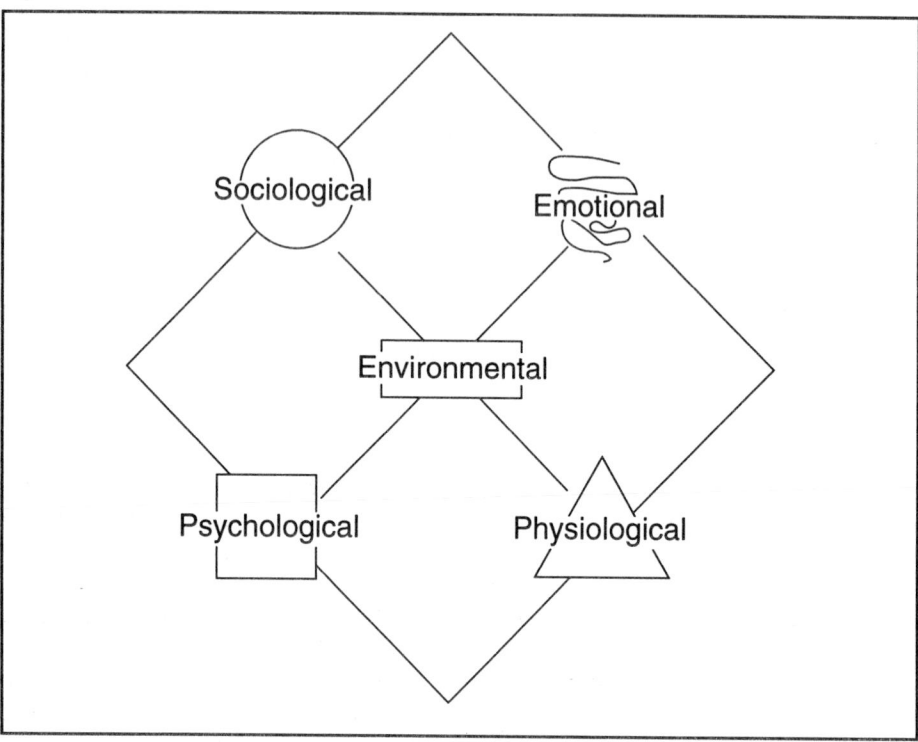

Although a person's personality characteristics may cluster with the description of one particular shape or learning preference, humans are neither all global nor all analytic, right-brained nor left-brained. Rather, individuals possess attributes across the hemispheres with specific preferences and needs for learning predominantly found in one or the other. Similarly, elements of style are found in each of the systems or domains.

In view of these hypotheses, a major question remains: is greater academic gain and improved attitude the result of matching teaching to learning style or to something else, such as added attention? To address this question, I explored a wide range of literature and found that information from physics and the neuroscience of consciousness, brain complexity, neural networks, self-constructed living systems, chaos and the edge of chaos, knowledge construction, complex adaptive systems and connectivism gave credence to the styles construct and helped explain it. A book covering these findings is in production, but the following brief overview helped answer the question for me.

SYSTEMS THEORY

Physics and biology are quantitative sciences based on measurements and mathematical data. Learning style, by comparison, pertains to qualities that describe an individual's preferences for learning new material. In spite of these differences, so long as the interconnecting conceptual models are logically consistent, biology, genetics, physics, and engineering can help explain conceptually, if not mathematically, why learning style instruction is effective.

Systems theory suggests that all things are connected in some way, that what happens to one system impacts other systems. This can be seen by dropping pebbles in a tub of water and watching the concentric circles bump into one another. It is also seen among systems of the body: humans are composed of many individual systems and subsystems that interrelate with interdependence upon each other. Heart disease, for example, not only clogs blood vessels, it can reduce physical stamina and weaken respiration – spin off results in other systems. Learning systems – emotional, social, cognitive, physical, and environmental – seem to work in the same way. What impacts one 'bumps into' and effects the others. When emotionally or physically stressed, cognitive functioning is impaired as anyone who ever experienced emotional pain can verify. By contrast, when involved in a loving relationship, that glow is reflected physically in quickness of step, body posture, facial expressions. No bodily system can work independent of the other systems and the body would perish without all its systems. Interdependence of learning systems also seems to exist, but among them the emotional learning system may be far more critical to the learning whole than previously thought.

EMOTIONAL LEARNING SYSTEM

Traditional views hold that the cortex is the most important part of the brain for learning; however, recent research is beginning to recognise the importance of emotions. Emotions affect attention, sustained focus, interest, motivation, and judgment, yet most of us have very little understanding of why emotions are so powerful. The cognitive, rational part of humanness is highly prized in school and the workplace, yet to overcome the emotional system's power, it often has to work hard – metaphorically, make bigger waves. Why is this? A cursory overview of neuropeptides and brain structures that regulate emotions might make the relationship clear.

Based on her research with opiates, opiate receptors, and amino acids, Candace Pert (Moyer, 1993), a molecular biologist, reported that cells throughout the body have millions of dish-like receptors on their surfaces that await amino acids strung together in varying combinations and lengths to form peptides. Sixty different types of neuropeptides or natural drugs of the brain – the brain's hormones – play several messenger roles: they build protein, control the opening and closing of blood vessels in the face, and, more important, they allow systems of the body to talk to each other (Moyer, 1993, p. 187). In their talking, peptides serve as psychosomatic communication networks that mediate intercellular communication and link the mind and body. This communication process between the neuropeptides and the structures that produce electrochemical responses support the pebble metaphor and the application of systems theory to learning. The importance of neuropeptides led Pert to conclude: 'everything you do is run by your emotions' (Moyers, 1993, p. 187).

Fig. 5

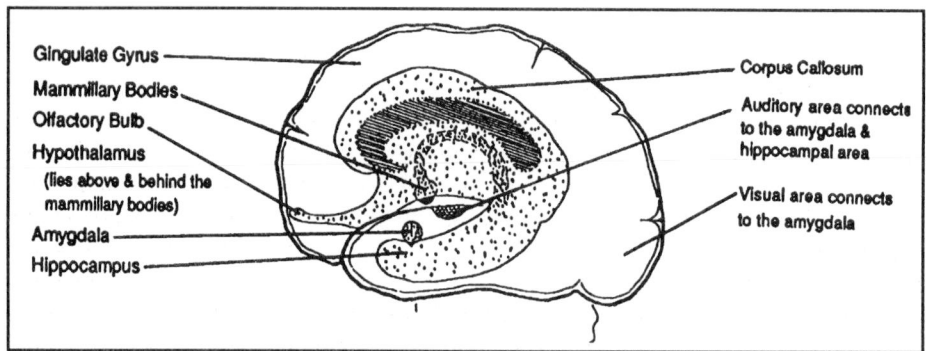

At a structural level, the limbic system (figure 5), a bagel-like structure with a bite taken out, sits immediately above the brain stem and below the cortex or cognitive brain. There are far more nerve connections going from the limbic system to the cortex than the other way around, and different parts of the limbic system decide what messages are sent to the cortex from inside and outside the body. Robert Sylwester (1993) said the limbic system has 'librarian-like' qualities in the selection and classification of incoming information for long-term memory storage and retrieval. Like a librarian, he stated, its decisions are based on the value it places on information received. The emotional role of the limbic system is critically important, because the cortex cannot contemplate, problem solve, or remember information not sent to it.

Whether a child engages in the learning process, therefore, is contingent upon emotional factors involved with the task. Emotional factors involved as a result of matching instruction to learning-style preferences, such as comfort level and task ownership, appear to account for the increased academic benefits derived from implementation of various learning style models.

IMPLICATIONS FOR TEACHING

As presented earlier, learning style models vary. Consequently, instruction based on specific models show variety. Is there a 'best" learning style model in terms of instruction that emphasises emotional involvement? Four learning style proponents have clearly defined instructional procedures and supporting reference materials: Butler (1986); Carbo (1986); Dunn and Dunn (1993, 1994), and McCarthy (1987). All provide:

- Rationale for specific recommendations,
- guiding principles for implementation, and
- sample lesson and unit plans.

McCarthy and Butler focus on teachers developing a thorough understanding of learning and teaching styles rather than formal identification of student styles. They believe that teachers must philosophically and practically obtain an in-depth understanding of their own styles in various contexts before they are sufficiently grounded to observe style preferences in students. By contrast, Carbo and the Dunns assess students directly with paper and pencil or computer-driven learning style inventories. They believe that youngsters are empowered to take ownership of learning when they can articulate to themselves and others how they learn. They believe that knowledge of style helps students take responsibility for homework and for working effectively in environments incompatible with their style, and that awareness of different styles helps establish rapport among diverse groups of learners.

For almost two decades, instruction based on each of these models has been adopted, adapted, and analysed for children, adolescents and adults attending on-campus academic programs for students with learning difficulties. The program, Operation Breakthrough, was designed for small group instruction where careful observational records of implementation could be kept. Students attended academic classes either twice a week for fourteen weeks for two and a half hours each session or three hours a day, four days a week for six weeks in the summer. We found that when youngsters and adults had an introductory understanding of learning styles and systems, they were more enthusiastic about assignments and more aware of how to take charge of their learning in comparison to that knowledge remaining solely with the teacher. Students of all ages enjoyed using learning style terms and they identified instructional approaches that felt more comfortable than others. Students were more willing to experiment with alternative ways of learning when they thought of the experience as stretching to someone else's style.

Differentiation of content to be learned from the teacher's teaching style encouraged students to reorganise information in ways that fit their self-identified styles. Before moving to new material, the same information was reorganised in several ways for different purposes: note taking, concept attainment, public speaking, and writing to communicate. The recursive nature of several reorganisations resulted in retention without drill and practice. Students were often surprised about the extent of learning that occurred while they were having fun putting new information into a musical rap, a play, or bogus report.

Follow-up data revealed that interest and enthusiasm for learning was sustained in classes where the receiving teachers were knowledgeable and enthusiastic about learning styles instruction, and where parents encouraged their children to reorganise and complete their homework according to preferred style. Youngsters appeared to need an on-going dialogue about the learning process to sustain interest in it.

One contribution of learning styles instruction was that it responded to the emotional needs students had for self-direction and ownership of their learning. Style-responsive instruction empowered students to take responsibility for doing as well as or better than they did prior to learning-style intervention (Dunn and Dunn, 1993,1994). Since youngsters had control over the manner in which they demonstrated competencies, teachers were encouraged to design lessons with options compatible with different modality preferences. Further, learning styles instruction encouraged students to set learning goals, to reflect on their accomplishments, and to establish new goals.

Thematic units and projects allowed for a variety of learning style alternatives for acquisition of knowledge and skills. Reading assignments were tape-recorded following Carbo's guidelines for auditory students. Traditional essays were alternated with musical compositions, riddles, poems, fairy tales, or documentaries for demonstration of knowledge acquisition. Projects included opportunities for building, writing, drawing, performing or conducting research. With thematic units it was easy to arrange choices for working alone, with one other or in a small group.

Choices of informal or formal seating with bright or dim lighting were all easily accommodated with minor room arrangements at no extra cost. Manipulative materials, informal seating, and a projects orientation with choice activities allowed students to work in ways compatible with how they preferred to learn. The mind map by Nancy Margulies (1991), author of *Mapping Inner Space*, highlights a range of ideas for addressing individual learning styles. [See figure 6.]

Fig. 6

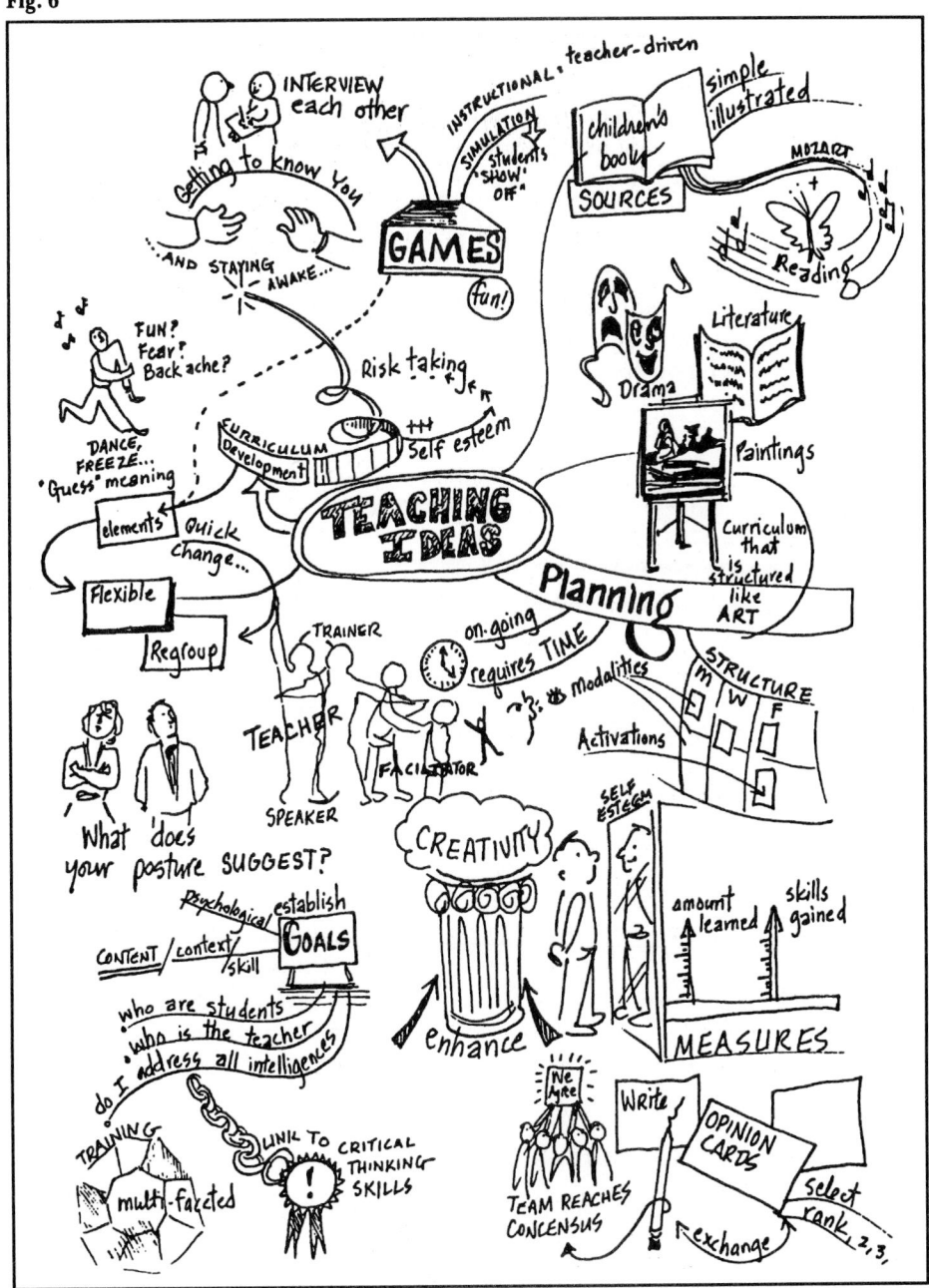

SUMMARY

The question at the outset was 'why does teaching that honours individual learning style produce high academic gains?' In this chapter, I presented five interdependent reasons: 1) humans have at least five major learning systems, 2) learning systems interrelate and communicate with each other, 3) the biochemistry of learning is highly dependent upon the learner's emotional state, 4) teaching that honours learning style preferences can build high levels of comfort and ownership of the learning process, and 5) high levels of comfort and ownership can produce positive learning states and subsequent academic achievement. Clearly, teaching that matches individual learning style preferences enhances academic attainment. Thus, alternative teaching procedures should receive deep consideration in relationship to all learners and especially to students who exhibit learning difficulties.

REFERENCES

Andrews, R. (1990, July-September). The development of a learning styles program in a low socioeconomic, underachieving North Carolina elementary school. *Journal of Reading. Writing. and Learning Disabilities International.* 6(3), 307-314.

Barbe, W. and Swassing, R. (1979). *Teaching students through modality strengths: Concepts and Practices.* Columbia, OH: Zaner-Bloser.

Boo, K. (1995, February 12). The tower girls. *The Washington Post.* pp. Al, A18, Al9.

Brandt, D. (1983). *Overcoming disappointment in an age of diminished expectations.* New York, NY: Pocket Books.

Brunner, C. and Majewski, W. (1990, October). Mildly handicapped students can succeed with learning styles. *Educational Leadership.* 48, 21-23.

Butler, K. (1986). *Learning and teaching style: Theory and Practice.* Columbia, CT: The Learner's Dimension.

Carbo, M., Dunn, R., and Dunn, K. (1986). *Teaching students to read through their individual learning styles.* Reston, VA: Prentice-Hall.

Curry, L. (1987). Integrating concepts of cognitive or learning styles: A review with attention to psychometric standards. Ottowa, Ontario: Canadian college of Health Services Executives.

Curry, L. (1990). *Learning styles in secondary schools: A review of instruments and implications for their use.* Madison, Wisconsin: University of Wisconsin Centre for Education Research. ERIC: ED 317283.

Claxton, C. and Murrell, P. (1987). *Learning styles: Implications for improving educational practices.* College Station, TX: Texas A&M University Department of Educational Administration.

Davidson, L. (1981). Learning style: The myth, the panacea, the wisdom. *Phi Delta Kappan,* (9), 641-645.

Dellinger, S. (1989). *Psycho-geometrics: How to use geometric psychology to influence people.* Englewood Cliffs, NJ: Prentice Hall.

Dennison, P. and Dennison, G. (1989). *Brain gym: Teacher's Edition.* Revised. Ventura, CA: Edu-Kinesthetics, Inc.

Dunn, R. and Dunn, K. (1993). *Teaching secondary students through their individual learning styles: Practical approaches for grades 7-12.* Boston: Allyn & Bacon.

Dunn, R. and Dunn, K. (1994). *Teaching elementary students through their individual learning styles: Practical apraoches for grades 3-6.* Boston: Allyn and Bacon.

Dunn, R., Griggs, S., Gorman, B., Olson, J., and Beasley, M. (1995). A meta-analytic validation of the Dunn and Dunn model of learning-styles preferences, *Journal of Educational Research,* (July).

Elliot, I. (1991). The reading place. *Teaching K-8, 21* (3), 30-34.

Gadwa, K. and Griggs, S. (1985). The school dropout: Implications for counsellors. *The School Counsellor,* 33, 9-17.

Gardner, H. (1985). *Frames of mind: The theory of multiple intelligences.* New York: Basic Books.

Grasha, A. (February 1972). Observations on relating teaching goals to student response style and classroom methods. *American Psychologist.* 27,144-147.

Gregorc, A. (1982). *An adult's guide to style.* Columbia, CT: Gregorc Associates, Inc.

Grinder, M. (1991). *Righting the educational conveyor belt.* Portland, OR: Metamorphous Press.

Hannaford, C. (1995). *Smart moves: Why learning is not all in your head.* Arlington, VA: Great Ocean Publishers.

Hanson, F., Silver, H., and Strong, R. (1986). *Teaching styles and strategies: Manual #2 in the dealing with diversity series.* Moorestown, NJ: Hanson Silver Strong and Associates, Inc.

Kaufman, A. and Kaufman, N. (1984). *Kaufman sequential or simultaneous: Leader's guide.* Circle Pines, MN: American Guidance Service.

Keefe, J. (1987). *Learning style: Theory and Practice.* Reston, VA: National Association of Secondary School Principals.

Keirsey, D. and Bates, M. (1984). *Please understand me: Character and temperament types.* Del Mar, CA: Prometheus Nemesis Book Company.

Klavas, A. (1993). In Greensboro, North Carolina, learning style program boosts achievement and test scores. *The Clearing House,* 67(3),149-151.

Kolb, D. *Experiential learning: Experience as the source of learning and development.* Englewood Cliffs, NJ: Prentice-Hall, Inc.

Lemmon, P. (1985). A school where learning styles make a difference. *Principal,* 64 (4), 26-29.

Letteri, C. (1976). Cognitive style: Implications for curriculum. In Molnar, A. and Zahorik, J. (Eds.), *Curriculum Theory* (64-69). Washington, DC: Association for Supervision and Curriculum Development.

Margulies, N. (1991). *Mapping inner space: Learning and teaching mind mapping.* Tucson, AZ: Zephyr Press.

McCarthy, B. (1987). *The 4mat system: Teaching to leaning styles with right/left mode techniques.* Barrington, IL: Excel, Inc.

Moyers, B. (1993). *Healing and the mind.* New York, NY: Doubleday.

Myers, I., and Briggs, K. (1976). *Myers-Briggs type indicator.* Palo Alto, CA: Consulting Psychologists Press, Inc.

Orsak, L., (1990, July-September). Learning styles and love: A winning combination. *Journal of Reading, Writing and Learning Disabilities International,* 6(3), 343-347.

Presseisen, B., Sternberg, R., Fischer, K., Knight, C. and Feuerstein, R. (1990). *Learning and thinking styles: classroom interaction.* Washington, D.C.: National Education Association.

Reid, G. (1994). *Specific learning difficulties (dyslexia): A handbook for study and practice.* Edinburgh, Scotland: Moray House Publications.

Renzulli, J. and Smith, L. (1978). *Learning style inventory: A measure of student reference for instructional techniques.* Creative Learning Press.

Silvernail, D. (1986). *Teaching styles as related to student achievement.* Washington, D.C.: National Education Association.

Snider, V. (1992). Learning styles and learning to read: A critique. *Remedial and Special Education,* 13 (1), 6-18.

Stone, P. (1992, November). How we turned around a problem school. *The Principal,* (2), 34-36.

Sylwester, R. (1993). What brain research says about paying attention. *Education Leadership,* 50 (4), 71-75.

Sylwester, R. (1994). How emotions affect learning. *Education Leadership.* (2), 60-65.

Witkin, H. (1976). Cognitive style in academic performance and in teacher-student relations. In Messick, S. (Ed.), *Individuality in learning.* San Francisco: Jossey-Bass.

LEARNING STYLES IN PRACTICE

MAGGIE NICHOLSON

LEARNING STYLES

In 'From Rage to Hope' (Kuykendall, 1992), the author expresses that if we are to teach students, we must first **reach** them. This can be achieved through the use of style-flexing strategies which can address the unique learning styles of each student. Valuing learning styles gives all children the opportunity to learn while appreciating and understanding the process of learning. Learning styles describe factors which influence all aspects of learning as well as the student's individual preferences for learning new material. Awareness of learning styles in assessment and teaching can facilitate effective learning for all, particularly for those experiencing learning difficulties.

Group knowledge of learning styles can also foster collaborative skills and reduce classroom conflicts because students gain a greater appreciation for different approaches to the same problems or ideas. This makes different perspectives acceptable rather than right or wrong. The key is to teach students about themselves so they can take responsibility for their own learning.

The ability to develop awareness and respond sensitively to learning styles takes time, experimentation, practice and planning. It benefits teaching in any subject and grade area regardless of the student's learning difficulties.

LEARNING STYLES IN PRACTICE

Summit Middle School, Frisco, Colorado provides an example of learning styles in practice. It is located in the heart of the Rocky Mountains, in a popular tourist destination; the population is diverse and growing rapidly. The school currently has an enrolment of six hundred students in grades six through eight (eleven through fifteen years old). It utilises a team model in which each grade works closely with teams of three teachers using an interdisciplinary approach. Benefits include on-going communication among staff, students, and parents. Interdisciplinary units providing a focus for academic subject areas, as well as with electives and exploratory courses such as Spanish, Technology and the Arts.

The philosophy of the school is that all students can learn and the school's role is to prepare the student for lifelong learning. The approach is student rather than curriculum centred emphasising the holistic needs of the child. Each student develops a portfolio highlighting examples of his/her work which is displayed upon completion of eighth grade.

Student abilities range greatly and are accommodated through various means. Student needs are assessed through group and individual means with the involvement of the school psychologist. A multi-disciplinary team meets to develop an Individual Education Programme (IEP) outlining student needs and the support services to be provided. The Learning Disabilities Programme at Summit Middle School offers a spectrum of services from individual/small group instructional assistance, collaborative support within the regular education classroom, inclusion (mainstreaming), instructional aide tutoring, consultation with staff, and modification of instructional materials .

RECOGNISING STUDENTS' LEARNING STYLES

A number of different methods can be used to assess the students' learning styles (Given, Lannen, Nicholson and Reid, 1995).

These include inventories, which are direct self report; structured and unstructured interviews; observations and checklists (see previous chapter) and analysis of learning achievements which involves asking students how they tackled and completed various projects (see Ayres, Chapter 7, and Morrison, Chapter 8. Vol. 1 Assessment Teaching and the Curriculum).

It is important to inform learners of learning style terminology through group and individual discussion, demonstrations and activities. For example, by asking students how they organise their wardrobe it is possible to discuss perceptions of left-handed students and aspects relating to concrete sequential learners who feel that everything should be orderly and in place. It is useful to find out to what extent the learner is practical, realistic, organised, efficient, factual, specific, detailed and structured. Listening to students' ideas, perceptions and experiences can provide an understanding of their learning preference.

LEARNING STYLES – LESSON PLANNING AND CLASSROOM APPLICATION

Acknowledging learning styles requires considerable planning. Madeline Hunter outlines elements of good lesson design which should be considered when planning a lesson. Instruction includes an anticipatory set, clearly stated objective, input, modelling, checking for understanding, guided practice and independent practice (Hunter, 1994) (see Fig. 1).

Fig. 1

LESSON DESIGN

1. **Anticipatory Set**
    Cue – a statement of what the learner will be learning shortly before learning occurs.
2. **Objective**
    A clear, observable goal the learner will accomplish before class is over. It helps the learner know what you expect of him/her. (The learner will draw (observable) a picture (content).
3. **Input**
    Breaking the objective down into smaller steps so learner can accomplish the objective. A series of small steps designed to lead the learner to accomplishing the objective.
4. **Model**
    Model desired objective. Teacher shows learner what is to be done or how it is to be done.
5. **Check for Understanding**
    Make certain the learner understands and can do the objective correctly.

6. **Guided Practice**

Allows the learner to practise with the teacher present so that errors may be corrected as early as possible. Learner does not practise incorrectly when work is checked early.

7. **Independent Practice**

Student practises alone to reinforce learning. Teacher is not present as an active helper (Homework, assignment, etc.).

Adapted from Mastery Teaching.
Hunter, M (1994).

The lessons allow opportunities for the student to pursue interest areas in independent study. The teacher acts as a model (listening, reading, speaking, writing, even thinking aloud.) All modalities are used (visual, auditory, tactile, and kinaesthetic) (see Fig. 2) and right-brain activities are balanced with left brain activities.

Fig. 2

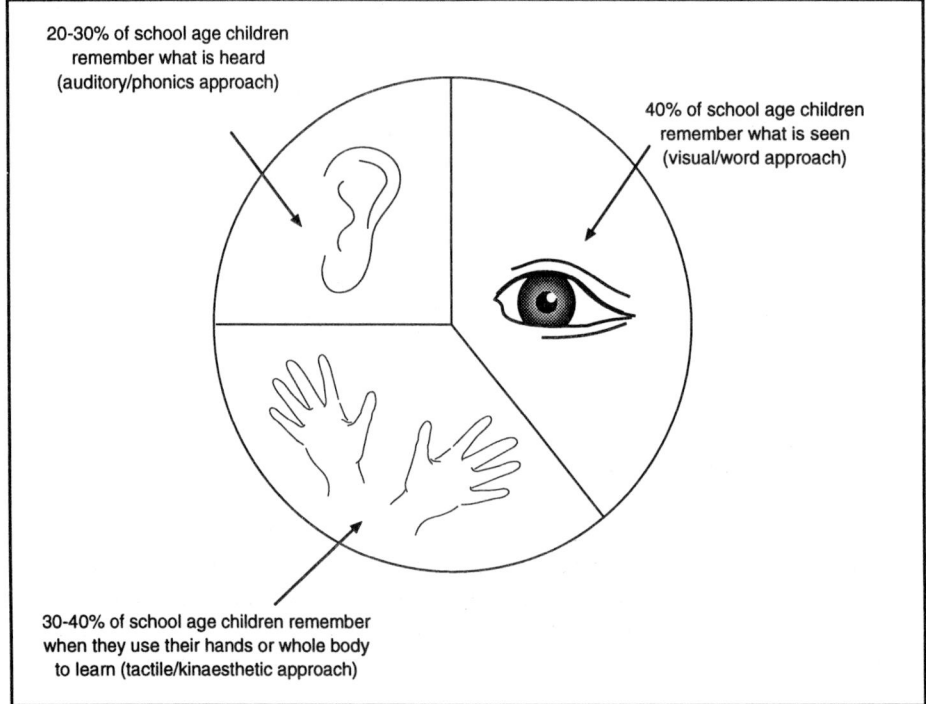

20-30% of school age children remember what is heard (auditory/phonics approach)

40% of school age children remember what is seen (visual/word approach)

30-40% of school age children remember when they use their hands or whole body to learn (tactile/kinaesthetic approach)

MODALITY STRATEGIES

AUDITORY MODALITY

oral report
panel discussion questions
debate
tape recording
song
poem
musical performance
puppet show
play
video tape
TV/radio show
slide show
verbal game on tape
travel lecture
tape a story and clap hands at
   each adjective
tell different ending
tell most humorous, exciting
share and ask:
   – most interesting
   – liked best
   – saddest
   – 'might have been' if something had been difficult

KINAESTHETIC MODALITY

survey
questionnaire
questions
test
game
machine
invention
proposed solution
start a campaign
musical performance
puppet show
dance
play
video tape
TV/radio show

pantomime
dramatise one character and what he did
floor maze or game
dress as one of the characters and play a part

TACTILE MODALITY

model
puzzle
learning kit
scrapbook
colouring book
artistic creation
sculpture
mobile
display
poster
collage
dress paper dolls as characters

VISUAL MODALITY

drawing
cartoons
computer
TV/video
designing posters/covers
story in pictures
collage
visual puzzles

Learning Styles can be a rewarding journey of discovery of your personal teaching style. This self-awareness can increase opportunities for identifying new strategies which can then be further adapted to different teaching situations. It is important to determine what works for you and to recognise the most comfortable style for you.

It is also important to be sensitive to global and analytic learners. The recognition of this helps facilitate pro-active intervention. It should however, be recognised that the same strategy may not work all the time. The success of a strategy is highly dependent on how, when, where, why and by whom it is used, although it is important to let students know that you expect them to succeed. Reinforcement through descriptive feedback to students about their performance is of great value and every effort should be made to relate students' past experiences to new learning.

Fig. 3: Modality strategies

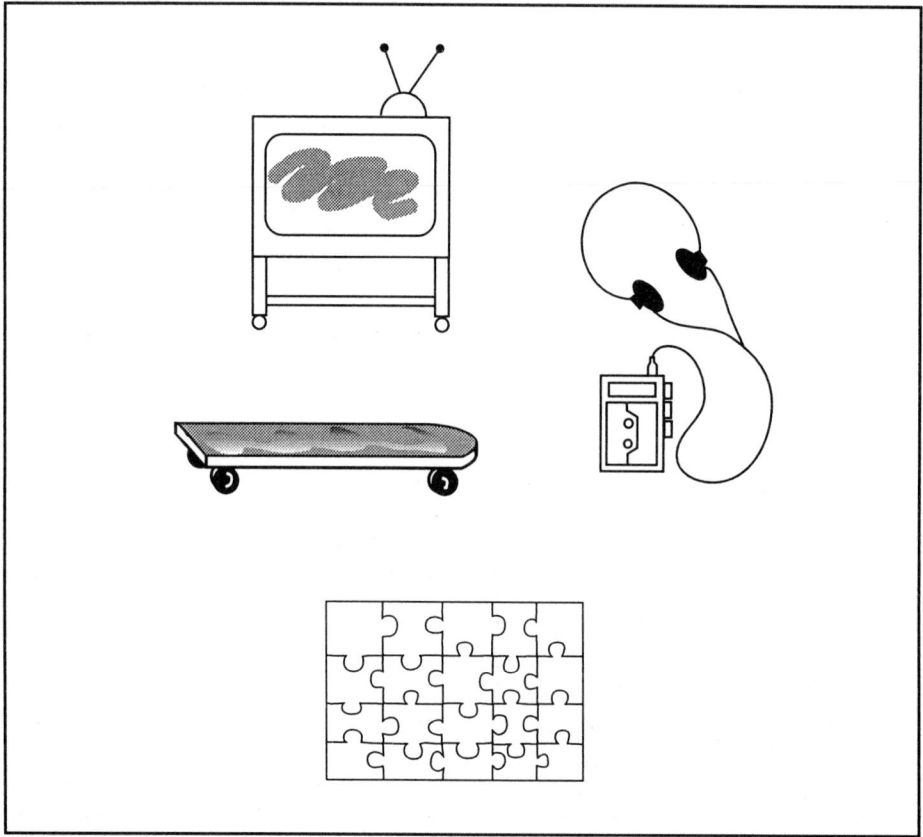

The following pages highlight some kinaesthetic activities for the learning styles classroom (Lewis, 1995) which illustrates how one modality can be used in a variety of ways.

TREASURE HUNT

A Treasure Hunt may be set up in the gym or classroom. Students use clues to locate different stations around the room. The student must complete the assigned activity at each station and be signed off by the teacher in order to move on to another station. When the student has completed and is signed off for all stations, he/she may retrieve the treasure (a snack or prize).

BALLOON WADDLE RELAY RACE

Divide the group into two teams. A player from each team receives a blown-up balloon with a review question tucked inside. Team members race against their opponents carrying the balloon between their knees from the starting line to the finish line. At the finish line each team member must break their balloon to retrieve their review question. The question must be answered correctly before the next member of the team begins to waddle toward the finish line with the balloon. The first team to finish wins!

LABEL YOUR PARTNER OR LABEL YOURSELF

To learn the parts of the body, (bones, parts of the brain, glands of the body), create stick on labels with the body part name (Index cards with tape work well as labels!). Students work alone or in pairs to correctly label their body parts. Teams with the most correct labels are the winners!

GOLF REVIEW

Arrange a miniature golf course around the classroom by arranging plastic or Styrofoam numbered cups lying on the floor. Review questions are placed inside the cups. Students must answer the review question correctly to advance to the next hole. Yardsticks may be used as golf clubs, a ping-pong ball or a wad of paper may be used as a golf ball.

IT'S NOT A TRIVIAL PURSUIT

Create a giant game board similar to the Trivial Pursuit Board on a plain vinyl tablecloth, large sheet of tagboard (laminated), or a plain vinyl shower curtain. Review questions are colour coded by subject. Students advance around the board by answering review questions correctly. This board is great for an integrated curriculum or end of the year exam review as many subjects may be reviewed in one game.

WHEEL OF FACTS

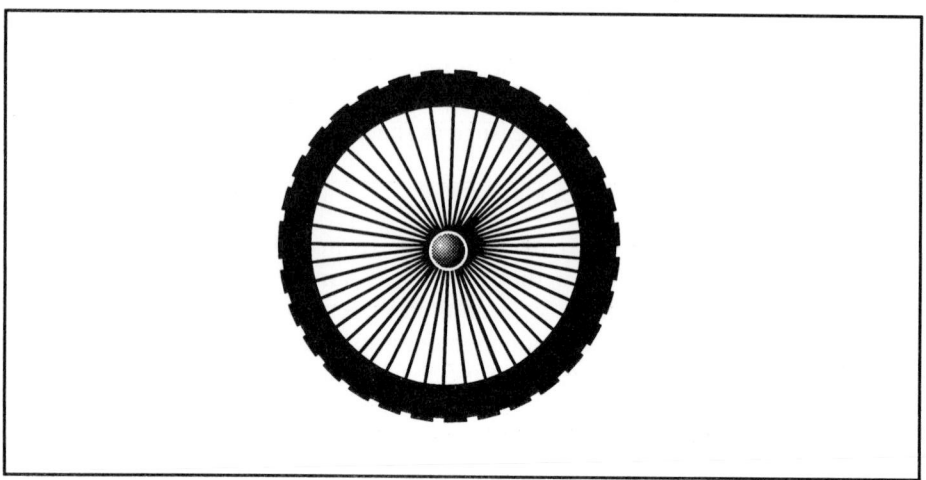

Based on an adaptation of the game show, Wheel of Fortune. Create a large cardboard or tagboard circle divided into 8-12 sections each with an adhesive pocket. Insert question cards into each pocket with answers written on the back of question cards. Money values may be assigned to each question section when questions are answered correctly. Player with the most money at the end of the game is the winner. (Also, players may use 'money' won to purchase small prizes if desired.) This game can be used again and again using different fact cards and is great for reviewing for end of year exams.

IT'S COMICAL

Enlarge comic strips frame by frame to teach lessons in sequencing and story building. Using comic strips cut from the newspaper, the teacher enlarges each frame on the copy machine and mounts the frame on coloured construction paper. The teacher mixes up the order of the frames and students try to place the frames in the correct order to tell the story. Frames may be numbered on the back in order, so that they become self-correcting.

FLOOR GRAPH MAT

Create a large floor graph on a shower curtain or vinyl tablecloth by dividing the area into numbered rows and columns. This mat may be used for a number of graphing activities.

1							
2							
3							
4							
5							
6							

Suggestions for using the graphing mat:

1. Comparing the number of boys and girls in the class. Students can actually stand on the squares.

2. Comparing dice rolls and probability. Place markers on squares on the mat according to the number rolled.

GONE FISHING

Cut large fish shapes from tagboard. Write a review question on each fish. Hook a metal paper clip or small self-sticking magnet to each fish. A hula-hoop placed on the floor becomes the pretend fish pond. A fishing pole can be created by attaching a magnet to a yard stick with a piece of string or yarn. Students keep the fish if they can answer the review question correctly, but most 'throw the fish back into the pond' if their answer is incorrect.

UP, UP AND AWAY WITH MY BEAUTIFUL BALLOONS

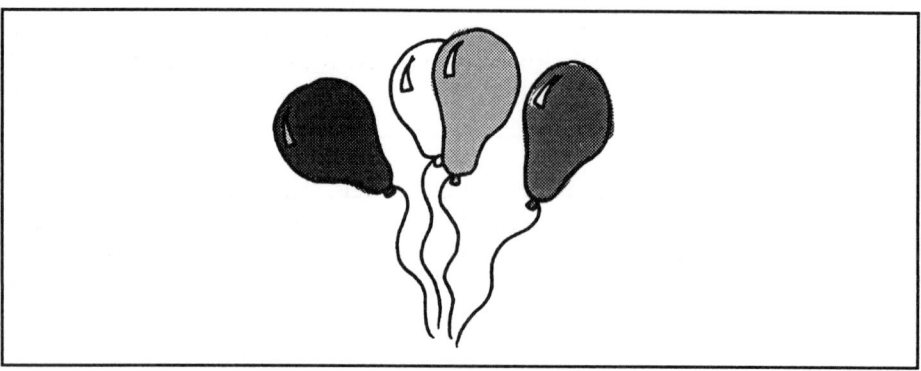

To help students practise their spelling words and to encourage creative writing, place a display of cardboard or real balloons taped to the wall in the classroom. Place a letter of the alphabet on one side of the balloon. Have students write a spelling or vocabulary word on the other side of the balloon to correspond with the initial letter. Following this activity, students may use the balloon words to create an original story.

ACCOMMODATING STUDENTS' LEARNING STYLES NEEDS

Dunn and Dunn (1993,1994) provide many examples of accommodating to student's Learning Styles, for example one teacher has a bathtub filled with pillows in her classroom in which a student may read.

A middle school teacher created a relaxing environment in which to read by filling a child's swimming pool with water, goldfish and plants surrounded by pillows and beanbags; the water relaxed some active students. A high school history teacher removed all desks and built a simulated camp fire using rocks and logs around which to discuss historical events. A geography teacher modelled her classroom around a rainforest theme complete with plants and hammocks. A Spanish teacher designed her classroom with a marketplace theme to simulate cultural activities. These examples show that the possibilities are exciting and unlimited. The teacher's sense of fun and enthusiasm will be reflected in the learners motivation and success.

Local resources provide rich learning materials for interdisciplinary teaching. The phone directory supplies a wealth of ideas including the use of local maps, alphabet activities, community awareness, communication skills and area information. Local newspapers can be adapted to projects in all subject areas through the use of sports sections, graphs, current events, weather information, entertainment guides and classified and other advertisements. Students can develop a budget, based on job, apartment, and consumer advertisements. These materials and activities can help to access the individual learning styles of each student.

Interdisciplinary thematic units can also be used to develop subject matter and student skills. Each year, Summit Middle School develops a schoolwide unit. For example, a unit on 'The Future' featured speakers, films, creative writing activities, and a futuristic fashion show. A Population unit integrated activities in ecology, biology, geography and statistics concluded by fieldtrips to compare population patterns in rural and urban areas. These also helped to accommodate the student's individual learning styles.

Student use of video equipment is a valuable tool which can be used in alternative assessment, co-operative learning and projects. Polaroid photographs can be used to supplement autobiographical activities. Collages can include personal photographs to illustrate experiences such as travel, family or interests.

In teaching foreign language, the suitcase can become an element of surprise into the classroom. For example, each pupil is asked to take a small suitcase of clothes into class and then describe each item in turn. Tactile stimulation is used based on the child's own clothes to make it more meaningful to the individual (Nicholson, 1994).

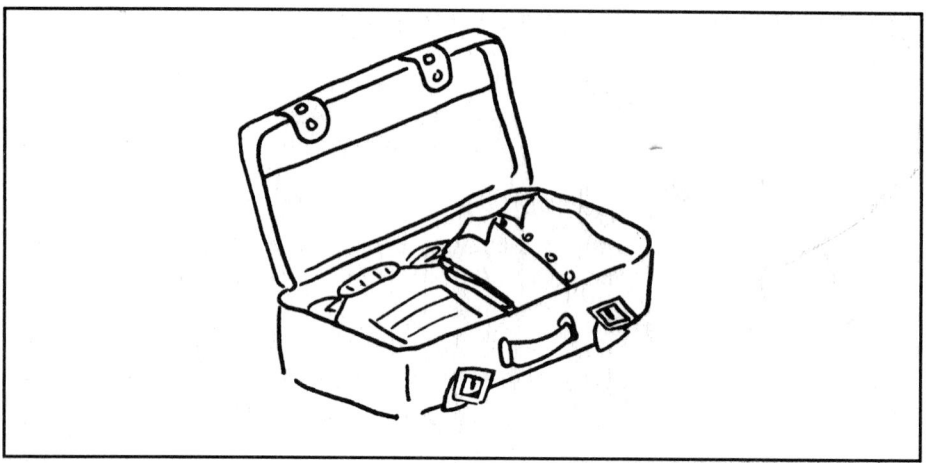

This kind of activity need not be restricted to clothes and can include items such as stuffed animals, groom items, school supplies, and holiday souvenirs. Culture capsules can be created in shoeboxes for specific information, such as making mate (South American tea), the Tuna (a type of Spanish musical group) and el Dia de los Muertos (a Mexican holiday).

Students can shine through their individual learning styles and strengths by individual or group classroom presentations.

CONCLUSION

A pro-active approach including staff in-service and modelling should help overcome the practical difficulties of implementing learning styles in the classroom. Staff discussion is very important and management support is necessary. Most of us function within our comfort levels but must be encouraged positively to accommodate to alternative methods.

The union between sound lesson planning and awareness to learning styles is a powerful educational tool. Teaching through a strong multi-sensory approach with carefully designed lessons can help children enjoy, respond to, and retain new learning. By believing they are valued as a learner, students will become empowered in their lives to become effective self-advocates: Learning Styles can therefore help students become lifelong, agile and successful learners.

REFERENCES

Ayres, D. (1995). Metacognitive assessment – reflections and strategies. In Reid, G. (Ed.) *Dimensions of Dyslexia, Vol. 1, Assessment, Teaching and The Curriculum*. Moray House Publications, Edinburgh.

Hunter, M. (1994). *Mastery Teaching*. Corwin Press, Inc. Thousand Oaks, CA. USA.

Given, B., Lannen, S., Nicholson, M. and Reid, G. (1995). Learning styles – unlocking potential. In *Links 2*. Vol. 1, No. 4., pp 26-31.

Kuykendall, C. (1992). *From rage to hope: strategies for reclaiming black and Hispanic students*. National Educational Service, 1610 W. Third Street, PO Box 8, Bloomington, Indiana, US.

Lewis, G. (1995). Kinaesthetic activities for the learning styles classroom. Buffalo Learning Styles Project. Bridge: Connecting Teaching and Learning, Buffalo, New York.

Morrison, K. (1995). Diagnosing the diagnosis: case studies in metacognition. In Reid, G. (Ed.) *Dimensions of Dyslexia, Vol. 1, Assessment, Teaching and The Curriculum*. Moray House Publications, Edinburgh.

Nicholson, M. (1994). Learning styles in practice. Paper presented to *Specific Learning Difficulties Annual Conference*. Moray House, Edinburgh, Scotland 1994.

ACCESS TO INDEPENDENT LEARNING THROUGH CURRICULUM DIFFERENTIATION

C. MORAG HUNTER-CARSCH

This chapter deals with two interrelated facets – curriculum differentiation and independent learning. They are interrelated because effective curriculum differentiation should enhance the opportunities for independent learning. It is the purpose of this chapter to outline what is meant by differentiation, provide a framework for differentiation and discuss how that framework can enable students with specific learning difficulties gain access to effective independent learning.

CONCEPT OF DIFFERENTIATION

It appears there are as many different ways of defining differentiation as there are of utilising the principles of differentiation in the classroom. It is interesting to examine the responses from groups of teachers on their perception of what is meant by differentiation.

Fig. 1

GROUPS' SUMMARIES OF DISCUSSION POINTS.

Group 1:

Differentiation is . . .

matching the task to the learner
access to the curriculum
variety of teaching methods
catering for the range of abilities
being creative with – staff, tasks, outcome, methods of recording
enabling each child to reach his/her potential
creating an environment where each child can feel good about themselves and valued by others

Group 2:

Differentiation is . . .

the process of delivering a curriculum for all, as all children are different, having different needs.
It is about the matching of knowledge, concepts, ideas, issues (of the curriculum) to all children's **skills,** interests, abilities, (background)

Differentiation can vary, in terms of differentiating by:
outcome (same task given to everybody, but different outcomes expected):
task (variety of tasks, but tackled at different levels):
organisation (e.g. peer tutoring, carousel, rainbowing)
A combination of these ways is beneficial for all including staff, parents (outsiders) and should be part of a whole-school policy.

Group 3:	**Group 4:**
Differentiation is . . .	*Differentiation is . . .*
a **process** in which **teaching/learning** is designed to match the **interests** of the learner based on **specific objectives** to ensure **breadth, balance, progression** and **continuity.**	1. A way to match the child to suitable tasks and targets 2. A way to assess the child's learning level 3. A way to identify deficit in learning 4. A way to focus on the special needs for both able and less bale

Strategies to achieve these objectives
process –   tasks
        –   outcome
        –   recognising individual differences through Individual Education Programmes if required
        –. groupings can be different depending on outcomes
        –   organisation of teaching
	5. A way of teaching one topic or set of facts to a group of mixed abilities
	6. A way of identifying similarities of attainment within like sub groups.
	
	Source: Hunter-Carsch (1995).

Clearly there are some common views from the responses of these different groups such as 'matching', 'accessing', 'catering for', 'assessing' and 'enabling'. However one might choose to view differentiation, the common elements from the above responses indicate that the **outcome** of differentiation may well be the facilitation of independent learning.

When I asked a different group of teachers (18 M.A. students) to analyse their definitions of differentiation, the three categories which emerged from this exercise centred on the areas of content, organisation and process (See Fig. 2). The **content** relates to 'what' differentiation is in practice, the **organisation** is 'how' it can be put into practice and the **process** relates to the 'effect' of differentiation on the learner. This is further outlined in Fig. 3 where the central factor – the curriculum – has a number of different influences relating to it such as the role of the individual learner, the teacher, group dynamics, method of assessment and the concept of differentiation. This emphasises the flexibility of differentiation and how a conceptual framework for differentiation can be adapted to deal with different types of learners and different learning situations.

A FRAMEWORK FOR CURRICULUM DIFFERENTIATION

To be sufficiently comprehensive, the framework for curriculum differentiation must take into account the range of variables highlighted in Figs. 1-3. (For further study reference should be made to Visser (1993), and subsequent NASEN publications on Curriculum Differentiation and to the work of contributors

Fig. 2

THE CONCEPT OF CURRICULUM DIFFERENTIATION
Analysis of definitions by a group of 18 MA students

CONTENT	ORGANISATION	PROCESS
What C.D. is/involves	whole class individual groups pairs	**listen** think and **write** (listen/think/**talk** (look and write share remember recall
❷ order of presentation		
❷ mode of presentation		
❷ learning style	◆ choice ◆ models ◆ prior experience knowledge ◆ constraints (social/cultural) physical comtact time ◆ expectations	(organise ideas (relate ideas (select ideas (prioritise modalities/VAKT
❷ pacing		
❷ rhythm/pattern (routines?)		
❷ personality dynamics		

to the 1993 special edition on the subject published by the British Psychological Society Education Review and to the 1995 BPS Review (Vol. 19 No. 1). Additionally, a vital contribution has been made by Norwich (1995) who addresses issues related to Socio-Cultural factors which affect assumptions about individual differences. The following section includes a brief report of the views of King and Spillman and further development of the writer's draft model of curriculum differentiation.

King's (1989) 'differentiation menu' included the following 23 factors to be differentiated in order to meet any pupils' special educational needs (i.e. not solely those of pupils with specific learning difficulties): 'aims/content/learning contexts/ breadth/depth/pace/language/materials/ teacher-pupil; pupil-teacher interaction/ forms of pupil recording/forms of pupil grouping/teaching styles/forms of classroom organisation/uses of support teacher/forms of assessment/kinds of marking/ resources for self-tudy/reinforcement/feedback/levels of motor skills/levels of confidence in oral work/levels of maturity of response.'

Fig. 3

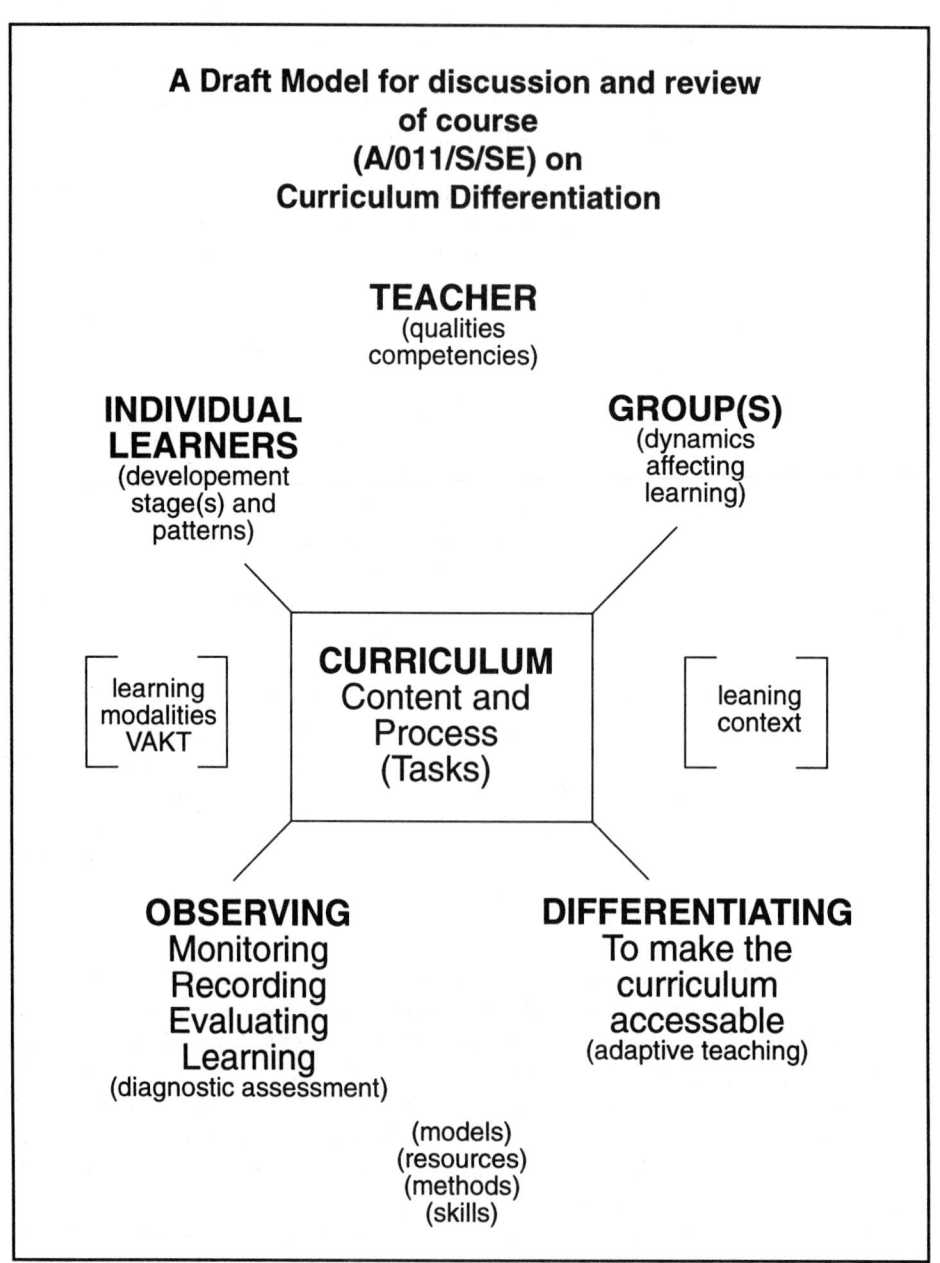

A Draft Model for discussion and review
of course
(A/011/S/SE) on
Curriculum Differentiation

TEACHER
(qualities
competencies)

**INDIVIDUAL
LEARNERS**
(developement
stage(s) and
patterns)

GROUP(S)
(dynamics
affecting
learning)

learning
modalities
VAKT

CURRICULUM
Content and
Process
(Tasks)

leaning
context

OBSERVING
Monitoring
Recording
Evaluating
Learning
(diagnostic assessment)

DIFFERENTIATING
To make the
curriculum
accessable
(adaptive teaching)

(models)
(resources)
(methods)
(skills)

Spillman (1991) provides a checklist of 'good practice' and suggests that 'the key to the differentiated curriculum is the flexible use by teachers of a wide range of activities and lesson organisations'. Differentiation is discussed in terms of classroom organisation and by the ways in which tasks are (a) introduced, (b) carried out, and (c) the kinds of outcomes which are required. The value of paired work and joining together of pairs into groups is illustrated.

An extensive combined list can be made of all the factors noted by King and by Spillman, (pp. 19-37); however, there remains the difficulty of priorities and how to translate into practice ways of bridging the gaps between 'the new literacy' (Willinsky, 1990) with its 'open' methods, and 'the structured approach' (often associated with teaching 'dyslexic' pupils; see also Hunter-Carsch, 1993) with its 'routine' and seeming 'inflexibilities'.

There are also complex theoretical issues to be taken into account in determining the underlying values which guide and inform teachers' decisions, attitudes and patterns for mediating learning. For more detailed discussion of these issues, readers are referred to Norwich (1995). The writer's attempt to devise a model for curriculum differentiation which would address both theoretical and practical issues, necessarily seeks to illustrate the fact that teachers need to operate at more than one level at any one time. It is here, perhaps, that the relative emphases of generalist and specialist most require to be shared.

A sufficiently comprehensive model would include the relationship between curriculum issues about WHAT has to be learned (content) and HOW it is to be learned (processes) (See Figs. 2 and 3), and the impact on these factors which is exerted by the teacher's employment of SUPPORT STRATEGIES which concern motivation and attitude. The balance of the whole picture is 'held in place' by MACROSTRATEGIES and MICROSTRATEGIES which can be employed by the class teacher or a collaborative teaching pair or team of teachers (see Hunter-Carsch, 1990).

In the 1990 model, the three 'macrostrategies' (wider concepts and stages in the process of meeting special educational needs for the individuals) were described as including firstly, *a series of steps towards meeting special educational needs*. The second involves an understanding and ability to make operational in the classroom *'a wider appreciation of the concept of "literacy" and relatedly the concepts of language'* and 'reading' in ways which connect them in the child's mind with human interest, curiosity, the will to communicate, to learn and to know, (see also Hunter-Carsch, 1995). The third involves *a dynamic system for recording* (making notes on) *the interaction between child and teacher* within a 'conferencing' situation (one-to-one tuition within the class).

The 'microstrategies' (factors to be adapted and controlled in terms of both the extent and the nature of learning problems) are listed below and discussed in relation to specific learning difficulties.

SPECIFIC LEARNING DIFFICULTIES

Microstrategies for adapting teaching and learning

The microstrategies involve adapting the following seven factors to meet individuals needs:

(i) Choice, (ii) challenge, (iii) space, (iv) time, (v) materials, (vi) relationships, (vii) methods. Additionally, adjustments may need to be made with reference to the way learning is mediated in terms of: (a) whole-part learning, (b) sequencing, (c) speed, and (d) accuracy.

Learning Support for the child with specific learning difficulties should be mediated in such a way as to provide empathy conveyed through understanding of the nature of the difficulties, encouragement which is unobtrusive, practical strategies and routines which facilitate learning, and ways of communicating which mobilise and sustain the child's interest, imagination and ability to think. Each of the 'microstrategies' is briefly described and illustrations provided below. Each variable can be adjusted to mediate learning more successfully for the child with specific learning difficulties affecting that particular aspect of his or her functioning.

(i) **Choice:** Some children with specific learning difficulties find if difficult to make choices. When faced with having to make a choice, for example between several activities, they become anxious and/or over-excited and appear to be unable to 'reason' or to consider each of the alternatives. For such children it is helpful to remove choice about work tasks, then gradually, to introduce limited choice, and eventually to open up the possibilities to include a range of tasks (choices). There should be no sense of punishment in the absence of choice at the initial phase. Rather, there is provision of a calm routine suggesting by the very way in which materials are laid out, that there is an order for proceeding and that the child can cope. For example – say to the child 'Start here. Do this one now. Show me when you finish it. Fine. Now this one, I'll show you how we do it. Start here, like this'. Explanations and negotiations should be avoided at this point and reassurance provided by the structuring of the activity itself.

For other children, there may be insufficient choice for them to feel able to adapt the work in ways that they can handle. In such cases, it is helpful to make clear by the visual layout of the tasks, how much choice (space laid out) there is and by, for example, putting the instructions on or in wavy lined paper 'clouds' to indicate flexibility for 'squaring up the edges'. The increments in extending choice for such children can be faster.

(ii) **Challenge:** This is related to choice, but also involves the amount of work which the child can be expected to complete in a given time, and the level of difficulty of the work. The tasks should not be so difficult that they reduce the child's resilience and will to tackle them with interest and enthusiasm. Nor should they be so easy that there is virtually no challenge. Getting the level exactly matched is likely to involve considerable prior observation of how the child gets into their work and their preferences for processing learning (e.g. VAKT (Visual Auditory Kinaesthetic Tactile) sequences) such as A (separately) and **then** KTV (together). Get to know the child over some time, particularly as children with specific learning difficulties often are erratic in their functioning even on the same kind of tasks, and on the same day. Start at a level which is predictably within the child's capabilities and through gradually escalating the challenge, build increasing confidence as well as the relevant knowledge or skills.

Through the management of both choice and challenge it can become possible to arrange the gradual decrease in teacher–directedness of the work and the corresponding increase of child-directedness. It is advisable to consult with the child regarding the increases in the length, complexity and nature of the challenge, once there is enough confidence built up on the basis of successful learning experiences. The child will be enabled to become more metacognitively aware as he or she sees the evidence of their successful learning. This is facilitated by providing a simple record-keeping system which involves the child in completing a part, if not all, of the record as each piece of work is completed. Through building up a visible/tangible note of successful learning, it becomes easier for the child to begin to generalise learning sufficiently to reduce the need to see, touch, check the 'evidence' of successful learning. As confidence is built up through seeing evidence of emerging competence, the necessary energy is also generated and the child's own direction of his/her learning can be gradually facilitated by the teacher's careful structuring.

(iii) **Space:** For some children, the size of the classroom (even a normal classroom not an open plan space) can seem to be a vast space that may feel oppressive or over stimulating. The child may dash about or else show the opposite kind of reaction and stand as if fixed and unable to organise himself comfortably within the space.

A gymnasium may present a context which generates an even greater sense of excitation or apprehension. This impedes the child's learning, whether his/her reactions are of a panic induced racing about or a rigid stillness. Adjustments of space can include the reduction of the gymnasium area initially by use of screens, and in the classroom creating a series of small working carrels (study-booths) in the classroom, either by use of freestanding heavy cardboard screening or by placing a desk/table against a wall and flanked by two screens/backs of library shelves or cupboards. The classroom 'offices' which are then created can be used as work places for scheduled 'office time' which all the children can enjoy for specified amounts of time, booked in advance. There should be no sense of punishment in being 'sent to the office'. Rather, this approach works in the opposite manner as the children are invited to 'sign up' and can be awarded extra office time to work quietly on their own, undisturbed, as a reward for specially good work as well as by choice as a routine part of classwork.

There are many ways in which the structuring of the space and placing of furniture can be employed to control the amount and direction of movement in the classroom. Relatedly, the aim is to avoid clutter and distraction from the current task. Open shelf units are to be avoided where possible in favour of closed doors. The open shelves invite the distractable child to explore them visually if not also by touch and movement. Where possible the surroundings should be functional but not fussy (e.g. avoid mobiles and too many dazzling, busy illustrations). The aim is to slow down active children, to avoid creating enticing corridors or bottlenecks and to relate the space clearly to the kind of work to be done in each of the spaces.

The establishment of routines about what is done in which area can also be helpful in the building of an external order which appears to affect the learners' internal ordering of experiences. (Control from outside seems to lead to 'control from within' – see also Redl and Wineman (1952)).

(iv) **Time:** Time may be a very difficult concept for some children if they have no awareness of, for example, what three minutes feels like. Their seeming anxiety in 'drowsiness' or 'distractability' in some cases, and 'head in the cloudness' in others, may be related to their limited sense of the passage of time. For them to 'see' what time passing 'feels like', it is helpful to provide a visual picture of 'time passing' e.g. by use of attractive coloured sand-timers. Once the children have watched the sand run through a three minute egg timer, it can be suggested that they find out how much they can do in 3 minutes. The time for the task that is set for them to do in the office can then be based on 'numbers of eggs'. They are often both relieved that they can perceive that the task will be 'finishable' (both because it has been designed to be within their capabilities and because it does not require more than an estimated amount of three minute spans which they see and check by using the timer). An individualised timetable (or simply a list of two or three tasks) can be drawn up for the child in a way which indicates (by illustrations) how many 'eggs" are allocated for each task.

It may be necessary to start with a single task of less than three minutes duration, in order to reinforce success and the chance for the child to 'rest' while watching until the sand has completely run through the timer. Their need for 'rest times' may not be sufficiently appreciated as for them, the strain of sustained attention appears to be greater, especially until routines and relaxation with concentration are achieved. This may also require relaxation training. The idea of pacing themselves becomes the easier in such circumstances and the sense of accomplishment is the greater if a record of successful timed tasks is maintained. Perhaps as few as two three minute tasks per day; one in the morning and one in the afternoon, can bring about an increased sense of self worth and turn a child's attitude from one of self doubt to one of willingness to try and hopefulness that there can be a better future, with increasingly successful learning.

On the basis of successful work in the office with timed individualised tasks, there is often rapid transfer of success to working on a timed basis in other places in the classroom perhaps with the use of the timer at first then gradually the classroom wall clock and/or digital or other watches. By building into the task plan an increasing range of 'free choice' times as competence to deal with choice develops, there is likely to be increasing confidence and length of time 'on task'.

(v) **Materials:** The structured approach seeks to assist the child to concentrate only on those features in the environment that are relevant to the particular aspect of learning that is the concern of the moment. Once the immediate surroundings are 'controlled' by making them as distraction free as possible (i.e. using an 'office'), it is easier to direct and hold the child's interest by using materials which are attractively presented. The resources the child uses are more easily memorable if they are tailored to the child's preferred learning styles and extend the child's interests. They might include exercise books covered in the child's favourite colour, colour-coded, monogrammed folders with the child's timetable, and attractively prepared tasks for the short work session in the office. Technology can play a special role here. Commercially produced programmes, audio tape recorders and word processing facilities, published schemes, kits, or teacher-made resources (or materials made by children), may be employed for developing learning through pre-set, specially integrated tasks.

The special nature of the materials should be closely linked to the methods of using them. A tape recorded programme made by the teacher and with invitations to the child to participate in various 'game-like' tasks, can provide the basis for a move from teacher-directed work to more independent work if the child follows the taped instructions which can extend work to include gradually more challenging tasks. The use of headphones can individualise the work and avoid the sounds becoming a distraction to others. The child can be taught how to use the tape recorder to record messages for the teacher or others and in this way manage to continue to work independently, but retain the means of requesting assistance. There is the possibility also of designing tasks for paired-work, also possible in some offices, and for work moving from the structure of the office to other locations.

(vi) **Relationships:** The structuring of relationships between teacher and pupil, or indeed pupil and pupil, does not imply anything ominous or 'cold' or seemingly 'uncaring'. It involves respecting the child's need for calm and detachment from emotional demands so that all the necessary effort can be direct into the learning which is intended. If the child is already aware of having learning difficulty, it is not always a kindness to draw attention to the child's efforts by being effusive. A 'low-key', more matter-of-fact tone and routine is frequently appreciated and felt to be less intrusive. A quieter voice, slower pronunciation and shorter rather than longer interactions may provide the basis for a relationship which gradually can accept more energetic praise and extended interactions. The importance of home-school relationships cannot be underestimated. The value of the growing trust through the structured approach in school can be extended to small amounts of work at home with the shared understanding between teachers and parents (see also Home-Help, Hunter-Carsch (1991).

(vii) **Methods:** This is perhaps the most complex variable as it can be regarded as an overriding approach, thus subsuming the other six variables, or , as intended here, as the way in which the materials are used within the carefully structured context. With reference to the teaching and learning of reading, Goodman (1975) commented, 'essentially reading is a matter of **getting it together**'. He added that, 'the children who have reading difficulties are those who experience difficulty in getting it together'. For them, a structured approach such as that of Stott (1962) which was based on a distillation of 'good practice' of experienced class teachers, may not be sufficiently differentiated to support the learning of individuals who require reinforcement of each tiny step mediated through their preferred modality or combination of modalities and orchestrated with reference to pacing and spacing uniquely designed to meet their needs. It is thus a professionally sophisticated and demanding challenge to discern how to interrelate the components from each of the variables noted above and to provide an individually adapted version of, for example, 'multi-sensory methods'.

ACCESSING INDEPENDENT LEARNING

Effective differentiation, therefore, even if through activities including group or paired learning should facilitate independent learning. This may involve a number of teacher tasks (See Fig. 4) such as observing that the basis for self-organisation for all students is available, the facilitation of self-study skills as well as designing and providing materials and resources. Additionally, the learner needs to self-reflect and evaluate both teaching and learning. Some of the strategies which can be utilised are also highlighted in fig. 4. Both teacher tasks and teacher strategies are mediated by aspects such as motivation, attitude, availability of information, models of learning and skills required and skills to be enhanced through learning. The progressive shift from 'outer-directed learning' (teacher-directed) towards 'inner-directed learning' (Student's own-choice, control and self-study) requires skilled teaching of a kind that employs 'the rhythm of education' described by Whitehead (1932) in terms of the sequence of phrases or stages: (i) of 'romance' (becoming interested in ideas); (ii) 'precision' (learning the skills) and (iii) 'generalisation' (appropriately applying the knowledge and skills).

Fig. 4

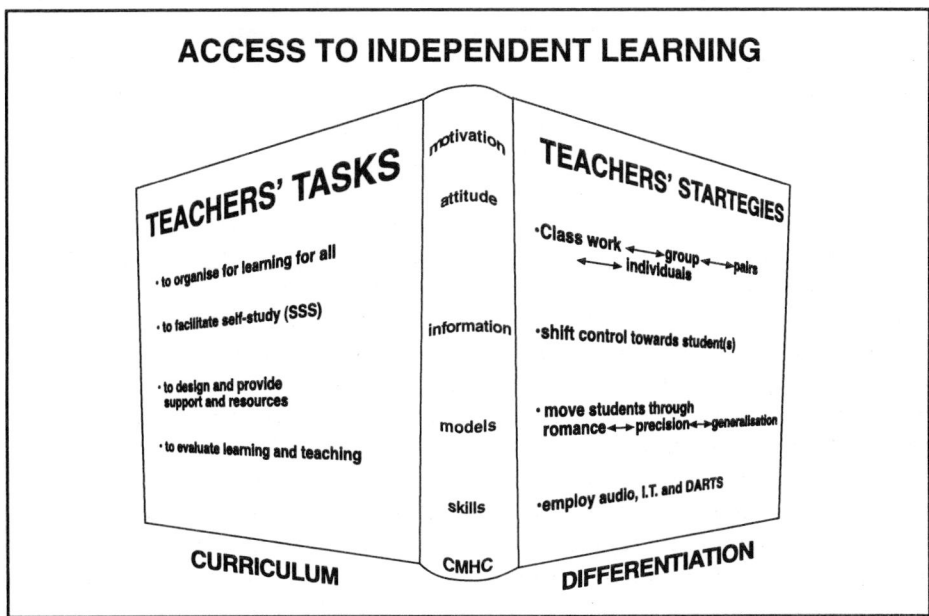

Fig. 5 highlights some of those teacher strategies which can be utilised for various aspects of differentiation. It concerns development of ideas based on the early work of Lunzer and Gardner (1978), Morris and Stewart Doré (1984) and Tonjes (1991).

Fig. 5

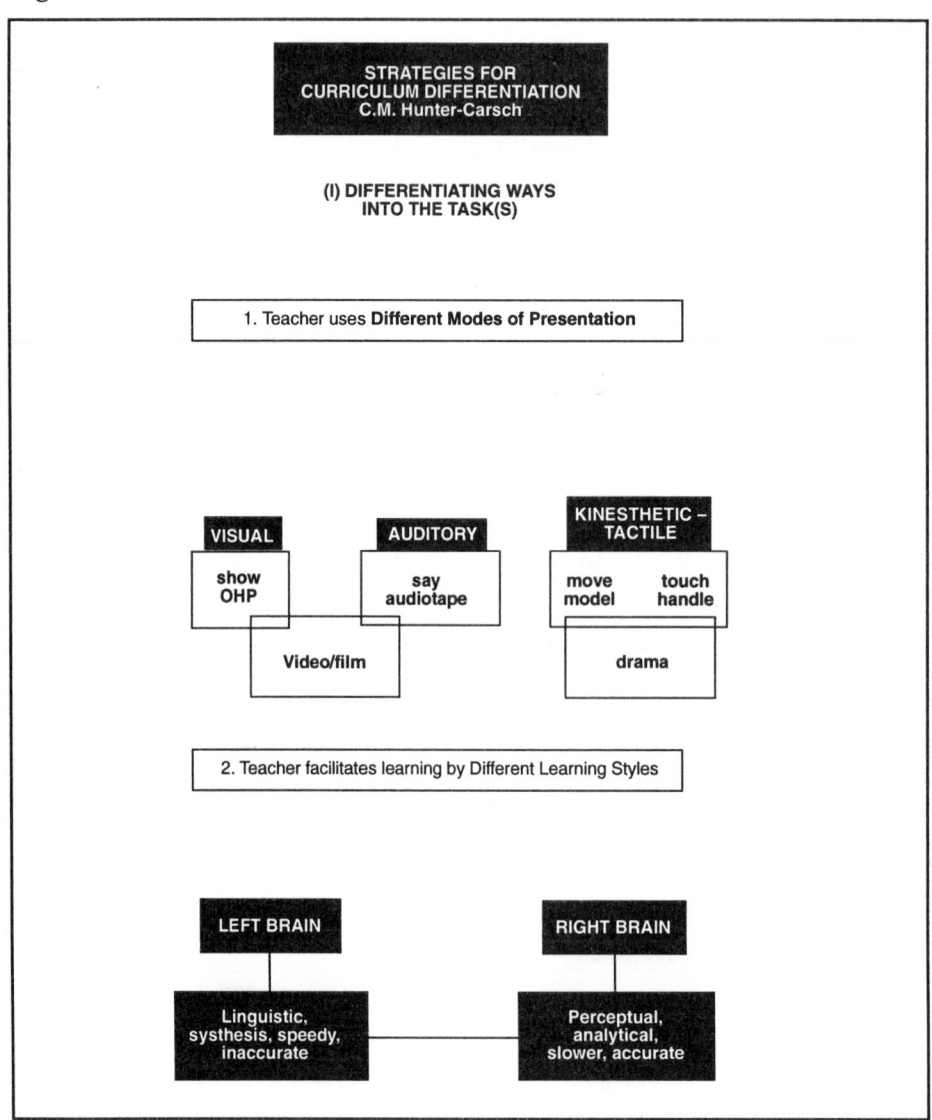

Fig. 5 (cont.)

3. Teacher provides Different Degrees of Challenge

- scope
- independence
- amount of content
- complexity of concepts
- access to support

4. Teacher provides choice of:

- tasks
- methods of working
- grouping (pairs, clusters)

5. Teacher uses Different Approaches to help with Preparation for Learning

- Langer's model; PREP
- A.O. (Advanced Organisers)
- Brainstorming
- Spider diagrams
- Q.O. Sessions (Questions only)

Fig. 5 (cont.)

**(II) DIFFERENT WAYS OF SUPPORTING STUDY
(ON TASK) AND RECORD KEEPING**

Teachers devise Strategies for

- identifying ideas
- selecting
- understanding

> **1. Use DARTS**
> **(Directed Activities Related to Text)**
> **for tasks requiring**

- reading
- oracy
- written work

Pupils use Different DARTS

- Glossing/Underlying
- Labelling
- Sequencing
- Prediction
- Cloze
- Modelling
- SQ3R (Survey, Question, Read, 'Recite', Recall)
- Diagrams
- Group Reading for Different Purposes

Fig. 5 (cont.)

---

2. Ways of assisting with Extracting Points and Processing Information

- audiorecorder
- strategies for notemaking
- Systematic Drafting and Redrafting (R Binns)
- I.T.

3. Ways of Translating Information for different audiences

- younger learners
- different genres

4. Ways of Communicating Information to different audiences

- newspapers
- radio
- television

CONCLUSION

The problem of how to differentiate the curriculum to meet the special educational needs of children with specific learning difficulties in the normal classroom has been discussed in relation to accessing independent learning. The desirability of sharing a conceptual framework within which a range of factors are taken into account by both the class teacher and the specialist teacher is an important factor. It is also suggested that the factors which relate to effective differentiation are not discrete but relate to each other in a dynamic manner (see also Hunter-Carsch, 1981, A Matrix for Diagnosing Inappropriate Learning Strategies: range and dynamics of specific language/reading differences). The matrix charts the interface between factors on three discussions:

(i)   Psycho-neurological factors,
(ii)   psycho educational factors and
(iii)   psycho-dynamic factors affecting learning style.

For the child with specific learning difficulties who requires individualised teaching, there is a need for a practical approach to literacy learning which permits tuition to be mediated within a structured context and employing structured teaching methods. If this can be provided within the ethos of an open approach to learning, in which the locus of control is increasingly felt by the child to be within himself or herself, there is the greater likelihood that the child will be able to learn successfully and go on learning. The necessary 'learning how to learn' can be facilitated through 'systematic drafting and redrafting', through writing about experiences and using subject content which matters to the child (Binns, 1980; Hunter-Carsch, Binns and Sobey, 1991).

The material that constitutes the content of the writing then renders the written communications the more easily memorable, meaningful and envisageable by directing the imagination rather than by 'capturing' it. This, while sharing and enjoying the flexibility of the 'new literacy' along with members of the peer-group, the child can be offered highly structured teaching within a safe, clearly delimited 'office' space, during specified times and with the shared professional support which derives from both specialist and generalist teacher working co-operatively together in the classroom. It is suggested that in this way, the child becomes more in 'control' of his or her learning and by recognising this, can get 'around' if not 'over' the hurdles which are presented by his or her specific learning difficulty. Effectively the child thus gains access to independent learning.

REFERENCES

Binns, R. (1980). A teaching technique for developing written language. In Clark, N. M. (Ed.) Reading and writing for the child with difficulties. *Education Review Occasional Publications*. University of Birmingham.

British Psychological Society Education Section Review (1993). Special edition on curriculum Differentiation distributed by NASEN, Stafford, and also BPS Education Section Review, Vol. 19, No. 1, (1995) pp 19-37.

Hardy, M. (1992). *Talking together, language and learning*. Vol. 4, July, pp 22-25.

Hunter-Carsch, C. M. (1981). Unpublished paper presented to British Psychological Society Cognitive Section International Conference on Dyslexia in Manchester University, February 1981, and briefly reported as Reading and learning difficulties: relationship and responsibilities. In Hendry, A, (1982), *Reading: The key issues*. London, Heinemann Educational Books.

Hunter-Carsch, C. M. (1990). 'Learning strategies for pupils with literacy difficulties: motivation, meaning and imagery.' In Pumfrey, P. and Elliot, C. *Children's difficulties in reading, spelling and writing*. London, The Falmer Press.

Hunter-Carsch, C. M. (1991). 'Home help.' In *Special children*, October 1991, pp 12-14.

Hunter-Carsch, C. M.; Binns, R. and Sobey, J. (1991), 'Creating young writers.' In *Language and learning*, 5, Feb. 1991, pp 9-12.

Hunter-Carsch, C. M. (1993). Reason, rhythm, relaxation and the new literacy: Implications for curriculum differentiation to meet the special needs of pupils with specific learning difficulties. In Wright, S. F. and Groner, R. (Eds.) *Facets of dyslexia and the remediation*. Amsterdam, North Holland, Elsevier Science Publishers.

Hunter-Carsch, C. M. (1993). 'Prerequisites for the teaching of reading to dyslexic children in mainstream classes: degrees of structuring learning.' In Hornsby, B. (Ed.) *Literacy 200*, London, Hornsby International Centre.

Hunter-Carsch, C. M. (1995). 'Stance, meaning and voluntary reading'. In Owen, P. and Pumfrey, P. (Eds.) *Emergent and developing reading: messages for teachers*. Vol. 1. London. The Falmer Press.

King, V. (1989). 'Support teaching: differentiation menu'. *Special Children*. Vol. 33, October 1989. Practice Papers 11.

Langer, J. (1981). 'From theory to practice: A pre-reading plan'. In *International Reading Association Journal of Reading*, 25, p 152-156.

Lloyd, D. (1989). 'The puppet theatre: a forum for innovation and inspiration'. In Hunter-Carsch, M. (Ed) *The Art of Reading*. Oxford, Basil Blackwell.

Lunzer, E. and Gardner, K. (1979). *The Effective Use of Reading*. London, Heinemann.

Morris, A. and Stewart-Doré, N. (1984). *Learning to learn from text*. North Ryde NSW, Addison Wesley.

Norwich, B. (1994). 'Differentiation: resolving tensions between basic social values and assumptions about individual differences'. Paper delivered at British Psychological Society Conference in December 1994 and to be published in 1995 in *Curriculum Studies*.

Redl, F. and Wineman, D. (1952). *Controls from within: techniques for the treatment of the aggressive child*. NY Free Press.

Spillman, J. (1991). 'Decoding differentiation'. *Special Children*. January 1991, pp 7-10.

Stott, D. H. (1962). *Programmed reading kit*. Glasgow, Holmes McDougall.

Stott, D. H. (1978). *Helping children with learning difficulties*. Ward Lock Educational.

Tonjes, M. (1991). *Secondary reading, writing and learning*. Boston, Allyn & Bacon.

Visser, J. (1993). *Differentiation: making it work*. Stafford, National Association for Special Educational Needs (NASEN).

Whitehead, A. N. (1932). *The aims of education*. London, Williams & Norgate.

Willinsky, J. (1990). *The new literacy*. London, Routledge.

SECTION 6

SOCIAL AND
EMOTIONAL CONSIDERATIONS

THE EMOTIONAL WORLD OF SPECIFIC LEARNING DIFFICULTIES

STEWART BIGGAR
and JENNIFER BARR

It is the Wimbledon final. The players have won a set each. The newcomer is leading 4:1 in the final set. She loses the match.

Sports commentators can talk of an athlete having (or lacking) the self-belief and confidence that helps them to reach peak performance at the crucial moment. From another tack, people with a disability are often described as overcoming obstacles, showing great courage and determination. Are these mere colloquialisms? Or do self-belief and confidence, courage and determination, have psychological validity in the context of the everyday achievements of children? How are these achieved? By what processes? What can help and what may hinder?

In this chapter, we argue that emotional factors lie at the heart of the experience of specific learning difficulties, and we offer a tentative model of some of the processes involved. We hope to show that each child's view of him or herself – the unique, individual self-concept – is crucial to the way in which the child responds to and deals with their learning difficulty, and we describe some of the ways in which other children and adults can affect this self-view. It will be helpful first to highlight some key ideas.

SKILLS AND STRATEGIES

The work of Piaget (1971) and of Vygotsky (1962) has had a powerful influence on the way that psychologists see children's development. Piaget maintained that learning of all kinds involves the gradual altering of a mental model of the world, so that it fits with new information as it is gathered. The mental construction must accommodate to new knowledge as it is assimilated, and this adapted model then guides the search for additional data. Piaget talked of the process as being driven by the child's desire to achieve active mastery.

One of Vygotsky's contributions was to show how important other people are for a child's learning. Learning is a social and interactive process. In day-today life, as in formal schooling, adults pick out for children those things which are important, they confer meaning on events and define what is to be learned; that is, they transmit cultural knowledge and values.

Wood (1989) offers an excellent discussion of these ideas and describes recent thinking. It is useful, he suggests, to think of learning as the development and refinement of skills and strategies. We do, quite literally, learn how to learn. This applies equally to playing football, having a conversation or reading a book. We refine our skills through using them, whether they be physical, social, or academic, and we develop higher order strategies as we practise them in different contexts. Fisher (1990) provides a useful account of the translation of such ideas into practice.

Bryant and Bradley (1985) and Goswami and Bryant (1990) argue that an important source of reading difficulties lies in the way a child approaches the task of reading. The job for the practitioner is to enable the child to understand the purposes and processes of literacy and thus to develop new and more effective strategies. It is not that a child who is failing to read does not use strategies, but that the strategies used are ineffective in enabling the learner to extract meaning from print: not learning to read or write conventionally is **also** a product of learning.

There seem to be many routes both to success and failure at reading. Bryant and Impey (1986) proposed the notion that children with dyslexic problems develop and rely on their own individual strategies just as normal children do. Seymour (1987), comparing case studies of normal and dyslexic readers, concluded there is little homogeneity in either group. Szeszulski and Manis (1987) compared the word recognition strategies used by dyslexic children and normal children matched for reading age. They found the strategies to be essentially similar, with the more advanced dyslexics indistinguishable from normals. The difficulties for the younger reading age dyslexics lay in the area of grapheme-phoneme correspondence rules.

Learning correspondence rules is important in the early stages of reading, but they can be fully used only by a child who already knows a good deal about literacy. Garton and Pratt (1989) describe important skills of pre-literacy. One of these, the child's level of phonological awareness, has been claimed to be the best single predictor of later reading success that we have (Bradley and Bryant, 1983; Goswami and Bryant, 1990). Skilled reading is a complex task depending on perceptual, cognitive and linguistic processes. Hall (1989) argues that readers do not proceed in strict sequence from basic perceptual units to overall interpretation of a text:

"Rather, the skilled reader derives information from many levels simultaneously, integrating graphophonemic, morphemic, semantic, pragmatic, schematic and interpretive information simultaneously . . . The skilled reader is purposive and a continuous monitor of his or her own comprehension."

(1989; 160)

SELF-CONCEPT

Johnston (1985) describes the extensive verbal reports of three adult disabled readers and concludes:

" . . . we need to consider more seriously explanations which stress combinations of anxiety, attributions, maladaptive strategies, inaccurate or non-existent concepts about aspects of reading, and a huge variety of motivational factors. "

(1985: 174)

Increasingly it is being recognised that even subtle influences on self-esteem can matter in children's learning. The interactive effects of self-esteem and skill development are, of course, unavoidable. There must of necessity be an interaction of some kind. Children who are confident and who acquire important skills easily can enjoy the benefit of a positive interplay between self-esteem and attainment. Other children, who may not have developed some crucial pre-literacy or social skills, and for whom the start of school becomes daunting and even frightening, may experience failure early on in their school careers.

What are the emotional consequences for a child who has been unable to develop effective skills and strategies in certain key areas of the curriculum and who is exhibiting specific learning difficulties? Searching for a model of the emotional processes involved in coping with specific difficulties, we considered the stages by which people often come to terms with other information – any information – that has a profound impact on their sense of self (there are useful parallels in thinking of a gay person 'coming out', or of a person assimilating the knowledge that they have contracted a serious illness). There can be an initial period of fear and confusion, where what the person expects of themselves is not what in practice it seems possible to achieve. Then there can be a stage of accurate identification and 'naming' of the difficulty, accompanied by a sense of relief that there is a reason, there is an explanation and it is not a question of fault or blame. As self-confidence is slowly restored, the sympathetic understanding of at least one other person may be crucial. At a certain point, the person may feel strong enough, or sure enough that 'this is who and how I am', that they are able to go public with the information. How well the reactions of others are handled at this stage depends both on the quality of available support, and on the emotional strength and confidence of the individual.

A study was undertaken in Dumfries and Galloway by one of the authors (Biggar, 1993). In the research, a sample was constructed of twenty children of primary or secondary school age from across the Region, who had been identified as having specific learning difficulties (dyslexia). Information about the history and circumstances of the children was gathered from four sources:

- From the case psychologist or from case notes;
- from interviews with parents, who described their experiences in trying to make sense of the problem and in seeking help;
- from interviews with teachers, covering areas such as teaching methods, specialist training and resource allocation; and
- from interviews with the children, exploring their feelings. These interviews included assessments of self-concept using Battle's Self-Esteem Inventory (1981).

These sources offer quite different perspectives on the experience of specific learning difficulties, and a fuller account is available from the author. Here, we shall concentrate on the children's own experiences, and examples drawn from the case studies are presented under the headings of finding out, moving on, and going public. The final sections look at factors which appear to hinder and factors which foster good emotional progress.

FINDING OUT

The children in the study whose specific difficulties were in the area of reading often seemed to be the ones most affected by their own realisation of failure. Children who were old enough and willing to reflect on their early years at school, claimed to have realised their difficulty before it became an issue for the adults. No doubt based on perceptions of their own performance up to that time, and their experience of developing mastery, the children assumed that they would continue to progress comparably with their peers. This expectation was made explicit by some children who had transferred to school with friends from playgroup or nursery. They reported becoming aware that they were not learning things which their peers seemed to find easy, and their first response was almost always to conceal or deny it.

It was this feeling of confusion and lack of understanding which the children reported they found most distressing. Certainly they tried to conceal their difficulty from friends, because friends – who also do not understand the problem – can 'section you out as being stupid', 'tease and humiliate you'. But there were also elements in many cases of concealment from self, of avoiding opportunities where failure might be experienced and of diversionary behaviour. There is no doubt that it was very painful for some children to admit their difficulty to themselves, and this could involve considerable self-blame. A young man John* could remember problems before P3, but in P3 he found that he 'could not read (his) own writing'. During that year John had four different teachers in succession. He reported thinking that they had each left because of him – this was his fault. During the following year it became clear to John that he was falling behind at nearly everything. He did not understand and he did not know what to do; he became quite anxious.

Literacy is highly valued in our culture and, as the medium for a great deal of the school curriculum, it has a prominent role. The rate at which children learn to read sometimes appears to be used as a measure of their overall ability to learn. While true for certain youngsters, this can be a damaging assumption for those whose specific learning difficulties mean that though poor at reading, they are otherwise able. They may be driven to different forms of avoidance or concealment, and can be subject to a variety of definitions by teachers. In the sample, two of the twenty children were first referred to the Psychological Service because of behaviour problems, though later these came to be regarded as stemming from specific learning difficulties. Moreover, in several cases where poor attainments **were** the stated reason for referral, these came with reports of associated behavioural patterns, including inattention, distractibility, laziness, immaturity and/or defiance.

Children themselves do not use these terms. Children talk of 'having a mental block', of 'stopping and starting', of 'facing a page of letters that make no sense' and of 'freezing'. They report feelings of embarrassment, humiliation, shame, anxiety and guilt. They can feel stupid, useless, frustrated and angry. They lose confidence in themselves as learners, and often they lose their friends.

Feelings of this kind were evinced by all but two of the sample. The longer such feelings were carried, the more serious an issue their difficulties became. It looks as if becoming trapped in this desperate, private and lonely emotional state can delay the possibility of more useful learning. One pupil, Peter, held himself in very low esteem. He had little confidence socially (as measured by Battle's Inventory) and he thought poorly of his academic ability. He did not believe his

---

* **Note:** In this chapter, names of children from the study are replaced by pseudonyms.

parents understood in the least how he felt. Peter's measured reading and writing attainments on leaving school at sixteen were lower than they had been at age nine, despite several years of learning support. He emanated an air of great sadness, and yet he was reflective and articulate. Peter is now fully employed in a skilled trade.

MOVING ON

Starting to make sense of the difficulty for oneself seems to be an important step forward. The crucial role of peer relations is suggested by the case of Fiona, a twelve year old girl. She had managed until P5 to conceal the extent, if not the fact of her problem with maths. Her friends seem to have accepted that she would ask them questions and copy their answers, and to this extent they colluded with her. Fiona's social confidence was reflected in other areas of her self-concept: she reported being teased 'a little bit' but it had not disturbed her. She described some of the techniques she had used to avoid doing sums in public, and she was clearly skilled at changing the subject and deflecting attention from herself on to others. Her difficulty was eventually discovered by her mother only when she was unable to count the change after a shopping trip.

Other children testified to the relief they felt at having even one or two friends who understood that they found some things difficult, and whom they could openly ask for help. Having someone who did not tease them helped them to bother less about those who did. This remained important whether or not the children felt supported and understood by adults.

An element central to the children's construction of their difficulties is the way they think that they – and their difficulties – are perceived by others. Michael described the friendship that developed with his learning centre teacher at primary school. Attending the centre brought taunts from his peers, he recalled, but being there was relaxing, purposeful and relieved his stress. His teacher did not define him as lazy or stupid, and she did not pressurise him to complete work. Michael understood that what she demanded of him was that he try his best. He emphasised the importance of support by someone you feel comfortable with. (We may note in passing that the importance of a close relationship with a trusted adult is highlighted by Marie Clay in the Reading Recovery Programme (1985).) Michael described how his teacher's sympathetic approach had helped him see his difficulty more clearly, and so had reduced his fear and anxiety.

Ian, the youngest child in the sample, had benefited from the identification of his motor learning difficulty pre-school, and felt supported by his parents and teachers. When he was also slow to begin reading, his difficulty was recognised early and appropriate learning support began. At the time of the study, Ian was only seven, but he was able to say:

"Teachers say it'll never go away, but I'll be able to work round it. I don't seem to be able to work round it now. I think I've got round something then it comes back and stands in my way."

Ian was strong enough to be able to say of those who called him handicapped, 'I think they're just horrible people', but clearly he will need on-going sympathetic support to maintain this positive approach to his difficulties.

GOING PUBLIC

The differences across the sample on measures of self-esteem were very large. In fact, these children's scores covered the full range from very high to very low on all three subscales of Battle's Inventory, that is on measures of social confidence, feelings about school and perceived parental support.

In general, those with difficulties in less restricting areas such as spelling saw themselves quite positively, especially if they believed that their difficulties had been recognised and were being tackled. Nevertheless, there were two children in the sample whose reading attainments exceeded their chronological age, yet who still regarded themselves as academically poor due to their spelling difficulties. There were other children whose academic attainments were actually poorer but who achieved greater confidence.

There is a stage beyond this, where children not only manage to make sense of their problem and to hold a positive approach to it, but become successful in overcoming feelings of public embarrassment. Michael, described earlier, was placed in a segregated, low-ability class on transfer to secondary school. He knew that he did not belong there but reported 'it took time to prove I wasn't different in other ways'. He did rejoin mainstream, and by third year 'everyone had forgotten'. His difficulty, which persists to the present day, was no longer an issue to him socially; having once felt different from others, Michael now felt normal. 'It is hard work and it wears you down.' The main benefit to him, however, was that the problem was now in the open, and it was in perspective.

By contrast, Gordon felt he had done all the coping by himself. He did not acknowledge any particularly significant others. In spite of a learning difficulty severe enough to merit the preparation of material on audiotape in class and SEB examination concessions, Gordon now attends a degree course at college. His parents had sought an independent assessment of his difficulties when he was thirteen. He recalled being told he was dyslexic and that he could either 'lie down and accept it' or else work very hard. Prior to this, he had been exhibiting school phobia and complaints of illness which had no identifiable physical cause. In Gordon's case, the use of the dyslexic label had provided a useful explanation which reduced both his and his parents' confusion and distress. His parents no longer accepted (though previously they had) the school's assertion that he was a daydreamer who did not try. He himself no doubt benefited from his parents' reappraisal, and from the specialist support he started to receive, but what he regarded as more important personally was his own courage in declaring his difficulty and his determination to overcome it.

We have tried to draw common themes from the testimony of the children interviewed, even though each of their experiences was unique. Those who have succeeded in forming a view of their difficulties which, on the one hand, does not distort their sense of worth and, on the other, enables them to make progress, have done so by different routes and with different kinds of help. Those who have not been able to move on seem to have been hampered by similarly diverse factors. An interplay between self-image and academic progress is clearly evident from this study, and even more crucial the importance of alleviating a child's feelings of guilt and self-blame as a pre-condition for progress. Children require help to reach a personal reconciliation with the fact of their difficulties, and their chances of positive academic outcomes are improved when this help is prompt, sympathetic and on-going.

FACTORS WHICH HINDER EMOTIONAL PROGRESS

It is possible to identify several factors in the cases of these twenty children which seem to be associated with continued or exacerbated difficulties. The largely qualitative nature of the research does not permit any claims about causal relationships, though some may be suggested (Robson, 1993). These are discussed under three general headings.

1   Inappropriate attributions

It has been noted that in many cases the poor attainments of children were attributed to behavioural patterns of inattention, distractibility, laziness, immaturity and/or defiance. Parents generally regarded teachers as the experts and, to an extent, believe and act upon such definitions. In eight of the twenty cases, parents described the scenes of anger and distress which followed their attempts to apply pressure on their children to complete homework or extra assignments. The parents themselves became impatient and angry and the children became upset. For children who already feel confused and guilty, this increased pressure is not helpful: it may serve to damage the sense of alliance and support they have a right to expect from their parents, and it can hinder the process of reaching a true understanding of their difficulty.

For some children, the further failure they experienced was sufficient signal to their parents that explanations in terms of laziness were not adequate. Others, like Gordon, began to exhibit behaviour of a neurotic kind before the perceptions of parents and teachers changed significantly. A few have carried these unfortunate labels throughout their school careers. If the only explanation offered to children who are failing is that the responsibility is theirs – that they are stupid or lazy or both – then in time they may come to believe it. What action can they take in self-defence?

2   Disagreement between adults

Avoiding, if we can, any questions of which view is 'correct', it was clear that in over half of the twenty cases the explanations of specific learning difficulty held by parents and teachers were at odds. This is consistent with the findings of the team from Stirling University (Riddell *et al.*, 1993). If we take the children's self-esteem measures as an outcome and relate them to parent reports of disagreements with school, some interesting patterns emerge.

In cases where the disagreement has been particularly strong, there is a tendency for children to feel that neither home nor school is on their side. Perhaps the problem turns into a focus on the dispute between home and school, such that neither is able to offer the confident reassurance which children so need. One exception was a fourteen year old girl, Kathryn, who scored very high on the measure of perceived parental support. However, she had been removed from school on the grounds that she was making no progress and was being bullied. Her scores on the academic and social confidence subscales were both very low. Kathryn's parents seem to have supported her general self-esteem but she was more emotionally dependent on them than a girl of this age might normally expect to be. She has not so far found ways to develop her own sense of worth or independent confidence. In purely academic terms, her difficulties were not severe, perhaps equivalent to those of Fiona.

However, Fiona's outcomes have been quite different. Not only did her mother state specifically that she had tried to avoid any suggestion of blame or pressure towards her daughter, she also said she had withheld her doubts over the school's explanation for her lack of progress. When Fiona was diagnosed independently as being dyslexic, her mother resisted this label also, on the grounds that it might cause dissent with the school. Her mother strove for solutions for Fiona's difficulty; she did not allow her own opinion or anxieties to confuse her primary aim of reaching a consensus in the approach of home and school. That she largely succeeded is suggested by her daughter's high (at times very high) scores on different aspects of her self-concept, taken at the end of P7. Fiona appeared more defensive than most children her age, but not so as to cast doubt on her clear statement that she expected to do well in secondary school. Her attainments have improved markedly.

Fiona's success reinforces the suggestion that conflicts between home and school may be one cause of poor outcomes. In this example, the flexibility of Fiona's mother helped to create a positive ethos, but it might equally be the case that in different circumstances it is the professionals who may need to conciliate. Prompted by their understanding of the emotional world of learning, there may be occasions (e.g. where parents already hold strong views) that the professionals could make genuine and unpatronising attempts to seek common ground and workable compromise, even if this means moderating their own judgements for a time.

3   Verbal abuse

The effect of teasing by peers on a child with specific learning difficulties probably depends on that child's emotional resilience. All the children who were interviewed reported having been teased on account of their difficulties, but the importance of this was by no means the same for them all. Some of the children discussed earlier had been able to come to terms with their difficulty personally and socially, and for them teasing had either stopped or become unimportant. Others reported that it was serious and on-going. They remained defensive and secretive at school to avoid opportunities for ridicule. One of these was Shirley, a girl of fourteen. She described her frustration at not feeling able to admit the extent of her difficulty in class, and therefore not getting help as she required it. Shirley's self-esteem was uniformly low, even though she had skills that were well-developed in art, music and drama, and these were important to her.

Shirley volunteered that her social and vocational skills course at secondary school had included a series of talks on various handicapping conditions. Why, she suggested, could this syllabus not be extended to include specific learning difficulties? Verbal abuse, or the fear of it, is at best unpleasant and, for emotionally vulnerable or exposed children, potentially quite damaging. An element of guided class discussion may indeed be useful.

FACTORS WHICH FOSTER EMOTIONAL PROGRESS

The preceding discussion suggests that a child's chances of emotional progress are best when certain conditions can be met:

- Where there is an accurate description of the child's abilities and difficulties, uncluttered by anxiety or prejudice;

- where those adults who are significant for the child agree about the nature of the problem and how to tackle it;

- where they offer a construction or rationalisation which makes sense to the child, and which both preserves a sense of value, and anticipates progress; and

- where the child feels understood by a trusted adult.

Piaget writes of a child's desire to achieve active mastery, of wanting to understand and to be able to do things. Faced with failure, children's attempts to understand often result in doubts about their competence, and so damage their confidence. If the situation continues, the effects are compounded. For example, poor readers need both courage and encouragement to abandon strategies for learning which are ineffective. At the outset, they have no first-hand evidence that better strategies can be found and so they may resist the attempts of others to teach them new skills.

There is an importance placed on literacy in our society, and difficulties with skills in this area can arouse strong feelings in parents. Children who are looking for some explanation or understanding of their lack of ability are sensitive to the heightened emotions of others. They may even, in their own minds, assume responsibility for having caused the upset themselves.

Without exception, the single most frightening event which poor readers reported was being asked to read aloud in class. It served no useful purpose in their eyes. Such children need to be helped to build their confidence. They are entitled not to be made anxious, not to be humiliated and not to be forced by another to disclose their difficulty in public.

There does not seem to be any single formula by which the needs of all children who have specific learning difficulties can be met, but this study does stress the importance of what Vygotsky called the 'better informed adult'. The children whose measured outcomes were better all round enjoyed a relationship of trust with someone who they were confident understood. Sometimes this was a parent, sometimes a teacher. Peers have also been an important source of support. If treated and respected as individuals, children do seem to be better at putting their difficulties into a wider perspective, and thus coming to terms with them. The requirements on a supportive adult seem to be:

- To be honest and open;
- to remove guilt or blame;
- to hold feeling for the child;
- to preserve the dignity of the child;
- to help the child to feel safe;
- to maintain positive regard;
- to value the child;
- to act as the child's advocate.

The circumstances of every child are different and the pattern of events which leads to the identification of a learning difficulty will always be unique. A child's emotional world is also a highly individual and personal place. In order to offer effective help, an adult needs some appreciation of how it feels for this child to have this difficulty. What we are arguing for in this chapter is a differentiation of the interpersonal to match the differentiation of the curriculum.

REFERENCES

Battle, J. (1981). *Culture-free SEI: self-esteem inventories for children and adults.* Seattle: Special Child Publications.

Biggar, S. (1993). *Specific Learning difficulties: A qualitative case study approach.* Unpublished project, University of Strathclyde.

Bradley, L. and Bryant, P. E. (1983). Categorising sounds and learning to read – a causal connection. *Nature,* 301, 419-421.

Bryant, P. E. and Bradley, L. (1985). *Children's reading problems.* Oxford: Blackwell.

Bryant, P. E. and Impey, L. (1986). The similarities between normal readers and developmental and acquired dyslexics. *Cognition,* 24, 1212-137.

Clay, M. M. (1985). *The early detection of reading difficulties.* 3rd edn. Auckland, NZ: Heinemann Education.

Fisher, R. (1990). *Teaching children to think.* Oxford: Basil Blackwell.

Garton, A. and Pratt, C. (1989). *Learning to be literate.* Oxford: Basil Blackwell.

Goswami, U. and Bryant, P. E. (1990). *Phonological skills and learning to read.* Hove, Sussex: Erlbaum.

Hall, W. S. (1989). Reading comprehension. *American Psychologist,* 44, (2), 157-161.

Johnston, P. H. (1985). Understanding reading disability: a case study approach. *Harvard Educational Review,* 55, (2), 153-176.

Marshall, C. and Rossman, G. B. (1989). *Designing qualitative research.* London: Sage.

Millar, R., Crute, V. and Hargie, O. (1992). *Professional interviewing.* London: Routledge.

Piaget, J. (1971). *Biology and knowledge.* Edinburgh: University of Edinburgh Press.

Riddell, S., Duffield, J., Brown, S. and Ogilvy, C. (1993). *Specific learning difficulties: policy, practice and provision.* Department of Education, Stirling University.

Robson, C. (1993). *Real world research: a resource for social scientists and practitioner-researchers.* Oxford: Blackwell.

Seymour, P. H. K. (1987). Individual cognitive analysis of competent and impaired reading. *British Journal of Psychology,* 78, 483-506.

Szeszulski, P. A. and Manis, F. R. (1987). A comparison of word recognition processes in dyslexic and normal readers at two reading-age levels. *Journal of Experimental Child Psychology,* 44, 364-376.

Thomson, M. E. and Watkins, E. J. (1990). *Dyslexia: a teaching handbook.* London: Whurr.

Vygotsky, L. S. (1962). *Thought and language.* Cambridge, Mass.: The MIT Press.

Wood. (1989). *How children think and learn.* Oxford: Blackwell.

SUPPORTING THE SYSTEM – DYSLEXIA AND TEACHER STRESS

GAVIN REID
JOHN W. HINTON

This chapter focuses on teacher supports within the school system. It is suggested that a supportive school system is necessary to provide the structure to minimise psychological stress induced by work (teacher stress) and provide a more favourable education climate for pupils (Proctor, 1993). It is also suggested that dyslexic children are particularly vulnerable to psychological stress in schools and that teachers dealing with dyslexic children also experience high levels of psychological stress (Hales, 1991; Reid, 1991; Biggar and Barr, 1993; Lipinski, 1995; Jordan, 1995).

The psychological stress experienced by dyslexic pupils and teachers of dyslexic pupils can be set against a background of increased stress in the teaching profession in general highlighted by the increasing demands being placed on teachers (EIS, (1994); Badger, 1994; Proctor, 1993; and Johnston, 1993). In a survey of 570 teachers (Johnston, 1993) which examined workload diaries of teachers, the picture which emerged was of 'an occupational group putting in on average an extra day of work each week in a quiet period of the year; reporting between three and four occasions of stressful feelings in that week; and registering high scores on an indicator of occupational stress'. It is therefore important that teachers should feel supported by the school system particularly if they are to offer effective support to pupils with special needs.

Dyslexic children can present both a challenge and a threat to the professional competence of teachers. This was evident from responses in a survey of specialist teachers with responsibilities for the teaching of dyslexic children (Jordan, 1995). Some of the comments which describe the teachers' feelings include 'inadequate'; 'upset for the child'; 'frustrated'; 'where do I start'; and 'feel I lack the skills required'. These responses are symptomatic of high 'perceived coping incapacity' and 'non-satisfaction of needs', both indicators of psychological stress as defined by Hinton and Burton (1992). This state would very likely be exacerbated if the teachers' were also experiencing additional excessive and conflicting role demands in school. It is, therefore, appropriate to investigate causes and responses to teacher work stress in relation to the network of supports within the school system.

CAUSES OF TEACHER STRESS

Many different factors contribute to teacher stress. Dunham (1992) cites ten major sources of stress in teaching including lack of support, constant changes, imposed curriculum innovation and lack of non-contact time. These factors could have implications for teachers of dyslexic pupils.

Boyle, Borg, Falzon and Baglioni (1995), in a comprehensive survey of 700 primary school teachers found four distinct dimensions in relation to teacher stress – pupil behaviour: time/resource difficulties; professional recognition needs and poor colleague relations. This supports the view that teacher stress is multi-dimensional and further emphasises the need to tackle teacher stress within a school systems framework.

Hinton and Burton (1992) propose that psychological stress (psystress) results from an imbalance between 'perceived demands' and 'perceived capabilities' and this occurs through 'cognitive appraisal'. According to this model, perceived coping incapacity (PCI) is the primary stress generation factor, combined with perceived non-satisfaction of needs. These are important considerations in accounting for and dealing with teacher work stress. This model shows that psychological stress (psystress) can be manifested physiologically, emotionally, cognitively and behaviourally. This model, therefore, quite appropriately considers the systematic factors affecting individuals within organisations. This is a particularly appropriate model for stress research since it acknowledges the role of social supports, responsibility and concern and environmental factors. This thoroughly researched transactional model therefore emphasises the importance of supporting the system which in turn supports the teacher, who can then offer support to the pupil. (see Fig. 1)

Fig. 1: Model of Potential Supports (Reid, 1995)

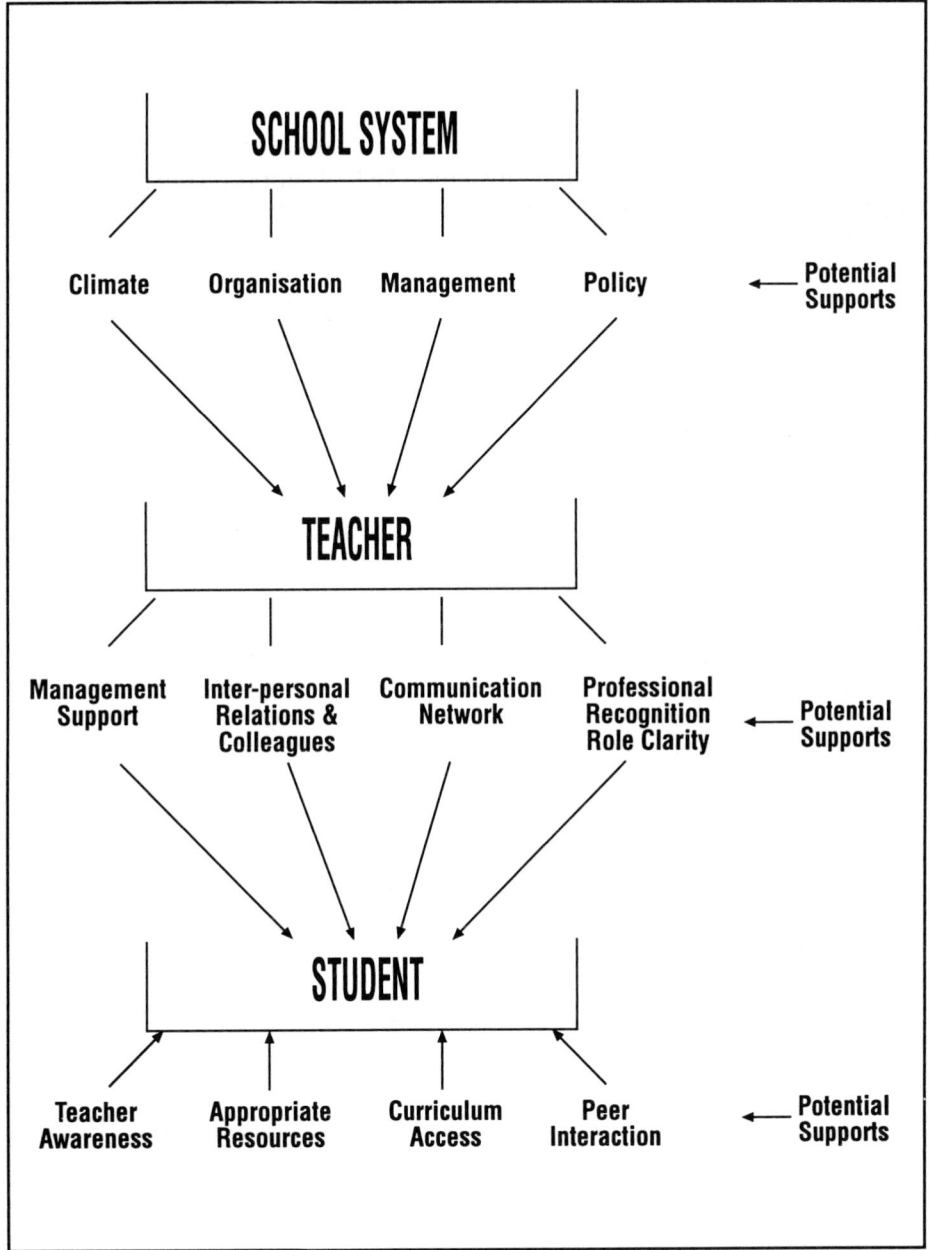

STRESS AND DYSLEXIA

Dyslexic students, from the early years in primary school to further education and beyond, require special consideration due to their vulnerability to psychological stress. Fawcett (1995) singled out the likelihood of the dyslexic child failing within the present school system as a major factor responsible for stress experienced by dyslexic children. Additionally, there are other sources of stress for dyslexics which can arise from the home situation and other factors at school. Fawcett argues that the considerable effort dyslexic children need to expend to 'keep pace with life' is very significant in the generation of psychological stress. Fawcett and Nicolson (1990) show that dyslexic children need to work harder in **all** aspects of learning, not only literacy skills, to achieve the same level of performance as other children.

It has been hypothesised (Fawcett, 1995) that much of the stress experienced by dyslexic children could be alleviated if the education system was more supportive to their needs and teachers more aware. Thus, lack of training, resulting in a lack of awareness of the needs of dyslexic children and how these can be met not only contributes to the stress experienced by dyslexic children, but also to that experienced by teachers. This in turn adds pressure and tension to the existing educational system.

Stanovich (1986) refers to the 'Matthew Effect' in relation to dyslexic children (a reference to the Biblical passage 'But from him that hath not shall be taken away even that he hath' Matthew XXV, 29). This statement can be used to refer to the cumulative effect of the failure to achieve literacy and how a difficulty in one aspect of literacy has a knock-on effect to other aspects of literacy and learning in general. This makes it more difficult for the dyslexic child to realise the potential of those skills which he/she actually does possess: and these skills can be eroded due to difficulties in other areas. This 'Matthew Effect', therefore, can be damaging to the child's self-concept as well as to potential achievement, and can clearly lead to the dyslexic child experiencing psychological stress.

Dyslexic children often display discrepancies between the verbal and performance sub-scales of the Wechsler Intelligence Scale (Lannen and Lannen, 1995; Turner, 1994; Gardner, 1994). This can result in 'cognitive tension', resulting in feelings of anxiety which can prevent them from functioning to their full capacity. This type of tension can also be experienced by high achieving dyslexic students (Lannen, 1990) and can produce considerable psychological stress.

Duane (1991) indicates that dyslexic children are more prone to 'conduct disorders' and depression and Fawcett (1995) provides some detailed examples of this with reference to case study research. These highlight the life-long difficulties of dyslexic children and their vulnerability in experiencing some form of psychological stress.

Thomson (1995) shows how difficulties in other areas apart from literacy can affect the dyslexic child at school. She argues that many dyslexic children are lost in both space and time, which makes it difficult for them to function well in the school environment and can cause on-going anxiety for them throughout the school day.

Chinn and Crossman (1995) cite a number of good examples which highlight the difficulty dyslexic adolescents have with social skills. They feel that social skills, like turn-taking and game participation, may provide difficulties which can arise because of the dyslexic child's lack of awareness or confusion with rules. This can lead to the child's actions being misunderstood.

Saunders (1995) describes how having a dyslexic child in the family can become a real emotional experience for everyone in the family. It follows, therefore, that having a dyslexic child in the class can also be an emotional experience for the teacher. Just as family supports are required to help the dyslexic child and family members, school supports are also necessary to help the teacher.

DYSLEXIA AND TEACHER STRESS

Studies involving groups of support teachers from different geographical locations with responsibility for teaching children with specific learning difficulties (dyslexia) revealed that these teachers experienced high levels of work stress compared to other teachers in the same schools (Reid, 1990, 1992). Follow-up interviews suggested some reasons for this. The teachers felt that children with specific learning difficulties presented additional dimensions not present to the same extent among other children, even among those with other types of learning difficulties. This included an unpredictable learning pattern which required the teacher to re-adjust in terms of teaching methodology and expectations; pupil demotivation; in some cases, limited experience and lack of training in teaching children with specific learning difficulties; lack of pupil progress; teacher self-doubt; limited management appreciation of the difficulty and factors relating to role conflict, work load and responsibility. This considerable list emphasizes the need for, and the attention which should be given to, the development of supports within schools to help teachers cope with difficulties such as these presented by dyslexic children.

THE NEED FOR SUPPORT

The model of 'psystress' (Hinton and Burton, 1992) views 'perceived coping incapacity' as the result of perceived demands being in excess of perceived capabilities. It is important, therefore, to provide some supports for teachers in relation to both demands and capabilities. Perceived demands can arise from a number of different areas such as school management; colleagues; parents and pupils themselves. How can the specialist teacher be supported to cope with these demands? Individual counselling or stress management programmes may help but it is unlikely that these will tackle the underlying difficulties since many of these difficulties are embedded in the system. Key personnel, therefore, such as head teachers, other members of the school management teams and colleagues need to be involved in any stress management programme if it is to be fully effective. The headteacher and school management have some control over timetabling, and school communication and can show an understanding and appreciation of the importance of supports with school.

ROLE FACTORS

It is important to consider the relationship between school supports and teachers' perceptions of their occupational roles. Many studies investigating teacher stress have singled out role factors as being particularly significant (Trendall, 1989; Capel, 1989; Dunham, 1992 and Reid, 1991). Role factors can be seen in terms of role demands, role ambiguity, role overload and role conflict.

In relation to teaching children with specific learning difficulties teachers felt that role demands were considerable, particularly in cases where only minimal training had been provided (Reid, 1991). In some cases, demands appeared to be incompatible with personality aspects and personal preferences of the teachers in relation to one-to-one teaching, small group teaching or team teaching in the whole-class situation. This also related to role conflict where there was some uncertainty regarding approaches in relation to direct tuition and co-operative teaching. This provided a dilemma for the teachers concerned and each group within the school had their own particular views on this matter and indeed on the role of specialist teachers. This clearly added to the existing pressure on teachers. This dilemma can be seen as a result of educational innovations and some uncertainty, perhaps controversy, on the most effective methods of teaching and providing for the needs of pupils with specific learning difficulties (Pumfrey and Reason, 1991).

WHOLE-SCHOOL APPROACH

The recognition of role factors as a contributory aspect of teacher work stress among learning support teachers underlines the view that in order to deal effectively with teacher stress, a whole-school approach is necessary (Tollan, 1987; Proctor, 1993). Individual stress management strategies, involving 'palliative' or 'direct action' methods (Kryciacou, 1989) may well have a function in dealing with individual difficulties of individual teachers, but may be rendered ineffective if the root cause is within the school organisation and system. An effective and healthy organisational climate in schools can therefore support teachers both in terms of work overload and role factors, such as role conflict. This is reinforced in a study by Cox (1988) which describes an individually orientated approach as 'detraction from the important role that the organisation plays in determining teachers' experiences and can play in resolving their problems' (p. 354). It is apparent therefore that within school factors such as the school communication network, inter-personal staff relations, organisational procedures, management concern for teachers' welfare, democracy in decision making and encouragement in relation to professional development are important considerations and need to be addressed.

Study of major curriculum innovation in Scotland was conducted by Badger (1994) (the 5 - 14 Development programme). The author reported that innovation was a source of considerable stress in the teaching profession. He suggested that a reappraisal of the organisational support and the pacing of innovation at school and national levels be undertaken. This study also highlighted the importance of management practice in dealing with change in schools.

DEVELOPING SUPPORTS

Schools are continually facing curricular and administrative changes, the latter being accelerated by devolved management of responsibility for school resources and policy. In view of the evidence on school supports, it is important that schools' in-service programmes considers the importance of school organisation in relation to teacher stress.

Such a programme could include the following factors:

- Personal Organisation.
- Classroom management.
- School Organisation.
- Management and administration.

Research by Reid (1991, 1992, 1993) and Proctor (1993) shows that the following aspects are significant in examining teacher stress and school supports:

- Perceived non-satisfaction of needs.
- Social support within school.
- Motivation.
- Job challenge.
- Staff involvement in organisational decisions.
- School administration.
- Readiness to innovate.
- Role of school management.

A framework for a whole-school programme taking into account these aspects is shown in Fig. 2.

Fig. 2: School Supports – An In-service Framework

Personal Organisation
- time management
- planning and preparation
- diary and record keeping
- information gathering/general awareness

School Organisation
- organisational components
- organisational models
- vulnerable aspects of organisations
- staff interaction within organisational structures

Inter-Personal Support within Organisations
- nature of inter-personal support
- features of a supportive organisation
- interpersonal support and teaching

Organisational Climate
- role of management
- organisational climate dimensions
- assessing climate

An in-service programme which considers this kind of framework should help to develop an awareness of the different aspects of school supports and school organisational climate. Additionally, such a programme should help to combine organisational factors and personal and school supports and also identify and highlight constructive aspects of personal and organisational factors in school. This, it is hoped, would minimise work stress, the effects of which are clearly evident in schools in the current climate of major curricular and administrative changes and particularly help teachers in relation to teaching groups of pupils with specific needs such as dyslexic children.

CONCLUSION

Whole-school programmes to reduce work stress not only address the issue of developing a supportive school system and communication network, but also deal with mis-matched perceptions of staff. A particular situation may be stressful to one teacher but not to another – personal perception, therefore, of the balance between perceived capabilities and perceived demands can vary from individual to individual. Reid (1991) found that differing perceptions between teaching staff and management was a significant issue in the work stress levels of one school: teaching staff felt management were not supportive and showed little awareness of classroom factors and of the implications and effect on the staff of 'overload' due to curricular innovations. Management, on the other hand, perceived themselves as very supportive and believed they provided staff with a supportive form of consultancy. Such a mis-match can be addressed in a whole-school programme.

Within this whole-school framework there is little doubt that the difficulties associated with dyslexia require special consideration. Dyslexic children can provide the teacher with a considerable challenge but this can be met by specialist and trained teachers. If the school system, however, is not supportive, this challenge can seem insurmountable adding to teacher work stress, but with adequate school supports the difficulties associated with teaching dyslexic children can be overcome.

REFERENCES

Badger, W. (1994). 5-14 Programme and teacher stress. In *Education in the North*, New Series, No. 2 1994 pp. 31 - 39.

Biggar, S. and Barr, J. (1993). The emotional world of specific learning difficulties. In Reid, G. (Ed.) *Specific Learning Difficulties (Dyslexia) Perspectives on Practice*, Edinburgh. Moray House Publications.

Boyle, G. J., Borg, M. G., Falzon, J .M. and Baglioni, Jr, A. J. (1995). A Structural Model of the Dimensions of Teacher Stress. in *British Journal of Educational Psychology* Vol. 65, Part 1, pp 49-67.

Capel, S. (1989). Influences and Incidence of Stress and Burnout. In *Secondary School Teachers. British Journal of Educational Psychology* p.57, 279-288.

Cox, T. (1988). Psychological Factors in Stress and Health. In *Handbook of Life Stress* (Eds. Fisher, S. and Reason, J.), London, Wiley.

Dunham. J. (1992). *Stress in Teaching* (2nd ed.). London, Routledge.

EIS (1994). Stress at Work – *Educational Institute of Scotland Research Report.*

Fawcett, A. (1995). Case studies and some recent research: In Miles, T. R. and Varma, V. (Eds.) *Dyslexia and Stress.* Whurr Publishers, London.

Gardner, P. (1994). Diagnosing dyslexia in the classroom: A three-stage model. In Hales, G. *Dyslexia Matters.* Whurr Publications.

Hales, G. (1990). Personality Aspects of Dyslexia. In Hale, G. (Ed.) *Meeting Points in Dyslexia. Proceedings of the First International Conference of the British Dyslexia Association*, Reading. BDA.

Hinton, J. W. and Burton, R. F. (1992). Clarification of the concept of psychological stress ('PSYSTRESS') *International Journal of Psychosomatics.* 39, (1-4), 42-43.

Johnston, M. (1993). Time and Tasks: Teacher Work Load and Stress. In *S.C.R.E. Spotlights,* 44pp., 1 - 5. Scottish Council for Research in Education, Edinburgh.

Jordan, E. (1995). Teachers Perceptions of Specific Learning Difficulties. In *Bridges,* Vol. 2, No 2, Spring 1995, p 34.

Kryrciacou, C. (1989). The Nature and Prevalence of Teacher Stress. In Teaching and Stress (Ed.) Cole, M. and Walker, S. Milton Keynes: Open University Press.

Lannen, S. and Lannen, C. (1995). Psychological assessment and the WISC-R: *Unpublished study.* Psychological Services, Riyadh, Saudia Arabia.

Lannen, S. (1990). *Personal correspondence.*

Lipinski, B. W. (1995). Dyslexia in Poland in *Bridges,* Vol. No. 2, Spring 1995. p. 35.

Nicolson, R. I. and Fawcett, A. J. (1990). Automaticity: a new framework for dyslexia research? In *Cognition* 30: 159-82.

Proctor, J. (1993). Occupational Stress Among Primary Teachers – Individuals. Organisations. Unpublished Ph.D. Thesis, University of Aberdeen.

Pumfrey, P. D and Reason, R. (1991). *Specific Learning Difficulties (Dyslexia): Challenges and Responses.* Routledge, London.

Reid, G. (1991). Stress factors in teaching children with specific learning difficulties. Paper presented at *Second International Conference, British Dyslexia Association,* Oxford 1991.

Reid, G. (1992). Teaching Stress –The Roles of Perceived Organisational Change, Personal Planning and Perceived Responsibility and Concern. Study in part fulfilment Ph.D. University of Glasgow.

Reid, G. (1993). Examinations of the Relationship Between Stress Variables and Dimension of the School Organisational Climate. Study in part fulfilment of Ph.D. University of Glasgow.

Reid, G. (1995). Organisational Climate and School Supports – A Whole School Programme. Part fulfilment of Ph.D. University of Glasgow.

Stanovich, K. E. (1986). Matthew effects in reading: Some consequences of individual differences in the acquisition of literacy. In *Reading Research Quarterly,* 21:360-407.

Tollan, J. (1987). An Investigation into the Causes and Means of Ameliorating Stress in Primary School Teachers in one Scottish Region. Unpublished M.App.Sci. Thesis. University of Glasgow.

Trendall, B. (1989). Stress in teaching and teacher effectiveness: A study of teachers across mainstream and special education. In *Educational Research*, 31 (1) 52- 58.

Turner, M. (1994). Quantifying exceptionality: issues in the psychological assessment of dyslexia. In Hales, G. *Dyslexia Matters.* Whurr Publications.

Thomson, P. (1995). Stress factors in early education. In Miles, T. R. and Varma, V. *Dyslexia and Stress.* Whurr Publications.

SECTION 7

PERSPECTIVES

EMPOWERING STUDENTS WITH SPECIAL NEEDS: ASSESSMENT AND CLASSIFICATION REVISITED

Every way of seeing is a way of not seeing. (Thayer, 1973)

LORI R. MUSKAT

INTRODUCTION

Few sights on this earth reflect the sheer wonder of humanity better than a new classroom full of four and five year old children. Active, spontaneous, curious, driven intrinsically by the joy of mastery – these tiny people often exude the awe that we older, larger beings frequently find elusive.

If one recalls one's very own first day at school, the image is ever clearer. For many, those first tentative steps away from our families and into the classroom represented the beginning of an exciting journey. With luck and hard work, the miracle of formal education would empower us and facilitate our transformation from dependent youngsters into autonomous, independent and functional young adults.

This romantic view of formal education, however, may begin to tarnish with even a brief visit to a 'mainstream' third grade classroom in the United States of America in 1995. Still wondrous in many regards, such a classroom begins to reflect pitfalls in the educational process. In any 'regular' education classroom of 25 children, one will probably observe that approximately two to five (i.e. 10 - 20%) students are not mastering basic reading, writing and maths skills at 'expected' rates (Shaywitz, Shaywitz, Fletcher and Escobar, 1990; Shaywitz, Fletcher and Shaywitz, 1995; Lyon, 1995a; Cohen, 1985; Bailin and Mann, 1988).

Often aware of their own inability to perform on par with their peers, these students frequently feel defective. For many, spontaneity, curiosity, and joy of mastery are replaced by self-consciousness, trepidation, and fear of failure. Further, this gradual strangulation of the child's life force does not cease when he or she exits the classroom. Indeed, it may be a spectre which frequently haunts the child and permeates outside activities, even in areas in which he or she may be gifted.

As parents and/or teachers become increasingly concerned about the welfare of struggling students and engage the formal educational system to explore and address these concerns, this subgroup of children enters the world of 'special education'. There, a different type of transformation often begins to occur – an unsettling metamorphosis in which socio-political factors cause the child to be viewed less as an individual and more as a 'problem'.

Often, despite the intention to provide a uniquely tailored program of education for the child, the very practices which allegedly exist to **identify, assess, classify,** and **provide intervention** end up doing the opposite. Frequently, they slap a label on a child which may be more limiting than illuminating in that it may not capture the essence of the child's specific learning difficulties at all. Yet, it may influence the way in which that child will be viewed by others henceforth within his or her educational world and beyond. Moreover, the label will most likely be incorporated by the child as part of his or her enduring identity (Cohen, 1985).

About this chapter

The purpose of this chapter is to outline the factors which presently serve to undermine the empowerment of learning disabled children in the United States of America. 'Empower', as used here, means to 'give power or authority to . . . to give ability to' (Neufeldt, 1994, p. 445). A multi-dimensional portrait of current issues and problems that affect the identification, assessment and classification of children with learning disabilities in the United States will be provided. It is hoped that the illustration of these issues may provide useful information to professionals in countries that are newer to the development of 'special' education laws and practices (see Table 1). To the extent that similar pitfalls may be avoided, education may facilitate rather than undermine empowerment of affected children.

The empowerment of children with special educational needs presents a complex dilemma. In order for students to be empowered, they must be viewed as individuals. As educators, we must maintain sight of and pay respect to the integrity of each individual child who is affected by learning problems. Yet, schools must also be empowered to meet the needs of these students. In order to do so, sound practices must be established and enacted which facilitate the identification and classification of students with learning difficulties. The dilemma, then, is: how can we identify and classify children in a way that preserves their individuality, thereby empowering them, while simultaneously empowering the schools that seek to educate them?

SPECIAL EDUCATION LAWS AND PRACTICES AMONG MEMBER COUNTRIES OF THE EUROPEAN DYSLEXIA ASSOCIATION

COUNTRY	SPECIAL EDUCATION LAWS	ARE THE SIGNS OF DYSLEXIA LOOKED FOR?
Austria	None	No
Belgium	1970. 'Specific education' law passed outlining organisation of special education for primary schools. Children with LD grouped under 'Type 8,' which covers dyslexics from the age of 6 to 15 years.	Yes. Risk signs of dyslexia looked for through testing. All children tested before starting primary school at age 5.
Croatia	Sub-Acts of the Education Laws give dyslexic students a right to full protection, but identification of these chldren is not effective. Sub-Acts under the Regulations of the Education of Children with Developmental Disorders; dyslexia is listed as a learning disorder.	No
Denmark	June, 1943. First circular for Special Teaching of Children with Reading Difficulties. Act on the Folkeskole, 1990. Legal Notice of Folkeskole's Special Education and other Special Education Assistance, 1990.	No
France	None. An 'advice' from the National Education, not obliged to be followed.	No
Germany	Schleswig-Holstein and Mecklenburg Vorpommern consider dyslexia as a specific problem and demand 'protection' in marks in dictation and German as foreign languages.	No
Great Britain	1981 Education Act 1991 Children Act 1993 Education Act	Not usually. Children have developmental checks by doctors and health visitors. Early signs will remain unrecognised in many cases.
Greece	420130.5.197 (Official Bulletin No. 86), Article #9. Dyslexics are permitted to take oral examinations at high school and special oral examinations to enter university.	No
Hungary	1970 law. A pupil can be exempted from a subject if a request is made.	During the last kindergarten year.
Ireland	A new law is under consideration.	No
Netherlands	Yes. Dyslexic students at secondary school are considered handicapped. Allowed certain concessions with examinations such as the use of computers, oral examinations and extra time.	No
Norway	Norwegian School Law (1975) establishes the right of all students to be taught in accordance with their abilities, or disabilities.	Occasionally
Poland	None, but legislation is planned.	Sometimes
Spain	Logse law, 1992. Recognised need for language disabled students to receive special help inside school.	No
Switzerland	Aargav School Law, 1982, specifies that speech therapy must be part of teaching at school.	No

(Adapted from Salter and Nielson, 1995)

In an effort to address this dilemma, this chapter is subdivided into three sections: (1) socio-political factors; (2) assessment and classification revisited; and, (3) advocacy efforts.

THE PROBLEM OF DEFINITION

Lyon (1993) and others (Keogh, 1994; Shaywitz *et al.*, 1995; Levine, 1987) have stated that the problem of imprecise definition presents a serious impediment to the furthering of knowledge in the field of learning disabilities. Inadequate definition leads to inappropriate classification. The impact of this situation becomes clear when we consider that in all research conducted involving learning disabled children, one must assume that a fair number of children have been classified incorrectly. This calls into question the soundness of the very foundation of our knowledge base in the field at this time.

FACTORS AFFECTING THE IDENTIFICATION AND CLASSIFICATION OF DYSLEXIC STUDENTS

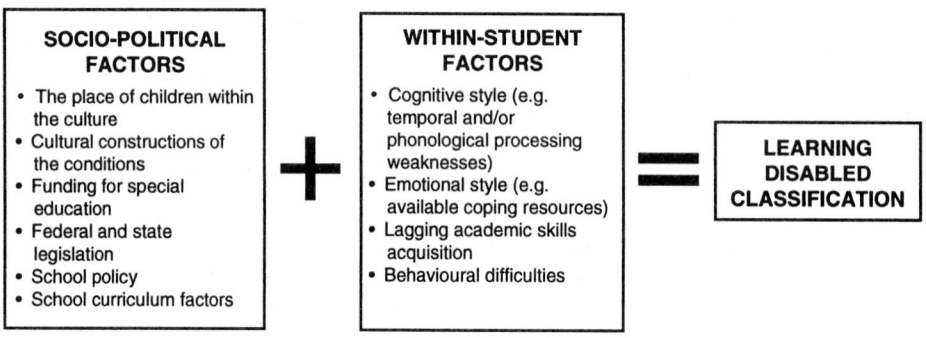

Generally, the conceptual issues addressed herein are applicable to assessment and classification practices which affect all children who face challenges within the regular education system. Children with specific learning difficulties, i.e. dyslexia, will be referred to most directly herein. For the purposes of clarity, 'dyslexia' is used here in accordance with the following definition set forth by the Orton Dyslexia Society in November, 1994. This definition has been chosen because it seems to be admirably clear and integrates recent research findings:

> *"Dyslexia is a neurologically-based, often familial, disorder which interferes with the acquisition and processing of language. Varying in degrees of severity, it is manifested by difficulties in receptive and expressive language,*

including phonological processing, in reading, writing, spelling, handwriting, and sometimes arithmetic. Dyslexia is not a result of lack of motivation, sensory impairment, inadequate instructional or environmental opportunities or other limiting conditions, but may occur together with these conditions. Although dyslexia is lifelong, individuals with dyslexia frequently respond successfully to timely and appropriate intervention."

(Rawson, 1995).

SOCIO-POLITICAL FACTORS

'Special' Education and the Concept of Context

Children classified as 'learning disabled' comprise one-third of all those receiving special education services in the United States. Yet, this group of children remain among the least understood. Lyon (1993) asserts that our body of knowledge has been based on fragmentary evidence, typically derived from technically inadequate measurement instruments and interpreted within the context of theoretical and conceptual frameworks that have not been clinically or scientifically validated. Further, the bulk of evidence suggests that current classification models used to categorise children with learning disabilities are ineffective in providing clinicians and researchers with useful information in order to improve their ability to make predictions or enhance communication. This state of affairs is unacceptable, given the deleterious impact that learning disabilities have upon the educational and social well-being of developing children.

In considering these critical issues so that we may make responsible decisions for the future, we must focus specific attention upon factors which are most often camouflaged between the lines when a parent meets with a team of school administrators to discuss concerns about his or her particular child. Key among these factors is that **a country's educational system does not exist within a vacuum**. It exists within a dynamic, multidimensional, political, economic context. Its very existence, as well as its functions and goals, is governed by the ever present, underlying values and philosophies that permeate and define the culture. In turn, these forces 'trickle down' and pervade the development of specific educational practices (i.e. identification, assessment, diagnosis/classification, etc.). Any child labelled as having special educational needs bears the mark of this hidden agenda.

Educators in many other parts of the world – Europe, South America, South Africa, Israel, to name but a few – are intensely aware of the cultural and political context of education (Salter, 1995; Weingrod, 1995; Strong, 1995; Welshman,

1995). We, in the United States, however, seem to be less aware of the politics underlying our educational practices. Nonetheless, they are there – and they have implications far beyond our own borders. To the extent that our practices (i.e. educational policies, assessment procedures, testing instruments, etc.) have been adopted by other countries, the politics and values in their very fabric exert an influence on other educational systems as well.

In view of the fact that education is associated foremost with a nation's children, one must first examine the greater place of children within that context. In the United States, current political rhetoric provides us with images of 'family values' and, implicitly, the plight of children. Zigler and Finn-Stevenson (1987), Moats and Lyon (1993) and others, however, inject sobering reality that social, medical, and educational services for children in the United States have never been a priority. Since children themselves do not vote or contribute money to political campaigns, their needs receive lip service in rhetoric but are frequently overlooked when the time comes to set priorities and dole out funding. Many of the children in our inner cities grow up in conditions remarkably similar to that of third world countries. In 1993, funds allotted for national defence totalled an estimated 289.3 billion dollars whereas the combined allotment for education, training, employment and social services totalled an estimated 52.3 billion dollars (Statesman's Yearbook, 1994).

Within the last decade, we have witnessed a decline in our nation's commitment to educational programs for children with disabilities, including learning disabilities. One illustration of this is the decrease in federal willingness to share special education costs. In 1981, federal funds subsidised 12% of excess state costs for special education. By 1992, funding dipped to 10%. Further, recent overtures calling for educational reform have completely ignored the needs of children with learning disabilities (Martin, 1993). At the national level, such factors operate to obscure the needs of any individual child.

The socio-political context and classification

Within a given culture, Keogh (1994, p. 313) states that 'findings of incidence, prevalence, and even expression of problem conditions are influenced by social and political conditions and pressures, not just by the nature of the condition itself'. The very conditions we choose to focus upon, as well as the way in which they are conceptualised and defined, reflect a society's views of difference and deviance. Learning disabled classification is no exception. A confluence of social, political, economic, professional and institutional factors have created a climate which dictates the fact that learning disabilities are being focused upon with increasing intensity as well as the way in which they are thought about more generally and functionally defined (Keogh, 1994; Lyon, 1994).

For example, 'dyslexia', as previously defined, is viewed as a 'disorder' - a common theme in most definitions. Yet, Speece (1993) states that decades of research on environmental factors continue to be ignored, and the field of learning disabilities remains entrenched in the notion that learning disabilities are due to within-child deficits.

Thus, most educational and medical research that has examined differences between dyslexics and 'normal' readers has viewed dyslexic learner's differences as being deficits. Findings regarding likely 'biological bases' and genetic factors underlying dyslexia have fuelled this view. It is important to bear in mind, however, that eye colour, hair colour, height, etc., are all human traits which, while biologically determined, hardly constitute disorders or deficits. Along these lines, Levine, Hooper, Montgomery *et al.* (1993) emphasise that the study of learning disabilities is really inseparable from the study of normal learners, gifted learners, and child development in general.

Cohen (1985) points out that dyslexia as well as other types of learning problems may contribute to accelerated or precocious development in other psychological and cognitive abilities. A number of studies have shown dyslexics to have superior talents in various non-verbal areas such as art, architecture, and athletics (Geschwind, 1982, 1983; Porac and Coren, 1981). Geschwind (1982) believed that dyslexia may result from genetic factors that are evolutionarily advantageous in some way. Nonetheless, the social political climate shapes the way in which dyslexia is viewed, i.e. as a disorder. Consequently, relatively little research which seeks to define areas of strength in dyslexic learners has been attempted. This is a critical point because, as shall be addressed further below, in order to empower an individual, it is important to know as much about areas of strength as areas of weakness.

In addition, social-political factors often inform classification decisions more than scientific factors do. This is significant because this set of circumstances impedes a meaningful empirical investigation of the condition. A clear illustration of this is provided by Mehan, Miehls, Hatwick and Croudes (1981) who studied referrals and service procedures in a California school district. They found that the number of pupils referred for assessment and classification varied relative to: (1) availability and caseloads of school psychologists; (2) the building principal's attitudes and beliefs about special education services; and (3) the nature of available alternative programs.

With factors such as these frequently at play, it is difficult to determine how many 'real' students with learning disabilities are represented within a given population (Keogh, 1993; p. 315). Further, how can the needs of any given child be explored and met effectively within such a climate?

Context and interdisciplinary boundaries

Lyon (1995a) states that a major impediment to the scientific development of the learning disabilities field is that many different academic disciplines focus on different issues. Educators, psychologists, speech pathologists, neurologists, neuropsychologists, optometrists, and psychiatrists are among the different disciplines involved in the study of children with learning problems. In addition, each discipline has its own vocabulary. Often, one can sit at a table of representative experts who carry on a heated debate only to find that semantics have obscured the fact that they are really in agreement (Griffin, 1995). Levine *et al.* (1993) assert that a key goal of future research should be to yield a vocabulary and approach that can transcend traditional disciplinary boundaries and barriers. These communication gaps are most unfortunate for the struggling students whose needs are overlooked or misunderstood because of them.

The politics of classification and assessment

Within the United States, the most powerful force in the development of legislation and service delivery systems for learning disabled children has been parents and advocacy groups whose purpose has been to secure services for affected youngsters; science has **followed** these decisions (Keogh, 1994). Implicit within this set of arrangements are the greater factors affecting advocacy. Generally, advocacy efforts tend to be costly endeavours. Therefore, in most instances, people with access to financial resources are more likely to have the greatest clout in advocacy via political lobbying, etc.

In view of this, one must consider the possibility that successful advocacy efforts may be more likely to reflect the agenda of those who have some access to resources. Perhaps the growing emphasis on learning disabilities as a condition in the United States functions to benefit some of the more powerful factions of United States society at present (e.g. Coles (1987) attributes the rise and popularity of the 'learning disabled' classification to the increasing social problems affecting middle class citizens during the post World War II years). A look at aspects of our legislation suggests, at the least, that classification and assessment practices have been shaped in a way that proliferates Anglo-American standards (Dana, 1993).

Legislative pitfalls

Regarding legislation most relevant to special education in elementary through to secondary school, a key outcome of advocacy efforts has been the passage of Public Laws 94-142, the Education of All Handicapped Children Act, and Public Law 101-476, the Individuals with Disabilities Education Act (Zigmond, 1995). At the college level and in the workplace, however, the Rehabilitation Act of 1973 and the Americans with Disabilities Act of 1990 govern the classification of learning disabilities (Olivier, 1994).

Despite their intent to the contrary, the path to obscurity for many children with special needs in the United States begins with these laws. Key elements of PL94-142 and PL101-476 mandate: that **states** provide appropriate public education to all students with disabilities; that each child with special needs has an **individualised educational program** (I.E.P.); that services be delivered in the **least restrictive environment**; that due process procedures be established; and, that identification, diagnostic and assessment procedures be free of racial and cultural bias.

While ambitious in scope and admirable in intent, the application of these laws is problematic. Each state must adhere to the general guidelines, but individual states may implement their own procedures in so doing. Thus, practices vary from one state to another. At the community level, schools are primarily funded through local taxes. Therefore, schools in affluent areas have access to considerably more resources than those in lesser advantaged areas. Notions of equality or of education as a common denominator pale as one considers that schools in less advantaged areas probably need more funding and actually get less (Moats and Lyon, 1993). Further, in terms of classification practices, a child may be classified as learning disabled in one state and not in another.

Equally as confusing for students and parents is that an individual may not meet criteria for learning disabled classification in his or her secondary school years – but may be classifiable in college and in the work place. This is because the conditions of PL94-142 and PL101-476, laws governing classification of school aged children, are somewhat different than those of the Rehabilitation Act of 1973 and the Americans with Disabilities Act of 1990, the laws governing adults. In general, the latter laws tend to be less specific and not tied to the 'discrepancy model' which will be addressed below.

Individualised Educational Plan

At the individual school level, implementation of mandated practices is complicated. Take, for example, the **individualised educational plan**. Law dictates that each I.E.P. contain: present levels of academic performance; annual goals; short term objectives; educational services to be provided; the participation of the child in the regular education program to the extent that he or she is able; the date of the initiation and anticipated length of services; and, procedures for evaluating progress toward stated objectives (Zigmond, 1995).

School personnel, in a noble effort to abide by the law, find themselves drowning in a sea of paperwork. Parents attending required review meetings find themselves buried beneath a landslide of minutiae and jargon. Concerned with the plight of one's treasured child who is struggling with reading, most find little solace in I.E.P. goals such as 'Johnny will decode regular three letter consonant-vowel-consonant words with 85% accuracy'. Moreover, many professionals are not even sure what this actually means in practice.

Further, I.E.P. guidelines are remarkably myopic - consisting of annual goals and short term objectives. What about the bigger picture, the long term? What is it that we are ultimately helping the child to accomplish? If Carla can, indeed, only decode words with 75% accuracy but cannot reason abstractly or in novel situations, perhaps it might make more sense to focus upon teaching her practical skills that may one day translate into some type of vocational placement; decoding may be more appropriately remediated only to the extent necessary for her to attain independence in activities of daily living.

The fallacy of 'intelligence' and the 'discrepancy model'

The aforementioned example addresses another problematic aspect of the I.E.P. In the United States, the prevalent mode of identifying children with special educational needs is the 'discrepancy model' (Zigmond, 1995; Danielson and Bauer, 1978; Brumbach, 1995; Lyon, 1995b). This refers to an attempt to quantify the imbalance between a student's **academic achievement** (i.e. performance on an individually administered achievement test which typically examines isolated basic skills levels) and his or her **intelligence** or intellectual potential (i.e. performance on an individually administered 'intelligence' test).

First, the notion of 'intelligence' bears discussion. In essence, the word 'intelligence' has been raped by the psychometric testing community. In the vernacular, 'intelligence' tends to be a broad and meaningful concept that alludes to one's mental ability to learn or understand from experience, acquire and retain knowledge, respond quickly and successfully to a new situation, and reason in order to solve problems (Neufeldt, 1994). Assaulted, the term most often emerges in psychological and educational literature only to mean one's score on a test composed of a variety of tasks whose relevance to real life functioning continues to be a healthy topic of debate.

A substantial body of literature exists elsewhere that addresses problems in the current conceptualisation of 'intelligence' and the shortcomings of the measures that are currently widely used to assess it (e.g. Sternberg, 1988). Common sense, however, may be equally as enlightening. If one were to be shipwrecked on a deserted island with seven other people, which seven people would one choose? What would the traits of each individual be and why? In considering this dilemma, the multi-dimensionality of the concept of intelligence becomes rather apparent.

As with other issues affecting our educational system, the continued use of the lame concept of intelligence would appear to be politically ordained. Dana (1993) asserts that the continued use of intelligence tests that provide for a rank ordering of persons against an Anglo-Saxon criterion must be recognised as part of a societal demand for acculturation and acceptance of Anglo-American standards. This demand can only be modified or changed by political decisions that result from realignments of power following from shifts in the population composition. Within school settings, however, teachers, psychologists, and administrators daily use these politically defined, inadequate, unitary measures of 'intelligence' as the last word in defining a child's potential. Such practices brand children in ways that are often more limiting than illuminating.

The concept of intelligence is a cornerstone of the 'discrepancy model'. Unfortunately, this model continues to be mandated by law despite the significant body of evidence which suggests that it is invalid (Fletcher and Foorman, 1994; Fletcher and Morris, 1986; Siegel, 1989; Stanovich, 1991; Lyon, 1994). Stanovich (1993, p. 286) eloquently questions:

> *"How could the field of learning disabilities venture so far down the road of resting its conceptual foundations on discrepancy measurements from IQ when it is so difficult to distinguish poor readers on the basis of discrepancy? . . . it is surprising that for so long the concept of intelligence received so little discussion in the learning disabilities literature. Researchers and practitioners in the field seem not to have realised that it is a foundational concept for the very idea of reading disability. As currently defined, IQ is a superordinate construct for the classification of a child as having a reading disability.*

Without a clear conception of the construct of intelligence, the notion of a reading disability as currently defined, dissolves into incoherence."

The 'least restrictive environment' and 'inclusion'

PL94-142 requires that a student be educated in the **least restrictive** environment in which his or her needs can be met effectively. This refers to the fact that in the United States, special education services are offered along a continuum ranging from those least segregated from the mainstream to those most segregated.

An example of a 'least restrictive' environment would be a pull-out program such as resource room. A child receiving this service would spend most of his or her time in the mainstream class and be pulled out occasionally (i.e. one - five times per week) for remedial services. A more highly restrictive environment would be a 'self-contained' class for learning disabled students. A child placed in this program would be segregated from the mainstream for most academic subjects; he or she may join mainstream students for special subjects or electives such as art, physical education, music, etc.

Faced with growing numbers of children classified as learning disabled and dwindling funds to provide services for such students, the most recent trend in special education has been to extend the notion of 'least restrictive environment' to a practice called 'inclusion'. This refers to informal public policy enacted at the federal and state levels which 'encourages' the education of learning disabled students within mainstream classrooms (Martin, 1993; Gallagher, 1993). The theory behind inclusion is that it is more conducive to a child's development for him or her to have as 'normal' an educational experience as possible.

Thus, for example, rather than the child being taken out of the room to attend remedial reading, the reading teacher may come to the mainstream classroom and meet with a small group of children there. This set of arrangements raises the issue of the viability of educating children, many of whom are more vulnerable to distractibility, in an environment where there is a high level of competing background sound. Nonetheless, this scenario is preferable to the one which occurs more often in which special needs children are placed in mainstream classes with teachers who have no specialised training. These educators frequently feel frustrated and overwhelmed that there is no support within the school system to assist them in meeting the needs of these students.

While the theory behind inclusion is admirable, the practice is less so. Baker and Zigmond (1990) state that in order for inclusion to be a viable philosophy, changes have to be made in current educational practices. Key among these is improved teacher training which fosters the expansion of the teaching methods repertoire as well as more flexible formatting of classroom activities.

The implementation of the I.E.P., along with its reliance on the flawed 'discrepancy model' and the changing notion of 'least restrictive environment', is but a small example of the way in which a child loses his or her individuality and sense of empowerment within the special education system; countless others exist and have been addressed elsewhere. While certainly a bleak picture in some regards, perhaps the practice of special education in the United States stands ready to transform as it enters its second generation. If this, indeed, is the case, then it is of paramount importance that we re-visit the concept and practices of assessment and classification as well as implications thereof for advocacy.

ASSESSMENT AND CLASSIFICATION RE-VISITED

In addition to socio-political factors at play in the conceptualisation, identification, and classification of learning disabilities in the United States, intra-individual factors are also contributory. Most scientists, educators, clinicians, parents and affected individuals themselves conclude that there seems to be a group of people whose reasoning and problem-solving abilities range from intact to very strong but who also demonstrate weaknesses in one or more specific modalities of information processing. Of the numerous conditions that could potentially fall into this category, dyslexia is the one that has received the most attention.

For the individual who has a 'dyslexic learning style' (Saunders, 1994) that impedes his or her ability to acquire academic skills or express him or herself, appropriate identification, classification and intervention are potentially empowering processes. The critical issue is: how can schools establish practices and procedures that facilitate empowerment rather than undermine it as current practices seem to do?

This section will examine: (1) school contexts and their current assessment practices; (2) more appropriate directions for assessment; (3) the dilemma of classification; and (4) recommendations for advocacy.

School Contexts

Assessment practices in public schools

Currently, in the United States, children having learning difficulties are most often initially identified by parents and teachers. Physicians may also be involved in the process, but many remain alarmingly uninformed about early indications of learning problems as well as risk factors. In school aged children, concerns most typically focus upon lagging acquisition of academic skills, language weaknesses, difficulty completing work within allotted time limits, distractibility and/or behavioural difficulties.

Once these concerns are brought to the attention of school administrators, a 'pupil personnel team' or 'child study team' meeting is arranged. This meeting is usually attended by a school administrator from the local Board of Education, the child's teacher, the school principal, the parents, the school psychologist and other specialised personnel as deemed appropriate (i.e. school social worker, speech/language therapist, psychiatrist, etc.). Parents are also permitted the option of bringing a private consultant to the meeting as well as having their child evaluated by a private practitioner. Private evaluations must be conducted in a format similar to that of public school evaluations in order for findings to be reviewed, approved and accepted by the public school.

Observations and concerns are presented by parents and members of the team. Based on these, an assessment plan is formulated for the purposes of determining whether the child meets classification criteria and is eligible for services. Most assessments include a psycho-educational evaluation which is comprised of a standardised intelligence test, some measure of visual motor integration, projective tests to screen emotional factors and examination of basic skills acquisition in isolated areas of decoding, spelling and maths. In addition, if specific concerns are expressed about language development, a speech and language evaluation may also be administered. Other evaluation services available include occupational therapy, physical therapy, psychiatry, and social work. Consulting psychiatrists and neurologists may also be called in by the school system if deemed necessary.

Once the prescribed evaluations have been carried out, the team reconvenes to discuss findings and develop an individualised educational plan if the child has been found to be eligible for services. By law, the I.E.P. must be reviewed and re-formulated yearly by the school team pending parental approval. Children must be re-evaluated to some extent yearly in order to provide updated documentation for eligibility of services. 'Intelligence' tests must be re-administered triennially. If the child is found to be ineligible for services and the parents wish to contest this decision, they have a right to a hearing under due process in order to appeal the determination.

Generally, unless children present as obviously and significantly multiply handicapped, initial assessment procedures are rather cursory and superficial. Most are formulated to determine whether or not a child fits the 'discrepancy model'. Further, most public school personnel are far more intimately acquainted with federal and state laws which govern the provision of special education services than they are with the rapidly accumulating body of scientific knowledge in the field of learning disabilities; there is presently little, if any, connection between research findings of the past 15 years and current educational practices.

The case of independent schools

The situation in independent (i.e. 'private') schools is different. These institutions are free to set admissions criteria, screen their own students, and to implement practices according to the more general laws governing education. In the United States, independent schools vary widely in their composition of students, awareness of learning problems and services they provide to students having difficulties. On one end of the continuum are special schools for children with learning disabilities. On the other end of the continuum are rigorous, traditional college preparatory schools, many of which assert that they have no children with learning disabilities.

This latter group of schools pose a particular challenge to the education of higher functioning dyslexic students. Since many deny that they have such students enrolled, they offer no services. In reality, many of these institutions lack appropriate knowledge of dyslexia and other learning disabilities; therefore, their admissions screening is ill-equipped to identify these students at the outset.

When students in these environments begin to face struggles, they are usually provided with individual tutoring for which families must pay themselves. This tutoring most often involves a review of course content or basic skills presented in a one-to-one format. In many instances, intervention is provided by teachers who have limited, if any, knowledge in the area of learning disabilities. It is also common for families to locate their own private tutors referred by word of mouth.

By law, parents are entitled to request testing through their public school system if they so choose; this would be enacted in the manner outlined above. Many parents of independent school students opt to incur the significant expense of a private evaluation. If the need for services is determined, it is also common for families to locate their own private tutors by word of mouth referral.

If the aforementioned actions do not result in improved academic performance of the child in the private school setting, he or she is likely to be 'counselled out' of the school. Although the trend in independent schools seems to be increased awareness of learning problems, the process has been slow and the path fraught with resistance in most instances. For individual children caught in this struggle, many are placed in the negatively reinforcing position of being asked to leave schools to which they either: (1) never should have been accepted in the first place; or (2) at which they could ultimately be successful if school personnel were more knowledgeable or policies and procedures more flexible. Unfortunately, many students understandably internalise school rejection as their own failure when, in fact, it is often the school that has failed the child.

Empowering students and schools: toward more appropriate assessment

In essence, our current practice of assessment, rooted in the 'discrepancy model' is narrow and limiting. It equates performance on designated tests with 'achievement' and 'intelligence'; it focuses on deficiencies, overlooks strengths, and reduces the child into component parts omitting, most conspicuously, any notion of him or her as a whole entity with a soul (Leibell, 1995).

Despite the glaring shortcomings inherent in current practices in public as well as private schools, however, growing numbers of educators are interested in meeting the needs of dyslexic students more effectively. With widely held assessment and classification practices dictated by inadequate laws, well meaning and conscientious school administrators are frequently frustrated in their efforts to help struggling students.

A path to empowering assessment

Levine (1987) emphasises the uniqueness of all children and cites this factor as posing an additional challenge in the education of learning disabled children more specifically. He also highlights, as does Speece (1993), the need for careful consideration of school contexts and their implication for the child with problems. In essence, empowering assessment should function to capture the 'truth' of the child's information processing style as precisely as possible, as well as its implications in the particular school context, family setting, etc. In order to do this, schools must be empowered by law to change their assessment practices at the socio-political level.

In addressing the needs of individual children, a good beginning may be for assessment practices to be broadened so as to be more comprehensive in nature. Cordoni (1995) asserts that evaluating children with learning problems and associated developmental dysfunctions should challenge the thoroughness, sensitivity, and eclectic breadth of the evaluator. Many researchers (Levine, 1987; Rawson, 1995; Fennel, 1995; Moats, 1994) echo her sentiments and emphasise the importance of the examiner's comprehensive knowledge base and the use of broadly based assessment practices.

Current research findings: the missing link

The definition of dyslexia as a biologically based disorder affecting language functioning pre-dated 'hard' physiological evidence (Orton, 1937). Recent research efforts in a number of different areas, however, have provided compelling indications that this appears to be the case. Shaywitz *et al.* (1995) have identified deficits in phonological processing to be at the root of reading problems. Along these lines, Denckla and Rudel (1976), Wolf (1984) and Korhonen (1995) have found that measures of rapid naming can be quite effective in identifying children at risk for later reading and language difficulties.

Tallal (1991) and her colleagues (Miller, 1995; Tallal, Miller and Fitch, 1993) have found evidence that slow temporal processing (i.e. inability to integrate sensory information that converges in rapid succession in the central nervous system) may underlie the deficits in phonological processing that are observed in language and reading disorders. Further, Tallal's work strongly suggests that slow temporal processing may be pansensory, i.e., it may affect processing across multiple sensory modalities. The implications of this work are compelling and far reaching in view of the visual types of errors (i.e. visual configural confusions, word insertions and substitutions) that characterise the oral reading of many dyslexic students.

In addition, some early risk factors have been identified. The more common of these include a family history of learning problems, mild to more significant birth and pregnancy complications, an early history of frequent ear infections (i.e. from birth through age four years), tactile defensiveness, fine and gross motor weaknesses (Cordoni, 1995). Knowledge about risk factors and etiology must be incorporated into current assessment practices.

The importance of a developmental framework

In order for more broadly based assessment techniques to be effective in empowering learning disabled children as well as the schools that are attempting to educate them, assessment must be conducted within a developmental framework (Levine, 1987; Levine *et al.* 1993; Fletcher and Foorman, 1994). Different processes need to be focused upon in different ways, depending upon the child's stage of development. For example, isolated skill areas such as sound blending and application of phonics may be more appropriate to examine in children in earlier elementary school grades. In contrast, it may be more relevant to examine the ability to organise language, take notes, synthesise, summarise, etc., in middle and upper school students.

Essential ingredients in assessment

Although current views of effective assessment differ, many researchers and clinicians agree about certain fundamentals that need to be examined (Johnson, 1995; Levine, 1987; Fennel, 1995; Rourke, 1994; Cordoni, 1995). These involve informal observation and diagnostic interviewing as well as formal testing. Major areas to be covered include: (1) a comprehensive developmental history; (2) thorough formal testing; (3) investigation of the school context and curriculum practices.

In terms of a developmental history, this should be comprehensive in nature. Areas covered should include: investigation of gestational conditions, birth history, medical history, developmental milestones, academic history, family history, social and emotional stressors (Cordoni, 1995; Fennell, 1995).

Regarding formal testing, current researchers focus upon anywhere from six to 11 different domains. These include: attention; auditory and visual memory under varied conditions; fine motor skills; oral language; alpha-numeric symbols; executive functions (i.e., planning, monitoring, organisation, regulation, metacognition); social/emotional (i.e., affect, social cognition, interactional skills, motivation); cognition (i.e., level of abstraction, reasoning and problem solving); reading (i.e., accuracy of decoding and sight word recognition, rate, comprehension); and writing (Berninger and Abbott, 1994).

Rourke (1994), a proponent of a neuropsychologically based model, emphasises that tests and measures should vary along several different continua. These include: (1) degrees of complexity and difficulty; (2) degrees of rote versus novel requirements; (3) tasks requiring information processing within a single modality to those that involve the processing and integration of stimuli within several modalities.

Meltzer (1994) and others (Torgesen, 1990; Feuerstein, 1979) emphasise the importance of dynamic, interactive strategies based assessment. Such processes examine the process by which children arrive at solutions. They also allow for the opportunity to teach a child new strategies in order to determine the extent to which he or she is able to incorporate them.

Also included in the assessment process should be the provision of feedback. Each student should be educated in a developmentally appropriate manner as to the nature of his or her learning difficulties.

In addition to comprehensive developmental history, formal evaluation of information processing and psychological adjustment, the school context must also be taken into account. It is important for the examiner to be aware of the curriculum demands and expectations to which the child is subject.

The type of assessment practice described herein may certainly represent an arduous and costly undertaking. It is by no means impossible, however, nor is it new. This practice has been in use for a few decades in the field of rehabilitation psychology (i.e., the discipline involved in treating individuals who have suffered traumatic brain injury). In fact, it is in this setting that the neuropsychological model of assessment of which Rourke (1994) writes was formulated and applied.

In rehabilitation settings, it has long been the practice to evaluate the individual's cognitive profile as well as his or her context/environment. On the basis of comprehensive assessment, Prigatano (1985) states that the model of cognitive retraining in brain injured individuals has involved three goals: (1) the use of compensation to get around a deficit; (2) use of substitution to solve a problem that the brain is able to solve, but by different methods; and (3) attempts to retrain specifically impaired functions directly.

In most instances, similar goals have been applied to the teaching of learning disabled children. This type of approach can only be successful, however, if the student's **strengths** as well as weaknesses have been identified. More thorough knowledge on the part of school personnel and more comprehensive assessment techniques are likely to result in more precise identification of a child's abilities as well as deficits areas. In **describing** these areas in detail, one could present a highly individualised profile of the student's cognitive as well as personality style and make specific recommendations as to the way in which the child learns best. This method would seem to present the best opportunity for preserving the individuality of a given child within a school.

The Dilemma of Classification

Revising current classification schemes seems somewhat more complex than revising assessment practices. With assessment, provided that the examiner is well trained and uses comprehensive methods but does not over-test, he or she is unlikely to cause damage to a student by accurately describing the child's strengths and weaknesses. With classification, however, one is determining a student's eligibility for services and, most often, placing a label upon the child for identification purposes. The potential for damage in this domain is much greater. Labels have a powerful force in shaping how a child is viewed by others as well as how he or she views him or herself in school as well as other domains. Denying services to a deserving student or labelling a student when it is inappropriate, thereby invalidating the truth of his or her academic experience, can have far reaching deleterious effects.

Lack of agreement regarding subtyping and precise definition of 'learning disability' and 'dyslexia', incomplete knowledge of the etiologies of these conditions, and the unclear relationship between some psychometric tests and their functional academic implications makes it extremely difficult to come up with sound, fair and reliable criteria by which to classify children (Lyon, 1995b). In essence, while classification is necessary in order to facilitate service delivery to children who are struggling academically, we seem to lack appropriate knowledge by which to do so at present; as previously stated, socio-political factors have informed policy more than science has. In continuing to apply inappropriate criteria, we run the risk of potentially hurting as many children as we help.

Another issue which is likely to pose a dilemma, even once we have more precise information and a more sound scientific knowledge base, is that of a black and white 'cut-off' point for determining eligibility. Shaywitz *et al.* (1990; 1995) have stated that disabled readers constitute the lower end of a continuum which also includes non-disabled readers. Determination of which point along this continuum to use as a cut-off for eligibility is a very sensitive and complex issue. If we are going to deny services to children falling close to the cut-off, we had better be certain that the criteria used to set this point are valid and reliable.

New directions for classification in the elementary school years

Similar to assessment, classification practices must be considered within a developmental framework. Criteria in the elementary school years may not be appropriate to apply in middle and upper school years. Along these lines, Fletcher and Foorman (1994) have stressed the importance of early intervention. They cite a study in which Strag (1972) looked at improved performance in learning disabled students relative to their grade at the time of intervention. When remedial intervention occurred in either 1st or 2nd grade, 82% of students could be brought up to grade level. When intervention occurred in 3rd grade, 46% of students could be brought up to grade level. In contrast, when intervention first occurred in grades five through seven, only 10 - 15% of students could be brought to grade level. Early intervention has implications far beyond the early grades.

Internationally, there is agreement that dyslexia affects between 10 - 20% of the population. Given this fact, together with the efficacy of early intervention, a logical solution may be to eliminate classification completely in grades kindergarten through to three for children who appear to have specific learning difficulties (i.e. in contrast to multiply handicapped children and children with more serious language disorders or developmental delays who are likely to be identified during the pre-school years). Although this recommendation bears some similarity to the notion of inclusion, it differs in that wide scale changes in our educational practices, particularly in the early elementary school years, would have to be implemented.

A first step in this process would be in areas of teacher training and school policy. Elementary schools could plan in advance, based on the estimation that approximately 15% of their students will experience difficulties acquiring basic reading and writing skills. For new teachers in training, it would probably make most sense for all teachers of pre-school through to elementary school grades to be required to have certification in special education practices. Elementary school teachers already on the job could be provided with intensive continuing education. Funds saved as a result of eliminating classification procedures could be used to enact training of current employees.

Within mainstream classrooms, students could be identified in much the same way as they are now – through informal means. Teachers with specialised training would be better equipped to identify and group these children within the classroom according to their abilities as well as to apply appropriate teaching methodologies.

In terms of a specific teaching curriculum for dyslexic students, a phonological awareness model would seem to hold the most promise based on current research findings (Brady, Fowler, Stone and Winbury, 1995). A specific model that could be considered is the Orton-Gillingham approach which has been used with success by many in instructing dyslexic students as to how to read and also in familiarising them with the underlying structures of language (i.e. a problematic area, as well, for most of these students) (Bailin and Mann, 1988; see Footnote 1). Children who acquire basic skills more easily could be placed in higher level reading and language arts groups, as is done currently, and offered a less intensive Orton Gillingham approach.

By training elementary school teachers and incorporating an intensive Orton Gillingham approach into mainstream classroom reading and language arts curricula in grades kindergarten through, three, we would be providing every student with a fair opportunity to receive early intervention and to function up to his or her potential. We would also be normalising the condition of dyslexia by making academic provisions for it in advance and empowering dyslexic students from the very beginning. Since children who are identified early seem to have the best outcomes in later years, intensive early intervention may also decrease the numbers of students who require special education services in middle and upper school.

Beyond the early elementary years

While it seems plausible, based on current research findings, that this type of approach may be the most effective for the broadest range of learning disabled students, no singular approach is a panacea. By the end of third grade, it is likely that some students will continue to falter significantly. At this point, it would be more appropriate to employ the type of broad based assessment discussed earlier in order to gain a more specific profile of the child's strengths and weaknesses and to make finer discriminations.

As far as classifying students beyond grade three, Fletcher, Francis, Rourke *et al.* and Stanovich (1994) have suggested that a modified discrepancy model may be beneficial. In this approach, relative discrepancies and unevenness among a student's academic skills or cognitive skills (e.g. reading comprehension in comparison with listening comprehension) rather than 'intelligence'/achievement discrepancies would serve as a criterion for classification. This may be a viable avenue to pursue at present through continued research.

Another research area that seems imperative to explore is that of temporal processing which builds upon the work of Tallal *et al.* (1993). In the central nervous system, temporal processing supersedes phonological processing. By focusing too narrowly on phonological processing deficits, we run the risk of missing the larger picture if, in fact, deficits in temporal processing are what underlie them as seems to be the case at this juncture. Greater understanding and more specific assessment of temporal processing may present a promising new frontier with exciting implications for classification practices.

As complex and elusive as it may be, it will also be important to pursue the formulation and measurement of a multi-dimensional, culturally fair concept of 'intelligence' that rests on a firm foundation of scientific knowledge. If we cannot measure a student's abstract reasoning and problem-solving ability, we cannot formulate an appropriate curriculum for that child. Nor can we plan in a long term, proactive way for students who need education geared toward achieving independence in activities of daily living. At the most basic level, how can we empower a student to realise his or her potential if we have little idea of what it is. Similarly, every child with special educational needs deserves to be **described** in a multi-dimensional way. Before we brand a child, we had better be certain that that symbol captures something about the essence of that child and fosters increased understanding. If it does not, we have no right to use it.

ADVOCACY EFFORTS

In order to advocate effectively, parents, educators and other interested individuals must hold tightly to the philosophy of **education as empowerment**, i.e., it exists to facilitate the development of children into autonomous and independently functioning adults. Pragmatically, this means that we must not allow our vision to be limited by the inadequate vocabulary and the myopia with which laws and cultural biases encumber us. It is a complex undertaking, but the first steps seem straightforward.

First, advocates must act to bridge the gap between current research findings and educational practices. On the social political level, this means staging a far-reaching effort to educate legislators in an attempt to get our laws changed. Along these lines, due to the rapidly accumulating body of new research findings, provision must be made through law that classification practices be re-evaluated at pre-determined intervals (i.e. every five years) in order to determine their continued relevancy. At present, the laws that require classified students to be re-evaluated triennially are undermined by the continued application of irrelevant criteria.

On a more personal level, advocates must educate the educators. This means providing current information to school personnel in an effort to make them aware of the inappropriateness of current special educational practices.

Second, individual families can effect change by knowing the right questions to ask. Every parent of a child with special educational needs deserves to know in plain, conversational language: what is my child capable of doing socially as well as academically? What should he or she be capable of doing relative to same age peers? What are his or her relative strengths and weaknesses? How can his or her strengths be used to augment weaknesses? How will his or her progress be monitored? How does this relate to his or her longer term ability to function as an independent adult? On what basis has all of the aforementioned been determined?

CONCLUDING REMARKS

This chapter has sought to illustrate that the identification and classification of learning disabled children is influenced by an array of factors, political as well as in the United States and in other countries with differing educational and mental practices.

In the United States, social factors as outlined herein have left an indelible mark on identification, assessment and classification practices. This situation serves to disempower the children identified as learning disabled as well as the schools who endeavour to educate them. By including such children in a category whose definition is inadequate and largely unsupported by recent research findings, the needs of these children as individuals are frequently obscured.

A combination of improved training for professionals, a broadly based assessment practices, a revised classification system and advocacy efforts aimed at changing federal legislation and school policy is recommended. Through these means, it may be increasingly possible to preserve the individuality of each learning disabled child while simultaneously empowering the schools whose mission it is to educate him or her.

The lessons of history repeatedly teach us that the power of politics frequently distracts us from the essence of issues. Nonetheless, it is a challenge we must face if, as educators and advocates, we are to effect social change in order to empower children with 'special' educational needs.

FOOTNOTES

Footnote 1. In the Orton-Gillingham approach, letters and sounds are taught first in isolation through auditory, visual and kinaesthetic linkages, then blended together to form words for reading and spelling. These words are then put together into meaningful units to form sentences. In addition to learning phonetic elements, students must understand and apply the rule structure of the language (i.e., rules for syllable division, spelling rules, acoustic principles leading to changes in pronunciation, and rules for developing or changing grammatical constructions) (Bailin and Mann, 1988).

REFERENCES

Bailin, A. and Mann, M. (1988). *Explaining dyslexia: the Orton point of view.* NY: The Orton Dyslexia Society.

Baker, J. M. and Zigmond, N. (1990). Are regular education classes equipped to accommodate students with learning disabilities? *Exceptional Child,* 56(6), 515-526.

Berninger, V. W. and Abbott, R. D. (1994). Redefining learning disabilities: moving beyond aptitude-achievement discrepancies to failure to respond to validated treatment protocols. In Lyon, G. R. (Ed.) *Frames of reference for the assessment of learning disabilities: new views on measurement issues* (pp. 163-184). Baltimore: Paul H. Brookes Publishing Co.

Blashfield, R. K. (1993). Models of classification as related to a taxonomy of learning disabilities. In Lyon, G. R., Gray, D. B., Kavanaugh, J. F. and Krasnegor, N. A. (Eds.) *Better understanding learning disabilities: new views from research and their implications for education and public policies* (pp. 17-26). Baltimore: Paul H. Brookes Publishing Co.

Brady, S., Fowler, A., Stone, B., and Winbury, N. (1994). Training phonological awareness: a study with inner-city kindergarten children. *Annals of Dyslexia,* 44, 26-59.

Brumbach, R. A. (1995). Special supplement on learning disabilities – why? *Journal of Child Neurology,* 10(1), S1.

Cohen, J. (1985). Learning disabilities and adolescence: dual considerations. In Feinstein, S. C. (Ed.) *Adolescent psychiatry: developmental and clinical studies* (pp. 177-196). Chicago: University of Chicago Press.

Coles, G. (1987). *The learning mystique.* NY: Fawcett Columbine.

Cordoni, B. (1995). Psycho-educational assessment for learning disabilities. Journal *of Child Neurology,* 10(1), S31-S36.

Dana, R. H. (1993). *Multi-cultural assessment perspectives for professional psychology.* Boston: Allyn and Bacon.

Danielson, L. C. and Bauer, J. N. (1978). A formula-based classification of learning disabled children: an examination of the issues. *Journal of Learning Disabilities,* 11, 50-63.

Denckla, M. and Rudel, R. (1976). Rapid 'automatised' naming (R.A.N.): dyslexia differentiated from other learning disabilities. Neuropsychologia, 14, 471-479.

Fennel, E. B. (1995). The role of neuropsychological assessment in learning disabilities. *Journal of Child Neurology,* 10(1), S36-S41.

Feuerstein, R. (1979). *The dynamic assessment of retarded performers: the learning potential assessment device, theory, instrument and techniques.* Baltimore: University Park Press.

Fletcher, J. M. and Foorman, B .R. (1994). Issues in definition and measurement of learning disabilities: the need for early intervention. In Lyon, G. R. (Ed.) *Frames of reference for the assessment of learning disabilities: new views on measurement issues* (pp. 185-200). Baltimore: Paul H. Brookes Publishing Co.

Fletcher, J. M. and Morris, R. D. (1986). Classifications of disabled learners: beyond exclusionary definitions. In S. Ceci (Ed.) *Handbook of cognitive, social, and neuropsychological aspects of learning disabilities* (Vol. 1, pp. 55-80). NJ: Lawrence Erlbaum Associates.

Fletcher, J. M., Francis, D. J., Rourke, B. P., Shaywitz, S. E. and Shaywitz, B. A. (1993). Classification of learning disabilities: relationship with other childhood disorders. In Lyon, G. R. (Ed.) *Frames of reference for the assessment of learning disabilities: new views on measurement issues* (pp. 27-55). Baltimore: Paul H. Brookes Publishing Co.

Gallagher, L. S. (1993). *Inclusion, reform, restructuring and practice.* PA: Learning Disabilities Association of America.

Geschwind, N. (1982). Why Orton was right. *Annals of Dyslexia,* 32, 13-30.

Geschwind, N. (1983). Biological association of left-handedness. *Annals of Dyslexia,* 33, 29-40.

Griffin, M. (1995). Personal communication. June 1.

Johnson, D. J. (1995). An overview of learning disabilities: Psycho-educational perspectives. *Journal of Child Neurology,* 10 (1), S2-S5.

Keogh, B. K. (1993). Linking purpose and practice: social, political and developmental perspectives on classification. In Lyon, G. R., Gray, D. B., Kavanaugh, J. F. and Krasnegor, N. A. (Eds.) *Better understanding learning disabilities: new views from research and their implications for education and public policies* (pp. 311-323). Baltimore: Paul H. Brookes Publishing Co.

Korhonen, T. T. (1995). The persistence of rapid naming problems in children with reading disabilities: a nine-year follow-up. *Journal of Learning Disabilities,* 28,(4), 232-239.

Levine, M. D. (1987). *Developmental variations and learning disorders.* MA: Educator's Publishing Service, Inc.

Levine, M. D., Hooper, S., Montgomery, J., Reid, M., Sandler, A., Swartz, C. and Watson, T. (1993). Learning disabilities: an interactive developmental paradigm. In Lyon, G. R., Gray, D. B., Kavanaugh, J. F. and Krasnegor, N. A. (Eds.) *Better understanding learning disabilities: new views from research and their implications for education and public policies* (pp. 229-250). Baltimore: Paul H. Brookes Publishing Co.

Lyon, G. R. (1995a). *Research in learning disabilities at the National Institute of Child Health and Human Development.* Washington, D.C.: National Institute of Child Health and Human Development.

Lyon, G. R. (1995b). Research initiatives in learning disabilities: contributions from scientists supported by the National Institute of Child Health and Human Development. *Journal of Child Neurology,* 10(1), S120-S126.

Lyon, G. R. (1994). Critical issues in the measurement of learning disabilities. In Lyon, G .R. (Ed.) *Frames of reference for the assessment of learning disabilities: new views on measurement issues* (pp. 3-13). Baltimore: Paul H. Brookes Publishing Co.

Lyon, G. R. (1993). Preface. In Lyon, G. R., Gray, D. B., Kavanaugh, J. F. and Krasnegor, N. A. (Eds.) *Better understanding learning disabilities: new views from research and their implications for education and public policies* (pp. xvii-xix). Baltimore: Paul H. Brookes Publishing Co.

Martin, E. W. (1993). Learning disabilities and public policy: myths and outcomes. In Lyon, G. R., Gray, K. B. Kavanaugh, J. F. and Krasnegor, N. A. (Eds.) *Better understanding learning disabilities: new views from research and their implications for education and public policies* (pp. 325-342). Baltimore: Paul H. Brookes Publishing Co.

Mehan, H., Miehls, J. L., Hartweck, A. and Crowdes, M. J. (1981). Identifying handicapped students. In Bachrach, S. T. (Ed.) *Organisational behaviour in school and school districts* (pp. 381-427). NY: Praeger.

Miller, S. (1995). *Temporal processing deficits and language-based learning disorders.* Presentation delivered at the 22nd Annual Meeting of the Orton Dyslexia Society, April, 1995, New York, NY.

Moats, L. C. and Lyon, G. R. (1993). Learning disabilities in the United States: advocacy, science and the future of the field. *Journal of Learning Disabilities,* 26(5), 282-294.

Moats, L. C. (1994). Strategy assessment in perspective. In Lyon, G. R. (Ed.) *Frames of reference for the assessment of learning disabilities: new views on measurement issues* (pp. 607-614). Baltimore: Paul H. Brookes Publishing Co.

Neufeldt, V. (Ed.) (1994). *Webster's New World Dictionary.* NY: Simon & Schuster.

Nielsen, G. S. and Salter, R. (1995). *Dyslexia: primary school provision in Europe.* London: European Dyslexia Association.

Olivier, J. (1994). *Learning disabilities and the law.* Presentation delivered at Eagle Hill School, December, 1994, Greenwich, CT.

Orton, S. T. (1937). *Reading, writing and speech problems in children.* NY: W. W. Norton.

Porac, C. and Coren, S. (1981). *Lateral preferences and human behaviour.* NY: Springer.

Prigatano, G. P. (1986). Cognitive re-training in perspective. In Prigatano, G. P. (Ed.) *Neuropsychological rehabilitation after brain injury* (pp. 51-66). Baltimore: John Hopkins University Press.

Rawson, M. (1995). Dyslexia over the lifespan. MA: Educator's Publishing Service, Inc.

Rourke, B. P. (1994). Neuropsychological assessment of children with learning disabilities: measurement issues. In Lyon, G. R. (Ed.) *Frames of reference for the assessment of learning disabilities: new views on measurement issues* (pp. 475-514). Baltimore: Paul H. Brookes Publishing Co.

Salter, R. (1995). *International Panel.* Presentation delivered at the 22nd Annual Meeting of the Orton Dyslexia Society, March, 1995, New York, NY.

Saunders, R. (1995). Personal communication. April, 1994.

Shaywitz, S. E., Shaywitz, B. A., Fletcher, J. M. and Escobar, M. D. (1990). Prevalence of reading disability in boys and girls. *Journal of the America Medical Association*, 264(8), 998-1002.

Shaywitz, B. A., Fletcher, J. M., Shaywitz, S. E. (1995). Defining and classifying learning disabilities and attention deficit/hyperactivity disorder. *Journal of Child Neurology,* 10 (1), S50-S57.

Siegel, L. S. (1989). I.Q. is irrelevant to the definition of learning disabilities. *Journal of Learning Disabilities,* 25, 618-629.

Speece, D. L. (1993). Broadening the scope of classification research: conceptual and ecological approaches. In Lyon, G. R., Gray, D. B., Kavanaugh, J. F. and Krasnegor, N. A. (Eds.) *Understanding learning disabilities: new views from research and their implications for education and public policies* (pp. 57-72). Baltimore: Paul H. Brookes Publishing Co.

Spring, E. and French, L. (1990). Identifying reading disabled children from listening and reading discrepancy scores. *Journal of Learning Disabilities,* 23, 53-58.

Stanovich, K. E. (1991). Discrepancy definitions of reading disability: has intelligence led us astray? *Reading Research Quarterly,* 26, 1-29.

Stanovich, K. E. (1993). The construct validity of discrepancy definitions of reading disability. In Lyon, G. R. (Ed.) *Understanding learning disabilities: new views from research and their implications for education and public policies* (pp. 273-307). Baltimore: Paul H. Brookes Publishing Co.

Stanovich, K. E. (1988). Exploring the differences between the dyslexic and the garden variety poor reader: the phonological core variable difference model. *Journal of Learning Disabilities*, 21, 590-604.

Statesman's Yearbook (1994). 131st Edition. NY: St. Martin's Press.

Sternberg, R. J. (1988). The triarchic mind: a new theory of human intelligence. NY: Penguin.

Strag, G. A. (1972). Comparative behavioural ratings of parents with severe mentally retarded, special learning disabled, and normal children. *Journal of Learning Disabilities,* 5, 52-56.

Strong, L. (1995). *International Panel.* Presentation delivered at the 22nd Annual Meeting of the Orton Dyslexia Society, March, 1995, New York, NY.

Symes, J. S. and Rapoport, J. L. (1972). Unexpected reading failure. *American Journal of Orthopsychiatry*, 42, 82-91.

Tallal, P. (1991). *Neurological correlates of learning and language disorders.* Presentation delivered at conference on Neuroscience of Learning Disorders, Columbia University, November, 1991, New York, NY.

Tallal, P., Miller, S. and Fitch, R. H. (1993). Neurobiological basis of speech: a case for the pre-eminence of temporal processing. *Annals of the New York Academy of Sciences.* June 14, 1993.

Thayer, L. (1973). *Communication and communication systems.* Illinois: Richard D. Irwin, Inc.

Torgesen, J. K. (1990). *Cognitive and behavioural characteristics of children with learning disabilities.* Austin, TX: Pro-Ed.

Weingrod, B. (1995). *International Panel.* Presentation delivered at the 22nd Annual Meeting of the Orton Dyslexia Society, March, 1995, New York, NY.

Welshman, M. (1995). *International Panel.* Presentation delivered at the 22nd Annual Meeting of the Orton Dyslexia Society, March, 1995, New York, NY.

Wolf, M. (1984). Naming, reading and the dyslexias: a longitudinal overview. *Annals of Dyslexia,* 34, 87-136.

Zigler, R. E. and Finn-Stevenson, M. (1987). *Children: developmental and social issues.* MA: D.C. Heath & Co.

Zigmond, N. (1995). Models of delivery of special education services to students with learning disabilities in public schools. *Journal of Child Neurology,* 10(1), S86-S91.

SPECIFIC LEARNING DIFFICULTIES, LEARNING SUPPORT TEACHERS AND THE IMPACT OF CHANGING POLICY

SHEILA RIDDELL, SALLY BROWN and JILL DUFFIELD

INTRODUCTION

Between 1990 and 1992, a research team based at the Department of Education, University of Stirling, undertook a research project commissioned by the Scottish Office Education Department to investigate policy, practice and provision for children with specific learning difficulties. From the start, it was clear that we were investigating an area in which feelings run high. Even the term 'special learning difficulties' was disliked by some of those with whom we would be working; for them, 'dyslexia' was the problem to be addressed and other labels were educationalists' jargon. This is not a matter of mere semantics; it goes to the core of how people conceptualise these kinds of difficulties, what they see as rational policy and how they believe the needs of these children should be met.

The views of learning support teachers, parents, voluntary organisations and education authority personnel on the nature of specific learning difficulties, ways of identifying children with these difficulties and appropriate forms of provision, were sought. This paper explores learning support teachers' ways of construing specific learning difficulties and the type of assistance they considered necessary. It then contrasts these views with those of education authority personnel and parents, reported in detail elsewhere (Riddell, Duffield, Brown and Ogilvy, 1992), and highlights the shifting conceptualisation of learning difficulties over the past twenty years from a child-deficit to a curriculum- and school-deficit model.

Within this context of changing ideas, learning support teachers have been encouraged to redefine their role, focusing on consultancy and co-operative teaching rather than individual tuition. This new role, however, has tended not to be welcomed by parents of children with specific learning difficulties, who have emphasised the needs of their individual child and argued that these cannot be met within normal classroom provision. Since government policy has continued to emphasise not only the new role for learning support staff, but also the rights of parents as consumers of educational services, there is potential for conflict between education professionals and parents of children with specific learning difficulties, as they struggle over competing definitions of the nature of the problem and its treatment.

Before turning to a discussion of the research findings which map out these tensions, we set the scene by looking at the relevant ideas embedded in two reports which have had a major influence on policy and thinking over the last decade and a half.

THE POLICY CONTEXT

The Warnock Report, the Progress Report of Scottish HMI and the SCOSDE guidelines

A central theme of the Warnock Report (DES, 1978) was the need to replace statutory categories of handicap with the notion of a continuum of special educational needs. Warnock maintained that there was no sharp dividing line between children with learning difficulties and others and that it was important to recognise the interaction between an individual and his or her environment as the source of learning difficulties. Modifying a child's learning environment, therefore, was likely to be an effective means of tackling their difficulties. Although envisaging a continuing role for special schools, Warnock indicated that most children with special needs should receive their education in mainstream schools.

The rejection of a child-deficit model was also evident in the report by Scottish HMI, published in 1978 and entitled **The Education of Pupils with Learning Difficulties in Primary and Secondary Schools in Scotland.** Inappropriate curricula and teaching methods were identified as the root cause of many pupils' learning difficulties:

> *"Many learning problems arise because the demands being made by schools are still too great for the linguistic competence of some of their pupils."*
> (SED, 1978, para 4.9, p. 124)

HMI pointed to some of the dangers of withdrawing pupils for individual tuition, the traditional means of providing teaching support. It was argued that difficulties were likely to arise when pupils were re-integrated into their mainstream class, since they might have lost touch with the general work of the group. De-contextualised drilling in particular skills was seen as unlikely to be of long-term assistance since pupils might well be unable to apply what they had learnt. Practice in specific skills was preferred and these skills should be context-specific and undertaken in mainstream classes. The report emphasised that the ultimate responsibility for dealing with children's learning difficulties lay with subject or class teachers.

> *"Pupils with learning difficulties should be taught, as far as possible, by class and subject teachers. If they are unable to give the proper kind of help, then the pupils involved should be given the additional support of a remedial teacher. That fact, however, does not reduce the class or subject teacher's responsibility for the pupils, or absolve him (sic) from continuing his (sic) own endeavours."*
>
> (SED, 1978, para 4.11, p. 25)

This emphasis on the paramount responsibility of the class or subject teacher had implications for the continued existence of an autonomous remedial department. HMI commented:

> *"There has been a steady trend towards the establishment of separate 'remedial departments' in which they (remedial teachers) offer separate courses. Such a trend appears to be at odds with the indicators of our survey which suggest that remedial education is a whole-school responsibility and an inherent element of the work of subject departments."*
>
> (SED, 1978, para 4.17, p. 27)

More than a decade later, the Scottish Committee for Staff Development in Education (SCOSDE, 1990) published a document entitled **Guidelines for Diplomas in Special Educational Needs** which clarified and modified the recommendations of the HMI Report. Summarising the roles of learning support teachers, it suggested that they should be concerned:

(a) Through consultation and collaboration, in helping class and subject teachers to plan and develop responses to the range of learning difficulties;

(b) through consultation and collaboration, in the development of a differentiated curriculum at whole-school and department levels to meet the range of learning difficulties found in mainstream classes;

(c) in supporting individual learners, either through direct teaching or through co-ordinating support from visiting teachers, parents or specialist services;

(d)   in working with management on the formulation and implementa-
       tion of whole-school or college policy;

(e)   in initiating and contributing to staff development related to their
       other roles.

Of particular interest to the research reported here, was the brief emphasis
put by the Guidelines on learning support teachers being able to offer specialised
individual help to children 'with specific learning difficulties, including those of a
dyslexic kind' (para 4.1, p. 22). No elaboration of this point was provided,
however.

Our research was carried out, therefore, in a policy context where the
Warnock Report, the 1978 Progress Report of Scottish HMI and the SCOSDE
guidelines had instigated a shift in emphasis in provision for children with
learning difficulties. Rather than seeing these children as the prime responsibility
of the remedial teacher, the class teacher was seen as fulfilling the most important
role in meeting their needs. The newly-styled learning support teacher was cast
in a consultancy role, with individual tuition seen as less important than curriculum
modification. Both Warnock and the SCOSDE guidelines recognised that children
with specific learning difficulties might require individual tuition, but the
implications of this not being in line with the general changes in policy were not
pursued.

THE IMPACT OF POLICY DEVELOPMENTS ON THE PRACTICE OF LEARNING SUPPORT

What has been the impact of this change in policy, especially those parts
which relate to the underlying causes of learning difficulties and the role of
learning support teachers? The study conducted by Allan, Brown and Munn
(1991) is one of the few pieces of research which has considered the implementation
of the HMI's recommendations. Their work in one Scottish region identified
problems that had arisen as a result of tensions within the views expressed by HMI
on the role of the learning support teacher. On the one hand, it was argued that
the new responsibilities, particularly consultancy and co-operative teaching, were
considerably more exacting than the traditional work of small group and individual
tuition. On the other hand, the HMI report implied that remedial teachers (now
learning support teachers) no longer had prime responsibility for children with
learning difficulties and did not require a departmental base from which to
operate. It was unclear, therefore, whether the status of learning support teachers
was being enhanced or downgraded and this had led to confusion in practice, as
learning support and mainstream teachers attempted to delineate their respective

functions and areas of responsibility. In secondary classrooms, there was a danger that the mainstream teacher either handed over all responsibility for children with learning difficulties to the learning support teacher, or attempted to retain complete control, interpreting any autonomous action on the part of the learning support teacher as a challenge to their own professional autonomy. The message of this research was that effective co-operative teaching and consultancy were not easily achieved.

A number of commentators south of the border have also noted weaknesses in the these kinds of approaches to learning difficulties. In her research on the work of learning support teachers, Bines (1988) found that teachers simply did not have enough time or resources to provide individual help and implement a more detailed and specialised approach to learning. She suggested that the goal of meeting the individual needs of all children was unrealistic and possibly misplaced. Rather, she suggested, teachers should tackle at an institutional level factors which led some children to be regarded as educational failures and accorded lower status:

> *"This could involve attempting to change conceptions of 'achievement', stressing the common rather than the different nature of teaching and learning processes for all pupils and also developing the social as well as the academic goals of the school."* (p. 157).

Dyson (1990) has also expressed reservations, not least because the existence of learning support staff has led mainstream teachers to label some pupils as 'special' and hence someone else's responsibility. He has suggested that the learning support teacher should redefine his or her role as an effective learning consultant. Initial steps to achieving this would be the renunciation of the learning support department, the abandonment of the special needs label and the abdication of the specialist teaching role. The weakness in Dyson's argument is its neglect of the fact that merely renaming learning support teachers is unlikely to change mainstream teachers' view of their function. What is clear is that both Bines and Dyson are advocating a shift even further away from the notion of the learning support teacher meeting the needs of children with difficulties on an individual basis.

Not all commentators, however, have agreed that learning support teachers should regard consultancy as their most important role. Moses, Hegarty and Jowett (1987), reporting on external support services to mainstream schools, found a marked evolution in the work for children with special educational needs. While the service's earlier role had concentrated on individual reading support, by 1984 they were dealing with a wider range of difficulties, in both primary and secondary schools and, significantly, were offering an advisory service to teachers as well as working directly with children. The authors of the report expressed reservations, however, about the new emphasis on consultancy rather than direct work with individual pupils.

Moses, Hegarty and Jowett were also interested in the question of **where** individual tuition should take place. They were aware that the practice of withdrawal from class had been the subject of considerable criticism, though not always for sound reasons. A new orthodoxy seemed, they suggested, to have been established in some quarters in which help inside the mainstream class-room is seen as the **only** solution and withdrawal was regarded as undesirable (p. 113) Despite its unpopularity among official policy makers, however, withdrawal has remained popular with junior school teachers. Gipps, Gross and Goldstein (1987) found that teachers regarded withdrawal as the most useful type of help that could be provided for children with learning difficulties and felt it should be extended to more pupils. Moses, Hegarty and Jowett (1987) concluded:

> *"Advisory and support services who wish to move away from this model of support may face a distinct lack of enthusiasm, if not actual opposition from schools and they need to be very clear about their reasons for rejecting this popular practice"* (p. 113).

Payne (1991) also defended withdrawing children from the mainstream class for individual tuition on an occasional basis. He claimed that teachers who practised this form of support had been led over recent years to feel like 'accomplices to some form of educational apartheid'. On the basis of interviews with pupils who had experienced both support in the mainstream class and temporary withdrawal for individual tuition, he found that they generally favoured the latter. He also stressed the need for a clear distinction to be drawn between temporary withdrawal and permanent segregation in a remedial or special class and listed the advantages of withdrawal identified by Gipps, Gross and Goldstein (1987).

The findings of Payne's research suggested that children withdrawn from the mainstream class for learning support worked harder on more appropriate work and developed a better relationship with the teacher. Other advantages arose from the support teachers' expertise and the privacy of the activity; these helped to avoid:

"The distressing spectacle of a child forced to read aloud in a stumbling parody of fluency to a teacher who is intent on maintaining in the rest of the room, that very silence which is increasing the child's discomfort at his own obvious inabilit" (p. 62).

The debates on the nature of learning difficulties and the role of the learning support teacher have had major implications for children with specific learning difficulties. Although Warnock and the 1978 HMI Report acknowledged that individual tuition may still be helpful for some children, the central thrust of policy was to blur distinctions between categories of difficulty, focus on within-school rather than within-child factors as the source of difficulties, and concentrate intervention at the classroom and the school level rather than withdrawing the individual child. Some commentators have argued for an even tighter focus on systemic intervention rather than endeavouring to remediate individual children's difficulties (Dessent, 1987). A contrasting view, however, could argue that the reasons for rejecting the notion of difficulties residing within the child and abandoning individual tuition have been rooted in orthodoxy rather than sound educational judgement. Certainly, this is the view of many parents of children with specific learning difficulties (see Riddell, Brown and Duffield, 1994) who continue to demand that the particular difficulties of their children are recognised and remedied by expert tuition delivered on a one-to-one basis.

But how do learning support teachers construe the nature of specific learning difficulties and appropriate focus of provision? It is to the views of this critical group of providers that we now turn.

THE RESEARCH FINDINGS

The nature of the learning support teachers' sample

In this strand of our research, 400 questionnaires were distributed to learning support teachers in eleven Scottish regional authorities and six divisions of one large authority. An overall response rate of 59 per cent provided 206 completed questionnaires and 30 blanks. All but one of the 17 Scottish regions and divisions were represented. The response rate in different areas appeared to relate to the dominant view of specific learning difficulties within the region. In two regions, an earlier interview study had revealed strong opposition to the use of categories of learning difficulties (including specific learning difficulties) and here the response rate was particularly low.

In general, those who replied were highly experienced teachers, with only 19 of the 206 having less than 10 years' total teaching experience. The Diploma in Special Educational Needs was held by 36 per cent and these were significantly more likely to be secondary than primary teachers.

Learning support teachers' conceptualisation of specific learning difficulties and dyslexia.

An open-ended question asked learning support teachers to provide a definition of specific learning difficulties. More than a third (37 per cent) attached no particular meaning to the term and suggested that almost any learning difficulty might be described in this way:

> Any specific factor preventing full access to the curriculum.

> Problems due to medical, cognitive, developmental or acquired difficulties.

> Some learning problem that can be identified and worked on.

However, 40 per cent indicated that specific learning difficulties were characterised by literacy difficulties and a discrepancy between attainment in this area and general ability. Although about a quarter agreed with the statement that children with specific learning difficulties were likely to have higher than average achievements in some areas, more than half suggested that children throughout the ability range might experience specific difficulties.

When asked whether they would ever use the term 'dyslexia' to describe a learning difficulty, 70 per cent indicated that they would, and those with ten or more years of teaching experience were more likely to use that term than their less experienced colleagues. Of those who used the term, the majority defined it as difficulty in decoding symbols, a much tighter definition than they had given to specific learning difficulties. A substantial number expressed reservations about use of the term dyslexia, however, suggesting that they would only use it with certain groups of people such as colleagues or the educational psychologist. Teachers who said they did not use the term explained that it was 'too generalised', that it referred to 'many difficulties, not one' and that it was 'too convenient a label'. A number of these answers conveyed irritation with parents 'latching on to the word' and 'wanting to call every learning difficulty, dyslexia'.

On the matter of group distinctiveness of children with specific learning difficulties, we found an interesting difference between learning support teachers and other educationalists. Our interviews with education authority personnel had indicated a split between those who regarded children with specific learning difficulties as a discrete group (25 per cent of respondents) and those who felt their difficulties, although distinctive, should be seen as part of a general continuum (50 per cent). The remaining 25 per cent had also subscribed to the notion of a continuum of learning difficulties but had been opposed to the recognition of particular categories of difficulties within it. When the learning support teachers were asked whether children with specific learning difficulties formed a discrete group who were distinct from others with learning difficulties, however, two thirds agreed with this statement and a third disagreed.

In response to a question on the degree of priority attached to meeting the needs of children with specific learning difficulties, our respondents were almost equally split, with almost half saying they attached high priority to meeting their needs and the others claiming that it was impossible to say – they determined priorities on an individual rather than a group basis. A very small minority suggested that low priority was attached to meeting the needs of such children. However, comments written in the final open section of the questionnaire conveyed learning support teachers' anxiety as they attempted to establish priorities between the needs of children with global learning difficulties and specific learning difficulties. Such dilemmas were particularly acute in areas with high levels of social deprivation. One teacher commented:

> *"The problems are also found in a much larger group of children [than those diagnosed specific learning difficulties] who do not have 'higher than average achievements in other areas'. These pupils often benefit greatly from a structured individual approach but rarely get it . . . They have not the necessary pre-reading skills before they are required to begin learning to read and write . . . These children often come from language-deprived homes and live in socially deprived areas. Children who are diagnosed as having specific learning difficulties are almost always, in my experience, from socially advantaged backgrounds with parents who can effectively ask for help. Children from disadvantaged backgrounds with similar difficulties are unlikely to get specific help; the difficulties are blamed on their home background and lack of parental skills; schools and education authorities seem to think there is little they can do."*

In attempting to summarise the views of this sample of learning support teachers, two findings are especially striking. First, a much higher proportion appeared to be conversant with (and ready to use) the term 'dyslexia' than with 'specific learning difficulties'. Secondly, they were much more likely than policy makers and managers to see specific learning difficulties (or dyslexia) as qualitatively different from global learning difficulties and to attach a high priority to meeting the needs of the former. In some ways, therefore, their stance might be seen as midway between that of local authority personnel and parents – almost all the parents in the research sample believed their children should be described as dyslexic and quite distinct from those with more global learning difficulties.

We have to be cautious, however, about claiming this as a generalisation across learning support teachers in Scotland. As we indicated in our comment on the response rate to the questionnaire, we suspect that those teachers who are opposed to any categorization of learning difficulties (and so to specific learning difficulties as a category) are under-represented in the sample. Given this caveat, we might also infer from these findings a certain lack of confidence about how to deal with children with these kinds of difficulties. On the one hand, those who come from privileged backgrounds may have parents who interfere in ways that are seen by the teachers as unhelpful. On the other hand, those from disadvantaged backgrounds may either not have their specific difficulties picked up (the assumption is made that social deprivation signals **global** learning difficulties) or receive inadequate support in the home.

If learning support teachers appear not to be confident at this general level of thinking about specific learning difficulties, can we expect things to improve as they get down to the more specific practical tasks of identification and assessment of those difficulties?

Learning support teachers' accounts of appropriate forms of identification and assessment.

Less than half of learning support teachers (42 per cent) expressed substantial confidence in their ability to identify children with specific learning difficulties, but a further 50 per cent reported some confidence. Teachers who used the term dyslexia and had more than ten years experience in learning support work were more likely to express confidence than others. Because dyslexia was defined more tightly than specific learning difficulties, it was not surprising that these teachers were more confident in their ability to recognise the phenomenon.

About 70 per cent of primary and 50 per cent of secondary learning support teachers claimed their school had systematic procedures for the identification of children with specific learning difficulties. In both primary and secondary schools, a team approach was used in identifying children with specific learning difficulties; however, class teachers in primary were more likely to be involved in this process than subject teachers in secondary. This suggested that the view advocated by HMI that children with learning difficulties are the prime responsibility of the mainstream teacher was less established in secondary than primary. Three quarters of the respondents said that formal diagnostic testing was used in their schools, either administered by themselves or the educational psychologist; about a third also used informal testing and observation to diagnose problems. This diagnosis was carried out mostly at primary school: 40 per cent of children were identified in P1-P3 and 40 per cent in P4-P7.

Overall, the learning support teachers conveyed feelings of confidence in their ability to identify children with specific learning difficulties and diagnose their problems. This was in marked contrast, however, with the perceptions of the sample of parents who singled out assessment as one of their major areas of dissatisfaction, complaining that the methods used by the learning support teachers were imprecise and inaccurate, and schools were often reluctant to arrange an assessment by an educational psychologist. Furthermore, they felt that formal assessment was often conducted too late in a child's career for effective remedial action to be taken.

Location of provision

Moving on from the identification of specific learning difficulties to the meeting of needs, learning support teachers were asked where such children generally received their education. The most frequent response indicated this was in the mainstream class with some withdrawal. Education in the mainstream class without withdrawal was also common, particularly in the secondary school. Just under 10 per cent of the teachers reported that children would spend some time in a reading centre and 3 per cent identified withdrawal to a special class within the mainstream school.

Teaching methods and the role of the learning support teacher

In the context of the changing official conception of the role of the learning support teacher to one of greater consultancy and co-operation, together with parental anxiety about the lack of individual tuition for their children, how did the learning support teachers conceptualise their role? The teachers were asked to rank order the following aspects of their role: acting as a consultant to other members of staff; working co-operatively with class/subject teachers; direct teaching for individual pupils outwith the normal class; contributing to a range of special services within and outwith the school for pupils with learning difficulties; and providing and arranging staff development in relation to learning difficulties. **Figure 1** shows the numbers of learning support teachers who regarded particular aspects of their role as being of prime importance. Co-operative teaching was regarded as most important by 42 per cent followed by consultancy, (23 per cent); only 20 per cent saw individual tuition as the most important aspect of their role.

Primary learning support teachers saw individual tuition as much more salient for their work than did secondary teachers.

When given the opportunity to comment, teachers indicated that they had responded in different ways to requests to rank the different aspects of their role. For some, it appeared that priorities were clear-cut. One teacher for example, expressed a direct antipathy towards the role of individual tutor, commenting 'I have no time or inclination to tutor'. Another, however, who ranked individual tuition as the least important part of his work, was far more ambivalent. He wrote of 'a constant anxiety' as to whether withdrawing pupils for direct support should be promoted to greater importance.

Overall, it appeared that most of these learning support teachers had accepted Scottish HMI's re-definition of their role as consultants and co-operative teachers rather than individual remedial tutors. However, given the view of the majority of the teachers in our sample that children with specific learning difficulties have very distinctive needs, it is not surprising that some teachers experience conflict between different aspects of their role. One teacher expressed this conflict vividly:

> "I am sole learning support teacher in a school of just over 600 pupils. Eleven children with Records of Needs, nine for specific learning difficulties. Various other pupils with less severe specific difficulties not recorded. Two pupils with severe specific learning difficulties have Reading Centre help two periods a week; the rest are the school's and my total problem. We also have traditional slow learners, a boy with muscular dystrophy and a boy with moderate learning difficulties. We rely on whole-staff awareness and push to support these pupils. I am also involved in staff development and curriculum development. A tutu and fairy wand definitely required."

The combination of learning support teachers endeavouring to follow official policy on their new role, and the enormous practical pressures on them in schools, is generally bad news for parents of children with specific learning difficulties who are looking for individual tuition.

Guidelines and teaching materials for children with specific learning difficulties

By this time it will be clear that the learning support teachers were not at their most self-assured when thinking about specific learning difficulties. What, therefore, did they have to hand in the way of advice or material resources for this aspect of their work? Our respondents were asked whether they had any guidelines on appropriate teaching methods for children with specific learning difficulties. About 60 per cent said that they did and secondary teachers were more likely than primary to report that they had received guidelines from voluntary organisations. Those working in primary, however, were more likely to report an awareness of regional guidelines.

About 70 per cent of respondents said that they had teaching materials designed for tackling specific learning difficulties, but only 27 per cent regarded these as significantly different from those recommended for other learning and literacy problems. The minority who claimed that they used distinctively different materials said that these focused on structured approaches, repetition, breaking down outcomes into manageable sections, use of phonics, visual or auditory targeting, emphasis on hand-eye co-ordination and multi-sensory methods. An important feature was that the interest level was aimed at an older age group than the reading content. The majority who did not use special materials for children with specific learning difficulties said that all children benefited from carefully structured techniques and that there was no need to allocate scarce resources for distinctive items:

"The cost of supplying special material would be prohibitive. It is the teacher's approach that makes the difference."

Again, there was a marked contrast between the views of parents and teachers. Whereas a majority of the learning support teachers defended their use of a common approach for all children with learning difficulties, parents argued strongly for a distinctive approach for those with specific learning difficulties.

Learning support teachers' assessment of their effectiveness

In general, learning support teachers expressed a moderate degree of confidence in their ability to assist children with specific learning difficulties in overcoming their problems and in advising colleagues about the most effective courses of action. The number of years' experience as a learning support teacher seemed to be a crucial element in the overall level of confidence, with those who had worked in this area for ten years or more expressing a significantly greater degree of confidence. Parents, however, took a much more critical view of the effectiveness of school provision. Although the progress report of HMI had established a new direction for learning support provision, the controversy remained particularly with regard to the scepticism among parents about the effectiveness of co-operative teaching and consultancy in comparison with individual tuition. Specific learning difficulties is an area where such controversies are likely to be in evidence since parents, supported by voluntary organisations, have been clear in their demand for an individualised programme delivered by expert learning support teachers outwith the mainstream class. Such demands have cut across the view not only of HMI, but also of regional authority policies, which emphasise the whole school approach based on the delivery of a differentiated curriculum within the mainstream class.

DISCUSSION OF THE FINDINGS

In this paper we have drawn attention to two major strands of policy and thinking about learning difficulties which would be expected to have had a major impact on practice: new ways of conceptualising learning difficulties and new roles for learning support teachers. The report of the research has concentrated, therefore, on learning support teachers' perspectives on these two strands together with some comparisons with the views of policy makers/managers and parents. The distinctiveness of the research is its setting in the context of specific learning difficulties rather than special educational needs more generally.

Turning first to how learning support teachers think about the nature of specific learning difficulties, there was little evidence of consensus among the group. A significant minority seemed unfamiliar with the particular meaning of the term (and used it to refer to any learning difficulty), less than half were in line with the most widely accepted description (a difficulty, often in literacy, which is not reflected in achievement in other areas) and two thirds were at least as comfortable with the term 'dyslexia' as with 'specific learning difficulties'.

Despite the apparent uncertainty about the concept, two thirds of the sample of teachers saw children with specific learning difficulties as forming a discrete group with problems that are qualitatively different from those of children with more global learning difficulties. A rather smaller proportion of the teachers (about half) felt that this group should be given priority treatment; most of the others were committed to deciding priorities on the basis of the needs of individual children rather than the nature of their difficulties.

How do these perceptions match official policy? The findings from another part of our research suggested that the dominant view in regional authorities reflected that of Warnock and Scottish HMI reports in conceptualising a continuum of special educational needs. Specific learning difficulties were seen as lying along this continuum, according to their severity, and as being catered for within existing provision. Ideas of a discrete group of children and terms like dyslexia tended to be eschewed by regional personnel.

In contrast, the sample of parents of children with specific learning difficulties argued strongly that their difficulties were qualitatively different from those experienced by children of generally low ability. Furthermore, in the light of what they saw as their children's distinctive problems, they insisted that individual teaching delivered by expert tutors with specially designed materials was essential. They were unimpressed by notions of co-operative teaching in mainstream settings. (See Riddell *et al.* in press, for a further discussion of parents' and local policy makers' perspectives.)

Learning support teachers, therefore, seemed poised between local authority personnel and parents. They were more likely than the former to recognise children with specific learning difficulties as a discrete group, but divided as to whether they should be accorded the high priority status requested by parents and unwilling to designate teaching materials as suitable only for children with specific learning difficulties – all those children with manifestation of difficulties in basic literacy could, many of them argued, benefit from such resources.

Turning to the second strand of policy and thinking, a new role for the learning support teacher, we found interesting differences between the primary and secondary teachers' ways of construing this area of special needs. In comparison with the secondary teachers, the learning support teachers in the primary sector expressed greater self-confidence in the systematic identification of children with specific learning difficulties, a more collaborative approach to the assessment of needs, a higher regard for withdrawal for individual tuition of pupils (and more frequent use of it) and a sharper awareness of regional guidelines on teaching methods in this area.

It seems likely that the primary teachers' confidence, in identifying these difficulties and undertaking withdrawal for individual tuition in the face of at least some official disapproval, stems from two factors. First, **all** primary school teachers see themselves as having responsibility (and appropriate training) for the development of basic literacy and numeracy and for becoming familiar with ways of picking up and then dealing with these problems. Secondly, collaborative approaches in general, and those reported by these teachers for the identification of children with specific learning difficulties in particular, characterise the ethos of many primary schools. The opportunities to discuss the problems, methods of identification and ways of meeting needs, and to hear from others about documents (such as regional guidelines) or materials that are available, are much greater within the collegial atmosphere of the (usually) small staff of the primary school. An environment of this kind is likely to foster close links between mainstream class teachers and learning support staff.

The circumstances in which the secondary learning support staff found themselves were rather different. Confidence in the identification of specific learning difficulties and in the value of withdrawal for individual tuition were less apparent. There was a sense that identification and assessment of needs was seen as most appropriately carried out in the early years before secondary school, and that any learning difficulties persisting into the later years would be less amenable to remediation. Mainstream subject teachers characteristically see their main responsibility as teaching their subject. In relation to our research this seems to have had two effects. Firstly, they tended to leave the learning support teachers to deal with any problems that arose; to a large extent, they seemed not to have moved on from the notion of the learning support teacher as the 'remedial expert'. Within this framework, learning support teachers could establish their own priorities but were likely to experience a degree of professional isolation. Secondly, the subject teachers were less favourably inclined towards withdrawal than were the primary teachers; children who are withdrawn are in danger of losing touch with the mainstream subject curriculum, and that curriculum is the subject teacher's first priority.

One of the implicit contrasts in this comparison of the primary and secondary sectors is between the way the mainstream primary class teachers and the mainstream secondary subject teachers view the role of learning support staff. The primary teachers may well be more ready to accept the recasting of the old remedial specialist into the learning support teacher who is expected to engage primarily in activities to enhance the work of the class teacher rather than to provide alternative programmes. The mainstream class teachers are prepared for this 'working-alongside' mode since they see the development of children's literacy as part of **their** role (just as it is for learning support teachers) and, as other research (Allan, Brown and Munn, 1991) has shown, primary teachers tend to be optimistic about the likelihood of remediation of young children's problems. Secondary subject teachers, however, seem to see things differently. They may (though some do not) accept the official conceptualisation of learning difficulties which rejects the idea that the child's inherent problems are the prime cause of failure and instead focuses attention on the possibility of inappropriate curricula or teaching methods.

They may also accept that old style remedial classes may exacerbate rather than alleviate children's learning difficulties, and that learning support teachers should operate largely in mainstream classrooms. What some, at least, find difficult is to abandon the notion that it is they who are in overall charge of the class, on account of their subject knowledge, and that the learning support teacher should be making use of his or her special expertise by supporting the lowest achievers (individual tuition within the mainstream classroom). The notion of equal partnership with the learning support teacher, or facilitation of that teacher's consultancy role, are often hard to sustain. Prognoses of the resolution of learning difficulties once a young person has reached secondary school tend to be much more pessimistic than in the primary; this pessimism nourishes the idea that the subject teacher should get on with stimulating the other children and leave the learning support teacher to deal with those who are having real problems.

The disparity between the primary and secondary sector, in the way mainstream teachers view the role of learning support teachers, reflects a general tension and lack of consensus which characterises this area. As our review of the literature showed, the value of the shift in role continues to be debated. On one side, there are calls for greater change so that learning support teachers become learning consultants. On the other, there is concern that the value of individual tuition has been too readily dismissed and that the research findings on the so-called failure of remedial education have been inconclusive.

This debate has particular relevance for specific learning difficulties. Whereas the parents of such children press for more individual tuition, policy makers at local authority level defend the importance of co-operative teaching and consultancy. The conflict seems likely to continue with learning support teachers occupying the uncomfortable middle ground with a sense of role uncertainty and insecurity. Few of our sample were aware of regional guidelines on provision which could be straightforwardly implemented as a way of avoiding the conflict; where such guidelines were available, they were sometimes regarded as unhelpful. There was some awareness, especially among secondary teachers, of guidelines from voluntary organizations. Since these tended to emphasise expert individual support, in line with parents' views, but the actual provision was overwhelmingly in mainstream classrooms with co-operative teaching and only some withdrawal, the resulting tensions were likely to have increased learning support teachers' unease about this aspect of their work.

Our survey has indicated that these learning support teachers feel themselves to be the victims of excessive expectation from both the education establishment and parents of children with specific learning difficulties. What can be said about the future of this piggy-in-the-middle state of affairs? In speculating about this, we turn to the document on staff development **Support for Learning: Special Needs within the 5-14 Curriculum** put out by the Scottish Consultative Council on the Curriculum in collaboration with the Scottish Office Education Department. In particular, we ask what it has to say about the conceptualisation of special educational needs and the role of the learning support teacher – the two issues upon which this final section of our paper has focused.

It is clear that the idea of a 'continuum of special educational needs which requires to be met through a range of provision' (part 1, p 5) is still a central idea. Quite what this is a continuum **of** is still not entirely clear. Since 'Pupils have special education (**sic**) needs when they face difficulties in, or barriers to, learning' (part 1, p 5) maybe it is a continuum of difficulties (more/less severe?) or barriers (harder/easier to overcome, or just one after another?). What the continuum does not tell us about is the diversity in the **nature** of the needs (or difficulties or barriers) that have to be faced. Perhaps this is because 'The special educational needs of the majority of pupils relate to problems in a particular aspect of the curriculum' (part 1, p 5) and so the continuum looks rather like the continuum of attainment targets in the 5-14 curriculum itself.

Beyond this, it is acknowledged that some pupils have special educational needs because of 'specific problems', but we are reminded that the 'system of labelling pupils has been replaced with a description of their learning needs' (part 1, p5). What are parents of children with specific learning difficulties to make of this? Well quite a lot, as it happens, since a diagram showing 'learning difficulties considered from the standpoint of individual problems' (part 1, p 6) includes 'specific learning difficulties' as one distinct element. What its significance is difficult to say since the 'code' of the diagram is almost indecipherable, but it has a prominent position which it did not have before.

Turning to the role of the learning support teacher, we are given five main elements (in this order): consultancy, teaching and tuition, co-operative teaching, specialist services and staff development. In comparison with the SCOSDE guidelines cited earlier, three things might be said: consultancy still retains its central role, specialist services are included for the first time and teaching and tuition seemed to have gained prominence (by putting this second in the list the alphabetical order is broken). Both the 'specialist services' and the 'tuition' open the door on one-to-one work rather wider. Furthermore, teaching and tuition includes 'providing special programmes in reading and writing for pupils with dyslexia'. Not only is central government recognising a special case here, it is conceding a change in nomenclature from 'specific learning difficulties' (back) to 'dyslexia'.

How parents and voluntary organisations will react to this remains to be seen. They may be content to rest their case or they may reject it as inadequate and simply a fudge to placate them. The document itself, in several places, reminds them of the power that parents now have, not just to be kept informed but also to be much more active in the decision making. Teachers are reminded that 'In partnership with parents they can decide what is to be taught and how it is to be taught'. Schools are advised to consider the following in planning pathways.

"Parents of pupils with special educational needs should be fully involved in the planning process. Their views will be of particular importance in specifying programme aims and in analysing decisions about the selection of curriculum content " (part 1, p 16)

The luckless learning support teacher may still be caught between the other two powerful forces and schools will have to consider ways of reducing this pressure. That might be done by putting more emphasis than there seems to be at present on their consultancy role, ensuring they play a major part in the decisions about provision for children with special needs (including specific learning difficulties) and providing support for them in interactions with parents so they are not left unaided to shoulder the public responsibility for unpopular decisions. However, the reality is that the more time learning support staff devote to consultancy, management and decision making, the less time there will be for individual tuition and that is unlikely to help relationships with parents of pupils with specific learning difficulties.

Figure 1

Learning support teachers' view of the most important aspect of their role (numbers).

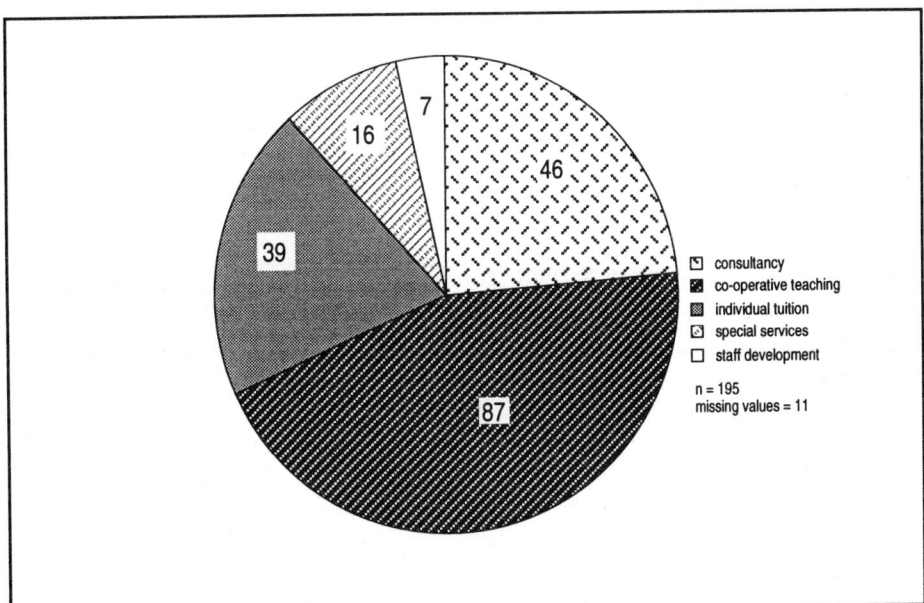

consultancy
co-operative teaching
individual tuition
special services
staff development

n = 195
missing values = 11

Table 1: Confidence in advising teachers about SLD reported by more or less experienced learning support teachers. (Result of chi-square test).

	Confident	Sometimes	Not Confident	Total
1 - 9 years experience	22 (21.4)	71 (68.9)	10 (9.7)	103 (53.9)
10 or more years experience	39 (44.3)	43 (48.9)	6 (6.8)	88 (46.1)
Total	61 (31.9)	114 (59.7)	16 (8.4)	191 (100.0)

p < .001   Missing values = 15

REFERENCES

Allan, J., Brown, S. and Munn, P. (1991). *Off the Record: Mainstream Provision for Pupils with Non-Regarded Learning Difficulties in Primary and Secondary School.* Edinburgh, Scottish Council for Research in Education.

Bines, H. (1988). 'Equality, community and individualism: The development and implementation of the "Whole School Approach" to Special Educational Needs' in Barton, L. (Ed.) *The Politics of Special Educational Needs.* London: The Falmer Press.

Department of Education and Science (1978). *Special Educational Needs* (The Warnock Report). London: HMSO.

Dessent, T. (1987). *Making the Ordinary School Special.* Lewes, Falmer Press.

Dyson, A. (1990). 'Effective learning consultancy: a future role for special needs co-ordinators?' *Support for Learning* 5, 3, 116-127.

Gipps, C., Gross, H. and Goldstein, H. (1987). *Warnock's 18%: Children with Special Needs in Primary School.* Lewes, Falmer Press.

Moses, D., Hegarty, S. and Jowett, S. (1987). *Meeting special educational needs: support for the ordinary school.* Educational Research 29, 2, 108-115.

Payne, T. (1991). 'It's cold in the other room', *Support for Learning* 6, 2, 61-65.

Riddell, S., Duffield, J., Brown, S. and Ogilvy, C. (1992). *Specific Learning Difficulties: Policy, Practice and Provision.* Department of Education, University of Stirling.

Riddell, S., Brown, S. and Duffield, J. (1994). 'Conflicts of policies and models: the case of specific learning difficulties' in Riddell, S. and Brown, S. (Eds.) *Special Educational Needs Policy and Practice in the 1990s: Warnock in the market-place.* London: Routledge, 113-139.

Scottish Education Department (1978). *The Education of pupils with Learning Difficulties in Primary and Secondary Schools in Scotland. A progress Report by HM Inspectors of Schools.* Edinburgh: HMSO.

Scottish Committee for Staff Development in Education (1990). *Award Bearing Courses within the Three Tier Structure: Guidelines for Diplomas in Special Educational Needs.* Edinburgh: SCOSDE.

Scottish Consultative Committee on the Curriculum (1993). *Support for learning: Special Needs within the 5-14 Curriculum.* Dundee: SCCC.

A FRAMEWORK FOR PRACTICE

LINDA CUMMING

INTRODUCTION

In order to meet pupil needs satisfactorily within the area of specific learning difficulties, it is important to focus attention upon aspects other than the most obvious one of the individual child or young person and his immediate learning and teaching requirements. The delivery of a service to such pupils involves not only a system of provision but also good inter-agency liaison, staff development organisation, material resources availability and a willingness to communicate with, and involve, parents at every stage. Somehow, all of these aspects have to amalgamate into a recognisable structure which will profit the pupil, satisfy his parents and which is realistic and manageable for schools and the authority.

Most practices have evolved over time and in response to a variety of stimuli. Most recently, perhaps, the 5-14 Development Programme has emphasised to all working in the field, the importance of pupil access to the normal curriculum and, equally, the requirement in many cases to amend and adapt programmes to suit individual needs. Computer technology, for example, has had a huge impact especially in the area of word processing, and as hardware and software packages become even more sophisticated so teaching approaches and staff training needs continue to change and develop.

STAFF DEVELOPMENT

While formal methods of staff development and information dissemination certainly have a place in the scheme of things, much valuable work is done through on-going contact between learning support, class and subject teachers and staff of Advisory and Psychological Services. Teachers who have experience of pupils with specific learning difficulties will have learned much from case discussions with staff of these services. School staff obtain advice, for example, on appropriate teaching strategies, as well as on materials and professional books which are available either through School Library Services or the Psychological Service if the pupil in question has been referred to that Service. Some Library Services are fortunate in having special needs departments and specialist librarians.

Formal staff development opportunities are usually available to specialist and learning support staff through college-based diploma courses or local in-service. Increasingly though, there is a need to train class and subject teachers in a more structured way, and at a level beyond what might be assimilated if they happen to be working closely with learning support or specialist colleagues. Although planned activity time has decreased of late, some schools will have taken the opportunity to invite local Psychological Service or Advisory staff to give presentations. Equally, if special educational needs in its most general sense is a priority within authorities, then opportunities may present themselves for specific learning difficulties of a dyslexic nature to be on the agenda. Such staff development exercises can only be at the awareness-raising level but if they are backed up by straightforward written information, including definitions and indicators, suggestions for further reading and local authority contacts, then the exercise will have been worthwhile.

There is a need, therefore, for concrete information on identification, further assessment, teaching strategies and resource suggestions to be developed centrally and to be disseminated to class and subject teachers through learning support staff. If there are good links, for example, between staff of the Psychological Service and the Advisory Service, then there are distinct possibilities for collaborative work in this respect. Small working groups, for example, of senior learning support teachers, are another source of expertise to be tapped to the benefit of colleagues.

Staff who have used the many computer programs and packages on the market will be aware of their value as motivators and as alternative methods of recording. In addition to regional in-service opportunities, every school appears to have at least one in-house computer buff who is usually only too eager to help a colleague in (technological) distress!

INTERVENTION PROCEDURE

Pupils may not only encounter difficulties in different areas of the curriculum, they may also show different levels of difficulty. Intervention procedures therefore have to attempt to cater for these factors by trying to ensure that school and specialist personnel are involved at the most appropriate stages.

In order to meet the needs of pupils with learning difficulties, it may be necessary to formalise intervention procedures by trying to ensure that staff at each stage of the identification, assessment and teaching process are aware of their responsibilities and of Authority expectations. These are that class and subject teachers, perhaps in consultation with learning support staff, should be capable of identifying a pupil with specific learning difficulties and that they will, thereafter, become jointly responsible, at a level appropriate to the degree of difficulty encountered, for some form of direct intervention. Further assessment will undoubtedly take place and the learning support teacher will contribute to planning and delivering a programme which takes account of the demands of the 5-14 guidelines.

Experienced learning support staff should feel confident in their assessment of pupil needs, and it may not be necessary to involve either Advisory or Psychological Service or other agencies. If there are serious concerns, schools may have access to Advisory Teachers who may be able to offer suggestions for further work or who may suggest a referral to the Psychological Service. It is very probable, in any case, that the school psychologist will be aware of the pupil through regular consultation with school staff.

Staff should be encouraged also to involve parents in their plans for the pupil and to deal sympathetically with parent concerns.

It can be a source of some concern to professionals that parents are often quite determined in requesting Psychological Service intervention at a stage long before which school and Advisory staff would deem it desirable or even necessary, and during which pupils are, in fact, making good progress. For that reason and, in any case in this more accountable age, authorities may be considering formalising school-based assessment and intervention procedures so that parents know what can be made available within school and what may be necessary in the future by way of specialist provision. Staff, too, can then be aware of their obligations in the process.

SPECIALIST PROVISION

Beyond the in-school procedure, which will certainly have involved class and learning support teachers and may have included parent help, it may be thought necessary to formally involve the Psychological Service.

More specialised provision will vary tremendously among authorities but is possible that if pupils are referred to the Psychological Service, specialist teachers, dealing principally with pupils with specific learning difficulties, will work with individual pupils either directly, or in a staff and resource support role on a long-term basis.

Authorities are now prepared to consider the opening of a Record of Needs for pupils with specific learning difficulties. Additional resources can be made available for pupils with severe difficulties and these often take the form of dictaphones, word processors and other forms of computer technology. In a very few instances, Supervisory Assistants may have been appointed to help support, in their local school, pupils with severe difficulties who require help with organising their workload and with reading texts. They may also tape materials and scribe for the pupil.

CASE STUDIES

Difficulties can and do occur at various stages of the intervention process as this brief case study illustrates. It particularly highlights how slow progress can be when a widely discrepant profile emerges, and how difficult and time consuming it can be for staff to support an anxious parent.

Case Study 1 – Louise

Louise was first assessed by a clinical psychologist when she was seven years old. Her parents had referred her to their GP because of concerns regarding Louise's very slow progress at school and behaviour problems at home, although the school, a very sympathetic one, had already identified difficulties and support was being provided.

She was referred on to the Psychological Service some months later. She had presented as a fairly lively and chatty girl whose pre-school development had been normal. A fine hand tremor was noted but neurological investigation yielded nothing of note. Her performance on BAS sub-tests was very variable – average and above average in some verbal tests and in digit span, but extremely poor in non-verbal sequencing tasks and in construction/jigsaw type activities. A WISC-R gave a similar profile. Overall, Louise's attainments and ability profile were characteristic of a younger child but with some strengths which suggested a specific learning difficulty. Handwriting and drawings were very immature. On the Neale Analysis of Reading Ability her reading skills seemed only mildly delayed but she had little by way of blending skills for spelling.

The school psychologist and specialist teacher made arrangements to meet with the class teacher and learning support teacher to plan a programme. General advice on specific learning difficulties was given to the class teacher. The programme for Louise aimed to improve her reading skills by accessing taped stories and through paired reading, to develop her blending skills through use of a well known structured scheme and tapes, and to increase her self-confidence and reduce anxiety by minimising the level of written work required and by carefully grading her programme of work. Louise's mother agreed to undertake the paired reading at home.

Louise made slow progress and her mother became even more anxious. At age 8, the parents requested that a Record of Needs be opened. Further assessment at this stage yielded a similar pattern to that obtained previously, although her learning and other behaviours were more mature and she displayed less anxiety in the school situation. She was reading at around the seven year level and spelling skills were around the six year level.

In the event, a Record was not opened, as it was judged that support could be adequately provided in the existing setting. Louise received input from the school learning support teacher and the specialist teacher regularly visited on a consultative basis.

Louise is now in P6, a happier and more confident girl who in language work is functioning as a member of a class group, albeit at a level below that of most of her classmates. Although there are difficulties still in following instructions and in comprehension, she is altogether a more organised and more motivated child, though still seeming immature for her years. Reading fluency has improved and she is able to identify and correct her spelling errors.

The learning support teacher, in consultation with the class teacher, organises most of Louise's language work. Her aim is to make Louise and her group more independent by, for example, ensuring that they have been taught simple reference skills. The work programme, though, is still very well organised and structured so that success at each stage is assured. The involvement of the specialist teacher is now minimal.

As important as the progress Louise has made is the fact that her mother recognises that progress, and has come to terms now with the fact that this is, and will continue to be, slow. All the staff concerned have worked hard, not just in terms of planning and teaching and evaluating Louise's progress but also in supporting an occasionally very demanding parent.

Case Study 2 – Ewen

This case study illustrates a fairly common pattern among pupils with specific learning difficulties and is an example of a successful in-school intervention programme.

Ewen's difficulties, particularly in written work, had been for some time the subject of discussion between his mother and staff of his small, rural school. The school found Ewen to be a likeable, lively and enthusiastic pupil whose performance in maths was satisfactory, whose oral reading had taken some time to develop and was still not considered to be fluent, and whose spelling and written work were felt to be 'careless' and 'slapdash'. His oral reading was still hesitant but he was able to gain meaning from what he read. The school felt that the parents' hectic lifestyle was somewhat responsible for Ewen's poor reading performance in that there had not been sufficient practice at home and promises to help with homework tasks were often not fulfilled.

The school had a small amount of learning support input per week but this had always been targeted at two pupils with poor overall attainments.

The Headteacher contacted the Advisory Service with a view to helping to assess Ewen's difficulties. The learning support teacher had already carried out standardised tests as follows:

Chronological Age:		7 years 9 months
Neale Analysis of Reading Ability (old version)	Accuracy	7 years 8 months
	Comprehension	8 years 4 months
Schonell Graded Word Spelling		7 years 0 months

An informal assessment of Ewen's written work showed that he wrote the minimum possible when required to do functional or creative writing tasks even on topics which he enjoyed, and that he displayed a tendency to spell unknown words phonetically. He was right-handed and most letters were correctly formed although his handwriting was not neat. A check of phonic skills showed Ewen to be competent at blending simple three and four letter words but having great difficulty with vowel diagraphs and common irregular words.

A meeting with his mother confirmed that there had been no concerns regarding early development and that Ewen enjoyed good health. His mother was concerned that Ewen might be dyslexic because of a family history of learning difficulties.

The learning support teacher, having had an opportunity to observe and work with Ewen, was now well aware of the discrepancies between his performance in reading and writing tasks and his apparently well-developed verbal skills and competence in maths. It was agreed that she would work with Ewen for two short spells during the morning she was at the school, one to work on re-drafting a piece of the previous week's writing and to prepare the spelling tasks for the week ahead, and the other to work on reading.

A structured spelling programme was used and, in addition, personal words required for writing were written on small cards to be studied using the look, cover, write and check approach. These were to be kept in an envelope while being learned and transferred to another once mastered. It was hoped that this approach would boost Ewen's confidence in spelling and, moreover, could be checked by a class-mate if necessary. He was encouraged to increase his writing output gradually, and his teacher encouraged not to correct every misspelling, but to select only a few words per week for further study. Computer games were used to reinforce spelling tasks and Ewen was able to use the word processing facility on occasion to type up particularly good pieces of writing.

Some in-service work on spelling difficulties was done with staff since it was felt that other pupils might benefit from a more structured approach in this area.

Ewen remained on the same reading scheme, but decoding skills were practised using games. Oral and written activities designed to improve his use of context cues were also used.

Ewen was brought to the notice of the school psychologist and it was decided that a referral was not necessary at this point. His parents agreed to assist with spelling work at home. This input was somewhat erratic but nonetheless, even in a few months, Ewen was showing improvements. He was responding to the attention of the learning support teacher and to a carefully structured programme continued by his class teacher. It should be possible, given parental support for the programme in hand, for Ewen to continue to make gains.

CONCLUSION

Although Louise and Ewen presented as two very different children in terms of their assessment profiles and learning styles, they were both considered to have specific learning difficulties. Both benefited from very structured programmes which focused on those difficulties while taking account of curricular and personal strengths. The strategies and resources used differed according to need and much thought was given to those which would boost their confidence in tackling particular areas of the curriculum.

Consideration was given to planning within the framework of the 5-14 Development Programme, making justifiable amendments and adaptations as required.

Both general and specific advice was given to staff and parents, and the help of the latter was solicited in both cases.

Specific learning difficulties continue to enjoy much media attention. While this is the case school and local authority staff will sometimes have difficulties convincing parents of the worth of their recommendations. Only continuing support and staff development will ensure that all staff have the confidence to assure parents that their children's needs are in fact being met. Good local authority links with a local branch of the Dyslexia Association can be helpful in this respect, as the Association can give information to parents and, most importantly, can encourage parent/school discussion of the difficulties.

*   The views in this chapter are the author's and do not necessarily represent those of Central Region Education Authority.

PARENTS' PERSPECTIVES

SHEILA AIRTH AND
GILLIAN THOMSON MBE

The first part of this chapter will attempt to encompass the points of view from a selection of parents throughout Scotland who have a child or children with dyslexic problems.

These parental opinions have been collected as a result of a survey (Roxburgh, 1995) conducted on behalf of the Scottish Dyslexia Association.

Recent research (Riddell, Duffield, Brown and Ogilvy, 1992) shows that parents are usually the first to notice the delay in their child's ability to learn the skills in literacy or numeracy. However, parents consider this to be the responsibility of the educationist, whom they regard as the expert in this field.

This chapter will cover the areas causing parents anxiety, frustration, stress and strain often leading to similar symptoms occurring in their dyslexic child.

Considerations such as early identification, communications, and the art of 'listening' are given as examples to improve relationships between 'the family' and 'the school'.

The main recognition for help lies in the requirement for teacher training in dyslexia. Parents feel that until the classroom teacher gains knowledge of dyslexia and the learning support teacher gains specific expertise, the one cannot support the other to produce the most effective result for the child.

The second part of this chapter is devoted to 'teaching tactics', with special attention to the parents' requests for help. Priority 'pleas' concern help in the primary and secondary classroom and appropriate support within the home. Preparation for 'life after school' and the future for the dyslexic pupil is also important.

PARENTS PAIN

Roxburgh's study (1995) shows that parents become exasperated by communication problems with schools and an apparent reluctance to diagnose dyslexia. This, as the comments below show, can result in parents becoming anxious, frustrated and stressed.

"My son was not given a test. I went to the school on numerous occasions and asked that he be tested for dyslexia."

"I have an 11 year old boy whose school is trying to be helpful but resources and time are limited. The boy is struggling but is proud at school and cries a great deal at home."

"Once my son's dyslexia was recognised it took over a year to really get things moving. I think teachers could be more aware of signs that point to dyslexia enabling earlier diagnosis."

"Now that our son is at secondary school and has many different teachers, it is much more difficult for us to assess his progress or even to find out exactly what help he receives."

This survey appeared to confirm the results of an earlier research study (Riddell *et al.* 1992) which stated that 'parents dissatisfaction focused on inadequate tuition, lack of recognition of the child's learning difficulties and lack of expertise among teachers.'

Some comments made by parents in the Roxburgh (1995) study which confirm these earlier findings include the following:

"Class teachers don't seem to be able to recognise the dyslexic child. More training is needed to help them."

"All class teachers should attend a compulsory course in the recognition and teaching of dyslexic children."

One parent suggested that:

*"A structured means of communication and support should be made available to parents. A structured programme should be initiated as soon as these children are identified, which parents should be informed of. Biggest challenges are not knowing what to **expect** in the way of learning support for your child*

*now and in the **future** and what **ought** to be done in order to secure **future** learning support. Often this leads to feelings of isolation and insecurity re child's **future**."*

In summarising the parent's opinions expressed in the Roxburgh study, it is clear that on the whole, parents are the first source of information concerning their child's development. Ostensibly, they are the people who know their child best. Parents recognise when a child has difficulties at school. This is most likely to be the onset of emotional inadequacies in how to deal with the situation at home. Some parents are aware of the signs and symptoms shown in dyslexic children. But for most the lack of knowledge and understanding is a great disadvantage to them. Once the parents know the causes of dyslexic problems, and that specific help can alleviate these problems, the load of worry, frustration, stress and strain is lifted from their mind. This will help parents to obtain a positive attitude and willingness to 'help at home' and to gain an understanding of dyslexia. This will be greatly enhanced through effective communication between home and school. The link of communication provides for mutual co-operation and the parents can become the 'teacher's best friend'. Parents recognise that supportive help is essential in the classroom. They need to be reassured that their child is being dealt with sensitively.

'Teaching tactics', the second part of this chapter, deals with the anxieties experienced by parents who need to know that their child is receiving the positive help that only an enlightened and understanding teacher can give.

THE PARENTS' SIDE OF THE COIN

Most parents who have brought up a dyslexic child could write a book on the parents' point of view. However, as this is only a small section of what will be a comprehensive book for teachers it must, be as clear and concise as possible.

Probably the saddest aspect of all is listening to the heartfelt pleas for help from parents, especially mothers, who are not being invited by school staff to work together to help the dyslexic youngster.

Making the most of the child's natural abilities and the resources available both at home and in school requires an understanding of the many facets of dyslexia and how it affects the learning process.

Most dyslexic people have a thirst for knowledge which cannot be satisfied by conventional methods of education and it must be recognised that these are the pupils who must be taught the way **they** can learn.

Two of the areas in which these children lack ability are in sequencing and short-term memory. This means that they will have difficulty both in remembering certain information and in putting it together in the correct order. They may therefore find it hard to make little skills into big ones. Despite this, often they will have no difficulty understanding and retaining certain very advanced information.

GROWING UP NOT BRINGING UP

There is not an education system in the world that fully prepares parents in the skills of bringing up their children. Each stage brings its own surprises and challenges and this is especially true for the parents of dyslexic children. Apart from the toddlers who have obvious difficulties before starting school, most five year olds set out joyfully on their new adventure, waved away by proud, optimistic mums and dads who have high hopes for their young charges. Sadly, for some, these hopes are dashed before very long as they watch a bright and happy toddler turn into a sad, frustrated boy or girl. In many cases, these children have been as good if not better than their peers in many of the pre-school activities in which they have been involved and parents begin to wonder why such obvious change for the worse has taken place.

Relatively few Primary 1 and 2 teachers are trained to recognise dyslexia so most of these pupils drift through the first years of school becoming less successful and consequently lose most of their self-esteem. These children drag their unhappiness and dislike of school home with the same sort of air that others drag a school bag full of difficult homework

Much soul-searching and often recriminations go on at home into the reasons for the child's behaviour and lack of achievement. Whose fault is it? Perhaps it is because there's a new baby, a family quarrel, bereavement, single parent, immature, dreamer or hyperactivity. Many explanations are put forward for the lack of progress but all too seldom is it recognised that the solution lies in understanding how each child learns and then teaching him in that way.

What is life like with a dyslexic child at home?

Often it is a constant struggle to get him (#) through the routine of the day. With his penchant for poor sequencing, patchy concentration and inability to forward plan, the time between getting out of bed and out to school is a minefield of obstacles which creates all sorts of mayhem for those trying to play 'happy families'.

Add to this the monumental task of persuading the hapless offspring that school is good for him and it becomes obvious that the mothers (and fathers) who succeed in getting their child to school each day deserve a medal.

If their child is apparently under-achieving at school, parents usually assume that it is their responsibility to help him 'catch up' at home. This means that instead of looking forward to a relaxed and happy time between school and bed, the child knows that it's going to be 'more of the same' with instructions to spell, read or write as best he can. Sadly his 'best' is rarely recognised as such and he may get very little credit for the effort he has made.

Homework sessions can be horrific and can often last from 4 o'clock until bedtime, destroying any potential quality time the family might have hoped for.

It is of the utmost importance that agreement is reached between school staff and parents on an acceptable time tor homework and that the time for favourite hobbies and TV programmes is sacrosanct.

One of the most difficult situations that parents can find themselves in is when the 'hunches' they feel become strong enough to do something about. Courage is plucked up to speak to the teacher about their concerns. In such a discussion, some reasons for his difficulty may include the following:

- He is just immature.
- He will catch up when he is ten.
- He can read so he cannot be dyslexic.
- He is just lazy, not interested.

Valuable time may be lost while the parents go off home and spend a very worrying time wondering if there is something seriously wrong with their judgement or with the child's health. Their next option is to turn for help and support to someone outside school. This can come from well intentioned, but possibly ill-informed relatives and friends, or from voluntary organisations, the members of which are not always highly qualified professionally, but have knowledge and understanding of the parents' needs, which can be an invaluable source of help.

This is an extremely anxious time for parents, and teachers can prevent situations like this from developing by sharing their concerns and working together to find a formula that is right for the child.

HELP IN SCHOOL

Parents wish that there could be specialist teachers, trained to recognise and teach dyslexic pupils in every school and that unlimited funds were available for whatever extra help was required, but are realistic enough to know this is not possible.

However there are plenty of inexpensive ways in which a dyslexic child can be helped.

The following suggestions should help the dyslexic child both in the classroom and at home.

- Instructions must be short. Pitch them at his understanding, not yours.

- Let him use fat pencils and/or grips. Mark on the page where to start. Lined paper may help; coloured paper (e.g. cream) might be better than white. Experiment with coloured plastic overlays (different colours are available from office supply shops).

- Discuss what the dyslexic child sees when he tries to read. Does the print jump about, slide off the page etc. Often he will miss out the first syllable in longer words, is this because he does not see it?

- Copying from a book is very difficult as he often cannot remember what has to be written as he concentrates so hard on remembering how the letters are shaped and their order in the words. Copying from the blackboard is almost impossible.

- Avoid a potentially fraught situation by giving him the information another way e.g. photocopied notes or orally. He may learn quite well by listening.

- Spelling is never consistent so do not ask for mistakes to be written out several times. Each word will probably be spelt differently. Highlight errors with a green pen not a red one.

- Let him miss out on reading aloud as this can be a nightmare. Often these children enjoy the world of books and the spoken word so read to them and give them access to talking books.

- Dyslexic children should have the opportunity to master keyboard skills.

- Tape recorders are useful for dictated homework. Essential information can be put on tape e.g. tables, maths definitions, chemical formulae, foreign languages. At secondary school level, text-book summaries can be taped along with key words from each chapter.

- If it is possible to give a pupil his own textbook then important parts of it can be highlighted.

- As these youngsters are often very astute, observant, resourceful and imaginative, their ideas and opinions should be listened to and taken into consideration when deciding what action is necessary.

- Where scribing is recommended, time should be allowed for both the pupil and the scribe to practise with each other.

Prior to moving to and the first day at Secondary School

- Check that records have been received from the Primary School.

- Ensure that all subject teachers know of any difficulties and previous recommendations of help.

- Make sure that the youngster knows to whom and where he should go if he needs help.

- Have printed copy of the timetable and arrange for the class teachers to have their names, subject and classroom numbers printed on workbooks and jotters. This will avoid the dreaded situation of possibly having to copy from the blackboard as soon as the pupil is in the door.

- Arrange for photocopied notes if necessary.

What advice can a teacher give to parents at home?

- Encourage chat and make a real effort to listen and HEAR what their offspring have to say.

- Allow time for the development of natural talents.

Observations by dyslexic youngsters who have completed their school career.

- Teachers' attitudes are as important as their qualifications.

- It is essential that the Head-Teacher is enlightened.

- The best teacher was the one who wanted to help and went about it in the correct way.

- The next best was the department which was keen to help but was not sure how best to do so.

PARENTS' ASSOCIATIONS

Parents may find it of help to know of organisations connected with dyslexia to whom they could go for assistance.

The Dyslexia Association was born out of the need by parents for support and information. It is over 25 years since the first branch was established and there are now well over 1,000 members throughout Scotland.

A very high percentage of enquiries are from parents who find that their children are either getting no help at all, or are getting help that is completely inadequate for their needs.

Voluntary Dyslexia Associations in Scotland may offer a variety of services ranging from:

- Meetings at which there are opportunities to talk and exchange views between families with dyslexic children.
- The offer of information and advice on a number of topics.
- Open meetings and conferences to hear speakers on the subject of dyslexia.
- Some Associations may also provide private psychological assessment and specific tutoring.

Teachers must look upon the use of outside agencies such as these organisations as a help and an added support to the child and encourage co-operation between themselves, the school and the family.

It must be realised that 'dyslexia' should not be used as an 'excuse' for not doing homework, for not trying at work, or for poor work.

In conclusion it is hoped that the views expressed by parents together with the suggestions in this chapter will help to heighten awareness amongst teachers of the very real needs of dyslexic pupils and their parents.

(#) 'Him' is used to refer to 'him' or 'her'.

REFERENCES

Roxburgh, I. (1995). *Parents' Perceptions*, unpublished study, Scottish Dyslexia Association.
Riddell, S., Duffield, J., Brown, S. and Ogilvy, C. (1992). *Specific Learning Difficulties (Dyslexia) Policy, Practice and Provision*. Scottish Office Education Department.

USEFUL ADDRESSES

The Scottish Dyslexia Association has now established a national head office.

Unit 3,
Stirling business Centre,
Wellgreen,
Stirling,
FK8 2DZ.
Tel: 01786 446650.

Calibre (Talking Books),
Aylesbury, Buckinghamshire.
HP20 1HU.
Tel: 01296 - 432339

Mr Peter Wilkes,
"Better Books & Software",
3 Paganel Drive,
DUDLEY,
DYl 4AZ

Mr Roy Hardman, SEN (Marketing)
9 The Close,
Church Aston,
NEWPORT,
TFl 0 9JL

The Scottish Council for Educational Technology,
Mr. Tom Nisbet, Co-ordinator,
74 Victoria Crescent Road,
GLASGOW, G12 9JN.

CONTRADICTORY MODELS: THE DILEMMA OF SPECIFIC LEARNING DIFFICULTIES

ALAN DYSON and DAVID SKIDMORE

MODELS AND CHANGE IN SPECIAL NEEDS EDUCATION

It is tempting to regard the history of special needs provision in mainstream schools as one of unequivocal and unidirectional progress towards more effective teaching and more enlightened attitudes. As schools and teachers become more sophisticated, we suppose, so outdated segregatory approaches are replaced by powerful integrationist techniques which enable pupils with special needs to learn effectively within a common curriculum and alongside their peers in ordinary classrooms.

There may be, however, an alternative interpretation of history which is less committed to explanations in terms of 'progress'. Such an interpretation would see change in special needs provision as the successive hegemony of a series of *models* of provision. These models can be understood as having a *technological* aspect; that is, they take the form of strategies and techniques for intervening in children's learning and organising educational provision. However, they also have an *assumptional* aspect: that is, they are structured around sets of assumptions about the nature of learning, the nature of children's difficulties in learning, the aims of intervention and so on. To this extent, models of special needs provision can be seen as analogous to (though clearly on a smaller historical scale than) the paradigms which Kuhn (1970) suggests dominate the practice of natural science.

Changes in special needs provision, therefore, can be understood as changes in the models of provision. In other words, they are not simply changes in technology (brought about, perhaps, by increasing sophistication), but changes in both technology and assumptions. As models succeed each other, they do not so much achieve similar aims in increasingly more effective ways, as set about addressing very different aims based on different assumptions with different technologies. Whether one model constitutes 'progress' *vis a vis* its predecessors, therefore, depends on some assessment of its foundational assumptions. It is a question, ultimately, of values.

Looking at the development of special needs education in ordinary schools from this perspective, the seminal 1978 HMI progress report (SED, 1978) marks a transition in the Scottish education system from one such model of special needs provision to another. In the 1970s, provision in mainstream schools was, as the report makes clear, dominated by a remedial model. Based on a predominantly psychological perspective (Tomlinson, 1982), this model saw children who were experiencing difficulties at school as suffering from particular weaknesses in cognitive functioning. However, although these weaknesses might form part of an overall intellectual limitation, they could nonetheless be diagnosed and, to a greater or lesser extent, remedied. In particular, a good deal of work went into the diagnosis and remediation of difficulties in reading (e.g. Tansley, 1967), since there appears to have been an unspoken assumption that reading was the key both to the curriculum and also to later effective functioning in adulthood. Not surprisingly, therefore, HMI found special needs provision dominated by the 'remedial' teaching of reading in a situation which constituted both locational withdrawal from the classroom and educational withdrawal from the curriculum offered to the majority of children.

The alternative model which HMI proposed was to go on – in the form of 'Learning Support' or the 'whole-school approach' (Dessent, 1987) – to dominate special needs provision in mainstream schools for well over a decade and still forms the basis of much official guidance offered to schools (SOED, 1994). It is not enough, HMI argued, to address children's difficulties in reading through specialist interventions delivered by specialist teachers. Children who have such difficulties are likely to have difficulties right across the curriculum which may be related to their inability to manage the linguistic and conceptual content of the curriculum as much as to any particular problems with reading. What they need, therefore, are forms of teaching that respond to their needs right across the curriculum – 'appropriate, rather than remedial education' (p.31) as HMI put it. 'Appropriate education' thus becomes 'a responsibility of the whole school, whether remedial staff are employed or not' (p.22), and the proper role of special needs specialists includes supporting both children in the mainstream curriculum and their teachers in the development of appropriate styles of curriculum delivery.

Although space does not permit a fuller explication and critique of this 'new' model, it is important to note some of the assumptions which underpin the HMI progress report:

- Children who have learning difficulties are assumed to have difficulties right across the curriculum; HMI argue explicitly against a 'narrow' conception of remedial education as being solely about addressing difficulties that are *specific* to the area of reading.

- Access to a broad curriculum is assumed to be a major educational aim; schools are explicitly warned against withdrawing children from areas of the curriculum where they might experience success in order to 'remediate' their difficulties. This characteristic of learning support and the whole-school approach, of course, has latterly been much reinforced by the advent of a curriculum framework viewed as an entitlement for all pupils.

- 'Appropriate' teaching for children with learning difficulties is assumed to be something of which all teachers are and should be capable, albeit with advice and support from specialists. It is, therefore, implicitly (though this has subsequently often been made explicit) assumed to be a subset of 'good' teaching for all children.

It is these assumptions and the hegemony which the HMI model has exercised over special needs provision in mainstream schools which forms the context for the emergence in recent years of specific learning difficulties as a rapidly expanding form of special need. It is salutary, therefore, to set alongside the HMI progress report this definition of dyslexia:

> *"Dyslexia can be defined as a specific difficulty in learning, constitutional in origin, in one or more areas of reading, spelling and written language, which may be accompanied by difficulty in number work. It is particularly related to mastering and using written language (alphabetic, numerical and musical notation) although often affecting oral language to some degree."*

> (Crisfield & Smythe, 1993, p.8)

or this definition of specific learning difficulties:

> *"Specific Learning Difficulties can be identified as distinctive patterns of difficulties relating to the processing of information, within a continuum from very mild to severe, which result in restrictions in literacy development and discrepancies in performances within the curriculum."*

> (Reid, 1994, p.3)

It is immediately apparent that we are dealing here with a set of assumptions which are significantly different from those which informed the HMI progress report. Specific learning difficulties are assumed to be just that – specific to certain areas of functioning, and most definitely not generalised across the whole curriculum. In particular, problems in reading are assumed to constitute the most significant of these difficulties rather than being one set of difficulties amongst many. 'Appropriate' teaching, therefore – at least if that means adapting the *conceptual* content of the curriculum – is unlikely to be quite so appropriate for children whose difficulties lie not in handling conceptual complexity but in information and language processing.

Given these assumptions, it is scarcely surprising that the forms of provision which are frequently advocated for children with specific learning difficulties sit somewhat uneasily with the orthodoxies of learning support and the whole-school approach. The literature on specific learning difficulties is full of recommendations for teaching programmes and approaches. However, these programmes frequently take the form of individualised interventions which are aimed at children's supposed 'underlying' difficulties, and which, therefore, as Reid puts it, 'cannot naturally and easily be accommodated within the school curriculum and the mainstream class' (Reid, 1994) p. 91). Indeed, some of these interventions are not, strictly speaking, educational at all, but more properly belong to the world of para-medical therapies (e.g. Dennison & Hargrove, 1985; Stone & Harris, 1991). Not surprisingly, many programmes, therefore, cannot be delivered by class and subject teachers with only minimal levels of support. Instead, they demand specialist teachers who are trained not merely in special needs generally, but in specific learning difficulties as such – which is why, of course, some specific learning difficulties organisations feel it is essential to deliver or accredit their own training courses for teachers.

In other words, what we are faced with is a 'model' of specific learning difficulties provision which differs in terms both of its assumptions and its technology from the 'model' of learning support and the whole-school approach. This inevitably faces schools with a dilemma: on the one hand, they are, by and large, committed to an approach to learning support which has been powerfully advocated at national level, and which appears to have important benefits for children with 'general' learning difficulties. On the other hand, there is growing pressure for them to adopt a somewhat different approach which is claimed to be more effective for children with specific learning difficulties, but which does not sit easily with their established learning support provision. This dilemma, we suggest, gives rise to three specific issues with which schools are faced:

- How should they reconcile their existing commitment to curriculum access and development as a major strategy for meeting special needs with the requirement for extra-curricular interventions which specific learning difficulties seem to carry ?

- How should learning support teachers reconcile their existing commitment to collaborative teaching and consultation with mainstream colleagues with the 'new' demand that they become trained specific learning difficulties specialists working directly with individual pupils ?

- How should schools manage their limited resources equitably so that they are able to meet the needs of both an established population of pupils with 'general' learning difficulties and an apparently growing population of pupils with 'specific' learning difficulties for whom individualised, extra-curricular and specialist provision may prove relatively costly in resource terms ?

These issues are made more complex for schools by the nature of the existing literature and guidance on specific learning difficulties. The emphasis within learning support on issues of mainstream pedagogy and curriculum development and on questions of school organisation has produced for schools a substantial literature which is of immediate use to head and principal teachers in the management of provision. However, the model underpinning specific learning difficulties provision focuses much more on questions of assessment, diagnosis and individual intervention. It has, therefore, relatively little to say on how provision within mainstream schools might be organised and managed. Pumfrey and Reason's (1991) comprehensive review of research, for instance, contains only one brief chapter on the management of provision, and that confines itself to a rehearsal of standard learning support strategies. Although, therefore, a few accounts are now beginning to appear of how schools are organising themselves to respond to specific learning difficulties (Brown, 1993; Lewis, 1995), there is a substantial gap in the literature which leaves schools somewhat bereft of guidance.

A MODEL FOR SPECIFIC LEARNING DIFFICULTIES PROVISION

It is in the light of this perceived gap that the Special Needs Research Group in the Department of Education, University of Newcastle upon Tyne, has been undertaking a series of linked studies of emerging forms of provision in secondary schools. Principal amongst these has been a study, sponsored by the Scottish Office Education Department, of provision in 27 schools across 5 Regions in Scotland (Dyson & Skidmore, 1994). In parallel with this was a smaller study of 14 schools in England. Finally, there have been two studies sponsored by English LEAs : in a study sponsored by Cleveland LEA, four schools took part in a cost-benefit analysis of their specific learning difficulties provision (Dyson, 1995); and a survey of provision in all the middle and high schools in a further English LEA (Dyson & Wood, 1994). The schools included in these studies do not constitute a nationally representative sample (in either Scotland or England); indeed, in all but the LEA-wide survey, schools were selected precisely because of their unusually well-developed approaches to specific learning difficulties. Nonetheless, we believe that these studies together allow us to describe secondary schools' emerging responses to specific learning difficulties with far greater confidence than has hitherto been possible. They also, we suggest, usefully complement the important study undertaken by Sheila Riddell and colleagues at the University of Stirling (Riddell, Duffield, Brown, & Ogilvy, 1992).

Rather than setting out the findings of each study in detail, what we propose to do is to describe a common model which we believe underpins provision across many of the schools we investigated. This model is like other models of special needs provision outlined in the preceding section in that it comprises both technological and assumptional components. Like those models too, its implementation in detail varies considerably from school to school and the assumptions upon which it is based are not necessarily made explicit by the schools. In other words, it is a model which can be *inferred* from schools' practice and teachers' accounts of that practice, rather than an explicit blueprint upon which those schools have deliberately sought to build their provision. Nonetheless, it does offer a means of accounting for the forms of provision we found as rational responses to specific learning difficulties and it therefore offers other schools a means of reviewing and developing their own provision in some rational manner. The model is represented diagrammatically in figure 1.

The model comprises three levels which link its assumptional and technological components. It is founded upon a distinctive *conceptualisation* of specific learning difficulties which is somewhat different from that frequently found in the literature. This gives rise to a *rationale* for the school's response to specific learning difficulties, and it is around this that the detailed features of *provision* are organised.

Fig. 1

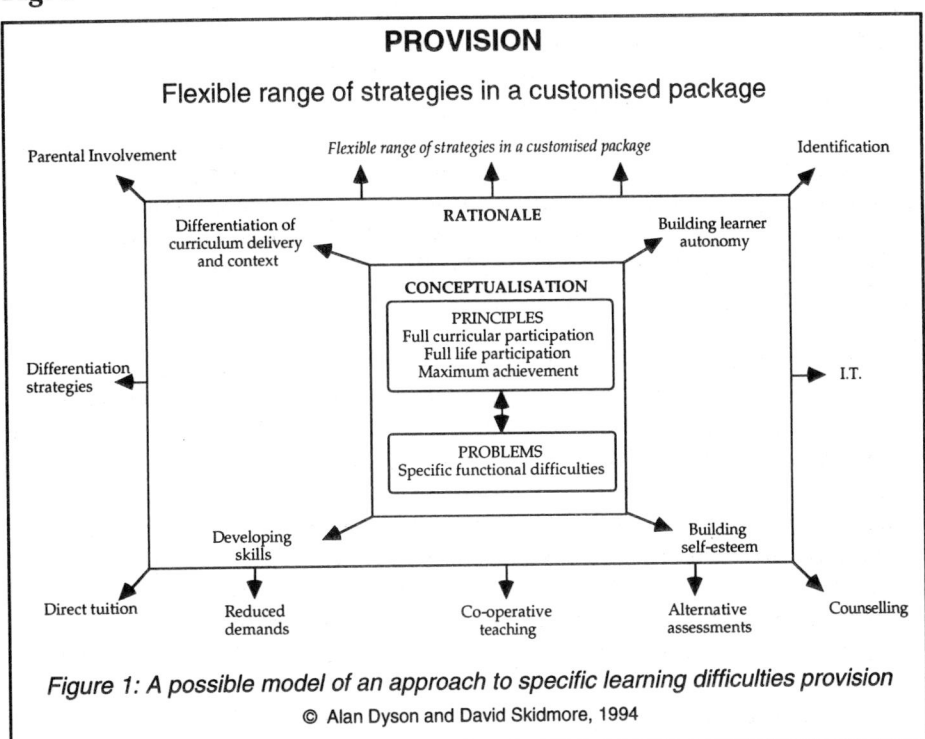

PROVISION

Flexible range of strategies in a customised package

Parental Involvement   *Flexible range of strategies in a customised package*   Identification

Differentiation of curriculum delivery and context   **RATIONALE**   Building learner autonomy

CONCEPTUALISATION

PRINCIPLES
Full curricular participation
Full life participation
Maximum achievement

PROBLEMS
Specific functional difficulties

Differentiation strategies   I.T.

Developing skills   Building self-esteem

Direct tuition   Reduced demands   Co-operative teaching   Alternative assessments   Counselling

Figure 1: A possible model of an approach to specific learning difficulties provision
© Alan Dyson and David Skidmore, 1994

CONCEPTUALISATION

Within the current literature, as we have seen, specific learning difficulties tend to be conceptualised from a psychological or psycho-medical perspective, in terms of information-processing deficits or phonological or other linguistic weaknesses. Within this model, however, specific learning difficulties are conceptualised much more as a series of *functional* problems which prevent the realisation of certain educational and social entitlements. Children are seen as entitled to participate in a common curriculum, to experience educational achievement and ultimately to enjoy a fulfilling adult life. Some of them have weaknesses in specific areas of functioning which threaten their social and educational entitlements. 'In other words,' as one school put it, 'there is a discrepancy between what a pupil can do and understand and what he/she can show he/she can do and understand.' In such a situation, the aetiology and diagnosis of those weaknesses are seen as less important than their impact on participation and achievement.

RATIONALE

This conceptualisation leads directly to the rationale upon which provision is based. So long as the focus is on the aetiology of children's weaknesses, then provision is likely to be concerned with the remediation or amelioration of those weaknesses – as is the case with many of the programmes advocated in the specific learning difficulties literature. However, if specific learning difficulties are conceptualised in terms of threats to educational and social entitlements, then the rationale for provision is likely to be the *delivery* of those entitlements.

NB

The following are typical of the sorts of rationales which the schools we studied were able to provide for their provision:

> Our rationale is: to provide access to the mainstream curriculum; improvement in basic skills; appropriate means of circumventing specific learning difficulties in order to enable pupils to achieve their maximum potential and, where appropriate, access to further and higher education; and to raise self-esteem and confidence.

Or again:

> We hope that pupils are able to show what they are capable of, despite their specific difficulties. We hope to give them a range of coping strategies and a sense that they are valued as individuals, and can achieve without undue frustration. We want them to take full part in the life and work of the class and the school.

These rationales, in common with many others, de-emphasise the notions of diagnosis, intervention and remediation in favour of notions of circumvention, coping, participation and achievement. In particular, they indicate four broad aims which provision should fulfil:

- **Differentiation.** If pupils are to participate in a common curriculum despite their functional difficulties, then that curriculum has to be delivered in ways which are differentiated to take account of those difficulties.

- **Building self-esteem.** If pupils are to achieve their potential in education and beyond, they need to see and value themselves as potential learners and potential achievers. They should be helped, therefore, to move beyond the negative views of themselves which an exclusive focus on their difficulties might create.

- **Building learner autonomy.** If pupils are to participate in a common curriculum without massive (and ultimately disabling) levels of support, then they need to learn how to function autonomously, drawing on their strengths and circumventing their weaknesses.

- **Developing skills.** If pupils are weak in certain skill areas, then some attempt might be made to address those weaknesses directly. However, such attempts have to take place alongside the three other aims of provision, and therefore do not form the basis for a full-blown return to 'remedial' education.

These four aims constitute a synthesis of 'established' and 'novel' approaches characteristic of the schools in our studies. The notion of differentiation (as opposed, perhaps, to its practice) is 'established' in that it has been at the centre of the whole-school approach. Similarly, the aim of skills-development has an even longer history in remedial education, and appears to be enjoying something of a revival within schools' approaches to specific learning difficulties. Building autonomy and building self-esteem, on the other hand, mark a crucial boundary between rationales for specific learning difficulties provision and those for learning support. The latter has historically been concerned with generalised difficulties and has often tended to focus on devising and delivering what our respondents called a 'restricted' or 'reduced and/or adapted' curriculum. This is probably still the case, even where the notion of 'curriculum adaptation' has been replaced by the rhetoric of 'differentiation' (Hart, 1992; Thompson & Barton, 1992). However, such restriction is not viewed as necessary for children who have significant strengths to offset their weaknesses, and therefore, in the words of one learning support teacher:

"Children with specific learning difficulties are given access to the full curriculum."

Given this approach, it is essential that such children are able to capitalise on their strengths and circumvent their weaknesses. It follows that the building of autonomy and self-esteem are not the desirable – but optional – extras they may perhaps have been in Learning Support, but are absolutely central to effective responses to specific learning difficulties.

PROVISION

This four-fold rationale directly informs provision in the schools in our samples. Given what we said in the preceding section about the synthesis of established and novel approaches within schools' rationales, it is significant that many of the forms of provision which schools are using are drawn from the repertoire of learning support. Many schools are happy to base their provision on the established role of the learning support teacher and to draw on standard techniques of assessment, co-operative teaching, the production of differentiated materials and so on. However, specific learning difficulties provision appears in our model as distinctive in three particular respects:

Eclecticism

Because the aim of provision is to enable the child to function effectively in the full curriculum, schools tend to draw on anything which might be helpful in this respect. As one teacher put it, 'We try anything !' Standard learning support techniques are, as we have indicated, prominent; however, other, more distinctive forms of provision are also in evidence: some of the psycho-medical interventions advocated in the specific learning difficulties literature; programmes of counselling as means of developing pupils' self-esteem; programmes of thinking skills and problem-solving, aimed at developing learner autonomy; the provision of lap top computers, spell-checkers and other IT aids for the same purpose; and so on.

Pragmatism

Significantly, in a field which is frequently characterised by ideological conflict, learning support teachers in our studies tend to select the particular techniques and forms of provision they wish to use on a pragmatic basis. They are, in the words of one Learning Support teacher, 'Not greatly impressed by theories.' The criterion for using a particular technique, therefore, is not whether it conforms to some theory about the aetiology and treatment of specific learning difficulties as such, but whether it is of immediate use in enabling a particular child to function effectively in the curriculum.

An example of this fundamental pragmatism can be seen in the attitude which many teachers take towards the issue of withdrawing pupils from ordinary lessons. Withdrawal is, in many ways, the battle ground between the older remedial approach to special needs provision, with its emphasis on tackling pupils' areas of weakness directly, and the newer Learning Support approach, with its emphasis on access to a differentiated curriculum. By and large, the teachers who responded to us subscribe to neither of these positions, seeing withdrawal as simply one more technique which might – or might not, depending on individual circumstances – be helpful in furthering the aim of effective functioning in the full curriculum. One respondent summarised the paradox in this way:

"Pupils have an entitlement to access the curriculum but they do not have to be physically in the classroom at all times."

Or, as another teacher put it:

"It all depends on the balance of advantage for the child."

Customisation

This pragmatic tendency directly informs a highly individualised approach to the structuring of provision for particular pupils. Learning support has, of course, traditionally stressed individualisation at the level of access to the curriculum. However, the strategies it has relied upon to achieve this (differentiation, co-operative teaching, curriculum adaptation and so on) have – by dint of the numbers of pupils involved – tended to be applied in much the same way to all. However, the strategies for specific learning difficulties provision tend much more to be assembled into customised packages for particular pupils. 'We wouldn't,' one teacher explained, 'do the same thing with two pupils.'

Moreover, a significant consideration in assembling these packages is the child's own wishes; if a pupil is happy to use a lap-top, for instance, s/he is given one, but if s/he feels out of place using one in class, then the lap-top is withdrawn. In other words, provision is determined not simply by what the child is believed to 'need' but also by what s/he wants.

A MODEL FOR RECONCILIATION?

We suggested earlier that the dominant model of specific learning difficulties stands in contradiction to the model which informs learning support and the whole school approach. Moreover, the emergence of specific learning difficulties as an issue faces schools with three crucial dilemmas : how to reconcile the aim of curriculum access with the need for extra-curricular interventions; how to reconcile a collaborative teaching role with a more specialist role; and how to manage limited resources equitably across different groups of children with special needs. It is important to determine, therefore, the extent to which the model we have described as emerging in schools actually resolves these issues.

We believe there is an important sense in which this model does offer some way out of the dilemmas which schools face. By reconceptualising specific learning difficulties in terms of curriculum access rather than psycho-medical deficits, it offers a way to connect schools' approaches to specific learning difficulties with their wider educational concerns, particularly in respect of pupils with other forms of special need. Hence, strategies drawn from the specific learning difficulties literature – individual extra-curricular programmes, intervention by specialist teachers, and so on – find a place as part of a wide range of strategies whose ultimate aim is to enable pupils to function within the curriculum. The *ideological* conflict which has beset specific learning difficulties provision is thus resolved at the level of *pragmatic* decisions about means of ensuring access and achievement for particular children.

The model also goes some way towards resolving resourcing dilemmas. In the first place, it draws heavily upon other sorts of learning support resources and expertise which are already well-established in schools. By and large it does not require a massive re-skilling of learning support teachers nor an investment in new materials and equipment. Moreover, the emphasis on curriculum access and effective functioning rather than on curative interventions gives a defined focus to provision. There is no open-ended commitment to working with a child until s/he is 'cured' of specific learning difficulties; neither is there any suggestion that such children will need highly specialised teaching right across the curriculum. Rather, the aim of curriculum access offers a criterion for determining how much special provision is necessary and what form that provision should take. As one teacher put it:

"There's no reason to interfere with a child's learning if they're coping."

In other words, intervention is only necessary when and insofar as a particular pupil is not functioning effectively within the curriculum, and its aim is limited to restoring such effective functioning.

This, coupled with the customising approach described above, allows schools to structure a staged response to specific learning difficulties rather than relying on a high level of 'blanket' provision. For some children, very little more will be necessary than a sympathetic response from class teachers and the offer of specific support as and when needed; indeed, schools reported a number of pupils who very much preferred this 'hands-off' style of provision. For other children, much more intensive forms of intervention and support will be necessary – though even in these cases, the focus on curriculum access and the use of standard techniques drawn from learning support means that much of this provision will be made by subject and class teachers working within ordinary classrooms.

There are, however, some slightly more problematic aspects of this proposed model. Although schools are currently finding its resource demands more or less manageable, the customising of provision does nonetheless make such demands.

On the whole, these are probably higher than the demands made by established forms of learning support and, moreover, relate to a groups of pupils who are only just beginning to attain prominence within schools. As one teacher somewhat wryly commented:

"The more you look, the more you find."

In consequence, some schools in our samples are finding that the demands made by this emerging group are beginning to divert resources away from other pupils with special needs, and that the school's capacity to sustain both high-quality learning support provision and specific learning difficulties provision based on the model we have outlined is becoming increasingly stretched. In some cases, this diversion of resources is exacerbated by the success of parents and lobby groups in the area in persuading or compelling local authorities and schools to place particular emphasis on provision for pupils with specific learning difficulties.

What is evident is that the viability of the model depends either on a balance being maintained between the level of demand and the level of available resources, or on a significant increase in resources to match the growing level of demand. We shall return to this point on our concluding section.

SPECIFIC LEARNING DIFFICULTIES : A WAY FORWARD?

We suggest that there are some important points which emerge from the foregoing discussion, and which may offer a way forward in respect of specific learning difficulties:

Models and debate in special needs education

We wish to begin with what may appear to be a theoretical issue, but which nonetheless, we suggest, has major practical implications. We regard much of the debate which takes place within the field of special needs education as impoverished by its uni-dimensionality. A whole series of debates – withdrawal *versus* in-class support, integration *versus* segregation, common curriculum *versus* alternative curricula, and, of course, specific learning difficulties *versus* the whole-school approach – have been conducted as though a resolution of the issues they raised was possible at the purely *technological* level. In other words, it has been assumed that evidence could be found to show that one form of provision was unequivocally 'better' than the other. The concept of 'special need' as something which is self-evident in any assessment of a particular child serves, of course, to rationalise this style of debate by implying that the 'meeting of needs' is an unproblematic touchstone which can be used to evaluate competing approaches.

Our contention, on the other hand, is that such debates have a significant *assumptional* component. The different positions which engage with each other rest on often unspoken assumptions about the nature of special needs and the purposes of education. It is the incompatibility of competing assumptions, we believe, which often makes such debates somewhat fruitless. The notion of 'models' of provision seems to us much more productive. By focusing on the conjunction of particular technologies with particular assumptions, it makes it possible for the full implications of a proposed form of provision to be explicated with an open acknowledgement that values and beliefs are inextricably bound up in the positions adopted by parties to the debate.

In the field of specific learning difficulties in particular, we suggest that some of the impasses between the 'dyslexia lobby' and its 'opponents' (Riddell, Brown, & Duffield, 1994) could be opened up if there was an acknowledgement that each was operating on the basis of a different *model* of provision. The debate is often conducted as though determining whether or not dyslexia 'exists' and whether or not it has a distinctive symptomatology and aetiology would *ipso facto* reveal what an appropriate educational response should be. In fact, as we have seen, much of the psychological literature on dyslexia and specific learning difficulties makes an unspoken assumption, about the centrality of curative intervention as an aim of provision, which ought itself to be the subject of debate. An alternative model along the lines that we have described is, however, at least equally defensible. Such a model has little to say on the 'existence' or otherwise of dyslexia because it is founded on assumptions about the centrality of curriculum access and maximal achievement as educational goals. It is not that these assumptions are necessarily more valid than any others, but that opening them up to debate and acknowledging the way they inform the conceptualisation of specific learning difficulties and the preferred form of intervention may offer a more fruitful way forward than the conflicts which currently characterise this field.

The model and school self-review

One of the investigations which contributed to the development of the model was a survey of specific learning difficulties in all the middle and high schools of one English LEA (Dyson & Wood, 1994). The results were extremely worrying: many schools had no clear conceptualisation of specific learning difficulties, had little or no idea of how many of their pupils had such difficulties, and could point to no differentiation between the provision for general and for specific difficulties. In such a situation, it is scarcely surprising if concerned parents come to distrust schools and to press for alternative forms of provision.

We believe, therefore, that there is much to be gained if schools use our model as the basis for a review of their current provision. This is particularly the case in view of the flexibility inherent in the model, which avoids committing schools in very different contexts to a uniform response. What matters is that each school develops, in a way which matches its available resources and preferred styles of working, means of realising the four aims of the rationale. This ought to be a realistic possibility for all schools which have an established approach to learning support since the model draws heavily on such approaches.

Moreover, the increasing emphasis in government policy on parental rights, and the increasing activity of the 'dyslexia lobby', together with the educational justifications for parental involvement, mean that schools need to be in a position to justify publicly their approaches to specific learning difficulties. We suggest that the model provides a basis for such justifications, enabling schools to propose to parents and their associations an educationally-meaningful alternative to the highly individualised and remedially-oriented provision which they may (understandably) see as the only possible response to their child's needs.

The model and government policy

This leads us, inevitably, to the implications of our model for government policy. We regard a significant strength of the model we have described as being its incorporation into the concept of specific learning difficulties of some notion of educational aims and purposes. It is this notion – however ill-defined – which allows schools to consider rationally the point at which a relative weakness in some area of functioning becomes a 'learning difficulty', and to begin to determine the sort of intervention which might be necessary if educational aims are to be realised for this child.

We note that the concept of 'special educational needs' and the government policy which is based on that concept do not appear to contain any equivalent articulation of educational aims. It is not surprising, then, that, as the government's own agencies have pointed out (Audit Commission & HMI, 1992), there seems to be no rational way of determining what needs for what interventions arise from what learning characteristics. It is similarly unsurprising that, in the field of specific learning difficulties, there are problems in deciding who has what special needs as a result of such difficulties, and what resources they are entitled to on the basis of such needs. We anticipate similar problems occurring as other 'new' forms of special need, – Attention Deficit Disorder (Reid, Maag, & Vasa, 1993; Cooper & Ideus, 1995) seems to be the current leader – begin to emerge, and we predict that the necessary balance between demand and resources will become increasingly difficult to maintain.

Our view is that such issues are always problematic, that hard decisions about resource-deployment are inevitable, and that easy solutions are not available. Nonetheless, we also believe that rational debate on these issues and rational decision-making in particular cases will only be possible when some explicit notion of educational aims is set alongside the concept of educational needs. The introduction of national curricula of differing sorts in both Scotland and England has gone some way towards achieving this. It may well be, however, that if the demand from specific learning difficulties and other 'new' forms of need increases, such a move will be essential if the education system is not to collapse under the strain. In this case, the model we have described and similar models that emerge from the practical decision-making undertaken by schools, might prove a useful starting point for debate.

REFERENCES

Audit Commission and Her Majesty's Inspectorate (1992). *Getting in on the Act: Provision for Pupils with Special Educational Needs: the National Picture.* (London, HMSO).

Brown, M. (1993). Supporting learning through a whole school approach, in: Reid, G. (Ed.), *Specific Learning Difficulties (Dyslexia): Perspectives on Practice.* (Edinburgh, Moray House Publications).

Cooper, P., and Ideus, K. (1995). Is attention deficit disorder a Trojan Horse?, *Support for Learning,* 10(1), 29 - 34.

Crisfield, J., Smythe, I. (Ed.) (1993). *The Dyslexia Handbook* 1993/4 (Reading, British Dyslexia Association).

Dennison, P. E., Hargrove, G. (1985). *Personalised Whole Brain Integration* (California, Educational Kinaesthetic).

Dessent, T. (1987). *Making the Ordinary School Special* (London, Falmer).

Dyson, A. (1995). *Provision for Pupils with Specific Learning Difficulties in Cleveland Secondary Schools: A Cost Benefit Analysis.* Special Needs Research Group, University of Newcastle upon Tyne for Cleveland LEA.

Dyson, A., Skidmore, D. (1994). *Provision for Pupils with Specific Learning Difficulties in Secondary Schools: A Report to SOED.* Special Needs Research Group, Department of Education, University of Newcastle upon Tyne.

Dyson, A., Wood, B. (1994). *A Survey of Provision for Pupils with Specific Learning Difficulties in Middle and High Schools Maintained by [One] LEA.* Special Needs Research Group Department of Education, University of Newcastle upon Tyne.

Hart, S. (1992). Differentiation – way forward or retreat ? *British Journal of Special Education,* 19(1), 10 - 12.

Kuhn, T. S. (1970). *The Structure of Scientific Revolutions* (2nd. ed.) (London, University of Chicago Press).

Lewis, J. (1995). The development of a unit for dyslexic children in a British comprehensive school, *Dyslexia,* 1(1). 12 - 18.

Pumfrey, P. D., and Reason, R. (1991). *Specific Learning Difficulties (Dyslexia): Challenges and Responses.* (Windsor, NFER-Nelson).

Reid, G. (1994). *Specific Learning Difficulties (Dyslexia): A Handbook for Study and Practice.* (Edinburgh, Moray House Publications).

Reid, R., Maag, J. W., Vasa, S. F. (1993). Attention Deficit Hyperactivity Disorder as a disability category: A critique, *Exceptional Children*, 60(3), 198-214.

Riddell, S., Brown, S., Duffield, J. (1994). Conflicts of policies and models: The case of specific learning difficulties, in: Riddell, S. and Brown, S. (Eds.), *Special Educational Needs Policy in the 1990s: Warnock in the Market Place*. (London, Routledge).

Riddell, S., Duffield, J., Brown, S., Ogilvy, C. (1992). *Specific Learning Difficulties: Policy, Practice and Provision: a Report to SOED*. Department of Education, University of Stirling.

Scottish Education Department (SED) (1978). *The Education of Pupils with Learning Difficulties in Primary and Secondary Schools in Scotland: A Progress Report by HM Inspectors of Schools*. (Edinburgh, HMSO).

Scottish Office Education Department (SOED) (1994). *Effective Provision for Special Educational Needs: A Report by HM Inspectors of Schools* (Edinburgh, SOED).

Stone, J., Harris, K. (1991). These coloured spectacles: what are they for?, *Support for Learning*, 6(3), 116-118.

Tansley, A. E. (1967). *Reading and Remedial Reading*. (London, Routledge and Kegan Paul).

Thompson, D., Barton, L. (1992). The wider context: a free market, *British Journal of Special Education*, 19(1), 13 - 15.

Tomlinson, S. (1982). *A Sociology of Special Education*. (London, Routledge and Kegan Paul).

THE 'OTHER SIDE' OF DYSLEXIA

GAVIN REID

Jane Healy (1994) provides an interesting insight into the potential of dyslexic children. She illustrates how difficulties in one area of learning should not prevent success in other areas. Dyslexic children may well have considerable difficulties in the processing of language and decoding the written word but these difficulties can be compensated for by accessing right hemisphere skills. It has been well documented that the right hemisphere skills of dyslexic children and adults can become a significant strength, provided appropriate learning opportunities are present (Healy, 1994; Galaburda, 1993; Bell, 1992). Skills, therefore, in visual and spatial processing and in comprehension and problem-solving may be heavily utilised by dyslexics when processing information. Additionally, these right hemisphere skills can also facilitate creativity. These skills and in particular creativity, need to be nurtured and encouraged, since success in learning for dyslexics may result from the use of right hemisphere skills rather than logical, sequential left hemisphere processing. While it must be recognised that the dyslexic learner requires considerable support and structure in language processing, this should not be at the expense of creativity or the development of other right hemisphere skills.

West (1991) presents a valuable insight into this 'other side' of dyslexia, particularly the alternative means of processing information which may be more natural for dyslexic people. West explains how the explosion of learning materials such as educational television, video and audio tapes has changed how people learn, and this 'explosion', as well as benefiting dyslexic people, has also helped to change attitudes to learning from a rigid, narrow, traditional focus to an inventive, flexible and imaginative one. Utilising the 'explosion' of learning materials does not represent a sidetracking of tackling the principal difficulties of dyslexic children but rather, carefully presented, these can be more effective than traditional means of learning.

It should also be recognised that dyslexic children and adults can develop extremely effective strategies to access and retain new learning including, for example, visual mnemonics or mind mapping strategies (Buzan, 1994; Reid,

1994; Margulies, 1990). Susan Hampshire, the well-known actress who is also dyslexic, devised a personal system of visual cues to help her learn scripts. Dyslexic people, therefore, rather than feel restricted by their difficulties in literacy can in fact be exceptionally creative. West (1991) coined a very appropriate phrase to describe dyslexic learners – for them he suggested 'the easy is hard and the hard is easy'. The implication of this statement is that the information processing pattern of dyslexics can be quite effective in areas such as problem-solving, although the strategies used may seem unusual and unconventional. West concluded that perhaps dyslexic individuals should learn to give themselves more credit for 'their ability to understand and use sophisticated concepts'. This fits in well with theories of creativity which suggest that there is no accepted pattern or formula for creativity, but instead is marked by its endless variety. Creativity is the free spirit of learning, with limitless potential.

As educationists, we all have a responsibility to ensure that creativity is encouraged and not restricted in any way. It is important that we become aware of the abilities, personality and learning style of the individual dyslexic learner. I found it interesting that after a presentation to a group of parents and teachers, I was approached rather apprehensively by a lady who introduced herself as a specialist teacher in art. She approached me to express an interest in obtaining specialist training in dyslexia and was of the opinion that such training would be valuable in her classroom practice and help her understand dyslexic children. It is interesting that she also felt such training would be appropriate, even though all her teaching took place in the art room. She clearly felt that art could help develop creativity and self-expression in dyslexic children. Her apprehension, I suppose, rested not in her own views, but those of others, perhaps colleagues who may be of the opinion that advanced specialist training in dyslexia would be under-utilised in the art classroom. How wrong they would be! The art class can help the dyslexic child develop creativity, achieve success and provide a foundation and springboard for other areas of learning in other classes. I felt, therefore, that the art teacher rather than be apprehensive, should be applauded.

West describes a number of attributes which may be seen in some dyslexic people which represent skills in creativity and visual thinking. These include:

- Talents in spatial, mechanical and related right hemisphere skills.
- Preference to draw, even though the same person may have poor handwriting.
- An especially good 'musical ear'.
- Ability to visualize images in the mind.

The research by Galaburda (1990), on hemispheric symmetry, supports West's description. Galaburda's research shows that while the brains of most people have a dominant hemisphere, usually the left, the brains of many dyslexics have symmetrical hemispheres. Additionally, Galaburda's research suggests that the pattern of connections between the two hemispheres is different in dyslexics, and this produces a different pattern of communication between the two hemispheres. The implication of this is that in tasks which require rules of logic the performance of dyslexic people may be less competent than their performances in those tasks requiring innovation and creativity. Creativity, therefore, may provide the foundation and impetus for the development of the learning skills of the dyslexic person. If this is the case, therefore, the art specialist who showed an interest in undertaking a course in dyslexia, showed considerable insight into how the abilities of dyslexic children can be fostered.

Thomas West sums this view up very effectively when he says:

"We ought to begin to pay less attention to getting everyone over the same hill using the same path. We may wish to encourage some to take different routes to the same end. Then we might see good reasons for paying careful attention to their descriptions of what they have found. We may wish to follow them some day." (West, 1991).

In order to steer the dyslexic child on the most appropriate path, it is important that empathy and support from others is present. This two volume text highlights the range of skills of professionals and parents who have the capabilities and the understanding to help the dyslexic learner achieve fulfilment and success in learning. Those who have been in some way connected with dyslexia, either through a relative, friend or student ,are well placed to provide support and show a clear insight into the difficulties experienced by the dyslexic person.

It is hoped this volume highlights the skills and understanding of professionals involved in the field of dyslexia. It is uplifting to talk to parents, relatives, friends and teachers of dyslexic people and share this empathy and concern which they openly acknowledge for dyslexic individuals. This kind of support is invaluable.

This chapter highlights the potential creativity of dyslexic people and the need for others to show awareness and understanding of their needs and skills. It is appropriate therefore that this chapter and this volume should close with two poems especially written for this publication, which generate messages of success and empathy. These, I feel, show an understanding of dyslexic people and acknowledge the 'other side of dyslexia'.

SUCCESS
by Catherine McDonald

I know this may seem absurd
But when it came down to writing a word
My eyes just went blurred
And I'd write what I'd heard
The result being a laughable scramble

A scramble and tangle of letters
I knew that I could do better
I'll explain it here in this letter . . .

It all started when I was at school
Or maybe it was at skool
The teacher said I was a fool
Or perhaps I was a ful

I could sing
I could dance
I could swim
But when it came down to handing the essays in
I would shrink from sniggers and laughter

The teacher said I was dreaming
I tried screaming
I was not
I had just forgot
How to spell or spel
The same way as tell
The result a written disaster

Book became buk
Read became reed
Write was right
And right rite

So I prayed and even prade
Every nite or was it night
And still it all
Did not come rite
Or right

I studied
I swatted
Long into the nights
In the traditional fashion
Not getting the formula right

SUDDENLY!

 I stopped

Whilst visualising
I began realising
I was moving

 in the wrong direction

So I

 mapped out a new route in my mind . . .

NOW

 Happily

I am strolling along

 Successfully

On a creative pathway
With learning styles of my own.

THE CHAMELEON
by Rob Merson

Chameleons crouching in the leaves of books,
Words that deceive us with their looks,
They stalk through the branches of library shelves
Mutably showing and hiding themselves,
In still rivers of print the chameleon reflected
But wind-ruffled ripples are all I detected,
If I try to explain, I'm the subject of mirth
A colour description to those blind since birth,
But I am determined to capture my prey,
I will hunt the chameleon and catch it one day.

REFERENCES

Bell, N. (1991). Gestalt Imagery; A Critical Factor In Language comprehension. Reprint from *Annals Of Dyslexia,* Vol. 41, Baltimore, Orton Dyslexia Society.

Buzan, T. (1993). *Radiant Thinking*. London BBC Books.

Galaburda, M. (1990). *Neuroscience issues in dyslexia research*. Paper presented Orton Dyslexia Society Annual Conference.

Healy, J. (1994). Your child's growing mind: a practical guide to brain development and learning from birth to adolescence (new edition) Double Day Publishing, New York.

Margulies, N. (1991). Mapping inner space. Tucson, AZ, Zephyr Press.

Reid, G. (1994). *Specific Learning Difficulties (dyslexia): a handbook for study and practice*, Edinburgh, Moray House Publications.

West, T. (1991). *In the mind's eye: Visual thinkers, gifted people with learning difficulties, computer images and the ironies of creativity*. Prometheus Books. Buffalo, New York.

NOTES ON CONTRIBUTORS

* **Sheila Airth** is qualified as a Primary and Physical Education teacher who learned about dyslexia through trying to help one of the family survive and succeed within the educational system. After receiving encouragement and support from the Glasgow branch of the Dyslexia Association, she ultimately set up a branch in Central Region in March 1989. After four years with Dyslexia Central, she was then appointed Chairman of the Scottish Dyslexia Association. In August 1995, the new national office of the SDA was opened at Unit 3, Stirling Business Centre, Wellgreen, Stirling.

* **Dr Jean Alston** was formerly employed in the Department of Special Educational Needs, on the Crewe Campus, of what is now the Manchester Metropolitan University. She has extensive experience of teaching in Manchester and Cheshire schools, and in the Derbyshire Language Support Service. She has conducted research, written, and lectured extensively, on the subject of handwriting and general writing skills. She is now an independent psychologist, writer and lecturer, and is employed as a consulting psychologist by the Dyslexia Institute.

* **Dr Jenni Barr** qualified in Scotland as an educational psychologist before embarking on four years of research with Margaret Clark in Birmingham, looking at aspects of policy and provision for pupils with learning difficulties. For the last twelve years, she has been employed in a variety of educational psychologist posts in Central and Fife Regions, and as a senior lecturer at Strathclyde University concerned with psychologist training. She remains committed to the generic work of an educational psychologist and to the importance of educational research in local authority settings.

* **Dr Stewart Biggar** is an educational psychologist with Tayside Region Psychological Service having recently completed post-graduate training in educational psychology at Strathclyde University. He has accumulated a range of experiences in areas of research, university-tutoring, training and adult basic education.

* **Pat Brown** is the Depute Headteacher of Hermitage Park Primary School, Edinburgh. Prior to that she was in charge of a Reading Unit in Lothian Region which specialised in teaching pupils with Specific Learning Difficulties. Her

interest in metacognition first developed whilst studying for a Masters degree at Edinburgh University. She has presented seminars and workshops on aspects of metacognition at both local and national levels.

* **Linda Cumming** has worked in primary learning support and as a specialist teacher with Central Regional Psychological Service. She is now Advisory Teacher (Primary Learning Support) and is concerned mainly with policy, curriculum and staff development issues as they relate to pupils experiencing a wide range of learning difficulties.

* **Dr Adrian Dighe** is a Senior Clinical Medical Officer working at the Child Development Centre, Southlands Hospital, Shoreham on Sea, West Sussex. During his previous post with the Medway NHS Trust in Kent, he developed an interest in children with specific learning difficulties, especially those with motor planning problems.

* **Fernando Almeida Diniz** is Head of Department at Moray House Institute of Education, Heriot-Watt University and Chairperson of the Advisory Committee for the Centre for Specific Learning Difficulties. After teaching in special and mainstream schools, he lectured at the University of Greenwich, London, where he was Head of Division and Reader in Special Needs in Education. He has extensive international experience and has held visiting professorships at universities in Germany and Spain.

* **Sheila Dobie** was Head of Department Movement Studies at Moray House Institute, Heriot Watt University. She initially trained in physical education followed by studies at the Laban Centre. A specialist interest led to an Advanced Diploma in Severe and Profound Learning Difficulties at Cambridge University and an MEd (SEN) at Stirling University. She is an Associate of the Institute of Neuro-Physiological Psychology and was awarded an OBE in the New Year's Honours 1991.

* **Dr Morag Donaldson** is a lecturer in the Department of Psychology, University of Edinburgh. Her teaching and research interests lie mainly in the area of language development in pre-school and primary school children. She is author of *Children's Explanations: a Psycholinguistic Study.* (Cambridge University Press, 1986).

* **Jill Duffield** is a Research Fellow at the Department of Education, University of Stirling, and a former modern studies teacher. As well as the specific learning difficulties research she has taken part in the evaluation of pilot primary foreign

language projects in Scotland. She is currently investigating how schools support the progress of lower achieving pupils, with Sally Brown and Sheila Riddell.

* **Professor Alan Dyson** is Professor of Special Needs Education and Co-Director of the Special Needs Research Group in the Department of Education, University of Newcastle upon Tyne. He is engaged in research into a wide range of issues in special needs. Along with other members of the Special Needs Research Group, he has recently completed a national survey of developments in special needs provision in mainstream schools (the report of which is published as *Innovatory Practice in Mainstream Schools for Special Educational Needs* by HMSO), and a survey of provision for pupils with specific learning difficulties for SOED. He is currently undertaking research into the role of SENCOs in mainstream schools and into the service needs of young adults with complex physical disabilities. He is co-editor of *Rethinking Special Needs in Mainstream Schools* (with Charles Gains) and *Towards Inclusive Schools* (with Catherine Clark and Alan Millward) – both published by David Fulton. He previously worked for 13 years as a special needs teacher and co-ordinator in mainstream and special schools.

* **Elizabeth Fairgrieve** was, until her recent retirement, Head Occupational Therapist (Children's Service), Tayside. She has worked in a variety of situations and with a wide range of childhood conditions, in Canada and the United Kingdom. She has a particular interest in motor-learning difficulties (the combination of motor problems and specific learning difficulty) and has worked co-operatively with several well-known contributors to this field e.g. conducting a study in the use of the 'Test of Motor Impairment' (Sheila Henderson) and its use as part of an assessment package for motor-learning difficulties. She currently (in association with Liz Stephenson) designs, teaches and assesses postgraduate courses on the subject for therapists and education professionals.

* **Eileen Francis** initiated the Specific Learning Difficulties Project at Moray House Institute. Until 1991 she was a Senior Lecturer at the Institute and contributed to courses provided by the Department of Curriculum and Support Studies. She is a member of the College of Speech and Language Therapists and of the Scottish Institute of Human Relations. Currently she is working independently on research and training projects.

* **Dr Barbara Given** is Director of the Education and Counselling Services within the Graduate School of Education at George Mason University, Virginia, USA. She is also co-chairperson of the South East Regional Learning Styles Centre which is one of five in the Learning Styles Centres National network. She has written extensively for national and international journals and made major

presentations throughout the United States and Europe. Barbara has been the keynote presenter at a number of conferences and workshops held by the Moray House Centre for Specific Learning Difficulties. She holds a number of positions as executive board member on national and international education bodies and is the newsletter editor for the International Alliance for Learning. Barbara has received a number of awards of distinction for her services to education and the community and appeared in recent editions of *Who's Who of American Women* and *Foremost Women of the Twentieth Century*.

* **Dr Jane Healy** is a teacher who has worked with all ages from pre-school to graduate school. Her major research interest has been in finding practical links between neuropsychology and developmental theory. She holds a master's degree in reading from John Carroll University and a Ph.D in educational psychology from Case Western Reserve University. Her many years of experience as a parent, classroom teacher, reading/learning specialist, college professor, and elementary administrator have helped her become an internationally-recognised author, lecturer, and consultant in applying brain research to practical classroom and parenting situations. She has received national media coverage, including an appearance on the 'Today Show', for her ideas about the impact of television on children's brain development. She is currently working as a learning specialist at the Vail Mountain School in Colorado and holds an appointment as adjunct assistant professor at Cleveland State University. Her award-winning books have been translated into eight languages: *Your Child's Growing Mind; A Guide to Learning and Brain Development from Birth to Adolescence; Endangered Minds; Why Children Don't Think and What We Can Do About It*, and *How to Have Intelligent and Creative Conversations with Your Kids*. Although Jane has received many honours, including being twice named the 'Educator of the Year' by Delta Kappa Gamma, she claims that she and her husband have learned most of what they know from the process of raising three sons.

* **Dr Cyril Hellier** is a senior educational psychologist in Tayside. He trained as a Primary Teacher in Dundee and has worked in both mainstream and special education. His post-graduate work was based on his experience as both teacher and psychologist. He has worked in Scotland, Canada and Australia; currently he is involved in developing the use of Reading for Sure, a system devised in Australia to prevent literacy failure. He has published and presented papers on various aspects relating to special education.

* **Dr John Hinton** is Honorary Senior Research Fellow and Head of the Stress Research Unit in the Psychology Department, University of Glasgow. He has developed an international network on work stress research and has actively

collaborated with the university of Dresden over the last 13 years. He is Scientific Co-ordinator of the European Research Network on the development of Bio-social indices of work stress. He is particularly interested in the development of psychological stress theory and its relevance to psycho-physiological methods of monitoring work stress.

* **Meg Houston** has worked in Edinburgh for 30 years as a Primary Teacher, a Remedial Teacher, a Learning Support Teacher and as Principal Support Teacher attached to Psychological Services. She is currently a Neighbourhood Support Officer in Lothian Region.

* **C. Morag Hunter-Carsch** is a Lecturer in the University of Leicester School of Education. She is a Primary Tutor, co-ordinates the Post-Graduate Teacher Training Junior (7-12 years) Course, contributes to the Primary English course and runs specialist teacher training courses in teaching pupils and post-16 learners with specific learning difficulties (dyslexia). Her teaching experience includes work in Scottish, English and Canadian schools. She is a chartered psychologist and was a lecturer in Psychology at the University of Strathclyde and lecturer on the Reading Diploma at the Open University. Her research on reading and literacy difficulties includes projects supported by SCRE, Schools Council, The Paul Hamlyn Foundation, the DES and ALBSU. Amongst her publications are two books which she edited for the UK Reading Association of which she was president in 1988-89. She has been a keynote speaker at 13 national and international conferences.

* **Janet Hunter** is a learning support teacher at Abercorn as well Riccarton Primary School. She has considerable experience in the area of dyslexia and is engaged in promoting whole-school aspects of assessment and teaching of children with learning difficulties. She has undertaken a P.G. Certificate in Specific Learning Difficulties at Moray House.

* **Dr Rhona Johnston** gained her B.A. and Ph.D. in Psychology at the University of Hull. She then trained as a primary school teacher at Dundee College of Education, and worked for two years as a secondary school remedial teacher in Fife schools. Since 1979 she has been a lecturer in Psychology at University of St Andrews.

* **Gillian Kettles** gained her MA in Psychology at the University of St Andrews in 1987 before completing her post-graduate training in primary education at Moray House College of Education. She subsequently spent a year working for the Queensland Department of Family Services in Australia before returning to

Edinburgh to work as a primary school teacher. Gillian completed her professional training in educational psychology at University College London in 1992 and has since worked for the Kent Educational Psychology Service in Chatham.

* **Mary Kiely** taught initially in a rural primary school. After a break to bring up a family, she taught in a psychiatric unit and a unit for severely maladjusted pupils before her present post as a Principal Teacher in the Learning Support Department of Dumfries Academy.

* **John Landon** is a Senior Lecturer at Moray House Institute/Heriot-Watt University and Co-ordinator of the Institute's Modular Master's Scheme. He has many years experience of teacher training in bilingual development in UK, Australia, Canada and Japan and has produced a number of teachers' guides and training packs. He is currently tutor of post-qualifying modules: Bilingualism and Special Education and Bilingualism and Literacy.

* **Marcia P. Mann** received a B.S. degree from New York University and an M.A. from Stanford University School of Medicine, both in the field of Speech Pathology and Audiology. She holds the Certificate of Clinical Competency in Speech Pathology from the American Speech-Language-Hearing Association, and is a Founding Fellow of the Academy of Orton-Gillingham Practitioners and Educators. As a student of Margaret Byrd Rawson, she began her work in the field of dyslexia in 1960. Since that time she has worked as a practitioner, lecturer, and trainer of others in the U.S., in Europe and the Middle East, and has been an active participant in the Orton Dyslexia Society. Currently, she is the Director of Bailin-Mann Associates, a private Learning Center in Brooklyn, New York.

* **Dr Lori Muskat** is a staff psychologist at Eagle Hill Diagnostic Clinic, affiliated with Eagle Hill School, a school for learning disabled students located in Greenwich, Connecticut, USA: she also has a private practice in New York City. In clinical practice, her areas of expertise include paediatric neuropsychology, neuro-psychological assessment and consultation, medical psychology, and the differential diagnosis of learning and emotional disorders. Research interests include social and political aspects of classification, diagnosis and treatment, processes involved in the creative arts, and international special education; the power of context is a frequent focal point of her work. She has taught on the faculties of the University of Pennsylvania and Pace university and has provided staff training at a number of New York area hospitals and educational institutions.

* **Marysia Nash** is a speech and language therapist specialising in dyslexia and specific developmental language disorders in children. She is currently working

part-time at Edinburgh Sick Children's NHS Trust and studying for a PhD in the Department of Psychology, University of Edinburgh. Her research interest is vocabulary deficits in language impaired children.

* **Maggie Nicholson** is a Spanish and Special Education teacher at Summit Middle School, Frisco, Colorado, USA. During the last 25 years, 16 of which have been at Summit Middle School, she has also taught English as a second language to students from kindergarten to grade 12 and Spanish to adult students. She is also currently a tutor in Spanish adult education at Colorado Mountain College. She has a MA degree in Learning Disabilities and a BA degree in Spanish. She has considerable experience in consultancy, having participated in numerous education and school committees. She presented a paper on learning styles at the Moray House conference in Edinburgh in 1994.

* **Diane Pepper** has worked in Lothian for 25 years as an Educational Psychologist. She trained as Primary Teacher at Homerton College, Cambridge. Her PhD was taken at Cambridge where she researched Young Children's Language Development.

* **Gavin Reid** is Co-ordinator of the Moray House Centre for Specific Learning Difficulties (Dyslexia) and Course Leader for the Post-Graduate Awards in Specific Learning Difficulties. He has been instrumental in the development of the M.Ed Award in Specific Learning Difficulties and is the author of the course text 'A Handbook for Study and Practice' and editor of this two-volume course reader 'Dimensions of Dyslexia'. He has made a number of presentations at conferences and universities, both in the UK and the United States; published journal articles and is a member of a number of national consultancy groups. He has had lengthy experiences as a class teacher and as an educational psychologist.

* **Jennifer Reid** is a speech and language therapist who has specialised in the treatment of pre-school and primary school children with specific language impairment. She is currently working as a research fellow in the Department of Psychology, University of Edinburgh.

* **Dr Sheila Riddell** is a lecturer in the Department of Education, University of Stirling. Having graduated from Sussex University in 1976, she worked as an English teacher for seven years before enrolling for a Ph.D at Bristol University in 1984. The topic of her research was gender and option choice in rural comprehensive schools. She moved to Scotland in 1988 and took up the post of Research Fellow in the Department of Education, University of Edinburgh, working on a project in the area of special educational needs. Since moving to

Stirling University in 1989, she has continued to research and write in the areas of special educational needs, gender and education and school effectiveness and improvement.

* **Nicola Robinson** is a speech and language therapist, currently employed by East/Mid Lothian NHS Trust and working in a Language Unit. She trained at Queen Margaret College in Edinburgh and has worked with a range of speech and language disorders with adults and children. She has developed an interest in the provision of services for children with written and spoken language disorders. Her chapter on the role of the speech therapist is based on a presentation which she made at the Annual Conference of the Edinburgh and South East Dyslexic Association in September 1991.

* **David Skidmore** is Lecturer in the Department of Education Studies and Management, University of Reading, and formerly member of the Special Needs Research Group, University of Newcastle upon Tyne.

* **Liz Stephenson** is Senior Occupational Therapist at Royal Aberdeen Children's hospital. Within a very varied caseload (ranging from acute physical conditions to child and family psychiatry), she has developed her particular interest in motor-learning difficulties (the combination of motor problems and specific learning difficulty). She has written two widely used booklets on motor-learning difficulties, and several papers and book chapters. She also (in association with Elizabeth Fairgrieve) designs, teaches and assesses postgraduate courses on the subject for therapists and education professionals.

* **Gill Thomson MBE** is a trained teacher, married, with four children, two of whom are dyslexic. In 1968 she co-founded a voluntary association for Dyslexia in Scotland, and in 1970 the British Dyslexia Association in England and Wales. Her experiences cover provision for professional help for children, students and adult dyslexics, parents and the public at local and Government levels.

* **Dr Keith Topping** develops and researches methods for non-professionals (such as parents or peers) to tutor others in fundamental skills (e.g. reading, spelling, writing) and higher order learning (science, maths, etc.), for use across a wide age range in many different contexts. He is the Director of the Centre for Paired Learning at the Department of Psychology, University of Dundee, where he also directs the postgraduate professional training course in educational psychology and the Higher Education Effective Learning Project.

* **Linda Watson** was a nursery teacher at Moray House Nursery for 15 years. She is currently a nursery and infant teacher at Leith Primary School.